Lecture Notes in Computer Science 16784

Philipp Neumann · Michael J. Puma ·
Michael H. Lees · Derek Groen ·
Jack J. Dongarra · Peter M. A. Sloot

Editors

Computational Science – ICCS 2026

26th International Conference
Hamburg, Germany, June 29 – July 1, 2026
Proceedings, Part II

 Springer

Editors
Philipp Neumann [iD]
DESY
Hamburg, Germany

Michael H. Lees [iD]
University of Amsterdam
Amsterdam, The Netherlands

Jack J. Dongarra [iD]
University of Tennessee
Knoxville, TN, USA

Michael J. Puma [iD]
Columbia University
New York, NY, USA

Derek Groen [iD]
Brunel University of London
Uxbridge, UK

Peter M. A. Sloot [iD]
University of Amsterdam
Amsterdam, The Netherlands

ISSN 0302-9743   ISSN 1611-3349 (electronic)
Lecture Notes in Computer Science
ISBN 978-3-032-29923-9   ISBN 978-3-032-29924-6 (eBook)
https://doi.org/10.1007/978-3-032-29924-6

Preface

Welcome to the 26th International Conference on Computational Science (ICCS 2026 - https://www.iccs-meeting.org/iccs2026/), held from 30 June to 1 July 2026 at DESY (Deutsches Elektronen-Synchrotron), in Hamburg, Germany.

This 26th edition, jointly organized by the University of Amsterdam (UvA) and the University of Tennessee at Knoxville (UTK), was a fully in-person event—as was the previous edition in Singapore. Despite the many challenges of our present times, we have strived to keep the ICCS community as dynamic, creative, and productive as possible. We are proud to present these proceedings as a testament to that effort.

Founded in 1959, DESY is a publicly funded research center of the Helmholtz Association and one of the world's leading accelerator centers. With 3000 staff members, of whom 1300 are scientists, DESY conducts ground-breaking matter research, leveraging DESY research infrastructures, such as the X-ray radiation source PETRA III, but also its international involvement, for example, in CERN experiments. This very data-intensive strand of research builds upon efficient data-centric computing and data streaming infrastructures, in particular DESY's Interdisciplinary Data & Analysis Facility (IDAF), and upon matter-oriented computing and data management research and development. This interplay of infrastructures, research, and development enables unprecedented scientific insights into more than 200 PBs of data that are being managed by DESY—from the interaction of elementary particles to nanomaterials and biomolecular processes. With these capabilities and capacities, DESY has become a magnet for thousands of guest researchers and was particularly happy to welcome ICCS participants in 2026!

The International Conference on Computational Science is an annual conference that brings together researchers and scientists from mathematics and computer science as basic computing disciplines, as well as researchers from various application areas who are pioneering computational methods in sciences such as physics, chemistry, life sciences, engineering, arts, and humanitarian fields, to discuss problems and solutions in the area, identify new issues, and shape future directions for research.

The ICCS proceedings series has become a primary intellectual resource for computational science researchers, defining and advancing the state of the art in this field.

We are proud to note that this 26th edition, with 23 workshops (the Workshops on Computational Science), and over 300 participants, kept to the tradition and high standards of previous editions.

The theme for 2026, **"At the Forefront of Science through Computation and Data"**, highlighted the role of Computational Science in assisting multidisciplinary research. This conference was a unique event, focusing on recent developments in scalable scientific algorithms; advanced software tools; computational grids; advanced numerical methods; and novel application areas. These innovative novel models, algorithms, and tools drive new science through efficient application in physical systems, computational and systems biology, environmental systems, finance, and others.

ICCS is well known for its lineup of keynote speakers. The keynotes for 2026 were:

- **George Karniadakis**, Brown University, USA
- **Amanda Randles**, Duke University, USA
- **Luis M. Rocha**, Binghamton University - State University of New York, USA
- **Christian Schroer**, DESY | University of Hamburg, Germany
- **Hareesha Narayana Shirankallu**, Bosch Global Software Technologies GmbH, Germany
- **Estela Suarez**, Jülich Supercomputing Centre | University of Bonn, Germany

This year, the main track of ICCS registered 177 submissions, of which 59 were accepted as full papers, and 35 as short papers. There were on average 2.1 single-blind reviews per submission.

We would like to thank all committee members from the main track and workshops for their contribution to ensuring a high standard for the accepted papers. We would also like to thank *Springer, Elsevier,* and *Intellegibilis* for their support. Finally, we appreciate all the local organizing committee members for their hard work in preparing this conference.

We hope you enjoyed the conference and the beautiful city of Hamburg.

July 2026

Philipp Neumann
Michael J. Puma
Michael H. Lees
Derek Groen
Jack J. Dongarra
Peter M. A. Sloot

Organization

Program Committee - General Chair

Derek Groen — Brunel University of London, UK

Program Committee - Local Chair at DESY

Philipp Neumann — DESY|University of Hamburg, Germany

Program Committee – Main Track

Michael H. Lees — University of Amsterdam, The Netherlands
Michael J. Puma — Columbia University, USA

Program Committee – Chairs Emeritus

Peter M. A. Sloot — University of Amsterdam, The Netherlands
Jack J. Dongarra — University of Tennessee, USA

Sponsorship Chair

Alan Serrano — Brunel University of London, UK

Early Career Engagement Chair

Valeria Krzhizhanovskaya — University of Amsterdam, The Netherlands

Program Committee – Workshops on Computational Science - Chair

Maciej Paszynski — AGH University of Krakow, Poland

Program Committee – Workshops on Computational Science

Amanda S. Barnard   Australian National University, Australia
Yongjie Jessica Zhang   Carnegie Mellon University, USA

Reviewers

Nura Tijjani Abubakar   Brunel University of London, UK
Julen Alvarez-Aramberri   University of the Basque Country (UPV/EHU),
                               Spain
Faris Alwzinani   Brunel University of London, UK
Philipp Andelfinger   Nanyang Technological University, Singapore
Adrian Bekasiewicz   Gdańsk University of Technology, Poland
Philipp Birken   University of Lund, Sweden
Matthias Bolten   Bergische Universität Wuppertal, Germany
Kerstin Borras   DESY and RWTH Aachen University, Germany
Alexander Breuer   Friedrich Schiller University Jena, Germany
Nik Brouw   University of Amsterdam, Netherlands
Roland V. Bumbuc   University of Amsterdam, Netherlands
Pedro J. S. Cardoso   Universidade do Algarve, Portugal
Lock-Yue Chew   Nanyang Technological University, Singapore
Ana Cortes   Universitat Autònoma de Barcelona, Spain
Daan Crommelin   CWI Amsterdam, Netherlands
Carlo Cunha   Northern Arizona University, USA
Bartosz Czaplewski   Gdańsk University of Technology, Poland
Vitor Duarte   Universidade NOVA de Lisboa, Portugal
Mariusz Dzwonkowski   Medical University of Gdańsk, Poland
Nahid Emad   Paris-Saclay University, France
Roberto R. Expósito   Universidade da Coruna, CITIC, Spain
Christos Filelis-Papadopoulos Democritus University of Thrace, Greece
Ruy Freitas Reis   Universidade Federal de Juiz de Fora, Brazil
Wlodzimierz Funika   AGH University of Krakow, Poland
Paweł Gepner   Warsaw University of Technology, Poland
Alex Gerbessiotis   New Jersey Institute of Technology, USA
Maziar Ghorbani   Brunel University of London, UK
Konstantinos Giannoutakis   University of Macedonia, Greece
Jorge González-Domínguez   Universidade da Coruña, Spain
Michael Gowanlock   Northern Arizona University, USA
George Gravvanis   Democritus University of Thrace, Greece
Derek Groen   Brunel University of London, UK
Loïc Guégan   UiT the Arctic University of Norway, Norway

Sebastian Götschel	Hamburg University of Technology, Germany
Laura Harbach	Brunel University of London, UK
Philipp Heuser	DESY, Germany
Rafiazka Hilman	University of Amsterdam, Netherlands
Mladen Ivkovic	Durham University, UK
Alireza Jahani	Brunel University of London, UK
Piet Jarmatz	Helmut Schmidt University, Germany
Zhong Jin	Chinese Academy of Sciences, China
David Johnson	Uppsala University, Sweden
Christopher Kadow	German Climate Computing CenterDKRZ), Germany
Armin Kashefi	Brunel University of London, UK
Takahiro Katagiri	Nagoya University, Japan
Sotiris Kotsiantis	University of Patras, Greece
Sergey Kovalchuk	ITMO University, Russia
Sebastian Kuckuk	Friedrich-Alexander-Universität Erlangen-Nürnberg, Germany
Michael Kuhn	Otto von Guericke University Magdeburg, Germany
Jaeyoung Kwak	Nanyang Technological University, Singapore
Michael Lees	University of Amsterdam, Netherlands
Jacek A. Litka	Gdańsk University of Technology, Poland
Lukasz Madej	AGH University of Krakow, Poland
Tomas Margalef	Universitat Autònoma de Barcelona, Spain
Paula Martins	University of Algarve, Portugal
Pedro Medeiros	Universidade Nova de Lisboa, Portugal
Marianna Milano	Università Magna Graecia Catanzaro, Italy
Francisco J. Moreno-Barea	Universidad de Málaga, Spain
Leonid Moroz	Warsaw University of Technology, Poland
Matthias Möller	Delft University of Technology, Netherlands
Philipp Neumann	DESY and University of Hamburg, Germany
Marcin Paprzycki	IBS PAN and WSM, Poland
Anna Paszynska	Jagiellonian University, Poland
Maciej Paszynski	AGH University of Krakow, Poland
Alberto Perez de Alba Ortiz	University of Amsterdam, Netherlands
Dana Petcu	West University of Timisoara, Romania
Dirk Pleiter	University of Groningen|KTH Royal Institute of Technology, Netherlands | Sweden
Paweł Poczekajło	Koszalin University of Technology, Poland
Gary Polhill	James Hutton Institute, UK
Michael Puma	Columbia University, USA
Alexander Pyayt	EPAM Systems, Russia

Rick Quax	University of Amsterdam, Netherlands
Amir Raoofy	Leibniz Supercomputing Centre, Germany
Anne Reinarz	Durham University, UK
Sophie Robert	LIFO - Université d'Orléans, France
Daniel Rodriguez	University of Alcalá, Spain
Daniel Ruprecht	Technische Universität Hamburg, Germany
Bertil Schmidt	University of Mainz, Germany
Martin Schreiber	Université Grenoble Alpes/Inria/Laboratoire Jean-Kuntzmann, France
Joaquim Silva	Nova School of Science and Technology - NOVA LINCS, Portugal
Mateusz Sitko	AGH University of Krakow, Poland
Tomasz Sluzalec	AGH University of Krakow, Poland
Sucha Smanchat	King Mongkut's University of Technology, Thailand
Alexander Smirnovsky	Peter the Great St. Petersburg Polytechnic University, Russia
Maciej Smołka	AGH University of Krakow, Poland
Diana Suleimenova	Brunel University of London, UK
Wen Jun Tan	Nanyang Technological University, Singapore
Benjamin Uekermann	University of Stuttgart, Germany
Tobias Weinzierl	Durham University, UK
Lars Wienbrandt	Kiel University, Germany
Maciej Woźniak	AGH University of Krakow, Poland
Yani Xue	Brunel University of London, UK
Marcin Łoś	AGH University of Krakow, Poland

Contents

ICCS 2026 Main Track Short Papers

ICCS 2026 Main Track Full Papers

Hybrid Two-Dimensional Wildfire Growth Model for High Resolution Environments

Silvan Wiedmer[1,3]([✉]) [iD], Stefano Balestra[2,3] [iD], and Ralf-Peter Mundani[2,3] [iD]

[1] Swiss Institute for Information Science, Chur, Switzerland
`silvan.wiedmer@fhgr.ch`
[2] Institute for Data Analysis, Artificial Intelligence, Visualization and Simulation, Chur, Switzerland
[3] University of Applied Sciences of the Grisons, 7000 Chur, Switzerland

Abstract. This paper introduces a novel wildfire growth model designed for rapid, slope-driven wildfires in Switzerland. By combining raster- and vector-based approaches, the model leverages raster efficiency and vector prediction accuracy. As a result, the new model utilises high-resolution landscape data available in Switzerland, overcoming a key limitation of established wildfire simulation models. The proposed model builds on the raster-based Cell2Fire simulator, allowing direct comparison with the baseline in diverse landscapes. Comparisons against idealised reference fire perimeters show a significant F_1-Score improvement over the baseline, even with larger simulation time steps. These findings indicate that raster-based models can incorporate the proposed extension to improve predictions with minimal additional computational cost.

Keywords: Wildfire Simulation · Time of Arrival Computations · High Resolution Data

1 Introduction

The first half of 2025 has already seen multiple record-breaking wildfires in both the United States and parts of Asia. The Los Angeles fires caused at least 27 deaths, and resulted in an economic loss of more than 250 billion USD [16]. Wildfires in South Korea and Japan burned approximately 7778 hectares of forest, likely caused by exceptional meteorological conditions influenced by climate change [6]. In addition to those current events, there is also a clear increase in wildfires when compared to historical records. Canada, for example, experienced a significant increase in wildfires during 2023, which was primarily due to record-breaking temperatures throughout the year [3]. This tendency also increases the risk of severe wildfires in central Europe, which was traditionally considered a low-risk region for wildfires, demonstrating the need for fire management [13]. Switzerland too is experiencing a growing risk of wildfires, particularly in the Locarnese region (Canton Ticino, Switzerland) [1]. This increase in wildfire risk,

© The Author(s), under exclusive license to Springer Nature Switzerland AG 2026
P. Neumann et al. (Eds.): ICCS 2026, LNCS 16784, pp. 3–17, 2026.
https://doi.org/10.1007/978-3-032-29924-6_1

caused by climate change, is expected to increase the frequency of extreme fire events [4].

To minimize the potential damage caused by wildfires, reliable and operational wildfire simulations are essential for fire management actions and suppression strategies [21]. These simulations enable authorities to respond effectively by implementing preventive measures and deploying efficient real-time countermeasures to protect cities, wildlife, and suppress wildfires.

Since the behaviour of wildfires is largely dependent on the environment, wildfire simulation software, such as FARSITE [9] in the United States and Prometheus [20] in Canada, are highly specialized and parametrized towards their respective regions. This work investigates the advantages of wildfire simulation approaches based on high resolution data (as available in Switzerland, e.g.) and proposes a new simulation model to address specific regional requirements that are not met by existing well-established models.

Given the country's distinct environmental conditions and the availability of high-resolution datasets (cell resolutions of $0.5\,\mathrm{m} \times 0.5\,\mathrm{m}$), there is a clear need for a highly optimised model that maintains state-of-the-art accuracy. Although the model is designed with future parallelisation in mind to conform to the computational requirements, it is not yet parallelised. The results of this work have both theoretical and practical significance as the developed model provides a foundation for future wildfire simulations in Switzerland and contributes to ongoing research on hybrid modelling approaches.

The remainder of this paper reviews related work, describes the proposed model, presents the results, and concludes with a discussion.

2   Related Work

Various approaches exist for wildfire simulations. The extensive review by [17–19] showed that simulations intended for operational use are primarily done using specialized simulation models. Such models have existed for many years and have been applied in various environments. FARSITE, for example has been specifically designed for the United States and is generally regarded the state of the art in terms of fire perimeter accuracy [10]. The two common modelling strategies are raster- and vector-based approaches. Raster models are typically much faster than vector models, but are lacking in the accuracy domain. Therefore, newer models like Cell2Fire [14] and Pyros [21] try to combine these approaches to get a best-of-both-worlds approach, which offers comparable accuracy to vector models with much improved simulation efficiency.

When it comes to wildfire simulations, there is a clear distinction between wildfire behaviour and wildfire growth modelling, with the latter being the focus of this work. It has to be noted that wildfire propagation is sometimes used as a synonym for fire growth in the literature, whereas fire spread may substitute fire behaviour. Fire behaviour refers to models that calculate the Rate of Spread (ROS) as well as the fire intensity, based on homogeneous landscape and weather conditions. The ROS defines how fast the fire front moves in a particular direction and has the unit [m/min] [2,9]. Specifically, these metrics are calculated mainly based on both fuel type and moisture, wind velocity, and slope [14]. Fire growth models, on the other hand, use the homogeneous fire behaviour predictions and grow the fire perimeter over heterogeneous landscapes including terrain, fuel and weather changes [11]. These models commonly rely on the assumption that the fire front of two-dimensional fires can be represented as an ellipse when all factors affecting fire behaviour are spatially and temporally constant (homogeneous) [9].

The complex three-dimensional process of wildfires is represented by the use of multiple fire behaviour models [9]. These models independently describe surface fire, crown fire, spotting, and rate of spread acceleration. Surface fires burn up fuels in contact with the ground like grass, shrubs, or downed wooden fuels, while crown fires describe the combustion of tree canopies. Another important phenomenon is spotting, which can rapidly advance wildfires by igniting new fires well ahead of the current fire perimeter. It is caused by firebrands transported by the wind, travelling many kilometres and even crossing firebreaks. Lastly, fire acceleration describes the rate at which the ROS of the fire front can adjust to new environmental conditions.

Evaluating wildfire simulations remains challenging as the use of an experimentally validated Rate of Spread (ROS) model does not inherently ensure the validity of the resulting fire perimeter [5]. To address this, many authors, such as [15,21], tend to incorporate idealised and historical fires for model evaluation. The simulation result is often represented as a binary raster grid, allowing cell-wise comparison with reference data in a confusion matrix framework [14,21]. In the context of operational wildfire management, type II errors are considered more critical than type I errors, as they represent burned areas that were not predicted as such [21].

The overview of key wildfire growth models highlights two important aspects. First, the well-established vector models, FARSITE and Prometheus, remain widely used due to their state-of-the-art accuracy [10]. Second, newer models such as Cell2Fire and Pyros tend to use raster-based or hybrid approaches to achieve significantly faster computational times while maintaining fire perimeter accuracy comparable to FARSITE and Prometheus. Here, it is important to note that the use of local elliptical spread, as used by Cell2Fire, does not make the model a hybrid approach, as the model propagates the fire using local neighbourhood rules and exports the final fire perimeter in raster format.

The current literature suggests that raster-based and hybrid models are the most viable options to meet the computational demands required by faster than real-time simulation in high resolution environments. These models demonstrate significant performance improvements over the traditional vector models FARSITE and Prometheus while maintaining comparable accuracy. Notably, both Pyros and Cell2Fire simulate fire spread using elliptical shapes but represent the final fire perimeter using raster cells. In Pyros, each fire agent expands its ellipse across multiple cells, which assumes uniform environmental conditions during a single time step. To satisfy this assumption in heterogeneous environments, the time step must be reduced so that the fire spread only occurs in homogeneous conditions. This constrains the spread to local neighbourhoods, similar to Cell2Fire, and therefore reduces the benefits of the hybrid approach implemented in Pyros, particularly in high-resolution, heterogeneous environments.

3   Implementation

The simulation model developed in this work excludes fire behaviour models other than surface fires, suppression activities, and the incorporation of weather data. As Pyros already uses a hybrid approach determined to be non-optimal for high resolution environments, the Cell2Fire model serves as basis for model development. This allows for a direct assessment of the computational overhead created by the new model as well as possible accuracy improvements.

3.1   Reference Simulation Model

The baseline model uses an elliptical spread which is calculated in each timestep based on the fire behaviour and the time since cell ignition. When this ellipse reaches the centre of a cell in its Moore neighbourhood it ignites it (see Fig. 1). To ignite a cell, its state is changed from *Available* to *Burning*. Next to that there are also states for *Burned*, *Treated*, and *NonFuel*.

To verify the re-implementation of the model, we performed a plausibility check against idealized fire scenarios. Our results demonstrated a high degree of convergence with other raster-based simulators found in the literature across both flat and sloped terrain [15].

3.2   Model Development

Both Cell2Fire and Pyros propagate the fire front using some form of vector approach, but they still represent the final perimeter in the raster format. Depending on the size of a cell, there is the potential to incorrectly classify a relatively large area especially when using cells of $25\,\mathrm{m} \times 25\,\mathrm{m}$, which is generally used by operational models [9,20,21]. Therefore, the idea of the new hybrid approach is to extract the vector-based fire front from the local spread ellipses when exporting the fire perimeter. This is done at the end of the simulation or at user-specified export intervals (for visualisation of intermediate time steps) and does not change the propagation logic.

While this extension helps to improve the accuracy of the fire perimeter, it does not entail large computational overhead. As the spread is still based on the local ellipse as used in Cell2Fire, there is no need for the expensive crossover removal used in vector models like FARSITE, thus avoiding one of the main weaknesses of the vector based approach [9,15].

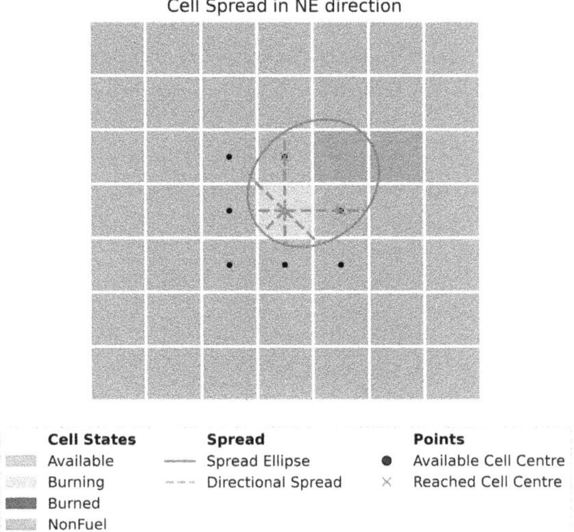

Fig. 1. Local Cell-to-Cell propagation in the north-east (45°) direction, as proposed by [14]. Each burning cell expands a local fire spread ellipse and checks if the cell centres of the *Available* cells in its Moore neighbourhood are within this ellipse. If so, the cell gets ignited in the next time step.

Vector Front Extraction (V1). The idea for the first version of the model (V1) is to store the directional spread distance for each burning cell during simulation. Since this value must be computed for each burning cell in every iteration, the already calculated spread distances are stored in a one-dimensional vector for each cell. Since the fire can spread from a single cell to every cell in its Moore neighbourhood, the vector has eight entries.

To get the fire perimeter, the simulation must first find the edge of the fire front. This is done by looping over all the available cells in the simulation grid and checking if the cell has at least one neighbouring cell which has the state *Burning*. By looping over all edge cells, the previously stored directional spread distances can be extracted from cells that are *Burning*. The extracted point can then be used to create the vector fire perimeter.

Exact Time of Arrival Calculation (V2). During the development of Version 1, the possibility of a further improvement was found which uses the stored spread distances to optimise the local propagation rules. In V1, the fire spread ellipse of a cell is determined by calculating the cells ROS and multiplying it by the time the cell has been burning for. This burning time is calculated by subtracting the ignition time from the current simulation time. The issue with this approach is that the ignition time is set to the next time step, even when the actual ignition is closer to the previous iteration. This results in the fire spread ellipse of the newly ignited cell being too small in every case except an exact match between the directional spread and the cell distance. The idea of this optimisation is that the model can achieve the same accuracy as before while using much larger time steps, potentially reducing execution time.

As both the distance to each cell and the directional spread are calculated to check whether the fire has reached a cell centre, it can also be used to calculate the exact time of arrival of the fire in the cell centre and use this time as the actual ignition time of the first ignition. Using the directional spread distance and dividing it by the time step size returns the ROS for the spread along this axis. The ignition time t_{ign} is then calculated using the following equation

$$t_{ign} = t + \frac{d}{ROS} \tag{1}$$

where t represents the ignition time of the cell that is currently burning, d the distance between the cells, and ROS the directional spread rate calculated beforehand.

Vector Fire Perimeter. The raster-based perimeter points must be converted into a vector fire perimeter. A simple approach is to use the convex hull of the spread-direction points from the edge cells. This is however only valid for idealised cases with a single fire in a uniform, unobstructed landscape. Real fire perimeters are often concave due to obstacles and may contain non burnable islands (see Fig. 2b).

To solve this, a new approach is developed relying on a sub-cell-level raster implementation. The idea is that each edge cell creates a convex hull within itself, using the directional spread points from its neighbours as well as the cell boundary points (see Fig. 2a). Then, the newly generated geometries are rasterized at sub-cell resolution, setting the state of all touched sub-cells to *Burning*. The vector perimeter can now be exported from the sub-cell resolution grid using the contours of the features (cells that are either *Burning* or *Burned* are *ones* and everything else *zeros*) in the landscape (see Fig. 2b).

4   Results

In the following, we present first results obtained with our new simulation model. The simulations were conducted on a 2023 M3 Pro Mac Book Pro with 36 Gb of Unified Memory. Since type II errors are critical for operational fire management [21], recall is used for type II error assessment, precision for type I errors, and the F_1-Score to quantify the overall similarity between two fire perimeters.

4.1   Idealised Fires

For evaluation, both the baseline and developed models are first compared to idealised fire scenarios including circular fire spread and slope driven spread. These scenarios, using homogeneous wildfire spread ellipses, are defined on a 100×100 cells simulation grid with a cell size of 30×30 m. To ensure the gains

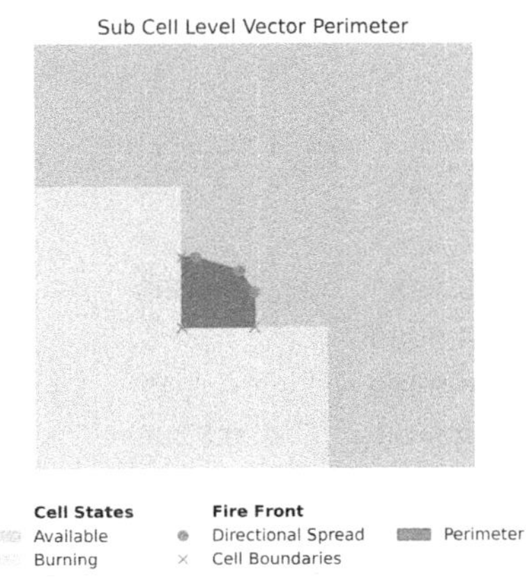

Sub Cell Level Vector Perimeter

(a) Cell based vector fire front.

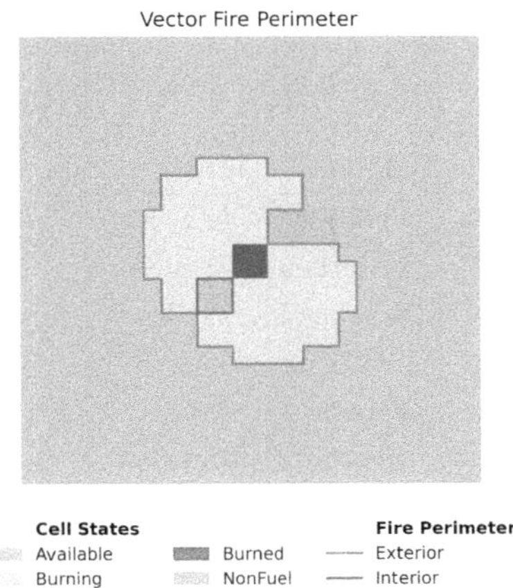

Vector Fire Perimeter

(b) Vector Representation of raster based fire front.

Fig. 2. Vector fire perimeter calculation using the sub-cell level raster implementation. Each cell calculates a local convex hull around its interior spread points (a) and rasterises the result on a sub-cell level grid. The resulting fire perimeter (b) is represented both in raster format and can be exported as a vector using the contours of the raster perimeter.

from the vector-based perimeter are measurable, the evaluation grid is set to a resolution of 200×200 cells, which splits the original cells into four new cells. The F_1-Score, precision, and recall scores for the three models are listed in Table 1.

The results show that V2 achieves substantially higher recall than both the baseline and V1, while precision remains comparable across models. This suggests a slight over-prediction of the fire perimeter, but an overall improvement, as the new model misses fewer actively burning cells and misclassifies fewer non-burning cells. Overall, V2 outperforms the original Cell2Fire implementation in both scenarios. The F_1-Score differs markedly between simulations with and without slope, and while incorporating the vector perimeter in V1 yields minor gains over the baseline, the main performance improvements come from the exact time-of-arrival calculation.

4.2 Parameter Studies

The results on idealised fire scenarios show a small part of the model performance. To assess how time step size affects prediction accuracy and how perimeter export frequency impacts execution time a parameter study is included.

Time Step Size. Similar to the Courant-Friedrichs-Lewy (CFL) condition in computational fluid dynamics, a restriction is placed on the time step size such that the simulation does not advance further than its adjacent cells per time

Table 1. Evaluation scores for the different models on idealised fire scenarios (with and without slope). The simulation time was set to 50 min, with a time step size Δt of 60 s and a ROS value of 10 m/min.

Model	Idealized Fire	F1 Score	Precision Score	Recall Score
Cell2Fire	No Slope	0.8725	0.9950	0.7769
Version 1	No Slope	0.8752	0.9985	0.7790
Version 2	No Slope	**0.9486**	**0.9987**	**0.9032**
Cell2Fire	Slope	0.7493	**0.9989**	0.5995
Version 1	Slope	0.7493	**0.9989**	0.5995
Version 2	Slope	**0.9025**	0.9893	**0.8298**

step. Although the time step size of 60 s does not break this restriction enforced by Cell2Fire, it could still be considered coarse, as there are only three time steps required to reach the centre of a cell in the Neumann neighbourhood when assuming circular spread. Figure 3 presents the time step parameter study for both slope and no-slope scenarios.

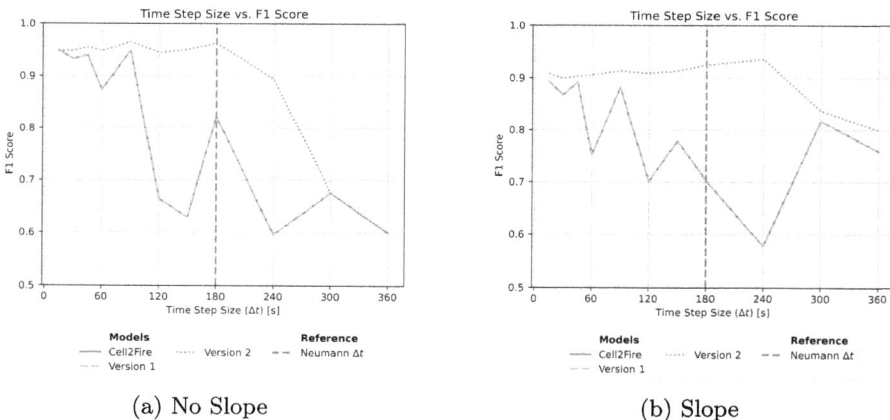

(a) No Slope
(b) Slope

Fig. 3. Time step size parameter study on idealised fires without slope (a) and with slope (b), using time step sizes ranging from 15 to 360 s. The study used a fixed ROS value of 10 m/min and a constant grid resolution of 30 m. The red vertical line indicates the time step at which the fire reaches the centre of the Neumann Neighbourhood cells within a single time step when using circular spread. (Color figure online)

As the extension of the baseline model is designed for large time steps, it is to be expected that all three models perform similar when using a small time step size regardless of the scenario. Taking a closer look at the fire perimeters simulated by the parameter study reveals some interesting insights.

All models fail to create a circular shape on flat terrain when the time step size is 240 s or greater. The Cell2Fire reference implementation and V1 are however much worse at predicting both the shape and size of the circle than V2. This is due to the time of arrival approach correcting for the error caused by the coarse time step. When using small time steps on sloped terrain, all model predictions are similar in size and shape, while the additional vector-front of the newer models seems to over-predict the backing fire. This problem of the vector-front remains for all the tested time steps, which is in agreement with the slightly lower precision scores shown in Table 1.

The results show that V2 is much better at predicting a perimeter shape close to the expected shape. All models suffer from the perimeter distortions due to limited spread directions which is known to be a significant challenge for raster-based models [21]. Finally, the new model can achieve accuracy comparable to the base model while using larger time steps, which can drastically improve the computational time required. The results further support the findings from the scores in Table 1 that the use of only the vector front does not drastically improve accuracy.

Execution Time. The impact of the new model adaptation in regard to execution time was also assessed. As the vector-based fire perimeter must be calculated from the current state of the raster-based spread, it is expected to impact performance based on the number of exports to be made. It should be noted that the model is not extensively optimised for sequential execution speed.

The study was conducted by running multiple simulations per model and altering the time between each export. The run-time of the baseline model remains relatively constant, showing only a slight increase in simulation time. This result is expected, as the model can simply store the simulation grid without any further processing. Both versions, V1 and V2 can have a negative performance impact in comparison to the baseline model but this solemnly depends on the user-defined export interval.

4.3   Reference Model

To evaluate the model under heterogeneous conditions, it is tested against FARSITE using a simplified scenario. To do so a new idealised wildfire scenario is created with no slope, where a small area of fuel is set to a different type from the rest resulting in a concave shape. Other influence factors such as wind and point source fire acceleration are turned off in FARSITE for this comparison. It should be noted that FARSITE was used as part of the FlamMap software package [12] for this evaluation.

Even after turning off these relevant features, such as wind, and point source fire acceleration, the simulation using the same value for simulation time (t) resulted in a fire perimeter much bigger than the perimeter predicted by FARSITE. This suggests that the previous adjustments made to ensure comparability are insufficient for an exact match between the models. Therefore the simulation time was set to a value that approximately matches the size of the reference shape and the results are only assessed visually.

The inspection of the resulting perimeters (Fig. 4) show the perimeter distortions of both models when compared to FARSITE. However, V2 is much closer in the general shape of the fire than the Cell2Fire implementation.

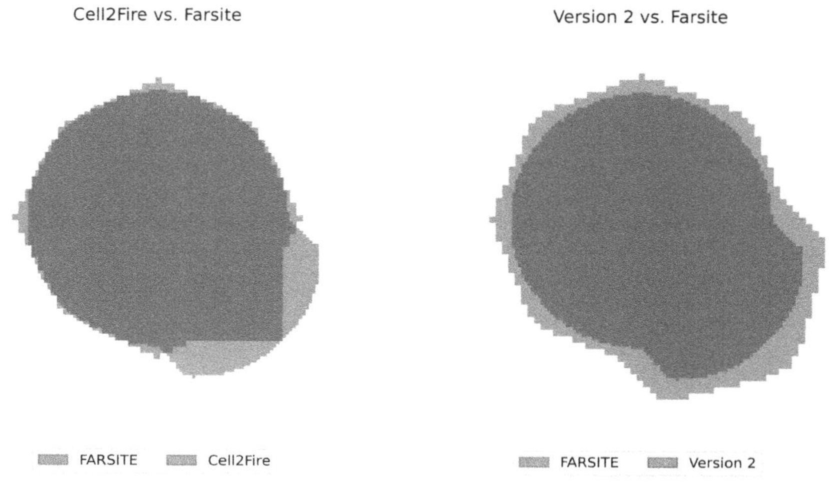

(a) Cell2Fire fire perimeter comparison against FARSITE

(b) V2 fire perimeter comparison against FARSITE

Fig. 4. Comparison of Cell2Fire (a) and V2 (b) to FARSITE on heterogeneous fuels. The landscape has no slope, and wind is not included.

4.4 Proof of Concept Simulation

The proof of concept simulation was run on real data to show the general performance of the model without optimization. The landscape used for this simulation consists of a single *swissALTI3D* [8] chunk with an area of 1×1 km and a cell resolution of 0.5 m, resulting in a 2000×2000 cell simulation grid. The according forest mix rate [7], which is used to determine which cells are capable of burning, can be seen in Fig. 5a.

As it has been found to perform best, Version 2 was used for this simulation. Simulating the fire for $t = 6$ h took 195 s ≈ 3.25 min on the specified hardware, while only exporting after the simulation has finished. Figure 5b shows the result of the proof of concept simulation.

5 Discussion

The results show that V2 significantly outperforms the baseline and V1 when tested under ideal conditions. This improvement is mostly attributed to the

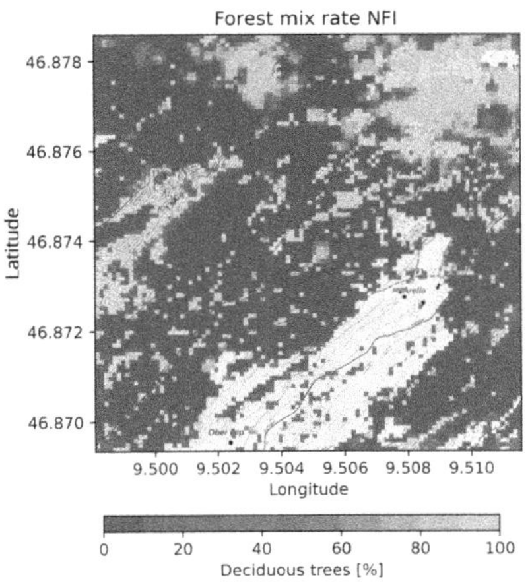

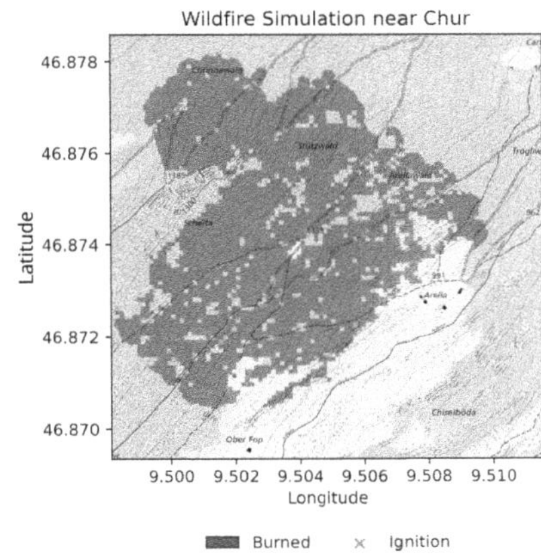

(a) Forest mix rate around Chur, Switzerland

(b) Proof of concept simulation around Chur, Switzerland

Fig. 5. The forest mix rate (a) and the result of the proof of concept simulation (b) around Chur, Switzerland.

exact time of arrival calculation in the local propagation logic. Version 2 also performs significantly better in matching the shape and size of the expected fire perimeter, which results in a higher recall score, especially important for wildfire simulation models [21]. In addition, the model remains stable in the F_1-Score metric, when the time step size is increased, allowing the model to use much coarser time steps while achieving similar results to the baseline model. While model performance scales with the user-defined export frequency, the computational overhead remains manageable because expensive perimeter calculations are triggered only during export events.

This study showed that the novel extraction of a vector perimeter from local fire spread ellipses can improve the accuracy of raster-based simulators. To the best of the authors knowledge, this is the first hybrid model that extracts the vector-based perimeter from the raster-based simulation in addition to the exact time of arrival calculation, while preserving parallelisability. Although the perimeter extraction alone does not improve the results significantly, the combination with the calculation of the exact time of arrival leads to much better results. Crucially, these advances are achieved without breaking the inherent parallelisability of raster-based simulations, while further avoiding complex vector-based crossover removals.

5.1 Interpretation and Implications

The work confirms the conclusion reached by [21] about the effectiveness of the hybrid approach. They found that their hybrid model achieved both promising accuracy as well as the computational performance required for faster-than-real-time simulations in the operational context.

After a careful review of the original paper and source code of Cell2Fire, it seems that the model does not use an exact time of arrival calculation similar to this work, but instead relies on small time steps to achieve state-of-the-art accuracy of over 90%. This aligns with the conducted time step parameter study, which showed that the models perform similar on small time step sizes.

These results have both theoretical and practical implications. It is shown, that existing models can be extended to be using the calculation of the exact time of arrival. As this extension has the possibility to drastically improve the time step size required for accurate simulations, it also has implications for practical use. The model achieves faster-than-real-time performance on a 2000×2000 grid using a single-threaded implementation on consumer-grade hardware. Scalability tests on the same hardware demonstrate that a 7-day wildfire event can be simulated in less than real-time even on 10000×10000 grid [in 24 min] and 20000×20000 grid [in 40 min]. Beyond these dimensions, performance was limited by available RAM and storage capacity rather than computational throughput. The current implementation has not been extensively optimized for sequential execution nor parallelized. These results highlight the significant potential for even greater acceleration in an optimized or parallelized version of the approach.

5.2   Limitations

The scope of this research excluded many different wildfire growth features, which would be required for operational simulations. This includes the integration of different fire behaviour models apart from surface fires, the inclusion of suppression activities, and the effects of weather. The combination of these limitations excludes the developed model from being used apart from experimental studies, and also makes evaluating the model performance with real-world scenarios a difficult task.

The choice of expanding an existing model resulted in better comparability and faster development, but it also includes the assumptions of the extended Cell2Fire model. The assumption that may affect the results of this study the most is that the ROS values of the burning cell are used until the fire reaches the centre of the neighbouring cells [14]. This can result in distorted perimeters, especially when using cell resolutions of 25 m.

The new model performs particularly well when using large time step sizes. This assumes, however, that all the environmental influences on fire behaviour (except fuel model) remain constant during this time step. This results in a situation where wildfires in fast-changing weather environments can only benefit from the exact time of arrival calculation when the fire can spread to a neighbouring cell during constant weather influences. Consequently, the model reverts to the Cell2Fire functionality due to smaller time steps required. Besides that, the model continues to exhibit clear distortions along the flanks of the fire perimeter, highlighting opportunities for further improvement.

Other limitations include the lack of a direct comparison with FARSITE in realistic wildfires, which is essential for building trust in the model [15].

Despite these limitations, the results still remain valid. Furthermore, the issues related to the assumption that fire spread depends solely on the current cell environment, as well as the need to reduce time step size due to rapidly changing weather conditions, are less critical within high resolution environments.

5.3 Future Work

To transition the current model into a robust operational tool, several functional extensions are planned. These include integrating more detailed surface fire behaviour models, accounting for crown fire transitions and spotting phenomena, and coupling the system with dynamic weather data. Furthermore, we aim to incorporate the specialized burned cell conditions utilized in Cell2Fire. Beyond these practical considerations, future research will explore the structural advantages of the Pyros architecture. A key distinction of Pyros is the use of vector-based ignition points rather than fixed cell centres. Expanding this feature would allow the model to bypass the limited spread directions inherent in traditional raster-based simulators, potentially enhancing accuracy without sacrificing the efficiency of the underlying grid. Finally, while the current implementation demonstrates strong sequential performance, parallelization of the propagation logic will be explored to enable even faster simulations.

5.4 Conclusion

A new hybrid wildfire growth model tailored to the environmental conditions found in Switzerland was developed. By extending the already performant Cell2Fire model, the new model significantly improved the fire perimeter predictions on idealized fires, while allowing for much larger time step sizes with minimal accuracy loss.

Although the current model excludes several critical features such as crown fire behaviour, spotting, suppression activities, and weather coupling, it still provides a foundation for further development of wildfire modelling in Switzerland.

Looking forward, the integration of the excluded features describes the most critical part, next to the implementation of parallel computation techniques, to make the model not only usable but future proof. Given the rising threat of wildfires in Switzerland this work represents a crucial step in providing the computational resources required to support effective decision-making and management strategies for Swiss authorities.

References

1. Bardsley, A.M., Bardsley, D.K., Conedera, M., Pütz, M., Robinson, G.M., Weber, D.: Wildfire, environmental risk and deliberative planning in the Locarnese region of Switzerland. Environ. Manage. **68**(6), 785–801 (2021). https://doi.org/10.1007/s00267-021-01523-5

2. Byram, G.M.: Combustion of forest fuels. In: Davis, K.P. (ed.) Forest Fire: Control and Use, pp. 61–89. McGraw-Hill, New York, NY (1959)

3. Chen, H., Zhang, W., Sheng, L.: Canadian record-breaking wildfires in 2023 and their impact on US air quality. Atmos. Environ. **342**, 120941 (Feb 2025). https://doi.org/10.1016/j.atmosenv.2024.120941, https://www.sciencedirect.com/science/article/pii/S1352231024006162

4. Conedera, M., Feusi, J., Pezzatti, G.B., Krebs, P.: Linking the future likelihood of large fires to occur on mountain slopes with fuel connectivity and topography. Nat. Hazards **120**(5), 4657–4673 (2024). https://doi.org/10.1007/s11069-023-06395-y

5. Duff, T.J., Chong, D.M., Tolhurst, K.G.: Indices for the evaluation of wildfire spread simulations using contemporaneous predictions and observations of burnt area. Environ. Modell. Softw. **83**, 276–285 (Sep 2016). https://doi.org/10.1016/j.envsoft.2016.05.005, https://www.sciencedirect.com/science/article/pii/S1364815216301360

6. Faranda, D., Alvarez-Castro, M.C., Alberti, T., Cazzaniga, G.: March 2025 Japan and South Korea wildfires have been fueled by meteorological conditions likely strengthened by human-driven climate change (Mar 2025). https://doi.org/10.5281/zenodo.15083384

7. Federal Office for the Environment FOEN: Forest mix rate NFI (Oct 2023). https://www.geocat.ch/geonetwork/srv/eng/catalog.search#/metadata/b07a4589-159b-4c3a-b1e7-dbdad11f7e62

8. Federal Office of Topography swisstopo: swissALTI3D (Aug 2024). https://www.swisstopo.admin.ch/de/hoehenmodell-swissalti3d

9. Finney, M.A.: FARSITE: Fire Area Simulator-model development and evaluation. Tech. rep., U.S. Department of Agriculture, Forest Service, Rocky Mountain Research Station (1998). https://doi.org/10.2737/rmrs-rp-4, http://dx.doi.org/10.2737/RMRS-RP-4

10. Papadopoulos, G.D., Pavlidou, F.-N.: A comparative review on wildfire simulators. IEEE Syst. J. **5**(2), 233–243 (2011). https://doi.org/10.1109/JSYST.2011.2125230

11. Ghisu, T., Arca, B., Pellizzaro, G., Duce, P.: An optimal cellular automata algorithm for simulating wildfire spread. Environ. Modell. Softw. **71**, 1–14 (Sep 2015). https://doi.org/10.1016/j.envsoft.2015.05.001, https://www.sciencedirect.com/science/article/pii/S1364815215001322

12. Finney, M., McHugh, C.: FlamMap (Aug 2024). https://research.fs.usda.gov/firelab/products/dataandtools/flammap, computer Software, Version 6.2

13. Miller, J., Böhnisch, A., Ludwig, R., Brunner, M.I.: Climate change impacts on regional fire weather in heterogeneous landscapes of central Europe. Natural Hazards Earth Syst. Sci. **24**(2), 411–428 (2024). https://doi.org/10.5194/nhess-24-411-2024, https://nhess.copernicus.org/articles/24/411/2024/

14. Pais, C., Carrasco, J., Martell, D.L., Weintraub, A., Woodruff, D.L.: Cell2Fire: a cell-based forest fire growth model to support strategic landscape management planning. Front. Forests Global Change **4** (2021). https://www.frontiersin.org/journals/forests-and-global-change/articles/10.3389/ffgc.2021.692706

15. Peterson, S.H., et al.: Using HFire for spatial modeling of fire in shrublands. Tech. rep., U.S. Department of Agriculture, Forest Service, Pacific Southwest Research Station (2009). https://doi.org/10.2737/psw-rp-259
16. Qiu, M., Chen, D., Kelp, M., Li, J., Huang, G., Yazdi, M.D.: The rising threats of wildland-urban interface fires in the era of climate change: The Los Angeles 2025 fires. The Innovation **6**(5) (May 2025). https://doi.org/10.1016/j.xinn.2025.100835, publisher: Elsevier
17. Sullivan, A.L.: Wildland surface fire spread modelling, 1990-2007. 1: Physical and quasi-physical models. Int. J. Wildland Fire **18**(4), 349–368 (2009). https://doi.org/10.1071/WF06143
18. Sullivan, A.L.: Wildland surface fire spread modelling, 1990-2007. 2: Empirical and quasi-empirical models. Int. J. Wildland Fire **18**(4), 369–386 (2009). https://doi.org/10.1071/WF06142
19. Sullivan, A.L.: Wildland surface fire spread modelling, 1990-2007. 3: Simulation and mathematical analogue models. Int. J. Wildland Fire **18**(4), 387–403 (2009). https://doi.org/10.1071/WF06144
20. Tymstra, C., Bryce, R., Wotton, B., Taylor, S., Armitage, O.: Development and structure of Prometheus: the Canadian wildland fire growth simulation model. Natural Resources Canada, Canadian Forest Service, Northern Forestry Centre, Information Report NOR-X-417.(Edmonton, AB) (2010)
21. Voltolina, D., Cappellini, G., Apuani, T., Sterlacchini, S.: Pyros: a raster–vector spatial simulation model for predicting wildland surface fire spread and growth. Int. J. Wildland Fire **33**(3) (2024). https://doi.org/10.1071/WF22142

Comparative Study of Numerical Analysis and Wind Tunnel Experiments on the Flight Behavior of a Quadcopter Drone Under Disturbance Winds

Kaisei Nomura[1]([✉]) [iD], Ayato Takii[2] [iD], Masashi Yamakawa[1,3,4] [iD], Yusei Kobayashi[1,4] [iD], Takahiro Ikeda[3,4] [iD], Shinichi Asao[5] [iD], and Seiichi Takeuchi[5]

[1] Kyoto Institute of Technology, Matsugasaki, Sakyo-ku, Kyoto 606-8585, Japan
kaikai6262nom.you@gmail.com
[2] Kobe University, 1-1, Rokkodai-cho, Nada-ku, Kobe 657-8501, Hyogo, Japan
[3] Center for the Possible Futures, Kyoto Institute of Technology, Matsugasaki, Sakyo-ku, Kyoto 606-8585, Japan
[4] High-Performance Simulation Research Center, Kyoto Institute of Technology, Matsugasaki, Sakyo-ku, Kyoto 606-8585, Japan
[5] College of Industrial Technology, 1-27-1, Amagasaki, Hyogo 661-0047, Japan

Abstract. This study presents a computationally efficient framework for early-stage design evaluation of next-generation air mobility systems. A coupled fluid–rigid body motion analysis combining the Moving Computational Domain (MCD) method with a multi-axis sliding mesh technique was quantitatively validated against wind tunnel experiments of a quadcopter subjected to frontal disturbance winds. An inviscid fluid formulation was employed while preserving dynamic motion coupling. The results demonstrate that the predicted pitch angle under disturbance winds (0–5 m/s) agreed with experimental measurements within a maximum error of $1.56°$, accurately reproducing the aircraft's dynamic equilibrium response. Rotor rotational speeds were predicted with an average relative error of approximately 10%, and their variation with wind velocity exhibited strong correlation with experimental trends. These findings confirm that the proposed framework provides practical predictive capability with significantly reduced computational cost, making it suitable for rapid behavior assessment during early design stages. The present study represents a step toward the realization of a scalable physics-based digital twin for multirotor aircraft. Future work will focus on improving rotor thrust prediction accuracy through refined geometric modeling.

Keywords: CFD · Quadcopter Drone · Flying Car · Validation

1 Introduction

In recent years, the development of flying cars (eVTOLs) and unmanned aerial vehicles (UAVs) equipped with multiple rotors has accelerated worldwide as next-generation air mobility solutions aimed at addressing serious societal challenges such as urban traffic

P. Neumann et al. (Eds.): ICCS 2026, LNCS 16784, pp. 18–33, 2026.
https://doi.org/10.1007/978-3-032-29924-6_2

congestion and aging infrastructure [1]. These vehicles are anticipated as new transportation systems utilizing near-ground airspace that has not traditionally been used by conventional aircraft. However, because they operate at low altitudes in close proximity to people, they require an extremely high level of safety exceeding that of existing aircraft. The development of new airframe designs and control systems entails enormous costs and time. Consequently, computational fluid dynamics (CFD) simulations are expected to play a crucial role in reducing risks and improving efficiency during the early stages of the development cycle.

Research on the aerodynamic characteristics of multirotor aircraft has progressed through multifaceted approaches. Previous studies have covered a wide range of topics, from evaluating the characteristics of individual rotors [2, 3] to investigating ground effects [4] and the influence of interference flows on vehicle stability [5]. In this context, our research group proposed the concept of a "digital flying car" [6] and has conducted studies aimed at reproducing high-fidelity flight phenomena in a virtual environment. Specifically, we have investigated the effects of takeoff downwash on the ground [7], turning maneuvers [8], and aircraft behavior during propeller failure emergencies [9], based on assumed flight dynamics of a flying car. Furthermore, to address wind disturbances encountered in real-world operations, forward and turning flight simulations under strong wind conditions were performed [10], demonstrating the impact of wind on aircraft behavior.

However, these studies have primarily focused on comparisons within numerical simulations and on understanding the behavior of idealized models. Direct validation of the numerical methods through comparison with detailed experimental data obtained from actual aircraft has not yet been conducted. In particular, small quadcopters have relatively low inertia compared to large aircraft and are therefore highly susceptible to external wind disturbances [11]. Clarifying the mechanisms of attitude recovery and control response to such disturbances in small aircraft provides a fundamental basis for safety assessments when scaling up to flying cars in the future, as both share the common flight principle of multi-rotor configurations. Therefore, reproducing realistic flight conditions within the computational domain without constraining the airframe and elucidating the overall system behavior remains a critical challenge in next-generation mobility development.

Accordingly, this study performed numerical flight simulations using an inviscid fluid model. Although inviscid calculations have been reported to show good agreement with experimental data within a certain high angle-of-attack range during early-stage aerodynamic evaluations of aircraft [12], the validity of the inviscid approximation under dynamic flight conditions of multirotor aircraft, which are characterized by complex rotor–rotor interactions and abrupt attitude changes, requires further verification. To address this complex moving boundary problem, a numerical framework combining the Moving Computational Domain (MCD) method [13], based on an unstructured moving-grid finite volume method [14], with a multi-axis sliding mesh method [15] was adopted. The MCD method strictly satisfies geometric conservation laws while avoiding grid failure associated with large aircraft attitude changes, making it suitable for describing large-amplitude motions. Furthermore, the simulations were performed in a parallel computing environment using unstructured grids [16]. The originality of this study lies in the first quantitative validation of the proposed analytical method. This was accomplished by comparing the dynamic response of the entire system, in which the aircraft autonomously adjusts its attitude to reach an equilibrium state under external wind disturbances, with wind tunnel experimental results obtained using an actual aircraft, while inheriting the analytical framework established in previous studies. For validation, an experimental aircraft installed in a wind tunnel was used to precisely measure the propeller rotational speeds and aircraft attitude angles while maintaining hover against frontal disturbance winds. In the simulations, identical external wind speed conditions were imposed. By comparing the numerical predictions of the aircraft response with the experimental data, the prediction accuracy of the method and the associated sources of error were evaluated. This approach represents a pioneering step toward establishing a practical digital twin capable of reproducing the dynamic behavior of real aircraft in a virtual environment, thereby contributing to reduced design time and enhanced reliability.

2 Experimental Overview

2.1 Test Aircraft

The experiments were conducted using ACSL's small aerial photography drone "SOTEN" [17]. The main specifications of the aircraft are summarized in Table 1. With the battery and all onboard sensors installed, the total takeoff weight of the aircraft is 1.72 kg, and its external dimensions with the arms extended are 0.560 m × 0.637 m. In this study, the direction corresponding to the 0.560 m dimension was defined as the forward direction of the aircraft for both the experiments and the numerical analysis. The propulsion system adopts a quadcopter configuration equipped with four 10.5-in. propellers. Flight data were acquired using the onboard measurement system. An exterior view of the aircraft is presented in Fig. 1.

Table 1. SOTEN specifications

Total aircraft weight	1.72 kg
Aircraft sizes(x,y,z)	0.560 m, 0.153 m, 0.637 m
Propeller size	10.5 in. (0.2667 m)
Number of propeller blades	2
Number of propellers	4

2.2 Definition of Coordinate Systems and Aircraft Configuration

Figure 2 illustrates the coordinate system and aircraft configuration definitions consistently used throughout the experiments and numerical analyses in this study. A right-handed coordinate system is adopted, with the aircraft center of gravity as the origin,

Fig. 1. Appearance of SOTEN

the forward direction as the x-axis, the vertically upward direction as the y-axis, and the right-wing direction as the z-axis. The definitions of positive and negative rotation angles about each axis are as follows:

- Roll angle: Rotation about the x-axis. When viewed from the rear of the aircraft, a downward deflection of the right wing is defined as positive, and that of the left wing as negative.
- Pitch angle: Rotation about the z-axis. The horizontal attitude is defined as $0°$, with nose-up rotation taken as positive and nose-down rotation as negative.
- Yaw angle: Rotation about the y-axis. When viewed from above, clockwise rotation is defined as positive and counterclockwise rotation as negative.

In addition, the arrangement and rotational directions of the four propellers are defined. The propellers located at the front right and rear left positions (Rotors 1 and 3) rotate counterclockwise (CCW) when viewed from above, whereas those at the front left and rear right positions (Rotors 2 and 4) rotate clockwise (CW).

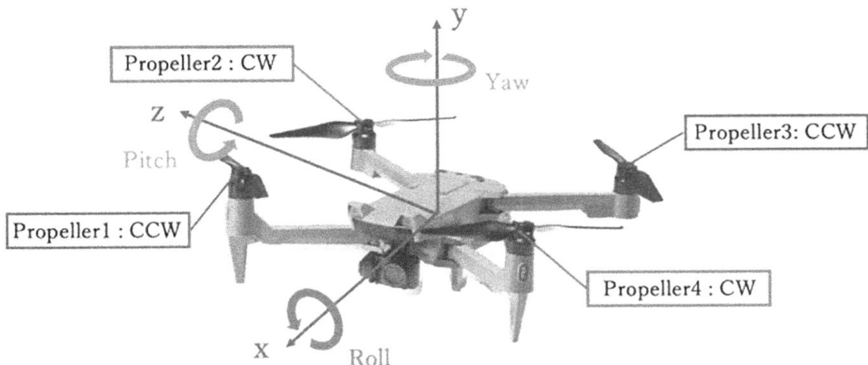

Fig. 2. Coordinate system and aircraft and propeller rotation directions

2.3 Wind Tunnel Facility

This experiment was conducted using the wind tunnel facility at the Fukushima Robot Test Field (RTF) [18]. The wind tunnel has a square test section with a cross-sectional area of 3.0 m × 3.0 m, providing sufficient spatial clearance for the test aircraft. Figure 3 shows the exterior view of the wind tunnel facility.

Fig. 3. Appearance of the wind tunnel

2.4 Experimental Conditions

The configuration of the wind tunnel test in this study is shown in Fig. 4. The test aircraft was positioned 3500 mm downstream of the wind tunnel outlet and maintained in hover at the mid-height of the outlet cross-section. During the flight tests, the aircraft was controlled to maintain a fixed hovering position regardless of wind speed variations by combining the onboard self-positioning control system with visual corrections provided by the operator. Figure 5 shows the actual flight test setup.

In the experiment, the wind speed was incrementally increased from zero (0 m/s) to 5 m/s in 1 m/s increments. At each wind speed condition, after confirming that the aircraft had reached a sufficiently stable flight state, data were recorded for 10 s. The experimental values used for comparison with the numerical analysis are the time-averaged values obtained during this 10-s measurement period. The data sampling rate was 50 Hz.

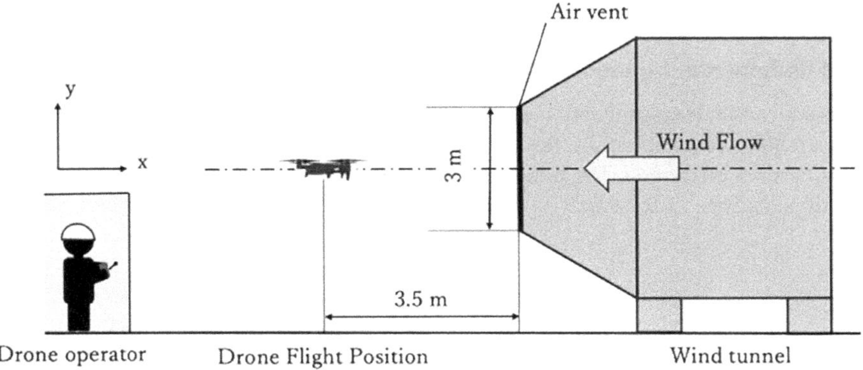

Fig. 4. Wind tunnel test configuration

Fig. 5. Flight test overview

3 Numerical Approach

3.1 Fundamental Equation of Fluid Dynamics

In this study, the three-dimensional Euler equations, which govern inviscid compressible flow, are adopted to solve the flow field around the drone model with an emphasis on computational efficiency. The nondimensionalized form of the three-dimensional Euler equations is given as follows.

$$\frac{\partial q}{\partial t} + \frac{\partial E}{\partial x} + \frac{\partial F}{\partial y} + \frac{\partial G}{\partial z} = 0, \tag{1}$$

$$q = \begin{pmatrix} \rho \\ \rho u \\ \rho v \\ \rho w \\ e \end{pmatrix}, E = \begin{pmatrix} \rho u \\ \rho u^2 + p \\ \rho uv \\ \rho uw \\ u(e+p) \end{pmatrix}, F = \begin{pmatrix} \rho v \\ \rho uv \\ \rho v^2 + p \\ \rho vw \\ v(e+p) \end{pmatrix}, G = \begin{pmatrix} \rho w \\ \rho uw \\ \rho vw \\ \rho w^2 + p \\ w(e+p) \end{pmatrix} \tag{2}$$

Here, q denotes the vector of conserved variables; E, F, and G represent the inviscid flux vectors in the x-, y-, and z-directions, respectively; ρ is the fluid density; u, v, and w are the velocity components in the x-, y-, and z-directions; and e is the total energy per unit volume. The pressure p in Eq. (2) is the gas pressure, which is determined from the ideal gas equation of state given in Eq. (3), assuming an ideal gas.

$$p = (\gamma - 1)\left[e - \tfrac{1}{2}\rho\left(u^2 + v^2 + w^2\right)\right] \tag{3}$$

Here, γ is the specific heat ratio, and in this study, γ was set to 1.4, the standard value for air at room temperature. For temporal discretization, a second-order Crank-Nicolson scheme was applied. For time integration, a pseudo-time inner iteration method based on an explicit two-stage rational Runge-Kutta scheme [19] was adopted, considering computational cost and stability. For spatial accuracy, a second-order extrapolation method was employed, combining gradient evaluation based on the Green-Gauss theorem with a vanLeer-like limiter function [20].

3.2 Fundamental Equation of Rigid Body

To describe the translational and rotational motion of the drone in three-dimensional space, the three-dimensional Newton–Euler equations are adopted as the governing equations for rigid-body dynamics. The three-dimensional Newton–Euler equations are expressed as follows.

$$m\ddot{r} = f \tag{4}$$

$$I\dot{\omega} + \omega \times I\omega = \tau \tag{5}$$

Here, m is the mass of the rigid body; r and f denote the position vector and the external force vector in three-dimensional space, respectively. I is the moment of inertia tensor, and ω and τ represent the angular velocity vector and the torque vector, respectively. Based on the above relationships, the six degrees of freedom associated with the rigid body's translational and rotational motions are described.

3.3 Moving Computational Domain Method

This study employs the Moving Computational Domain (MCD) method [13], in which the computational domain moves in accordance with the motion of the object. Figure 6 presents a conceptual illustration of the MCD method. This approach is based on an unstructured moving-mesh finite volume method, enabling the simulation of free motion without constraints imposed by the computational domain while strictly satisfying the geometric conservation law. Furthermore, to reproduce the relative motion of multiple rotating axes, such as the four independently rotating propellers considered in this study, the MCD method is combined with a multi-axis sliding mesh method [15].

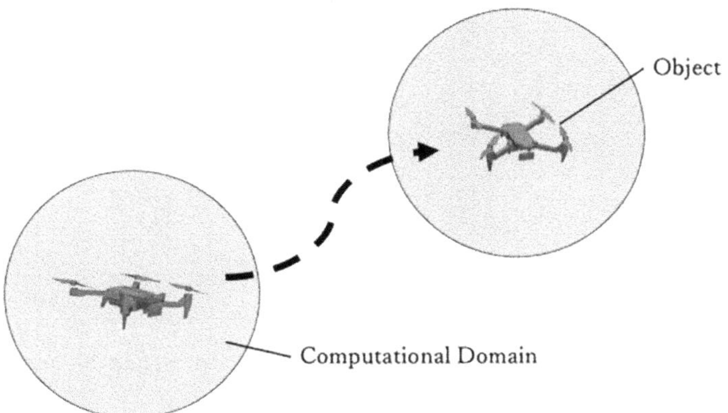

Fig. 6. Moving Computational Domain Method

4 Simulation Overview

4.1 Computational Grid

Figure 7 illustrates the computational domain and mesh configuration around the aircraft used in this study. The computational domain was defined as a spherical region with a radius approximately 15 times the aircraft length to adequately account for the propeller-induced downwash and its interaction with the surrounding flow field. As shown in Fig. 7, a hierarchical mesh structure was adopted, with the grid progressively refined toward the vicinity of the aircraft. This approach captures the steep flow gradients around the object while optimizing computational cost. Figure 8 presents the surface mesh of the analyzed quadcopter drone. The aircraft model was developed based on the specifications of ACSL's small aerial photography drone, "SOTEN" [17]. Figure 9 shows the computational grids and their dimensions for each rotor region corresponding to the four propellers. The representative length used in this study is defined as the maximum aircraft width, including the distance between the propeller tips. The computational model was generated using the unstructured mesh generation software MEGG3D [21,

22], resulting in a total of 1,269,880 cells in the entire domain. Each of the four independent rotor regions consists of 166,400 cells and has a diameter of 0.28 m. The minimum cell size on the rotor surface is approximately 1.5 mm.

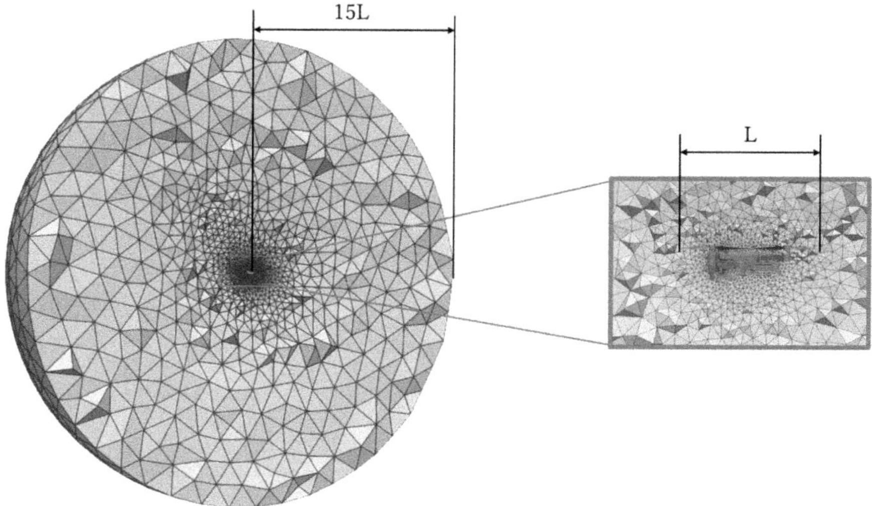

Fig. 7. Computational domain and grid configuration around the aircraft

Fig. 8. Surface mesh of the quadcopter drone

4.2 Computational Conditions

Table 2 summarizes the initial and boundary conditions used in the analysis. To replicate the headwind conditions anticipated during actual flight, the velocity components v and w were set to 0 m/s. For the streamwise component u, six inflow velocity cases were defined,

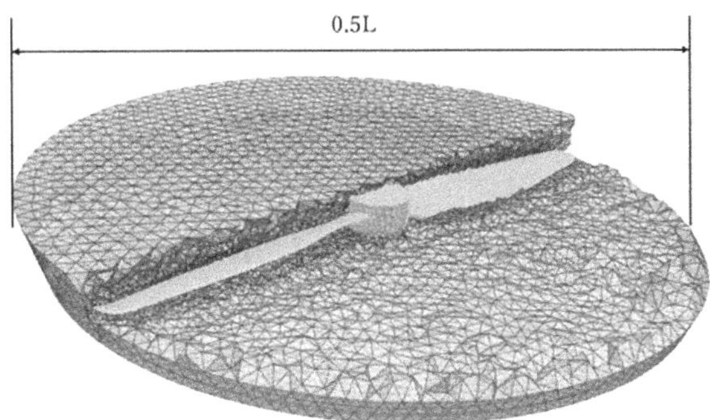

Fig. 9. Computational mesh of the propeller region and its size

ranging from 0 m/s to -5 m/s in increments of 1 m/s. Three types of boundary conditions were applied: slip wall conditions, Riemann invariant boundary conditions, and sliding mesh interfaces. Furthermore, in this analysis, all variables were nondimensionalized using representative values. The representative length was defined as the total aircraft length, $L = 0.56$ m; the representative density was set to the air density, $\rho = 1.247$ kg/m^3; and the representative velocity was taken as the speed of sound, $V = 340.29$ m/s. The dimensionless time step was set to $dt = 2.0 \times 10^{-3}$.

Table 2. Initial and Boundary conditions

u	$-5 \sim 0$ m/s
v	0 m/s
w	0 m/s
Drone body surface	Slip wall condition
Outer boundary	Riemann invariant boundary condition
Propeller domain	Sliding mesh interface

4.3   Flight Simulation Conditions

In this study, simulations were conducted under six wind speed conditions ranging from 0 m/s to -5 m/s in 1 m/s increments, corresponding to the wind tunnel experiments. As the initial condition, either a quiescent state or a uniform flow in the negative x-direction was imposed throughout the computational domain, from which the aircraft motion was initiated. The following control conditions were applied to maintain the aircraft's position and attitude. Along the y-axis, the rotor rotational speed was adjusted so that the rotor thrust balanced gravity, thereby maintaining the target altitude. Along the x- and z-axes, the target ground speed of the aircraft was set to 0 m/s relative to the headwind entering from the +x direction. Under these conditions, the attitude angles required to sustain hovering were computed. This procedure reproduces the flight behavior in which the aircraft autonomously adjusts its attitude to counter external wind disturbances while attempting to maintain a fixed position. The computational results were time-averaged over approximately 1 s of physical time after the aircraft motion reached a dynamic equilibrium state and then compared with the experimental data.

5 Comparison of Experimental and Numerical Results

5.1 Qualitative Evaluation of the Flow Field

To qualitatively evaluate the flow field obtained from the numerical analysis, the velocity vectors around the aircraft and the pressure distribution on the aircraft surface are presented in Fig. 10. Figure 10a shows the results under no-wind conditions (0 m/s), whereas Fig. 10b shows the results under headwind conditions (5 m/s). Compared with the no-wind condition in Fig. 10a, the velocity vectors in Fig. 10b clearly indicate a uniform inflow from the front of the aircraft. This inflow accelerates downstream as it passes through the propellers, forming a downwash that extends beneath the aircraft. Furthermore, examination of the surface pressure distribution confirms that the pressure is lower on the upper surface and higher on the lower surface of each propeller. These results indicate that the fundamental aerodynamic characteristics of rotating wings are appropriately reproduced in the present analysis.

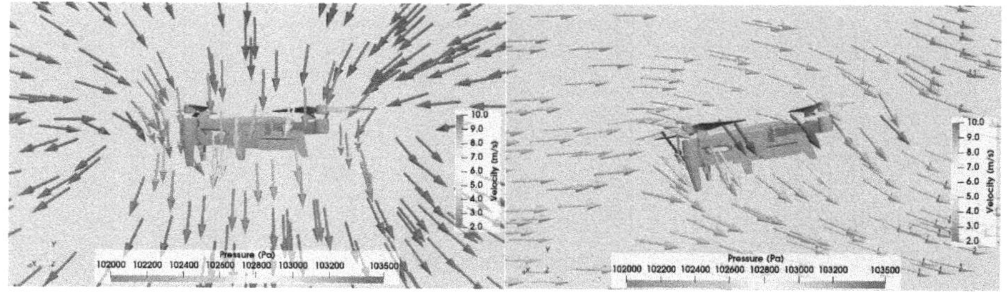

(a) No wind condition (0 m/s)   (b) Headwind condition (5 m/s)

Fig. 10. Velocity vectors around the aircraft and surface pressure distribution

5.2 Comparison of Attitude Angles

Figure 11 shows the variation in the aircraft's attitude angles with wind speed. The horizontal axis represents the headwind speed, and the vertical axis represents the attitude angle. As shown in Fig. 11, both the experimental and numerical results indicate that the pitch angle increases in the negative direction as the wind speed increases. This increase in forward tilt reflects the aircraft's response to maintain stationary hovering. To counteract the rearward aerodynamic drag induced by the headwind, a thrust component in the upwind direction is required. The quadcopter generates a horizontal propulsive component by tilting the aircraft forward, thereby redirecting part of the rotor thrust. Consequently, a larger forward tilt angle becomes necessary as the wind speed increases.

A detailed comparison of the pitch angle shows that the experimental values changed almost linearly from $0°$ under calm conditions to $-8.29°$ at a wind speed of 5 m/s. Similarly, the numerical results varied from $0.17°$ under no-wind conditions to $-9.85°$ at 5 m/s, generally reproducing the behavior of the actual aircraft. The absolute error in pitch angle at the maximum wind speed of 5 m/s was within $1.56°$, demonstrating that this method provides sufficient accuracy for predicting the aircraft system's response to disturbance winds.

In contrast, discrepancies between the experimental and numerical results were observed for the roll and yaw angles. The roll angle remained close to $0°$ across all wind speeds, showing good agreement between experiment and analysis. The yaw angle, however, exhibited noticeable fluctuations in the experimental data. Under ideal conditions with a perfectly symmetrical airframe model and uniform inflow, the numerical analysis should theoretically yield zero yaw and roll angles in a headwind. The observed yaw deviations in the experiment are likely attributable to asymmetries in the experimental environment, such as minor structural distortions of the aircraft frame and slight nonuniformities in the wind speed distribution within the wind tunnel test section. These yaw deviations may cause the flight control system to adjust individual propeller rotational speeds to maintain attitude. Consequently, this effect may have contributed to the discrepancies between analytical and experimental results observed in the comparison of rotor rotational speeds discussed in Sect. 5.3, potentially influencing the accuracy of the pitch angle prediction. Future work should focus on identifying subtle disturbance factors in the experimental environment and refining the analytical model to account for these effects.

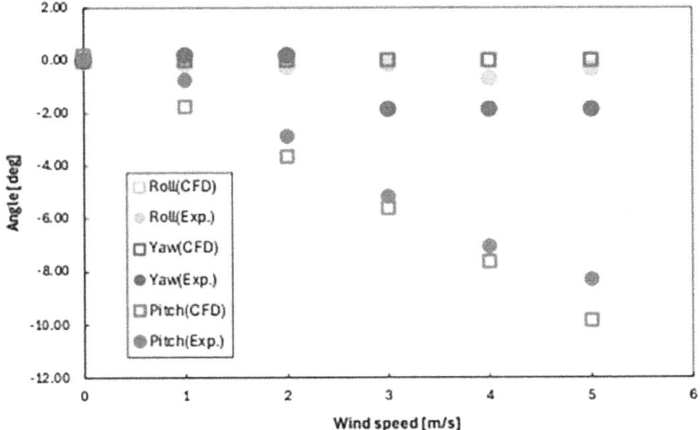

Fig. 11. Comparison of attitude angles with respect to wind speed

5.3 Comparison of Rotor Rotation Speeds

Figure 12 illustrates the variation in the rotational speed of each rotor with wind speed. The horizontal axis represents the wind speed, and the vertical axis represents the rotational speed. Here, P1 and P4 correspond to the front rotors, whereas P2 and P3 correspond to the rear rotors. The figure indicates that, in both the experimental and numerical results, the rotational speeds of the front rotors decrease as the wind speed increases, while those of the rear rotors increase or remain at relatively high levels. This trend supports the generation of a pitch-down moment that raises the rear of the aircraft, thereby forming the forward-leaning attitude described in Sect. 5.2.

A comparison between the experimental and numerical results shows that the numerical values are consistently higher than the experimental values over the entire wind speed range. To quantitatively assess this difference, the relative error ε was calculated using the following equation, taking the experimental values as the reference.

$$\varepsilon = \frac{N_C - N_E}{N_E} \tag{6}$$

Here, N_C represents the rotor rotational speed obtained from the numerical analysis, whereas N_E denotes the rotor rotational speed measured in the wind tunnel experiments. Table 3 summarizes the range of relative errors for all rotors at each wind speed. The relative error ranged from 7.6% to 11.1% under no-wind conditions and from 4.1% to 14.9% at the maximum wind speed. One possible contributing factor is the underestimation of thrust in the numerical analysis. As a result, the thrust generated at a given rotational speed was predicted to be smaller than that of the actual aircraft. It is therefore inferred that, in the analysis, the control system set higher rotational speeds than those of the actual aircraft in order to maintain position while supporting the aircraft weight.

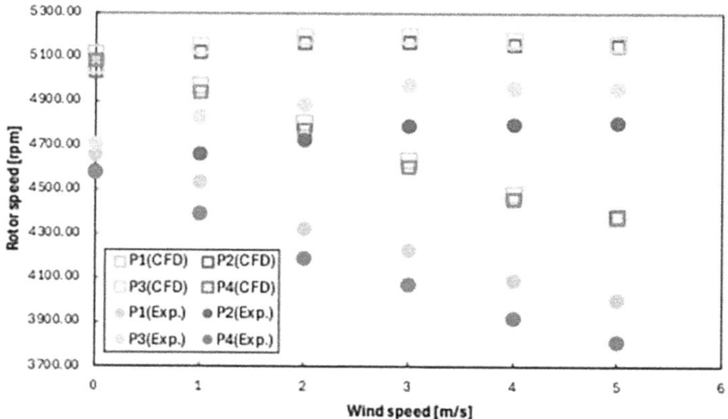

Fig. 12. Comparison of individual rotor speeds with respect to wind speed

Table 3. Relative error of rotor speed at each wind speed

Wind speed (m/s)	Propeller1 (%)	Propeller2 (%)	Propeller3 (%)	Propeller4 (%)
0	9.8	9.9	7.6	11.1
1	9.7	9.9	6.7	12.5
2	11.1	9.3	6.2	13.8
3	9.5	7.9	4.4	13.0
4	9.5	7.5	4.4	13.7
5	9.4	7.2	4.1	14.9

6 Conclusions

This study verified the validity of a coupled fluid–rigid body motion analysis combining the MCD method with a multi-axis sliding mesh method. By comparing numerical results obtained from an inviscid fluid model with wind tunnel experimental data for quadcopter behavior under disturbance winds, the following findings were obtained.

First, with respect to attitude angle reproducibility, the proposed method was confirmed to accurately capture the aircraft's forward-tilting response to disturbance winds. Specifically, the pitch angle error remained within $1.56°$ at the maximum wind speed, demonstrating sufficient accuracy in predicting the aircraft's dynamic equilibrium state. However, slight deviations in the roll and yaw angles were found to cause discrepancies in propeller rotational speeds, potentially affecting the accuracy of the attitude angle prediction. Furthermore, the rotational speed profiles of each rotor indicated that the numerical results were approximately 10% higher overall than the experimental values. This discrepancy is primarily attributed to the underestimation of thrust in the numerical analysis. Nevertheless, a very high correlation was observed between the experimental and numerical results in terms of the rotational speed trends with increasing wind speed. Based on these results, the present method employing an inviscid fluid model can be regarded as an effective approach for constructing a digital twin capable of rapidly predicting the dynamic response of an actual aircraft with practical accuracy.

To further improve the prediction accuracy of rotor rotational speeds, which remains a challenge identified in this study, it is necessary to introduce a model that accounts for mesh resolution on the propeller blade surfaces. In addition, more advanced modeling that incorporates detailed airframe geometry and potential asymmetries in the experimental environment is expected to enhance prediction accuracy under more complex and realistic flight conditions.

Acknowledgments. This paper is based on results obtained from a project, JPNP14004, subsidized by the New Energy and Industrial Technology Development Organization (NEDO).

References

1. Zhijun, M. et al.: eVTOL aircraft for the low-altitude economy: a review of development history, core technologies, and future trends. Case Stud. Transp. Policy. **22**, 101629 (2025)
2. Ruiz, M.C., Scanavino, M., D'Ambrosio, D., Guglieri, G., Vilardi, A.: Experimental and numerical analysis of multicopter rotor aerodynamics. In: AIAA Aviation 2021 Forum. AIAA 2021-2539 (2021)
3. Gordillo, P. et al.: Numerical and experimental estimation of the efficiency of a quadcopter rotor operating at hover. Energies. **12**(2), 261 (2019)
4. Tanabe, Y., Sugawara, H., Sunada, S., Yonezawa, K., Tokutake, H.: Quadrotor drone hovering in ground effect. J. Robot. Mechatron. **33**(2), 339–347 (2021)
5. Herz, S., Atte, A., Seth, D., Rauleder, J., McCrink, M.: Effects of rotor-rotor and rotor-body interactions on quadrotor vehicle performance for multiple flight configurations. Aerosp. Sci. Technol. **158**, 109873 (2025)
6. Kyoto Institute of Technology: Trademark "Digital Flying Car" (Registration No. 6705590), registered June 8 (2023)
7. Gomi, R., Takii, A., Yamakawa, M., Asao, S., Takeuchi, S., Nishimura, M.: Flight simulation from takeoff to yawing of eVTOL airplane with coaxial propellers by fluid-rigid body interaction. Adv. Aerodyn. **5**(1), 2 (2023)
8. Takii, A., Gomi, R., Yamakawa, M., Tsubokura, M.: Turning flight simulation with fluid-rigid body interaction for flying car with contra-rotating propellers. In: ICCS 2023, pp. 566–577 (2023)
9. Takahashi, N., Gomi, R., Takii, A., Yamakawa, M., Asao, S., Takeuchi, S.: Numerical simulation of the Octorotor flying car in sudden rotor stop. In: ICCS 2023, pp. 33–46 (2023)
10. Magata, T., Takii, A., Yamakawa, M., Kobayashi, Y., Asao, S., Takeuchi, S.: Effects of wind on forward and turning flight of flying cars using computational fluid dynamics. In: ICCS 2024, pp. 3–18 (2024)
11. Azid, S.I., Kumar, K., Cirrincione, M., Fagiolini, A.: Wind gust estimation for precise quasi-hovering control of quadrotor aircraft. Control. Eng. Pract. **116**, 104930 (2021)
12. Ferreira, D., De Paula, A.A., Secco, N.R., Galdino da Silva, R.: Validation of inviscid CFD analysis for the Generic Future Fighter. In: 27th Brazilian Congress of Thermal Sciences and Engineering. COB2023-1927 (2023)
13. Yamakawa, M., Mitsunari, N., Asao, S.: Numerical simulation of rotation of intermeshing rotors using added and eliminated mesh method. Procedia Comput. Sci. **108**, 1883–1892 (2017)
14. Yamakawa, M., Takekawa, D., Matsuno, K., Asao, S.: Numerical simulation for a flow around body ejection using an axisymmetric unstructured moving grid method. Comput. Therm. Sci. **4**(3), 217–223 (2012)
15. Takii, A., Yamakawa, M., Asao, S., Tajiri, K.: Six degrees of freedom flight simulation of tilt-rotor aircraft with nacelle conversion. J. Comput. Sci. **44**, 101164 (2020)
16. Yamakawa, M., Kita, Y., Matsuno, K.: Domain decomposition method for unstructured meshes in an OpenMP computing environment. Comput. Fluids. **45**(1), 168–171 (2011)
17. ACSL Inc: Homepage. https://www.acsl.co.jp/. Last accessed 20 Jan 2026
18. Fukushima Robot Test Field: Homepage. https://rtf.f-rei.go.jp/. Last accessed 20 Jan 2026
19. Wambecq, A.: Rational Runge-Kutta methods for solving systems of ordinary differential equations. Computing. **20**(4), 333–342 (1978)
20. Hishida, M., Hashimoto, A., Murakami, K., Aoyama, T.: A new slope limiter for fast unstructured CFD solver FaSTAR. In: Proceedings of the 42nd Fluid Dynamics Conference/Aerospace Numerical Simulation Symposium 2010 JAXA Special Publication, JAXA-SP-10-012. Japan Aerospace Exploration Agency (JAXA) (2011)

21. Ito, Y., Nakahashi, K.: Surface triangulation for polygonal models based on CAD data. Int. J. Numer. Methods Fluids. **39**(1), 75–96 (2002)
22. Ito, Y.: Challenges in unstructured mesh generation for practical and efficient computational fluid dynamics simulations. Comput. Fluids. **85**(1), 47–52 (2013)

Advanced Computational Modelling of Pollution Dispersion in the North Sea

Nafea Lachhab[1]([✉]), Mohammed Seaid[2], Mofdi El-Amrani[1], and Nabil El Moçayd[3]

[1] Laboratory of Mathematics and Applications, FSTT, Abdelmalek Essaadi University, Tangier, Morocco
nafea.lachhab@etu.uae.ac.ma

[2] Department of Engineering, University of Durham, South Road, Durham DH1 3LE, UK
m.seaid@durham.ac.uk

[3] College of Agriculture and Environmental Sciences, University Mohammed VI Polytechnic, Benguerir, Morocco
nabil.elmocayd@um6p.ma

Abstract. This study develops a robust three-dimensional computational model to predict the transport and dispersion of marine pollutants in the North Sea. Coastal vector datasets are first employed to generate a high-resolution computational mesh spanning $51.0°$N-$60.0°$N and $4.5°$W-$13.1°$E. Subsequently, sea-surface current fields at $(1/4)°$ resolution, incorporating both wind-driven and geostrophic components, are assimilated to reconstruct velocity profiles throughout the full water column. A stochastic Lagrangian particle-tracking method is then introduced to simulate crude oil releases ($40°$ API) from the Forties Oil Field ($57.0°$N, $1.0°$E). The simulations indicate that particles travel an average distance of 500–600 km over a 30-day period. Moreover, dispersive processes account for approximately 60% of the total transport distance relative to advective contributions. Seasonal variability plays a decisive role in contaminant pathways; consequently, predicted spatial distributions differ substantially by release month, although comparable trends are observed for both surface and subsea discharge scenarios. The results further suggest that releases from the Forties Oil Field pose a limited coastal threat, with an estimated 3% probability of shoreline impact along the United Kingdom, given the predominantly eastward wind forcing.

Keywords: North Sea · Pollutant transport and dispersion · Stochastic Lagrangian particle tracking · Oil spill modelling · Monte Carlo analysis

1 Introduction

The North Sea is among the most intensively studied and economically exploited coastal regions worldwide. It hosts numerous oil and gas fields and plays a pivotal role in the European energy sector. In addition, its geographic site supports

P. Neumann et al. (Eds.): ICCS 2026, LNCS 16784, pp. 34–48, 2026.
https://doi.org/10.1007/978-3-032-29924-6_3

major commercial fisheries, seabird conservation areas, tourism, and dense shipping routes [8]. As offshore hydrocarbon development expanded, the construction of terminals and drilling platforms accelerated; consequently, concerns emerged regarding ecological degradation and accidental contaminant release. Prior to 1984, environmental monitoring of seawater surrounding offshore installations was not mandatory, and early detection efforts were therefore limited in scope and consistency. In 1984, the UK Prevention of Oil and Pollution Act (1971) was amended to require structured monitoring programs at offshore drilling sites [7]. Nevertheless, contaminant detection remained heavily dependent on chemical techniques, many of which were still under development at the time. Meanwhile, operational discharges from drilling activities continued to generate long-term environmental pressures. In response to these challenges, hydrodynamic modelling methods began to emerge. For example, the SlikMap stochastic model, introduced in 1984 [17], sought to quantify environmental risks to coastlines and marine ecosystems in Norwegian waters. These early studies demonstrated that current-field modelling provides substantial value for environmental monitoring and risk assessment.

Subsequent advances in ocean modelling have enabled the prediction of velocity, temperature, and salinity throughout the full water column. These improvements have been driven by expanded observational datasets, enhanced computational capacity, and satellite remote sensing. For instance, the Geostrophic and Ekman Current Observatory (GEKCO) product [20], developed by the Centre for Topographic Studies of the Ocean and Hydrosphere (CTOH), employs satellite altimetry to estimate surface currents. Similarly, the Danish Meteorological Institute (DMI) operates a three-dimensional advective-dispersive ocean model that underpins an operational oil-spill forecasting service applied to both Greenlandic waters and the North Sea [12]. However, many existing hydrodynamic models remain inaccessible, computationally intensive, or costly to implement. Moreover, comparatively few studies have focused specifically on the environmental implications of oil spills within the North Sea region. Accordingly, this study presents the development of a computational approach to estimate three-dimensional current velocities in the North Sea and west of Shetland. The methodology builds upon earlier approaches reported in [12, 17]. Specifically, the objectives of this work are (i) to implement a problem-specific modelling method and employ a validated third-party software platform; (ii) to evaluate model predictions against historical datasets; and (iii) to quantify and document predictive reliability.

The remainder of this paper is structured as follows. Section 2 introduces the governing oceanographic equations together with the underlying theoretical framework. Subsequently, Sect. 3 describes the computational methodology adopted for simulating pollutant dispersion in the North Sea, including the numerical discretisation strategy and particle-tracking formulation. The results and their validation against observational and reanalysis datasets are then presented and discussed in Sect. 4. Finally, Sect. 5 summarises the principal findings of the study and outlines directions for future research.

2   Mathematical Modelling of Pollution Dispersion

This section presents the mathematical framework used to simulate pollutant transport in the North Sea. The formulation combines the governing equations of ocean motion with Ekman and geostrophic dynamics, a logarithmic representation of near-bottom flow, and a stochastic random-walk model for dispersive transport. In this way, both advective and turbulent-diffusive mechanisms are incorporated within a unified three-dimensional framework.

The motion of seawater is governed by the momentum equation

$$\frac{D\boldsymbol{v}}{Dt} - \nu\nabla^2\boldsymbol{v} + \frac{1}{\rho}\nabla p = -2\Omega \times \boldsymbol{v} + \boldsymbol{g} + \boldsymbol{F}_r, \tag{1}$$

where $\boldsymbol{v} = (u, v, w)^\top$ denotes the Cartesian velocity vector (m/s) in spatial coordinates $\boldsymbol{x} = (x, y, z)^\top$ (m), ρ is the seawater density (kg/m^3), ν the kinematic viscosity (m^2/s), p the pressure (Pa), $\Omega = 7.29 \times 10^{-5}$ rad/s the Earth rotation rate, $\boldsymbol{g} = (0, 0, 9.81)^\top$ m/s^2 the gravitational acceleration, and $\boldsymbol{F}_r$ the wind forcing vector. Under the Boussinesq approximation, seawater may be treated as incompressible for large-scale ocean circulation [19], so that mass conservation reduces to

$$\frac{\partial u}{\partial x} + \frac{\partial v}{\partial y} + \frac{\partial w}{\partial z} = 0. \tag{2}$$

Wind forcing is a major driver of surface circulation. Assuming constant eddy viscosity, the Ekman solution for the wind-induced velocity components is written as

$$u_e + iv_e = |\boldsymbol{v}_e|_{z=0} \, e^{az} e^{i\left(\frac{\pi}{4}+az\right)}, \tag{3}$$

where $\boldsymbol{v}_e = (u_e, v_e, w_e)^\top$ is the wind-induced velocity (m/s) and a (m^{-1}) is the decay constant. The Ekman boundary-layer depth d_e is estimated by

$$d_e = \frac{7.6}{0.0068} \, |\boldsymbol{v}_e|_{z=0}\,, \tag{4}$$

from which $a = \frac{\pi}{d_e}$. The associated redistribution of surface waters modifies the sea-surface topography and generates horizontal pressure gradients. Neglecting acceleration in (1), the geostrophic velocity components are then given by

$$u_g = -\frac{1}{f\rho}\frac{\partial}{\partial y}\int_{-h}^{0} g(\varphi, z)\rho(z)\,dz + \frac{g}{f}\frac{\partial\eta}{\partial y}, \tag{5}$$

$$v_g = -\frac{1}{f\rho}\frac{\partial}{\partial x}\int_{-h}^{0} g(\varphi, z)\rho(z)\,dz + \frac{g}{f}\frac{\partial\eta}{\partial x}, \tag{6}$$

where u_g and v_g are the geostrophic velocities in the x and y directions (m/s), φ is the latitude, $f = 2\Omega \sin\varphi$ the Coriolis parameter (rad/s), h the water depth (m), and η the sea-surface elevation (m). The sub-surface contribution is approximated from geopotential anomaly differences $\Delta\phi$ between two locations $n1$ and $n2$ separated by a distance l as

$$\frac{\Delta\phi_{n1} - \Delta\phi_{n2}}{2\Omega l \sin\varphi}. \tag{7}$$

Near the seabed, bottom friction modifies the current structure. To represent this effect, the logarithmic law of the wall is adopted for the bottom boundary layer [16]:

$$\frac{\bar{u}}{u_*} = \frac{1}{\kappa} \ln\left(\frac{h}{ez_0}\right), \tag{8}$$

where $\bar{u}$ is the depth-averaged velocity (m/s), u_* is the friction velocity (m/s), $\kappa = 0.4$ is the von Kármán constant, e is the base of the natural logarithm, and z_0 is the roughness length (m).

Contaminant dispersion is represented through a stochastic random-walk formulation, in which the release is discretised into particles that undergo advective transport and turbulent spreading [13]. The particle displacement is written as

$$\boldsymbol{X}_{t+\Delta t} = \boldsymbol{X}_t + \boldsymbol{v}_t \Delta t + \sqrt{2\boldsymbol{D}\Delta t} \cdot \boldsymbol{\xi}, \tag{9}$$

where $\boldsymbol{X}_t$ and $\boldsymbol{X}_{t+\Delta t}$ denote the particle positions at times t and $t + \Delta t$, respectively, $\boldsymbol{v}_t$ is the advective velocity (m/s), Δt is the time step, $\boldsymbol{D}$ is the dispersion coefficient matrix (m^2/s), and $\boldsymbol{\xi}$ is a random variable with zero mean and unit variance. The second term in (9) represents advection, whereas the third term accounts for dispersive spreading. Following [10], the dispersion tensor is extended to three-dimensional flow as

$$D_{zx} = D_{xz} = \frac{(a_l wu - a_t uw)h\sqrt{g}}{v_s C},$$

$$D_{zy} = D_{yz} = \frac{(a_l wv - a_t vw)h\sqrt{g}}{v_s C}, \tag{10}$$

$$D_{zz} = \frac{(a_l w^2 + a_t uv)h\sqrt{g}}{v_s C},$$

where a_l and a_t are the longitudinal and turbulent dispersivities, set to 5.93 and 0.23, respectively; C is the Chezy bed roughness coefficient (70 m$^{1/2}$/s) [6], and v_s is the depth-averaged flow speed.

When the transported particles represent oil droplets, vertical buoyant rise is incorporated through the terminal velocity

$$w_t = \sqrt{\frac{2\,gV_p(\rho_p - \rho)}{c_d \rho a_p}}, \tag{11}$$

where ρ_p is the particle density, V_p is the particle volume, a_p is the particle projected area, and c_d is the drag coefficient, taken as 0.47 for a spherical droplet. This term allows the model to account for the combined effects of advection, turbulent dispersion, and buoyancy-driven vertical motion in the transport of marine pollutants.

3   Computational Method for Pollution Dispersion

In our simulations, the computational domain over the North Sea extends from 51.0°N to 60.0°N in latitude and from 4.5°W to 13.1°E in longitude. This spatial

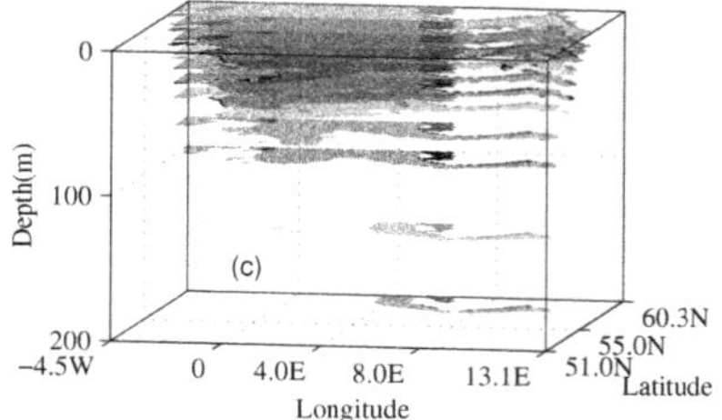
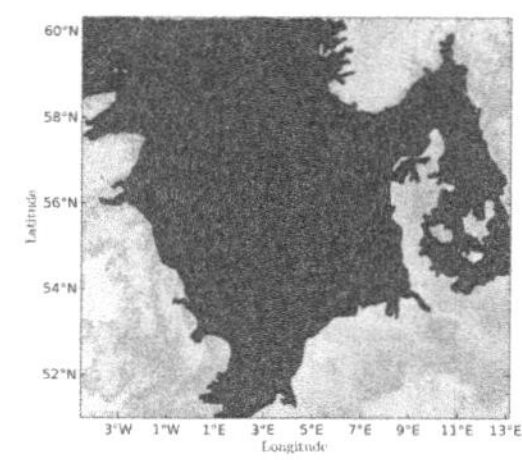

Fig. 1. Illustration of the computational meshes employed in the present study: the left plot displays the vertically structured meshes corresponding to the 14 discrete depth layers, whereas the right plot shows the sea-surface mesh used in the present study to resolve flow dynamics and particle transport.

configuration encompasses the principal dynamical features of the basin, including shallow coastal regions, deeper central areas, and the complex bathymetric gradients that strongly influence the circulation patterns. For the numerical simulation of the governing flow equations, we adopt a multi-layer approach for the vertical discretization [15]. In this framework, the three-dimensional system (1)-(2) is decomposed into a sequence of coupled two-dimensional problems defined on horizontal layers. Each layer is then solved using a semi-Lagrangian finite element method [9], which ensures numerical stability under relatively large time steps while retaining high accuracy in the advection-dominated regime. Consequently, the method provides an efficient and robust strategy for resolving stratified flows in shelf-sea environments. The vertical structure is represented by 14 discrete layers along the z-direction. These layers are defined according to characteristic depth levels derived from the bathymetric distribution of the North Sea, namely $z = 0$ (sea surface), 5, 10, 15, 20, 50, 60, 80, 100, 150, 200, 100, 150, 200 m. Each layer includes all mesh nodes satisfying $h \geq z$, where h denotes the local water depth and z the prescribed layer depth. Thus, the vertical discretization naturally adapts to spatial bathymetric variability such that shallow regions are represented by fewer active layers, whereas deeper offshore areas retain the full vertical resolution. In this manner, the approach balances computational efficiency with the need to capture vertical shear and stratification effects. Figure 1 depicts the computational meshes employed for each vertical layer, together with the sea-surface mesh used in the simulations. To ensure numerical reliability, a mesh convergence analysis was conducted. The results indicate that a mesh of 17065 elements with an area constraint of $20\,\mathrm{km}^2$ provides an optimal compromise between accuracy and computational cost. Accordingly, this resolution is adopted throughout the present study. Bathymetric data are obtained from the GEBCO dataset and interpolated onto the generated triangular mesh using a thin-plate spline procedure, see Fig. 2. This interpolation technique guarantees a smooth and consistent representation of bottom topography across elements. As a result, spurious gradients induced by discretization artifacts are minimized, thereby enhancing the stability and physical fidelity of the simulated flow fields.

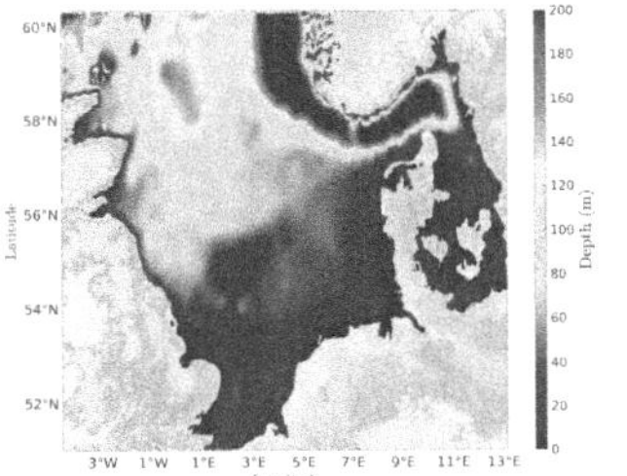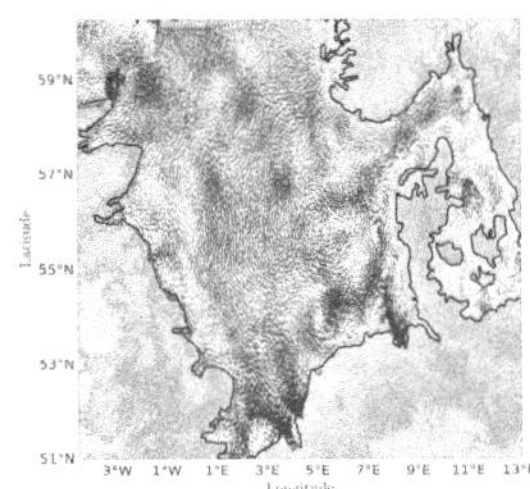

Fig. 2. Snapshot of the model bathymetry (left plot) used in the simulations and the corresponding sea-surface velocity field (right plot), illustrating the spatial variability of bottom topography and its dynamical influence on the surface circulation.

Once the bathymetry-conforming meshes are generated for all vertical layers, the velocity fields are computed on each layer and evaluated against observational and reanalysis products. Figure 2 presents an example of the simulated sea-surface velocity field, while Table 1 summarises the external datasets employed in the modelling framework. Surface-current validation is performed using both OSCAR and GEKCO. In particular, GEKCO is adopted as the primary reference because it combines Ekman currents at 15 m depth with surface geostrophic currents and provides daily fields, whereas OSCAR supplies 5-day averages.

Ekman currents are computed using the Ekman depth and decay constant defined in (4). For the geostrophic component, temperature and salinity fields are interpolated onto all mesh nodes across the vertical layers, and pressure, in-situ density, and specific volume anomaly are then evaluated from the thermodynamic equation of state for seawater [14]. These quantities are introduced into (7) to estimate the sub-surface geostrophic velocities. The Ekman and geostrophic components are then combined to obtain the horizontal velocity components u and v. The vertical velocity component w is derived by integrating the continuity equation (2) over the water column, with boundary conditions $w = 0$ at the sea surface ($z = 0$) and at the seabed ($z = h$), ensuring mass conservation and consistency with the theoretical framework in [19]. To represent the bottom boundary layer, the depth-averaged velocity is parameterised as one-half of the surface current magnitude. A bottom roughness length $z_0 = 0.002$ m is adopted from [18]; the friction velocity is then computed from (8) and used to construct a logarithmic near-bed velocity profile.

The initial position of each contaminant particle is prescribed within the three-dimensional computational mesh. For a particle located at $(x_p, y_p, z_p)^\top$, the nearest mesh node in the horizontal plane is first identified, and the vertical coordinate z_p is then used to determine the two adjacent layers that bound the particle location. Let d_a and d_b denote the depths immediately above and below the particle, respectively. For each of these layers, the surrounding nodal velocities are averaged to obtain layer-specific estimates v_a and v_b. The particle

Table 1. Overview of model data sources used in the present study, including their origin, temporal coverage, spatial resolution, and key variables analyzed.

Source	Data set	Resolution	Increment
Natural Earth	Coastal vector data [1]	10 mi	NA
SIO, UCSD	Bathymetry [4]	$(1/240)°$	NA
CTOH	GEKCO currents [2]	$(1/2)°$	Daily
NOAA	OSCAR currents [5]	$(1/3)°$	5 days
NCEP	GODAS temperature [3]	$(1/3)°$ $(1/3)°$	Monthly
	GODAS salinity [3]		Monthly

velocity is then linearly interpolated as

$$v = f v_b + (1 - f) v_a, \tag{12}$$

where the interpolation factor is

$$f = \frac{z_p - d_a}{d_a - d_b}. \tag{13}$$

This interpolation ensures a smooth variation of velocity with depth and avoids artificial discontinuities at layer interfaces. The same neighbouring nodes are also used to interpolate the local bathymetric depth h, preventing spurious particle penetration below the seabed. Repeating this procedure at each time step yields dynamically updated trajectories consistent with the evolving three-dimensional flow field. The resulting coupling between Eulerian velocities and Lagrangian particle tracking provides a stable framework for simulating contaminant transport in a stratified shelf-sea environment.

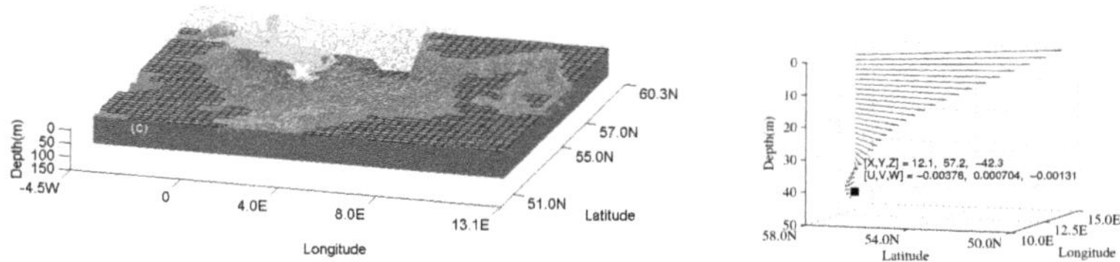

Fig. 3. Three-dimensional velocity field within the computational domain (left plot) and the corresponding vertical velocity profile at the contaminant release location (right plot), highlighting the local shear structure and depth-dependent flow characteristics governing initial particle transport.

4   Results and Discussion

In the numerical simulations, a total of 500 particles are released at the seabed from a fixed point located at latitude 57.7°N, longitude 1.01°E, and a depth of

90 m. The temporal resolution is set to a constant time step of $\Delta t = 1$ hour; accordingly, each simulation is integrated over a period of 30 days. To account for seasonal variability, simulations are initialised at the beginning of each month for the years 2011–2013, using the corresponding hydrodynamic conditions for each period. In this way, inter-annual and intra-annual differences in circulation and stratification are systematically incorporated into the transport analysis. The released contaminant is crude oil of $40°$ API gravity, with a density of $825\,\mathrm{kg/m^3}$. The mean droplet diameter in seawater is estimated to lie within the range 10–100 μm [12]. Based on these characteristics, the rising velocity of the oil droplets is computed using (11), yielding physically realistic ascent speeds between 0.01 and $0.1\,\mathrm{m/s}$. Consequently, buoyancy-driven vertical transport competes with advective and shear-induced dispersion during the early stages following release. The source location corresponds to the Forties Oil Field in the North Sea, while the designated risk area extends from $56.7°\mathrm{N}$ to $58.7°\mathrm{N}$ and from $2.0°\mathrm{E}$ to $2.5°\mathrm{E}$. Figure 3 presents the three-dimensional flow structure together with the vertical velocity profile at the release site. Under the simulated conditions, the relative geostrophic component is found to be weak; therefore, the circulation exhibits predominantly barotropic characteristics, with geostrophic velocities displaying minimal depth dependence. An examination of hydrographic data for the period 2011–2013 indicates that salinity varies between 33 and 35 ppt, whereas temperature ranges from $6°\mathrm{C}$ to $17°\mathrm{C}$. As a result, seawater density remains approximately constant at about $1027\,\mathrm{kg/m^3}$, leading to a small geopotential height gradient across the domain. This limited density contrast further explains the subdued baroclinic contribution to the geostrophic flow. Boundary layer diagnostics reveal that the bottom boundary layer thickness is approximately one-third of the total water depth h. For representative depths of 40 m and surface current velocities between 0.05 and $0.15\,\mathrm{m/s}$, the associated friction velocity ranges from 0.01 to $0.05\,\mathrm{m/s}$, corresponding to a boundary layer thickness of roughly 15 m. This estimate lies well within the commonly reported range of 5–60 m for large-scale ocean circulation [22], thereby supporting the physical consistency of the parameterization. Furthermore, the Ekman layer depths computed from (4) vary between 40 and 70 m. During summer months, enhanced wind variability tends to produce a shallower Ekman layer, typically around 40 m. In addition, the decay constant a assumes values between 0.03 and 0.05, implying an integrated current rotation of approximately $70°$–$90°$ across the water column. Taken together, these dynamical characteristics delineate a circulation regime in which wind-driven processes dominate vertical structure, while density-driven effects remain comparatively weak.

To assess model performance, the simulated flow fields are systematically compared with independent datasets, namely GEKCO, OSCAR, and available moored current meter observations. Through this multi-source validation strategy, both large-scale circulation patterns and local velocity structures are evaluated. In parallel, the error associated with the dispersion model (9) is quantified by decomposing it into two principal components namely, the advective error arising from uncertainties in the current field and the parameterised dispersion error. This separation enables a clearer interpretation of the respective contributions of resolved flow dynamics and subgrid-scale mixing processes. The statistical agreement between model results and reference datasets is evaluated using the Willmott Index of Agreement (WS) [23], defined as

$$\text{WS} = 1 - \frac{\sum_{i=1}^{72} (U_{G,i} - U_i)^2}{\sum_{i=1}^{72} \left(|U_{G,i} - \overline{U}| + |U_i - \overline{U}| \right)^2}, \tag{14}$$

where U denotes the simulated velocity magnitude (m/s) or direction (°), U_G represents the corresponding GEKCO reference values, and $\overline{U}$ is the annual mean of the simulated velocity magnitude or direction. The summation extends from $i = 1$ to 72, reflecting the 5-day averaged temporal resolution provided by GEKCO, which yields 72 data points per year. The index ranges between 0 and 1, with WS = 1 indicating perfect agreement and WS = 0 denoting the absence of predictive skill. In the present simulations, WS values of 0.41 for velocity magnitude and 0.52 for velocity direction are obtained when compared with GEKCO and OSCAR datasets. These values indicate moderate agreement, particularly in directional representation, while highlighting residual discrepancies in current intensity. Furthermore, the reliability of the reference datasets themselves is considered. It is worth noting that GEKCO and OSCAR have both been independently validated against moored current meters and surface drifters. Reported correlations are approximately 0.7±0.1 for GEKCO [21] and 0.5±0.1 for OSCAR [11]. Hence, GEKCO demonstrates comparatively stronger agreement with in-situ observations. This finding is consistent with previous analyses [11], which indicate that OSCAR amplitude predictions tend to degrade at latitudes exceeding 10°. In light of these validation statistics, the advective error in the present model is conservatively estimated at approximately 30%, based on the reported GEKCO correlation with surface drifters. Accordingly, this value is adopted as a representative uncertainty bound for the resolved current field. Through this layered validation approach, combining statistical skill assessment, cross-dataset comparison, and reference-data evaluation, the robustness and limitations of the simulated flow and dispersion fields are quantitatively established.

Figure 4 presents the velocity fields and corresponding particle trajectories at selected days following release for December 2011 and June 2013, thereby highlighting the pronounced seasonal variability in transport pathways and dispersion patterns. For clarity of presentation, only a localized subregion of the computational domain surrounding the release site is displayed; nevertheless, the depicted dynamics remain representative of the broader circulation regime. The horizontal dispersion coefficients D_{xx} and D_{yy} are evaluated for representative current magnitudes of 0.05–0.15 m/s at depths of 50 m and 100 m. At 50 m depth, the resulting values are $D_{xx} = 3 \times 10^3$ cm^2/s and $D_{yy} = 2 \times 10^4$ cm^2/s. At 100 m depth, the coefficients increase to $D_{xx} = 5 \times 10^3$ cm^2/s and $D_{yy} = 3 \times 10^4$ cm^2/s. These magnitudes are consistent with classical estimates of

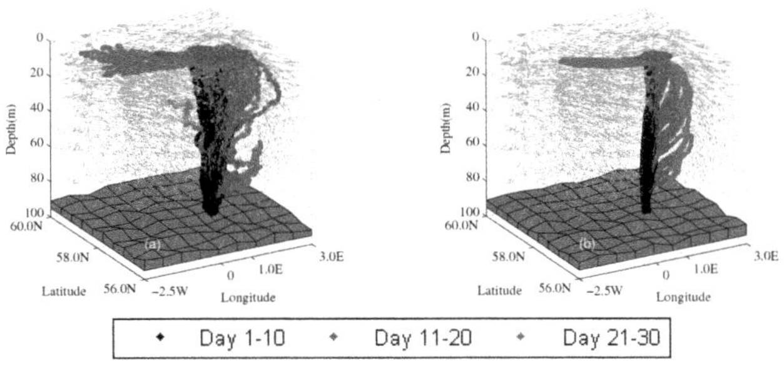

Fig. 4. Velocity fields and corresponding particle trajectories at selected days following release for December 2011 (left plot) and June 2013 (right plot), illustrating the seasonal variability in transport pathways and dispersion patterns. For improved visual clarity, only a localized subregion of the computational domain surrounding the release site is shown.

mixing coefficients reported in the literature. However, whereas classical parameterizations predict a decrease in mixing intensity with height above the seabed, the present estimates exhibit a moderate increase with depth. This difference reflects the local shear structure and wind-driven variability characteristic of the North Sea during the considered period. The simulated contaminant distributions after 30 days demonstrate a strong dependence on the month of release. In particular, particles advect with mean speeds of approximately $0.2\,\mathrm{m/s}$ during summer months and $0.26\,\mathrm{m/s}$ during winter months, indicating enhanced transport under stronger winter circulation. For a given release month, the ratio of advective to dispersive transport rates, corresponding to the second and third terms in (9), is approximately 0.4. Thus, although advection governs large-scale displacement, dispersion contributes substantially to the spatial spreading of the contaminant plume. Because the dispersive term in (9) is stochastic, each simulation is repeated 1000 times as part of a Monte Carlo uncertainty analysis. The ensemble mean particle position is computed for each month, and the deviation of individual realisations from this mean is quantified. The standard error associated with stochastic dispersion is estimated as σ/N, expressed as a percentage of the ensemble mean, where σ denotes the standard deviation and $N = 1000$ the number of realisations. The resulting percentage uncertainty due to dispersive variability is approximately 5% across all particles and release months, thereby indicating robust ensemble convergence. To estimate the total model uncertainty, advective and dispersive errors are subsequently combined. Assuming that an average particle travels approximately $750\,\mathrm{km}$ over the simulation period and adopting a representative dispersion-advection ratio of 0.4, the displacement attributable to advection and dispersion is approximately $300\,\mathrm{km}$ and $450\,\mathrm{km}$, respectively. Incorporating the estimated uncertainties yields distances of $300 \pm 60\,\mathrm{km}$ for advection and $450 \pm 10\,\mathrm{km}$ for dispersion, leading to a combined displacement of $750 \pm 90\,\mathrm{km}$. Consequently, the aggregate model uncertainty is approximately 17%. This quantitative error assessment provides a transparent measure of predictive reliability and strengthens confidence in the simulated transport patterns under the considered seasonal conditions.

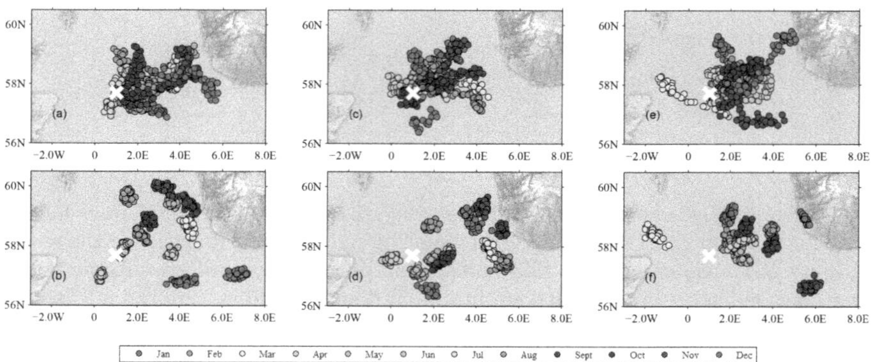

Fig. 5. Spatial distributions of contaminant particles for each monthly release illustrating the seasonal variability in transport pathways, surface spreading, and shoreline exposure risk. Here, each plot corresponds to a separate release month and shows particle positions after the 30-day simulation period, thereby enabling a comparative assessment of the influence of changing hydrodynamic conditions on dispersion patterns for 2011 (a), 2012 (c) and 2013 (e) in two-dimensional releases and 2011 (b), 2012 (d) and 2013 (f) in three-dimensional releases.

A detailed depiction of particle distributions for each monthly release during 2012 is presented in Fig. 5. These results reveal a pronounced seasonal dependence in transport pathways. In most cases, particles drift eastward following release; however, the April simulation exhibits a marked westward displacement. Consequently, this scenario suggests a temporary shift in circulation patterns that could pose a potential threat to the Norwegian coastline within approximately one to three months after release. During the April experiment, the oil droplets with the highest prescribed rising velocity (0.1 m/s) reach the sea surface in just under 10 days. This ascent time is longer than anticipated and likely reflects a scaling inconsistency in the vertical velocity parameterization. Ideally, the rise time should range from several hours to a few days, consistent with field observations reported in [12]. Nevertheless, once the oil droplets reach the surface, horizontal advection by surface currents becomes increasingly dominant, as evidenced by the enhanced lateral spreading visible in Fig. 5. The ensemble-averaged trajectories further illustrate the distinction between purely advective transport and combined advective-dispersive motion. In general, wind-driven (Ekman) currents exhibit greater temporal variability than geostrophic currents, particularly during summer months, with magnitudes fluctuating between 0 and 0.1 m/s. By contrast, the geostrophic component, linked to sea-surface height gradients influenced in part by tidal dynamics, displays a comparatively stable and predictable structure. However, because the considered wind magnitude and direction frequently dominate the total surface flow, the net transport of contaminants is typically directed eastward. The prevailing eastward drift observed in Fig. 5 can be attributed to anomalies in both the magnitude and direction of the surface current components. Specifically, GEKCO data indicate a substantial increase in geostrophic current magnitude during mid-to-late April 2012, rising from approximately 0.07 m/s to 0.23 m/s. Simultaneously, the Ekman component maintains speeds near 0.1 m/s. Importantly, the directions of both components during much of April exhibit an east-to-west orientation, thereby favouring westward contaminant transport and explaining the April outcome. Such a reversal in flow direction appears to be relatively uncommon within the analysed period. Indeed, only one out of the 36 monthly simulations (three years, twelve releases per year) resulted in westward transport posing a potential risk to the United Kingdom, corresponding to approximately 3% of cases. Therefore, although episodic circulation anomalies may temporarily alter transport pathways, the statistical likelihood of significant westward contaminant drift from the Forties Oil Field toward the UK coastline remains low under the examined hydrodynamic conditions.

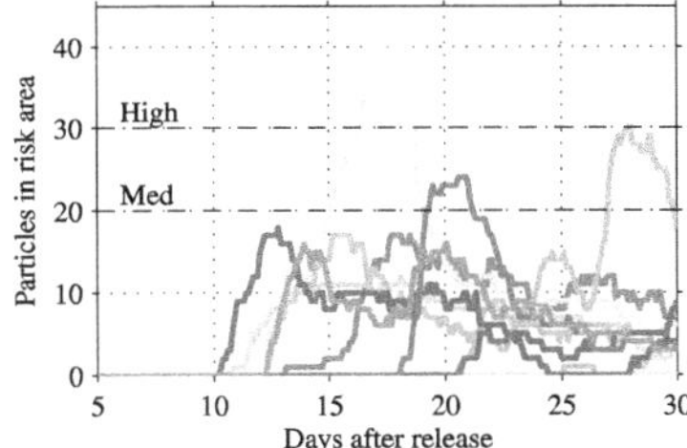

Fig. 6. Temporal evolution of the number of particles entering the defined risk area for each monthly release scenario. The curves illustrate the cumulative particle count within the specified geographic bounds over the 30-day simulation period, thereby quantifying the relative exposure under varying seasonal circulation conditions. Here, the legend and corresponding colour scheme are consistent with those presented in Fig. 5.

For the risk assessment, the number of particles entering the predefined risk area is quantified for each monthly release during 2012, as presented in Fig. 6. This metric provides a direct measure of potential shoreline exposure under varying seasonal circulation regimes. The results indicate that contaminant particles do not enter the risk area immediately after release; rather, they typically arrive approximately 10 days post-release, having travelled a distance of roughly 200 km. This delay reflects the combined effects of horizontal advection, vertical ascent, and lateral dispersion. Consequently, short-term coastal exposure within the first week following a release appears unlikely under the simulated hydrodynamic conditions. The predefined medium-risk threshold of 20 particles is exceeded during July and November, whereas the high-risk threshold of 30 particles is surpassed in April. These exceedances underscore the importance of seasonal variability in circulation patterns, as changes in wind forcing and current structure substantially alter transport pathways and accumulation rates within the risk zone. Furthermore, particles characterised by slower rising velocities remain within the risk area for extended durations. In some cases, approximately 10% of the released particles persist within the defined bounds at the final of the 30-day simulation period. This prolonged residence time increases the potential for sustained environmental exposure, particularly when combined with recurrent or episodic releases. Taken together, these findings demonstrate that both the timing of release and the vertical ascent characteristics of the contaminant critically influence coastal risk levels. Accordingly, accurate representation of seasonal hydrodynamics and buoyancy-driven processes is essential for reliable impact forecasting in offshore spill scenarios.

Finally, an analysis of the computational cost associated with a single 30-day simulation involving 1000 particles indicates that the dominant contribution to total CPU time arises from the computation of the hydrodynamic velocity field. This component includes the solution of the multilayer flow equations and the associated interpolation procedures required to provide velocity inputs for particle tracking. Consequently, the Eulerian flow solver constitutes the principal computational bottleneck of the modelling method. In contrast, the numerical integration of the stochastic advection-dispersion equations governing particle motion accounts for approximately 24% of the total CPU time. Although the Lagrangian particle-tracking component involves repeated evaluation of interpolated velocities and random dispersive increments, its computational demand remains secondary to that of the flow-field simulation. An additional 6% of the total computational time is primarily devoted to post-processing tasks, including particle counting within the risk area and graphical output generation. Therefore, only a relatively small fraction of resources is allocated to analysis and visualisation compared with the core hydrodynamic computations. Because the simulation horizon is fixed at 30 days for all scenarios, the total runtime remains largely unchanged across experiments. Accordingly, variations in computational cost are influenced more strongly by the complexity of the velocity field calculations than by differences in release month or particle behaviour. This performance assessment demonstrates that the proposed modelling method achieves a balanced compromise between physical fidelity and computational efficiency, rendering it suitable for repeated ensemble simulations and uncertainty quantification studies.

5   Conclusions

This study developed an advanced computational model to simulate pollution dispersion in the North Sea by integrating physics-based hydrodynamic modelling with observational data for currents and bathymetry. Oceanographic equations of motion were applied to estimate sub-surface currents, with vertical structure represented through a turbulent boundary layer parameterization. The resulting velocity fields were subsequently coupled to an advective-dispersive random walk model, enabling probabilistic prediction of contaminant transport and quantification of shoreline impact risk following a hypothetical release from the Forties Oil Field. The simulations indicate that the probability of contaminant landfall along the UK coastline is low, approximately 3%, with the overwhelming majority of simulated releases advected eastward toward the Norwegian coast. This dominant eastward transport is primarily driven by prevailing wind forcing. On average, particles travelled approximately 600 km over a 30-day period and seasonal variability was found to exert a significant influence on dispersion characteristics, with higher particle velocities and enhanced transport observed during winter months. Model performance was encouraging, with error estimates on the order of 17%. Nevertheless, several sources of uncertainty remain, particularly in the estimation of dispersion coefficients and in the representation of complex current structures. The principal opportunity for model enhancement lies in refining the hydrodynamic component of the method. Future work will focus on implementing a baroclinic modelling approach using the Hamburg Shelf Ocean Model (HAMSOM). Coupling this methodology with the North-West European Shelf (NWES) system would improve boundary condition representation and enable explicit treatment of volume fluxes entering and leaving the computational domain. Such an approach would allow externally driven currents, including the Shetland Current, to be incorporated more realistically into circulation estimates. Atmospheric forcing and sea-surface topography datasets (e.g., GEKCO) would provide input to HAMSOM, replacing daily current fields while preserving the particle-tracking simulation and post-processing methodology developed in this study. In summary, this work demonstrates the feasibility of combining deterministic hydrodynamic modelling with stochastic dispersion techniques to produce robust, risk-based assessments of offshore contaminant transport. Based on improved circulation modelling and boundary coupling, the method has strong potential to evolve into a comprehensive predictive tool for environmental risk management in the North Sea.

Acknowledgments. We would like to thank the Moroccan Ministry of Higher Education, Scientific Research and Innovation and the OCP Foundation who funded this work through the APRD research program.

References

1. Coastline Vector Dataset. http://www.naturalearthdata.com
2. Geostrophic and Ekman Current Observatory. http://www.legos.obs-mip.fr
3. Global Ocean Data Assimilation System. http://www.esrl.noaa.gov/psd/data/gridded/data.godas.html
4. Global Topography Tool. http://topex.ucsd.edu
5. Ocean Surface Current Analyses - Realtime. http://www.oscar.noaa.gov
6. Anzani, H.S., Kantoush, S.A., Kobayashi, S.: Impact of bed roughness configurations on flow dynamics and hydraulic resistance in open-channel flows. Sci. Rep. **16**, 3614 (2025)

7. Beyer, J., Ellingsen, K.E., Yoccoz, N.G., Buhl-Mortensen, P., Bakke, T.: Environmental effects monitoring of offshore oil and gas activities on the Norwegian continental shelf: a review. Mar. Environ. Res. **209**, 107166 (2025)

8. Carpenter, A.: Oil pollution in the North Sea: the impact of governance measures on oil pollution over several decades. Hydrobiologia **845**, 109–127 (2019)

9. El-Amrani, M., Seaid, M.: An essentially non-oscillatory semi-Lagrangian method for tidal flow simulations. Int. J. Numer. Meth. Eng. **81**(7), 805–834 (2010)

10. Falconer, R.A., Ismail, A.: Numerical modelling of tracer transport in a contact tank. Environ. Int. **23**, 763–773 (1997)

11. Johnson, E.S., Bonjean, F., Lagerloef, G.S.E., Gunn, J.T., Mitchum, G.T.: Validation and error analysis of OSCAR sea surface currents. J. Atmos. Ocean. Technol. **24**, 688–701 (2007)

12. Keramea, P., Spanoudaki, K., Zodiatis, G., Gikas, G., Sylaios, G.: Oil spill modeling: a critical review on current trends, perspectives, and challenges. J. Mar. Sci. Eng. **9**(2), 181 (2021)

13. Kitanidis, P.K.: Particle tracking equations for the solution of the advection-dispersion equation with variable coefficients. Water Resour. Res. **30**, 3225–3227 (1994)

14. Millero, F.J., Huang, F.: The density of seawater as a function of salinity and temperature. Ocean Sci. **5**, 91–100 (2009)

15. Sari, S., Rowan, T., Seaid, M., Benkhaldoun, F.: Simulation of three-dimensional free-surface flows using two-dimensional multilayer shallow water equations. Commun. Comput. Phys. **27**(5), 1413–1442 (2020)

16. De Serio, F., Mossa, M.: Streamwise velocity profiles in coastal currents. Environ. Fluid Mech. **14**(4), 895–918 (2014). https://doi.org/10.1007/s10652-014-9338-3

17. Skognes, K., Johansen, O.: Statmap: a 3-dimensional model for oil spill risk assessment. Environ. Model. Softw. **19**(19), 727–737 (2004)

18. Stanev, E., Dobrynin, M., Pleskachevsky, A., Grayek, S., Gunther, H.: Bed shear stress in the southern North Sea as an important driver for suspended sediment dynamics. Ocean Dyn. **59**, 183–194 (2008)

19. Stewart, R.H.: Introduction To Physical Oceanography. Department of Oceanography, Texas AM University (2005)

20. Sudre, J., Maes, C., Garcon, V.: On the global estimates of geostrophic and Ekman surface currents. Limnol. Oceanogr. Fluids Environ. **3**, 1–20 (2013)

21. Sudre, J., Morrow, R.A.: Global surface currents: a high-resolution product for investigating ocean dynamics. Ocean Dyn. **58**, 101–118 (2008)

22. Trowbridge, J.H., Lentz, S.J.: The bottom boundary layer. Ann. Rev. Mar. Sci. **10**, 397–420 (2018)

23. Willmott, C.J., Robeson, S.M., Matsuura, K.: A refined index of model performance. Int. J. Climatol. **32**(13), 2088–2094 (2012)

Implementation of an Admission Control in SDN Network

Adam Skorecki, Jakub Dutkiewicz, Bartłomiej Radziun, Wiktor Hoffmann, Grzegorz Kaczorek, and Magdalena Młynarczuk[(✉)]

Gdańsk University of Technology, Faculty of Electronics, Telecommunications and Informatics, Narutowicza 11/12, 80-233 Gdańsk, Poland
magmlyna@pg.edu.pl

Abstract. The rapid growth of network traffic and the increasing complexity of multi-vendor infrastructures pose a significant challenge to traditional network management. Software-Defined Networking (SDN) has emerged as the leading architectural solution to these problems by separating the control plane from the data plane and introducing centralized programmability. Although the SDN was originally designed to optimize packet-switched environments, inherent limitations of packet networks, such as unpredictable packet traffic spikes, require the implementation of robust oversight mechanisms. This paper presents the integration of Admission Control (AC) function with SDN architecture to guarantee the quality of service for different classes. For the first class, it was essential to provide both throughput and loss probability, whereas for the second class, only throughput needed to be guaranteed. These parameters were measured on the SDN network demonstrator with the AC function. The proposed demonstrator was implemented using the Mininet environment, the Ryu controller, and a Django-based application, which evaluates incoming service requests based on real-time network services. The results of the research show that the centralized AC mechanism effectively prevents resource exhaustion and enables guaranteed quality of service for packet flow, proving that Admission Control in the SDN network is essential for maintaining performance integrity in modern telecommunications networks.

Keywords: Software-Defined Networking · Admission Control · Quality of Service

1 Introduction

Modern telecommunication networks are facing a dynamic surge in traffic volume and escalating architectural complexity, largely driven by the growing number of network devices from multiple vendors. These factors amplify the challenges associated with network orchestration and management, leading to significant operational inefficiencies. The continued reliance on manual configuration of network elements, resulting in increased service provisioning delays, directly contributes to diminished user satisfaction and degraded Quality of Experience (QoE).

© The Author(s), under exclusive license to Springer Nature Switzerland AG 2026
P. Neumann et al. (Eds.): ICCS 2026, LNCS 16784, pp. 49–61, 2026.
https://doi.org/10.1007/978-3-032-29924-6_4

Software-Defined Networking (SDN) [1] has emerged as the leading paradigm to address these systemic issues by fundamentally restructuring network architectures. The core objective of the SDN is the functional decoupling of the control plane from the data (forwarding) plane, which enables the direct programmability of the network resources. Resource orchestration is centralized and executed by a dedicated network element, the SDN controller.

Decisions regarding network reconfiguration in the SDN network can be driven by applications that monitor the overall network state in real-time. This approach enhances operational flexibility through automated control and mitigates hardware interoperability issues across multi-vendor environments.

The SDN network was initially designed for packet-switched environments, and current traffic dynamics and evolving user expectations necessitate the implementation of robust supervisory mechanisms, such as the Admission Control (AC) function. However, there has been little discussion on implementation of Admission Control function in the SDN network within testbed environments. The integration of AC is vital for effective resource management and ensuring Quality of Service (QoS). This research focuses on the realization of an AC application designed for the SDN-based architecture, supporting two classes of service with specific requirements.

The results of the realization of the SDN demonstrator with AC function are described in this paper, which is organized as follows. Section 2 contains information about admission control function and work related to its subject. Section 3 describes the concept of the SDN demonstrator with the AC function. Section 4 outlines the AC function test scenarios. Section 5 contains the tests results. Section 6 summarizes the paper and presents further work.

2   Admission Control Function and Related Work

Admission Control (AC) is a preventive mechanism designed to preserve Quality of Service (QoS) integrity within packet-switched environments. The mechanism evaluates whether a new service request aligns with the established traffic contract and ensures that the mandatory performance objectives can be sustained for the new connection. This decision-making process entails an assessment of the network's capacity to satisfy throughput and QoS metrics, such as packet loss probability, according to the Service Level Agreement (SLA). By validating the requested traffic profile against real-time resource availability, the AC function prevents resource exhaustion and ensures that admitting new flows does not compromise the performance bounds guaranteed to all concurrent active sessions. Such a proactive approach is critical for mitigating network congestion and maintaining quality for different classes of service.

The problem of Admission Control (AC) in Software-Defined Networks (SDN) has been extensively discussed in recent literature. The methods employed to study this issue can be broadly categorized into three main groups: methods based on advanced machine learning algorithms, mathematical traffic optimization models, and implementations within simulation environments.

A significant portion of contemporary research focuses on the use of Artificial Intelligence for traffic prediction and AC decision-making. In [2], the authors proposed the use of Graph Neural Networks (GNN) in Beyond 5G networks, arguing that Deep Learning-based solutions handle topology complexity better than traditional methods. Similarly, in [3] the authors used a DeepAR probabilistic model to forecast traffic for managing network slices. These methods require substantial computational power and training data, which may hinder their deployment in smaller, dynamically managed environments.

The second group of studies concentrates on theoretical optimization algorithms. The paper [4] analyzes online algorithms for centralized admission control, evaluating their performance compared to offline solutions. Meanwhile, in [5] Partially Observable Markov Decision Processes (POMDPs) were applied, specifically for media delivery networks, where video quality is the critical parameter. Although mathematically robust, these approaches often focus on specific use cases or theoretical performance bounds, frequently overlooking the aspect of interaction with network administrators.

In the context of practical implementation and scalability, [6] presented an analysis of AC mechanism scalability using the Mininet environment and the OpenDaylight controller. However, most Mininet-based solutions focus primarily on the infrastructure layer, rarely integrating control logic with external management applications accessible to the end-user.

In contrast to the previously mentioned works, which rely on complex predictive models, purely theoretical analysis, or remain confined to the controller environment, this paper proposes a pragmatic approach to Admission Control. The novelty of the proposed solution is implementation of the AC as an application in the application plane of the SDN network. The application is based on a mathematical model to determine packet loss probability. Simultaneously, dedicated HTB (Hierarchical Token Bucket) mechanism is implemented in the data plane to guarantee the required throughput. The implemented system integrates the Ryu controller with a Django-based web application, providing QoS guarantees (packet loss probability) and throughput. Such a solution allows for the flexible definition of policies in real-time without the computational overhead characteristic of AI-based methods, while providing satisfactory results in order to guarantee quality for differentiated service classes. Our approach offers a lightweight, Django-integrated solution, making it suitable for real-time computing environments.

3 Network Demonstrator

The experimental environment was designed as a comprehensive SDN-based demonstrator to validate the effectiveness of the Admission Control (AC) function. The architecture follows the standard of the SDN paradigm, logically decoupled into three functional planes: the data plane, the control plane, and the application plane. The architecture of the demonstrator is shown in Fig. 1.

The data plane was emulated using Mininet [7], a high-fidelity network emulation tool. The topology consists of five switches interconnected as shown in Fig. 2. To support differentiated Quality of Service (QoS), the Hierarchical Token Bucket (HTB) queuing discipline was implemented at the egress ports of the switches. This allows for precise bandwidth management and traffic separation between two defined classes: a Class 1 with guaranteed throughput and packet loss probability, and a Class 2 with guaranteed throughput. The use of HTB ensures that flows of the Class 1 are protected from the interference caused by Class 2, while the OpenFlow protocol, on southbound interface, enables control of packet forwarding in the data plane.

The control plane is managed by the Ryu SDN controller [8], which operates in a proactive mode. The Ryu controller was selected for its modularity and robust support for the OpenFlow v1.3 protocol [9]. The controller serves as the intermediary between the network hardware and the management logic. It is responsible for maintaining an up-to-date view of the network topology and pushing flow entries (FLOW_MOD messages) to the switches. Furthermore, the controller exposes a northbound interface (NBI) based on the REST (Representational State Transfer) architecture, allowing external applications to retrieve real-time port statistics and flow data in JSON format.

The application plane consists of a dedicated network management system developed using the Django web framework [10]. This layer implements the core Admission Control logic and provides a user-friendly interface for service provisioning. Communication between the Django application and the Ryu controller is realized through asynchronous HTTP requests to the REST API. The application periodically polls the controller to monitor link utilization. When a new service request is submitted via the web interface, the AC module calculates the remaining capacity and evaluates the impact of the new flow on the current network state.

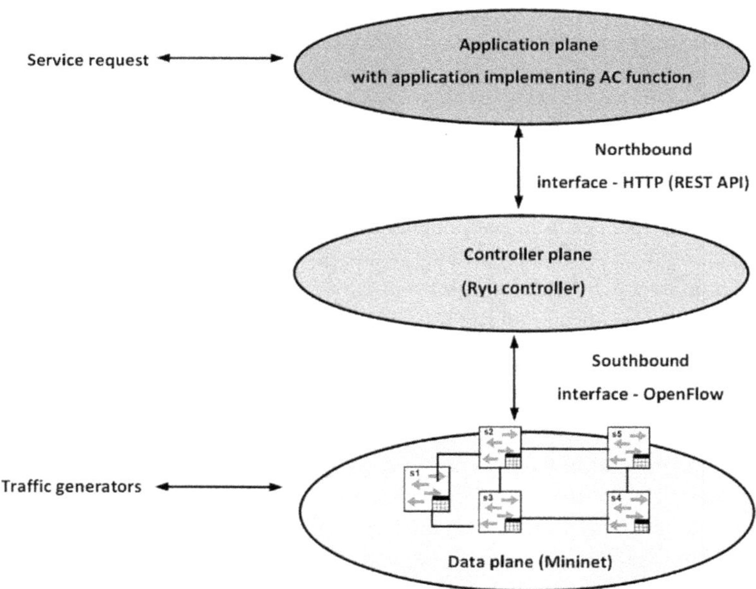

Fig. 1. SDN network demonstrator architecture.

If admitted, the AC application triggers the controller to update the flow tables in the data plane, thereby establishing a connection with the requested QoS parameters.

To verify the performance and functional validity of the demonstrator, iPerf traffic generators were used to simulate traffic load of Class 1 and Class 2, while Wireshark was used for deep packet inspection.

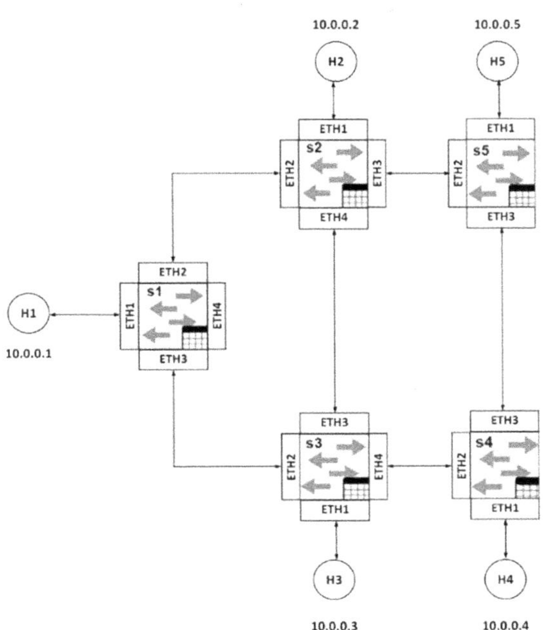

Fig. 2. Mininet network topology.

3.1 SDN AC Application

The core of the proposed system is a web-based application developed using the Django framework, which serves as the application plane in the SDN architecture. The selection of Django was motivated by its modularity, robust Object-Relational Mapping (ORM) system, and seamless integration with HTTP-based libraries, which are essential for communicating with the controller via the northbound interface.

The application's architecture, presented in Fig. 3, comprises several key functional modules:

- Statistics Module,
- Authentication and Authorization Module,
- Admission Control Logic,
- Flow Manager,
- User Interface and Administrative Dashboard.

The Statistics Module component is responsible for the continuous monitoring of the network state. It utilizes REST API queries to the Ryu controller to retrieve port statistics and flow data in JSON format. Based on this information, the module calculates real-time link utilization.

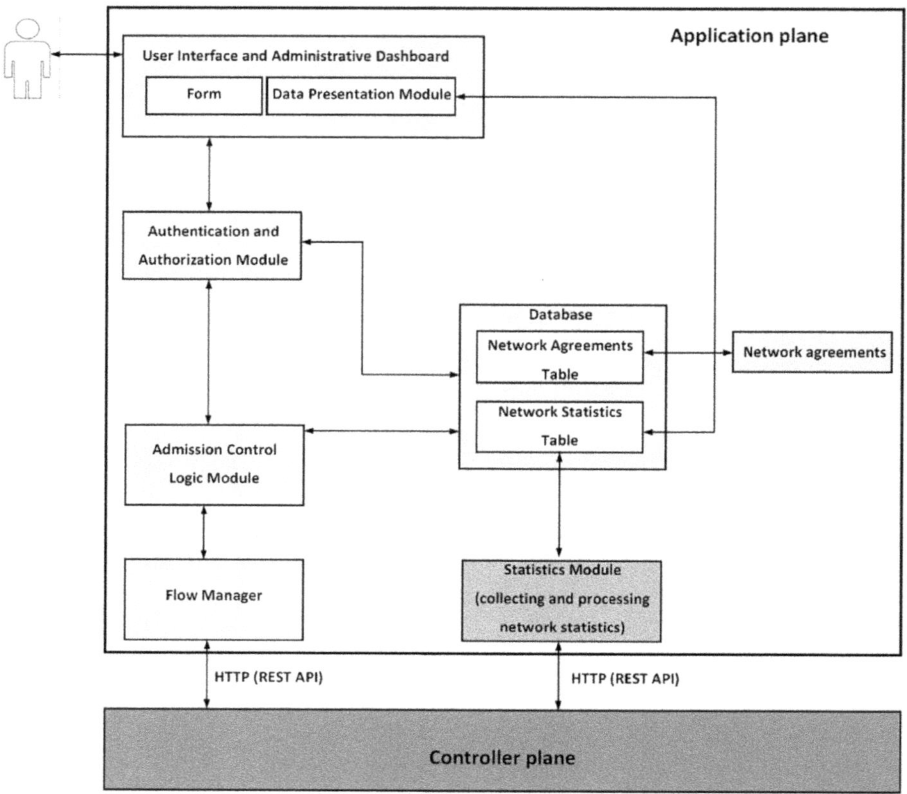

Fig. 3. Application architecture.

The Authentication and Authorization Module confirms the declared identity of the user, verifies the SLA related to the user and ensures SLA compliance, checking if the user has permission to request a specific capacity.

Admission Control Logic Module, acting as the decision-making engine, performs a verification for every incoming service request (req_bw) submitted via the web interface. The service request is rejected if occupied capacity is beyond the *UTILIZA-TION_TRESHOLD*, there is insufficient bandwidth or calculated loss probability for Class 1 (*p_loss_e2e*) exceeded *LOSS_TRESHOLD*. If degradation of the Class 1 is allowed in the service request, the bandwidth of the Class 2 is used if available.

The flows are removed from flow tables after the hard timeout defined in FLOW_MOD messages, corresponding to *req_duration* in the service request.

The pseudocode of AC function in the Admission Control Logic Module is presented in Table 1.

Table 1. The pseudocode of AC function.

 # --- AC Module Logic ---

Set ac_reject_reason = NONE

#--- CONDITIONS FOR AC ---
If capacity_occupied >= (*UTILIZATION_THRESHOLD* * *C*):
   ac_reject_reason = "Utilization threshold exceeded"
Else if *req_bw* > *available_bw*:
   ac_reject_reason = "Insufficient bandwidth"
Else if requested_class == CLASS_1 AND p_loss_e2e exists:
   If *p_loss_e2e* >= *LOSS_THRESHOLD*:
      ac_reject_reason = "Loss threshold exceeded"

#--- DECISION: ACCEPT ---
If ac_reject_reason == NONE:
   Reserve throughput for requested_class
   Schedule throughput release after *req_duration*
   Exit()

 # --- REJECT OR DEGRADATION ---
If degrade_enabled AND requested_class == CLASS_1:
   Compute available bandwidth for CLASS_2
   If *req_bw* > *available_bw_class2*:
      Show ERROR: "Not enough bandwidth for degradation"
      Exit()

 # --- DEGRADE TO CLASS 2 ---
Reserve throughput for CLASS_2
Schedule throughput release after *req_duration*
Exit()

#--- REJECT (no degradation possible) ---
Show ERROR message with ac_reject_reason
Exit ()

Flow Manager is responsible for sending HTTP POST request to the SDN controller after a positive admission decision. This module generates the necessary instructions in JSON format for the SDN controller. As a result, FLOW_MOD messages are sent through the southbound interface in order to update the flow tables of the data plane switches, installing the required forwarding rules with the associated QoS parameters.

User Interface and Administrative Dashboard is a module in which the application provides a web-based form for users to define request service parameters. Simultaneously, it offers a monitoring dashboard for administrators, providing view of the flow table entries and network statistics.

4 Tests

The research environment was established using a topology consisting of five OpenFlow switches and five hosts serving as traffic generators and receivers. The experiments were conducted on a workstation equipped with an Intel Core i7–8700 (3.7 GHz) processor and 64 GB of RAM. The Mininet and Ryu controller virtual machines were each allocated 16 GB of RAM and 5 threads.

To implement differentiated traffic handling in service systems, the Hierarchical Token Bucket (HTB) [11], one of the most widely used mechanisms for rate limiting, was provided. The mechanism was configured on each switch output interface. The total capacity was limited to 20 Mbps, with a 5 Mbps guarantee for the Class 1 (VoIP, RTP, Stream) and 15 Mbps for the Class 2 (Data). Traffic was generated using the iPerf tool with UDP streams. The experimental evaluation was divided into three scenarios.

Scenario 1: Operation for a Single Traffic Class 1
Test conditions. The experimental setup involves host H1 acting as the traffic generator and host H4 as the receiver. The application initiates a service request for Class 1 – VoIP (req_bw = 4.5 Mb/s, guaranteed throughput = 5 Mb/s, traffic load for Class 1 = 0.9). Traffic of Class 1 is generated using iPerf with source H1 to H4. In Admission Control Logic Module the following parameters are given:

- UTILIZATION_TRESHOLD = 0.8,
- capacity = 20 Mbps
- LOSS_THRESHOLD = 0.001,
- req_duration = 120 s.

Scenario 1 objectives. The primary objective of the first scenario is to evaluate the efficiency of the Admission Control (AC) mechanism for the Class 1 under traffic load 0.9 for this class. The specific objectives include an investigation of the impact of HTB parameters (buffer length (k) and the burst size) on packet loss probability and determining the minimum acceptable buffer and burst sizes required to maintain *LOSS_TRESHOLD*. The burst is defined as the amount of bytes that can be burst at the maximum rate at which a class can send, in excess of the configured rate [12].

By systematically adjusting k and burst parameters within the Mininet environment, and measurement the resulting end-to-end packet loss probability, it is necessary to verify decision-making logic when a flow operates near its maximum guaranteed throughput limit.

Scenario 2: Operation for Traffic Class 1 and Class 2
Test conditions. The experimental setup involves host H1 acting as the traffic generator and host H4 as the receiver. The application initiates a service request for:

- Class 1: VoIP (req_bw = 4.5 Mbps, guaranteed throughput = 5 Mbps, traffic load for Class 1 = 0.9),
- Class 2: Data (req_bw = 13.5 Mbps, guaranteed throughput = 15 Mbps, traffic load for Class 2 = 0.9).

Traffic sources of Class 1 and Class 2 are generated using iPerf with source H1 to H4. In Admission Control Logic Module the parameters are given as in Scenario 1.

Scenario 2 objectives. The primary objective of the second scenario is to evaluate how the parameters of the Class 2 traffic source affect the quality of service experienced by the Class 1. Moreover, the research specifically examines the impact of the buffer length k and burst parameters on Class 1 while the network is under significant Class 2 load. By systematically adjusting these parameters within the Mininet environment, it is necessary to verify end-to-end packet loss probability for the Class 1. This scenario is designed to verify separation of traffic classes and to ensure that the quality for Class 1 remains uncompromised by Class 2.

Scenario 3: Multi-path and Variable Load Conditions
Test conditions. The experimental setup involves host H1, H3 and H4. In this configuration, hosts H1 and H3 act as simultaneous traffic generators sending data with high Class 1 (p1 and p2) to a common receiver, host H4, as presented in Fig. 4. The application initiates a service request for:

- Class 1: p1 (traffic load 0.3, 0.5, 0.7, 0.9),
- Class 1: p2 (traffic load 0.3, 0.5, 0.7, 0.9).

In Admission Control Logic Module the parameters are given as in Scenario 1. In Mininet HTB parameters are as follow: k = 5, burst = 12000 B.

Scenario 3 objectives. The research focuses on the behavior of the AC mechanism when Class 1 requests are received for different network routes that may share common bottlenecks. The primary objective of the scenario is to determine the precise threshold at which the AC module begins rejecting new service requests to prevent violation of the maximum packet loss probability threshold. This scenario validates the system's capacity.

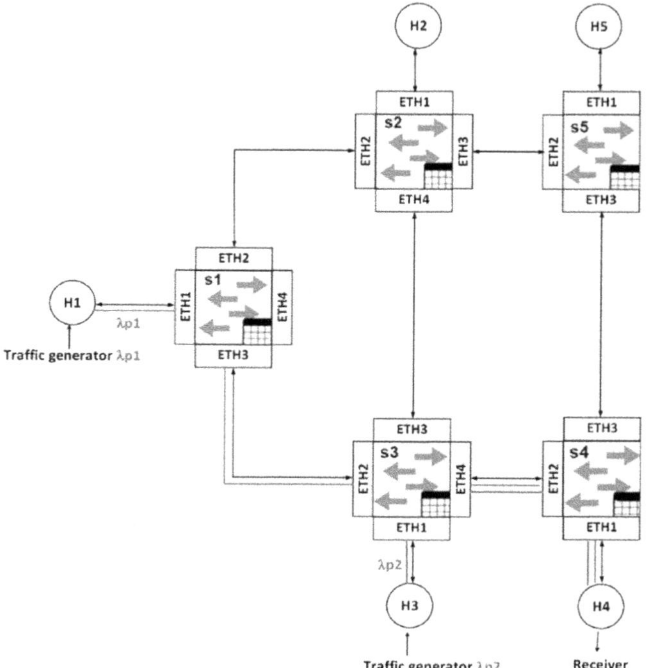

Fig. 4. Multi-path and Variable Load Conditions.

5   Results

The verification of the proposed system was conducted through a multi-stage process encompassing functional software evaluations and empirical research based on the previously defined scenarios. Initial functional tests confirmed the seamless operation of the application layer and its integration with the SDN infrastructure. The Authentication and Authorization module successfully filtered incoming requests by validating them against SLA contracts stored in the database. Deep packet inspection using Wireshark further verified the southbound communication, confirming that the Ryu controller correctly translated application-level decisions into FLOW_MOD messages for the Mininet switches. Additionally, the HTB queue structure and associated filters were validated using the *tc* command, ensuring that traffic was appropriately mapped to the correct service classes based on destination ports.

The research for the first scenario confirmed the correct operation of the AC function. The service request was accepted. The end-to-end packet loss probability in the AC module was computed considering buffer length (k) only, excluding the burst parameter,

As illustrated in Table 2, the burst parameter emerged as the primary factor influencing network stability. At a low value of 5000 B the system was unable to compensate for instantaneous traffic spikes, leading to significant packet loss even as buffer sizes were increased. Conversely, increasing the burst to 12000 B successfully eliminated all observed packet loss probabilities proving that adequate traffic shaping is essential for meeting the QoS requirements of Class 1. The buffer length, k, only provided measurable improvements when the burst size was sufficient to mitigate the initial spikes in packet count.

Table 2. Results of the first scenario - packet loss probability for Class 1.

k/burst (B)	5000	9500	12000
1	0.01039604	0.002084962	0
5	0.0082074	0.001323802	0
10	0.00312662	0	0
20	0	0	0
50	0	0	0
100	0	0	0

The second scenario evaluated the quality of the Class 1 under Class 2 load, confirming the effective separation provided by the HTB mechanism. While for Class 2 90% of its 15 Mbps allocation was occupied, the Class 1 maintained a loss probability consistent with the trends observed in the single-flow scenario, as shown in Table 3. This results demonstrate that Class 1 flows remain independent of background data transmissions (Class 2), if appropriate burst size is provided (Table 3).

Table 3. Results of the second scenario - packet loss probability for Class 1.

k/burst (B)	5000	9500	12000
1	0.00990099	0.002084419	0
5	0.00672225	0.001302762	0
10	0.00366610	0.000781657	0
20	0.00216427	0	0
50	0.00136802	0	0
100	0	0	0

Finally, the third scenario tested the system's capacity to prevent network over-subscription across multiple traffic generators and paths. The experimental results, summarized in Table 4, indicate that the Admission Control module successfully maintains its functionality as the cumulative load approaches capacity limits. The system consistently blocked new call service requests sent via application plane once the predicted packet loss probability, calculated in AC Module Logic, exceeded the 0.001 threshold, particularly for flows requiring 70% or more of the guaranteed bandwidth on shared links. These findings confirm the preventive capability of the AC function.

Table 4. Comparative analysis of the Admission Control function within the third scenario.

Priority class p1	0.3	0.5	0.7	0.9
Priority class p2	0.3	0.5	0.7	0.9
Dropped s1-eth3	0	0	Blocked by SDN AC application	Blocked by SDN AC application
Sent s1-eth3	7664	12766	Blocked by SDN AC application	Blocked by SDN AC application
Dropped s3-eth4	0	17	Blocked by SDN AC application	Blocked by SDN AC application
Sent s3-eth4	7664	24953	Blocked by SDN AC application	Blocked by SDN AC application
End-to-end packet loss probability	0	0.0006808	Blocked by SDN AC application	Blocked by SDN AC application

6 Conclusions

The primary outcome of this research project is the successful implementation of the SDN network demonstrator, featuring a functional Admission Control function that supports two service classes. The experimental environment was established using the Mininet emulator, where a specific network topology was defined alongside Hierarchical Token Bucket (HTB) queues to ensure guaranteed bandwidth for various class services.

In the control plane, the Ryu controller was integrated to facilitate the transmission of real-time network statistics to the management application and to enable the dynamic modification of flow tables within the emulated switches. The statistics were used in order to verify the load traffic in the network. The application plane, developed using the Django framework, effectively executes both Admission Control (AC) and Authentication and Authorization (AA) functions. Furthermore, the system provides a centralized interface for managing network agreements, submitting service requests, and monitoring critical network data, including port statistics and flow table contents. The conducted studies confirmed the correct operation of the implemented Admission Control function. The implemented SDN AC application successfully denied a service request that could not meet the required Quality of Service (QoS). As a result, the most important parameters were indicated. Utilizing Django framework and Ryu enhances the integration and deployment of the proposed solution within academic and experimental testbeds.

While the current Admission Control function is based on throughput and packet loss probability, future development should aim to incorporate additional Quality of Service parameters, such as end-to-end delay. Expanding the demonstrator's capabilities to include dynamic routing protocols is also recommended to enhance its performance and adaptability in more complex network scenarios.

Acknowledgments. This work was supported by the Gdańsk University of Technology under the grant DEC-25/1/2023/IDUP/I3b/Ag within the Argentum Triggering Research Grants – "Excellence Initiative - Research University" program.

Disclosure of Interests. The authors have no competing interests to declare that are relevant to the content of this article.

References

1. ITU-T Recommendation Y. 3300: Framework of Software-Defined Networking (2014)
2. Messaoudi, S., Ksentini, A., Messaoudi, F., Bonnet, C.: GNN-based SDN Admission Control in Beyond 5G Networks. In: GLOBECOM 2023 - 2023 IEEE Global Communications Conference, pp. 6103–6108, Kuala Lumpur (2023)
3. Jiang, W., Zhan, Y., Zeng, G., Lu, J.: Probabilistic-Forecasting-Based Admission Control for Network Slicing in Software-Defined Networks. IEEE Internet Things J. **9**(15), 14030–14047 (2022)
4. Leguay, J., Maggi, L., Draief, M., Paris, S., Chouvardas, S.: Admission control with online algorithms in SDN. In: NOMS 2016—2016 IEEE/IFIP Network Operations and Management Symposium, pp. 718–721, Istanbul (2016)
5. Cao, H., Yin, B., Cao, J., Shi, H., Lu, X.: Analysis of admission control in SDN-based media delivery network. In: 2016 35th Chinese Control Conference (CCC), pp. 2443–2448, Chengdu (2016)
6. Erel, M., Teoman, E., Özçevik, Y., Seçinti, G., Canberk, B.: Scalability analysis and flow admission control in mininet-based SDN environment. In: 2015 IEEE Conference on Network Function Virtualization and Software Defined Network (NFV-SDN), pp. 18–19, San Francisco (2015)
7. Mininet Project Contributors: Mininet. http://mininet.org. Last accessed 16 Feb 2026
8. Ryu SDN Framework: https://ryu-sdn.org. Last accessed 16 Feb 2026
9. Open Networking Foundation: ONF TR-502: SDN Architecture, Issue 1 (2014)
10. Django: The web framework. https://www.djangoproject.com. Last accessed 16 Feb 2026
11. Yan, J., Jin, D.: VT-Mininet: Virtual-time-enabled Mininet for scalable and accurate software-define network emulation. In: Proceedings of the 1st ACM SIGCOMM Symposium on Software Defined Networking Research (SOSR '15), Article 27, pp. 1–7. Association for Computing Machinery, New York (2015)
12. Tc-htb(8): Linux man page. https://man7.org/linux/man-pages/man8/tc-htb.8.html. Last accessed 28 Mar 2026

Topology-Aware Communication Optimization for CFD Simulations in OpenFOAM

Jonas Sieberer[1]([⊠]), Clemens Gößnitzer[2], Andreas Schröder[1], and Robert Elsässer[1]

[1] Universität Salzburg, 5020 Salzburg, Austria
{jonas.sieberer,andreas.schroder,robert.elsaesser}@plus.ac.at
[2] Large Engines Competence Center LEC, 8010 Graz, Austria
clemens.goessnitzer@lec.tugraz.at

Abstract. Parallel computational fluid dynamics (CFD) simulations are commonly executed on modern high-performance computing systems with hardware topologies, where communication costs vary significantly across memory hierarchies and network links. OpenFOAM, a widely used open-source CFD framework, provides a scalable MPI-based parallel infrastructure. However, its default process placement and communication strategies are largely topology-agnostic, which can lead to suboptimal performance on NUMA-based cluster architectures.

We present a topology-aware communication optimization for OpenFOAM that targets both local and global communication in iterative linear solvers. Local communication is optimized by reassigning MPI ranks to physical cores based on the communication structure induced by the domain decomposition and the underlying hardware topology. In addition, a custom global reduction schedule is introduced that aligns collective communication with the hierarchical organization of compute nodes, NUMA domains, and NUMA nodes.

Our experimental results show a substantial redistribution of communication toward faster hardware paths, leading to better runtime with the largest improvements observed for communication-intensive solver configurations. These findings demonstrate that topology-aware communication strategies can significantly enhance the performance of OpenFOAM on modern HPC systems.

Keywords: Computational fluid dynamics · Finite volume method · OpenFOAM · Non-uniform memory access hierarchy

1 Introduction

Computational fluid dynamics (CFD) simulations [18] are an essential tool in modern scientific and engineering research, with applications ranging from aerodynamics and weather prediction to combustion and energy systems. As simulation models grow in size and complexity, CFD applications increasingly rely on high-performance computing (HPC) systems to achieve acceptable runtimes [13]. The open-source CFD framework OpenFOAM (Open Source Field Operation and Manipulation) [21] is widely used in both academia and industry[1]. OpenFOAM employs the finite-volume method (FVM)

---

[1] We used OpenFOAM-12 by "The OpenFOAM Foundation", https://openfoam.org/release/12/.

© The Author(s), under exclusive license to Springer Nature Switzerland AG 2026
P. Neumann et al. (Eds.): ICCS 2026, LNCS 16784, pp. 62–77, 2026.
https://doi.org/10.1007/978-3-032-29924-6_5

to discretise the underlying partial differential equation, which results in large (and sparse) systems of linear equations. These systems are typically solved using iterative methods on large HPC machines. Parallel execution in OpenFOAM is based on domain decomposition and MPI-based inter-process communication [19]. Although this approach makes simulations highly scalable in theory, the performance of the corresponding solvers is strongly influenced by the amount of local and global communication arising during the computation.

Modern HPC systems exhibit hierarchical hardware topologies, including compute nodes, NUMA domains, and cache-coherent core groups, where communication costs vary significantly across levels. OpenFOAM assigns MPI ranks by default sequentially without taking into account the underlying hardware structure. Thus, communication patterns are not aligned with the hardware topology, causing a substantial fraction of communication to be mapped onto slower hardware paths instead of low-latency ones.

We present a topology-aware communication optimization for OpenFOAM that targets both, local and global communication in iterative linear solvers. We improve local communication by assigning MPI ranks to physical cores based on the communication structure induced by the domain decomposition and the hardware topology. We also introduce a hardware-aware global reduction schedule to better align communication with the hierarchical organization of the system. The proposed approach is implemented as a preprocessing step and does not modify OpenFOAM's numerical algorithms. Our experimental results show that these topology-aware strategies lead to (partly significant) runtime improvements on modern HPC systems. While implemented for Open-FOAM, the methodology can possibly be extended to other applications and architectures.

Our main goal is to reduce communication overhead in OpenFOAM, which is a key bottleneck for its scalability [2]. Improving the efficiency of various other parallel applications by exploiting hardware topology has been widely studied. In particular, local [7] and global communication [8] were optimized in MPI applications through rank-to-core binding and rank reordering. In [16] a related approach was used to optimize data communication in ccNUMA systems for a parallel social network application. Further work on reducing communication in NUMA architectures includes thread and memory migration strategies [6], and the reduction of cache coherence traffic [1]. How OpenFOAM currently deals with the hardware architecture is described in Sect. 4.

The paper is organized as follows. Section 2 outlines FVM and its parallel execution in OpenFOAM. Section 3 describes the relevant hardware characteristics of modern HPC systems. Section 4 presents our topology-aware communication optimizations. Experimental results are given in Sect. 5, followed by the conclusions in Sect. 6.

2   The Finite-Volume-Method in OpenFOAM

This chapter presents an overview of the implementation of the finite-volume method in OpenFOAM. First, the discretisation of the computational domain and the mesh structures used are described. Then the discretisation of PDEs and their transformation into a system of linear equations is briefly explained for the sequential workflow. Subsequently, the parallel workflow in OpenFOAM is discussed, with a particular focus on the communication between processes. Special attention is given to the local and global communication steps required during the execution of iterative linear solvers.

2.1 Mesh Structure and Finite-Volume Discretisation

In OpenFOAM, the three-dimensional computational domain $\Omega \subset \mathbb{R}^3$ is discretized into a finite number n of non-overlapping polyhedral control volumes V_i, also called cells, that together form the discretized domain Ω_D. A control volume is bounded by a set of flat faces; the collection of cells and faces defines the computational mesh [9].

Faces shared by two control volumes are referred to as internal faces, while faces on the boundary of Ω_D are boundary faces. By convention, the cell with the smaller index is designated as the owner of a face, while the adjacent cell is referred to as the neighbor. Boundary faces are grouped into boundary patches, allowing different boundary conditions to be applied to different parts of the domain boundary. The faces belonging to these boundary patches are conventionally placed at the end of the face index range. Each face f_r is associated with a face area vector S_r, which is normal to the face and points outward from the owner cell. Each control volume V_i is associated with a representative calculation point x_i, typically chosen as the cell centroid [9].

OpenFOAM operates internally on three-dimensional meshes. Two-dimensional problems are represented by using a single cell in the third direction by assigning empty boundary conditions to the corresponding faces. Figure 1a illustrates a simple two-dimensional 3×3 mesh together with the associated face area vectors.

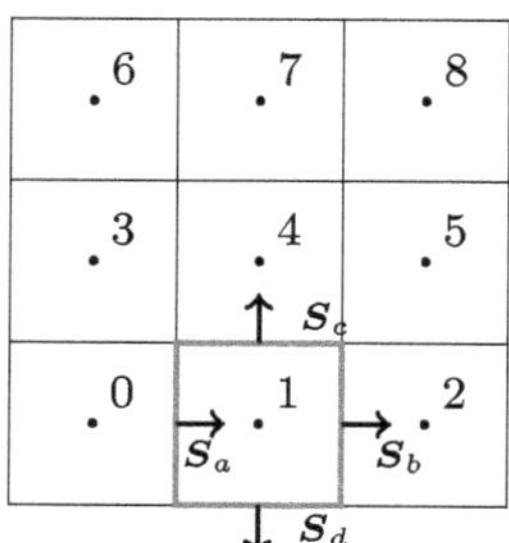

(a) 3×3 mesh over $[0, 1]^2$ with cell indices.

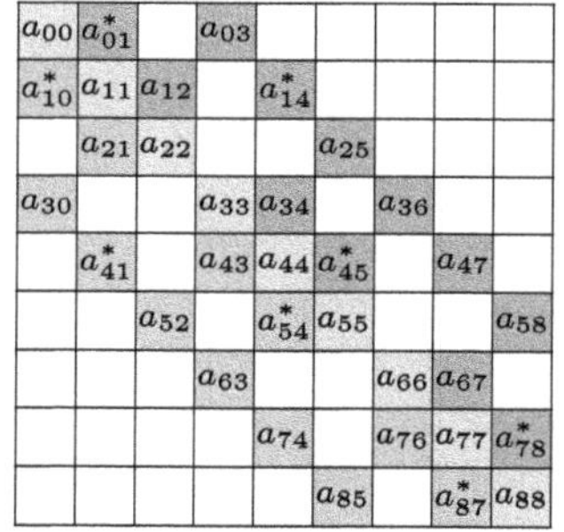

(b) Finite volume Matrix A for the left mesh.

Fig. 1. Structured 3×3 example mesh with marked faces $f_a, \ldots, f_d$ of cell V_1 and corresponding sparse finite-volume matrix. (Some matrix elements are marked with $*$, they represent the coefficients lying on the processor patches, see explanation in Fig. 2b)

Let the partial differential equation be defined over Ω_D. In the finite-volume method, the equation is integrated over each control volume. Applying the divergence theorem [15] one can transform volume integrals into surface integrals over the faces of the cell. The resulting face fluxes are approximated using discretisation schemes provided by OpenFOAM [4]. Internal faces give rise to coupling terms between neighbouring control volumes, while boundary faces contribute according to the prescribed boundary conditions.

Each control volume therefore leads to a linear equation containing contributions from neighbouring cells as well as source and boundary terms collected on the right-hand side. Assembling the contributions from all faces yields a system of linear equations of the form $A\phi = b$, where $A \in \mathbb{R}^{n \times n}$ is a sparse matrix whose non-zero off-diagonal entries correspond to internal faces and encode the mesh connectivity.

In many practical applications, the underlying PDEs are nonlinear. In OpenFOAM, such cases are treated using iterative linearization techniques, where nonlinear terms are evaluated using previously computed solution values. This results in a sequence of linear systems of the above form, which are solved repeatedly until convergence.

Figure 1b shows the finite-volume matrix corresponding to the mesh in Fig. 1a. Diagonal entries collect all self-coupling and boundary contributions, while the right-hand side vector b contains source and boundary-condition terms.

Solving this system yields the values of the unknown field at the calculation points, which are assumed to be representative for the corresponding control volumes. Open-FOAM provides a range of iterative solvers for this task, and solving these linear systems constitutes the dominant computational cost in most simulations. Parallel execution reduces the size of the local systems but introduces communication between processes, as discussed in the following sections.

2.2 Domain Decomposition and Parallel Execution

When OpenFOAM is executed in parallel, the mesh is initially generated in the same way as for a sequential simulation. For a given number of processes $n_p \geq 2$, the parallel computation begins with a domain decomposition step, in which the global mesh is partitioned into n_p submeshes. The objectives of this decomposition are to obtain a balanced distribution of cells among the processes and a minimization of inter-subdomain interfaces, as these directly determine the amount of inter-process communication.

OpenFOAM provides several decomposition methods, including simple geometric partitioning as well as graph-based approaches using third-party libraries such as SCOTCH [12] and METIS [5]. During decomposition, each control volume V_i is uniquely assigned to exactly one MPI process P_k, with $k \in \{0, \ldots, n_p - 1\}$. Each process therefore obtains a subset of cells that form its local submesh.

Figure 2a illustrates a simple decomposition of a 3×3 mesh into two subdomains. After decomposition, each submesh is constructed locally on its assigned process. As in the sequential case, the submesh consists of points, faces, and cells, which are assigned new local indices. Addressing structures are created to map these local indices to the corresponding global indices of the original mesh. The original boundary patches are split accordingly and distributed among the submeshes.

For each pair of adjacent subdomains, a new boundary patch is introduced, referred to as a *processor patch*. These patches represent the set of faces between neighbouring MPI processes, which are appended to the list of boundary faces of each submesh. Each processor face corresponds to an internal face of the global mesh and therefore appears on exactly two processor patches, one on each adjacent process. The processor boundary condition defines the communication interface and ensures that the required field values are exchanged between neighbouring processes during the computation.

Once the submeshes have been constructed, all processes execute the same solver code in a distributed-memory parallel fashion. Apart from additional coordination and input/output tasks performed by MPI rank 0, all ranks participate symmetrically in the numerical computation and communication.

On each process P_k, a local linear system $A_k \phi_k = b_k$ is assembled for the corresponding submesh. The coefficients associated with internal faces and physical boundary faces are computed in the same manner as in the sequential case. For processor faces, the discretisation coefficients are determined analogously to internal faces. However, the required neighbour values are not locally available.

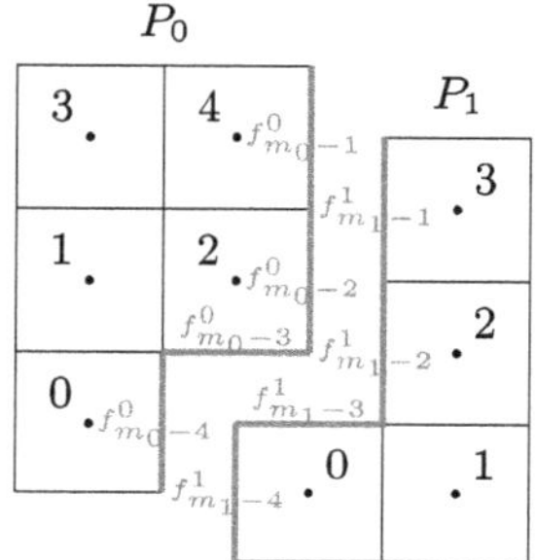

(a) Example decomposition into two subdomains (local cell indices).

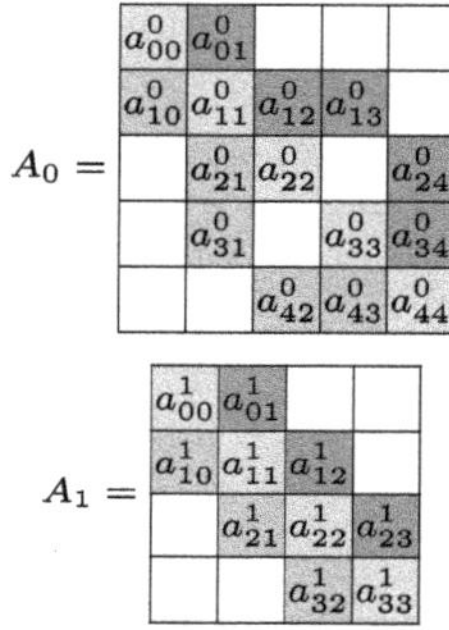

(b) Local matrices A_0 (top) and A_1 (bottom).

Fig. 2. Simple horizontal decomposition of 3×3 mesh. The faces $f^0_{m_0-4}, \ldots, f^0_{m_0-1}$ form the new processor boundary patch of P_0 and correspond to the global coefficients $a^*_{01}, a^*_{41}, a^*_{45}, a^*_{78}$ in Fig. 1b (where they are marked with $*$).

All coefficients associated with internal faces are contained in the local matrices, whereas those corresponding to processor faces are stored separately. Since processor faces do not introduce additional source terms, the local right-hand side vectors b_k and the initial solution values are direct subvectors of their global counterparts. Hence, the collection of local systems remains algebraically consistent with the global system. Figure 2b illustrates the resulting local matrix structures for our example.

To solve the global system iteratively, missing neighbor values associated with processor faces must be exchanged between processes. This neighbor communication is required, for example, in sparse matrix–vector products involving adjacent subdomains.

In addition, iterative solvers require global operations such as scalar products and norm evaluations, which involve collective communication across all processes. Although independent of processor-face data, these reductions require global synchronization and thus contribute to the overall communication cost. If a large number of processes are used, neighbor exchange and global reductions significantly influence the runtime. The structure of these communication patterns is discussed in the next section.

2.3   Local and Global Communication

Iterative linear solvers in OpenFOAM [4], including Krylov subspace methods such as the preconditioned conjugate gradient method (PCG), and multigrid solvers such as the geometric algebraic multigrid method (GAMG), repeatedly execute distributed linear algebra operations. Each iteration involves matrix–vector products, vector norms, and scalar products. In a parallel setting, these operations induce *local communication* between neighboring subdomains and *global communication* for collective reductions.

Local Communication. Local communication refers to data exchange between adjacent subdomains that share a processor boundary patch. Consider the local operation $u_k = A_k v_k$, where $A_k \in \mathbb{R}^{n_k \times n_k}$ denotes the local finite-volume matrix on process P_k and $v_k \in \mathbb{R}^{n_k}$ is the local vector, in which each entry represents the value of a cell in the corresponding submesh. While contributions associated with internal faces can be computed locally, those corresponding to processor faces require values of v owned by neighbouring processes. These values are referred to as halo values [20].

Since the vector v changes between successive executions of matrix-vector products, the required halo data must be exchanged after every iteration. For each processor patch, the relevant vector entries are packed, sent to the neighboring process, and the corresponding remote values are received in return. Thus, the communication volume depends heavily on the processor patches and the quality of the domain decomposition.

In OpenFOAM, this exchange is implemented via a two-stage update. First, communication is initiated for all processor patches, issuing send and receive operations through OpenFOAM's communication layer, which internally wraps MPI primitives. This allows local computations that do not depend on halo data to proceed during the send/receive process. Second, the solver waits for completion of the communication and incorporates the received halo values, completing the local matrix–vector product.

Global Communication. Global communication is required for operations that combine contributions from all processes, such as scalar products, vector norms, and other collective reductions. Each process computes a local partial result, which must be aggregated into a global value and redistributed to all ranks.

In OpenFOAM, reductions are handled within the Pstream communication layer. Depending on the configuration and implementation settings, OpenFOAM either delegates the operation to MPI collective routines or executes its own explicit reduction schedule based on point-to-point communication. When default OpenFOAM schedules are used, the corresponding deterministic reduction patterns are independent of the MPI implementation and operate solely on MPI rank indices. If the number of processes exceeds a certain predefined value, a tree-based reduction schedule is used, which is organized as a logical binary tree over the subdomain indices. At each level, processors are paired such that one process receives a partial result from its partner, performs a local reduction, and forwards the aggregated value to the next level. This continues until a root process accumulates the global result, which is then propagated back to all ranks.

As mentioned above, the schedule is constructed based on MPI rank indices and is independent of the hardware topology. Hence, communication steps may traverse

NUMA boundaries or network links unnecessarily, although faster paths exist. This also motivates the topology-aware communication optimizations given in the next sections.

3 Hardware Topology Background

Modern high-performance computing (HPC) systems are typically organized as clusters of interconnected compute nodes [11]. Each node is a shared-memory system containing multiple processor sockets, main memory, and a network interface for inter-node communication. Although all cores within a node share a global address space, the physical organization of processors, caches, and memory results in a hierarchical topology with non-uniform communication and memory-access costs.

At the highest level, communication between compute nodes is performed via dedicated interconnects such as InfiniBand. Inter-node communication usually incurs the highest latency and lowest bandwidth and is therefore the most expensive communication path. In this work, only the node-local topology is considered.

Within a node, cores are organized into NUMA (non-uniform memory access) domains, typically corresponding to CPU sockets. Each NUMA domain is directly connected to a portion of main memory. Memory accesses within the same domain exhibit lower latency and higher bandwidth than accesses to remote memory attached to other sockets, which require traversal of inter-socket interconnects.

At a finer granularity, each NUMA domain consists of multiple NUMA nodes, corresponding to individual cores or small core groups, which share partially the same cache resources. Modern processors provide a hierarchical cache subsystem, typically including private L1 and L2 caches at each core and a shared last-level cache (LLC) [3], see Fig. 3. Data served from cache is substantially faster than accesses to main memory, making intra-NUMA locality the most efficient communication path within a node.

The performance of parallel applications therefore depends on how well computation, memory placement, and communication are aligned with the hardware hierarchy. In particular, NUMA-aware process placement aims to exploit fast local communication paths while minimizing costly remote and inter-node data transfers [17].

Depending on the relative placement of two communicating processes, four distinct types of point-to-point communication can be identified, from fastest to slowest:

- *intra-NUMA-node*, cores on same NUMA-node
- *inter-NUMA-node*, cores in same NUMA-domain, but on different NUMA-nodes
- *inter-NUMA-domain*, cores on same compute node, but on different NUMA-domains
- *inter-node*, cores on different compute nodes

These latency differences arise from the underlying cache hierarchy, memory controllers, and interconnects, as illustrated in Fig. 3. This hierarchical structure directly motivates topology-aware communication optimizations.

3.1 Hardware Setup

The experiments were conducted on two HPC clusters with shared-memory compute nodes. The VSC-5 zen3_0512 system provides 128 cores per node across two sockets,

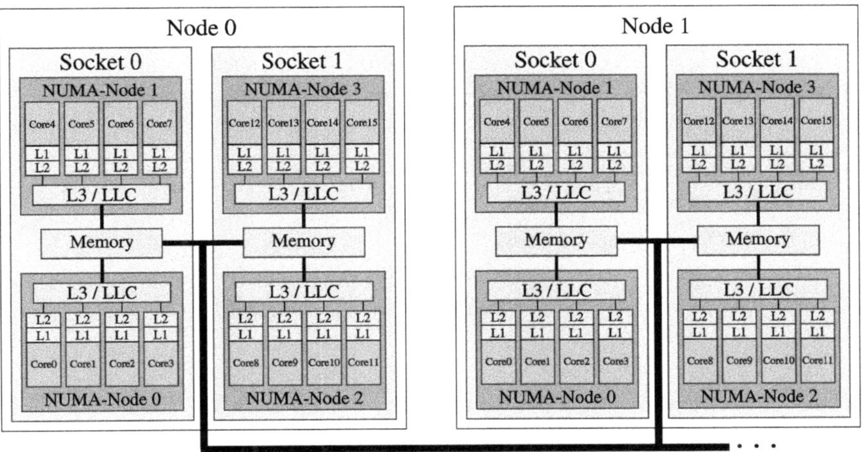

Fig. 3. Example hardware topology with two compute nodes, illustrating communication paths at different hierarchy levels. Thicker links indicate higher latency.

organized into a total 16 NUMA nodes[2]. The LEC hpc2 cluster is a private in-house system with 48 cores per node distributed over four sockets, with each socket corresponding to one NUMA node. The relevant hardware and software characteristics are shown in Table 1. In VSC-5, the compute nodes are connected via several InfiniBand switches. However, we do not consider this additional network hierarchy in our paper.

To quantify the impact of different communication paths, additional point-to-point communication times were measured using the OpenFOAM communication framework. In these tests, a list of scalar values is exchanged bidirectionally between all participating processes, and the corresponding round-trip time is measured. Depending on the placement of the processes within the hardware topology, different communication times can be observed, reflecting the respective communication layers. The size of these lists corresponds, in the parallel workflow, to the number of faces associated with processor patches. Accurate knowledge of the hardware topology seems to be essential, as incorrect assumptions about the mapping between cores, NUMA nodes, and NUMA domains can significantly degrade potential performance gains.

The measured mean communication times, summarized in Table 2, clearly reveal substantial latency differences between the communication path types. Although absolute times vary between nodes, especially on VSC-5 depending on their position, the relative cost ordering remains consistent, confirming the importance of prioritizing fast communication paths. However, for larger message sizes on VSC-5, inter-NUMA-domain communication can become slower than inter-node communication. This behavior depends on the specific hardware characteristics and on the processor-patch sizes occurring in a given simulation. Since both aspects vary across HPC systems and benchmark cases, we assume a fixed hierarchical ordering of communication paths in the present work. Future work could incorporate runtime communication

---

[2] See VSC-5: Vienna Scientific Cluster 5, https://docs.asc.ac.at/systems/vsc5.html.

Table 1. Hardware characteristics relevant for communication.

	VSC-5 zen3_0512	LEC hpc2
CPU	AMD EPYC 7713	Intel Xeon Gold 6126
Cores per node	128	48
Sockets per node	2	4
NUMA nodes per socket	8	1
Cores per NUMA node	8	12
Network	InfiniBand 200 Gbit/s	InfiniBand 100 Gbit/s
MPI	OpenMPI 4.1.4	OpenMPI 4.1.5

benchmarks to determine the effective hierarchy dynamically and adapt the optimization accordingly.

Table 2. Mean point-to-point communication time in μs.

	VSC-5				LEC hpc2		
Size	Intra-Nn	Inter-Nn	Inter-Nd	Inter-Node	Intra-Nn	Inter-Nn	Inter-Node
10	0.4	0.7	1.4	2.9	1.1	1.5	7.9
100	0.8	1.5	3.2	3.7	1.4	2.0	8.6
500	1.3	2.8	6.5	5.6	2.2	3.3	11.1
1000	3.1	5.0	11.4	8.0	3.6	5.8	11.8

4 Topology-Aware Communication Optimization

As discussed previously, the runtime of large-scale OpenFOAM simulations is dominated by iterative linear solvers, whose core operations induce substantial communication overhead. Since communication costs depend strongly on process placement within the hardware hierarchy, performance can be improved by aligning rank mapping and communication schedules with the underlying topology. In the following, we present a topology-aware optimization targeting both local and global communication.

Let P_k, $k \in 0, \ldots, n_p - 1$, denote the MPI process with rank k. By default, Open-FOAM employs a canonical, index-based rank assignment that is independent of both the mesh decomposition and the hardware topology.

For a simulation executed on N compute nodes with N_c cores each, resulting in $n_p = N \cdot N_c$ MPI processes, process P_k is placed on node $\lfloor k/N_c \rfloor$ and core ($k \bmod N_c$). This simple bottom-up strategy does not account for NUMA nodes, NUMA domains, or inter-process communication patterns. Consequently, neighbouring subdomains with high data exchange may reside on distant hardware resources, causing avoidable inter-socket or inter-node communication.

4.1 Optimized Processor Rank-to-Core Allocation

To overcome the limitations of the default OpenFOAM mapping, processes with high mutual communication are assigned to physically close cores, where proximity corresponds to faster communication paths in the hardware hierarchy. Since communication costs increase from intra-NUMA-node to inter-node transfers, the optimization minimizes communication hierarchically, beginning with the most expensive level.

Graph-Based Formulation. The communication structure induced by the mesh decomposition is modeled as a weighted graph, where each MPI process is a vertex and edges represent neighbouring subdomains defined by processor patches. The edge weights are equal to the number of faces on the corresponding processor patch and approximate the expected communication volume.

Minimizing inter-node communication reduces to a graph partitioning problem. The graph is partitioned into N parts of (almost) equal size N_c, such that the sum of edge weights between different parts is minimized. This problem is analogous to mesh decomposition and is solved using e.g. the SCOTCH graph partitioning library [12]. Since exact partition sizes cannot always be guaranteed, a lightweight post-processing step is applied to enforce balanced partitions. Figure 4 shows this approach for $n_p = 36$ subdomains on $N = 3$ nodes. Compared to the canonical OpenFOAM rank assignment, the optimized partitioning substantially reduces inter-node communication edges.

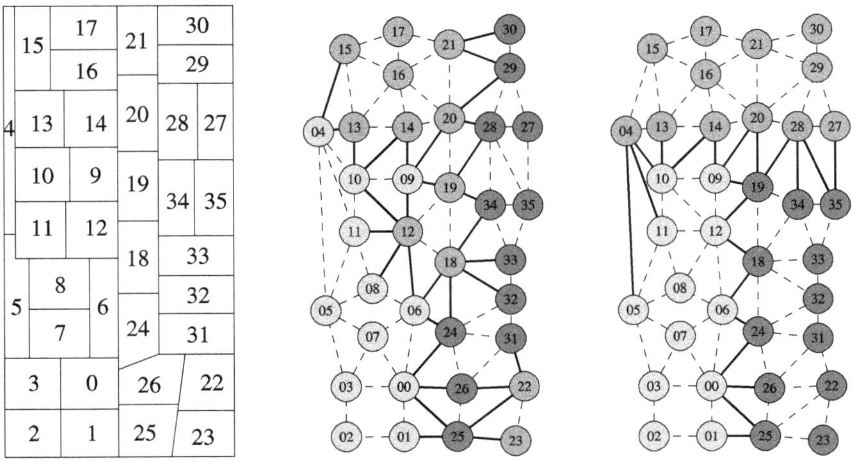

(a) Example decomposition obtained by SCOTCH

(b) Comm. graph with canonical rank-to-core assignment

(c) Comm. graph with optimized rank-to-core assignment

Fig. 4. A decomposition with two possible rank-to-core assignments shown in (b) and (c). Vertices with same color are located on the same compute node. Dashed edges show intra-node communication, while thick edges show inter-node communication.

Hierarchical Partitioning. After minimizing inter-node communication the same strategy is applied recursively to lower levels of the hardware hierarchy. Each node-level partition is treated as an induced subgraph and further partitioned into NUMA domains and subsequently into NUMA nodes with appropriate partition sizes.

This yields an explicit assignment of each process to a compute node, NUMA domain, and NUMA node. For reproducibility, ranks are renumbered so that rank 0 occupies the first core of the first node, with subsequent ranks ordered by increasing NUMA-domain and NUMA-node indices, preserving the communication structure.

Rank File Generation. From the optimized assignment, a rank file is generated that binds each MPI rank to a specific core. This requires a mapping of the physical cores to NUMA domains and NUMA nodes. Assuming a homogeneous cluster architecture, the mapping is identical across nodes and is stored in two arrays of length N_c. Combining these informations yields a rank file specifying a fixed target node and core slot for each rank. We implemented this procedure in a custom OpenFOAM preprocessing utility.

Optimizing only the rank-to-core assignment improves local communication but introduces a subtle drawback. The default tree-based global reduction in OpenFOAM operates solely on MPI rank indices. As a result, ranks with nearby indices communicate at lower tree levels, whereas distant ranks interact only at higher levels. Because OpenFOAM assigns ranks canonically in index order, independent of hardware topology, this default mapping implicitly aligns well with the index-based reduction tree.

When ranks are reassigned using a custom rank file, this implicit alignment between rank indices and the reduction tree is lost. As a result, the fixed index-based reduction tree may induce additional communication over slow hardware paths. Therefore, optimizing local communication alone is insufficient and must be complemented by a topology-aware global communication schedule.

4.2 Optimized Global Communication Schedule

To overcome the issue described above, the global reductions are reorganized to follow the hardware hierarchy. That is, reductions are first performed within NUMA nodes, then within NUMA domains, and finally across compute nodes. Using the known rank-to-core mapping and the hardware topology, a custom reduction tree is constructed. For each rank, exactly one successor (send target) and a list of predecessors (receive sources) are defined, with rank 0 serving as the root. The resulting schedule is written to an OpenFOAM dictionary and loaded once at the start of the simulation. Enabling custom schedules needs only minor modifications to the OpenFOAM communication layer. These changes and the implemented utility can be found in [14].

The optimized global communication schedule can be used either in conjunction with the optimized rank assignment or independently with the default OpenFOAM rank mapping, depending on the hardware and MPI implementation. The impact of the proposed optimizations on the performance is evaluated in the following section.

5 Experimental Results

The proposed topology-aware communication optimizations were evaluated using several OpenFOAM standard cases executed on the HPC systems described in Sect. 3.1. Each case was run in three configurations: (i) unmodified OpenFOAM, (ii) global optimization only, and (iii) combined local and global optimization.

The benchmarks include two- and three-dimensional cases with varying mesh sizes and solver types, representative for communication-intensive workloads, see Table 3. These cases can also be found in [14]. All experiments follow a strong-scaling setup with fixed problem size and increasing node counts. The preprocessing time ranges between 10–30 s (on both, LEC hpc2 and VSC-5). Since this utility is executed once per simulation setup, its cost is negligible w.r.t. the overall runtime.

Table 3. Overview of experimental benchmark cases and simulation parameters.

Case	System	Geometry	Cells	Solver	Timesteps
pitzDaily	VSC-5	2D	19,560,000	GAMG	300
pitzDaily	LEC hpc2	2D	11,002,500	GAMG	300
laplacianFoam	VSC-5	3D	30,000,000	CG	500
laplacianFoam	LEC hpc2	3D	11,250,000	CG	500
cavity2D	VSC-5	2D	20,250,000	GAMG	50
cavity2D	LEC hpc2	2D	9,000,000	GAMG	50
cavity3D	VSC-5	3D	20,796,875	GAMG	100
cavity3D	LEC hpc2	3D	8,998,912	GAMG	100

Communication Analysis. Using the generated rank files and reduction schedules, the distribution of communication across hardware levels was analyzed. Figure 5 shows the relative share of local and global communication across hardware paths for the *pitzDaily* case. For local communication, the mesh-induced communication graph is used, where edge weights correspond to processor-patch sizes. Based on the rank-to-core mapping, edges are assigned to hardware levels, and the communication volume of a single halo exchange is obtained by aggregating edge weights per level and normalizing by the total volume. For global communication, the reduction tree defines the communication pattern, with unit weights per edge. The relative share is obtained by counting edges per hardware level. Different trees are used for the standard and optimized configurations. The optimized configuration shifts communication predominantly toward fast intra-NUMA-node paths, while communication across NUMA domains is substantially reduced. Similar trends were observed across all cases and node counts.

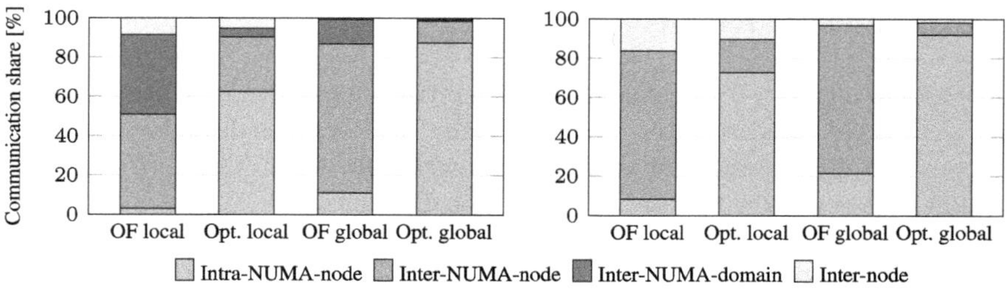

Fig. 5. Distribution of local and global communication across different hardware communication paths for *pitzDaily* on VSC-5 with six nodes (left) and LEC hpc2 with seven nodes (right) for OpenFOAM standard (OF) and the optimized versions (Opt.).

Runtime Results. To assess the performance improvements, runtimes were measured for increasing numbers of compute nodes. For each configuration, multiple runs were performed, outliers were removed, and mean runtimes were recorded (Fig. 6 shows the scaling behavior). We decided to present the data on a log–log scale in order to accommodate a wide range of runtime values and to highlight scaling trends and relative performance differences. For the corresponding runtime decrease, comparing (i) unmodified OpenFOAM and (iii) combined local and global optimization, see Table 4.

Table 4. Relative runtime decrease (%) of the local and global optimized OpenFOAM compared to the standard version on different amount of compute nodes (2–10). A negative value means that the runtime increases. LEC denotes the cluster LEC hpc2.

Case	System	2	3	4	5	6	7	8	9	10
pitzDaily	VSC-5	6.0	16.1	12.8	23.8	23.5				
	LEC	−0.8	7.9	7.1	9.6	7.9	6.6			
laplacian	VSC-5	18.1	35.4	53.7	70.6	85.3				
	LEC	0.5	1.3	2.7	3.8	4.1	2.9	1.9	6.4	5.0
cavity2D	VSC-5	11.0	21.7	21.1	23.4	30.1				
	LEC	0.8	14.2	16.9	17.6					
cavity3D	VSC-5	3.2	4.7	6.4	6.3	8.1				
	LEC	−0.2	4.5	8.8	9.2	9.7	8.9	6.3	6.9	8.4

Across all benchmarks, the combined local and global optimization consistently achieves the lowest runtime. On VSC-5, improvements are particularly pronounced, indicating that local communication dominates solver runtime on this architecture. On LEC, the difference between global-only and combined optimization is smaller, suggesting a comparatively stronger impact of global communication. On the LEC cluster, not all cases were executed up to ten nodes. Previous scaling studies showed performance degradation beyond moderate node counts for certain cases due to hardware and

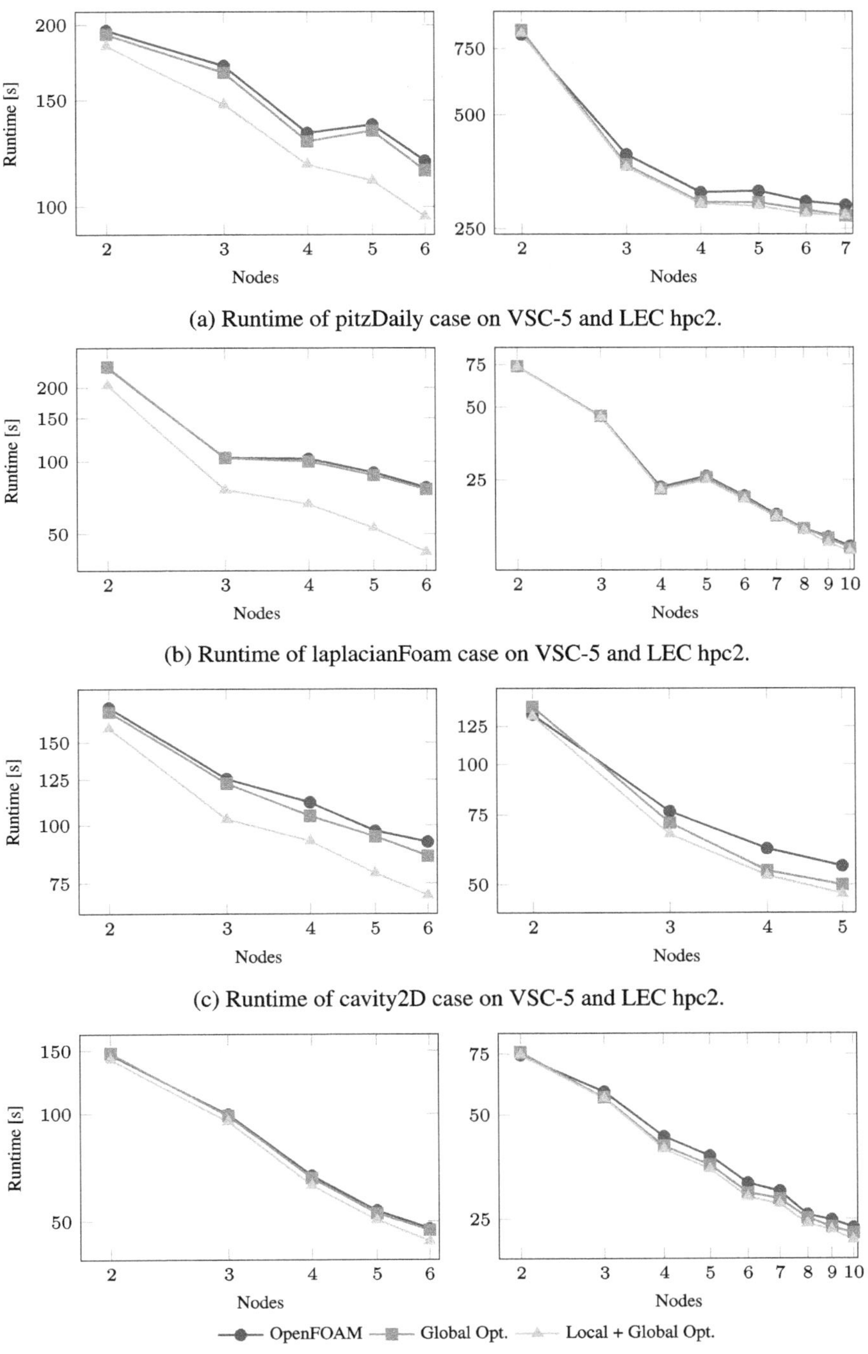

(a) Runtime of pitzDaily case on VSC-5 and LEC hpc2.

(b) Runtime of laplacianFoam case on VSC-5 and LEC hpc2.

(c) Runtime of cavity2D case on VSC-5 and LEC hpc2.

(d) Runtime of cavity3D case on VSC-5 and LEC hpc2.

Fig. 6. Runtime of all benchmark cases in the three configurations.

interconnect effects. To ensure meaningful comparisons, experiments were therefore restricted to configurations exhibiting stable scaling.

The observed performance differences between two- and three-dimensional cases are primarily determined by the communication characteristics of the iterative solver. In general, three-dimensional meshes involve more neighbouring cells and processor interfaces, leading to increased communication per iteration. However, the amount of communication per iteration also depends on the employed solver.

The two-dimensional cavity case exhibits larger speedups due to a higher number of iterations, resulting in increased communication, and thus greater optimization potential. The three-dimensional laplacian case setup also show significant improvements when the solver requires many iterations. Thus, the speedup depends on the mesh structure as well as solver characteristics. Although the magnitude of the speedup varies, all cases consistently show reduced runtime with topology-aware communication.

6   Conclusion and Future Work

This work demonstrates that topology-aware communication optimization can reduce the runtime of parallel OpenFOAM simulations. By optimizing process placement and reduction schedules w.r.t. the hardware hierarchy, communication in iterative linear solvers is shifted from slow inter-node and inter-socket paths to faster local links. Although we observe performance improvements across all benchmark cases, the achieved speedup depends on the hardware architecture and solver characteristics.

Future work will focus on extending the approach to dynamically changing decompositions. Possible directions include periodically recomputing rank placements and communication schedules based on updated processor patches, or incorporating communication-aware criteria directly into the mesh decomposition process.

Acknowledgments. We acknowledge the financial support of the "COMET - Competence Centers for Excellent Technologies" Program of the Austrian Federal Ministry for Innovation, Mobility and Infrastructure and the Austrian Federal Ministry of Economy, Energy and Tourism and the Provinces of Salzburg, Styria and Tyrol for the COMET Centre (K1) LEC GETS. The COMET Program is managed by the Austrian Research Promotion Agency (FFG). The computational results were partially achieved using the Austrian Scientific Computing (ASC) infrastructure. To improve the language and readability, we used GPT-5.2 of OpenAI [10].

Disclosure of Interests. The authors have no competing interests.

References

1. Caheny, P., Alvarez, L., Derradji, S., Valero, M., Moretó, M., Casas, M.: Reducing cache coherence traffic with a NUMA-aware runtime approach. IEEE Trans. Parallel Distrib. Syst. **29**(5), 1174–1187 (2018)
2. Culpo, M.: Current bottlenecks in the scalability of OpenFOAM on massively parallel clusters (2011). PRACE white paper to appear on http://www.praceri.eu
3. Garcia Flores, V.: Memory Hierarchies for Future HPC Architectures. Ph.d. dissertation, Universitat Politecnica de Catalunya, Barcelona, Spain (2017)

4. Greenshields, C., Weller, H.: Notes on Computational Fluid Dynamics: General Principles. CFD Direct Ltd, Reading, UK (2022)
5. Karypis, G., Kumar, V.: A fast and high quality multilevel scheme for partitioning irregular graphs. SIAM J. Sci. Comput. **20**(1), 359–392 (1998)
6. Laso, R., Lorenzo, O.G., Cabaleiro, J.C., Pena, T.F., Lorenzo, J.A., Rivera, F.F.: CIMAR, NIMAR, and LMMA: novel algorithms for thread and memory migrations in user space on NUMA systems using hardware counters. Future Gener. Comput. Syst. **129**, 18–32 (2022)
7. Mercier, G., Jeannot, E.: Improving MPI applications performance on multicore clusters with rank reordering. In: Recent Advances in the Message Passing Interface, pp. 39–49. Springer (2011)
8. Mirsadeghi, S.H., Afsahi, A.: Topology-aware rank reordering for MPI collectives. In: 2016 IEEE International Parallel and Distributed Processing Symposium Workshops (IPDPSW), pp. 1759–1768 (2016)
9. Moukalled, F., Mangani, L., Darwish, M.: The Finite Volume Method in Computational Fluid Dynamics - An Advanced Introduction with OpenFOAM and Matlab. Springer (2015)
10. OpenAI: ChatGPT-5.2 (2026). https://chatgpt.com/
11. Patterson, D.A., Hennessy, J.L.: Parallel Computer Architecture: A Hardware/Software Approach. Morgan Kaufmann (2011)
12. Pellegrini, F.: Distillating knowledge about SCOTCH. In: Combinatorial Scientific Computing. Dagstuhl Seminar Proceedings (DagSemProc), vol. 9061, pp. 1–12 (2009)
13. Severance, C., Dowd, K.: High Performance Computing. OpenStax CNX (2010)
14. Sieberer, J.: Topology-Aware Communication Optimization (2026). https://doi.org/10.5281/zenodo.19368569
15. Strang, G., Herman, E.: Calculus Volume 3. OpenStax (2016), Chapter 6: Vector Calculus
16. Szustak, L., Lawenda, M., Arming, S., Bankhamer, G., Schweimer, C., Elsässer, R.: Profiling and optimization of python-based social sciences applications on HPC systems by means of task and data parallelism. Future Gener. Comput. Syst. **148**, 623–635 (2023)
17. Tan, L., Yufei, R., Dantong, Y., Shudong, J.: Analysis of numa effects in modern multicore systems for the design of high-performance data transfer applications. Future Gener. Comput. Syst. **74** (2017)
18. Versteeg, H.K., Malalasekera, W.: An Introduction to Computational Fluid Dynamics - The Finite Volume Method. Pearson Education, Amsterdam (2007)
19. Walker, D.W., Dongarra, J.J.: MPI: a standard message passing interface. Supercomputer **12**, 56–68 (1996)
20. Wang, H.: Algorithm Design for High-Performance CFD Solvers on Structured Grids. Ph.d. dissertation, University of California, Irvine (2021)
21. Weller, H., Tabor, G., Jasak, H., Fureby, C.: A tensorial approach to computational continuum mechanics using object orientated techniques. Comput. Phys. **12**, 620–631 (1998)

Aggregating Columnar Data on Cluster File Systems

Jonas Hahnfeld[1,2]([✉]), Jakob Blomer[1], and Thorsten Kollegger[2]

[1] CERN, Geneva, Switzerland
`{jonas.hahnfeld,jakob.blomer}@cern.ch`
[2] Goethe University Frankfurt, Institute of Computer Science, Frankfurt, Germany
`kollegger@em.uni-frankfurt.de`

Abstract. Data in High Energy Physics (HEP) is primarily stored in binary columnar formats. This enables efficient reading of select columns for the physics analysis use case while employing transparent compression to reduce storage space. However, this combination of requirements makes it challenging to write HEP data in parallel. This has been partially addressed with multithreaded writing, but efficient usage in cluster environments remained an open question. In this paper, we extend the concepts to distributed scenarios and parallel writing of columnar data into a single file on cluster file systems. For this, we present different strategies based on a central aggregator, using MPI one-sided communication, and relying on synchronization with file locks. We evaluate the scalability of these approaches on two cluster file systems, and discuss the impact of different parameters on performance. Finally, we motivate a real-world use case for resource-intensive Monte Carlo simulation jobs.

Keywords: Distributed parallel writing · Cluster file systems · Columnar data format · High Energy Physics · ROOT

1 Introduction

The Large Hadron Collider (LHC) at CERN is currently the largest particle accelerator used for High Energy Physics (HEP) research. It hosts a number of experiments that record and analyze particle collisions to improve our understanding of the fundamental structure of the universe. This requires handling of data at exabyte scale, which commonly relies on the ROOT framework for storage and analysis [7].

After the currently ongoing Run 3, until 2030, the LHC will be upgraded to the High-Luminosity LHC (HL-LHC). This will enable even more collisions and consequently result in a steep increase of data rates. To prepare for this future, the HEP community is currently adopting the RNTuple format [6]. It was developed as an evolution of the presently used TTree columnar format. Early results confirm smaller file sizes and better performance when exploiting modern storage systems [5].

© The Author(s) 2026
P. Neumann et al. (Eds.): ICCS 2026, LNCS 16784, pp. 78–93, 2026.
https://doi.org/10.1007/978-3-032-29924-6_6

In previous work, we added support for scalable multithreaded parallel writing to RNTuple [13]. This has the potential to avoid the merge step for combining smaller files from multiple threads. The evaluation shows perfect scalability up to the storage bandwidth limit on a single server. This will be useful on traditional High Throughput Computing resources provided by the Worldwide LHC Computing Grid [4].

However, as data volumes and compute requirements grow, capacities are increasingly complemented by resources on existing High Performance Computing (HPC) systems. This requires efficient usage of cluster environments, with distributed parallelism and output to cluster file systems. A particular challenge is that distributed writers must be able to make independent progress without relying on collective operations. This is critical for load balancing between events of different sizes and varying processing times.

The main contributions of this work are as follows: In Sect. 3, we discuss concepts to aggregate columnar data on cluster file systems and possibilities to implement distributed parallel writing. We experimentally evaluate the scalability of the alternative implementation strategies in Sect. 4. In a second step, we study the best strategies on two different cluster file systems in Sect. 5. Finally, we present a possible use case of our work for Monte Carlo simulations in Sect. 6.

2   Related Work

There exist multiple formats and libraries to store scientific data on HPC systems: NetCDF was designed to exchange data in atmospheric research [17]. Its parallel interface PnetCDF is built on MPI-IO [14]. HDF5 supports flexible data models and parallel I/O via MPI [10]. However, neither of these two widespread libraries is suitable for parallel writing of HEP data as discussed in [13]: While NetCDF supports record variables with an unlimited dimension, it assumes they grow together which is impractical for nested data of variable size. For HDF5, resizing an extendible dataset is a collective operation, which would prevent independent writer progress. Variable-length array datatypes on the other hand are not supported at all with parallel writing.

More recently, ADIOS 2 tackles scalable storage of scientific data as part of the Exascale Computing Project (ECP) [11]. The library is based on MPI and the framework supports a number of *engines* and *transports*. ADIOS 2 *variables* allow for flexible data layouts, including different array sizes per rank needed to support nested data. However, the library is fundamentally built around *steps* which are collective synchronization points. Altogether, none of the existing libraries support distributed parallel writing of HEP data and a direct comparison is not possible.

MPI-IO refers to the set of I/O functions defined as part of the MPI standard [15]. It is portably implemented by ROMIO [21] and OMPIO [8], and underpins both PnetCDF and HDF5 mentioned before. MPI-IO can significantly improve application performance with data sieving and collective I/O [20].

However, this does not apply for columnar HEP data where events are processed in parallel and writers should progress without synchronization. Moreover, HEP data is grouped into clusters that are non-overlapping and several tens of megabytes in size.

Singh and Gabriel introduce parallel I/O directly on compressed files [19]. In contrast, we integrate distributed parallel writing for columnar data. This requires aggregating metadata to allow reading of individual columns as if the data was written sequentially. Furthermore, our solution focuses on independent write operations instead of collective writes.

Beyond multithreading, the ROOT framework also provides the two classes `TParallelMergingFile` and `TMPIFile`. They use incremental merging to produce a single output file, which was also adopted by the ATLAS experiment [18]. However, these approaches require sending all data to a server or collector rank, which does not scale as we will show. For this reason, we do not present an explicit comparison to these classes.

3 Aggregating Columnar Data

Columnar data formats are optimized for reading subsets of the stored columns. Notable examples include the original ROOT Trees [7] currently used by LHC experiments and Apache Parquet [22]. In this work, we focus on RNTuple, which is the designated successor of the TTree format [6].

3.1 Overview of Multithreaded Parallel Writing

All three columnar data formats mentioned above support nested data and transparent compression. As a result, rows (called *entries* in RNTuple) have variable size. This makes parallel writing challenging because data cannot be laid out in a regular grid. However, for HEP use cases, entries or *events* are often independent and can be reordered.

Based on this observation, we previously described concepts for parallel writing of columnar data [13]. The key contribution is the identification of relocatable *units of writing* that can be prepared and compressed independently. In the case of RNTuple, a *cluster* is a natural unit of writing, which spans a consecutive range of entries. This allows to implement parallel writing with cooperating threads: After the cluster size is known, a lock is taken and the writer reserves an appropriate buffer in the file. Finally, the metadata is updated to append the cluster and its entries to the dataset. We note that this approach trivially enables independent progress outside the critical section, and allows different number of clusters written per thread.

3.2 Distributed Parallel Writing with Aggregator

In this work, we aim to extend the concepts developed for multithreaded parallel writing to distributed environments. The goal is to have multiple *writers* produce a single file with columnar data on a shared file system. A naive strategy is to send compressed clusters to a single *aggregator* that serializes the write operations. In a potential implementation with MPI, this can be realized with a thread on a root rank. Doing so requires support from the MPI implementation and an application that is initialized with `MPI_THREAD_MULTIPLE`.

In the HEP context, an equivalent approach is used by the Athena framework of the ATLAS experiment [18]. However, for distributed environments, the approach has two disadvantages that limit scalability: First, it requires sending a large amount of data, where a single aggregator can become a bottleneck. Moreover, since writing is serialized at the aggregator, it is limited by the bandwidth of a single process. This means it cannot efficiently utilize the full potential of parallel cluster file systems.

A better approach is to send only the metadata, which is small compared to the total size of compressed cluster data. Nevertheless it is enough information for the aggregator to compute the cluster size and reserve a buffer in the file. It then returns the buffer's byte offset to the writer, which can flush out the cluster data. The advantage is that this approach allows distributed parallel writing from all processes into the assigned parts of the file. Still, all metadata is collected as before and written by the aggregator when closing the file.

For implementations, there are two important details to optimize performance: First, the container format may require anchor objects when reserving byte buffers. For example, ROOT files are organized on disk as a linked list of *keys*. Therefore, when embedding RNTuple data into ROOT files, each buffer is preceded by a `TKey` header. In a straightforward implementation, this header is directly written on the aggregator. However, this can introduce increased latency if other processes on the same node write at the same time. Alternatively, the aggregator can send the header to the writer, which can prepend it to the cluster data. We will demonstrate the advantage of this optimization in Sect. 4.2.

Additionally, cluster file systems may use striping to distribute a file to multiple storage servers. If multiple nodes write to parts of the file in the same stripe, this will result in lock contention. It may therefore be required to align the reserved buffers to improve performance. If the stripe size is small compared to a unit of writing, one method is padding to ensure alignment. While this introduces an overhead in file size, we found it acceptable compared to the gain in write bandwidth. We will discuss the performance impact of alignment for different cluster file systems in Sect. 5.

3.3 Maintaining a Global Offset Without Aggregator

In this section, we discuss concepts for distributed parallel writing without a central aggregator. The key insight is that metadata aggregation can be delayed until committing the dataset. Instead, each writer tracks its local metadata and the collective aggregation is done when closing the file. For the cluster data, the writers only need to reserve and write to buffers in the file. These can be linearly allocated using a global offset that is atomically incremented. The problem of implementing such global offset is similar to that of maintaining a shared file pointer in MPI-IO.

The authors of ROMIO mention different methods to implement shared file pointers [21]. One possibility is to have a central entity, either a thread or dynamic process, own the file pointer. A writer can access and update the value by communicating with this entity. However, such active entity is also able to directly aggregate the metadata as discussed in the previous section. For this reason, it is not useful to reduce the aggregator's role and only maintain the file offset.

A method without active involvement of the central entity is remote memory access, for example via MPI one-sided communication. It allows a process to share a "window" of its memory and either uses "active" or "passive" target synchronization. While the former explicitly involves the target process, the MPI standard mentions that the passive "communication paradigm is closest to a shared memory model" [15]. Using accumulate functions, it is then possible to implement a counter to maintain a global offset.

The final method used by some portable MPI-IO implementations relies on file locks [21]: They store the shared file pointer in a file and protect reads and atomic updates with advisory record locks. The same technique can be used for distributed parallel writing of columnar data. We note that instead of a second, separate file, it is also possible to identify a part of the final file that can be temporarily used.

When merging the metadata, implementations have to decide on the order of clusters. If appended by process, their order may not match the structure in the file. This can result in non-linear access patterns and seeking when reading the produced file. It is unclear if this has a measurable impact since each cluster is several tens of megabytes in size. If found important, a linear order can be restored by sorting based on buffer offsets when aggregating the cluster metadata.

4   Scalability of Distributed Parallel Writing

Based on the described approaches, we implement distributed parallel writing of columnar data in the RNTuple format. The prototype relies on MPI for easy integration into cluster environments on HPC systems. However, some aggregation strategies such as the metadata aggregator can also be implemented with other communication libraries. For example, some HEP experiment frameworks have a distributed architecture based on ZeroMQ [3,9].

In a first step, we evaluate the scalability of our prototype on the Vega supercomputer [2]. Each node of the system has two AMD Epyc 7H12 processors for a total of 128 physical cores, and 256 GB of DDR4-3200 memory. Nodes are interconnected with Infiniband HDR, which provides a bandwidth of up to 200 Gb/s. We build ROOT 6.36.06, the latest version with long-term support, from source with GCC 14.2.0. Our prototype is compiled using OpenMPI 5.0.9 and UCX 1.20.0 with support for `MPI_THREAD_MULTIPLE`. For execution, we use entire nodes allocated with SLURM and request two `cpus-per-task` to allow using hyperthreading for the aggregator on the root rank.

In the remainder, we use a variation of the synthetic benchmark described in our previous work [13]: Instead of threads, each MPI rank writes entries of random data into two fields, a 64-bit integer and a vector of `float`s. The vector size follows a Poisson distribution with $\mu = 5$ while the elements are uniformly distributed in $[0, 100)$. This results in a relatively small entry size of only 36 bytes on average. Unless noted otherwise, each rank writes 10 million entries, amounting to 360 MB before compression, in a weak scaling setup. The columnar data is staged in a 4 MiB buffer before being passed to the operating system. We experimented with bigger buffer sizes up to 32 MiB, but did not see improved bandwidths. For each data point, we repeat the benchmark five times and compute the arithmetic mean of the run times. Then we calculate the storage bandwidth based on the written data volume of all ranks. If compressing data using `zstd` (level 10), the bandwidth is based on the compressed data volume written to storage. Error bars are computed with one standard deviation of the measured run times.

4.1 Comparison of Aggregation Strategies

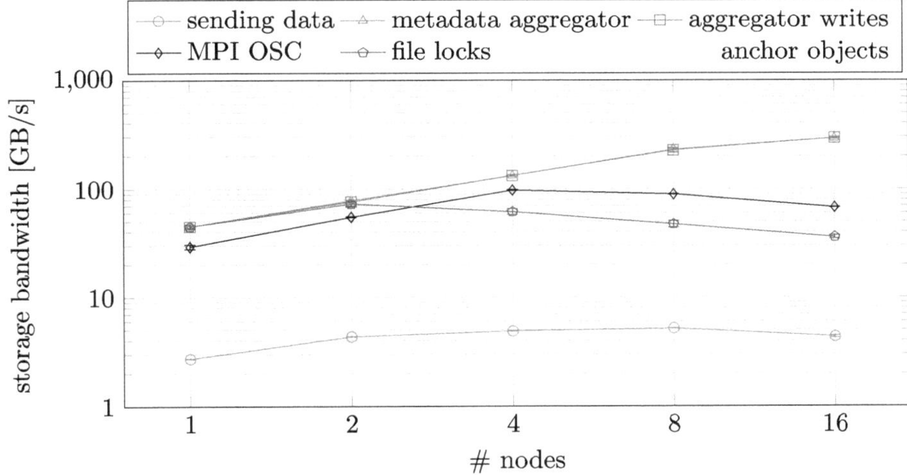

Fig. 1. Measured bandwidth writing to `/dev/null` without compression.

By writing to `/dev/null`, we compare the strategies for infinitely fast storage. This allows to assess their communication behavior when writing the data is not the bottleneck. Figure 1 shows the measured bandwidth without compression with up to 16 nodes and 128 ranks per node. The first strategy is to send all data to an aggregator rank using MPI. It is clear that this approach is the slowest, with a maximum bandwidth of 5 GB/s. This was measured in a strong scaling experiment at a constant total data volume of 46 GB, to reduce run time. In previous experiments, weak scaling with reduced repetition counts did not result in improved bandwidths.

For the second strategy, our prototype sends only metadata to the aggregator and will write data directly into the shared file. This approach scales much better and achieves more than 290 GB/s on 16 nodes. By default, writing is fully distributed and each rank writes the anchor objects necessary for its data. We evaluate this approach with a variation where the aggregator is instructed to write these anchor objects. In the case of writing to `/dev/null`, this does not make a difference since data is discarded by the operating system. This is why the two top lines (green triangles and blue squares) are perfectly overlapping.

We also implement two strategies to maintain a global offset as introduced in Sect. 3.3. The first option uses MPI one-sided communication (OSC) and reaches a maximum of 100 GB/s at four nodes, which is slower than the metadata aggregator. To also test synchronization via file locks, we maintain the global offset in a file on the Lustre file system and use byte-range locking via `fcntl`. In this case, the performance peaks at 70 GB/s with 2 nodes and then decreases with more nodes.

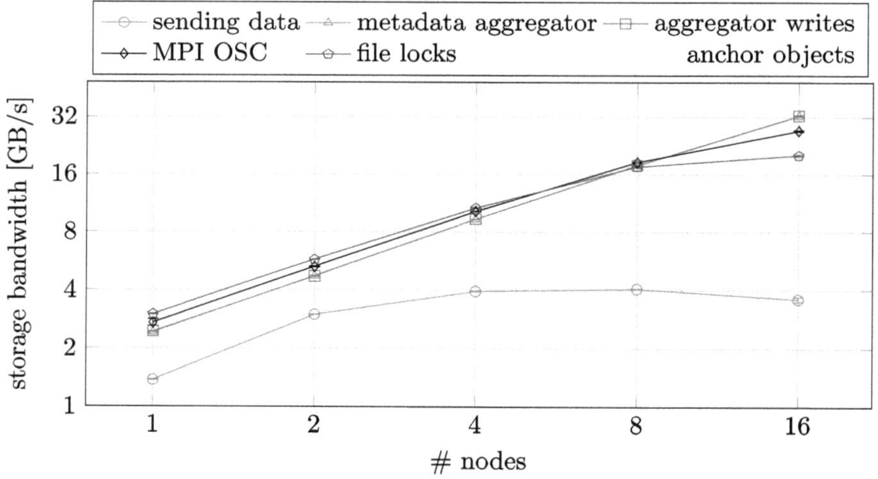

Fig. 2. Measured bandwidth writing to `/dev/null` with `zstd` compression.

Figure 2 shows the results when compressing the columnar data with `zstd`. While sending the data is still the slowest, the other strategies are limited by the compression throughput. This results in a maximum bandwidth of 32.5 GB/s with 16 nodes at a parallel efficiency of 68 % compared to a maximum bandwidth of 3 GB/s with a single node. It should be noted that these bandwidths are achieved with different strategies, as synchronization via file locks is the fastest for fewer nodes. This is because it uses the file system as additional external resource for synchronization. The metadata aggregator and OSC on the other hand need to compete for CPU resources.

4.2   Distributed Parallel Writing on Cluster File Systems

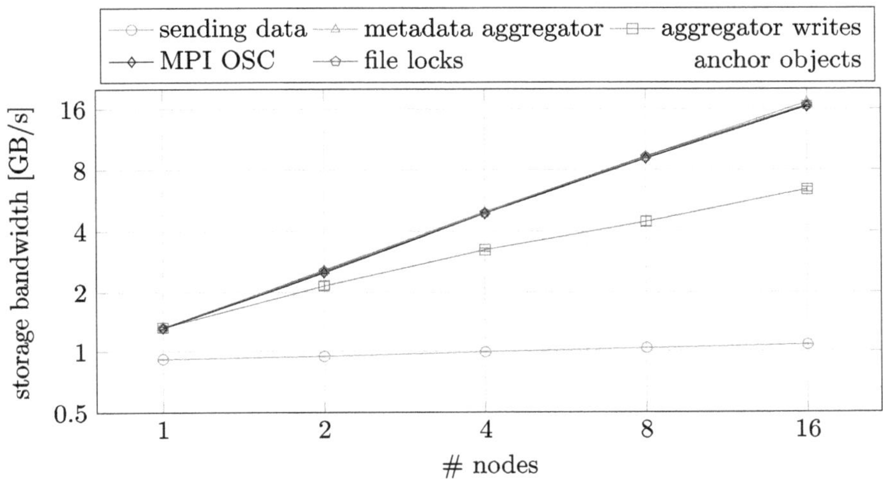

Fig. 3. Measured bandwidth writing to Lustre without compression.

Next, we write the RNTuple data into a single file on the Lustre file system provided on Vega. The file system is backed by 10 DDN Exascaler ES400NVX with NVMe disks, running version 2.15.2 of Lustre. In this section, we configure a write alignment of 1 MiB, matching the default stripe size, and a stripe count of 8. We will explore different choices for these parameters in Sect. 5.1 and discuss their impact. The measurements follow the same methodology as before, with a strong scaling setup for the first strategy that sends all data. For the others, the benchmark writes a constant amount of data per rank, and all results are plotted in Fig. 3. Writing to Lustre, the metadata aggregator achieves a maximum bandwidth of 17.2 GB/s. MPI OSC and file locks scale up to 16.4 GB/s and 16.6 GB/s, respectively. If the aggregator writes the anchor objects, the bandwidth is significantly lower with a maximum of 6.4 GB/s. As discussed before in Sect. 3.2, this is because of increased latency on the aggregator.

The results using `zstd` compression in Fig. 4 are similar to those without compression: Using the metadata aggregator, we measure a maximum bandwidth of 12.9 GB/s. Maintaining a global offset with MPI OSC or synchronizing via file locks is slightly slower at 11.9 GB/s and 11.6 GB/s, respectively. We conclude that these three strategies are able to make efficient use of cluster file systems for writing columnar data.

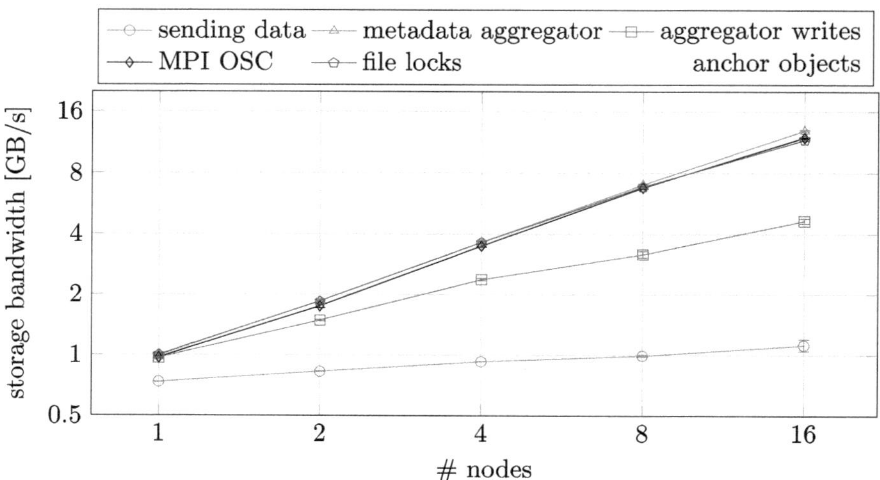

Fig. 4. Measured bandwidth writing to Lustre with `zstd` compression.

5 Performance Studies of Cluster File Systems

In this section, we continue to study the performance of the most scalable strategies as determined before. For that, we focus on the use case of writing compressed data because it is more relevant for the HEP community. Additionally, it involves some compute and is therefore closer to the real use of HPC resources. In the following, we look at the two file systems provided on the Vega supercomputer: Lustre and CephFS. We compare different write and file system configurations and measure their impact on the attained bandwidth.

5.1 Lustre

As a parallel file system, Lustre is able to *stripe* a file to multiple Object Storage Targets (OSTs). If used properly, this allows an application to achieve a higher bandwidth than a single OST can provide. Striping can be configured with two primary parameters: The stripe count prescribes how many objects are allocated on different OSTs. Data is written round-robin to each object according to the configured stripe size. In our measurements, we do not see an advantage for larger stripe sizes. We therefore keep this parameter at its default value of 1 MiB and set a matching write alignment. As before, data is staged in a 4 MiB buffer on the application side before being written.

For the Lustre file system, we already compared the different strategies in Sect. 4.2. We therefore restrict ourselves to the metadata aggregator and compare different configurations as shown in Fig. 5. The line with green triangles corresponds to the previous measurement using a stripe count of 8, with a maximum of 12.9 GB/s. When instead configuring a lower *stripe_count* = 1, the write bandwidth is limited to around 3 GB/s.

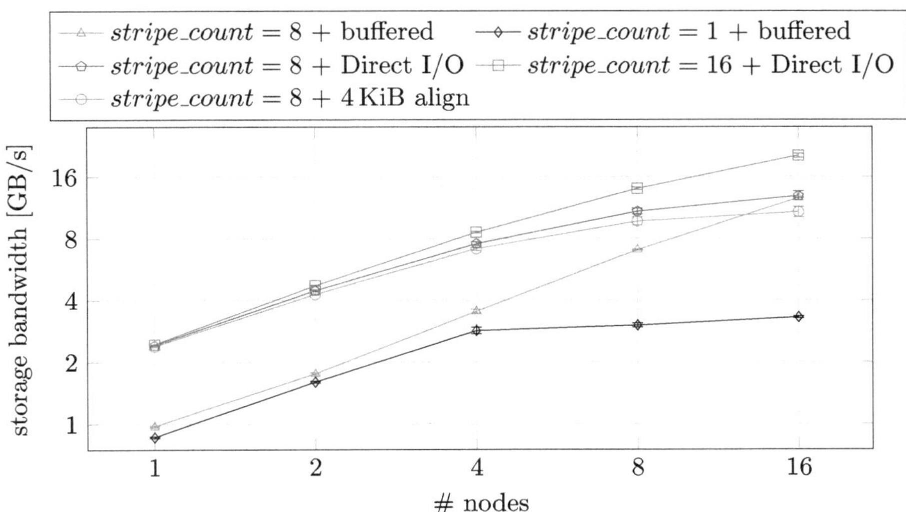

Fig. 5. Measured bandwidth writing to Lustre using the metadata aggregator and `zstd` compression, with different stripe counts and alignments.

The achievable bandwidth is not only limited by the hardware, but also by buffered writing and caching in software. This can be avoided by opening the file with the additional flag `O_DIRECT`. In previous work, we showed the benefit for multithreaded writing [12]. For distributed parallel writing to Lustre, it results in an increased bandwidth with fewer nodes and a stripe count of 8. This can be further improved to 20.3 GB/s with a stripe count of 16, which is not beneficial for buffered writing. We also tested increasing the application buffer to 32 MiB, which however does not change the measured bandwidths.

For the final measurement, we revert to a stripe count of 8 and decrease the write alignment to 4 KiB. This is lower than the stripe size of 1 MiB and results in contention when multiple ranks write into the same stripe. With Direct I/O, we measure a bandwidth of 10.8 GB/s, which is 16 % lower than 12.9 GB/s measured using an alignment of 1 MiB. For buffered writing, the effect is smaller and the bandwidth is only reduced to 12 GB/s, which we omit from the plot. A possible explanation is that writing with `O_DIRECT` is synchronous while buffering is able to hide latency resulting from contention.

5.2   CephFS

The second cluster file system available on Vega is CephFS. It provides a POSIX-compatible layer on top of the RADOS object storage. The installation on Vega is backed by 61 servers with HDDs and runs Ceph version 18.2.4. The object pool is erasure-coded with $m = 16$ data chunks and a default size of 4 KiB. This multiplies to a *stripe_width* of 64 KiB, which we choose as write alignment. On the CephFS side, we keep the default file layout with an object size of 32 MiB and *stripe_count* $= 1$. For all measurements, we bypass caching by opening the file with `O_DIRECT`. Otherwise, with buffered writing, we observed bad scaling behavior with more than one node.

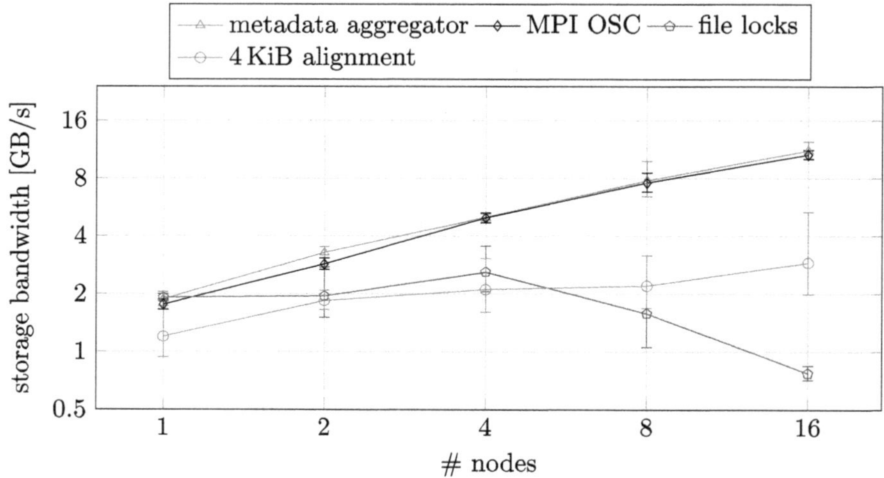

Fig. 6. Measured bandwidth writing to CephFS with `zstd` compression.

Figure 6 shows the bandwidths measured with different strategies writing compressed data to CephFS. Compared to previous results, the variation between runs is much larger, as reflected by the error bars. This is because the CephFS mount is also used for the home directories, which likely generates constant background load. Nevertheless, we measure up to 11.2 GB/s with the metadata aggregator and 10.6 GB/s with MPI OSC.

When synchronizing via file locks, the bandwidth does not scale beyond 2.6 GB/s. This can have multiple reasons, one of which is the general load on the Metadata Servers (MDS) from the home directories. More detailed measurements would be required to fully explain this bad scalability. Finally, we measure the metadata aggregator with a write alignment of 4 KiB. It is clear that the achieved bandwidth is much lower with a maximum of 2.9 GB/s.

6   Application: Monte Carlo Simulation

In this last section, we consider a possible real-world use case for distributed parallel writing: HEP experiments heavily rely on Monte Carlo simulations of the expected detector response. Then, physicists compare these predictions with actual detector data to find signals of new physics or precisely measure observables. To address the required computational needs, experiments would benefit from the ability to use HPC systems. However, this requires to make efficient use of cluster environments.

In the following, we consider the CMS experiment, one of the two general-purpose experiments at the LHC. Similar techniques will also be applicable for other experiments. Monte Carlo simulation in CMS is handled by its offline software framework CMSSW [1]. Recently, CMS framework developers started integrating RNTuple as an alternative to TTree. We build on this work and locally add our prototype as an option for distributed parallel writing. This requires an extension of our implementation to support writing multiple RNTuple datasets into a single file. We achieve this by starting one metadata aggregator per dataset and synchronizing buffer reservation on the root rank.

Table 1. Monte Carlo simulation steps of 1000 TTbar events using CMSSW with 1 process and 8 threads. The final row is a combination of the last two steps, directly outputting reconstructed events into the MiniAOD format.

Step	Run Time	Output File Size	Event Throughput
GEN-SIM	1199.2 s	787.2 MB	0.83 ev/s
DIGI	286.6 s	1269.3 MB	3.49 ev/s
RECO	163.5 s	123.0 MB	6.12 ev/s
MiniAOD	72.8 s	40.6 MB	13.73 ev/s
RECO → MiniAOD	172.3 s	40.5 MB	5.80 ev/s

Table 1 lists the steps of a Monte Carlo simulation using CMSSW: In a first step, collision events are generated and simulated in the detector. For this study, we choose to generate top-antitop pairs ($t\bar{t}$ or "TTbar"). Then the detector response is digitized and trigger information is added. The result are events in the same form as they would be recorded by the actual detector. Afterwards, the events are reconstructed by computing particle momenta and energies. Finally, the event content is reduced into the "MiniAOD" format for physics analyses [16].

The columns in Table 1 show the run time, the output file size, and the event throughput for handling 1000 TTbar events using a single process with 8 threads. It can be seen that the first GEN-SIM step takes the most time, while the output of the second DIGI step is the largest. We therefore use the latter to test our integration, generating 1.2 GB of output per rank. However, many analyses only require the reconstructed events in the smaller MiniAOD format, which is produced at a much lower rate. To cover this use case, we run a combination of the last two steps, reconstructing the events and directly producing MiniAODs. For our benchmarks, we run the generation, simulation, and digitization once ahead of time. We then reuse the produced sample as inputs where each MPI rank processes the same 1000 events in a weak scaling setup. While this neglects load balancing problems, it is sufficiently realistic to evaluate distributed parallel writing.

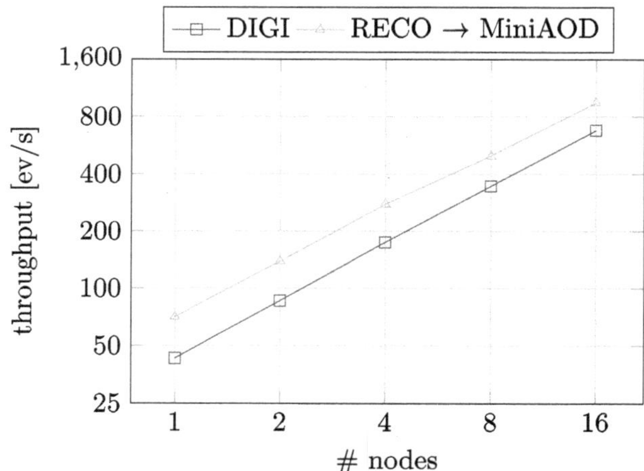

Fig. 7. Measured throughput of TTbar events using CMSSW with 16 ranks per node and 8 threads per rank.

Figure 7 plots the event throughput when scaling up to 16 nodes. As we configure 8 threads per rank, it is possible to fit 16 ranks per node on Vega. This results in 19.2 GB of output data per node for the DIGI step, and around 650 MB per node of MiniAOD. As the variation between runs is negligible at less than 5 % of the run time, we omit the error bars.

It can be seen that the event throughput increases almost linearly with the number of nodes. For the DIGI step, it scales from 43 events per second with one node to 678.4 events per second with 16 nodes. This corresponds to 256 ranks that write into a single output file of 327.2 GB at a sustained average bandwidth of 867 MB/s. When producing MiniAOD, the data volume is much lower with a total of 10.6 GB written by 256 ranks. The event rate increases from 70.7 events per second with one node to 946.6 events per second with 16 nodes. We note that in both cases, the achieved throughput is lower than the ideal extrapolation based on Table 1. However, scaling to multiple nodes works well with a parallel efficiency of 98.7 % and 83.7 % compared to one node, respectively.

7 Conclusions

In this paper, we introduced the concepts for distributed parallel writing of columnar data. We presented multiple strategies for aggregating columnar data on cluster file systems and compared their communication behavior. Using a synthetic benchmark, we studied their scalability and found that three approaches perform well: the metadata aggregator, maintaining a global offset via MPI one-sided communication and synchronizing via file locks.

We then looked into the performance of different configurations on two cluster file systems: First, we showed that opening the file with O_DIRECT increases the bandwidth when writing to Lustre. For best performance, it is necessary to tune the stripe configuration and ensure proper alignment. Additionally, we presented measurements on CephFS, where alignment is even more important. Further experiments should investigate the performance on other cluster file systems commonly used in HPC systems.

Finally, we tested our prototype for Monte Carlo simulation with the CMSSW experiment framework. This confirmed the feasibility of our approaches for aggregating realistic data in cluster environments. The results demonstrated good scalability for the studied use cases with up to 16 nodes. As such, the possibility of distributed parallel writing will be useful for efficiently exploiting computing resources during HL-LHC. Avenues for future research and development include fault tolerance and crash recovery not discussed in this work.

Acknowledgments. This work has been sponsored by the Wolfgang Gentner Programme of the German Federal Ministry of Education and Research (grant 13E18CHA). We acknowledge the EuroHPC Joint Undertaking for awarding this project access to the EuroHPC supercomputer LUMI, hosted by CSC (Finland) and the LUMI consortium, and Vega, hosted by the Institute of Information Science (Slovenia) and the HPC RIVR consortium. We thank Chris Jones and Matti Kortelainen from Fermilab for their work on integrating RNTuple into CMSSW that we built on.

Disclosure of Interests. The authors have no competing interests to declare that are relevant to the content of this article.

References

1. CMSSW – CMS Offline Software. https://github.com/cms-sw/cmssw. Accessed 24 Apr 2025
2. Vega. https://izum.si/en/vega-en/. Accessed 24 Apr 2025
3. Al-Turany, M., Klein, D., Manafov, A., Rybalchenko, A., Uhlig, F.: Extending the FairRoot framework to allow for simulation and reconstruction of free streaming data. J. Phys. Conf. Ser. **513**(2), 022001 (2014). https://doi.org/10.1088/1742-6596/513/2/022001
4. Bird, I., et al.: LHC Computing Grid: Technical Design Report. Technical report LCG-TDR-001, CERN, Geneva (2005). https://cds.cern.ch/record/840543
5. Blomer, J., et al.: ROOT's RNTuple I/O subsystem: the path to production. EPJ Web Conf. **295**, 06020 (2024). https://doi.org/10.1051/epjconf/202429506020
6. Blomer, J., Canal, P., Naumann, A., Piparo, D.: Evolution of the ROOT Tree I/O. EPJ Web Conf. **245**, 02030 (2020). https://doi.org/10.1051/epjconf/202024502030
7. Brun, R., Rademakers, F.: ROOT – an object oriented data analysis framework. Nucl. Instrum. Methods Phys. Res., Sect. A **389**(1), 81–86 (1997). https://doi.org/10.1016/S0168-9002(97)00048-X
8. Chaarawi, M., Gabriel, E., Keller, R., Graham, R.L., Bosilca, G., Dongarra, J.J.: OMPIO: a modular software architecture for MPI I/O. In: Cotronis, Y., Danalis, A., Nikolopoulos, D.S., Dongarra, J. (eds.) EuroMPI 2011. LNCS, vol. 6960, pp. 81–89. Springer, Heidelberg (2011). https://doi.org/10.1007/978-3-642-24449-0_11
9. Eulisse, G., Konopka, P., Krzewicki, M., Richter, M., Rohr, D., Wenzel, S.: Evolution of the ALICE software framework for run 3. EPJ Web Conf. **214**, 05010 (2019). https://doi.org/10.1051/epjconf/201921405010

10. Folk, M., Heber, G., Koziol, Q., Pourmal, E., Robinson, D.: An overview of the HDF5 technology suite and its applications. In: Proceedings of the EDBT/ICDT 2011 Workshop on Array Databases, AD 2011, pp. 36–47. Association for Computing Machinery, New York, NY, USA (2011). https://doi.org/10.1145/1966895.1966900

11. Godoy, W.F., et al.: ADIOS 2: the adaptable input output system. A framework for high-performance data management. SoftwareX **12**, 100561 (2020). https://doi.org/10.1016/j.softx.2020.100561

12. Hahnfeld, J., Blomer, J., Canal, P., Kollegger, T.: Direct I/O for RNTuple columnar data. EPJ Web Conf. **337**, 01034 (2025). https://doi.org/10.1051/epjconf/202533701034

13. Hahnfeld, J., Blomer, J., Kollegger, T.: Parallel writing of nested data in columnar formats. In: Carretero, J., Shende, S., Garcia-Blas, J., Brandic, I., Olcoz, K., Schreiber, M. (eds.) Euro-Par 2024: Parallel Processing, pp. 18–31. Springer, Cham (2024)

14. Li, J., et al.: Parallel netCDF: a high-performance scientific I/O interface. In: Proceedings of the 2003 ACM/IEEE Conference on Supercomputing, SC 2003, p. 39. Association for Computing Machinery, New York, NY, USA (2003). https://doi.org/10.1145/1048935.1050189

15. Message Passing Interface Forum: MPI: A Message-Passing Interface Standard Version 5.0 (2025). https://www.mpi-forum.org/docs/mpi-5.0/mpi50-report.pdf

16. Petrucciani, G., et al.: Mini-AOD: a new analysis data format for CMS. J. Phys. Conf. Ser. **664**(7), 072052 (2015). https://doi.org/10.1088/1742-6596/664/7/072052

17. Rew, R., Davis, G.: NetCDF: an interface for scientific data access. IEEE Comput. Graphics Appl. **10**(4), 76–82 (1990). https://doi.org/10.1109/38.56302

18. Serhan Mete, A., van Gemmeren, P.: Shared I/O developments for run 3 in the ATLAS experiment. In: Proceedings of 41st International Conference on High Energy Physics — PoS(ICHEP2022), vol. 414, p. 219 (2022). https://doi.org/10.22323/1.414.0219

19. Singh, S.P., Gabriel, E.: Parallel I/O on compressed data files: semantics, algorithms, and performance evaluation. In: 2020 20th IEEE/ACM International Symposium on Cluster, Cloud and Internet Computing (CCGRID), pp. 192–201 (2020). https://doi.org/10.1109/CCGrid49817.2020.00-74

20. Thakur, R., Gropp, W., Lusk, E.: Data sieving and collective I/O in ROMIO. In: Proceedings. Frontiers '99. Seventh Symposium on the Frontiers of Massively Parallel Computation, pp. 182–189 (1999). https://doi.org/10.1109/FMPC.1999.750599

21. Thakur, R., Gropp, W., Lusk, E.: On implementing MPI-IO portably and with high performance. In: Proceedings of the Sixth Workshop on I/O in Parallel and Distributed Systems, IOPADS 1999, pp. 23–32. Association for Computing Machinery, New York, NY, USA (1999). https://doi.org/10.1145/301816.301826

22. Vohra, D.: Apache Parquet, pp. 325–335. Apress, Berkeley, CA (2016). https://doi.org/10.1007/978-1-4842-2199-0_8

LLM-Assisted Credibility Scoring for Simulation Models from Raw Time-Series via Automatic Visualization and Interpretable Indicators

Ameya Shrikant[✉][iD], Philipp Andelfinger[iD], and Wentong Cai[iD]

Nanyang Technological University, Singapore, Singapore
`{ameya.shrikant,philipp.andelfinger,aswtcai}@ntu.edu.sg`

Abstract. Simulation credibility assessment traditionally relies on substantial human expert involvement, making the process time-consuming and difficult to scale. We propose AUTOCRED, an LLM-assisted framework that automates credibility assessment while preserving transparency and methodological rigor. The framework takes simulation time-series data and a textual problem description as input. From these inputs, the LLM constructs a structured conceptual model, generates credibility indicators with normalized weights, and produces deterministic scripts for diagnostic visualizations tailored to the simulation model. Evaluation is centered on these visualizations rather than raw time-series data. Structured insights derived from the plots are used to score indicators, which are then aggregated into a final credibility measure. A meta-validation module iteratively checks internal consistency among assumptions, indicators, weights, and scores. Experiments across multiple simulation domains show that AUTOCRED assigns high credibility to valid configurations and reliably detects inconsistencies with the stated model purpose. The approach enables scalable and interpretable simulation credibility assessment with reduced reliance on continuous human oversight.

Keywords: Simulation model validation · Model credibility · LLM-assisted reasoning · Time-series data

1 Introduction

Simulation models have become key tools in scientific understanding, engineering design, and policy decisions. Since simulation outputs frequently inform real-world action, the trustworthiness of a model for its intended purpose is a central concern. Establishing such credibility remains a demanding and largely expert-driven task [8,15]. Analysts typically inspect diagnostic plots, examine modeling assumptions, compare observed patterns with expected behaviors, and combine these observations into a final credibility judgment. While effective, this process

P. Neumann et al. (Eds.): ICCS 2026, LNCS 16784, pp. 94–108, 2026.
https://doi.org/10.1007/978-3-032-29924-6_7

requires substantial expert effort, scales poorly to large parameter studies, and may yield different conclusions across evaluators due to subjective interpretation.

Recent work aiming to reduce subjectivity and the required expert effort has explored partial automation. For example, quantitative learning approaches attempt to learn mappings from simulation outputs to credibility scores [19]. Although such methods reduce manual intervention, they rely on predefined indicators and domain-specific design choices, which can make adaptation to new simulation settings or revised modeling assumptions challenging.

In parallel, large language models (LLMs) have demonstrated the ability to summarize domain knowledge, generate structured explanations, and explicate their reasoning steps. They are pretrained on diverse text corpora that include descriptions of dynamical systems, statistical models, and domain conventions. This exposure suggests that they can reason about models of system evolution over time by relating observed behavior to stated assumptions and objectives, rather than relying solely on predefined numerical mappings. This observation motivates the central question of this paper: *Can the structured reasoning process used by experts in simulation credibility assessment be operationalized through LLM-generated intermediate artifacts, without task-specific training?*

To address this question, we propose AUTOCRED, an LLM-assisted framework that implements credibility assessment as a sequence of reasoning steps.

Fig. 1. Overview of the AUTOCRED workflow.

Taking simulation time-series data and a textual problem description as input, AUTOCRED structures credibility assessment into four stages (Fig. 1): conceptual formalization, evidence construction, evaluation, and validation. Each stage is executed using a large language model (represented by the robot icon) and produces inspectable intermediate artifacts, allowing the final credibility score to be traced back to observable patterns and documented reasoning steps.

AUTOCRED is implemented as a structured prompting workflow. In this context, the main contributions of this work are:

– An LLM-driven simulation credibility assessment framework implemented using structured prompting without additional training.

- A workflow that places diagnostic plots at the center of evaluation, using them as direct evidence for credibility scoring.
- An iterative meta-validation mechanism that enforces internal consistency in the credibility assessment process.

2 Background and Related Work

Simulation credibility assessment lies at the core of modeling and simulation practice, aiming to determine whether a model is sufficiently trustworthy for a specific context of use [8,15]. Within the verification and validation (V&V) literature, credibility is established from accumulated evidence rather than a single numerical metric [8,15]. Credibility requires both the adequacy of the model for its purpose and the alignment of its implementation with its specification.

2.1 Simulation Credibility as Structured Evidence

In classical V&V frameworks, credibility is established by iteratively carrying out the following steps [15]: checking the conceptual model, verifying the implementation, assessing operational behavior, and examining data validity. Evidence collected across these steps is combined into an overall expert judgment.

This process relies heavily on human experts for examining diagnostic plots, assessing modeling assumptions, and interpreting behavioral patterns in light of domain expectations. Formal standards such as NASA-STD-7009 and its Credibility Assessment Scale (CAS) decompose credibility into structured factors, emphasizing documentation and context [12]. CAS does not compute a single credibility value; instead, it structures evidence for evaluation by decision-makers.

2.2 Stylized Facts as Validation Targets

One common way to structure validation is through the use of *stylized facts*, which describe recurring patterns in a system's behavior while abstracting from minor variations [11]. They serve as behavioral targets when models aim to reproduce general tendencies rather than specific datasets, e.g., predator–prey oscillations in ecological systems or volatility clustering in financial time series [11].

Traditionally, stylized facts are expressed in natural language and assessed through expert interpretation supported by visualization, limiting reproducibility. Recent work aimed to address this limitation by formalizing stylized facts in a domain-specific language to enable rigorous statistical testing [18]. A challenge of this approach is the requirement for experts to agree on shared definitions of patterns and thresholds.

In contrast, AUTOCRED operates on natural language descriptions of stylized facts and employs structured LLM-driven reasoning to interpret them. Expected behaviors described in the simulation specification are evaluated through diagnostic visualizations and intermediate reasoning artifacts (cf. Fig. 1). This preserves interpretability while allowing systematic assessment.

2.3 Quantitative and Automated Credibility Assessment

To reduce manual effort, a nascent research thrust has begun exploring quantitative and learning-based approaches that map simulation outputs to credibility indicators or scores. The Quantitative Learning Method (QLM) [19] learns structured mappings from simulation outputs to credibility values from small numbers of expert-provided scores. Cheng et al. [3] extend this direction with an LLM-assisted framework that integrates metrics, visualizations, and expert preference signals to construct evaluation criteria and weights.

These approaches depend on predefined indicators, labeled data, or domain-specific metrics. Such dependencies can make transfer difficult when modeling assumptions, evaluation criteria, or domains change. AUTOCRED does not train domain-specific mappings. Instead, it uses a pretrained LLM to arrive at documented credibility assessments without requiring task-specific retraining.

2.4 Visualization-Centered Model Evaluation

Visualization plays a central role in simulation analysis. Diagnostic plots support validity checks, identification of behavioral patterns, and anomaly detection [15]. In Bayesian workflows, posterior predictive checks treat visualization as primary evidence for diagnosing model misfit and guiding refinement [5]. More recent work frames diagnostic visualizations as tools for explaining why models fail under certain conditions [6]. Similar perspectives appear in visual analysis of time-dependent observables in complex simulations, where visualization supports interpretation of dynamic behavior [4].

AUTOCRED builds on this perspective by placing diagnostic plots at the center of the credibility assessment (cf. Fig. 1). Visualizations to assess the model's credibility are generated automatically and serve as structured evidence from which insights are extracted and linked to credibility indicators.

2.5 LLMs and Structured Judgment

Besides producing end-to-end predictions, LLMs are capable of structured judgment tasks by identifying relevant features, generating intermediate representations, and articulating reasoning steps. For instance, work on modeling human moral judgment shows that LLMs can extract meaningful attributes and aggregate them through reasoning mechanisms [7].

A recent work made use of these capabilities to infer conceptual models from simulation code [13] to facilitate V&V efforts. In contrast, our work infers a conceptual model from natural language and uses it as an intermediate step, with the objective of determining overall credibility judgments automatically.

A well-known drawback of LLMs is their sensitivity to the prompting and the possibility of generating hallucinations stemming from the probabilistic nature of text generation and the diversity of the pretraining data. Self-reflection and refinement of previous outputs has been shown to ameliorate these issues [10]. AUTOCRED employs this idea through iterative consistency checks and potential correction of its credibility assessments.

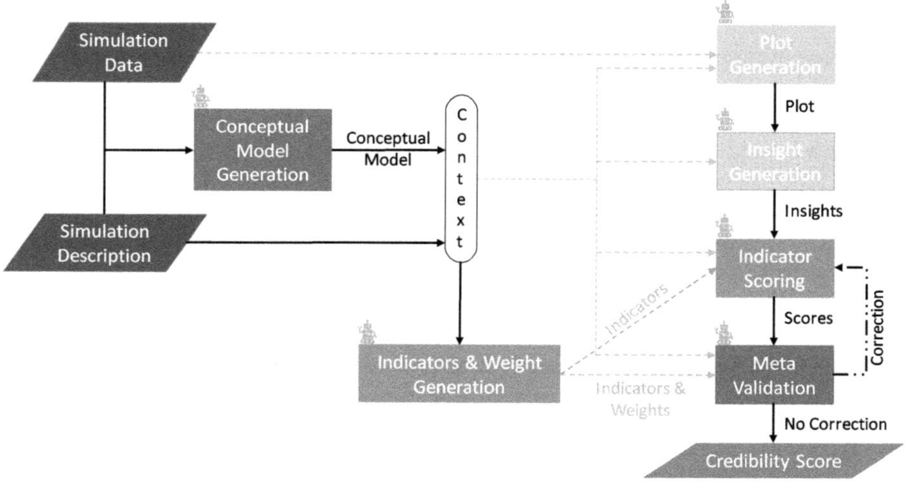

Fig. 2. AutoCred workflow. Parallelograms denote information entering or leaving the system. Solid arrows indicate the main forward reasoning flow. Dashed arrows denote contextual conditioning. The dotted feedback loop represents meta-validation refinement. The robot icon denotes LLM-driven steps. Colors correspond to Fig. 1.

3   Methodology

We designed AutoCred based on three key requirements:

1. **Context awareness.** The credibility evaluation must remain tied to the model's objectives, assumptions, and intended use.
2. **Evidence-based reasoning.** The evaluation must provide a transparent link between observable behaviors and the criteria used for assessment.
3. **Internal coherence.** Indicators, weights, and assigned scores must be logically consistent with one another and with the stated modeling assumptions.

Figure 2 presents the AutoCred workflow. AutoCred operates on two external inputs: (i) a simulation description, and (ii) multi-run simulation outputs.

The simulation description defines objectives, assumptions, and expected behaviors. The simulation time-series data provide observable realizations of the modeled system. From these inputs, AutoCred constructs a sequence of reasoning steps that lead to a credibility score.

The framework satisfies the above properties as follows: **1.** The conceptual model and description remain active conditioning inputs throughout the pipeline. **2.** Scores are derived exclusively from structured insights grounded in diagnostic visualizations. **3.** The meta-validation loop evaluates consistency among assumptions, indicators, weights, and scores before aggregation.

3.1 Input Preparation

AUTOCRED operates on two inputs: simulation description and simulation time-series data. The data consist of R independent runs, denoted by $\{X^{(r)}\}_{r=1}^{R}$, each containing T time steps. A short excerpt of the first run (e.g., the first 100 time steps) is provided during conceptual model construction to anchor variable semantics and numerical scale. The excerpt is not scored.

To account for potential stochasticity of the simulation model, an averaged reference run is constructed by taking the pointwise mean across runs. This averaged run is appended to the dataset and treated as run $R + 1$.

3.2 Reasoning Steps

AUTOCRED structures the credibility assessment into seven reasoning steps, all of which are carried out using a large language model, specifically OpenAI's ChatGPT-5.1 [14].

Step 1: Conceptual Model Generation

Inputs: simulation description and data excerpt.
Output: structured conceptual model (JSON schema).
The LLM converts the narrative description into a structured representation of entities, state variables, parameters, mechanisms, assumptions, and expected behaviors. This representation forms the conceptual model. The conceptual model and the simulation description are combined into a shared *model context* (see Fig. 2), which conditions all subsequent modules.

Step 2: Indicator and Weight Generation

Inputs: model context
Output: indicator set with normalized weights.
Indicators translate the model's stated expectations into measurable evaluation criteria. For example, in a flocking model, an indicator such as *collective alignment formation* captures whether agents converge toward a common heading. Each indicator corresponds to a clearly defined behavioral property derived from the model description. Associated weights reflect the declared importances.

Step 3: Visualization Generation

Inputs: model context and data excerpt.
Output: deterministic plotting module and standardized plots.
AUTOCRED constructs evidence through diagnostic visualization. The LLM generates a deterministic plotting script tailored to the simulation model. The visualization structure is fixed across runs, while the underlying data vary. Prompt templates steer the LLM towards plotting of model-relevant statistics rather than raw time-series columns. Figure 3 shows example plots from Sect. 4.4.

Step 4: Insight Generation

Inputs: model context and run-specific plots.
Output: structured insight set per run.

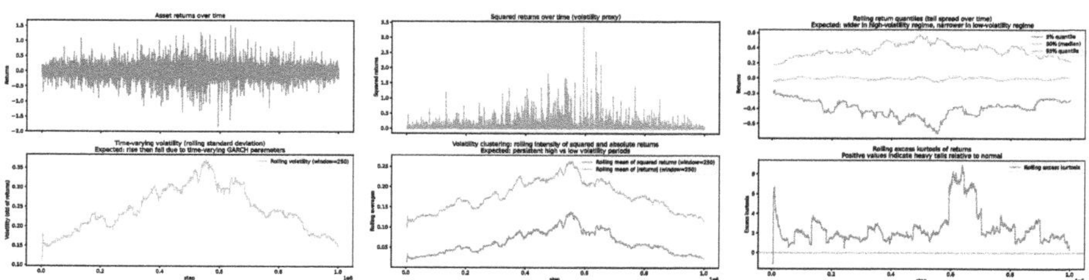

Fig. 3. Diagnostic plots from the GARCH(1,1) experiment. The plots were generated automatically using LLM-produced Python scripts.

Visual patterns are translated into explicit observations and resulting insights. The insights identify relevant patterns and explain their relevance with respect to the simulation description. They are directly tied to observations from the plots. All subsequent scoring decisions refer to these insights.

Step 5: Indicator Scoring

Inputs: *model context*, indicators, and run-specific insights.

Output: per-run indicator scores $s_k^{(r)} \in [0, 1]$.

For each run, the LLM assigns scores to the fixed set of indicators based on the structured insights derived from the plots. Scores vary across runs, while the indicator definitions and weights remain unchanged. Each assigned value is justified by reference to the corresponding insights, ensuring traceability from score to observed evidence.

Step 6: Meta-Validation

Inputs: model context, indicators, weights, and indicator scores

Output: confirmation or correction directive.

Meta-validation checks internal consistency by evaluating whether indicators match the conceptual model, whether weights reflect declared priorities, and whether scores align with observed evidence.

If inconsistencies are detected, corrections are applied and all runs are rescored until no further correction is required. The dotted feedback loop in Fig. 2 represents this process, after which the pipeline proceeds to aggregation.

Step 7: Credibility Aggregation

Inputs: indicator weights and per-run scores.

Output: overall credibility score.

Aggregation combines run-level scores into a final credibility measure. For each run,

$$A^{(r)} = \sum_{k=1}^{K} w_k \, s_k^{(r)}. \tag{1}$$

The overall credibility score is

$$C = \frac{1}{R} \sum_{r=1}^{R} A^{(r)}. \tag{2}$$

Here, $w_k \in [0,1]$ is the normalized weight of indicator k, with $\sum_{k=1}^{K} w_k = 1$ and $s_k^{(r)} \in [0,1]$ is the score assigned to indicator k for run r.

The aggregation step is deterministic. Each scalar value can be traced back to the corresponding indicators, insights, plots, and conceptual model elements. The credibility score therefore reflects the accumulated results of the preceding reasoning steps.

From a computational perspective, the cost of AUTOCRED is dominated by language model inference and increases linearly with the number of runs, at approximately 14.65 s per run, while remaining largely insensitive to time-series length.

4   Experimental Evaluation

This section evaluates AUTOCRED with respect to three specific questions:

1. *Can AUTOCRED replicate ground truth labels derived from human judgments on model behavior?*
2. *Can AUTOCRED distinguish intended model behavior from deliberately unrealistic parameter regimes?*
3. *Does the meta-validation loop detect and correct inconsistent indicator weights or scoring rules?*

All experiments were executed using the same pipeline configuration. No domain-specific tuning or prompt modifications were made. For each configuration, AUTOCRED was executed seven independent times. Repeated executions under identical configurations yield stable credibility ranges across runs, as reflected in Tables 3, 5, and 6.

4.1   Swarm Behavior Classification Against Ground Truth Labels

Objective. As our first experiment, we test whether AUTOCRED produces judgments consistent with ground truth labels assigned by human annotators.

Dataset. We use the *Swarm Behavior* dataset from the UCI Machine Learning Repository [1]. The dataset contains approximately 25,000 simulation-derived instances generated from a Boids model. Each instance represents a single timestep snapshot of agent positions and velocities, with no temporal sequence across snapshots.

Each snapshot is labeled independently by human annotators under three binary categories: *aligned, flocking,* and *grouping.* These labels were generated outside AUTOCRED and therefore provide an external reference.

Evaluation Procedure. Fifty instances were randomly sampled for evaluation. For each behavioral category, AUTOCRED outputs a probability estimate $\hat{p}$ indicating confidence that the snapshot exhibits the corresponding behavior.

Predictions are compared with ground-truth labels $y \in \{0, 1\}$ using binary cross-entropy (BCE):

$$\text{BCE}(y, \hat{p}) = -\left[y \log(\hat{p}) + (1 - y) \log(1 - \hat{p}) \right]. \tag{3}$$

BCE measures the divergence between predicted probabilities and true binary outcomes. A BCE of 0 indicates perfect agreement. In a balanced binary task, random guessing yields an expected BCE of approximately 0.69. Lower values indicate stronger probabilistic alignment (Table 1).

Table 1. Binary cross-entropy loss and random baseline on Swarm Behavior dataset

Class	BCE Loss	Random Baseline
Aligned	0.25	0.692
Flocking	0.15	0.686
Grouping	0.27	0.686

Results. All observed losses are substantially below the random baseline across the three independent behavioral dimensions. This indicates that AUTOCRED's evaluation of aligned motion, flocking, and grouping from snapshot-based evidence is consistent with externally curated labels.

This experiment also demonstrates adaptability. Although the Swarm Behavior dataset is structured around individual snapshots of simulation states, only minor preprocessing adjustments were required. The core reasoning steps of AUTOCRED remained unchanged, indicating that the framework does not require strictly time-series-structured input data to generate meaningful judgments.

4.2 Wolf-Sheep Predator-Prey Model

Objective. This experiment tests whether AUTOCRED distinguishes sustained predator-prey coexistence from parameter settings that lead to rapid ecological collapse.

Model Description. The NetLogo Wolf–Sheep model [16] simulates interacting predator and prey populations. The simulation description specifies sustained predator–prey coexistence as the primary credibility criterion.

Experimental Setup. Two parameter regimes were constructed with 30 runs and 300 time-steps per run: In the realistic regime, reproduction rates, energy transfer, and grass regrowth allow sustained coexistence over time. In the unrealistic regime, grass regrowth is set to zero and wolf energy gain is reduced, leading to early predator extinction and prey overpopulation (Table 2).

Table 2. Wolf-Sheep parameter configurations

Parameter	Realistic	Unrealistic
Initial number of sheep	100	100
Initial number of wolves	50	80
Sheep reproduce (%)	4	4
Wolf reproduce (%)	5	5
Sheep gain from food	4	4
Wolf gain from food	20	6
Grass regrowth time	30	0

Table 3. Credibility score ranges for the Wolf-Sheep experiment.

Configuration	Credibility range (%, [min, max])
Realistic regime	[93.8, 95.2]
Unrealistic regime	[9.1, 11.0]

Runs exhibiting sustained predator–prey oscillations received high credibility, whereas runs leading to early extinction received low credibility. The separation between regimes reflects the ecological criterion specified in the simulation description. This outcome confirms that AUTOCRED evaluates the model relative to the stated ecological objective.

4.3   Flocking Model (NetLogo)

Objective. This experiment tests whether AUTOCRED distinguishes stable flock formation from parameter settings that disrupt local interaction rules.

Model Description. The NetLogo Flocking model [17] implements three local rules: alignment (steering toward neighbors' headings), cohesion (steering toward neighbors' center of mass), and separation (avoiding crowding).

The simulation description defines credible behavior as the formation of at least one dominant locally aligned and cohesive group.

Experimental Setup. Five regimes were tested with 15 runs and 250 time-steps per run (Table 4):

The realistic configuration balances alignment, cohesion, and separation to produce stable flock formation. The distorted regimes isolate or exaggerate individual mechanisms: cohesion-only produces clustering without spacing, jitter produces unstable turning, no-interaction prevents collective formation, and separation-only prevents cohesive grouping.

Table 4. Flocking parameter configurations.

Parameter	Realistic	Cohesion-only	Jitter	No-interaction	Separation-only
Vision	5	7	7	0.5	5
Max separate turn	1.5	0.5	30	3	8
Minimum separation	1	0.2	1	1	5
Max align turn	5	0.44	30	5	1
Max cohere turn	3	8.41	32	3	1

Table 5. Credibility score ranges for the Flocking experiment.

Configuration	Credibility range (%, [min, max])
Realistic flocking	[93.8, 96.1]
Cohesion-only	[29.0, 31.3]
Jitter regime	[21.4, 22.9]
No-interaction regime	[24.7, 26.3]
Separation-only regime	[9.9, 11.5]

The realistic regime is clearly distinguished from the altered regimes. Configurations that prevent stable flock formation or produce unstable collective motion receive substantially lower credibility. The results are consistent across runs and reflect the interaction rules specified in the simulation description, confirming that AUTOCRED's evaluation conforms with the simulation description.

In addition, we conducted an ablation experiment for the realistic flocking configuration by removing the conceptual model from the model context. Under this modification, the generated credibility score decreased from 94.4% to 87.9%. This reduction demonstrates the benefit of explicitly formalizing expectations about model behavior, as the conceptual model provides structured guidance for interpreting observable patterns.

4.4 GARCH(1,1) Financial Time-Series Model

Objective. The GARCH model of asset volatility is defined by a simple recurrence relation. It allows us to study AUTOCRED's ability to generalize beyond commonly studied agent-based models.

Model Description. The GARCH(1,1) model [2] generates a time series of asset returns with time-varying volatility:

$$\sigma_t^2 = \omega + \alpha \epsilon_{t-1}^2 + \beta \sigma_{t-1}^2.$$

Here, σ_t^2 denotes the conditional variance (volatility) of returns at time t. The term ϵ_{t-1} represents the shock (unexpected return component) at time $t-1$, and ϵ_{t-1}^2 captures the magnitude of that shock. The term σ_{t-1}^2 is the previous period's conditional variance. The parameter ω controls the baseline variance level, α determines how strongly recent shocks affect current volatility, and β governs the persistence of past volatility over time. Our baseline configuration uses $\omega = 0.01$ with $\alpha, \beta \in [0.01, 0.09]$ with a linear increase to 0.09 and subsequent decrease to 0.01 over the course of the simulation.

In financial time series, an important modeling consideration is the *leverage effect*, according to which negative returns lead to larger increases in future volatility than positive returns of similar magnitude. GARCH(1,1) does not distinguish between positive and negative shocks, allowing us to test AUTOCRED's ability to capture the absence of this effect.

Experimental Variants. Four configurations were evaluated using 20 runs and one million time-steps per run:

1. *Default configuration:* Volatility evolves according to standard GARCH(1,1), producing volatility clustering without leverage asymmetry.
2. *Constant volatility:* The volatility recursion is removed, yielding fixed-variance returns.
3. *Imposed leverage requirement with explicit disclosure:* The simulation description states that the data were generated by a symmetric GARCH(1,1) model. At the same time, the evaluation demanded the presence of a leverage effect, which is incompatible with GARCH(1,1).
4. *Imposed leverage requirement without disclosure:* The same leverage requirement was imposed, but the simulation description did not state that the model was GARCH(1,1) or that it was symmetric. In this case, AUTOCRED must rely only on observed data patterns and the stated expectations.

Table 6. Credibility score ranges for GARCH(1,1).

Configuration	Credibility range (%, [min, max])
Default configuration	[96.1, 97.5]
Constant volatility	[20.6, 22.3]
Imposed leverage (disclosed)	[90.5, 92.6]
Imposed leverage (undisclosed)	[83.8, 86.9]

The GARCH experiment demonstrates that AUTOCRED evaluates the model in accordance with its stated assumptions. The default configuration, which exhibits time-varying volatility, received high credibility. The constant-volatility variant was penalized because it removes volatility clustering, a central property of the model.

More importantly, the two leverage variants illustrate how declared assumptions influence the evaluation. When the simulation description clearly stated that the data were generated by a symmetric GARCH(1,1) model, the imposed leverage requirement was recognized as incompatible with the model specification and did not substantially reduce credibility. When the simulation description did not specify that the data were generated by a symmetric GARCH(1,1) model, the missing leverage effect led to a lower credibility score. As in the previous experiments, AUTOCRED correctly evaluated the simulations according to the assumptions stated in the simulation description.

4.5   Meta-validation Consistency Test

Objective. This experiment tests whether the meta-validation loop detects and corrects inconsistent evaluation rules.

Setup. In the Flocking experiment (realistic configuration), the indicator weights were artificially set equal regardless of declared importance. Extreme scoring constraints were introduced (e.g., forcing scores above 0.96 or below 0.15 under arbitrary conditions).

Result. AUTOCRED correctly identified inconsistencies between weights, scores, and the simulation description. It proposed targeted corrective adjustments, restoring differentiated weights and coherent scoring behavior. For example, the system flagged that equal indicator weights contradicted the declared importance hierarchy in the simulation description and recommended restoring differentiated weights before rescoring.

Beyond this specific setup, meta-validation is triggered infrequently in practice, occurring in approximately one out of every twenty trials under identical data and configuration, indicating that the reasoning pipeline is largely stable. This further confirms that the meta-validation loop corrects inconsistent indicator weights and scoring rules before final aggregation.

4.6   Qualitative Analysis

In addition to aggregate scores, AUTOCRED produces structured reasoning artifacts. For the realistic flocking configuration, a representative run yielded the following LLM-generated indicators and scores:

collective-alignment-formation   (w=0.35,   s=0.96):   Alignment rises monotonically from near zero to $\sim$0.9 by step 250 and then stabilizes, matching the expectation that moderate/large vision and balanced turns yield highly aligned, coherent flock motion after transient reorganization.

spatial-cohesion-and-spacing   (w=0.30,   s=0.94):   Cohesion remains in a mid-high, bounded band with smooth oscillations and mean NN distance declines from $\sim$2.6 to $\sim$1.1 while stabilizing, which aligns with expectations of moderate, stable compactness without collapse or full dispersion under successful flocking.

collision-and-overlap-control   (w=0.20,   s=0.93):   Minimum NN distance stays low but nonzero ($\sim$0.05-0.3) and noisy without evidence of collapse, indicating rare and brief close approaches but no persistent overlaps, consistent with effective minimum-separation enforcement.

turn-rate-dynamics-consistency   (w=0.15,   s=0.95):   Mean turn rate shows a high spike at initialization then decays from $\sim$4.5 to $\sim$1.5 with residual variability, matching the expectation of elevated turning during transient reorganization followed by lower, stable values during established flocking.

These excerpts illustrate how indicator scores are directly grounded in observable patterns from the diagnostic plots. In one additional trial, a high BCE of 0.61 was observed for the flocking class. Our inspection of the data revealed that in these cases, the ground truth labels were erroneous and the classification produced by AUTOCRED was in fact correct [9]. This finding suggests an alternative use of AUTOCRED for auditing human-labeled simulation data.

Taken together, the results address the three evaluation questions: AUTOCRED aligns with external labels, distinguishes intended behavior from altered regimes, and meta-validation successfully detects and corrects inconsistencies.

5 Conclusion

We presented AUTOCRED, a framework that structures simulation credibility assessment as a reasoning process supported by a large language model. The framework processes a simulation description and simulation time-series data through a sequence of structured steps, producing inspectable artifacts that link credibility scores to observable evidence and stated modeling assumptions.

Across the experiments, several high-level insights emerge. First, AUTOCRED replicated human-labeled behavioral categories in the swarm dataset, demonstrating alignment with external ground truth. Second, it consistently distinguished realistic model configurations from unrealistic parameter combinations in both predator–prey and flocking simulations. Third, the GARCH experiment showed that contradictory and unsatisfied assumptions are identified correctly. Finally, the meta-validation experiments confirmed that inconsistencies in indicator weights or scoring rules are detected and corrected before aggregation.

Our framework and experiments represent a step toward a higher degree of automation in the validation of simulation models. Although AUTOCRED cannot replace human expertise and oversight, it provides a structured and transparent environment in which expert supervision can focus on reviewing indicators, weights, and meta-validation decisions. In this way, the framework reduces manual validation efforts while preserving interpretability and methodological rigor. Future work will focus on extending the framework to provide recommendations for repairing identified model defects.

Acknowledgements. This research was supported by the RIE2025 Industry Alignment Fund - Industry Collaboration Projects (IAF-ICP) (Award I2301E0026), administered by A*STAR, as well as supported by Alibaba Group and NTU Singapore through Alibaba-NTU Global e-Sustainability CorpLab (ANGEL).

References

1. Swarm Behaviour. UCI Machine Learning Repository (2020). https://doi.org/10.24432/C5N02J
2. Bollerslev, T.: Generalized autoregressive conditional heteroskedasticity. J. Econometr. **31**(3), 307–327 (1986)

3. Cheng, Q., et al.. LLM-based evaluation policy extraction for ecological modeling. arXiv preprint arXiv:2505.13794 (2025)
4. Cibulski, L., Haack, F., Uhrmacher, A., Bruckner, S.: Visual analysis of time-dependent observables in cell signaling simulations. arXiv preprint arXiv:2509.08589 (2025)
5. Gabry, J., Simpson, D., Vehtari, A., Betancourt, M., Gelman, A.: Visualization in Bayesian workflow. J. Roy. Stat. Soc. Ser. A: Stat. Soc. **182**(2), 389–402 (2019)
6. Kale, A., Guo, Z., Qiao, X.l., Heer, J., Hullman, J.: EVM: incorporating model checking into exploratory visual analysis. IEEE Trans. Visual. Comput. Graphics **30**(1), 208–218 (2024)
7. Kwon, J., Levine, S., Tenenbaum, J.B.: LLMs as automatic feature extractors, Neuro-symbolic models of human moral judgment (2023)
8. Law, A.M.: How to build valid and credible simulation models. In: 2022 Winter Simulation Conference (WSC), pp. 1283–1295 (2022)
9. Liu, Z., McArdle, R., Orlando, G.: Classifying the behaviors of BOID swarms. Inst. Artif. Intell. (2020)
10. Madaan, A., et al.: Self-refine: Iterative refinement with self-feedback. In: Oh, A., Naumann, T., Globerson, A., Saenko, K., Hardt, M., Levine, S. (eds.) Advances in Neural Information Processing Systems, vol. 36, pp. 46534–46594. Curran Associates, Inc. (2023)
11. Meyer, M.: How to use and derive stylized facts for validating simulation models. In: Beisbart, C., Saam, N.J. (eds.) Computer Simulation Validation. SFMA, pp. 383–403. Springer, Cham (2019). https://doi.org/10.1007/978-3-319-70766-2_16
12. National Aeronautics and Space Administration. Nasa standard for models and simulations. Technical report NASA-STD-7009, NASA (2008)
13. Neykova, R., Groen, D.: Reversed model verification by inferring conceptual models from simulation code. In: Lees, M.H., et al. (eds.) ICCS 2025. LNCS, vol. 15906, pp. 361–368. Springer, Cham (2025). https://doi.org/10.1007/978-3-031-97635-3_43
14. OpenAI. ChatGPT-5.1 (2025). https://openai.com. Large language model
15. Sargent, R.G.: Verification and validation of simulation models. J. Simul. **7**(1), 12–24 (2013)
16. Wilensky, U.: Netlogo wolf sheep predation model (1997). http://ccl.northwestern.edu/netlogo/models/WolfSheepPredation. Center for Connected Learning and Computer-Based Modeling, Northwestern University
17. Uri Wilensky. Netlogo flocking model (1998). http://ccl.northwestern.edu/netlogo/models/Flocking. Center for Connected Learning and Computer-Based Modeling, Northwestern University
18. Wilsdorf, P., Zuska, M., Andelfinger, P., Uhrmacher, A.M., Peters, F.: Validation without data-formalizing stylized facts of time series. In: 2023 Winter Simulation Conference (WSC), pp. 2674–2685. IEEE (2023)
19. Zhang, J., Laili, Y., Gong, J., Zhang, L., Ren, L.: A quantitative learning method for simulation model evaluation using l-shade optimized structured regression. In: Cai, W., Low, M., Tan, G., D'Angelo, G., Ta, D. (eds.) AsiaSim 2025. LNCS, vol. 2727, pp. 3–15. Springer, Cham (2025). https://doi.org/10.1007/978-981-95-4472-1_1

PINN-Cast: Exploring the Role of Continuous-Depth NODE in Transformers and Physics Informed Loss as Soft Physical Constraints in Short-Term Weather Forecasting

Hira Saleem$^{(\boxtimes)}$, Flora Salim , and Cormac Purcell

University of New South Wales, Sydney, NSW, Australia
{h.saleem,flora.salim,cormac.purcell}@unsw.edu.au

Abstract. Operational weather prediction has long relied on physics-based numerical weather prediction (NWP), whose accuracy comes at the cost of substantial compute and complex simulation workflows. Recent transformer-based forecasters offer efficient data-driven alternatives, however transformers are physics-agnostic models. Additionally, standard transformer encoders evolve representations through discrete layer updates that may be less suited to modeling smooth latent dynamics. In this work, we propose a continuous-depth transformer encoder for weather forecasting that integrates Neural Ordinary Differential Equation (Neural ODE) dynamics within each encoder block. Specifically, we replace discrete residual updates with ODE-based updates solved using adaptive numerical integration. We also introduce a two-branch attention module that combines conventional patch-wise self-attention with an auxiliary branch that applies a derivative operator to attention logits, providing an additional change-sensitive interaction signal. To further align forecasts with governing principles, we propose a customized physics-informed training objective that enforces physical consistency as a soft constraint. We evaluate the proposed method against a standard discrete transformer baseline and an existing continuous-time Neural ODE forecasting variant, demonstrating the importance of PINN-Cast in short term weather forecasting.

Keywords: Hybrid Computational Methods · Physics-Informed Machine Learning · Data-Driven Weather Forecasting

1 Introduction

Weather forecasting can be viewed as a continuously evolving physical process governed by time-dependent partial differential equations (PDEs) that describe the spatiotemporal evolution of key atmospheric variables (e.g., temperature, pressure, humidity, and wind). In operational settings, these governing equations

© The Author(s), under exclusive license to Springer Nature Switzerland AG 2026
P. Neumann et al. (Eds.): ICCS 2026, LNCS 16784, pp. 109–122, 2026.
https://doi.org/10.1007/978-3-032-29924-6_8

are solved numerically via large-scale simulation pipelines (numerical weather prediction, NWP), which require sophisticated discretizations, high-performance computing (HPC) resources, and careful management of computational cost [1, 2, 20].

While such full-fidelity NWP systems remain the foundation of operational forecasting, they are also complex to develop, expensive to run at scale, and difficult to iterate on rapidly when exploring new modeling ideas. Motivated by the broader goal of advancing computationally efficient scientific modeling, this work is positioned as an exploratory study which investigates whether (i) continuous-depth Neural ODE (NODE) dynamics inside transformer blocks and (ii) physics-informed soft constraints can improve learning stability and physical plausibility in data-driven forecasting at moderate resolution.

Recent advances in artificial intelligence (AI), particularly deep learning and transformer-based architectures particularly Vision Transformer (ViT) [9], have enabled data-driven weather forecasting models that achieve strong predictive accuracy and high throughput [3, 18, 19]. However, typical transformer encoders update hidden representations through a fixed number of discrete residual steps, which may be less suited to representing smoothly evolving dynamics. This motivates hybrid architectures that integrate continuous-depth dynamics into attention-based models.

To advance physics-aware forecasting within a computationally efficient transformer framework, we propose **PINN-Cast**, a continuous-depth transformer encoder for weather forecasting by integrating Neural Ordinary Differential Equation (NODE) [7] updates inside each transformer block. Specifically, we represent the hidden state evolution as an initial value problem, where $\frac{dh(t)}{dt} = f_\theta(h(t), t)$, and f_θ is parameterized by a neural network. In our implementation, f_θ is realized as a lightweight multilayer perceptron. These NODE [7] updates replace the conventional discrete residual transformations applied after attention and after the feed-forward network, yielding continuous-depth feature evolution within the encoder.

In addition, we propose a two-branch attention mechanism that augments standard patch-wise self-attention with an auxiliary derivative-based branch. The derivative branch computes finite differences of attention logits providing a complementary change-sensitive interaction signal. Finally, we incorporate physical constraints through soft penalties via a customized physics-informed loss derived from fundamental relationships associated with thermodynamics and kinetic energy. This objective discourages violations of established physical couplings between temperature and wind evolution, guiding learning toward forecasts that are not only data-consistent but also physically plausible. In summary, our contributions are as follows:

1. **Two-branch attention with derivative-based interaction:** We propose an attention module that fuses patch-wise self-attention with an auxiliary branch that applies a finite-difference operator to attention logits introducing a change-sensitive interaction signal.

2. **Continuous-depth transformer encoder via NODEs:** We introduce NODE layers within the transformer encoder to replace discrete residual updates with continuous-depth latent dynamics, yielding smoother and more stable representation evolution.
3. **Physics-informed soft constraints:** We design a customized physics-informed loss based on thermodynamic and kinetic-energy relationships to penalize physically inconsistent behavior during training.
4. **Evaluation:** We evaluate PINN-Cast on WeatherBench at 5.625° resolution against (i) a discrete-depth transformer baseline and (ii) a continuous-time Neural ODE-based forecasting variant, demonstrating the impact of ODE-based encoder updates and physical consistency on forecast accuracy.

2   Related Work

Currently, operational weather forecasting systems (IFS) [10] approximate atmospheric evolution by numerically discretizing and integrating the governing equations, while representing unresolved processes through physical parameterizations. While highly accurate, the forecast skill is bounded by initial-condition uncertainty, model error/parameterizations and high computational costs.

Meanwhile, recent data-driven forecasting models learn forecast operators directly from data and deliver competitive skill with substantially lower inference cost, motivating hybrid and physics-aware approaches alongside traditional NWP. FourCastNet [16,22] introduced operator-learning for global forecasting showing that Fourier based models can approximate atmospheric evolution with very fast inference. On the other hand, GraphCast [17] achieved state-of-the-art medium-range performance using multi-mesh graph neural networks. Utilizing transformer's long range dependency, weather forecasting models such as Pangu-Weather [4] demonstrated strong medium-range skill with a 3D Earth-specific transformer. Building on the need for broader generalization across variables and tasks, ClimaX [18] reframed forecasting as a foundation-model problem enabling flexible multi-variable, multi-task transfer. Subsequently, FengWu [5] and FuXi [6] advanced long-lead forecasting via large-scale architectures and multi-stage/cascaded strategies to control error growth. Stormer [19] further showed scalable transformer forecasters with improved robustness across lead times through training objectives for variable dynamics. ArchesWeather [8] revisited efficient attention and architectural priors to improve practicality without sacrificing accuracy.

Complementing these discrete space–time predictors, ClimODE [24] introduced a continuous-time, Neural ODE-based formulation to better reflect atmospheric transport dynamics (e.g., advection) and move forecasting toward smoother latent evolution, highlighting the promise of continuous-depth modeling even when peak accuracy still lags the largest discrete forecasters. Beyond purely data-driven evolution, NeuralGCM [15] moved further toward physics-consistent learning by coupling neural parameterizations with a differentiable dynamical core without sacrificing skill.

While the above models demonstrate impressive accuracy and scalability, a large subset of state-of-the-art neural forecasters still advance time through discrete rollouts and evolve internal features via discrete layer-wise residual updates, and in many purely data-driven designs physical consistency is learned only implicitly from data rather than being explicitly encouraged. In contrast, continuous-time and physics-aware directions such as ClimODE [24] and NeuralGCM [15] highlight the value of incorporating smoother dynamics and physical structure, but they also motivate the need for architectures that can retain transformer-level expressivity while integrating continuous-depth evolution and lightweight physics regularization. Addressing this gap, our work replaces discrete residual updates with Neural ODE dynamics solved via adaptive integration, augments standard attention with a change-sensitive two-branch mechanism (including a derivative-operator signal on attention logits), and introduces a custom physics-informed training objective as a soft constraint, together aiming to improve short-term forecast fidelity while better aligning learned dynamics with governing principles.

3   Methodology

3.1   Notation

Throughout this section, we use the following notation. B denotes the batch size, H and W denotes the Latitude-Longitude grid. V is the number of atmospheric variables. N the number of patch tokens, C the embedding dimension, N_h the number of attention heads, and $d_h = C/N_h$ the per-head dimension. $W_{\mathrm{qkv}} \in \mathbb{R}^{C \times 3C}$ is a learned linear projection that produces queries, keys, and values jointly.

3.2   Problem Formulation

Given an input multivariate weather field $X_t \in \mathbb{R}^{V \times H \times W}$ at time t. The goal is to learn a forecaster f_θ that predicts the future state at a lead time Δ (e.g., Δ hours). All forecasts are produced via a single forward pass. The model directly predicts the state at each target lead time Δ.

$$\hat{X}_{t+\Delta} = f_\theta(X_t, \Delta), \qquad \hat{X}_{t+\Delta} \in \mathbb{R}^{V \times H \times W}. \tag{1}$$

3.3   Two-Branch Attention with Neural ODE Integration

We extend the ClimaX variable-tokenization framework [18] by introducing a Two-Branch Attention mechanism paired with Neural ODE [7] based residual updates inside each transformer block. The complete architecture diagram is shown in Fig. 1. Our attention uses a single shared query-key-value projection, but applies it through two computational paths: (i) a patch-wise self-attention branch and (ii) a derivative-based attention branch. Although both branches are initialized from the same projected tensors (q, k, v), they achieve complementary roles because they apply different transformations and reshaping.

Given tokenized patch embeddings $x \in \mathbb{R}^{B \times N \times C}$, we compute a shared projection $[q, k, v] = W_{\mathrm{qkv}} x$ and reshape into multi-head form $q, k, v \in \mathbb{R}^{B \times N_h \times N \times d_h}$, where $C = N_h \cdot d_h$.

Patch Attention (PA): The first branch performs standard scaled dot-product attention over the patch tokens within each sample:

$$A^{\mathrm{pa}} = \mathrm{Softmax}\left(\frac{qk^{\top}}{\sqrt{d_h}}\right), \qquad \mathrm{PA}(x) = A^{\mathrm{pa}} v, \tag{2}$$

yielding $\mathrm{PA}(x) \in \mathbb{R}^{B \times N_h \times N \times d_h}$. This branch aggregates information across spatial patches, enabling each patch to attend to other regions of the same atmospheric state. It primarily captures spatial similarity and long-range dependencies, supporting global context and multi-scale pattern representation (e.g., coherent large-scale structures).

Derivative-Based Attention (DA): The second branch uses the same (q, k, v) but reinterprets the computation by reshaping across the combined sample/head axis at each patch index:

$$q_s, k_s, v_s \in \mathbb{R}^{N \times (B N_h) \times d_h}.$$

Similarity logits are computed as

$$S = \frac{q_s k_s^{\top}}{\sqrt{d_h}}, \tag{3}$$

followed by a first-order finite difference of the logits along the re-indexed attention axis obtained by merging the batch and head dimensions (i.e., the $(B \cdot N_h)$ index), implemented by subtracting consecutive slices and padding:

$$\Delta S = S_{:,2:} - S_{:,:-1}, \qquad \Delta S \leftarrow \mathrm{Pad}(\Delta S). \tag{4}$$

Attention weights and the branch output are then

$$A^{\mathrm{da}} = \mathrm{Softmax}(\Delta S), \qquad \mathrm{DA}(x) = A^{\mathrm{da}} v_s. \tag{5}$$

The result is reshaped back to $\mathbb{R}^{B \times N_h \times N \times d_h}$. Rather than using raw similarity scores, this branch operates on changes in similarity induced by the finite-difference operator. Consequently, it emphasizes relative variation in interaction strengths (i.e., where attention logits change sharply), providing a complementary change-sensitive signal to PA. This helps highlight transitions in patch relationships (e.g., boundaries or rapidly varying interaction patterns), even though the branch starts from the same shared (q, k, v) projections.

Fusion. The two branch outputs are concatenated and projected back to the embedding dimension:

$$\mathrm{TA}(x) = W_o[\mathrm{PA}(x) \, \| \, \mathrm{DA}(x)] \in \mathbb{R}^{B \times N \times C}, \tag{6}$$

matching the implementation where concatenation occurs along the per-head feature dimension, followed by an output projection.

3.4 Neural ODE-Based Residual Updates

The fused attention output is updated via residual updates formulated as initial value problems and approximated via adaptive numerical integration implemented as Neural ODEs. For a hidden state $h \in \mathbb{R}^{B \times N \times C}$, we define the ODE dynamics as an initial value problem:

$$\frac{dz(t)}{dt} = f_\theta(z(t), t), \qquad z(0) = h, \tag{7}$$

The input hidden state h is passed as the initial condition $z(0)$ to an ODE solver, which integrates the learned dynamics f_θ which is parameterized as a two-layer MLP with ReLU activation and hidden dimension matching the input dimension C. The solution is computed from $t \in [0, 1]$ using `odeint` with an adaptive solver (default `dopri5`) and specified tolerances. The output $z(1)$ serves as the updated hidden state.

$$\text{ODESolve}(h) = z(1). \tag{8}$$

One ODE-Transformer block then applies two ODE-governed residual updates: one to the normalized attention pathway and one to the normalized MLP pathway:

$$h \leftarrow h + \text{ODESolve}(\text{LN}(\text{TA}(h))), \qquad h \leftarrow h + \text{ODESolve}(\text{LN}(\text{MLP}(h))). \tag{9}$$

These continuous-depth updates replace discrete residual transformations, promoting smoother feature evolution through the continuous ODE formulation while retaining the standard transformer decomposition into attention and feed-forward components.

3.5 Latitude Weighted Physics Informed Loss Function

We use latitude weighted mean squared error to compute loss for the predicted variables.

$$L_{lat-weight} = \frac{1}{N \times H \times W} \sum_{n=1}^{N} \sum_{i=1}^{H} \sum_{j=1}^{W} (L_i)(\hat{X}_{t+\Delta t}^{n,i,j} - X_{t+\Delta t}^{n,i,j})^2 \tag{10}$$

where L_i accounts for Latitude weights:

$$L(i) = \frac{\cos(lat(i))}{\frac{1}{H} \sum_{i'=1}^{H} \cos(lat(i'))}$$

Additionally, we introduce two physics-motivated auxiliary penalty terms inspired by kinetic energy and temperature advection. Kinetic energy in atmospheric science refers to the energy associated with the motion of air masses. Thermodynamic balance equation describes the evolution of temperature in an air parcel due to processes like heat addition and pressure changes.

$$L_{kinetic} = \left| \frac{1}{2}(u_{pred}^2 + v_{pred}^2) - \frac{1}{2}(u_{true}^2 + v_{true}^2) \right| \tag{11}$$

where u is the eastward wind component (m/s) and v is the northward wind component (m/s).

We compute a thermodynamic balance penalty by forming first-order finite-difference approximations of the temperature tendency and spatial gradients, and then minimizing the mean squared residual of an advection balance.

$$L_{\text{thermo}} = \mathbb{E}\left[\left(\frac{\Delta T}{\Delta t} + u\frac{\Delta T}{\Delta x} + v\frac{\Delta T}{\Delta y} \right)^2 \right], \tag{12}$$

where $\frac{\Delta T}{\Delta t}$, $\frac{\Delta T}{\Delta x}$ and $\frac{\Delta T}{\Delta y}$ are first-order finite-difference approximations of the temperature tendency and spatial gradients computed on the native grid. The terms $\frac{\Delta T}{\Delta x}$ and $\frac{\Delta T}{\Delta y}$ approximate horizontal advection using the predicted wind components (u, v).

$$Loss_{physics} = L_{lat-weight} + \alpha \times L_{kinetic} + \beta \times L_{thermo} \tag{13}$$

where α and β are the weight factors for physics based loss. The resulting the loss function is inspired by physical principles, however it does not enforce strict physical laws but instead guides the model toward outputs that are consistent with physical expectations.

We compute finite differences on the native grid without explicit metric scaling; the penalty therefore encourages directional consistency rather than enforcing a dimensionally exact advection residual. Incorporating latitude-dependent grid spacing is a straightforward extension for future work."

We note that both kinetic energy and temperature evolve over time due to forcing, dissipation, and energy conversion. Our loss terms therefore do not enforce strict conservation laws. Rather, they act as physics-motivated auxiliary penalties on physically meaningful derived quantities, encouraging the model to produce forecasts whose wind-derived kinetic energy closely tracks the ground truth. Similarly, L_{thermo} penalizes the advection-equation residual evaluated on the predicted fields themselves, thereby promoting internal consistency between predicted winds and temperature gradients without requiring explicit modeling of diabatic source terms. Together, these terms provide a richer gradient signal than per-variable MSE alone and guide learning toward physically coherent outputs.

4 Experiments and Results

We train our model on ERA5 [12,13] at the resolution of 5.625° (32 × 64 grid points) provided by WeatherBench [23]. We compare our approach with discrete transformer network (non-pretrained ClimaX [18]) and physics informed continuous model ClimODE [24]. We evaluate at 5.625° to enable controlled comparison under limited compute, whether the observed gains persist at higher resolutions remains an open question for future work and is addressed in Sect. 5.

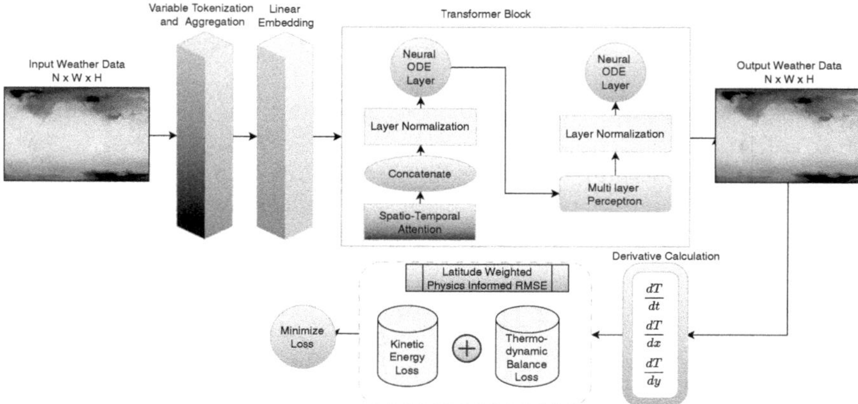

Fig. 1. Overall prediction pipeline. The model receives spatiotemporal weather fields as input, processes them through transformer encoder blocks containing two-branch attention and Neural ODE updates, and produces the forecast $\hat{X}_{t+\Delta}$. During training (dashed box), the physics-informed loss supervises the entire forward pass by combining latitude-weighted MSE with kinetic energy and advection consistency penalties

4.1   Training Details

We consider weather forecasting as a continuous spatio temporal forecasting problem i.e. a tensor of shape $N \times H \times W$ at time t is fed to the model as input and it outputs a tensor of $N' \times H' \times W'$ at future time step $t + \triangle t$. The complete set of hyperparameters are given in Table 1.

4.2   WeatherBench

We train PINN-Cast on hourly data with following set of variables: Land Sea Mask (LSM), Orography, 10-meter U and V wind components (U10 and V10) and 2-meter temperature (T2m) in addition to 6 atmospheric variables: geopotential (Z), temperature (T), U and V wind components, specific humidity (Q) and relative humidity (R) at 7 pressure levels: 50 250 500 600 700 850 925. We use data from 1979–2015 for training, 2016 for validation and 2017–2018 for testing phase. We compare STC-ViT with ClimaX, and ClimODE on ERA5 dataset at 5.625° resolution provided by WeatherBench [23]. To ensure fairness, we retrained ClimaX from scratch without any pre-training.

4.3   Evaluation Metrics

We used Root Mean Square Error (RMSE) and Anomaly Correlation Coefficient (ACC) to evaluate our model predictions. The formula used for RMSE is:

$$RMSE = \frac{1}{N} \sum_{k=1}^{N} \sqrt{\frac{1}{H \times W} \sum_{i=1}^{H} \sum_{j=1}^{W} L(i)(\hat{X}_{k,i,j} - X_{k,i,j})^2} \qquad (14)$$

Table 1. Training Hyperparameters

Hyperparameters	Meaning	Value
p	Patch size	2
Heads	Number of continuous attention heads	16
Depth	Number of Transformer layers	4
Dimension	Hidden dimensions	1024
Dropout	Dropout rate	0.1
batch_size	Batch Size	12
epochs	Training Epochs	50
norm	Normalization	z-score
lr	Learning Rate	5e−5
$\beta 1$, $\beta 2$	Decay Rate of AdamW optimizer	0.9, 0.999
ES	Early stopping	True
α	Kinetic Loss weight factor	0.1–0.5
β	Thermodynamic Loss weight factor	0.8

where $H \times W$ is the spatial resolution of the weather input and N is the number of total samples used for training or testing. L(i) is used to account for non-uniformity in grid cells.

$$ACC = \frac{\sum_{k,i,j} \hat{X}'_{k,i,j} X'_{k,i,j}}{\sqrt{\sum_{k,i,j} L(i)\hat{X}'^{2}_{k,i,j} \sum_{k,i,j} L(i) X'^{2}_{k,i,j}}} \tag{15}$$

where $\hat{X}' = \hat{X}' - C$ and $X' = X' - C$ and C is the temporal mean of the entire test set $C = \frac{1}{N}\sum_{k} X$

4.4 Results

Our model outperforms both approaches at all lead times which shows that replacing regular attention with two-branch attention in ViT architecture derives improved feature extraction by mapping the changes occurring between successive time steps. Additionally, enforcing physical constraints in the model lead to improved prediction scores. The RMSE and ACC results are shown in Table 2 (Fig. 2 and 3).

Table 2. RMSE and ACC results trained on ERA5 at 5.625° resolution

Variable	Lead Time (hrs.)	RMSE (Lower is better)			ACC (Higher is better)		
		Ours	ClimODE	ClimaX	Ours	ClimODE	ClimaX
T2m (K)	6	**0.87**	1.20	2.02	**0.98**	0.97	0.92
	12	**1.04**	1.44	2.26	**0.97**	0.96	0.90
	18	**1.13**	1.42	2.45	**0.97**	0.96	0.88
	24	**1.18**	1.40	2.37	**0.97**	0.96	0.89
	36	**1.42**	1.70	2.85	**0.96**	0.94	0.84
T850 (K)	6	**0.83**	1.16	1.64	**0.98**	0.97	0.94
	12	**0.99**	1.32	1.77	**0.97**	0.96	0.93
	18	**1.09**	1.47	1.93	**0.97**	0.96	0.92
	24	**1.19**	1.55	2.17	**0.97**	0.95	0.90
	36	**1.44**	1.75	2.49	**0.95**	0.94	0.86
u10 ($m\backslash s$)	6	**0.92**	1.44	1.58	**0.97**	0.91	0.92
	12	**1.11**	1.80	1.96	**0.96**	0.89	0.88
	18	**1.28**	1.97	2.24	**0.95**	0.88	0.84
	24	**1.46**	2.00	2.49	**0.93**	0.87	0.80
	36	**1.89**	2.25	2.95	**0.89**	0.83	0.70
v10 ($m\backslash s$)	6	**0.95**	1.53	1.60	**0.97**	0.92	0.92
	12	**1.15**	1.81	1.97	**0.96**	0.89	0.88
	18	**1.32**	1.95	2.26	**0.94**	0.88	0.83
	24	**1.50**	2.02	2.48	**0.93**	0.86	0.80
	36	**1.92**	2.29	2.94	**0.88**	0.83	0.70

4.5 Qualitative Results

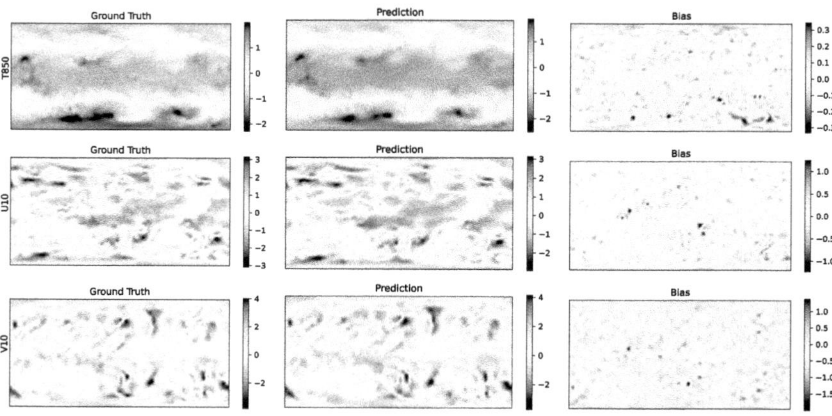

Fig. 2. 12 h forecast results

4.6 Ablation Studies

We perform ablation studies to isolate the contribution of each proposed component to overall forecast accuracy. The full PINN-Cast model combines both

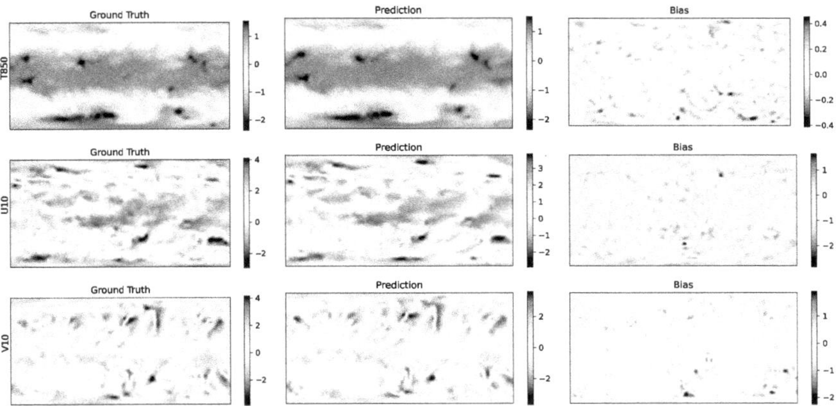

Fig. 3. 1 day forecast results

architectural modifications with the physics-informed loss, allowing us to assess whether the improvements stem from richer attention interactions, smoother continuous-depth dynamics, or physics-motivated supervision, and how these components interact when combined.

Vanilla ViT. We train a standard Vision Transformer with single-branch self-attention, discrete residual updates, and latitude-weighted MSE loss, serving as our base architecture.

Two-Branch Attention. We replace single-branch attention with our proposed two-branch attention module (PA + DA) to isolate the effect of the derivative-based interaction signal, while keeping discrete residual updates and MSE-only training.

Neural ODE. We replace discrete residual updates with ODE-governed updates in the encoder blocks to evaluate the contribution of continuous-depth dynamics, while retaining single-branch attention and MSE-only loss.

PINN-Cast (Full). Finally, we combine all three components: two-branch attention, ODE-governed residual updates, and physics-informed loss representing the complete proposed method. The addition of kinetic energy and advection consistency penalties on top of the architectural modifications further improves forecast quality, confirming that physics-motivated supervision provides complementary benefits beyond what the architectural changes alone achieve. The ablation results are shown in Figure 4.

4.7   Software and Hardware Requirements

We use PyTorch [21], Pytorch Lightning [11], torchdiffeq [7], and xarray [14] to implement our model. We use 4 NVIDIA Tesla Volta V100-SXM2-32GB for the training at resolution of 5.625° with complete training time just under 2 days.

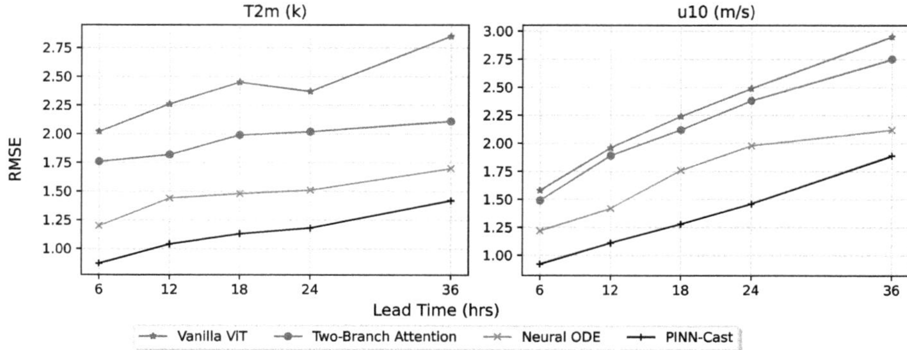

Fig. 4. Ablation studies highlight the results for different components of PINN-Cast individually. Each row isolates a component of PINN-Cast. Each component yields improvement over the base ViT, while combining all three components (two-branch attention, ODE-governed updates, and physics-informed loss) achieves the best overall performance.

5   Conclusion, Limitations, Future Work and Impact

Conclusion. We presented PINN-Cast, a transformer forecaster that integrates ODE-governed residual updates, a two-branch attention module with a derivative-based interaction signal, and physics-motivated auxiliary losses as soft constraints. Evaluation on WeatherBench at 5.625° resolution against ClimaX and ClimODE demonstrates that each component contributes to improved short-term forecast accuracy, with the full model achieving the best performance across all variables and lead times.

Limitations and Future Work. Our evaluation is limited to a single coarse resolution (5.625°) and a restricted set of baselines, whether the observed gains persist at higher resolutions and against pretrained or larger-scale forecasters remains an open question. The physics-informed penalties rely on unscaled finite differences and simplified advection proxies rather than dimensionally exact governing equations. Future work will extend to higher resolutions and additional variables, incorporate latitude-dependent grid scaling into the physics losses, broaden comparisons to recent forecasting models, and investigate how ODE dynamics and physics penalties shape learned representations.

Impact. This work provides a modular framework for integrating continuous-depth dynamics and physics-based regularization into transformer forecasters without hard-wiring constraints into the architecture. The approach offers a practical pathway toward data-driven weather models that balance predictive accuracy, physical plausibility, and computational efficiency across varying resource budgets.

Acknowledgments. This work was supported by SmartSAT Cooperative Research Center(project number P3-31s). We would like to acknowledge National Computational Infrastructure (NCI) (DOI: 10.26190/PMN5-7J50), a high performance computing center for providing us with the GPU resources and weather data collection (WeatherBench and ERA5) which enabled us to perform this research.

Disclosure of Interests. The authors have no competing interests to declare that are relevant to the content of this article.

References

1. Andersson, E.: Medium-range forecasts (2022)
2. Bauer, P., et al.: The ECMWF scalability programme: progress and plans. European Centre for Medium Range Weather Forecasts (2020)
3. Bi, K., Xie, L., Zhang, H., Chen, X., Gu, X., Tian, Q.: Pangu-weather: a 3D high-resolution model for fast and accurate global weather forecast. arXiv preprint arXiv:2211.02556 (2022)
4. Bi, K., Xie, L., Zhang, H., Chen, X., Gu, X., Tian, Q.: Accurate medium-range global weather forecasting with 3D neural networks. Nature 1–6 (2023)
5. Chen, K., et al.: FengWu: pushing the skillful global medium-range weather forecast beyond 10 days lead. arXiv preprint arXiv:2304.02948 (2023)
6. Chen, L., et al.: Fuxi: a cascade machine learning forecasting system for 15-day global weather forecast. NPJ Clim. Atmos. Sci. **6**(1), 190 (2023)
7. Chen, R.T., Rubanova, Y., Bettencourt, J., Duvenaud, D.K.: Neural ordinary differential equations. In: Advances in Neural Information Processing Systems, vol. 31 (2018)
8. Couairon, G., Lessig, C., Charantonis, A., Monteleoni, C.: Archesweather: an efficient AI weather forecasting model at 1.5 {\deg} resolution. arXiv preprint arXiv:2405.14527 (2024)
9. Dosovitskiy, A., et al.: An image is worth 16x16 words: transformers for image recognition at scale. arXiv preprint arXiv:2010.11929 (2020)
10. ECMWF: Ifs documentation cy48r1. ecmwf (2023)
11. Falcon, W.A.: Pytorch lightning. GitHub 3 (2019)
12. Hersbach, H., et al.: Era5 hourly data on single levels from 1959 to present [dataset]. copernicus climate change service (c3s) climate data store (CDS) (2018)
13. Hersbach, H., et al.: The era5 global reanalysis. Q. J. R. Meteorol. Soc. **146**(730), 1999–2049 (2020)
14. Hoyer, S., Hamman, J.: Xarray: ND labeled arrays and datasets in python. J. Open Res. Software **5**(1), 10–10 (2017)
15. Kochkov, D., et al.: Neural general circulation models. arXiv preprint arXiv:2311.07222 (2023)
16. Kurth, T., et al.: Fourcastnet: accelerating global high-resolution weather forecasting using adaptive fourier neural operators. In: Proceedings of the Platform for Advanced Scientific Computing Conference, pp. 1–11 (2023)
17. Lam, R., W., et al.: Learning skillful medium-range global weather forecasting. Science, eadi2336 (2023)
18. Nguyen, T., Brandstetter, J., Kapoor, A., Gupta, J.K., Grover, A.: Climax: a foundation model for weather and climate. arXiv preprint arXiv:2301.10343 (2023)

19. Nguyen, T., et al.: Scaling transformer neural networks for skillful and reliable medium-range weather forecasting. arXiv preprint arXiv:2312.03876 (2023)
20. Palmer, T., Shutts, G., Hagedorn, R., Doblas-Reyes, F., Jung, T., Leutbecher, M.: Representing model uncertainty in weather and climate prediction. Annu. Rev. Earth Planet. Sci. **33**, 163–193 (2005)
21. Paszke, A., et al.: Pytorch: an imperative style, high-performance deep learning library. In: Advances in Neural Information Processing Systems, vol. 32 (2019)
22. Pathak, J., et al.: Fourcastnet: a global data-driven high-resolution weather model using adaptive fourier neural operators. arXiv preprint arXiv:2202.11214 (2022)
23. Rasp, S., Dueben, P.D., Scher, S., Weyn, J.A., Mouatadid, S., Thuerey, N.: Weatherbench: a benchmark data set for data-driven weather forecasting. J. Adv. Model. Earth Syst. **12**(11), e2020MS002203 (2020)
24. Verma, Y., Heinonen, M., Garg, V.: Climode: climate forecasting with physics-informed neural odes. In: The Twelfth International Conference on Learning Representations (2023)

Instrumenting Lightweight, Modular Machine Learning Training and Inference in Parallel Solvers

Ayman Yousef[1]([✉]), Corey Wetterer-Nelson[2], Mengjiao Han[3],
Victor Mateevitsi[3], Joseph Insley[3], Silvio Rizzi[3], Janet Knowles[3],
Michael E. Papka[3,4], and Amanda Randles[1]

[1] Duke University, Durham, NC 27709, USA
`ayman.yousef@duke.edu`
[2] Atomic Industries, Denver, CO 80014, USA
[3] Argonne National Laboratory, Argonne, IL 60439, USA
[4] University of Illinois Chicago, 1200 West Harrison Street, Chicago, IL 60607, USA

Abstract. Recent advances in exascale computing have increased the resolution and fidelity of large-scale simulations, while rapid progress in deep learning has accelerated efforts to couple machine learning with physics-based solvers. We present a lightweight, modular in situ coupling methodology that embeds machine learning training and inference directly into simulation workflows using the ParaView and Catalyst APIs. The approach provides C++/Python interoperability via a solver-side data adaptor that packages simulation state into Conduit Nodes and a Catalyst-driven Python "bridge script" that converts solver fields into NumPy/PyTorch representations with minimal intrusion into the solver code. We describe the design and instrumentation required to integrate the framework and demonstrate it within a proxy (mini-app) of the HARVEY vascular flow solver. To illustrate practical usage, we implement both in situ training and in situ inference of a point-cloud autoencoder running concurrently with the solver. We report scalability and overhead characteristics and show that the approach enables distributed online ML workflows without language unification or major solver refactoring.

Keywords: In Situ · Machine Learning · HPC · Fluid Dynamics

1 Introduction

Machine learning (ML) is increasingly integrated into physics-based computational modeling, often as surrogate models or as augmentations to existing solvers [20]. These methods support digital-twin proxies for computationally intensive simulations [17] and solver adaptation through trainable recurrent or corrective models [8]. At the same time, the growing imbalance between compute capability and I/O throughput has motivated in situ workflows that analyze, compress,

P. Neumann et al. (Eds.): ICCS 2026, LNCS 16784, pp. 123–137, 2026.
https://doi.org/10.1007/978-3-032-29924-6_9

or visualize data during execution rather than post hoc by way of writing full simulation states to disk [2–4]. In situ execution is particularly well matched to ML training and inference because it can replace expensive solver-to-disk data movement with ephemeral, runtime data access, while also making model outputs available immediately for monitoring or feedback. The overall structure of the proposed coupling methodology is shown in Fig. 1.

Despite this potential, coupling simulation codes and ML models across heterogeneous programming languages remains challenging. Many approaches require unifying languages across solver and model [6,16], substantial solver refactoring [5,15], or building bespoke libraries [8,19]. In addition, many toolchains target only inference or only training, limiting practical adoption due to an under-instrumentation of these complementary workflows. Finally, existing studies often provide limited guidance on the code changes required to orchestrate a production solver, making it difficult for developers to reproduce or extend prior approaches. This paper addresses these gaps with the following contributions:

- **A lightweight, Catalyst-based framework** for embedding both in situ ML training and inference into parallel solvers via a solver-side adaptor and Python scripts.
- **An integration in a HARVEY mini-app**, providing a reproducible proxy that demonstrates solver-side instrumentation and data movement patterns.
- **Two end-to-end use cases** that exercise both training and inference using a distributed point-cloud autoencoder running concurrently with the solver.

2   Related Work

The coupling of ML models and scientific solvers often falls into two broad categories: those that homogenize the language across all codes in an experimental setup and those that employ intermediary APIs to handle data conversion between the two ends. The inception and development of online machine learning in the open-source computational fluid dynamics model OpenFOAM [11] is exemplary of the former category. The work of Maulik et al. [15,16] implements in situ machine learning in the OpenFOAM solver through two discrete approaches. Their preliminary work utilized TensorFlow's C API to load saved model "graphs" at runtime to enable concurrent inference [16]. These graphs were created before the simulation and stored offline. They further evolved their implementation, embedding a Python interpreter within the OpenFOAM solver to establish the PythonFOAM framework [15]. This approach facilitated direct data packaging in a Pythonic format to be used by models defined in Python through the Python/C API. PythonFOAM requires compiling with Python's C libraries and building functionality for data conversion from C++ to Python. This dependency, combined with the specificity of the use case, prompted concerns over invasiveness and generalizability. The work of Sun et al. [19] addressed some of the issues described by utilizing direct invocation of functions in Python

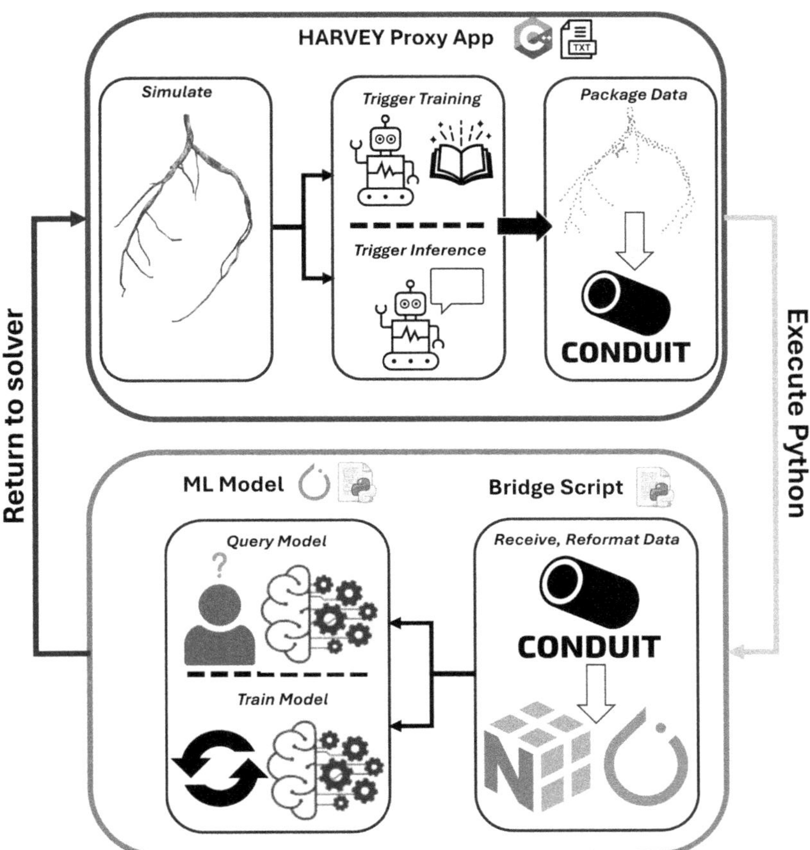

Fig. 1. In situ ML pipeline integrated into the HARVEY mini-app. Solver fields are packaged into a Conduit Node by a solver-side `CatalystAdaptor` and passed to Catalyst at runtime. Catalyst executes a Python "bridge script" (via ParaView) that converts Conduit views into NumPy/PyTorch tensors and invokes model-side training/inference routines. This separation keeps solver modifications minimal while enabling flexible Python-based ML workflows.

through the use of the CFFI Python module and dynamic link libraries. The ability to use a dynamic link library broadens the applicability of their proposed framework. However, the lack of a model training workflow, the use of a less established Python module, and the absence of demonstrable GPU usage limit the utility of the described in situ ML scheme.

Balin et al. [5], and Kurz et al.'s [12] implementations of in situ machine learning center around the SmartSim application, representing the latter of the two coupling strategies. Balin et al. [5] deployed the SmartSim and SmartRedis applications with the PHASTA fluid dynamics solver, performing supervised model training and inference in situ. Kurz et al. [12] similarly utilized the Smart-

Sim application to facilitate the recurrent training of an agent model tasked with optimizing eddy-viscosity coefficients of the FLEXI application. Although the SmartSim application is more mature than the presented orchestration, the need to build both SmartSim and SmartRedis APIs and compile the solver with SmartSim increases the cost of deployment. There is also the issue of having to redesign the method for solver deployment. SmartSim-based applications require the use of a Python-based driver script to handle both solver and model execution. The additional requirement of reformatting major aspects of the workflow to conform to API specifications (ex., simulation and machine learning codes must be instantiated via SmartSim's "Model" wrappers to interface with the API-specific "Experiment" object) further burdens the developer. What's missing are applications that require less extensive code refactoring and lower the barrier to integrating in situ ML workflows in scientific solvers. In contrast, our approach leverages a widely deployed in situ ecosystem to provide a minimally invasive path to both training and inference without requiring solver language unification or a new workflow driver.

3   Design Considerations

We designed the framework around three guiding requirements: (i) minimal solver intrusion, (ii) support for both training and inference in situ, and (iii) compatibility with existing HPC software ecosystems. Several coupling strategies were considered. Direct language unification (e.g., embedding Python or using C++ ML APIs) simplifies interoperability but introduces significant solver refactoring and dependency constraints. Middleware-based approaches (e.g., SmartSim) provide robust orchestration but require restructuring solver execution and introducing additional runtime services. We instead adopt a Catalyst/ParaView-based design [1,4], leveraging its widespread availability on leadership-class systems and its ability to decouple solver instrumentation from model execution. Conduit enables zero-copy data exchange through memory views, avoiding unnecessary duplication and reducing data movement overhead. This design prioritizes portability and low integration cost while still enabling distributed training and inference workflows within the solver execution context.

4   Implementation

We detail the three distinct components of the experimentation workflow: the proposed in situ machine learning framework, the solver in which it's integrated (termed solver-side), and the machine learning model invoked (termed model-side), with an overview of the framework in Fig. 1. On the solver-side, we present the minimal adaptations made to the HARVEY solver to enable in situ workflows. Similarly, we detail the small alterations to model scripting needed to accommodate the in situ environment. We present our approach of linking the distinct C++ and Python domains into a cohesive system through the employment of the Catalyst and ParaView APIs. The Pythonic capabilities of the two

APIs, in combination with the lightweight nature of Catalyst, its widespread availability on leadership-class systems, and amenability to middleman APIs, make the presented framework highly integrable within existing codebases.

4.1 Framework Overview

HARVEY: One of the first considerations made during the design process was the choice of computational solver. The fluid-structure-interaction software package HARVEY was chosen due to its scalability on leadership-class systems, portability, and prior amenability to in situ analysis methodologies [14,18,24]. HARVEY is a lattice Boltzmann method (LBM) based solver adept at modeling the blood flow of patient-derived geometries of extensive, complex vasculature [21]. As a result, simulations often scale to the size of billions of fluid points to accurately recover patient-specific hemodynamics. We specifically employ a mini-app of the HARVEY solver due to the private nature of the codebase and the desire to provide a reproducible example. While chosen as the representative, we believe the framework to be deployable with like-solvers. Outside of compatibility with Catalyst/Conduit data formatting specifications and correct builds, there is nothing exclusive about the HARVEY solver that enables it to perform in situ machine learning with the methodology presented.

Catalyst and ParaView: The crux of data handling and connectivity between the two code domains is the Catalyst and ParaView packages. Catalyst is a software package that provides functionality for interrogating scientific data producers and creating visuals in situ [4]. Previously, Catalyst was a library packaged with the ParaView visualization software [1,4]. As of ParaView v5.9, Catalyst is available as a standalone API. This "stub" is a bare-bones specification that provides the structure needed at compile time for instrumenting the necessary data adaptors. The ability to circumvent solver compilations with more complex packages like ParaView, instead allowing the use of dynamically opened libraries, ensures that the implementation is lightweight and portable. Compilation against the stub enables the use of Catalyst's three core functions: *initialize, execute, and finalize.* Catalyst handles the packaging of data from C to Python and interfaces with ParaView, whilst ParaView handles the execution of Python code. ParaView builds its own Python interpreter based on a provided base installation, providing the mechanism through which we are able to deploy machine learning models at runtime. Facility-maintained ParaView installations can be found across a multitude of leadership-class computing systems (e.g., Tuolumne, Frontier, Aurora), emphasizing the accessibility of the proposed framework. It is important to note that the inclusion of ParaView in the loop presents the prospect of using other synergistic functions. Native visualization capabilities and robust back-end compatibility are relevant advantages that can be co-opted to augment training workflows.

PyTorch: PyTorch is a seminal Python deep learning library that enables graph-based model programming [10]. The choice of PyTorch for model scripting over other similar APIs came down to its availability on leadership-class systems, popularity amongst developers, and native support for distributed workflows. To enable the use of PyTorch functionality, we utilize a separate virtual environment containing the necessary libraries. The ability to use virtual environment libraries in tandem with ParaView is a considerably new feature of the software. Given that the Python installation used for the build of ParaView matches that of the standalone virtual environment and the appropriate library paths are defined, the virtual environment can be employed by ParaView seamlessly without the need for rebuilds or package reinstallations.

4.2 Solver-Side Adaptations

To utilize the proposed framework for Python code execution, there are a small number of non-invasive adjustments to the solver of interest required in order to interface with Catalyst. These adjustments include the creation and termination of a Catalyst instance at the beginning and the end of the solver, respectively, and the definition of execution functions. Within HARVEY, these Catalyst functions are defined within a class named `CatalystAdaptor`. `CatalystAdaptor` defines functions that directly mirror and invoke Catalyst's three core functions, labeled Initialize, Execute, and Finalize, to reflect their Catalyst counterparts. The Initialize function sets up the paths to relevant libraries (Catalyst, ParaView) and the script it is to run, while the Finalize function handles resource de-allocation. From a developer's perspective, the instrumentation cost is intentionally small. In practice, solver-side changes are limited to adding a `CatalystAdaptor` wrapper (initialize/execute/finalize) and packaging selected fields into a Conduit Node at user-defined timesteps. Model-side changes are limited to defining training/inference entry points callable from a middleman script and initializing distributed state variables once per run.

`CatalystAdaptor`'s Execute routine encapsulates both the data packaging and the call to Catalyst's *execute* function, as highlighted in Fig. 2. Within this routine, HARVEY fluid data is converted to match the structure specified by the Conduit "Node" class [9]. Conduit provides a standard to describe computational simulation meshes through the definition of a mesh, a topology, and scalar fields in a hierarchical data structure similar to that of JSON or XML files (Fig. 2A and 2B). Values can either be copied or passed as pointers, a zero-copy approach that serves to further underscore the lightweight nature of the proposed approach and seamlessly enable bidirectional data movement needed for routines like model inference. Conduit is commonplace within the in situ community, utilized within seminal APIs like Ascent [13], SOMA [22], and Catalyst. The widespread adoption of Conduit as a means of describing solver data, along with exhaustive examples outlined within online documentation, speaks to the convenience of our instrumentation. Once a Node object is populated, it is passed as the lone input argument to Catalyst's *execute* function (Fig. 2C).

HARVEY   **Bridge Script**

```
conduit_cpp::Node exec_params;
auto state = exec_params["catalyst/state"];
state["timestep"].set(cycle);
state["time"].set(time);
state["bridge_time"].set(temp_ex);
state["model_time"].set(temp_ex);
state["multiblock"].set(1);
```
A.) Initialize Node object

```
channel["type"].set("mesh");
auto mesh = channel["data"];
mesh["coordsets/coords/type"].set("explicit");
mesh["coordsets/coords/values/x"] = coordX;
mesh["coordsets/coords/values/y"] = coordY;
mesh["coordsets/coords/values/z"] = coordZ;
```
B.) Setup mesh/fields

```
catalyst_status err = catalyst_execute(
    conduit_cpp::c_node(&exec_params));
if (err != catalyst_status_ok)
{
    std::cerr << "Failed to execute
    Catalyst: " << err << std::endl;
}
```
C.) Call bridge script

```
def catalyst_execute(info):
    global producer
    producer.UpdatePipeline()
    node = info.catalyst_params
    assert node.has_path("catalyst/state")
```
D.) Index Node in Python

```
fields=node["catalyst/channels/grid/data/fields"]
grid=node["catalyst/channels/grid/data/coordsets"]
xcoords=np.array(grid["coords/values/x"])
ycoords=np.array(grid["coords/values/y"])
zcoords=np.array(grid["coords/values/z"])
grid_=np.concatenate(xcoords,ycoords,zcoords)
```
E.) Extract mesh/fields

Bridge Side
```
    import autoenc_model
    autoenc_model.main(grid_and_vel)
```
Model Side
```
    def main(pythInput, cat_step):
        train_loop(train_loader)
```
F.) Call training script

Fig. 2. Representative instrumentation code. (A–C) Solver-side `CatalystAdaptor` initialization and execution: simulation fields are packaged into a Conduit Node and passed to Catalyst. (D–F) Bridge-script logic: Catalyst parameters are accessed, Conduit arrays are converted to NumPy arrays, and model-side routines are invoked.

The script directly run by Catalyst is a middleman Python file termed the "bridge script", as illustrated in Fig. 1. The script acts as the intermediary between the simulation solver and the machine learning model, tasked with handling the data conversion from the Conduit Node object to fit general Python routines. The path to the bridge script is passed as a command-line argument and set within CatalystAdaptor's Initialize function. We access the passed Node data within the bridge script through the "catalyst-params" field, which returns a reference to the arguments passed in the Execute call in the form of a Conduit Node (Fig. 2D). Conduit's Python specification defines Node objects as containers for C++ Node pointers. Conduit provides support for converting references to NumPy arrays through appropriate channel indexing (Fig. 2E).

In the current implementation, the bridge script also handles the integration of the virtual environment by augmenting the list of Python library paths with those of the virtual environment. Additionally, the invocation of the ML model occurs within the bridge script. As highlighted in Fig. 2F, we define our model Python script independently and load it in as a module within the bridge script. This compartmentalization allows the use of already defined model scripts, adding to the framework's versatility. Once data is passed and reformatted, training and inference functions defined by the model script can be called within the bridge script due to Python's modular programming.

4.3 Model-Side Adaptations

Model Instantiation and Distribution: The pervasiveness of model training and inference throughout the lifetime of the solver requires proper variable initialization. Model objects are initialized as global variables within model scripts across all studies, avoiding the need for additional data transfers and recurrent setup costs that characterize repeated setup. Alongside a model instance, we initialize rank, world size, and communication backend variables that are persistent throughout the lifetime of the simulation. Distributed training is supported using the PyTorch `DistributedDataParallel` (DDP) wrapper. MPI is used to obtain rank and world-size information (via the `mpi4py` library), while gradient synchronization is performed using PyTorch distributed collectives through the NVIDIA Collective Communications Library (NCCL) software layer. Each process calculates mini-gradients that are averaged across and passed back to all participating ranks to mimic the process of training a single model instance. We initialize an NCCL communication backend to enable the calculation and accumulation of gradients on GPUs. For training and inference, separate model instances are initialized per participating rank. Execution of the solver and ML routines occurs in a synchronized timestep-driven manner. This avoids race conditions by ensuring that data exchange occurs only at well-defined execution boundaries. Within the ML workflow, PyTorch DistributedDataParallel enforces synchronization of gradients across ranks using collective communication primitives, ensuring consistency across processes.

Training Paradigms: In situ execution enables multiple training schedules that differ from conventional offline workflows. A direct analogue to offline training is to accumulate samples during the run and train once near the end of the simulation; however, this can require substantial memory to store the dataset. This is especially true in time-series models that require substantial length scales of data. An alternative is streaming or dynamic training, where each invocation both adds new solver samples and performs one or more optimization steps on the evolving dataset [5]. This approach can reduce peak storage requirements and supports responsive updates that are useful for feedback-driven settings (e.g., reinforcement learning or adaptive surrogates) [12]. Because these trade-offs are often underspecified in prior work, we evaluate both a "train-at-end" schedule and a dynamic, periodically trained schedule within our framework.

Data Bidirectionality: A distinction between the training and inference routines is the data exchange between the model and solver. For inference, data has to be relayed back to the calling model in order to update states. Within our pipeline, this bidirectionality between model and solver is seamless thanks to the zero-copy attribute of Conduit. Predictions are returned to the bridge script as NumPy arrays (or tensors converted to NumPy), and the bridge script writes these values back to Node fields that already reference solver-allocated buffers. This setup enables in-place updates on the solver side when the corresponding Conduit arrays are constructed as views of solver memory.

5   Evaluation

To exhibit the presented framework and evaluate model performance, we carried out weak scaling studies to characterize scalability, profiled the overhead cost incurred as a result of in situ training, and disseminated two separate, distinct use cases of in situ machine learning focused on the training and query of a point cloud autoencoder. All testing occurred on the Polaris supercomputer (Argonne National Laboratory, NVIDIA). Across all experiments, we maintain a ratio of 1:1 between ranks and GPUs, with a total of 4 MPI ranks per node. Example model/bridge scripts and solver code can be found at the cited Github repository [23]. The primary sources of memory overhead arise from dataset buffering and model state replication across ranks.

5.1   Profiling Model Training Stability and Overhead

Given the novelty and prototypical nature of our pipeline, we began experimentation by first verifying the parallel training implementation. We constructed a point-cloud autoencoder model based on the work of [25] and trained it on fluid data generated by HARVEY to serve as a lossy compressor. An autoencoder model was specifically chosen for three reasons: its effectiveness at gauging the pipeline's capability of driving both model training and inference, the well-established utility of autoencoders as a means of lossy compression in LBM solvers [7], and its prevalence within in situ machine learning applications [5, 15]. We simulated steady velocity flow through the inlet of an idealized cylindrical domain across 64 ranks, performing in situ training throughout the simulation's lifetime. Training was invoked every 10 steps within the simulation's 100 timestep lifetime, with the fluid domain passed as training data (stacking with each subsequent training call) for the autoencoder. Training was performed for 10 epochs at each training call, with the training loss per epoch tracked across the simulation lifetime. Figure 3 showcases the convergence of training across the lifetime of training, with ranks converging at a similar loss value at ~50 epochs into training. This convergence verifies that the communication scheme provided by PyTorch's DDP wrapper is correct and that the communication setup, as specified with the model training script, works as expected.

To understand the additional overhead attributable to the proposed pipeline and to assess its scalability, we performed a set of weak scaling runs on up to 64 nodes (equivalent to 256 MPI ranks). We kept the fluid domain size roughly consistent, aiming for ~1 million fluid points per MPI rank. To fairly assess the nature of the pipeline, we set up a trivial training task, reducing the number of epochs per call to 1. We profiled the main portions of the framework to capture the overhead contribution of each aspect of the in situ pipeline, culminating in the results showcased in Fig. 4. The blue bar encapsulates all HARVEY's typical simulation kernels, the green bars are representative of the model training routine, and the purple bars are indicative of the setup and invocation of model training associated with the CatalystAdaptor and bridge codes, respectively. Across the board, model training and the accompanying synchronization were

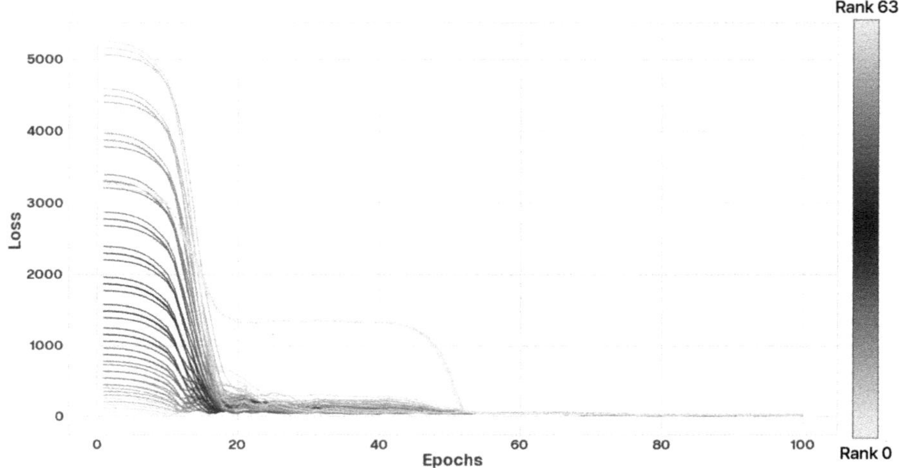

Fig. 3. Distributed in situ training stability. Training loss per epoch across ranks for an autoencoder trained concurrently with the solver. Convergence to a consistent loss across ranks indicates correct DDP synchronization and well-posed parallel training.

the most burdensome portion of the in situ training pipeline. The dominance of model synchronization is evident across all node counts past the single-node run. The data transit from solver to model proved significantly less costly across all simulation rank counts, with a maximum cost of $\sim$2.9 s. Initial results suggest that a majority of the runtime is concentrated on the first timestep, which involves the setup of the global variables and initializing kernels, with repeated calls to train inducing a much lower cost as a result.

5.2   In Situ Autoencoder Training on HARVEY Fluid Data

With confirmation of the training workflow, we sought to evaluate our methodology's ability to enable two distinct online machine learning workflows: online training/offline inference and offline training/online inference. For the former composition, we set out to investigate the two aforementioned training schemes in an online setting. The first mimics the generic offline training setup, training all at once with a stable dataset at the end of the simulation. The second explores training iteratively, with a dynamically populated training dataset that grows throughout the lifetime of the simulation. HARVEY simulation composition matched that of the verification experiment, albeit over a longer period of time to allow the fluid flow to fully develop. We simulated for a total of 1001 timesteps, with the first 800 timesteps dedicated to model training. This strategy reflects a potential use case in complex patient-specific fluid modeling. If effective, fluid data pre-convergence can be used to train a deep learning model on the task of accurately compressing domains at time points further along in the simulation. Fluid domain data was collected every 10 timesteps

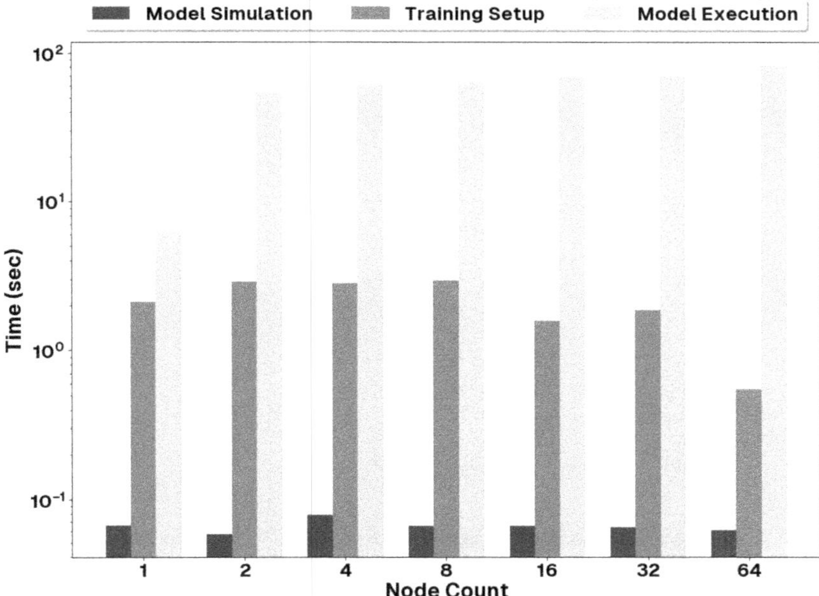

Fig. 4. Weak-scaling overhead attribution for in situ training. Total time is decomposed into solver compute (HARVEY kernels), model training (and synchronization), and framework overhead (data adaptation and bridge-script invocation). Training dominates at scale while solver-to-model linking remains comparatively small.

to populate a custom PyTorch dataset crafted to handle a continuous stream of data. The two in situ training paradigms explored required slightly different directives within the bridge script. For training executed in step with the data generator, the bridge script invoked training every 100 timesteps, with each call looping through 10 epochs for a total of 80 training epochs throughout the simulation lifetime. In contrast, training was invoked once at the last timestep when investigating the traditional training scheme. We launched in situ training on a scaling set of MPI ranks and inputs (on up to 32 ranks) for both considered paradigms. We present the training results for the 4 MPI rank training case in Fig. 5. Although the model is not overly performant, we compared training loss with a model trained with the same data offline, represented by the dotted yellow line, to ensure training was being performed correctly. Conventional training in situ outpaced iterative training, quickly reaching convergence within the first 10 epochs of training. Iterative training converged around the same loss value later in the lifetime of the model, proving the validity of the training scheme. Both in situ training schemes matched the performance of their offline counterpart, further verifying the fidelity of the solver-model coupling.

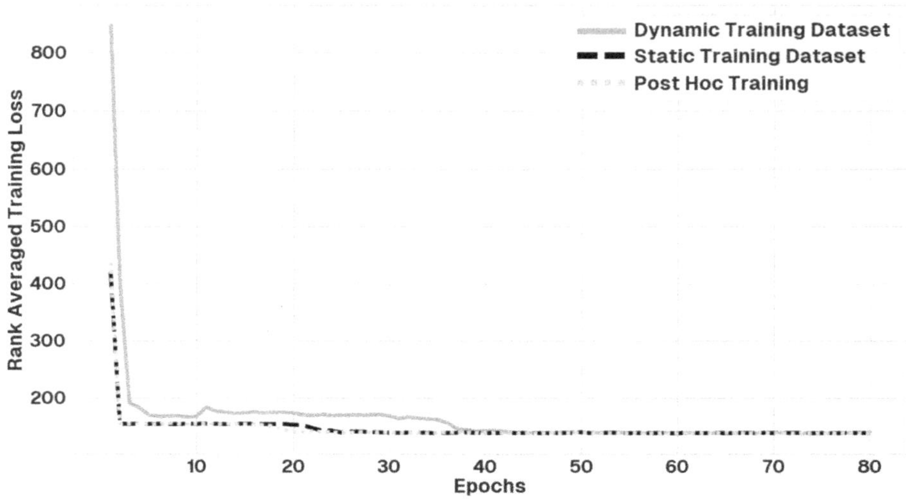

Fig. 5. Model loss curves generated across three separate training paradigms: in situ training with a static dataset, in situ training with an iteratively updated ("dynamic") dataset, and offline training. Loss curves were calculated based on the loss per epoch averaged across all 4 MPI ranks. Both in situ training schemes matched their offline training counterpart, with convergence around 10 epochs and 40 epochs, respectively.

5.3   Compressing HARVEY Data Through Online Model Inference

To evaluate the second of the two focused online machine learning workflows, we initialized and trained an autoencoder model offline for testing of online inference functionality. We evaluated the ability of the trained model to encode the solver-generated fluid grid and accompanying velocity field through inference, with the same split between training and prediction timesteps as detailed in the online training study. Mimicking the simulation composition used for in situ training evaluation, we simulated flow within a cylinder for a total of 1001 timesteps. The latter 200 timesteps were reserved for offline inference to mirror the previous training-based experiment. We performed model inference every 10 timesteps, encoding the spatial domain and velocity field and saving the latent vector on disk. After the fact, we investigated the accuracy of model encoding by decoding the saved latent vectors to recover the original solver-based grid representation. An example reconstructed fluid grid for a single rank simulation is shown in Fig. 6, visualized alongside the simulation-based ground truth. Although testing was performed in varying simulation sizes and rank sets, the serial experiment best illustrated the potential cost savings that lossy encoding can produce. The simulation domain was composed of a vector of size (21504, 4), while the latent encoded vector was composed of a vector of size (128, 1), leading to an effective compression rate of 672x. To evaluate reconstructive accuracy, we calculated both the relative Frobenius error (as defined in [5]) and the mean squared error (MSE). The reconstruction, illustrated in Fig. 6, had a relative Frobenius error of 0.0311 and an MSE of 2.441 and 8.667e−13 for the coordinates and velocity magnitude fields, respectively.

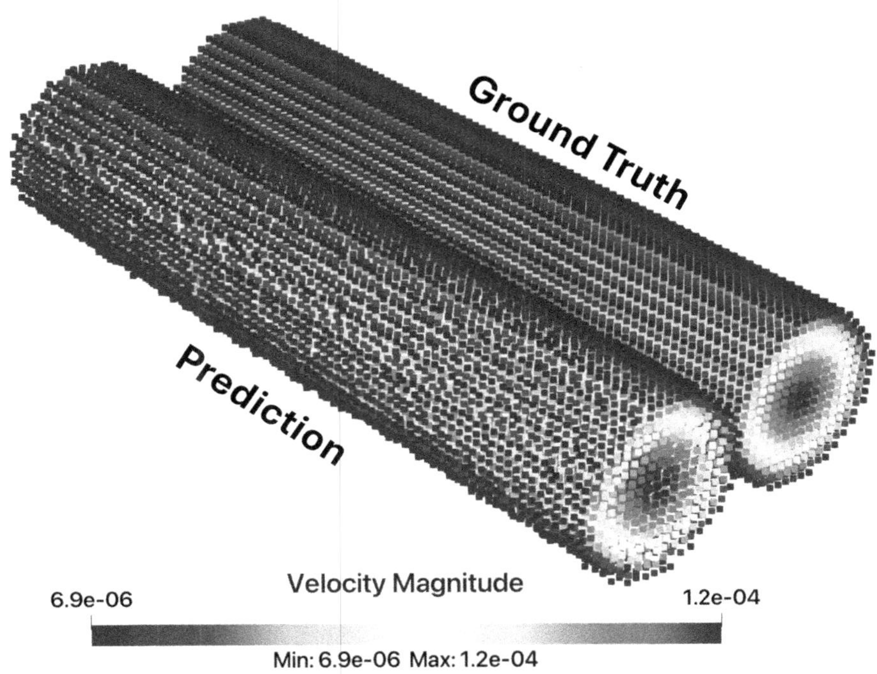

Fig. 6. Representative reconstruction from in situ inference. A pretrained autoencoder encodes solver state during the simulations and outputs latent vectors on disk. Post hoc decoding recovers the fluid-point coordinates and velocity magnitude, with the reconstructed field preserving the inlet-flow structure with minimal reconstruction error.

6   Conclusion

We presented a lightweight, modular framework for distributed in situ ML training and inference built on the Catalyst and ParaView software. By integrating the framework into the HARVEY mini-app, we demonstrated end-to-end coupling between a parallel fluid solver and Python-based ML workflows, including both in situ training and inference of a point-cloud autoencoder during solver execution. The design—compiling only against the Catalyst stub, using runtime-loaded libraries, and isolating ML logic in Python bridge/model scripts—provides a portable and minimally invasive path for adding ML capabilities to existing solvers without language unification or major refactoring.

Our evaluation verifies the correctness of distributed training, characterizes overhead and scalability to 256 ranks, and demonstrates two practical workflows: online training and online inference for lossy state compression. Future work will expand systematic comparisons across training schedules and comparable applications, explore bounded-memory streaming datasets, and integrate external data services to enable concurrent training across ensembles. More broadly, this orchestration provides a pragmatic bridge between parallel simulation and modern ML tooling, enabling adaptive, data-driven HPC applications and more responsive simulation environments.

Acknowledgments. This research used resources of the Argonne Leadership Computing Facility, a US DOE Office of Science user facility at Argonne National Laboratory, and is based on research supported by the US DOE Office of Science-Advanced Scientific Computing Research Program, under Contract No. DE-AC02-06CH11357.

References

1. Ahrens, J., Geveci, B., Law, C., Hansen, C., Johnson, C., et al.: Paraview: an end-user tool for large-data visualization. Vis. Handb. **717**, 50038–1 (2005)
2. Ahrens, J., Jourdain, S., O'Leary, P., Patchett, J., Rogers, D.H., Petersen, M.: An image-based approach to extreme scale in situ visualization and analysis. In: SC'14: Proceedings of the International Conference for High Performance Computing, Networking, Storage and Analysis, pp. 424–434. IEEE (2014)
3. Atzori, M., et al.: In situ visualization of large-scale turbulence simulations in Nek5000 with Paraview Catalyst. J. Supercomput. **78**(3), 3605–3620 (2022)
4. Ayachit, U., et al.: Paraview catalyst: enabling in situ data analysis and visualization. In: Proceedings of the First Workshop on in Situ Infrastructures for Enabling Extreme-Scale Analysis and Visualization, pp. 25–29 (2015)
5. Balin, R., et al.: In situ framework for coupling simulation and machine learning with application to CFD. arXiv preprint arXiv:2306.12900 (2023)
6. Bedrunka, M.C., Wilde, D., Kliemank, M., Reith, D., Foysi, H., Krämer, A.: Lettuce: PyTorch-based lattice Boltzmann framework. In: Jagode, H., Anzt, H., Ltaief, H., Luszczek, P. (eds.) ISC High Performance 2021. LNCS, vol. 12761, pp. 40–55. Springer, Cham (2021). https://doi.org/10.1007/978-3-030-90539-2_3
7. Chen, X., Yang, G., Yao, Q., Nie, Z., Jiang, Z.: A compressed lattice Boltzmann method based on ConvLSTM and ResNet. Comput. Math. Appl. **97**, 162–174 (2021)
8. Gonzalez-Sieiro, J., Pardo, D., Nava, V., Calo, V.M., Towara, M.: Reducing spatial discretization error on coarse CFD simulations using an OpenFOAM-embedded deep learning framework. Eng. Comput. 1–22 (2024)
9. Harrison, C., Larsen, M., Ryujin, B.S., Kunen, A., Capps, A., Privitera, J.: Conduit: a successful strategy for describing and sharing data in situ. In: 2022 IEEE/ACM International Workshop on in Situ Infrastructures for Enabling Extreme-Scale Analysis and Visualization (ISAV), pp. 1–6. IEEE (2022)
10. Imambi, S., Prakash, K.B., Kanagachidambaresan, G.R.: PyTorch. In: Prakash, K.B., Kanagachidambaresan, G.R. (eds.) Programming with TensorFlow. EICC, pp. 87–104. Springer, Cham (2021). https://doi.org/10.1007/978-3-030-57077-4_10

11. Jasak, H.: Openfoam: open source CFD in research and industry. Int. Naval Archit. Ocean Eng. **1**(2), 89–94 (2009)
12. Kurz, M., Offenhäuser, P., Viola, D., Resch, M., Beck, A.: Relexi–a scalable open source reinforcement learning framework for high-performance computing. Software Impacts **14**, 100422 (2022)
13. Larsen, M., Brugger, E., Childs, H., Harrison, C.: Ascent: a flyweight in situ library for exascale simulations. In: Childs, H., Bennett, J.C., Garth, C. (eds.) In Situ Visualization for Computational Science, pp. 255–279. Springer, Cham (2022). https://doi.org/10.1007/978-3-030-81627-8_12
14. Martin, A., et al.: Performance portability evaluation of fluid-structure interaction simulations on heterogeneous platforms. In: ISC High Performance 2025 Research Paper Proceedings (40th International Conference), pp. 1–11. Prometeus GmbH (2025)
15. Maulik, R., Fytanidis, D.K., Lusch, B., Vishwanath, V., Patel, S.: PythonFOAM: In-situ data analyses with OpenFOAM and Python. J. Comput. Sci. **62**, 101750 (2022)
16. Maulik, R., Sharma, H., Patel, S., Lusch, B., Jennings, E.: Deploying deep learning in OpenFOAM with tensorflow. In: AIAA Scitech 2021 Forum, p. 1485 (2021)
17. Pegolotti, L., et al.: Learning reduced-order models for cardiovascular simulations with graph neural networks. Comput. Biol. Med. **168**, 107676 (2024)
18. Randles, A.P., Kale, V., Hammond, J., Gropp, W., Kaxiras, E.: Performance analysis of the lattice Boltzmann model beyond Navier-Stokes. In: 2013 IEEE 27th International Symposium on Parallel and Distributed Processing, pp. 1063–1074. IEEE (2013)
19. Sun, X., Cao, W., Shan, X., Liu, Y., Zhang, W.: A generalized framework for integrating machine learning into computational fluid dynamics. J. Comput. Sci. **82**, 102404 (2024)
20. Tiwari, S.: The rise of intelligent machines: an introduction to artificial intelligence. In: Artificial Intelligence and Machine Learning in Drug Design and Development, pp. 1–22 (2024)
21. Vardhan, M., et al.: Diagnostic performance of coronary angiography derived computational fractional flow reserve. J. Am. Heart Assoc. **13**(13), e029941 (2024)
22. Yokelson, D., et al.: Soma: observability, monitoring, and in situ analytics for exascale applications. Concurr. Comput. Pract. Exper. **36**(19), e8141 (2024)
23. Yousef, A., Wetterer-Nelson, C., Han, M., et al.: Catalystml: in situ machine learning framework for parallel solvers (2026). https://github.com/aymanzyy/catalystml, gitHub repository
24. Yousef, A.Z., Draeger, E.W., Randles, A.: Low-cost post hoc reconstruction of HPC simulations at full resolution. In: 2023 IEEE 13th Symposium on Large Data Analysis and Visualization (LDAV), pp. 17–21. IEEE (2023)
25. Öngün, C.: Point cloud autoencoder. Github Repository (2020). https://github.com/cihanongun/Point-Cloud-Autoencoder

Uncertainty Propagation for Random Field Outputs Using Denoising Diffusion Models

Pavankumar Koratikere[1], Leifur Leifsson[1(✉)], Slawomir Koziel[2,3], and Anna Pietrenko-Dabrowska[3]

[1] School of Aeronautics and Astronautics, Purdue University, West Lafayette, IN 47907, USA
{pkoratik,leifur}@purdue.edu

[2] Engineering Optimization and Modeling Center, Department of Engineering, Reykjavík University, Menntavegur 1, 102 Reykjavík, Iceland
koziel@ru.is

[3] Faculty of Electronics Telecommunications and Informatics, Gdansk University of Technology, Narutowicza 11/12, 80-233 Gdansk, Poland
anna.dabrowska@pg.edu.pl

Abstract. Uncertainty propagation (UP) is a popular method for estimating randomness in model outputs by propagating input uncertainties through the model. Several methods have been proposed for UP through an expensive-to-evaluate model, including surrogate-based approaches. These methods rely on approximating input-output relation to create a fast-to-evaluate model which can then be used for UP. However, these approaches are limited by the curse of dimensionality and are not easily scalable to UP problems where the model output is a random field. To alleviate these challenges with quantifying random field outputs, this work proposes to utilize diffusion models to perform UP. Specifically, denoising diffusion probabilistic models (DDPMs) are used for tackling UP for random field outputs. DDPM is an unsupervised model, and hence, does not learn input-output mapping. Moreover, DDPMs have been shown to work well for complex high-dimensional distributions. The DDPM-based UP is demonstrated on two physics-based problems and is evaluated against direct Monte Carlo (MC) simulations. The DDPM-based approach is able to accurately learn the underlying distribution using small number of samples, while the MC simulation requires thousands of samples. These results indicate that DDPM can be an efficient tool for quantifying uncertainty in random output fields.

Keywords: Uncertainty propagation · random output fields · denoising diffusion probabilistic models · deep neural networks · diffusion models

1   Introduction

Uncertainty quantification (UQ) is a widely used tool in various science and engineering applications [9,13]. The primary aim of UQ is to determine the impact on model outputs due to the randomness in model parameters. It consists of three steps: (i) identifying the type of uncertainty in model parameters, (ii) using a mathematical framework to quantify this uncertainty, and (iii) uncertainty propagation (UP) (also known as forward UQ). The UP consists of propagating randomness in parameters through the model to quantify uncertainty in model output. This work focuses on UP, especially for the models that consists of random field outputs.

Monte Carlo (MC) methods are one of the most popular approaches for UP. It consists of sampling from the parameter uncertainty distribution and evaluating the model on the generated samples to obtain distribution for the model outputs [9]. This approach is not feasible when model is computationally expensive to evaluate. Alternatively, a fast and cheap-to-evaluate model can be constructed for evaluating a sample. Common models include Gaussian process regression [12], polynomial chaos expansion [15] (PCE), and neural networks [7] (NN). These methods approximate the mapping between input and output, and hence, are limited by the curse of dimensionality. Moreover, these methods are primarily designed for finite number of inputs and outputs, and may not always scale to random fields. However, dimensionality reduction approaches using PCE [6] and NNs [2] have been proposed for UP to alleviate the challenges posed by uncertain random field.

Recently, denoising diffusion probabilistic models (DDPMs) have gained a lot of interest, owing to their effectiveness in approximating complex high-dimensional probability distributions [1,4]. Specifically, DDPMs are a class of generative models that learn an underlying data distribution by training on samples from that same distribution. Note that DDPM is not modeling input-output relation, rather it approximates the unknown distribution. As a result, it is not limited by the number of uncertain parameters and can circumvent the input curse of dimensionality.

Owing to these advantages, this work proposes a novel method for utilizing DDPM for UP tasks, where the model output is a random field. The proposed method is demonstrated on UP task for two physics-based problems and is benchmarked against direct MC simulations. The results indicate that DDPM is able to accurately learn the underlying data distribution with a small number of samples.

The remainder of this paper is organized as follows: Sect. 2 provides an overview of DDPM and outlines the proposed method. It also provides a description of the deep neural network architecture used within DDPM. Section 3 presents the result of performing UP using DDPM. Lastly, Sect. 4 concludes this work, along with some recommendations for future work.

2   Methods

This section briefly introduces denoising diffusion models, followed by the proposed algorithm for performing UP using diffusion models. Lastly, it provides a detailed description of the deep neural network model used in this work.

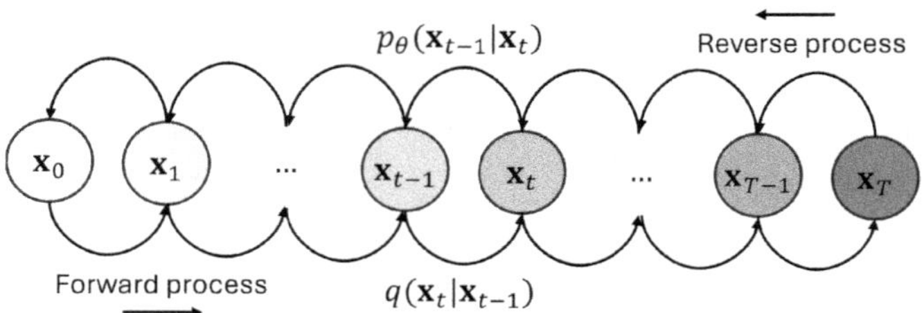

Fig. 1. Forward and reverse process within a diffusion model.

2.1   Denoising Diffusion Probabilistic Models

Denoising diffusion probabilistic model (DDPM) is an unsupervised generative model that learns a target probability distribution $p(\mathbf{x})$ using the samples from the same distribution. Specifically, DDPM approximates $p(\mathbf{x})$ with a parametric distribution $p_\theta(\mathbf{x}_0)$, where $\mathbf{x}_0$ is a sample from the original distribution [4]. Mathematically, it can be written as

$$p(\mathbf{x}) \approx p_\theta(\mathbf{x}_0) = \int p_\theta(\mathbf{x}_{0:T})d\mathbf{x}_{1:T}, \tag{1}$$

where $\mathbf{x}_1,\ldots,\mathbf{x}_T$ represent latent variables of the same dimension as $\mathbf{x}_0$. The joint distribution $p_\theta(\mathbf{x}_{0:T})$ is defined via a Markov chain and is written as

$$p_\theta(\mathbf{x}_{0:T}) = p_T(\mathbf{x}_T) \prod_{t=1}^{T} p_\theta(\mathbf{x}_{t-1}|\mathbf{x}_t), \tag{2}$$

where transition probability distribution follows a Gaussian and is given by

$$p_\theta(\mathbf{x}_{t-1}|\mathbf{x}_t) = \mathcal{N}(\mu_\theta(\mathbf{x}_t,t),\sigma_t^2\mathbf{I}). \tag{3}$$

The mean μ_θ and σ_t are written as

$$\mu_\theta(\mathbf{x}_t,t) = \frac{1}{\sqrt{\alpha_t}}\mathbf{x}_t - \frac{1-\alpha_t}{\sqrt{1-\bar{\alpha}_t}\sqrt{\alpha_t}}\hat{\boldsymbol{\epsilon}}_\theta(\mathbf{x}_t,t), \text{ and } \sigma_t^2 = \frac{(1-\alpha_t)(1-\bar{\alpha}_{t-1})}{1-\bar{\alpha}_t}. \tag{4}$$

As shown in Fig. 1, DDPM starts with a sample $\mathbf{x}_T$ from a standard gaussian distribution which is then progressively denoised to obtain a sample $\mathbf{x}_0$ from target distribution. Now, the primary task is to learn a noise predictor $\hat{\boldsymbol{\epsilon}}_\theta(\mathbf{x}_t,t)$.

To learn an appropriate noise predictor for this reverse process, a Markov chain is used to fully define a forward process that progressively corrupts $\mathbf{x}_0$ with Gaussian noise to obtain $\mathbf{x}_T$ [4,11]. This forward process is written as

$$q(\mathbf{x}_{1:T}|\mathbf{x}_0) = \prod_{t=1}^{T} q(\mathbf{x}_t|\mathbf{x}_{t-1}), \tag{5}$$

where the conditional distribution $q(\mathbf{x}_t|\mathbf{x}_{t-1})$ is assumed to be Gaussian so that it is of the same form as $p_\theta(\mathbf{x}_{t-1}|\mathbf{x}_t)$. Mathematically, it is written as

$$q(\mathbf{x}_t|\mathbf{x}_{t-1}) = \mathcal{N}(\sqrt{1-\beta_t}\mathbf{x}_{t-1}, \beta_t\mathbf{I}), \tag{6}$$

where $\beta_1, \ldots, \beta_T$ represents variance scheduler that controls how much Gaussian noise is added at each time step t. Based on this forward process definition, α_t and $\bar{\alpha}_t$ can be computed as

$$\alpha_t = 1 - \beta_t, \text{ and } \bar{\alpha}_t = \prod_{s=1}^{t} \alpha_s. \tag{7}$$

Using the properties of Markov chain and reparameterization trick [5], $\mathbf{x}_t$ can be directly computed from $\mathbf{x}_0$ using

$$\mathbf{x}_t = \sqrt{\alpha_t}\mathbf{x}_0 + \sqrt{1-\alpha_t}\boldsymbol{\epsilon}, \quad \boldsymbol{\epsilon} \sim \mathcal{N}(\mathbf{0}, \mathbf{I}). \tag{8}$$

For any given t and $\mathbf{x}_t$, the goal is to train $\hat{\boldsymbol{\epsilon}}$ so that the difference between forward and reverse process is minimized. Based on Ho et al. [4], a simplified version of negative log-likelihood of evidence lower bound is used as the loss function, which is written as

$$\mathcal{L}(\theta) = \mathbb{E}_{\mathbf{x}_0 \sim p(\mathbf{x}), t \sim U[1,T], \boldsymbol{\epsilon} \sim \mathcal{N}(\mathbf{0},\mathbf{I})}\left[\left\|\boldsymbol{\epsilon} - \hat{\boldsymbol{\epsilon}}_\theta[\mathbf{x}_t(\mathbf{x}_0, t)]\right\|^2\right]. \tag{9}$$

Algorithm 1. Training process for a diffusion model [10]

1: **input**: training data $\mathbf{x}_i, i = 1, \ldots, N$
2: **repeat**
3:     **for** $j \in \mathcal{B}$ **do**   ▷ for each sample index in batch
4:         $t \sim U[1, \ldots, T]$ ▷ sample t randomly
5:         $\boldsymbol{\epsilon} \sim \mathcal{N}(\mathbf{0}, \mathbf{I})$ ▷ sample noise
6:         $\mathcal{L}_j(\theta) = \left\|\boldsymbol{\epsilon} - \hat{\boldsymbol{\epsilon}}_\theta(\sqrt{\alpha_t}\mathbf{x}_j + \sqrt{1-\alpha_t}\boldsymbol{\epsilon})\right\|^2$ ▷ compute loss
7:     **end for**
8:     $\mathcal{L}(\theta) = \sum_j \mathcal{L}_j(\theta)$ ▷ accumulate losses
9:     take gradient of $\mathcal{L}$ with respect to θ
10:    update model parameters θ using gradient
11: **until** convergence
12: **output**: model parameters θ

Algorithm 2. Sampling process using diffusion model [10]

1: **input**: trained model $\hat{\boldsymbol{\epsilon}}_\theta$
2: $\mathbf{x}_T \sim \mathcal{N}(\mathbf{0}, \mathbf{I})$
3: **for** $t = T, \ldots, 2$ **do**
4:     $\boldsymbol{\mu}_{t-1} = \dfrac{1}{\sqrt{\alpha_t}} \mathbf{x}_t - \dfrac{\beta_1}{\sqrt{\alpha_t}\sqrt{1 - \bar{\alpha}_t}} \hat{\boldsymbol{\epsilon}}_\theta(\mathbf{x}_t)$ ▷ compute mean for next step
5:     $\boldsymbol{\epsilon} \sim \mathcal{N}(\mathbf{0}, \mathbf{I})$
6:     $\mathbf{x}_{t-1} = \boldsymbol{\mu}_{t-1} + \sigma_t \boldsymbol{\epsilon}$ ▷ next sample
7: **end for**
8: $\mathbf{x} = \dfrac{1}{\sqrt{\alpha_1}} \mathbf{x}_1 - \dfrac{\beta_1}{\sqrt{\alpha_1}\sqrt{1 - \bar{\alpha}_1}} \hat{\boldsymbol{\epsilon}}_\theta(\mathbf{x}_1)$ ▷ final sample
9: **output**: sample $\mathbf{x}$

Note that, in above equation, $\mathbf{x}_t$ is computed using (8). A deep neural network model, parametrized with θ, is used as a noise predictor. The loss function $\mathcal{L}$ is minimized with respect to θ to obtain the parameters of the network. In this work, adaptive moment (ADAM) optimization method is used for training the network with a learning rate of 0.0001. The network is trained for 5000 epochs with a batch size of 64. The total number of time steps T is set to 200. These optimization parameters are determined using manual trial and error process. Algorithm 1 and 2 summarize the training and sampling process used in this work, respectively. Refer to Ho et al. [4], Sohl-Dickstein at el. [11], and Lai C et al. [8] for a detail review of diffusion models.

2.2   Uncertainty Propagation Using DDPM

Consider a computationally expensive function $\mathcal{F} : \mathbb{R}^d \times \mathbb{R}^n \to \mathbb{R}^m$, where d is the number of uncertain variables, n is the number of deterministic variables, and m is the number of outputs. The function $\mathcal{F}$ can be written as

$$\mathbf{Y} = \mathcal{F}(\mathbf{X}, \boldsymbol{\varphi}), \tag{10}$$

where $\mathbf{X} \in \mathbb{R}^d$ is a random vector representing uncertain variables and $\boldsymbol{\varphi} \in \mathbb{R}^n$ denotes deterministic variables. In this work, $\boldsymbol{\varphi}$ is held constant and the focus is only on uncertain variables. Since input to the function $\mathcal{F}$ is uncertain, the output $\mathbf{Y} \in \mathbb{R}^m$ is also a random vector.

The UP problem consists of propagating the uncertainty in $\mathbf{X} \sim P_\mathbf{X}(\mathbf{x})$ through $\mathcal{F}$ to quantify the uncertainty in $\mathbf{Y} \sim P_\mathbf{Y}(\mathbf{y})$. Hence, the goal is to find the distribution $P_\mathbf{Y}(\mathbf{y})$ or some of the statistics of $\mathbf{Y}$, such as mean or standard deviation, induced by input uncertainty. This paper specifically deals with problems that have uncertain field outputs. Moreover, $\mathcal{F}$ can be computationally expensive and only a limited number of evaluations can be made.

DDPM is shown to approximate complex high-dimensional probability distributions [1,4]. Since the output of $\mathcal{F}$ is also a random field, this work proposes a method for approximating $P_\mathbf{Y}$ using DDPM. Algorithm 3 outlines the proposed

---

Algorithm 3. Uncertainty propagation using DDPM (this work)

1: **input**: $P_{\mathbf{X}}$, $\mathcal{F}$, φ, N
2: $\mathbf{x}_i \leftarrow$ generate N samples from $P_{\mathbf{X}}$
3: $\mathbf{y}_i \leftarrow$ compute output at $\mathbf{x}_i$ using $\mathcal{F}$
4: $\hat{\boldsymbol{\epsilon}}_\theta \leftarrow$ train DDPM using $\{\mathbf{y}_1, \ldots, \mathbf{y}_N\}$ $\triangleright$ c.f. Algorithm 1
5: generate samples from $P_{\mathbf{Y}}$ using $\hat{\boldsymbol{\epsilon}}_\theta$ $\triangleright$ c.f. Algorithm 2
6: compute mean and standard deviation using sampled points
7: **output**: samples from $P_{\mathbf{Y}}$, mean and standard deviation of $\mathbf{Y}$

---

method. The core idea is straight-forward: generate samples from the target distribution $P_{\mathbf{Y}}$ and use DDPM to approximate it. This is a fundamentally different approach to UP problem as compared to other methods. DDPM is not modeling an input-output relation, instead it learns the underlying distribution $P_{\mathbf{Y}}$. Moreover, this method is independent of the number of input variables (uncertain or deterministic), and hence, circumvents the input curse of dimensionality. DDPM also has a strong theoretical foundation via the Fokker-plank equation and the stochastic differential equation [8].

Meanwhile, there are certain challenges with the proposed approach. Firstly, it is assumed that sampling from $P_{\mathbf{X}}$ and then evaluating it using $\mathcal{F}$ will generate diverse sample set from $P_{\mathbf{Y}}$. This may not be true always. Secondly, even though training a DDPM is more stable than other unsupervised generative models, it is still difficult, especially given the number of hyperparameters. Lastly, depending on the complexity of $P_{\mathbf{Y}}$, DDPM might require a lot of samples to learn the underlying distribution which is not always feasible. However, it is worthwhile exploring DDPM for UP problems, given its effectiveness in approximating complex high-dimensional distribution.

2.3   Network Architecture

This section describes the architecture of the deep neural network model used in this work for noise prediction. As shown in Fig. 2a, a deep convolutional neural network is used. Note that this architecture is determined using manual trial and error process for the problems demonstrated in Sect. 3.

The model consists of a series of blocks that perform computation on the given input sample $\mathbf{x}$ at a time step t. A sinusoidal embedding method [1] is used to convert discrete time step t to a continuous representation that can then be used by the model. In this work, time step t is embedded into 128 dimensions. The input $\mathbf{x}$ is first processed by a 1D convolutional unit, followed by a nonlinear activation function. This convolution unit converts one input channel to 64 output channels. This is followed by 5 individual computation blocks, whose architecture is described in Fig. 2b.

Each block first applies a convolution operation to the given input, followed by adding time step information. The embedded time is processed through a one layer fully connected network (FCNN) before adding it to output channels of the convolution unit. This addition of time step information is crucial for

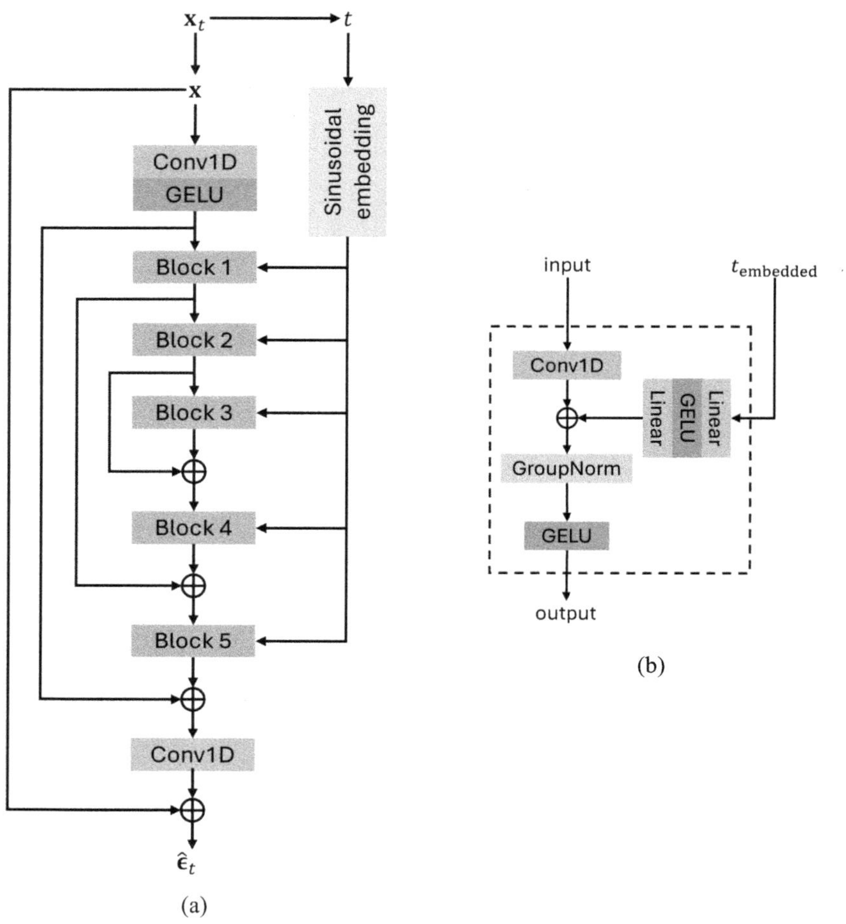

Fig. 2. Deep learning model used as noise predictor $\hat{\epsilon}_\theta$ within DDPM (a): full architecture and (b): single computation block used within the architecture.

Table 1. Architecture details for the individual blocks used within noise predictor $\hat{\epsilon}_\theta$ model.

Block	Convolution unit		Fully connected unit	
	in channels	out channels	1st linear	2nd linear
Block 1	64	128	128×128	128×128
Block 2	128	256	128×256	256×256
Block 3	256	256	128×256	256×256
Block 4	256	128	128×128	128×128
Block 5	128	64	128×64	64×64

the model to correctly predict noise ϵ at given t. The weights of FCNN are initialized using the He method [3]. Note that each block has its own FCNN. Next, the combined output is passed through a group normalization unit before passing it through a nonlinear activation function. This normalization prevents exploding gradient issues for the activation function and is shown to be better than batch normalization [14]. In this work, channels are divided into groups of eight for normalization.

Table 1 outlines the size of convolution and fully connected units across each of the five blocks. The block 1 and 2 expand the number of channels to 256 while block 4 and 5 contract the number of channels back to 64. After processing the input through each of the five blocks, a final convolution unit is used to further reduce the number of channels to one. There are also four connections that enable skipping some of the intermediate blocks to improve training efficiency and to prevent vanishing gradient issues, especially when using deep networks. Each convolution block used in this network has a kernel size of 15, padding of 7 and stride of 1. The model is built and trained using PyTorch framework on NVIDIA 3070.

3   Results

This section demonstrates UP using DDPM on two physics-based problems. The training set for DDPM consists of 250 samples for both problems, while 10000 points are sampled from the trained DDPM model. The direct MC simulation is also performed using 10,000 samples. The mean and standard deviation of the random field computed using DDPM samples are compared against the values obtained from direct MC simulation. It is important to note that the problems illustrated in this section are only for demonstrating the proposed method. The added value of DDPM for UP will be more clear in the scenarios that involve large number of uncertain input variables, such as uncertain boundary conditions.

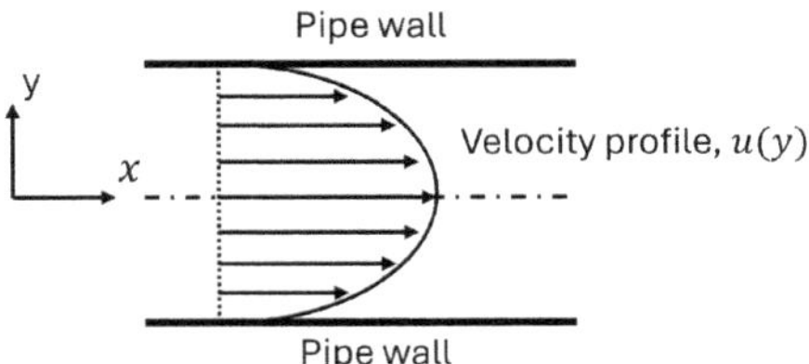

Fig. 3. A fully developed flow in a circular pipe.

3.1   Flow in a Circular Pipe

Consider fluid flow in a circular pipe as shown in Fig. 3. Under the assumption of incompressible, laminar flow and Newtonian fluid, an analytical expression can be obtained for this 1D flow. The fully developed velocity field can be computed as

$$u(y) = \frac{G}{2\nu}\left(\frac{d^2}{4} - y^2\right),\tag{11}$$

where $-d/2 \leq y \leq y/2$, G is the pressure gradient applied in the direction of flow, ν is the fluid viscosity, and d is the diameter of the pipe. Since the flow is 1D, the velocity u only varies in y direction. In this work, the fluid viscosity ν is considered to be uncertain, which follows a uniform distribution given by

$$\nu \sim U[7.5 \times 10^{-4}, 2.5 \times 10^{-3}].\tag{12}$$

This results in an uncertain $u(y)$ field that needs to be quantified. Hence, the goal is to train a DDPM to approximate the distribution of this uncertain field. For this problem, $\mathcal{F}$ is given by (11), $\mathbf{X}$ consists of viscosity ν and $\mathbf{Y}$ is the random velocity field $u(y)$. The $\boldsymbol{\varphi}$ consists of parameters G and d, which are fixed to $0.1\,\mathrm{Pa/m}$ and $0.1\,\mathrm{m}$, respectively. For this problem, the random field $u(y)$ consists of 100 linearly spaced collocation points between $-d/2$ and $d/2$.

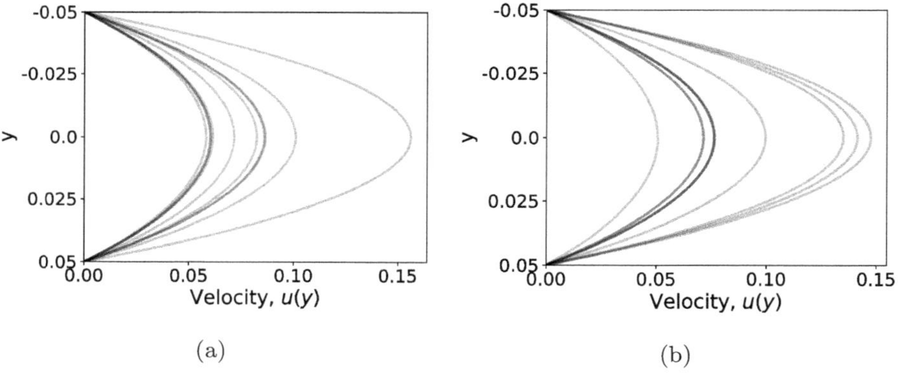

Fig. 4. Comparison of ten randomly generated velocity profile samples (a) from true distribution, and (b) using DDPM.

Figure 4 compares ten $u(y)$ samples generated from the true distribution and the trained DDPM. It should be noted that samples generated from DDPM has similar flow field features as the true samples. Specifically, the $u(y)$ field starts and ends at $0\,\mathrm{m/s}$, which is physically consistent with no-slip wall condition. Moreover, the $u(y)$ samples generated by DDPM are also symmetric about the center line. This points to the fact that DDPM is generating samples that are physically valid.

Figure 5 compares flow field statistics obtained from DDPM samples to that of direct MC samples. Specifically, 10th, 25th, 75th, and 90th percentile are compared, along with mean $u(y)$ field. It can be noted that samples from DDPM yield almost identical statistics as the direct MC samples. This indicates that DDPM is able to learn the true underlying distribution of $u(y)$ field.

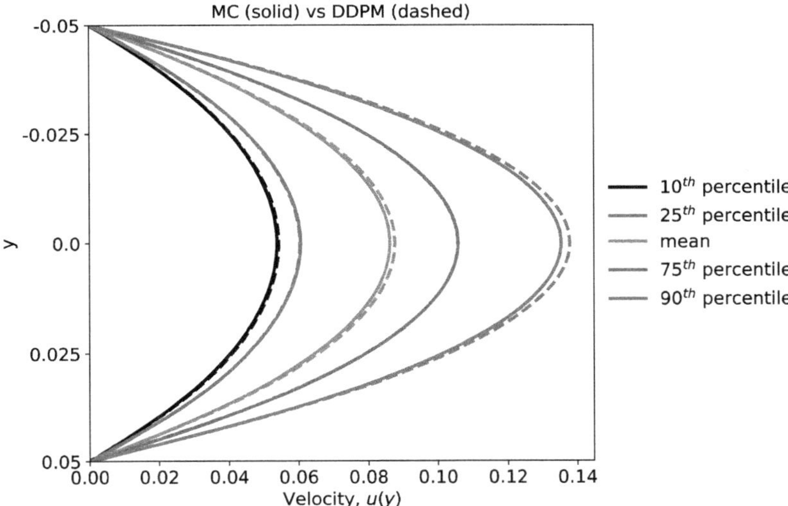

Fig. 5. Comparison of mean and 10th, 25th, 75th, and 90th percentile computed using Monte Carlo and DDPM-based approach

Figure 6 compares probability density function (PDF) of the center line velocity $u(0)$ obtained from DDPM and direct MC simulation. There is strong agreement between the PDFs with a slight mismatch around the peak. This shows that DDPM is able to capture the randomness in important flow field features, such as maximum velocity u_{max}. Lastly, Fig. 7 illustrates the evolution of a Gaussian noise to $u(y)$ sample within DDPM. At the start of reverse process ($t = 200$), the sample is just a Gaussian noise (blue line). As $t \to 0$, the noise is progressively removed to yield a smooth $u(y)$ field. These results indicate that DDPM is able to learn the distribution of $u(y)$ with just 250 samples, and hence, can be used to quantify uncertainty in $u(y)$.

3.2 Converging-Diverging Nozzle

This problem deals with compressible flow within a conical converging-diverging (CD) nozzle shown in Fig. 8. The geometry of the nozzle is governed by the inlet, outlet and throat radius, while the flow is driven by the back pressure p_b. There is no flow in the nozzle when p_b is same as the stagnation pressure p_0. As p_b decreases beyond a threshold, the flow accelerates to supersonic speeds through the throat and encounters a normal shock-wave in diverging part of the nozzle. This shock wave decelerates the flow to subsonic speeds as it exits the nozzle.

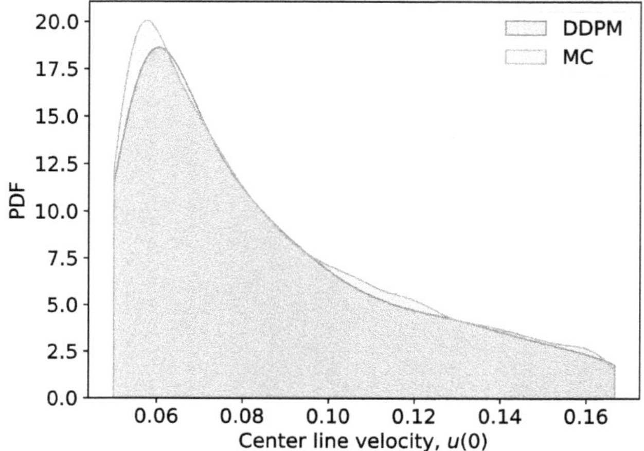

Fig. 6. Comparison of probability density function of the center line velocity, $u(0)$.

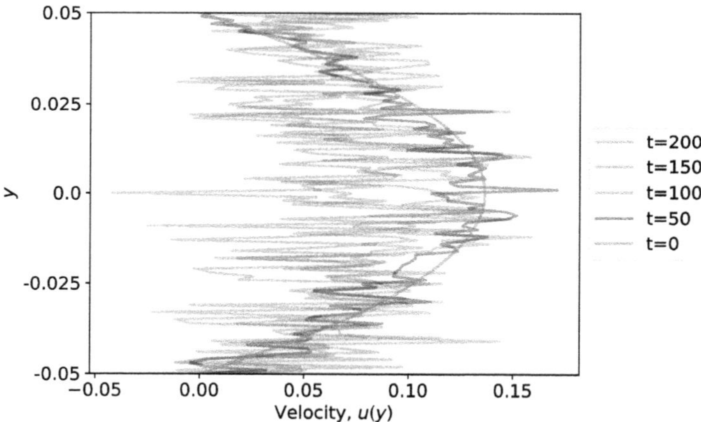

Fig. 7. Evolution of $u(y)$ within DDPM

In this work, the ratio of back pressure to stagnation pressure (p_b/p_0) and the ratio of specific heats (γ) are considered to be uncertain. Both these variables are distributed as

$$p_b/p_0 \sim \mathcal{N}(0.4, 0.02^2) \quad \text{and} \quad \gamma \sim U[1.15, 1.35]. \tag{13}$$

This results in an uncertain Mach number $M(x)$ field along the length of the nozzle. The goal is to use the DDPM model to quantify this uncertain distribution of $M(x)$. Note that $M(x)$ is a discontinuous field due to the presence of a shock wave. Moreover, there are regions where $M(x)$ is not affected by the variations in p_b/p_0. This makes it a challenging distribution for the DDPM to model.

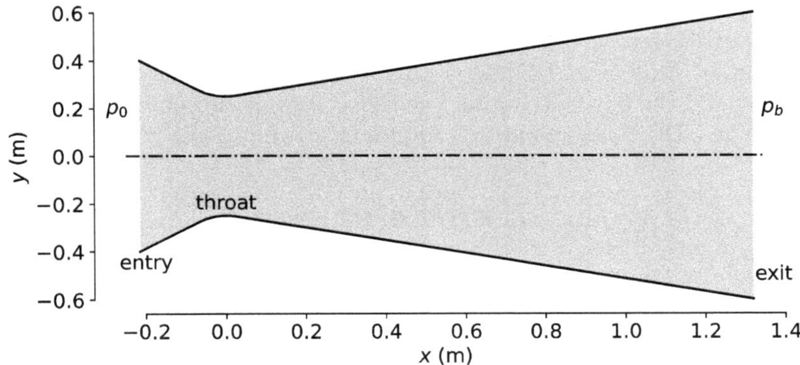

Fig. 8. Converging-diverging nozzle used in this work.

The $M(x)$ is governed by isentropic flow relations and normal shock wave equations, which are solved numerically to obtain $M(x)$ for any given condition. This work uses pygasflow[1] package, an open-source Python library for solving various compressible flow problems. The solver uses 114 linearly spaced collocation points from the nozzle inlet till the exit.

In this problem, $\mathcal{F}$ is the solver described earlier. The **X** consists of uncertain p_b/p_0 and γ, and **Y** is the random Mach field $M(x)$. The φ consists of various fixed parameters such as nozzle geometry variables. The inlet, outlet and throat radius is set to $0.4\,\mathrm{m}$, $0.6\,\mathrm{m}$, and $0.25\,\mathrm{m}$, respectively.

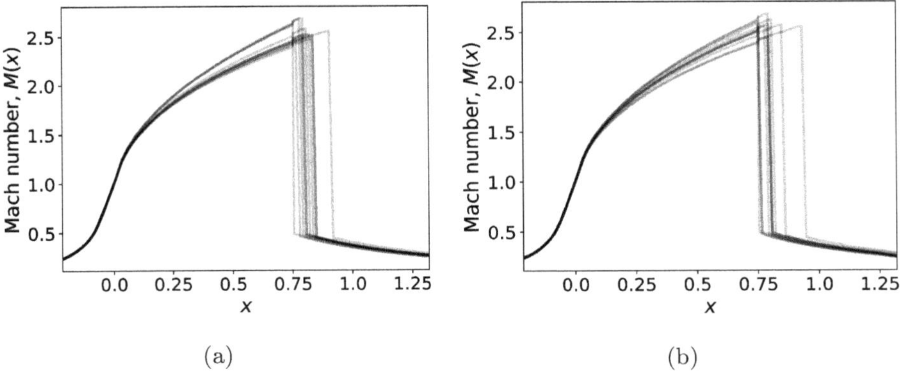

Fig. 9. Comparison of ten randomly generated Mach profile samples (a) from true distribution, and (b) using DDPM.

Figure 9 compares ten $M(x)$ samples generated from the true distribution and the trained DDPM. It should be noted that samples generated from DDPM

---

[1] https://pygasflow.readthedocs.io.

has similar flow field features as the true samples. Specifically, the $M(x) = 1$ at the throat of the nozzle, which is physically consistent as Mach number is equal to 1 at throat. Moreover, DDPM is able to generate shock waves without any smoothing, and the flow speed after the shock wave is subsonic. All these points indicate that DDPM is generating samples that are physically valid.

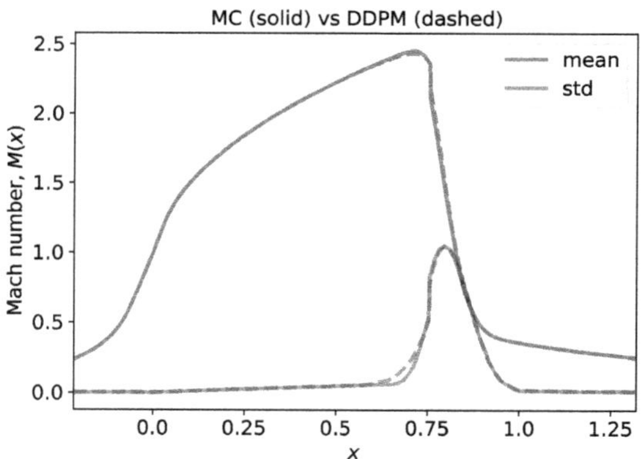

Fig. 10. Comparison of mean and standard deviation of random Mach field computed using Monte Carlo and DDPM.

Figure 10 compares flow field statistics from DDPM samples to that of direct MC samples. The mean and standard deviation of $M(x)$ field obtained from DDPM are almost same as the one obtained from direct MC simulation. Moreover, DDPM is able to identify regions in the field that have near-zero variability. This indicates that DDPM is able to learn the discontinuous random flow features of $M(x)$, while taking into account zero-uncertainty regions.

Figure 11 compares PDF of the shock wave location in the nozzle obtained from DDPM and direct MC simulation. The PDF obtained from DDPM is almost identical as the one obtained from MC, but with a slightly lower peak value. This indicates that DDPM is able to capture the randomness in important flow field features, such as the shock wave location.

Similar to the previous problem, Fig. 12 illustrates the evolution of a Gaussian noise to a $M(x)$ sample within DDPM. At the start of reverse process ($t = 200$), the sample is just a Gaussian noise (blue line). As $t \to 0$, the sample is progressively denoised to yield a valid $M(x)$ sample. These results indicate that DDPM is able to learn the distribution of $M(x)$ with just 250 samples, and hence, can be used to generate samples from it.

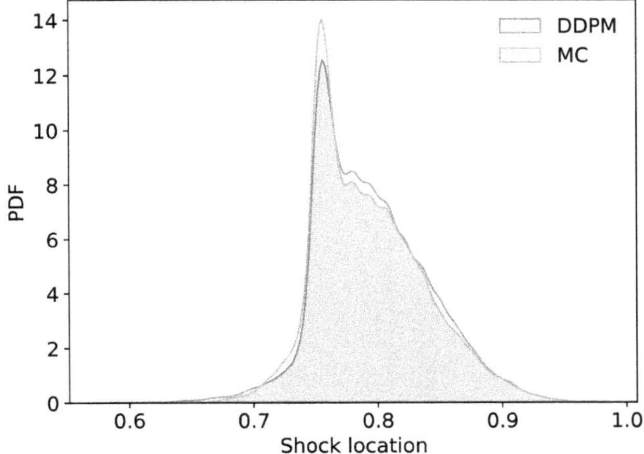

Fig. 11. Probability density function of shock location in the CD nozzle.

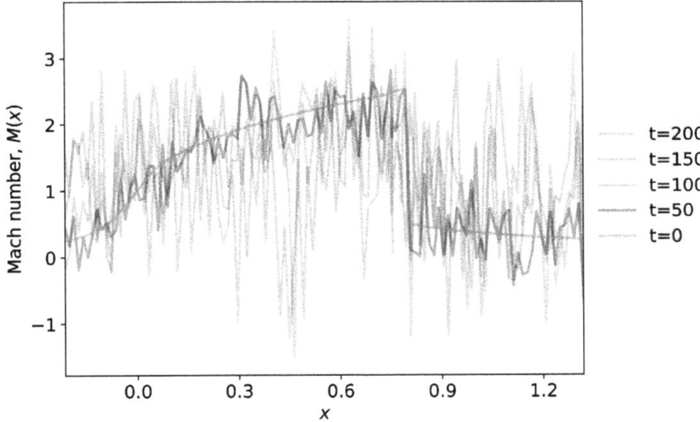

Fig. 12. Generation of a sample from random Mach field using DDPM.

4   Conclusion

This work proposes a novel method for tackling uncertainty propagation (UP) problems and to quantify randomness in output fields using diffusion models. Specifically, the proposed method consists of training a denoising diffusion probabilistic model (DDPM) to learn the underlying distribution governing the output random field. To demonstrate DDPM for UP, this work utilizes two physics-based fluid flow problems that consists of random field outputs induced by uncertain flow parameters. The results highlight that DDPM can learn the distribution of random field, while utilizing only a small number of samples. Hence, it can be a potent tool for UP through computationally expensive scientific models. Going forward, DDPM-based UP approach needs to be tested rigorously on problems involving 2D random fields. Moreover, latest state-of-the-art diffusion models, such as score-matching or flow-matching, can be utilized to further improve the sample efficiency.

Acknowledgements. This work is supported in part by the Icelandic Research Fund Grant 239858.

References

1. Dhariwal, P., Nichol, A.: Diffusion models beat GANs on image synthesis. In: Advances in Neural Information Processing Systems, vol. 34, pp. 8780–8794 (2021)
2. Dikshit, A., Koratikere, P., Leifsson, L.T., He, P.: Surrogate-based uncertainty propagation in aerostructural analysis of a wing in subsonic flow. In: AIAA SCITECH 2026 Forum, Orlando, Florida, p. 2398 (2026)
3. He, K., Zhang, X., Ren, S., Sun, J.: Delving deep into rectifiers: surpassing human-level performance on imagenet classification. In: Proceedings of the 2015 IEEE International Conference on Computer Vision (ICCV), pp. 1026–1034 (2015)
4. Ho, J., Jain, A., Abbeel, P.: Denoising diffusion probabilistic models. In: Advances in Neural Information Processing Systems, vol. 33, pp. 6840–6851 (2020)
5. Kingma, D.P., Welling, M.: Auto-encoding variational bayes. arXiv preprint arXiv:1312.6114 (2013)
6. Kontolati, K., Loukrezis, D., Giovanis, D.G., Vandanapu, L., Shields, M.D.: A survey of unsupervised learning methods for high-dimensional uncertainty quantification in black-box-type problems. J. Comput. Phys. **464**, 111313 (2022)
7. Koratikere, P., Leifsson, L.: Efficient airfoil geometric uncertainty quantification using neural network models and sequential sampling. In: International Design Engineering Technical Conferences and Computers and Information in Engineering Conference. American Society of Mechanical Engineers (2023)
8. Lai, C.H., Song, Y., Kim, D., Mitsufuji, Y., Ermon, S.: The principles of diffusion models. arXiv preprint arXiv:2510.21890 (2025)
9. Lee, S.H., Chen, W.: A comparative study of uncertainty propagation methods for black-box-type problems. Struct. Multidiscip. Optim. **37**(3), 239–253 (2009)
10. Prince, S.J.: Understanding Deep Learning. The MIT Press (2023)
11. Sohl-Dickstein, J., Weiss, E., Maheswaranathan, N., Ganguli, S.: Deep unsupervised learning using nonequilibrium thermodynamics. In: Proceedings of the 32nd International Conference on Machine Learning, vol. 37, pp. 2256–2265. PMLR (2015)
12. Tripathy, R., Bilionis, I., Gonzalez, M.: Gaussian processes with built-in dimensionality reduction: applications to high-dimensional uncertainty propagation. J. Comput. Phys. **321**, 191–223 (2016)
13. Wang, C., Qiang, X., Xu, M., Wu, T.: Recent advances in surrogate modeling methods for uncertainty quantification and propagation. Symmetry **14**(6), 1219 (2022)
14. Wu, Y., He, K.: Group normalization. In: Proceedings of the European Conference on Computer Vision (ECCV), Munich, Germany, pp. 3–19 (2018)
15. Xiu, D., Karniadakis, G.E.: Modeling uncertainty in flow simulations via generalized polynomial chaos. J. Comput. Phys. **187**(1), 137–167 (2003)

Dynamic Weighting and Aggregation in Multimodal Federated Learning for Disease Prediction

Ali Anaissi[1,2]([✉]), Lesley Manantan[1], Niushad Saeed[1], Jeevani Fernando[1], Manish Sharma[1], Puneykan Arora[1], Sai Dayakar Reddy Gollapudi[1], Weidong Huang[2], and Ali Braytee[2]

[1] University of Sydney, Camperdown, Australia
`ali.anaissi@sydney.edu.au`,
`{lman0453,nsae0696,sfer0786,msha94546,paro7137,`
`sgol0977}@uni.sydney.edu.au`
[2] University of Technology Sydney, Ultimo, Australia
`{weidong.huang,ali.braytee}@uts.edu.au`

Abstract. The advent of Natural Language Processing (NLP) and Large Language Models (LLMs) has transformed data-driven solutions in healthcare. However, significant challenges remain in managing the growing complexity and diversity of medical data under stringent privacy regulations. Traditional centralized models for disease prediction, which rely on data sharing, often face trade-offs between performance and patient confidentiality. These issues are further amplified in modern healthcare, where integrating multimodal data, such as medical images and clinical text, is critical for accurate and comprehensive diagnosis.

While federated learning frameworks address privacy concerns by keeping data decentralized, they often struggle with data heterogeneity and limited support for multimodal inputs. To address these limitations, this paper introduces a novel multimodal federated learning framework for disease prediction. The proposed framework employs ResNet-50 for image feature extraction and bidirectional LSTMs for clinical text analysis, enabling effective multimodal data fusion. Furthermore, an adaptive dynamic weighted aggregation algorithm is proposed to adjust client contributions based on data quality and model performance, thereby enhancing the stability and accuracy of the global model.

Evaluated on lung tumor datasets, the proposed approach outperformed state-of-the-art methods across multiple evaluation metrics, demonstrating its robustness, scalability, and strong potential for real-world healthcare applications.

Keywords: Federated Learning · Multimodel data · Dynamic aggregation algorithm

1 Introduction

In recent years, the application of deep learning in medical diagnosis, particularly for disease detection and prediction, has gained substantial traction [1]. However, the legitimate use of medical data remains a critical challenge. Traditional centralized training models rely on uploading raw data to a server, which often involves sensitive patient information. Strict data access restrictions within and across organizations lead to data silos, limiting the generalization of models and ultimately compromising their accuracy and performance [2].

Federated learning models offer a promising solution to address the data silo problem. This decentralized training approach eliminates the need for sharing raw data, instead enabling local model training while aggregating updates on a central server. Healthcare institutions train models locally on private data and share model parameters with a central server. The server aggregates these updates using methods such as weighted averaging, updates the global model, and redistributes the updated parameters. This iterative process improves the model's generalization capabilities while preserving data privacy, making federated learning a robust approach for healthcare data applications [3].

Despite its advantages, federated learning faces several challenges, particularly in aggregating multimodal data, such as medical images and clinical text, and designing adaptive aggregation algorithms. Integrating Natural Language Processing (NLP) and Large Language Models (LLMs) into federated learning frameworks can significantly advance these efforts. While visual data, such as medical images, captures anatomical features, clinical text provides crucial contextual information about patient history, diagnoses, and treatments. LLMs like BERT and GPT excel in processing unstructured text, extracting nuanced insights, and enabling the integration of multimodal data with visual features. However, federated learning systems often struggle to fuse such diverse data sources effectively, especially in Non-Independent and Identically Distributed (Non-IID) environments [4,5].

This study aims to address the limitations of current federated learning models in healthcare by introducing a novel framework that incorporates NLP and LLMs for multimodal data fusion. Specifically, we propose a federated learning architecture that combines the ResNet-50 model for medical image analysis with a bidirectional LSTM and LLM-based embeddings for clinical text processing. The multimodal features are then fused into a unified framework, enabling comprehensive disease prediction and diagnosis.

Additionally, we introduce a dynamic weighted aggregation algorithm that adjusts global model aggregation weights based on the magnitude of updates from individual clients. This adaptive approach enhances model stability, particularly in heterogeneous and complex data environments. Furthermore, integrating LLMs for text feature extraction ensures the effective representation of clinical text, addressing challenges associated with noisy and incomplete datasets. By leveraging these innovations, our framework offers a scalable solution for collaborative healthcare applications while maintaining stringent privacy standards.

The key contributions of this work are:

- Integration of NLP and LLMs with deep learning models to process both medical images and clinical text, addressing the challenge of multimodal data fusion in federated learning.
- Development of an adaptive aggregation method that improves model stability and performance in complex, Non-IID environments by leveraging client-specific contributions.
- Utilization of advanced NLP techniques and LLMs, such as BERT and GPT, to extract robust features from clinical text, enabling comprehensive analysis when combined with visual features.
- Providing practical guidance for cross-institutional learning with stringent privacy protection, advancing the application of federated learning in healthcare.

The paper is organized as follows: Sect. 2 reviews related work, providing an overview of prior research in the field and highlighting gaps addressed by this study. Section 3 outlines the proposed methodology, detailing the framework, algorithms, and techniques employed. Section 4 presents experimental results, including evaluations and comparative analyses. Finally, Sect. 5 concludes the paper, summarizing findings and discussing implications for future research.

2 Related Work

Federated Learning (FL) has gained significant traction in the medical domain as a transformative solution for addressing challenges related to data privacy, decentralized collaboration, and disease prediction. By enabling decentralized training, FL ensures sensitive patient data remains local, with only model updates shared to a central server. This approach mitigates privacy risks associated with traditional centralized models and fosters collaborative advancements across institutions. For instance, Google and the Mayo Clinic utilized FL for a cancer detection system, allowing model training on decentralized datasets without exposing sensitive information. Similarly, Owkin, a French biotech firm, deployed FL to analyze tumor data collaboratively, achieving enhanced diagnostic accuracy while maintaining patient confidentiality [1,6]. Such applications illustrate the dual benefits of FL in advancing medical diagnostics and upholding stringent privacy standards [7]. Specific use cases include Google Health's FL-based diabetic retinopathy detection using retinal images from multiple hospitals to improve prediction accuracy across diverse patient groups [8], and Intel's brain tumor detection model developed with the University of Pennsylvania, pooling data from 14 hospitals to achieve unprecedented accuracy in predictive modeling [9]. These implementations highlight FL's capacity to leverage distributed data for creating accurate and generalizable models while addressing privacy concerns.

The integration of multimodal data, combining medical imaging, genomics, and clinical records, has expanded FL's potential. Multimodal FL synthesizes diverse data types, enabling personalized diagnostics and treatment recommendations. For example, during the COVID-19 pandemic, multimodal FL integrated X-rays, ultrasound images, and clinical data to deliver tailored diagnoses and treatments [10]. These frameworks improve diagnostic generalization by incorporating extensive datasets from multiple institutions, as emphasized by Sheller [7], highlighting their critical role in advancing the robustness of medical models.

Despite its advantages, FL faces technical hurdles. Frequent parameter updates between clients and servers create communication bottlenecks, addressed through gradient compression [11], quantization [12], and asynchronous updates [13]. Uneven computing power among clients challenges model convergence, mitigated by adaptive task allocation and hierarchical aggregation [14,15]. Aggregation algorithms play a pivotal role; FedAvg is effective in stable environments, while FedProx incorporates regularization to manage data and computational heterogeneity, making it suitable for complex medical applications [16].

Building on this foundation, our work introduces several innovations to enhance FL in heterogeneous environments. A weight difference method reduces communication overhead by transmitting only model weight changes since the last update. Dynamic weight adjustment allocates aggregation weights based on client contributions, enabling clients with greater computational power to have a more significant influence on the global model. This adaptive approach ensures robust performance in diverse and complex environments. Additionally, the weight differential mechanism enhances privacy protection, reduces data leakage risks, and improves generalization capabilities. Together, these advancements address key challenges in FL, offering scalable and efficient solutions for collaborative healthcare applications while maintaining stringent data privacy.

3 Methodology

Recent advancements in Natural Language Processing (NLP) and Large Language Models (LLMs) have demonstrated transformative potential across various domains, including healthcare. These technologies enable sophisticated analysis and understanding of textual data, complementing deep learning techniques for image processing. Leveraging the power of NLP and LLMs, we propose a novel federated learning framework that integrates a multimodal model with an innovative dynamic aggregation algorithm. This framework is specifically designed to tackle the challenges posed by heterogeneous data distributions in federated learning, including the need for effective fusion of diverse data modalities such as medical images and clinical text. The proposed framework utilizes advanced NLP techniques and LLMs for text analysis, coupled with deep learning methods like ResNet-50 for image processing. These components are integrated into a robust dynamic aggregation algorithm that adapts to variations in client contributions, ensuring improved global model stability and accuracy. By decentralizing training and maintaining strict data privacy, the framework addresses key challenges in healthcare applications, enabling secure and efficient learning in decentralized environments while enhancing performance and scalability.

First, we will present the multimodal federated learning framework, and then we will cover our novel dynamic aggregation algorithm. The core of the multimodal model lies in its ability to process both image and text data, using distinct architectures tailored for each modality. Specifically, the framework employs a ResNet50 network for image processing and a bidirectional LSTM (Long Short-Term Memory) network for text processing. These components facilitate joint learning across modalities, enabling effective feature extraction and fusion to create a comprehensive representation of the multimodal data. ResNet50, a residual network architecture, is used for extracting deep visual features from images, making it particularly effective for tasks like medical image classification. On the other hand, the bidirectional LSTM captures context from both directions of the text sequence, enhancing the model's ability to understand complex semantic relationships in medical texts.

To address the challenges of heterogeneous data distributions due to the Non-IID (non-independent and identically distributed) problem and varying client capabilities in federated learning, we introduce an innovative, dynamic aggregation algorithm. This algorithm adjusts the contribution of each client to the global model based on the magnitude of changes in client model weights. The goal is to ensure stability by enhancing the robustness of the global model, especially in the presence of Non-IID data, and improve performance by mitigating degradation caused by uneven data distributions and computational resource disparities across clients. The server dynamically calculates client contributions during aggregation, enabling adaptive updates that enhance learning outcomes. To further improve system stability and ensure data privacy, the framework incorporates early stopping, which halts training when performance plateaus, and amplitude controls, which limit excessive weight changes during aggregation.

Figure 1 illustrates the overall architecture of the federated learning framework and the interaction process between its components. The system consists of multiple clients and a central server, with training occurring across multiple steps.

Step 1: Local Training by the Client: Each client trains the model locally using its multimodal dataset (e.g., Dataset D_1, D_2, ..., D_K). This ensures data privacy, as the data remains local to each client.

Step 2: Uploading Model Weights to the Server: After local training, the client uploads the updated model weights to the server.

Step 3: Server Aggregates Weights: The server dynamically aggregates the model weights from all clients using the dynamic weighting algorithm. Each client's contribution is weighted according to the magnitude of changes in its model weights during training.

Step 4: Server Distributes Updated Global Model: The server distributes the aggregated global model weights back to each client for the next round of local training.

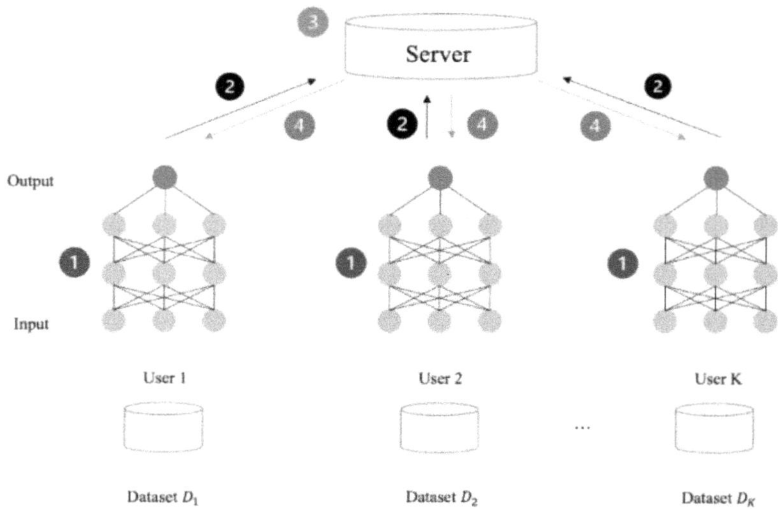

Fig. 1. Federated Learning Components and Processes

The server plays a central role in coordinating and aggregating the model updates from all clients. It starts by initializing a global model (e.g., a multimodal ResNet-LSTM model) and distributing it to the clients for initial local training. After each training round, the server collects the updated model weights from the clients, applies our proposed dynamic weighting algorithm to aggregate them, and sends the updated global model back to the clients. This process helps ensure the model converges quickly, even in environments with heterogeneous data.

The dynamic weighting algorithm offers a more precise and adaptable aggregation strategy than traditional federated learning methods such as FedAvg [17], which averages client weights without accounting for variations in client data distribution or computational contributions. Our approach ensures that clients with greater contributions to model training are given more influence in the aggregation process, enhancing the generalization ability and stability of the global model. The method is described in Algorithm 1 and operates as follows:

- *Local Weight Change Calculation:* After completing local training, each client calculates the changes in its model weights across all layers. These changes are aggregated to quantify the client's contribution during the training round.
- *Weight Coefficient Computation:* The server collects the weight change magnitudes from all clients and computes a weight coefficient for each. These coefficients are normalized based on the relative weight change ratios, ensuring that the influence of each client is proportional to its contribution.
- *Weighted Aggregation:* Using the computed coefficients, the server aggregates the weight changes for each layer, generating a weighted update that reflects the varying contributions of the clients.

– *Global Model Update:* The server applies the weighted update to the global model, resulting in an improved and updated global model.

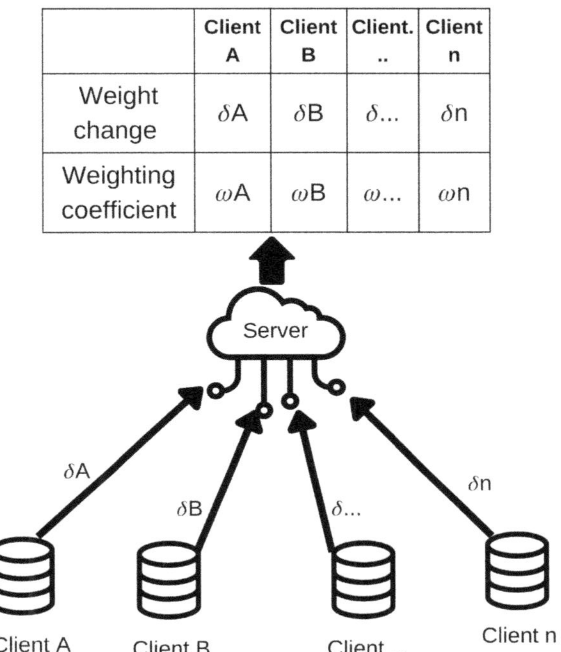

Fig. 2. Weighting coefficient calculation process

By dynamically adjusting the aggregation process based on client contributions, this algorithm ensures balanced and robust model updates, particularly in heterogeneous data and computational environments. The detailed steps are described below.

In each round of local training, client k trains the model using its local dataset and updates the weights of each model layer. For the i-th layer, the weight change of client k is computed as the difference between the weight of the subsequent layer and the current layer, representing the weight update generated during the current round of training, without involving weight changes from previous rounds. The weight change magnitude δ_k for client k is defined as the sum of the L_2-norms of the weight changes across all layers and is calculated as follows:

$$\delta_k = \sum_{i=1}^{L} \left\| W_k^{i+1} - W_k^i \right\|_2 \tag{1}$$

Here, L represents the total number of layers in the model, i denotes the index of each layer, and k identifies the specific client.

On the server side, after collecting the weight change amplitudes δ_k uploaded by all clients, the server first computes the total sum of these weight change amplitudes ($\sum_{k=1}^{K} \delta_k$). This sum is then used to normalize the weight coefficient for each client. The weight coefficient ω_k for client k is determined based on its weight change amplitude, reflecting its relative contribution to the global model aggregation. Specifically, ω_k is calculated as the ratio of the client's weight change amplitude to the total sum of weight changes, as shown below

$$\omega_k = \frac{\delta_k}{\sum_{k=1}^{K} \delta_k + \epsilon} \tag{2}$$

Here, ϵ is a small positive constant added to the denominator to prevent division by zero, ensuring numerical stability, and K is the total number of clients. The weight coefficient ω_k represents the relative influence of client k in the aggregation process. Clients with larger weight changes are assigned higher weight coefficients, significantly contributing to the global model update. These coefficients are subsequently used to perform a weighted average of the weight changes across all clients in the next step of the aggregation process. Figure 2 illustrates the process of calculating the weighting coefficients for each client during the aggregation phase.

The server then uses the weight coefficient ω_k of each client to perform hierarchical weighted aggregation on the weight updates of all clients, resulting in the final weight update ΔW_i for each layer of the global model. To further optimize communication efficiency and reduce the volume of transmitted data, the weight differential function is introduced in this step. The key idea behind the weight differential function is that clients upload only the weight changes for each layer from their local training rather than the complete weight values. This approach effectively minimizes the transmission bandwidth required for data exchange.

For each layer i of the model, the server computes the weighted aggregated weight change ΔW_i for the ith layer across all clients. The formula for this calculation is as follows:

$$\Delta W_i = \sum_{k=1}^{K} \omega_k \cdot \left(W_k^{i+1} - W_k^i \right) \tag{3}$$

Here, ω_k represents the weight coefficient of the client k, which is determined by the magnitude of the weight change amplitude for that client. The term within the parentheses denotes the weight update for the ith layer contributed by client k during the current round of local training, also referred to as the weight difference.

This formula shows that each client only needs to upload its weight updates (i.e., the differential values), enabling the server to compute the aggregated updates ΔW_i for each layer through a weighted summation of these updates. By introducing weight differentiation, clients transmit only the changes in weights rather than the complete weight information, significantly reducing communication overhead and improving efficiency. This also minimizes the risk of data leakage, as the transmitted updates do not directly expose sensitive information. Furthermore, by reducing transmission volume, the server's computational load during aggregation is decreased, allowing the process to complete more quickly.

The server then uses the weighted aggregate update ΔW_i for each layer to update the weights of the global model. This step integrates the training contributions of all clients to form an improved model. For each layer i of the model, the server updates the global model's weights using the following formula:

$$W_i^{t+1} = W_i^t + \Delta W_i \tag{4}$$

Here, t represents the training round of the global model, and i is the index of the layer. ΔW_i is the aggregated update for layer i, calculated in the previous step, representing the combined contribution of all clients to the weight change for that layer. This operation is performed independently for each layer, ensuring that every layer of the global model can absorb the training updates from all clients and complete the weight update for that round.

As shown in Table 1, each layer's weight update is calculated using a weighted aggregation of the updates from all participating clients. The weight coefficients $\omega_A, \omega_B, \ldots, \omega_n$ correspond to the clients' contributions based on their weight change magnitudes, ensuring that more influential clients have a higher impact on the global model.

Table 1. Global Model Weight Updates for Each Layer

Layer Index	Weighted Update Weights
1	$\Delta W_1 = \omega_A \cdot \Delta W_{A1} + \omega_B \cdot \Delta W_{B1} + \cdots + \omega_n \cdot \Delta W_{n1}$
2	$\Delta W_2 = \omega_A \cdot \Delta W_{A2} + \omega_B \cdot \Delta W_{B2} + \cdots + \omega_n \cdot \Delta W_{n2}$
$\vdots$	$\vdots$
n	$\Delta W_n = \omega_A \cdot \Delta W_{An} + \omega_B \cdot \Delta W_{Bn} + \cdots + \omega_n \cdot \Delta W_{nn}$

4 Experiments

4.1 Dataset Preparation and Preprocessing

We utilized two public multi-modal chest X-ray datasets to enhance predictive modeling. The IU-CXR dataset [18] includes 7,470 images and radiology reports linked to unique patient IDs. Over 100 disease labels from the *Problems* column were grouped into 14 clinically relevant categories and numerically encoded. Reports were preprocessed by merging *Findings* and *Impression* sections into a *notes* column, tokenized with a 10,000-word vocabulary, converted to integer sequences, and padded to length 100. CXR images were converted to RGB, resized to 224×224, normalized to $[0, 1]$, and stored for model input.

Algorithm 1. Our proposed framework

1: **Input:**
2:    K clients, each with local dataset D_k, $k \in [1, K]$
3:    Global model with L layers
4: **Output:** Aggregated global model weights
5: **for** each client $k \in [1, K]$ **do**
6:    Client k trains the model locally using dataset D_k
7:    For each layer $i \in [1, L]$, compute the weight change δ_k for client using Eq. 1
8: **end for**
9: Server collects the weight change magnitudes δ_k from all clients
10: Compute the total sum of weight change magnitudes using $\sum_{k=1}^{K} \delta_k$
11: **for** each client $k \in [1, K]$ **do**
12:    Compute the weight coefficient ω_k for client k using Eq. 2
13: **end for**
    Aggregation:
14: **for** each layer $i \in [1, L]$ **do**
15:    **for** each client $k \in [1, K]$ **do**
16:       Compute the weight update for client k for layer i using Eq. 3
17:    **end for**
18: **end for**
    Update global model:
19: **for** each layer $i \in [1, L]$ **do**
20:    Update global model weight for layer i using Eq. 4
21: **end for**
22: Return updated global model

The MIMIC-CXR dataset [19] contains 370,000 images and reports from 227,000 studies. Reports and images were preprocessed similarly to IU-CXR. Integrating textual and imaging data from both datasets enables robust multimodal modeling for tasks such as disease classification, report generation, and representation learning.

4.2   Results and Discussion

We evaluated the effectiveness of our proposed algorithm by comparing its performance with the FedAvg and FedProx algorithms, using identical model architectures and data allocations. Evaluation metrics, including accuracy, loss, and F1 score, were calculated and averaged across all clients to ensure fairness and minimize the impact of performance discrepancies. The final testing results were derived from the last validation round, providing a comprehensive comparison.

Figures 3a and 3b display the validation accuracy and loss trends for our algorithm compared to the traditional FedAvg algorithm using IU-CXR dataset. Both algorithms were trained using identical hyperparameters: 20 rounds, 10 epochs per round, and 3 clients. Results from the untrained global model at round 0 serve as a baseline. Our algorithm achieved a validation accuracy of 0.97, surpassing FedAvg's 0.93, and reduced the loss to 0.14, compared to FedAvg's 0.19, indicating faster convergence and superior overall performance. Using the

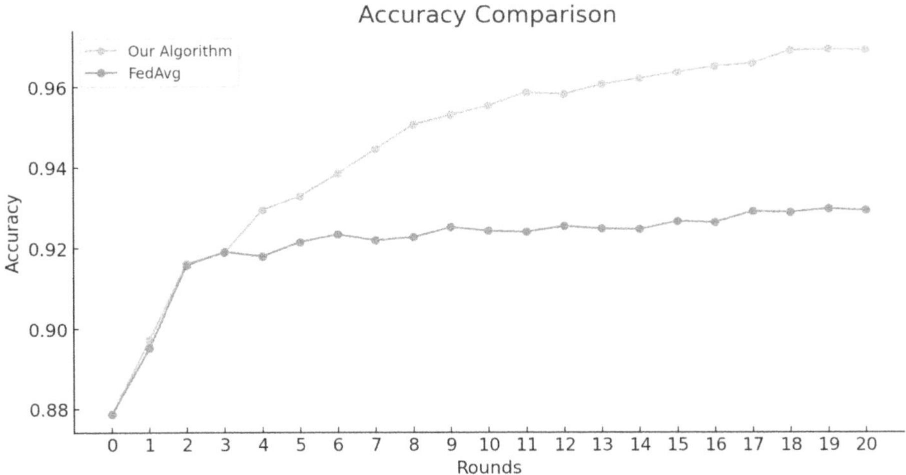

(a) Validation accuracy comparison between our algorithm and FedAvg.

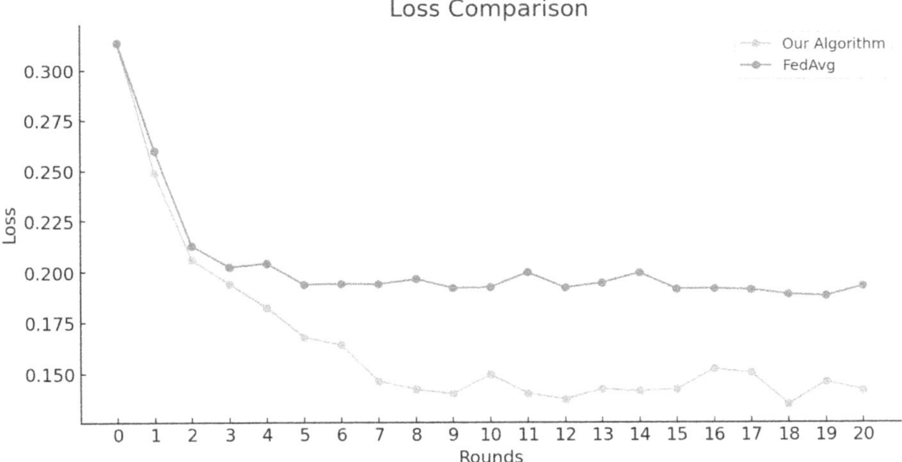

(b) Validation loss comparison between our algorithm and FedAvg.

Fig. 3. Comparison between our algorithm and FedAvg: (a) validation accuracy and (b) validation loss.

MIMIC-CXR dataset, our algorithm demonstrated similarly outstanding performance. Figures 3a and 3b show the trends in validation accuracy and loss during training. Our algorithm achieved a validation accuracy of 0.97, outperforming FedAvg's 0.94, and reduced the loss to 0.15, compared to FedAvg's 0.22. These results reaffirm the robustness of our approach in achieving faster convergence and superior predictive capabilities across diverse datasets.

Table 2 shows that our algorithm outperformed FedAvg across all metrics. Notably, it achieved a significantly higher recall (0.85 vs. 0.56 for FedAvg), indicating its superior sensitivity in identifying positive class samples, a critical factor in medical applications where missing diagnoses could have serious consequences. Furthermore, the higher F1 score reflects a better balance between precision and recall, highlighting our algorithm's ability to maintain both accuracy and robustness. Similar trends were observed with the MIMIC-CXR dataset, where our algorithm achieved a recall of 0.82, compared to FedAvg's 0.60, and an F1 score of 0.78, compared to FedAvg's 0.74.

Table 2. Performance comparison of FedAvg, FedProx, and proposed algorithm across datasets.

Metric	Dataset	FedAvg	FedProx	Proposed Algorithm
Recall	IU-CXR	0.56	0.60	0.85
	MIMIC-CXR	0.60	0.65	0.82
F1 Score	IU-CXR	0.72	0.75	0.88
	MIMIC-CXR	0.74	0.76	0.78
Loss	IU-CXR	0.19	0.18	0.14
	MIMIC-CXR	0.22	0.20	0.15
Accuracy	IU-CXR	0.93	0.94	0.97
	MIMIC-CXR	0.94	0.96	0.97

We also compared our algorithm's performance with FedProx, a widely used baseline in federated learning. Our algorithm outperformed FedProx, achieving a validation accuracy of 0.97 compared to FedProx's 0.94 using IU-CXR dataset. Moreover, our method demonstrated a more balanced performance across key metrics such as precision, recall, and F1 score. Similarly, with the MIMIC-CXR dataset, our algorithm achieved a validation accuracy of 0.97, compared to FedProx's 0.95. While the accuracy improvement was modest, the recall of our algorithm was significantly higher (0.82 vs. 0.65 for FedProx), ensuring fewer false negatives. This aspect is particularly crucial in applications like healthcare, where missing high-risk cases can have severe consequences.

Our results show that assigning higher weights to clients with larger model weight updates plays a critical role in accelerating convergence and improving model stability. By leveraging this dynamic weighting strategy, our novel federated aggregation algorithm not only achieves higher validation accuracy but also ensures a more balanced performance across key metrics such as precision, recall, and F1 score. These advancements are particularly valuable for integrating multi-center medical data, enhancing both the robustness and predictive accuracy of the global model.

This work further demonstrates the potential of federated learning for multimodal medical data fusion, combining innovative aggregation techniques with robust data processing to improve predictive performance. The proposed algorithm offers an adaptable, scalable solution for collaborative medical prediction tasks, with applications extending to cross-institutional collaboration in areas where data privacy is a major concern.

5   Conclusion

In this study, we presented a robust multimodal federated learning framework for disease prediction, integrating medical imaging and clinical text data using ResNet-50 and bi-directional LSTM models. The incorporation of a novel dynamic aggregation algorithm addressed challenges related to uneven data distribution and varying client contributions, significantly enhancing model convergence and stability. Our experimental results demonstrated that the proposed algorithm outperformed the standard FedAvg approach, achieving superior accuracy and recall rates, thereby highlighting its effectiveness in healthcare applications where accurate and reliable predictions are critical. The integration of machine learning and deep learning into federated learning frameworks marks a transformative step for cross-domain collaborations, particularly in healthcare, where data privacy remains a paramount concern. Additionally, the proposed dynamic aggregation algorithm offers scalability and adaptability, extending its applicability beyond healthcare to a variety of federated learning tasks. Despite certain limitations, this work lays a solid foundation for future research, aiming to refine federated learning methodologies and foster more secure, collaborative, and effective systems for disease prediction and medical decision support.

References

1. Pennisi, M., et al.: Feder: federated learning through experience replay and privacy-preserving data synthesis. Comput. Vis. Image Underst. **238**, 103882 (2024)
2. Yang, Q., Liu, Y., Chen, T., Tong, Y.: Federated machine learning: concept and applications. ACM Trans. Intell. Syst. Technol. (TIST) **10**(2), 1–19 (2019)
3. Li, T., Sahu, A.K., Talwalkar, A., Smith, V.: Federated learning: challenges, methods, and future directions. IEEE Signal Process. Mag. **37**(3), 50–60 (2020)
4. Baltrušaitis, T., Ahuja, C., Morency, L.-P.: Multimodal machine learning: a survey and taxonomy. IEEE Trans. Pattern Anal. Mach. Intell. **41**(2), 423–443 (2018)
5. Hochreiter, S.: Long short-term memory. Neural Computation MIT-Press (1997)
6. Guan, H., Yap, P.-T., Bozoki, A., Liu, M.: Federated learning for medical image analysis: a survey. Pattern Recogn. **151**, 110424 (2024)
7. Sheller, M.J., et al.: Federated learning in medicine: facilitating multi-institutional collaborations without sharing patient data. Sci. Rep. **10**(1), 12598 (2020)
8. Rieke, N., et al.: The future of digital health with federated learning. NPJ Digit. Med. **3**(1), 1–7 (2020)
9. Dayan, I., et al.: Federated learning for predicting clinical outcomes in patients with covid-19. Nat. Med. **27**(10), 1735–1743 (2021)
10. Xu, J., Glicksberg, B.S., Su, C., Walker, P., Bian, J., Wang, F.: Federated learning for healthcare informatics. J. Healthc. Inform. Res. **5**, 1–19 (2021)

11. Wang, H., Sievert, S., Liu, S., Charles, Z., Papailiopoulos, D., Wright, S.: Atomo: communication-efficient learning via atomic sparsification. In: Advances in Neural Information Processing Systems, vol. 31 (2018)
12. Bernstein, J., Wang, Y.X., Azizzadenesheli, K., Anandkumar, A.: signSGD: compressed optimisation for non-convex problems. In: International Conference on Machine Learning, pp. 560–569. PMLR (2018)
13. Xie, C., Koyejo, S., Gupta, I.: Asynchronous federated optimization. arXiv preprint arXiv:1903.03934 (2019)
14. Liu, L., Zhang, J., Song, S., Letaief, K.B.: Hierarchical federated learning with quantization: convergence analysis and system design. IEEE Trans. Wireless Commun. **22**(1), 2–18 (2022)
15. Siqi Luo, X., Chen, Q.W., Zhou, Z., Shuai, Yu.: HFEL: joint edge association and resource allocation for cost-efficient hierarchical federated edge learning. IEEE Trans. Wireless Commun. **19**(10), 6535–6548 (2020)
16. Li, L., Fan, Y., Tse, M., Lin, K.-Y.: A review of applications in federated learning. Comput. Ind. Eng. **149**, 106854 (2020)
17. McMahan, B., Moore, E., Ramage, D., Hampson, S., Arcas, B.A.: Communication-efficient learning of deep networks from decentralized data. In: Proceedings of the 20th International Conference on Artificial Intelligence and Statistics (AISTATS), pp. 1273–1282 (2017)
18. Demner-Fushman, D., et al.: Preparing a collection of radiology examinations for distribution and retrieval. J. Am. Med. Inform. Assoc. **23**(2), 304–310 (2016)
19. Johnson, A.E.W., et al.: MIMIC-CXR: a large publicly available database of labeled chest radiographs. arXiv preprint arXiv:1901.07042 (2019)

A Personalized Brain Atlas for Everyone: Unlocking New Frontiers for Individuals, Humanity, Science, and Artificial Intelligence

Wieslaw L. Nowinski[(✉)]

Sano Centre for Computational Personalised Medicine, Krakow, Poland
w.nowinski@sanoscience.org
https://www.wieslawnowinski.com

Abstract. The brain's enormous complexity, together with the high global prevalence of neurologic disorders, necessitate the development of comprehensive and advanced neuromarkers to enhance both brain understanding as well as disorder prevention, prognosis, diagnosis, and treatment. I propose a combined neuroimaging and neuromodeling multi-purpose, multi-model, multi-dimensional, and multi-modal neuromarker in the form of an electronic brain atlas. This special type of brain atlas is a personalized brain atlas for everyone (*pBAe*), capable of systematically accommodating the condition of one's brain over time.

The *pBAe* is defined as a time series of navigable and quantifiable pairs of (raw brain scans; reconstructed and annotated 3D brain models), and I here address its content, data acquisition and harmonization, software architecture, construction methodology, and development strategy.

The proposed *pBAe* content and functionality are illustrated through the author's personalized brain atlas, demonstrating 3D structure, cerebrovasculature, and cranial nerves fully parcellated by color and labeled.

When deployed globally, the *pBAe* will have a profound impact on individuals, society, science, and AI development. For individuals, it offers deeper insights into brain structure, function, and disorders; quantified brain health; lifestyle modifications; early screening with predictive capabilities; continuous brain status monitoring; and personalized medicine, including targeted therapies. Individual *pBAes* worldwide would collectively form a massive neurodatabase whose analyses could drive new discoveries leading to improved public health and human well-being. Ultimately, the synergy between the *pBAe* initiative and AI can create a self-reinforcing "virtuous circle" accelerating progress in both fields.

Keywords: Human brain · brain atlas · personalized medicine · software architecture · 3D modeling · neurodatabase · computer graphics · AI · NeuroAI

1   Introduction

A wide range of tests, measurable features, and biomarkers enable to monitor and evaluate a biological state or condition of the human body including anthropometric measurements (e.g., height and weight), physiological measurements (e.g., heart rate, blood

© The Author(s), under exclusive license to Springer Nature Switzerland AG 2026
P. Neumann et al. (Eds.): ICCS 2026, LNCS 16784, pp. 167–181, 2026.
https://doi.org/10.1007/978-3-032-29924-6_12

pressure, and body temperature), cognitive and psychological metrics (e.g., intelligence quotient and emotional intelligence), sensory capabilities (e.g., visual acuity and hearing sensitivity), and genetic and molecular biomarkers (e.g., blood type and genetic predispositions), among others. Moreover, some biometric features, such as fingerprints and iris patterns, serve for identification. Many biomarkers are simple, such as the blood type, which is fixed, and the height or pulse rate, which are variable. More advanced biomarkers in the form of biologically based predictive models have been used for screening, diagnosis, staging, prognosis, treatment selection, and monitoring in cancer [1] and heart diseases [2]. These types of biomarkers provide measures that can supplement clinical decision-making.

The human brain is the most complicated organ and neurologic disorders affect a considerable part of the global population. For instance, the Global Burden of Disease Study 2021 estimated nervous system health loss caused by 37 conditions between 1990–2021, founding that 3.4 billion individuals, i.e., 43.1% of the global population, were affected by neurologic disorders [3]. The brain's complexity and such a high prevalence of disorders worldwide demand comprehensive and advanced neuromarkers to enhance both brain understanding and disorder prevention, prognosis, diagnosis, and treatment. Some simple neuromarkers include intelligence quotient, emotional intelligence, memory capacity, and attention span. More advanced neuromarkers are needed in mental disorders and [4] outlines how the development of neuromarkers should occur in this field. A brain scan can be valuable as a neuromarker; however, normally, brain scans are only acquired in cases of head injury or symptomatic neurologic disorders.

To bridge this gap, I propose a combined neuroimaging and neuromodeling neuromarker in the form of an electronic brain atlas. This special type of brain atlas shall be a personalized brain atlas for everyone (in brief *pBAe*), progressively monitoring, capturing, and updating the information about the condition of one's brain over time. This work stems from our previous, three-decade-long human brain atlas development efforts, resulting in the creation of over 50 human brain atlas prototypes and 35 commercial products licensed to 67 companies and institutions and distributed in about 100 countries [5]. These atlases have been applied in neurosurgery, neuroradiology, neurology, human brain mapping, and neuroeducation. Here, I propose a novel type of ubiquitous brain atlas as a multi-purpose, multi-model, multi-dimensional, and multi-modal neuromarker applicable in a new niche, namely, serving as a tool for laymen, clinicians, and ultimately the global research community. To my best knowledge, this is a pioneering work as there is no personalized brain atlas yet created for anyone in the sense as defined here; fortunately, my personal 3D brain atlas extended to the head and neck [6, 7] partly meets the *pBAe* definition and, as an instance, is employed for illustration.

This work introduces the concept of the *pBAe*, outlines the materials, methods and tools enabling its development, illustrates its content and main functions as well as discusses its potential clinical, social, scientific, and technological impact.

2 Materials and Method

Here, I define the *pBAe*, determine its content, software architecture, discuss data acquisition and harmonization, and present the method for *pBAe* construction.

Definition. The human brain maps and atlases have been developed for more than 100 years, and the role and definition of brain atlases have evolved over time [8]. The brain atlas is commonly regarded as a neuroimage repository, brain database, or brain template. By several authors, brain atlases are considered: a research tool to make generalizations about localization of function and structure [9]; useful references and analytical tools as well as a framework for data sharing [10]; large-scale neuroimaging databases that capture the mean and variance in the population [11]; and tools to integrate in a topographically meaningful manner diversified information about numerous aspects of the brain [12]. I have earlier defined a multi-purpose, user-extendable, and reference human brain atlas as "a vehicle to gather, present, use, share, and discover knowledge about the human brain with a highly organized content, tools enabling a wide range of its applications, massive and heterogeneous knowledge database, and means for content and knowledge updating and growing by its user" [13].

The *pBAe* is an instance of this general definition. To make the *pBAe* definition more specific and compact, it must reflect that the *pBAe* shall contain time-related brain changes and serve both its owner and his/her healthcare provider (and, in the long term, the global research community). Brain changes over time can be obtained by the acquisition of multiple brain scans. To make these scans more "understandable" by a layman, they shall be converted to 3D models, which are subsequently annotated with structure and function. Hence, the *pBAe* is defined as a *time series of navigable and quantifiable pairs of (raw brain scans; reconstructed and annotated 3D brain models)*.

Atlas Content and Data Acquisition. I propose the *pBAe* to initially include structure, cerebrovasculature, and cranial nerves. The structure contains the main parts of the brain, including the cerebrum with the cerebral cortex, subcortical nuclei, and ventricular system; cerebellum; and brainstem. The cerebrovasculature comprises the arterial and venous systems. The cranial nerves contain 12 pairs of CN I – CN XII nerves.

The cerebral cortex, parcellated (subdivided) into lobes, gyri, and sulci, comprises the primary motor, somatosensory, auditory, and visual cortices as well as the association cortices involved in behavior and intellectual processes. The subcortical nuclei are involved in many functions, including the thalamus relaying sensory information from the body to the cerebral cortex, the hippocampus being involved in memory and learning, and the amygdala determining the emotional, motivational, and social significance of sensory inputs, among others. Moreover, the hippocampus as a neuromarker shows rapid loss of its tissue in the early stages of Alzheimer's disease [14], while the enlargement of the ventricular system is an indicator of brain atrophy or hydrocephalus.

The cerebrovasculature is critical regarding stroke, which is the second leading cause of death worldwide. In the case of ischemic stroke, the standard time window for intravenous thrombolytic treatment is 4.5 h from the stroke onset to therapy [15]. However, this time window for some individuals may be longer depending on collateral circulation, which provides the auxiliary vascular structures and alternative routes for blood flow to compensate for it when compromised due to stenosis or occlusion of the principal supplying arteries. Conversely, some vascular variants may reduce potential circulatory anastomoses, i.e., connections between blood vessels. Therefore, the knowledge of vascular collaterals and variants is vital. The main circulatory anastomosis is provided by the arterial circle of Willis located at the skull base, which interconnects the anterior circulation (through the internal carotid artery) with the posterior circulation (via the vertebral and basilar arteries).

The cranial nerves are involved in the senses, such as smell (CN I), vision (CN II), hearing and balance (CN VIII) as well as control of facial expressions (CN VII) and eye movement (CN III, IV, VI), among others.

The structure, vasculature, and cranial nerves can be imaged through magnetic resonance imaging (MRI). There are numerous MRI pulse sequences to image various features and tissues [16, 17]. The structure can be imaged employing T1-weighted images, especially MP-RAGE (magnetization-prepared rapid gradient echo), which is a 3D T1-weighted sequence. To image the arterial and venous systems, magnetic resonance angiography (MRA) and magnetic resonance venography (MRV) are employed, respectively. The TOF (time-of-flight) MRA sequence does not require contrast agents, whereas CE (contrast-enhanced) MRA involves contrast agents. SWI (susceptibility-weighted imaging) is suitable for imaging veins without contrast agents [18]. The SPGR (spoiled gradient-recalled echo) sequence images both structure and vasculature and is helpful to spatially register the structural with vascular scans. The cranial nerves can be imaged by employing T1-weighted, T2-weighted, and SSFP (steady-state free procession) sequences [19].

The use of MP-RAGE structural imaging to construct a 3D interactive and stereotactic atlas of the cerebrum, cerebellum, and brainstem is described in [20]. A 3D interactive and stereotactic cerebrovascular atlas reconstructed from TOF, SPGR, and SWI scans is presented and its validation discussed in [21]. A 3D interactive and stereotactic atlas of cranial nerves is featured in [22].

Atlas Construction. In general, a brain atlas is created in four major steps: data acquisition, data processing, application development, and validation. Data processing involves image segmentation, multiple scan registration, structure modeling, and structure parcellation (e.g., by color) and annotation or labeling (naming as well as assigning function and/or some parameters, such as vessel diameter). The design and development of human brain atlases have been covered in my previous work [7, 13, 23, 24].

There are many methods and tools developed to support brain mapping, which also facilitate atlas construction, and some of them have been featured in [13]. For example, visualization and registration are supported by the *Visualization Toolkit* (VTK) and the *Insight Toolkit* (ITK), respectively, and these toolkits have been integrated into the *Medical Imaging Interaction Toolkit* (MITK) [25]. *FreeSurfer* is a neuroimaging toolkit for processing, analyzing, and visualizing human brain MR images, including an automation of cortical and subcortical segmentation [26]. *BrainSuite* is a collection of open-source software tools that enable largely automated processing of MR images of the human brain, segment and label grey matter, and provide the ability to create and use custom brain atlases [27]. *FSL* is a library of analysis tools for functional, structural, and diffusion neuroimages [28].

The *pBAe* shall contain the personalized database with the scans and 3D models, prospective and retrospective data harmonization, and be able to convert the scans into 3D models by automatically performing segmentation, registration, modeling, and annotation. It shall be empowered with tools for atlas content navigation, exploration, and quantification by placing the scans and models in a stereotactic coordinate system and providing coordinates, distances, areas, and volumes of selected locations, regions, and structures. Besides the personalized database, a common database shall also provide useful information about the brain and its structure, function, and disorders. There are many public brain-related web resources. For example, the *Neuroscience Information Framework* catalogs and surveys the largest searchable collection of neuroscience data with about 2,000 databases, atlases, and the largest ontology for neuroscience on the web [29]. *BrainInfo* comprises 15,000 neuroanatomical terms along with hierarchical relations of each structure to its superstructures and substructures [30]. NOW*in*BRAIN is a repository of more than 8,600 3D reconstructed neuroimages organized in 12 galleries [31–33].

The software architecture of the *pBAe* is presented in Fig. 1.

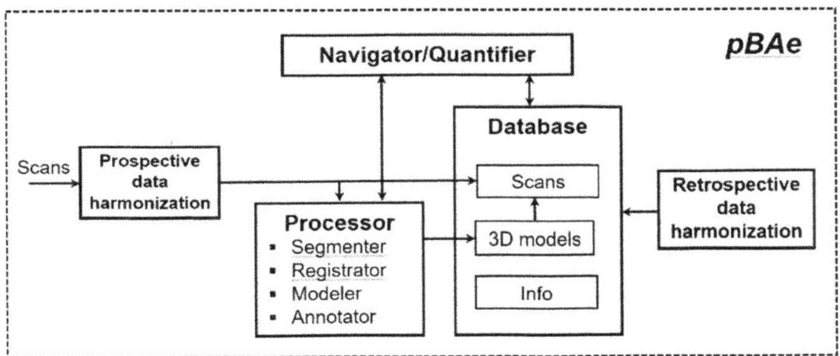

Fig. 1. The software architecture of the *pBAe*.

3   Results

To illustrate the potential of the *pBAe*, I use my personalized brain atlas [6], as to my best knowledge, this is the only existing advanced personalized brain atlas developed so far with about 3,000 3D components. Although it does not fully meet the atlas definition proposed here, it is sufficiently advanced to serve as an illustration.

The main components of the *pBAe* in 3D, i.e., the structure, cerebrovasculature, and cranial nerves, parcellated by color are shown in Fig. 2.

The structure, cerebrovasculature, and cranial nerves together parcellated by color and partly labeled with names are illustrated in Fig. 3.

The primary motor, somatosensory, and visual cortices parcellated by color and labeled with structure and function are demonstrated in Fig. 4.

The atlas guides and enhances scan interpretation, as illustrated in Fig. 5, where a 2D coronal MRI image is labeled with the hippocampus, which is also visualized in 3D.

The atlas is located in the stereotactic coordinate system and its structures can be quantified as illustrated in Fig. 6, where, e.g., the distance between the left and right temporal horns of the lateral ventricles is measured.

The complete and incomplete arterial circle of Willis is illustrated in Fig. 7.

An unruptured aneurysm of the basilar artery compressing the oculomotor nerve CN III and causing the oculomotor nerve palsy is presented in Fig. 8.

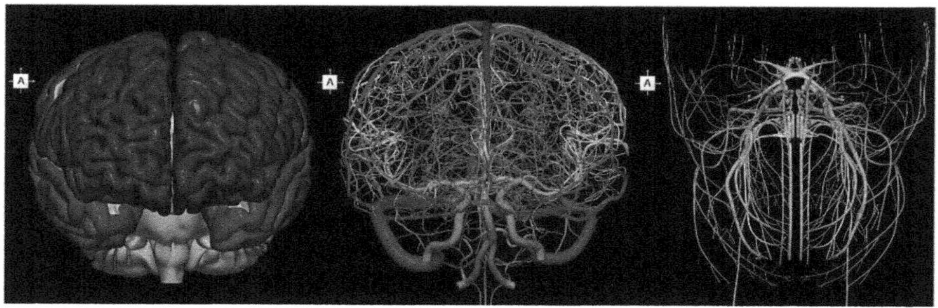

Fig. 2. Anterior view of the main components of the *pBAe* in 3D parcellated by color. Left) Structure. Center) Cerebrovasculature. Right) Cranial nerves.

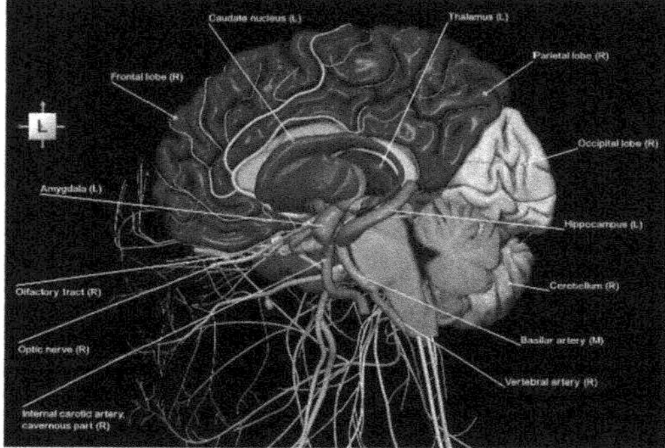

Fig. 3. Left view of the right structure (including the left subcortical nuclei), cerebrovasculature, and cranial nerves parcellated by color and partly labeled with names.

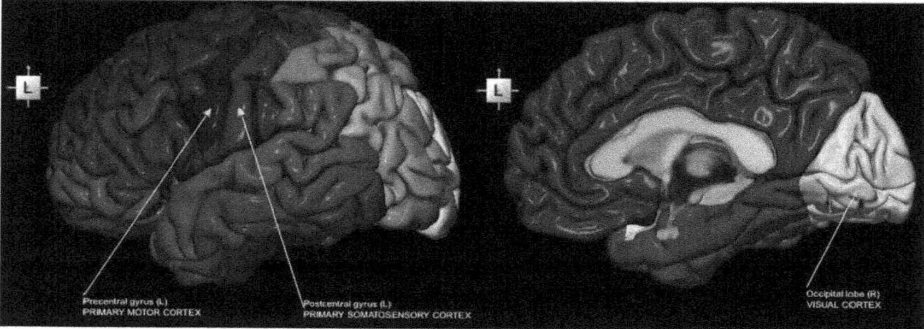

Fig. 4. Left view of the primary motor, somatosensory, and visual cortices parcellated and labeled with anatomic names and function. Left) The cerebral cortex parcellated into gyri with the precentral gyrus (the primary motor cortex) and the postcentral gyrus (the primary somatosensory cortex) labeled with names and functions. Right) The right cerebral hemisphere parcellated into lobes, and the occipital lobe (the visual cortex) labeled with name and function.

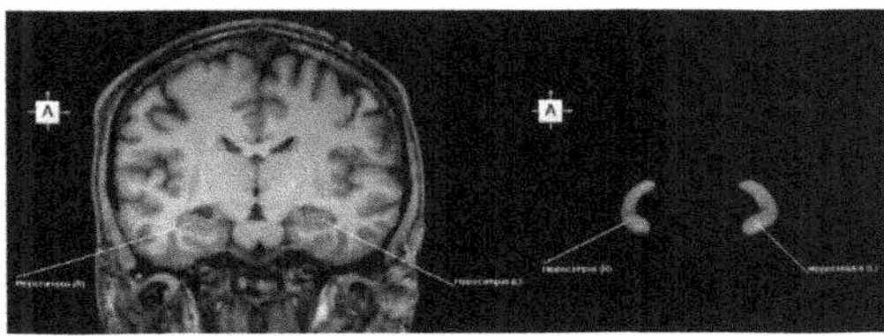

Fig. 5. Anterior view of the hippocampus. Left) An MRI coronal image with the hippocampus labeled by the atlas. Right) The hippocampus in 3D labeled.

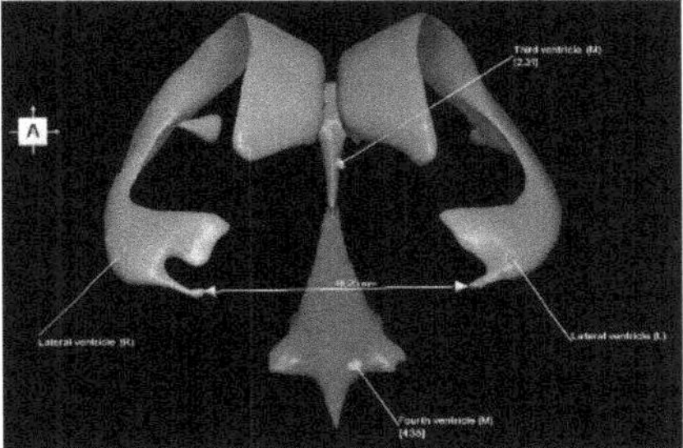

Fig. 6. Quantification of the ventricular system. The volume of the third and fourth ventricles (in cm^3) and the distance between the lateral ventricles' left and right temporal horns are measured.

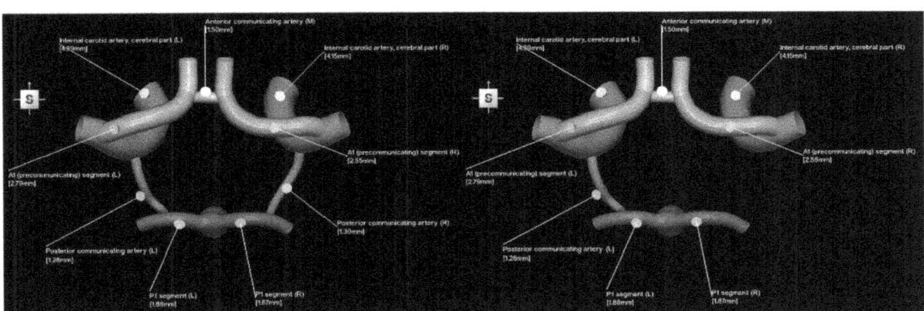

Fig. 7. The arterial circle of Willis. Left) The complete circle parcellated and labeled with vessel names and diameters. Right) An incomplete circle (absent right posterior communicating artery).

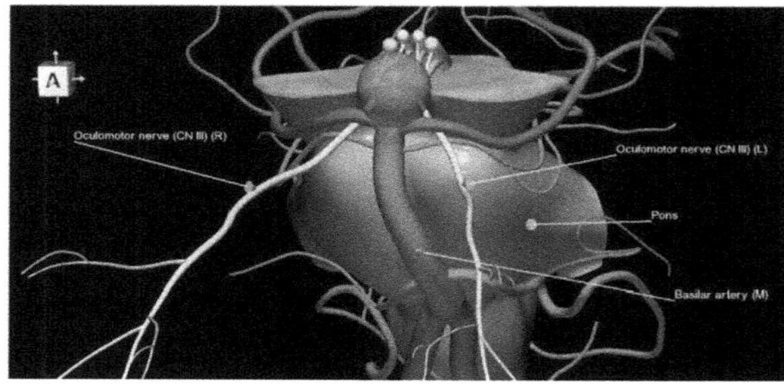

Fig. 8. The oculomotor nerve (CN III) compressed by an unruptured aneurysm (modeled as a ball) of the basilar artery causing oculomotor nerve palsy.

4 Discussion

I discuss the *pBAe* in terms of the feasibility of building, content extension, and impact.

Feasibility. The feasibility of building the *pBAe* has technical and economic aspects. Technically, several tools (see Sect. 2) assist in the automation of atlas creation, at least for the cerebral cortex and subcortical nuclei. However, there is not yet a solution for automatic and accurate segmentation, modeling, parcellation, and labeling of the cerebrovasculature and cranial nerves; though there are various methods for automated cerebral vessel segmentation based on skeletonization, thresholding, mathematical morphology, deformable models [34], expectation maximization [35], statistical model analysis with curve evolution [36], atlas [37] and AI [38]. They are mostly for segmenting TOF MRA scans and are not able to handle smaller vessels, e.g., such as collaterals.

The cost of atlas creation depends both on its content and processing. More frequent scanning improves the temporal resolution of the atlas at the expense of its increased cost. Processing-wise, creating a detailed and accurate brain atlas that is fully parcellated and completely labeled by applying a traditional approach is a long-term and tedious process. Even for the given automatically segmented models, checking, labeling, and validating multiple models, each with thousands of components, is very time-consuming. For instance, the atlas [6] employed here for illustration contains about 3,000 3D objects, including 630 cranial nerve segments and 1,500 vessels (1,300 for the intracranial and 200 for extracranial cerebrovasculature). The difficulty in the automated labeling of vessels results not only from their large number but also from their high variability, as the cerebral arteries and especially the cerebral venous system are highly variable with numerous variants [39]. An illustration of the development of a 3D interactive brain atlas of cerebral arterial variants is featured in [40].

Therefore, one of the main goals of future work shall be to develop rapid and robust AI technology for the automatic conversion of subject-specific scans to 3D segmented and annotated cerebral models embedded in a personal *pBAe*. An example of a rapid and robust AI-based method is *BRAVE-NET* [41]—a multiscale 3D convolutional neural network for fully automated TOF MRA arterial brain vessel segmentation (though it is still unable to perform automated vessel labeling). The *BRAVE-NET* deep learning architecture integrates the 3D Unet with multiscaling for better spatial information integration and deep supervision for improving model convergence. It is robustly validated on high-quality labeled data of 264 patients with cerebrovascular disease. *BRAVE-NET* is of high performance, and for clinically used data dimensions, the segmentations can be obtained within minutes on a standard CPU system (e.g., 2 min on AMD Ryzen 7 1700X), and the same data on a standard GPU (NVIDIA Titan Xp) system take 40 s.

Atlas Content Extension. The atlas content proposed in Sect. 2 is quite basic. The smaller the atlas content, the easier and cheaper the *pBAe* development is. Moreover, its brain function is realized through annotations, so functionally, such a basic atlas is not fully personalized. On the other hand, extending this content and building advanced versions of the *pBAe* increases its potential at the expense of cost.

Individual structure- and function-based brain parcellations facilitate understanding anatomical and functional variations among individuals. Brain function can be noninvasively measured by applying different techniques, such as functional MRI. In particular, resting-state functional MRI (rsfMRI) helps reveal the brain's functional organization [42]. Moreover, the integration of various modalities could provide a more comprehensive depiction of brain function and structural organization [43, 44].

Brain connections (the connectome) play a central role in understanding brain function, cognition, behavior, and neurologic disorders. Individual differences in intelligence, memory, and personality characteristics can be linked to variations in brain connectivity. So far, the human connectome has only been created at the macroscale by providing anatomical and functional connectivity [45, 46]. An example of a 3D interactive atlas of anatomical connectivity with parcellated and labeled white matter tracts is presented in [47]. The *MIDB Precision Brain Atlas,* developed by employing functional mapping, is a basic and clinical research resource with functional neural networks from over 9,950 individuals containing more than 53,00 network maps [48].

The extension of the *pBAe* with the spinal cord and spinal nerves is also vital, as they are part of the nervous system. Note that the prevalence of back pain resulting from various causes (such as musculoskeletal, nerve-related, lifestyle, and stress-related) increases with age, and low back pain is the leading cause of disability worldwide [49].

Modalities other than MRI can also be applied in the construction of a personalized atlas, such as cognitive tests, electroencephalography (EEG) to record the spontaneous electrical activity of the brain, and computed tomography (CT) enabling bone imaging. For instance, a cognitive test *Mini-Mental State Examination* (MMSE), a widely utilized tool for assessing cognitive function [50], can be employed to measure brain health [51]. EEG can also be used clinically to evaluate brain health [51]. CT is suitable for skull and spine imaging, and it facilitates, e.g., the detection and quantification of skull malformations (such as plagiocephaly, trigonocephaly, macrocephaly, and microcephaly). Having the skull and spine models included in the *pBAe*, makes them potentially useful in head and spine injuries as a pre-injury reference. An example of a 3D interactive and stereotactic skull atlas is described in [52, 53].

Impact. The impact of the *pBAe* concept can be tremendous at various levels, including individual, social, scientific, and technological for AI.

Individual human brains vary immensely in morphology, connectivity, function, and organization. For an individual, the *pBAe* is potentially beneficial in health prevention, prediction, diagnosis, disorder monitoring, prognosis, and treatment progression. In health, as the *pBAe* provides annotated scans (Fig. 5) as well as structures and cortical areas (Fig. 3), function description (Fig. 4), and quantification (Figs. 6 and 7), the atlas owner can educate him/herself about own brain's structure, function, and disorders. The brain health status can be monitored by MR imaging being a common method of brain health measurement by structural volumetric estimates, particularly those of total brain volume, total grey matter volume, grey matter volume of specific regions (such as the hippocampus and ventricular system), and the presence and volume of white matter hyperintensities [51]; additionally, cognitive tests and EEG also measure brain health [51]. Such knowledge shall motivate the atlas owner to pursue a suitable lifestyle and adopt a healthful diet to keep the brain (and the body) healthy.

Knowing brain health measurement facilitates prevention and enables prediction. For instance, the identification and quantification of white matter hyperintensities are useful in stroke occurrence assessment as they are associated with an increased risk of stroke [54] and its recurrence [55]. Similarly, the closeness of cranial nerves to unruptured aneurysms may predict neuropathy caused by nerve compression. Ischemic stroke is a leading cause of morbidity and mortality worldwide [56]. There are many methods for diagnosis and treatment of stroke, and under certain conditions, the standard 4.5-h treatment window for intravenous thrombolysis can be extended [57]. Collaterals and vascular variants are vital as collateral circulation plays a crucial role in sustaining blood flow to the ischemic regions. Good collateral circulation has demonstrated protective effects toward a favorable functional outcome and a lower risk of stroke recurrence [58], whereas poor collaterals are associated with larger ischemic infarcts and worse clinical outcomes as well as higher occurrence of hemorrhagic transformations [59]. The circle of Willis, the primary collateral circulation, has many variants and less than 50% of patients have a complete, symmetrical, and well-developed circle (see Fig. 7); these variants may considerably affect collateral blood flow, and they have been demonstrated to impact outcomes in ischemic stroke [59]. From the individual standpoint, knowledge about own collaterals is important, particularly in the case of poor collaterals, since regular exercise improves collateral circulation [60]. A potential application of a functionally parcellated *pBAe* in stroke is the decision-making in thrombolytic treatment. The risk of performing a thrombolytic procedure is the occurrence of hemorrhagic transformation, which may be fatal, so several conditions shall be checked [57]. For the atlas-assisted decision-making, brain atlases of anatomy and blood supply territories have been applied providing the complete list of anatomic structures and blood supply territories with their volumes and percentage of contributions to the infarct (i.e., damaged tissue) and penumbra (i.e., tissue at risk of progressing to infarction that is still potentially salvageable) [61, 62]. The personalized functional brain atlas would enhance this decision-making by considering the trade-off between the risk of treatment versus the loss of functions in the penumbra region if not being treated. Note that this decision process could include the patient's (or his or her family's) own preferences.

Personalized medicine [63] will benefit from the personalized brain atlas. Diagnostically, the process of *pBAe* construction and actualization acts as a sort of a screening mechanism. The scans could reveal, e.g., any non-symptomatic lesions or congenital malformations. In addition, 3D models could facilitate the detection of vascular and cranial nerve variations. As the *pBAe* is constructed as a time series, it monitors, quantifies, and documents the changes over time, such as brain atrophy and ventricular enlargement.

Therapeutically, in the case of head injury or brain intervention, the *pBAe* serves as a reference storing the brain state prior to intervention. Moreover, the knowledge of vascular and cranial nerve variations can impact surgical approaches.

Individual parcellation may enable precise targeting of therapeutic regions, for instance, in deep brain stimulation (DBS). A standard atlas employed in DBS procedures is anatomic, and our electronic brain atlases have been embedded in the surgical workstations of major companies, such as Medtronic, Brainlab, and Elekta [64, 65]. Probabilistic functional atlases derived from neuroelectrophysiology [66–68] and multimodal anatomic-functional-vascular atlas [69] can further enhance DBS procedures. An additional improvement of DBS is potentially feasible via individual surgical targets derived from white matter connectivity such as [70, 71] and embedded in the *pBAe*.

Scientifically, the *pBAe* can contribute to "population neuroscience". Assuming that even slightly more than 1% of the world's population were to possess the *pBAe*, and that each owner agreed to make his/her anonymized copy available for research, this would result in a huge, distributed database of approximately 100 million complete human brains. Such a massive and heterogeneous database would enable, among many others, the studies of brain organization, function, and diverse features in the entire brain and its numerous regions along with their variability in health and disease across various populations in terms of age, gender, ethnicity, lifestyle, education, job, living place, and nutrition; examine trends like temporal (development and aging) and geographic; and test various hypotheses (e.g., regarding behavior, cognition, personality, memory, emotion, language, and nature of creativity). These efforts would drive new discoveries leading to improved public health and the betterment of humankind. A better understanding of the brain's architecture, networks, functions, algorithms, and representations employed will expedite the development of more advanced neuro-related technologies, including AI, neuroprosthetics, and brain-computer interfaces.

A successful global deployment of such an enormous initiative requires the automated, rapid, and accurate conversion of brain scans to 3D parcellated and annotated cerebral models. AI appears to be the most promising technology capable of executing this task. Robust and rapid solutions, such as *BRAVE-NET* [41], able not only to segment but also to parcellate and annotate segmented 3D models, would facilitate the development of detailed personalized brain atlases such as [6] in minutes and not in years. Therefore, constructing increasingly advanced versions of the *pBAe* in progressively shorter timeframes along with the growing penetration of Earth's population will necessitate continual advances in AI capabilities. And reciprocally, the analysis of this immense neurodatabase, which would be continuously growing in the number of brains as well as the quality and complexity of brain models, would result in new brain discoveries and insights inspiring the growth of AI.

Hence the *pBAe*, considered a process and a global initiative of continuously increasing both atlas complexity and its population penetration, will influence AI advancements and, at the same time, be influenced by them. Therefore, the symbiosis between the *pBAe* initiative and AI can create a "virtuous circle" advancing both fields. Several authors have already addressed the convergence and complementarity of AI and neuroscience [72–75]. For instance, the role of neuroscience in advancing AI research along with the applications of AI for the advancement of neuroscience, has been discussed by a Nobel Prize winner (for his work on AI) Hassabis et al. [75].

Finally, future work on the *pBAe* advancement, besides involving AI, shall also integrate ongoing efforts on brain modeling and handling at the nanoscale [76–79].

Acknowledgments. This publication is supported by the European Union's Horizon 2020 research and innovation programme under grant agreement Sano No. 857533. This publication is supported by Sano project carried out within the International Research Agendas programme of the Foundation for Polish Science, co-financed by the European Union under the European Regional Development Fund. The publication was created within the project of the Ministry of Science and Higher Education "Support for the activity of Centers of Excellence established in Poland under Horizon 2020" on the basis of the contract number MEiN/2023/DIR/3796.

Disclosure of Interests.   The author has no competing interests to declare that are relevant to the content of this article.

References

1. Ludwig, J.A., Weinstein, J.N.: Biomarkers in cancer staging, prognosis and treatment selection. Nat. Rev. Cancer. **5**, 845–856 (2005). https://doi.org/10.1038/nrc1739
2. Braunwald, E.: Biomarkers in heart failure. N. Engl. J. Med. **358**, 2148–2159 (2008)
3. GBD 2021 Nervous System Disorders Collaborators: Global, regional, and national burden of disorders affecting the nervous system, 1990–2021: a systematic analysis for the Global Burden of Disease Study 2021. Lancet Neurol. **23**(4), 344–381 (2024)
4. Jollans, L., Whelan, R.: Neuromarkers for mental disorders: harnessing population neuroscience. Front. Psychiatry. **9**, 242 (2018). https://doi.org/10.3389/fpsyt.2018.00242
5. Nowinski, W.L.: Human brain atlasing: past, present and future. Neuroradiol. J. **30**(6), 504–519 (2017). https://doi.org/10.1177/1971400917739274
6. Nowinski, W.L., Chua, B.C., Thaung, T.S.L., Wut, Y.S.H.: The Human Brain, Head and Neck in 2953 Pieces. Thieme, New York (2015)
7. Nowinski, W.L.: 3D atlas of the brain, head and neck in 2953 pieces. Neuroinformatics. **15**(4), 395–400 (2017)
8. Nowinski, W.L.: Evolution of human brain atlases in terms of content, applications, functionality, and availability. Neuroinformatics. **19**(1), 1–22 (2021)
9. Roland, P.E., Zilles, K.: Brain atlases–a new research tool. Trends Neurosci. **17**, 458–467 (1994)
10. Boline, J., Lee, E.F., Toga, A.W.: Digital atlases as a framework for data sharing. Front. Neurosci. **2**(1), 100–106 (2008)
11. Evans, A.C., Janke, A.L., Collins, D.L., Baillet, S.: Brain templates and atlases. NeuroImage. **62**(2), 911–922 (2012)
12. Amunts, K., Hawrylycz, M.J., Van Essen, D.C., et al.: Interoperable atlases of the human brain. NeuroImage. **99**, 525–532 (2014)
13. Nowinski, W.L.: Towards an architecture of a multi-purpose, user-extendable reference human brain atlas. Neuroinformatics. **20**, 405–426 (2022). https://doi.org/10.1007/s12021-021-095 55-2
14. Rao, Y.L., Ganaraja, B., Murlimanju, B.V., Joy, T., Krishnamurthy, A., Agrawal, A.: Hippocampus and its involvement in Alzheimer's disease: a review. 3 Biotech. **12**(2), 55 (2022). https://doi.org/10.1007/s13205-022-03123-4
15. Hacke, W., Kaste, M., Bluhmki, E., et al.: Thrombolysis with alteplase 3 to 4.5 hours after acute ischemic stroke. N. Engl. J. Med. **359**, 1317–1329 (2008)

16. Runge, V.M., Heverhagen, J.T.: The Physics of Clinical MR Taught Through Images, 5th edn. Springer, Cham (2022)
17. Brown, R.W., Cheng, Y.-C.N., Haacke, E.M., et al.: Magnetic Resonance Imaging: Physical Principles and Sequence Design, 2nd edn. Wiley, Hoboken (2014)
18. Haacke, E.M., Xu, Y., Cheng, Y.C.N., Reichenbach, J.R.: Susceptibility-weighted imaging (SWI). Magn. Reson. Med. **52**(3), 612–618 (2004)
19. Romano, N., Federici, M., Castaldi, A.: Imaging of cranial nerves: a pictorial overview. Insights Imaging. **10**(1), 33 (2019). https://doi.org/10.1186/s13244-019-0719-5
20. Nowinski, W.L., Chua, B.C., Qian, G.Y., Nowinska, N.G.: The human brain in 1700 pieces: design and development of a three-dimensional, interactive and reference atlas. J. Neurosci. Methods. **204**(1), 44–60 (2012)
21. Nowinski, W.L., Chua, B.C., Puspitasari, F., et al.: Three-dimensional reference and stereotactic atlas of human cerebrovasculature from 7 Tesla. NeuroImage. **55**(3), 986–998 (2011)
22. Nowinski, W.L., Johnson, A., Chua, B.C., Nowinska, N.G.: Three-dimensional interactive and stereotactic atlas of cranial nerves and nuclei correlated with surface neuroanatomy, vasculature and magnetic resonance imaging. J. Neurosci. Methods. **206**(2), 205–216 (2012)
23. Nowinski, W.L.: Computational and mathematical methods in brain atlasing. Neuroradiol. J. **30**(6), 520–534 (2017). https://doi.org/10.1177/1971400917740362
24. Nowinski, W.L.: Brain atlasing: design principles, methods, tools and applications. In: Mityushev, V., Ruzhansky, M. (eds.) Analytic Methods in Interdisciplinary Applications, Springer Proceedings in Mathematics & Statistics, vol. 116, pp. 97–107. Springer, Cham (2015)
25. Wolf, I., Vetter, M., Wegner, I., et al.: The medical imaging interaction toolkit. Med. Image Anal. **9**(6), 594–604 (2005)
26. Fischl, B.: FreeSurfer. NeuroImage. **62**(2), 774–781 (2012)
27. BrainSuite: https://brainsuite.org/. Last accessed 3 Jan 2026
28. Jenkinson, M., Beckmann, C.F., Behrens, T.E., Woolrich, M.W., Smith, S.M.: FSL. Neuroimage. **62**(2), 782–790 (2012)
29. Neuroscience Information Framework: https://neuinfo.org/. Last accessed 3 Jan 2026
30. BrainInfo: http://braininfo.rprc.washington.edu. Last accessed 3 Jan 2026
31. Nowinski, W.L.: NOW*in*BRAIN: a large, systematic, and extendable repository of 3D reconstructed images of a living human brain cum head and neck. J. Digit. Imaging. **35**(2), 98–114 (2022). https://doi.org/10.1007/s10278-021-00528-0
32. Nowinski, W.L.: NOW*in*BRAIN 3D neuroimage repository: exploring the human brain via systematic and stereotactic dissections. Neurosci. Inform. **2**(3), 100085 (2022). https://www.nowinbrain.org. Last accessed 3 Jan 2026
33. Nowinski, W.L.: NOW*in*BRAIN public repository: 3D neuroimage galleries. Neuroinformatics. **23**, 42 (2025). https://doi.org/10.1007/s12021-025-09735-4
34. Suri, J.S., Liu, K.C., Reden, L., et al.: A review on MR vascular image processing: skeleton versus nonskeleton approaches: part II. IEEE Trans. Inf. Technol. Biomed. **6**(4), 338–350 (2002). https://doi.org/10.1109/TITB.2002.804136
35. Wilson, D.L., Noble, J.A.: An adaptive segmentation algorithm for time-of-flight MRA data. IEEE Trans. Med. Imaging. **18**(10), 938–945 (1999). https://doi.org/10.1109/42.811277
36. Gao, X., Uchiyama, Y., Zhou, X., et al.: A fast and fully automatic method for cerebrovascular segmentation on time-of-flight (TOF) MRA image. J. Digit. Imaging. **24**(4), 609–625 (2010)
37. Passat, N., Ronse, C., Baruthio, J., et al.: Region-growing segmentation of brain vessels: an atlas-based automatic approach. J. Magn. Reson. Imaging. **21**, 715–725 (2005)
38. Taher, F., Prakash, N.: Automatic cerebrovascular segmentation methods—a review. IAES Int. J. Artif. Intell. **10**(3), 576–583 (2021)
39. Rhoton, A.L.: Cranial Anatomy and Surgical Approaches. The Congress of Neurological Surgeons, Schaumburg (2003)

40. Nowinski, W.L., Thirunnavuukarasuu, A., Volkau, I., et al.: A three-dimensional interactive atlas of cerebral arterial variants. Neuroinformatics. 7(4), 255–264 (2009)

41. Hilbert, A., Madai, V.I., Akay, E.M., et al.: BRAVE-NET: fully automated arterial brain vessel segmentation in patients with cerebrovascular disease. Front. Artif. Intell. 3, 552258 (2020). https://doi.org/10.3389/frai.2020.552258

42. Blumensath, T., Jbabdi, S., Glasser, M.F., et al.: Spatially constrained hierarchical parcellation of the brain with resting-state fMRI. NeuroImage. 76, 313–324 (2013). https://doi.org/10.1016/j.neuroimage.2013.03.024

43. Glasser, M.F., Coalson, T.S., Robinson, E.C., et al.: A multi-modal parcellation of human cerebral cortex. Nature. 536(7615), 171–178 (2016)

44. Wang, C., Ng, B., Garbi, R.: Multimodal brain parcellation based on functional and anatomical connectivity. Brain Connect. 8 (2018). https://doi.org/10.1089/brain.2017.0576

45. Van Essen, D.C.: Cartography and connectomes. Neuron. 80, 775–790 (2013)

46. Coleman, C., Van Horn, J.D.: Towards comprehensive connectivity modeling. Neuroinformatics. 22, 225–227 (2024). https://doi.org/10.1007/s12021-024-09676-4

47. Nowinski, W.L., Chua, B.C., Yang, G.L., Qian, G.Y.: Three-dimensional interactive human brain atlas of white matter tracts. Neuroinformatics. 10(1), 33–55 (2012)

48. Hermosillo, R.J.M., Moore, L.A., Feczko, E., et al.: A precision functional atlas of personalized network topography and probabilities. Nat. Neurosci. 27(5), 1000–1013 (2024)

49. WHO: Low back pain. https://www.who.int/news-room/fact-sheets/detail/low-back-pain?utm_source=chatgpt.com. Last accessed 29 Oct 2025

50. Folstein, M.F., Folstein, S.E., McHugh, P.R.: "Mini-mental state." A practical method for grading the cognitive state of patients for the clinician. J. Psychiatr. Res. 12(3), 189–198 (1975)

51. Lee, A., Shah, S., Atha, K., Indoe, P., et al.: Brain health measurement: a scoping review. BMJ Open. 14(2), e080334 (2024). https://doi.org/10.1136/bmjopen-2023-080334

52. Nowinski, W.L., et al.: Three-dimensional stereotactic atlas of the adult human skull correlated with the brain, cranial nerves and intracranial vasculature. J. Neurosci. Methods. 246, 65–74 (2015)

53. Nowinski, W.L., Thaung, T.S.L.: A 3D stereotactic atlas of the adult human skull base. Brain Inform. 5(2), 1–9 (2018). https://doi.org/10.1186/s40708-018-0082-1

54. Moran, C., Phan, T.G., Srikanth, V.K.: Cerebral small vessel disease: a review of clinical, radiological, and histopathological phenotypes. Int. J. Stroke. 7(1), 36–46 (2012)

55. Kim, G.M., Park, K.Y., Avery, R., et al.: Extensive leukoaraiosis is associated with high early risk of recurrence after ischemic stroke. Stroke. 45(2), 479–485 (2014)

56. Feigin, V.L., Brainin, M., Norrving, B., Martins, S., Sacco, R.L., Hacke, W., et al.: World Stroke Organization (WSO): global stroke fact sheet 2022. Int. J. Stroke. 17, 18–29 (2022)

57. Nowinski, W.L.: Taxonomy of acute stroke: imaging, processing, and treatment. Diagnostics. 14(10), 1057 (2024). https://doi.org/10.3390/diagnostics14101057

58. Sharma, A., Agarwal, A., Vishnu, V.Y., et al.: Collateral circulation- evolving from time window to tissue window. Ann. Indian Acad. Neurol. 26(1), 10–16 (2023)

59. Maguida, G., Shuaib, A.: Collateral circulation in ischemic stroke: an updated review. J. Stroke. 25(2), 179–198 (2023). https://doi.org/10.5853/jos.2022.02936

60. Hung, S.H., Kramer, S., Werden, E., et al.: Pre-stroke physical activity and cerebral collateral circulation in ischemic stroke: a potential therapeutic relationship? Front. Neurol. 13, 804187 (2022)

61. Nowinski, W.L.: Human brain atlases in stroke management. Neuroinformatics. 18(4), 549–567 (2020). https://doi.org/10.1007/s12021-020-09462-y

62. Nowinski, W.L., Qian, G., Bhanu Prakash, K.N., et al.: Analysis of ischemic stroke MR images by means of brain atlases of anatomy and blood supply territories. Acad. Radiol. 13(8), 1025–1034 (2006)

63. Delpierre, C., Lefèvre, T.: Precision and personalized medicine: what their current definition says and silences about the model of health they promote. Implication for the development of personalized health. Front. Sociol. **8**, 1112159 (2023)

64. Nowinski, W.L.: Anatomical targeting in functional neurosurgery by the simultaneous use of multiple Schaltenbrand-Wahren brain atlas microseries. Stereotact. Funct. Neurosurg. **71**(3), 103–116 (1998)

65. Nowinski, W.L.: Anatomical and probabilistic functional atlases in stereotactic and functional neurosurgery. In: Lozano, A., Gildenberg, P., Tasker, R. (eds.) Textbook of Stereotactic and Functional Neurosurgery, 2nd edn, pp. 395–441. Springer, Berlin (2009)

66. Nowinski, W.L., Belov, D., Benabid, A.L.: An algorithm for rapid calculation of a probabilistic functional atlas of subcortical structures from electrophysiological data collected during functional neurosurgery procedures. NeuroImage. **18**(1), 143–155 (2003)

67. Nowinski, W.L., Belov, D., Pollak, P., Benabid, A.L.: Statistical analysis of 168 bilateral subthalamic nucleus implantations by means of the probabilistic functional atlas. Neurosurgery. **57**(4 Suppl), 319–330 (2005). https://doi.org/10.1227/01.neu.0000180960.75347.11

68. Nowinski, W.L., Belov, D., Thirunavuukarasuu, A., Benabid, A.L.: A probabilistic functional atlas of the VIM nucleus constructed from pre-, intra- and postoperative electrophysiological and neuroimaging data acquired during the surgical treatment of Parkinson's disease patients. Stereotact. Funct. Neurosurg. **83**(5–6), 190–196 (2005)

69. Nowinski, W.L., Chua, B.C., Volkau, I., et al.: Simulation and assessment of cerebrovascular damage in deep brain stimulation using a stereotactic atlas of vasculature and structure derived from multiple 3- and 7-tesla scans. J. Neurosurg. **113**(6), 1234–1241 (2010)

70. DiRisio, A.C., Avecillas-Chasin, J.M., Platt, S., et al.: White matter connectivity of subthalamic nucleus and globus pallidus interna targets for deep brain stimulation. J. Neurosurg. **139**(5), 1366–1375 (2023). https://doi.org/10.3171/2023.2.JNS222576

71. Patriat, R., Cooper, S.E., Duchin, Y., et al.: Personalized tractography-based parcellation of the globus pallidus pars interna using 7T MRI in movement disorder patients prior to DBS surgery. NeuroImage. **178**, 198–209 (2018)

72. Surianarayanan, C., Lawrence, J.J., Chelliah, P.R., Prakash, E., Hewage, C.: Convergence of Artificial Intelligence and neuroscience towards the diagnosis of neurological disorders-a scoping review. Sensors. **23**(6), 3062 (2023). https://doi.org/10.3390/s23063062

73. Macpherson, T., et al.: Natural and Artificial Intelligence: A brief introduction to the interplay between AI and neuroscience research. Neural Netw. **144**, 603–613 (2021)

74. The new NeuroAI. Nat Mach Intell. **6**, 245 (2024). https://doi.org/10.1038/s42256-024-00826-6

75. Hassabis, D., Kumaran, D., Summerfield, C., Botvinick, M.: Neuroscience-inspired Artificial Intelligence. Neuron. **95**, 245–258 (2017)

76. Nowinski, W.L.: Toward morphologic atlasing of the human whole brain at the nanoscale. Big Data Cogn. Comput. **7**(4), 179 (2023). https://doi.org/10.3390/bdcc7040179

77. Nowinski, W.L.: Storage estimation in morphology modeling of the human whole brain at the nanoscale. J. Comput. Sci. **81**, 102346 (2024). https://doi.org/10.1016/j.jocs.2024.102346

78. Nowinski, W.L.: On human nanoscale synaptome: morphology modeling and storage estimation. PLoS One. **19** (2024). https://doi.org/10.1371/journal.pone.0310156

79. Shapson-Coe, A., Januszewski, M., Berger, D.R., et al.: A petavoxel fragment of human cerebral cortex reconstructed at nanoscale resolution. Science. **384**(6696), eadk4858 (2024)

A Comparative Analysis of EEG Network Construction Strategies for Discriminating PNES

Ilaria Lazzaro[1]([✉]) [iD], Valeria Popello[1] [iD], Chiara Zucco[1] [iD],
Marianna Milano[2] [iD], Antonio Gambardella[3] [iD], and Mario Cannataro[1] [iD]

[1] Data Analytics Research Center and Department of Medical and Surgical Sciences,
University "Magna Græcia" of Catanzaro, 88100 Catanzaro, Italy
`{ilaria.lazzaro,valeria.popello,chiara.zucco,cannataro}@unicz.it`
[2] Department of Experimental and Clinical Medicine, University "Magna Græcia" of
Catanzaro, 88100 Catanzaro, Italy
`m.milano@unicz.it`
[3] Institute of Neurology and Department of Medical and Surgical Sciences,
University "Magna Græcia" of Catanzaro, 88100 Catanzaro, Italy
`a.gambardella@unicz.it`

Abstract. Network-based EEG analysis has recently attracted attention as a tool for studying alterations in the functional organisation of the brain associated with neurological conditions such as epilepsy and psychogenic non-epileptic seizures (PNES), which represent a diagnostic challenge due to their clinical similarity to epileptic seizures and the absence of epileptiform activity in EEG recordings. In this work, we propose a systematic framework for the construction and analysis of EEG-based functional brain networks, with the aim of evaluating the impact of phase-based connectivity estimators and graph construction strategies on network topology. Functional connectivity matrices were calculated using the phase lag value (PLV), phase locking index (PLI), and weighted phase locking index (WPLI) across multiple frequency bands. Brain networks were constructed using four binarisation and filtering approaches: median threshold, minimum connected component, minimum spanning tree, and orthogonal minimum spanning tree. Global and local graph-theoretic measures were analysed to characterise network organisation in healthy controls, epileptic patients, and PNES patients. The results demonstrate that methodological choices have a marked impact on network topology and critically affect the sensitivity of graph-theoretical measures in distinguishing between clinical groups.

Keywords: Electroencephalogram (EEG) · Functional connectivity · Networks Analysis · Graph theory

---

I. Lazzaro and V. Popello—Contributed equally to this work.

P. Neumann et al. (Eds.): ICCS 2026, LNCS 16784, pp. 182–196, 2026.
https://doi.org/10.1007/978-3-032-29924-6_13

1   Introduction

Psychogenic non-epileptic seizures (PNES) are events of psychological origin, often associated with stress or traumatic experiences, which can closely resemble epileptic seizures in their clinical manifestation. This similarity poses a significant diagnostic challenge, as patients are often unaware of the non-epileptic nature of their seizures [1]. In this context, electroencephalography (EEG) remains a fundamental tool for investigating brain activity, providing a non-invasive measure of neuronal activity. The EEG signal is non-stationary and is typically analysed within canonical frequency bands, conventionally defined as delta, theta, alpha, beta, and gamma, each associated with specific neurophysiological mechanisms [2]. In epilepsy, seizures are commonly accompanied by pathological EEG signatures, such as spikes or sharp waves, while PNES episodes generally do not present epileptiform discharges. Consequently, the current diagnostic gold standard for PNES is based on prolonged video-EEG monitoring, which integrates electrophysiological recordings. In recent years, the analysis of EEG signals has progressively adopted a network-based paradigm [3,4], modelling the brain as a graph of interacting regions to investigate functional organisation and dynamical properties of brain activity [5,6]. Numerous studies have applied this framework to brain disorders, reporting alterations in global and local network topology across multiple frequency bands using phase-based functional connectivity measures such as Phase Locking Value (PLV), Phase Lag Index (PLI), and Weighted Phase Lag Index (WPLI) [7,8]. Alongside connectivity estimation, the construction of functional brain networks represents a critical methodological step. Different strategies—including fixed or proportional thresholding, minimum spanning tree (MST)-based approaches or Minimum Connected Component (MCC), have been proposed to ensure network comparability and interpretability [9]. Recent works have shown that the choice of binarisation or graph construction method can substantially influence network topology and derived graph metrics [10,11]. However, most existing studies focus on single clinical populations, and systematic comparisons across epilepsy, PNES, and healthy controls remain scarce. In this context, we propose a systematic framework for the construction and analysis of EEG-based functional brain networks, aimed at evaluating the impact of phase-based connectivity estimators and binarisation strategies on network topology. Functional connectivity matrices are computed using PLV, PLI, and WPLI across multiple frequency bands. In addition to binarised networks, a weighted (non-binarised) functional network is also constructed; however, as these networks are fully connected, they are not considered for the extraction and analysis of graph-theoretical measures. Brain networks are then derived using four graph construction approaches: median thresholding (MED), Minimum Connected Component (MCC), Minimum Spanning Tree (MST), and Orthogonal Minimum Spanning Tree (OMST). Global and local topological measures, including global efficiency, local efficiency, degree, strength, and betweenness centrality, are analysed to characterise network organisation in healthy controls, epilepsy patients, and patients with psychogenic non-epileptic seizures. The rest of this paper is organised as follows. Section 2 presents the materials and methods, while Sect. 3 outlines the experimental results obtained and discusses the findings. Finally, Sect. 4 presents the conclusions and future work.

2 Materials and Methods

This section describes the methodological framework adopted in the study. After providing a brief description of the dataset and the EEG signal pre-processing pipeline, in detail, the construction of functional connectivity matrices and the procedures used for functional network binarisation are presented.

2.1 Dataset

EEG recordings were collected at the Neurology Unit of the Renato Dulbecco University Hospital, Catanzaro, Italy, from three groups of subjects in resting-state conditions: healthy controls (CNT), patients with psychogenic non-epileptic seizures (PNES), diagnosed through video-EEG evaluation in the absence of ictal activity, and patients with epilepsy (EPI). The acquisition protocol, clinical assessment, and data quality procedures followed the methodological framework previously described in [12].

In particular, for the present study, a balanced cohort of 69 subjects was considered, including 23 individuals for each group (CNT, PNES, and EPI). All procedures were conducted in accordance with the Declaration of Helsinki and approved by the local ethics committee. Signals were acquired using a 19-channel Ag/AgCl montage based on the International 10–20 System (Fp1, Fp2, F3, F4, F7, F8, Fz, C3, C4, Cz, P3, P4, Pz, T3, T4, T5, T6, O1, and O2) with a sampling rate of 256 Hz. Recordings were performed in a dimly lit room with participants seated comfortably, with a duration ranging from 10 to 20 min. Given the well-known susceptibility of EEG to physiological and environmental artefacts, the raw traces were first visually reviewed by expert neurologists to identify corrupted segments. An automatic preprocessing stage was subsequently applied, including the detection and removal of amplifier saturation events and severely noisy epochs. The cleaned signals were filtered using a Butterworth band-pass filter (0.1–70 Hz) together with a 50 Hz notch filter to attenuate power-line interference. Afterwards, the data were decomposed into five standard frequency bands—delta (0.5–4 Hz), theta (4–8 Hz), alpha (8–13 Hz), beta (13–30 Hz), and gamma (>30 Hz)—via dedicated digital filters. These band-specific signals constituted the basis for the computation of functional connectivity matrices and for the subsequent comparative framework adopted to evaluate different connectivity construction methods and binarization procedures.

2.2 Connectivity Matrix

Starting from pre-processed EEG signals, we calculated functional connectivity matrices using phase-based synchronisation measures.

These measures were selected to capture functional interactions between EEG channels while minimising spurious correlations arising from volume conduction and the use of a common reference. Specifically, the following connectivity metrics were employed:

- **Phase Locking Value (PLV)**: quantifies the degree of phase synchronization between two EEG signals by measuring the temporal stability of their phase difference. The PLV ranges between 0 and 1, with higher values indicating stronger synchronization between signal pairs.
  Formally, given two EEG signals $x(t)$ and $y(t)$, the PLV is defined as illustrated in Eq. 1 [13].

$$\mathrm{PLV}_{xy} = \left| \frac{1}{T} \sum_{t=1}^{T} e^{j\varphi_{xy}(t)} \right|, \tag{1}$$

where $\varphi_{xy}(t) = \phi_x(t) - \phi_y(t)$ denotes the instantaneous phase difference between the two signals at time sample t, T is the total number of samples, and j is the imaginary unit. Despite its simplicity and widespread use due to its high sensitivity and straightforward interpretability, the PLV is particularly susceptible to zero-lag interactions, which may be partially attributed to volume conduction effects or common source activity rather than true functional interactions [14].
- **Phase Lag Index (PLI)**: evaluates the asymmetry of the distribution of phase differences between two EEG signals by considering exclusively non-zero phase-lag interactions. By ignoring phase differences centered around zero, the PLI reduces the influence of volume conduction and common sources, thereby providing a more robust estimate of the functional interactions of genuine neurophysiological origin [15].
  The mathematical definition of PLI is defined in Eq. 2 [16].

$$\mathrm{PLI} = \left| \langle \mathrm{sign} \left(\sin(\phi_x(n) - \phi_y(n)) \right) \rangle \right|, \tag{2}$$

where $\langle \cdot \rangle$ denotes temporal averaging.
- **Weighted Phase Lag Index (WPLI)**: it represents an extension of the Phase Lag Index (PLI). In which the contribution of phase differences is weighted according to the magnitude of the imaginary component of the cross-spectrum. This weighting strategy improves the statistical stability of the measure and reduces its sensitivity to noise, thereby providing a more reliable estimate of functional connectivity in EEG data [17].
  The WPLI is formally defined as follows in Eq. 3 [18].

$$\mathrm{WPLI}_{xy} = \frac{\left| \frac{1}{N} \sum_{n=1}^{N} \left| \mathrm{Im} \left(S_{xy}^{n} \right) \right| \, \mathrm{sign} \left(\mathrm{Im} \left(S_{xy}^{n} \right) \right) \right|}{\frac{1}{N} \sum_{n=1}^{N} \left| \mathrm{Im} \left(S_{xy}^{n} \right) \right|}, \tag{3}$$

where $\mathrm{Im}(S_{xy})$ denotes the imaginary part of the cross-spectrum between signals x and y, and $\langle \cdot \rangle$ indicates temporal averaging.

2.3 Functional Network Construction Methods

Once the previously described functional connectivity matrices were obtained, brain networks were constructed by applying different binarisation strategies directly to the connectivity matrices [19], in order to compare alternative representations of network topology and to assess the impact of methodological choices on the extracted graph-theoretical measures. Specifically, binarisation procedures were employed to reduce the dependence of network metrics on the absolute distribution of connectivity weights, and to enable robust and reproducible inter-subject and inter-group comparisons. In this study, the binarisation methods considered include median-based thresholding, the Minimum Connected Component (MCC) criterion, the Minimum Spanning Tree (MST) and the Orthogonal Minimum Spanning Tree (OMST) are all applied to the functional connectivity matrices derived from the phase-based synchronisation measures. Specifically, the techniques for binarisation were employed:

- **Median Thresholding (MED)**: is set to the median connectivity weight in the matrix. Connections with weights exceeding the median are retained, while all remaining connections are discarded. This approach yields networks with comparable density across subjects and reduces the influence of extreme connectivity values [20]. However, it may be sensitive to the underlying distribution of connectivity weights and does not explicitly guarantee network connectedness [21].
- **Minimum Connected Component (MCC)**: determines the lowest connectivity threshold that guarantees the resulting binary network to be fully connected, i.e., that at least one path exists between every pair of nodes [22]. By explicitly enforcing global network connectedness, this method prevents fragmentation into disconnected components and preserves the integrative structure of the network, which is essential for the reliable computation of graph-theoretical measures that assume connected graphs. This adaptive property makes the MCC particularly suitable for EEG-based functional connectivity analyses, where inter-subject variability in overall connectivity strength is pronounced.
- **Minimum Spanning Tree (MST)**: constructs a connected and cycle-free subgraph that links all N nodes using exactly $N - 1$ edges, selected to maximise the overall connectivity strength. By definition, the MST enforces a fixed network density across subjects and groups, thereby eliminating potential confounding effects related to differences in edge density and enabling meaningful topological comparisons. Recent investigations have demonstrated that MST-based representations are effective in capturing disease-related alterations in network organisation, including disruptions in network integration and hub structure in neuropsychiatric and neurodegenerative conditions [23, 24].
- **Orthogonal Minimum Spanning Tree (OMST)**: extends the classical Minimum Spanning Tree (MST) framework by iteratively extracting multiple spanning trees that are mutually orthogonal, i.e., constructed on residual connectivity matrices after the removal of edges selected in the previous step

iterations. The final network is obtained by combining these orthogonal trees, thereby progressively increasing network density while preserving strict control over connectedness and sparsity [25].

2.4   Network Measures

Topological measures provide a quantitative characterisation of a network's structural organisation by describing how nodes and edges are interconnected. These measures are essential for assessing key properties of complex systems, including efficiency, robustness, and modular organisation, and are particularly relevant for the analysis of biological and brain networks [26,27]. In this study, both global and local topological measures were computed to comprehensively characterise network organisation at the whole-network and node-specific levels. The measures that we considered are:

- **_Local Efficiency_**: quantifies how efficiently information is exchanged among its neighbours when that node is removed.
  In Eq. 4, the mathematical details of the local efficiency are shown.

$$E_{loc} = \frac{1}{n} \sum_{i \in N} E_{loc,i} = \frac{1}{n} \sum_{i \in N} \frac{\sum_{j,h \in N; j \neq i, h \neq i} a_{ij} a_{ih} [d_{jh}(N_i)]^{-1}}{k_i(k_i - 1)}, \tag{4}$$

  where $d_{jh}(N_i)$ is the shortest path length between nodes j and h restricted to the subgraph formed by the neighbours of i. Local efficiency reflects the system's ability to sustain efficient information transfer within local clusters [28];
- **_Global Efficiency_**: provides an alternative but complementary view of integration.
  In Eq. 5 shows the mathematical formula of global efficiency.

$$E_{glob} = \frac{1}{n} \sum_{i \in N} E_i = \frac{1}{n} \sum_{i \in N} \frac{\sum_{j \in N; j \neq i} d_{ij}^{-1}}{n - 1}, \tag{5}$$

In general, global efficiency is high in networks that maintain short paths even between distant nodes, such as functional brain networks during task activation [29].
- **_Degree_**: it is defined as the number of edges connected to node i and the formula is illustrated in Eq. 6.

$$k_i = \sum_{j \in N} a_{ij}, \tag{6}$$

where N is the set of all nodes in the network, and a_{ij} denotes the presence (1) or absence (0) of an edge between nodes i and j. Nodes with high degree, known as *hubs*, are critical for maintaining network connectivity, while nodes with low degree (*non-hubs*) often play peripheral roles. The collection of all degree values defines the *degree distribution*, an important indicator of network organisation and growth [30].

– **Strength**: extends the concept of degree to weighted networks by taking into account the magnitude of the connections.

Node strength is defined as the sum of the weights of all edges connected to node i, as shown in Eq. 7.

$$s_i = \sum_{j \in N} w_{ij}, \tag{7}$$

where w_{ij} represents the weight of the edge between nodes i and j, and N is the set of all nodes in the network.

Strength reflects not only the number of connections a node has, but also the strength of these connections.

At the network level, the distribution of node strength provides important information about the organisation and heterogeneity of connection weights, complementing the degree distribution in unweighted graphs [31]

– **Betweenness Centrality**: quantifies the proportion of shortest paths that pass through a given node.

In particular, Eq. 8 illustrates the mathematical definition of betweenness centrality.

$$b_i = \frac{1}{(n-1)(n-2)} \sum_{h,j \in N; h \neq i, j \neq i} \frac{\sigma_{hj}(i)}{\sigma_{hj}}, \tag{8}$$

where n is the total number of nodes, σ_{hj} is the number of shortest paths between nodes h and j, and $\sigma_{hj}(i)$ is the number of such paths passing through node i. Nodes with high betweenness act as communication bridges and are often critical for information flow in the brain or metabolic networks [32,33].

3   Results and Discussion

After constructing functional brain networks from EEG connectivity matrices, we proceeded with the analysis by evaluating the global and local topological measures of the resulting networks. This analysis was designed to characterise the organisation of the functional brain network across multiple spatial scales, starting from EEG data from our clinical domain. The main objective of this study is to evaluate how methodological choices in network construction influence network analysis results, both in terms of connectivity metrics (PLI, PLV, WPLI) and binarisation and graph-construction strategies (MED, MST, MCC, OMST). The first set of metrics examined comprises global network measures, with a particular focus on global efficiency shown in Fig. 1; it summarises frequency bands, connectivity estimators, and graph construction strategies. The distributions of global efficiency reveal a strong dependence on both the frequency band and the connectivity matrix used to construct the network. In particular, networks constructed using PLV and WPLI in the alpha and theta bands show greater separation of groups (CNT, PNES, EPI). In contrast, PLI-based networks and gamma-band networks show largely overlapping distributions, suggesting limited discriminatory power of global measures in these configurations. Furthermore, when comparing binarisation and graph construction strategies, additional differences emerge: more conservative approaches, such as Minimum Spanning Tree (MST), tend to produce lower, more compressed global efficiency values, further reducing variability between groups. Conversely, denser and more informative strategies, including MCC and OMST, retain a greater proportion of functional connections and exhibit increased variability in global measures.

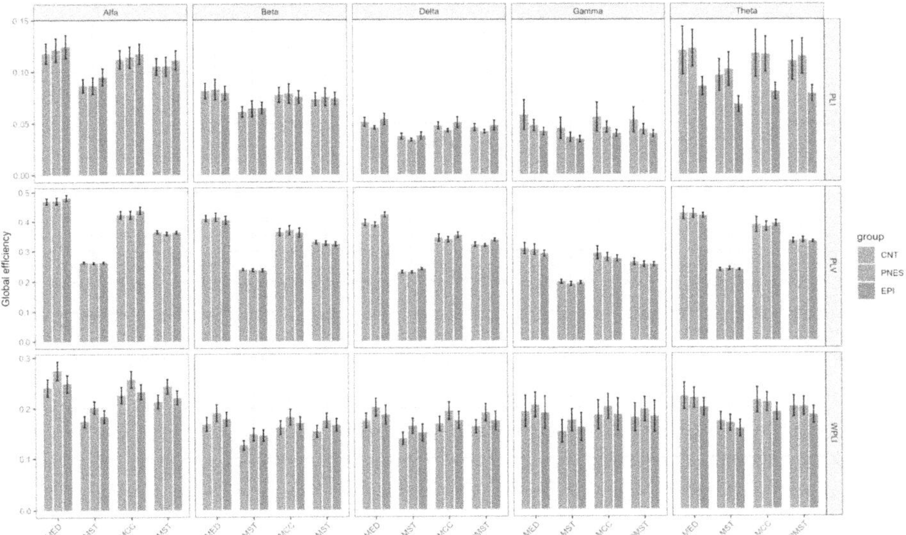

Fig. 1. Global efficiency across frequency bands, connectivity metrics, and graph construction strategies. No statistically significant differences were observed across groups, but results depend on the connectivity metric and graph construction method, with MCC and OMST showing greater variability than MST.

In contrast to global efficiency, local efficiency captures the efficiency of information within the neighbourhood of nodes, providing a measure of local segregation and short-range functional organisation. As shown in Fig. 2, local efficiency is strongly influenced by both the connectivity estimator and the graph construction strategy. Compared to MCC and OMST, MED-based networks exhibit reduced local efficiency values and limited between-group variability, whereas MST-based networks display strongly compressed or near-zero values, reflecting their tree-like topology and the absence of local clustering. In contrast, denser construction strategies such as MCC and OMST preserve local neighbourhood structure and consistently yield higher local efficiency values, particularly when combined with PLV and WPLI in the alpha, beta, and theta bands, where clearer group-level differences can be observed.

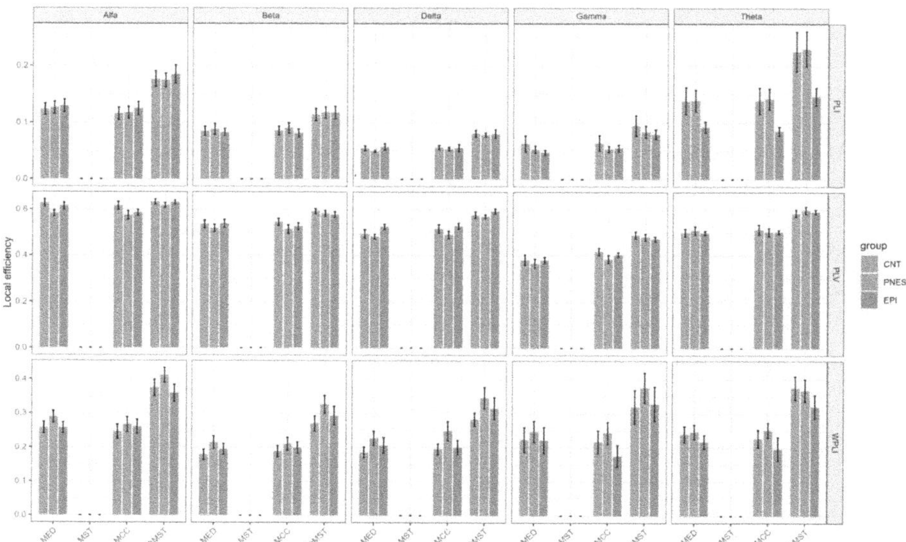

Fig. 2. Local efficiency across frequency bands, connectivity metrics, and graph construction strategies. No statistically significant differences were observed across groups, but MCC and OMST show higher values and variability compared to MED and MST.

Although no statistically significant differences were observed in the joint comparison across the three groups, pairwise analyses revealed significant effects under specific methodological configurations. As shown in Fig. 3, these effects are primarily observed in the delta and theta frequency bands, depending on the graph construction strategy adopted. In particular, the CNT vs PNES comparison did not show statistically significant differences in local efficiency across any of the evaluated configurations. This finding is consistent with previous reports indicating a substantial overlap in EEG-derived functional connectivity patterns between healthy controls and PNES patients, which may limit discriminability at the network level [34]. In contrast, for the CNT vs EPI comparison, significant effects were mainly observed in the delta band, emerging under graph construction strategies that preserve a broader set of connections, such as MED and OMST. In these configurations, EPI networks consistently exhibited higher local efficiency than CNT, suggesting increased local clustering and enhanced short-range information processing. These effects were most pronounced for PLV-based connectivity, indicating that phase synchronisation metrics are particularly sensitive to epilepsy-related alterations in local network organisation. Conversely, no significant differences were detected when MST-based graphs were employed, suggesting that overly sparse network representations may obscure group-specific topological alterations. In the theta band, the CNT vs EPI comparison revealed fewer but still discernible effects, again primarily associated with PLV connectivity combined with OMST filtering. This pattern suggests that theta-band alterations in epilepsy are more subtle and become detectable only when the graph construction strategy balances sparsity with the retention of redundant yet informative connections. A similar trend was observed in the comparison between PNES and EPI, where statistically significant differences emerged under specific graph construction strategies. In particular, with graphs constructed using MED, PNES networks tended to show lower local efficiency than EPI networks, suggesting less local segregation. Conversely, using the MCC strategy, PNES networks showed higher local efficiency than EPI networks, while maintaining the statistical significance of the comparison. This reversal suggests that the differences between PNES and EPI are not unambiguous but critically depend on the filtering criterion adopted, reflecting the varying balance between network density, control of inter-modular connections, and preservation of local topological structure. Overall, the presence of significant effects with both MED and MCC, albeit in opposite directions, suggests that the alterations in local efficiency observed in the PNES vs EPI comparison are sensitive to methodological choices, but at the same time confirms the existence of relevant topological differences between the two clinical conditions.

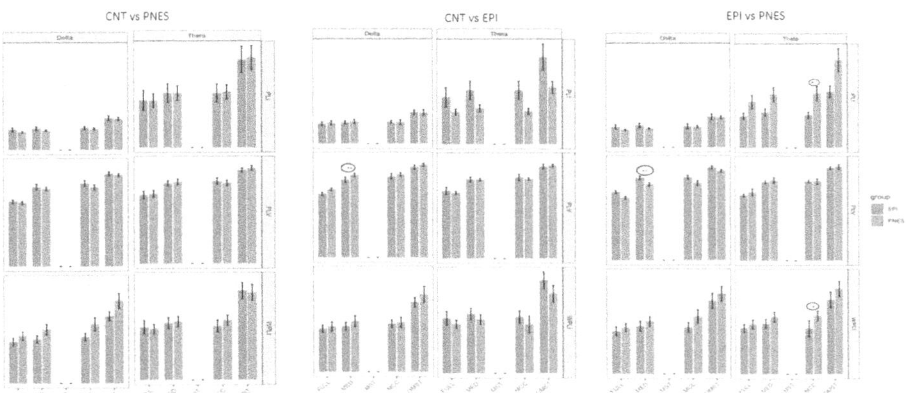

Fig. 3. Pairwise comparisons of local efficiency between clinical groups across delta and theta frequency bands.

After evaluating global efficiency (EG) and local efficiency (EL) across network configurations, the topographical distribution of node degree (node size) and node strength (colour coding) was analysed for all considered cases. Across all graph construction strategies, PLV-based networks exhibit higher and more spatially homogeneous degree and strength values. This behaviour reflects the sensitivity of PLV to zero-lag synchronisation, which tends to produce denser network representations. In contrast, PLI and WPLI yield more conservative and spatially heterogeneous nodal patterns. When comparing binarisation strategies, OMST-based networks show a marked reduction in redundant connections while preserving structurally meaningful hubs. This effect is particularly evident for the

OMST–PLI Fig. 4a and OMST–WPLI Fig. 4b configurations, EPI subjects tend to exhibit increased nodal strength in specific regions, consistent with enhanced local synchronisation, whereas CNT and PNES display more distributed connectivity patterns.

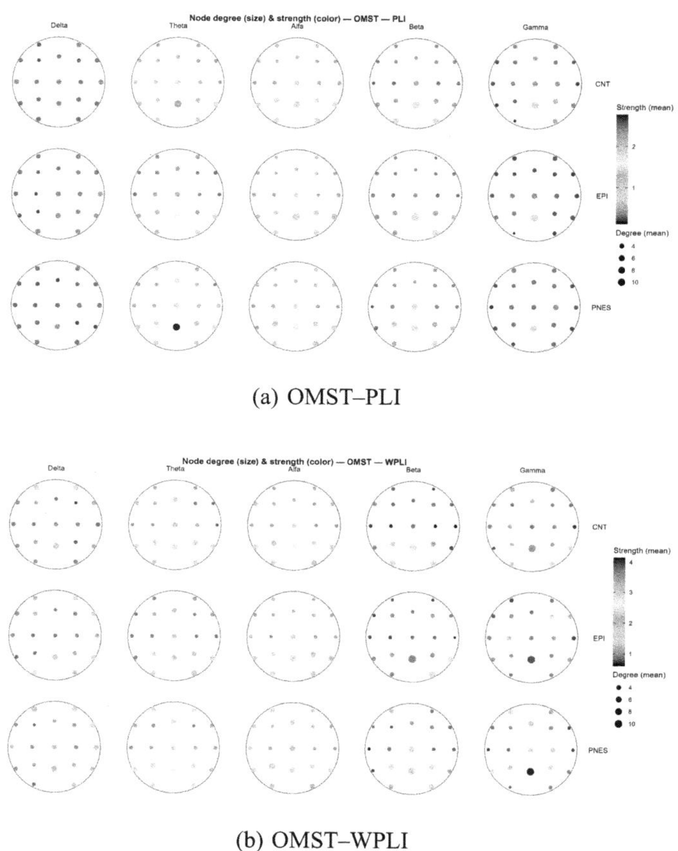

(a) OMST–PLI

(b) OMST–WPLI

Fig. 4. Topographical distribution of node degree (node size) and node strength (colour) for OMST-based networks constructed using PLI (a) and WPLI (b).

In addition, we also calculated betweenness centrality (BC) to reflect the topological role of a node within the network structure. In fact, PLV-based networks tend to generate dense networks due to their sensitivity to zero-delay synchronisation and have an inflated number of hubs. The PLI configuration partially mitigates this problem by discarding zero-delay interactions. In contrast, WPLI does not introduce additional information but removes spurious connections to a sufficient extent to make the betweenness centrality interpretable. The betweenness centrality (BC) measure was calculated to characterise the topological role of each node within the network structure. Topographic maps of BC were generated for all connectivity metrics and graph construction strategies; however, Fig. 5 shows only the WPLI-based comparison between EPI and PNES, as this configuration showed the most stable and interpretable effects among the filtering methods. Node-level BC values are projected onto the scalp using interpolated topographic maps, with warmer colours indicating higher BC values.

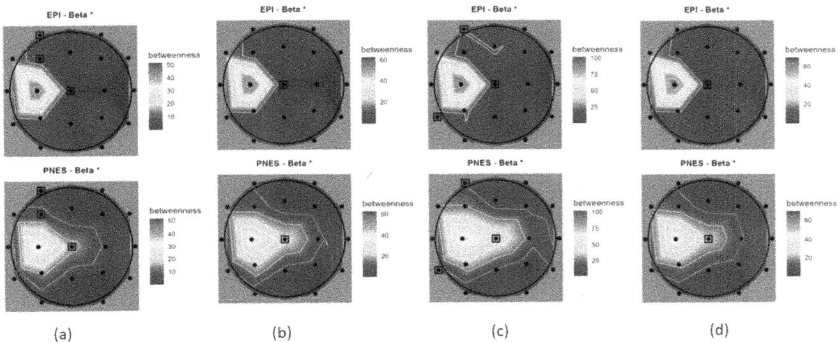

Fig. 5. Topographic maps of betweenness centrality (BC) in the beta band for the WPLI-based EPI vs PNES comparison across different graph construction strategies: (a) WPLI–MED, (b) WPLI–MCC, (c) WPLI–MST, (d) WPLI–OMST.

Specifically, in the WPLI-based comparison between EPI and PNES, the beta band consistently showed statistically significant differences in BC between the MED, MCC, MST and OMST configurations. These differences were visible not only at the global network level but also at the electrode level in the corresponding topographic maps. This convergence between frequency band, connectivity metric, and threshold strategy strongly suggests that the effects observed in the beta band are not determined by a specific filtering choice but are associated with clinical characteristics such as cortical integration, network stabilisation, and maintenance of functional states [34].

4   Conclusions

In this paper, we propose a systematic framework for the construction and analysis of EEG-based functional brain networks, aimed at assessing the impact of connectivity estimators and graph construction strategies on network topology. By combining phase-based connectivity measures (PLI, PLV, WPLI) with multiple binarisation approaches (MED, MCC, MST, OMST), the study highlights how methodological choices substantially influence the resulting network representations. The results indicate that global efficiency alone provides limited discriminative power, while local efficiency and nodal-level analyses offer more informative insights, particularly when denser and data-driven strategies such as MCC and OMST are adopted. Epilepsy-related alterations are more consistently detected in the delta and theta bands, especially when PLV-based connectivity is combined with graph constructions that preserve local clustering. In addition, betweenness centrality contributed to identifying network hubs and communication pathways that differ across clinical groups, providing indications on the reorganisation of information flow within functional brain networks. Despite the encouraging results, this study is limited by the use of a single resting-state EEG dataset and a relatively small sample size. Future work will focus on extending the proposed workflow to larger and more diverse datasets, exploring alternative brain network methodologies, and integrating machine learning approaches to enhance the clinical applicability of EEG-based functional network analysis.

Acknowledgments. This work was funded by the Next Generation EUItalian NRRP, Mission 4, Component 2, Investment 1.5, call for the creation and strengthening of 'Innovation Ecosystems', building 'Territorial R& D Leaders' (Directorial Decree n. 2021/3277)- project Tech4You- Technologies for climate change adaptation and quality of life improvement, n.ECS0000009. This work reflects only the authors' views and opinions, neither the Ministry for University and Research nor The European Commission can be considered responsible for them.

References

1. Brown, R.J., Reuber, M.: Psychological and psychiatric aspects of psychogenic non-epileptic seizures (PNES): a systematic review. Clin. Psychol. Rev. **45**, 157–182 (2016)
2. Subha, D.P., et al.: EEG signal analysis: a survey. J. Med. Syst. **34**(2), 195–212 (2010)
3. Milano, M., et al.: A computational approach to study age-related modifications of the genes involved in Parkinson's disease. Comput. Biol. Med. **196**, 110765 (2025)
4. Agapito, G., et al.: Ten practical tips and tricks to improve the effectiveness of biological network alignment. PLoS Comput. Biol. **21**(9), e1013386 (2025)
5. Lazzaro, I., et al.: A multilayer network-based method for brain connectivity analysis from EEG data. In: 2024 IEEE International Conference on Bioinformatics and Biomedicine (BIBM), pp. 6914–6920. IEEE (2024)
6. Roshanaei, M., et al.: EEG-based functional and effective connectivity patterns during emotional episodes using graph theoretical analysis. Sci. Rep. **15**(1), 2174 (2025)
7. Ortiz, E., et al.: Weighted phase lag index and graph analysis: preliminary investigation of functional connectivity during resting state in children. Comput. Math. Methods Med. **2012**(1), 186353 (2012)
8. Abadal, S., et al.: Graph neural networks for electroencephalogram analysis: Alzheimer's disease and epilepsy use cases. Neural Netw. **181**, 106792 (2025)
9. Abazid, M., et al.: Weighted brain network analysis on different stages of clinical cognitive decline. Bioengineering **9**(2), 62 (2022)
10. Chen, W., et al.: MDD brain network analysis based on EEG functional connectivity and graph theory. Heliyon **10**(17) (2024)

11. Subramaniyam, N.P., Thiagarajan, T.C.: A novel method for estimating functional connectivity from EEG coherence potentials. Sci. Rep. **15**(1), 10723 (2025)
12. Zucco, C., et al.: Resting-state EEG classification for PNES diagnosis. In: International Conference on Computational Science, pp. 526–538. Springer (2022)
13. Seal, A., et al.: DeprNet: a deep convolution neural network framework for detecting depression using EEG. IEEE Trans. Instrum. Measur. **70**, 1–13 (2021)
14. Gonuguntla, V., Kim, J.-H.: EEG-based functional connectivity representation using phase locking value for brain network based applications. In: 2020 42nd Annual International Conference of the IEEE Engineering in Medicine & Biology Society (EMBC), pp. 2853–2856. IEEE (2020)
15. Trinh, T.-T., et al.: PLI-based connectivity in resting-EEG is a robust and generalizable feature for detecting MCI and AD: a validation on a diverse multisite clinical dataset. In: 2023 45th Annual International Conference of the IEEE Engineering in Medicine & Biology Society (EMBC), pp. 1–6. IEEE (2023)
16. Wang, Z., et al.: Automated rest EEG-based diagnosis of depression and schizophrenia using a deep convolutional neural network. IEEE Access **10**, 104472–104485 (2022)
17. Imperatori, L.S., et al.: EEG functional connectivity metrics wPLI and wSMI account for distinct types of brain functional interactions. Sci. Rep. **9**(1), 8894 (2019)
18. Wang, B., et al.: Depression signal correlation identification from different EEG channels based on CNN feature extraction. Psychiatry Res. Neuroimaging **328**, 111582 (2023)
19. Jo, H.J., Lee, M.J., Lee, W.H.: Graph-theoretical analysis of EEG-based functional connectivity during emotional experience in virtual reality for emotion recognition. Sci. Rep. **15**(1), 39965 (2025)
20. Smith, K., Abásolo, D., Escudero, J.: Accounting for the complex hierarchical topology of EEG phase-based functional connectivity in network binarisation. PLoS ONE **12**(10), e0186164 (2017)
21. van Wijk, B.C.M., Stam, C.J., Daffertshofer, A.: Comparing brain networks of different size and density using graph theory. Hum. Brain Mapp. **31**(7), 1037–1053 (2010)
22. Vijayalakshmi, R., et al.: Minimum connected component-a novel approach to detection of cognitive load induced changes in functional brain networks. Neurocomputing **170**, 15–31 (2015)
23. Becske, M., et al.: Minimum spanning tree analysis of EEG restingstate functional networks in schizophrenia. Sci. Rep. **14**(1), 10495 (2024)
24. Ye, X., et al.: EEG-based minimum spanning tree analysis reveals network disruptions in Alzheimer's disease spectrum: an observational study. Front. Aging Neurosci. **17**, 1604345 (2025)
25. Adamovich, T., et al.: The thresholding problem and variability in the EEG graph network parameters. Sci. Rep. **12**(1), 18659 (2022)
26. Watts, D.J., Strogatz, S.H.: Collective dynamics of 'smallworld' networks. Nature **393**(6684), 440–442 (1998)
27. Rubinov, M., Sporns, O.: Complex network measures of brain connectivity: uses and interpretations. Neuroimage **52**(3), 1059–1069 (2010)
28. Gonzalez-Astudillo, J.: Development of network features for brain-computer interfaces. Ph.D. thesis. Sorbonne université (2022)
29. Latora, V., Marchiori, M.: Economic small-world behavior in weighted networks. Eur. Phys. J. B-Condens. Matter Complex Syst. **32**(2), 249–263 (2003)

30. Nykamp, D.Q.: The degree distribution of a network. Math Insight (2012)
31. Barrat, A., et al.: The architecture of complex weighted networks. Proc. Natl. Acad. Sci. **101**(11), 3747–3752 (2004)
32. Freeman, L.C.: Centrality in social networks conceptual clarification. Soc. Netw. **1**(3), 215–239 (1978)
33. Milano, M., Guzzi, P.H., Cannataro, M.: Network building and analysis in connectomics studies: a review of algorithms, databases and technologies. Netw. Model. Anal. Health Inform. Bioinform. **8**(1), 13 (2019)
34. Ahmadi, N., et al.: EEG-based classification of epilepsy and PNES: EEG microstate and functional brain network features. Brain Inform. **7**(1), 6 (2020)

Analysis of Parameter Settings for the Bat Algorithm Using Variance Evolution

Xin-She Yang$^{(\boxtimes)}$ and Mehmet Karamanoglu

Faculty of Science and Technology, Middlesex University, The Burroughs, London
NW4 4BT, UK
`x.yang@mdx.ac.uk`

Abstract. Parameter settings in evolutionary algorithms and meta-heuristics are important because such parameter values can influence the performance of algorithms under evaluation. For a given algorithm, there are many different numerical experiments to show that the algorithm can work well in practice; however, in most cases there is no theoretical analysis of parameter settings. In this work, we show that theoretical analysis using the theory of dynamical systems and evolution of population variance can give some good results in terms of parameter ranges for the bat algorithm. We also show that results from numerical experiments are consistent with theoretical bounds. Such analyses can provide good insights from different perspectives about the algorithmic characteristics such as variance evolution, transition between exploration and exploitation as well as convergence behaviour.

Keywords: Bat algorithm · Variance evolution · Nature-inspired computing · Optimization

1 Introduction

There are many algorithms and techniques for solving optimization problems in engineering and industrial applications. Most algorithms have algorithm-dependent parameters that may require a certain degree of tuning or parametric studies. As real-world design problems can be highly nonlinear and multi-modal, subject to multiple constraints [6,30], some traditional algorithms such as gradient-based algorithms cannot deal well with such nonlinear optimization problems. Nature-inspired algorithms are a class of algorithms that can have some advantages over traditional algorithms because they use some randomization components, which makes it more likely for algorithms to find the global optimal solutions. However, most nature-inspired metaheuristic algorithms tend to have more parameters than traditional algorithms [18,23,25,30], and their performance can be influenced largely by their parameter settings. Therefore, parameter tuning is important to metaheuristic algorithms.

Parameter tuning and parameter settings are important [11,16,17]. There are different ways for tuning parameters in algorithms, such as the Monte Carlo

P. Neumann et al. (Eds.): ICCS 2026, LNCS 16784, pp. 197–210, 2026.
https://doi.org/10.1007/978-3-032-29924-6_14

based methods [17] and others [11]. These methods can provide some great insights into the parameter value ranges and the best parameter values for a given algorithm for solving a set of optimization problems. Apart from parameter tuning methods, there are ways for analyzing algorithms to gain insights into their parameter settings, including the use of dynamical system theory [10] and the analysis of population variance [32]. In this paper, we will use the bat algorithm (BA) as the main focus to show that the evolution of population variance can obtain the same parameter ranges as other methods. In addition, the comparison of actual variance with theoretical predictions gives constant results, and the order of transition time from exploration to exploitation for a given problem is also consistent with theoretical analysis.

This paper is organized as follows. Section 2 briefly outlines the bat algorithm and parameter settings, whereas Sect. 3 presents the analysis of the variance evolution in the swarm population. Section 4 uses three benchmark functions to validate and compare the variance variations during iterations. Section 5 shows the parameter settings on acceptance probability of new solutions. Finally, Sect. 6 provides a summary with some discussion about future work.

2   Bat Algorithm and its Parameter Settings

The bat algorithm (BA) is a swarm intelligence based algorithms [29], which has been extended and applied to many applications [12, 21, 31]. For a swarm of n virtual bats at locations x_i^t with flying velocities v_i^t at iteration t, the main algorithmic equations of the BA can be rewritten as

$$\omega_i = \omega_{\min} + (\omega - \omega_{\min})\beta, \tag{1}$$

$$v_i^{t+1} = \rho v_i^t + (g - x_i^t)\omega_i, \tag{2}$$

$$x_i^{t+1} = x_i^t + v_i^{t+1}, \tag{3}$$

where g is the best solution found so far at iteration t among all the population x_i^t ($i = 1, 2, ..., n$). Here, ω_i is the frequency of bat i in the range from $\omega_{\min}$ to ω (maximum possible frequency), and β is a random number drawn from a uniform distribution [0, 1]. In addition, there are variations of pulse emission rate and loudness in the standard BA [29]. However, we will focus on the algorithmic equations only; therefore, there are two main parameters to be considered here: inertia weight ρ and the maximum frequency range ω.

To analyze the characteristics and iteration behaviour, fixed point theory based methods can usually work well for deterministic, gradient-based algorithms under certain assumptions. However, such methods do not work well for metaheuristic algorithms because randomization and random variables are used in metaheuristic algorithms [14, 19, 34]. Researchers have studied metaheuristic algorithms, such as particle swarm optimization (PSO), from different perspectives. For example, PSO has been analyzed using simplified dynamical system framework [10]. Genetic algorithms, differential evolution and other algorithms have been analyzed using Markov chains and other methods to gain insights about parameters and convergence [1–3,5,8,22,24,26,27].

For the bat algorithm, Chen et al. used both Markov chain framework and dynamical system [9] and obtained the appropriate ranges of the two parameters in the BA. They rewrote the BA as a dynamical system

$$v_i^{t+1} = \rho v_i^t + (g - x_i^t)\omega_i = -\omega x_i^t + \rho v_i^t + \omega g, \tag{4}$$

$$x_i^{t+1} = x_i^t + v_i^{t+1} = x_i^t + \rho v_i^t - \omega x_i^t + \omega g, \tag{5}$$

which can be expressed as a matrix form

$$Y^{t+1} = AY^t + Wg, \tag{6}$$

where

$$Y^t = \begin{pmatrix} x_i^t \\ v_i^t \end{pmatrix}, \quad A = \begin{pmatrix} 1 - \omega & \rho \\ -\omega & \rho \end{pmatrix}, \quad W = \begin{pmatrix} \omega \\ \omega \end{pmatrix}. \tag{7}$$

The stability theory of dynamical system requires both eigenvalues λ of A must satisfy $|\lambda| \leq 1$. Their analysis [9] concludes that

$$-1 \leq \rho \leq 1, \quad 0 \leq \omega \leq 2\rho + 2. \tag{8}$$

Though such analysis is insightful, however, it does not provide direct insight into how the population in the bat algorithm evolves during iterations. A different way of analyzing the population is to see how the population variance changes over time. For example, the population variance of differential evolution (DE) has been analyzed by Zaharie [32,33], which provides some insights about the influence of the mutation probability and variations of population variance in the DE.

For the BA, we can use a similar framework to analyze its variance evolution. In order to carry out such analysis and for the ease of notations for late analysis, we will drop the superscripts and use $z_i = x_i^{t+1}$, $y_i = v_i^{t+1}$, $x_i = x_i^t$, and $\omega_{\min} = 0$. Thus, we can rewrite the algorithmic Eqs. (2) and (3) as

$$y_i = \rho v_i + (g - x_i)\omega_i, \tag{9}$$

$$z_i = x_i + y_i = x_i + \rho v_i + (g - x_i)\omega_i, \tag{10}$$

where $\omega_i = \omega\beta$. This set of equations will be used for analysis in the next section.

3   Evolution of Variance

For a given random variable X with a mean of μ and a variance of σ^2, the mean of an arbitrary function $\phi(X)$ can be estimated by the Taylor expansion method [15,28] or the delta method in general [4,20].

$$\mathbb{E}\left[\phi(X)\right] = \phi(\mu) + \frac{\phi''(\mu)}{2}\sigma^2, \tag{11}$$

where ϕ'' is the second derivative of ϕ. The variance of $\phi(X)$ can be approximately by

$$\mathrm{Var}[\phi(X)] = [\phi'(\mu)]^2\sigma^2 + \frac{[\phi''(\mu)]^2}{2}\sigma^4. \tag{12}$$

3.1 Variance Evolution of the Bat Algorithm

Now we can carry out the theoretical analysis of the BA using a similar analysis for differential evolution [32,33]. For bat i, the updating Eq. (10) becomes

$$z_i = x_i + \rho v_i + (g - x_i)\omega\beta, \tag{13}$$

where β obeys a uniform distribution with a mean of β_0. When $\beta \sim U(0,1)$, we have $\beta_0 = 1/2$.

Similarly, the corresponding equation for bat j is

$$z_j = x_j + \rho v_j + (g - x_j)\omega\beta. \tag{14}$$

The differences of the preceding two equations give

$$(z_i - z_j) = (x_i - x_j) + \rho(v_i - v_j) - (x_i - x_j)\omega\beta, \tag{15}$$

which can be written compactly as

$$(z_i - z_j) = (1 - \omega\beta)(x_i - x_j) + \rho(v_i - v_j). \tag{16}$$

By squaring this equation, it becomes

$$(z_i - z_j)^2 = (1 - \omega\beta)^2(x_i - x_j)^2$$
$$+ \rho^2(v_i - v_j)^2 + 2(1 - \omega\beta)\rho(x_i - x_j)(v_i - v_j). \tag{17}$$

Though the population evolves with time, it is difficult to show if all bats or agents are completely independent in the statistical sense. However, as an approximation and for simplicity, we assume here that $(x_i - x_j)$ and $(v_i - v_j)$ are independent for a given population of size n. Thus, the expectation of the preceding equation becomes

$$\frac{2n}{(n-1)}\sigma_z^2 = (1 - \omega\beta_0)^2\frac{2n}{(n-1)}\sigma_x^2 + \rho^2\frac{2n}{(n-1)}\sigma_v^2. \tag{18}$$

where we have used

$$\mathbb{E}\left[(x_i - x_j)^2\right] = \frac{2n}{(n-1)}\sigma_x^2, \tag{19}$$

$$\mathbb{E}\left[(1 - \omega\beta)g(Z)\right] = \mathbb{E}\left[(1 - \omega\beta)\right]\mathbb{E}\left[g(Z)\right] \tag{20}$$

assuming β and $g(Z)$ are independent [4,32].

When the population size n is sufficiently large ($n \gg 1$), we have approximately $n/(n-1) \approx 1$ and

$$\sigma_z^2 = (1 - \omega\beta_0)^2\sigma_x^2 + \rho^2\sigma_v^2, \tag{21}$$

It should be sufficiently realistic to assume that $\sigma_v^2 = \sigma_x^2$ for the previous population at an earlier iteration because the variance of velocities is closely linked to the variance of positions. Then, Eq. (21) becomes

$$\sigma_z^2 = [(1 - \omega\beta_0)^2 + \rho^2]\sigma_x^2. \tag{22}$$

This is the change of variances in a single iteration. For $t \geq 1$ iterations, the new variance at iteration t becomes

$$\sigma_{z,t}^2 = \Lambda^t \sigma_0^2, \tag{23}$$

where σ_0^2 is the variance of the initial population. The factor is given by

$$\Lambda = (1 - \omega\beta_0)^2 + \rho^2 \leq 1. \tag{24}$$

The reduction of variance during the iteration requires that

$$\Lambda \leq 1. \tag{25}$$

At one extreme $\rho^2 = 1$ from $\rho = \pm 1$, it requires that

$$1 - \omega\beta_0 = 0, \tag{26}$$

or

$$\omega = \frac{1}{\beta_0} = 2, \tag{27}$$

for a uniform distribution in $[0, 1]$ with $\beta_0 = 1/2$. At the other extreme $\rho = 0$, Eq. (24) becomes

$$-1 \leq 1 - \omega\beta_0 \leq +1, \tag{28}$$

which gives

$$0 \leq \omega \leq \frac{2}{\beta_0} = 4. \tag{29}$$

This conclusion is consistent with the results, given in Eq. (8). That is

$$-1 \leq \rho \leq +1, \quad 0 \leq \omega \leq 4. \tag{30}$$

This shows that both the variance evolution and dynamical systems can obtain the same parameter value ranges for the BA.

3.2 Transition from Exploration to Exploitation

As the iterations and search for optimality continue, the overall population variance should gradually be reduced. Once the variances become sufficiently small, the diversity of the whole population may be limited, indicating potentially converged states.

There is a transition time constant $\tau = t_*$ when the population variance reduces to about $1/100 = 1\%$ of its initial variance. That is

$$\frac{\sigma_{z,t}^2}{\sigma_0^2} = \Lambda^{t_*} = [(1 - \omega\beta_0)^2 + \rho^2]^{t_*} = 0.01. \tag{31}$$

Taking the logarithm of both sides, we have

$$\tau = t_* = \frac{\ln 0.01}{\ln[(1 - \omega\beta_0)^2 + \rho^2]}. \tag{32}$$

In case of $\beta_0 = 1/2$ and $\omega = 2$, we have

$$\tau \approx \left\lceil \frac{4.6}{-\ln[(1 - 2 \times 1/2)^2 + \rho^2]} \right\rceil = \left\lceil \frac{2.3}{-\ln \rho} \right\rceil. \tag{33}$$

For $\rho = 0.9$, we have $\tau \approx 22$ after rounding up to the nearest integer. In practice, the transition can occur between τ to 2τ (or about 22 to 44 iterations for $\rho = 0.9$).

It is worth pointing out that the choice from the initial variance to $1/100$ of the initial value is rather arbitrary. If a different value such as $1/1000$ is used, the time constant τ only changes by a factor of $\ln 0.001 / \ln 0.01 = 1.5$, and this factor does not affect the results significantly. Thus, the transition time constant should be viewed as an approximate timescale for the transition from exploration to exploitation, which can be estimated by $O(-1/\ln \rho) = O(1/\ln(1/\rho))$.

Even the variance does not change much after this transition, the objective values continue to reduce (or improve) for minimization problems because the moves are mostly local refinements. However, if the transition occurs too early, it may lead to premature convergence of the population. Therefore, ρ cannot be too small. In practice, $\rho \in [0.7, 0.97]$ is the appropriate range, as indicated from our empirical parameter studies.

4   Numerical Experiments

To validate the above theoretical results and compare with the actual variations of variances for the BA, we will use three test benchmarks: the sphere function, the Rosenbrock function and the spring design benchmark. The sphere function is convex and separable, whereas the Rosenbrock function is non-convex and non-separable. The spring design problem is a nonlinear constrained design problem.

4.1   Sphere Function

For the D-dimensional sphere function

$$f_1(\boldsymbol{x}) = \sum_{i=1}^{D} x_i^2, \quad x_i \in \mathbb{R}, \tag{34}$$

we can use the BA to find its minimum $f_{\min} = 0$ at $(0, 0, ..., 0)$. For a population of size $n = 20$, the number of iteration is set to be $t_{\max} = 100$. For $D = 3$ and different values of $\rho = 0.7, 0.8, 0.9$ with $\omega = 2$, the theoretical prediction of the population variances with the actual population variance in simulation are shown in Fig. 1.

The transition from a quick variance reduction to a slower rate occurs between $\tau = 22$ to $2\tau = 44$ iterations, as seen in Fig. 1. After this transition period, even the variance does not change, the objective values continue to reduce for minimization problems, which shows that the search moves are mostly local refinements at later iterations.

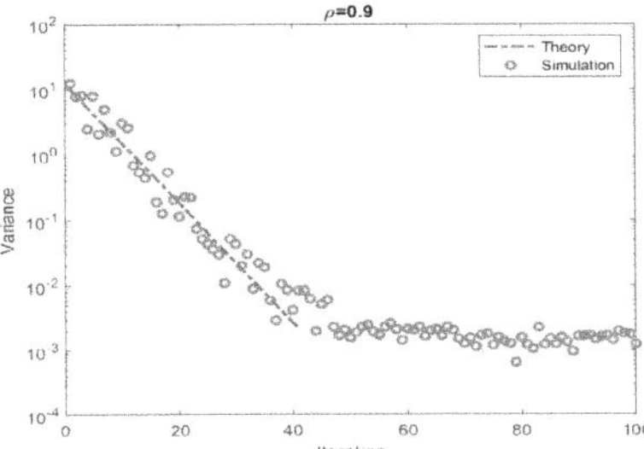
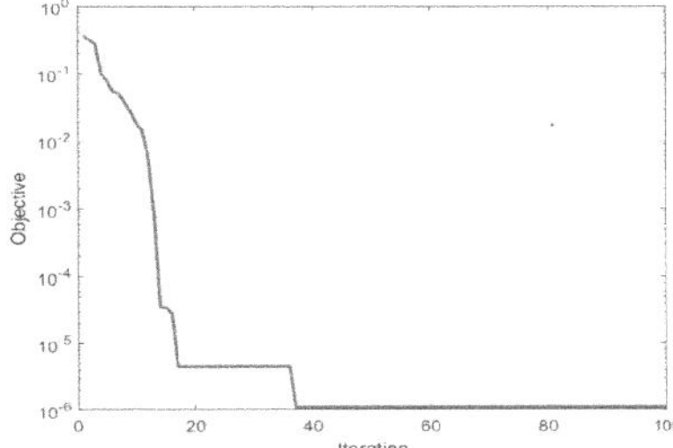

Fig. 1. Variation of population variance of the bat algorithm with $\rho = 0.9$ for the sphere function where the dashed line is the prediction from theory and the data are obtained from simulation (left). The variations of the objective values $f_{\min}$ are shown on the right.

Similarly, variances for $\rho = 0.8$ and $\rho = 0.7$ are also shown in Fig. 2. As we can see, the predictions are quite accurate at the earlier iterations for $\rho = 0.9$ and $\rho = 0.8$. When ρ gets smaller, the prediction is less accurate.

In addition, at later iterations, the predictions are very different, which may indicate that the BA becomes more exploitation focused. In this case, the search move and update of solutions are mainly local, and the acceptance rate of new moves becomes low. Thus both, the variances and the objective values become slow varying as see in the flat part of the curves.

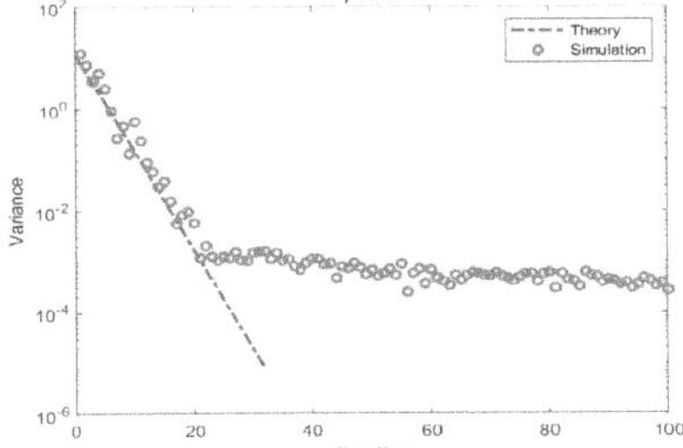
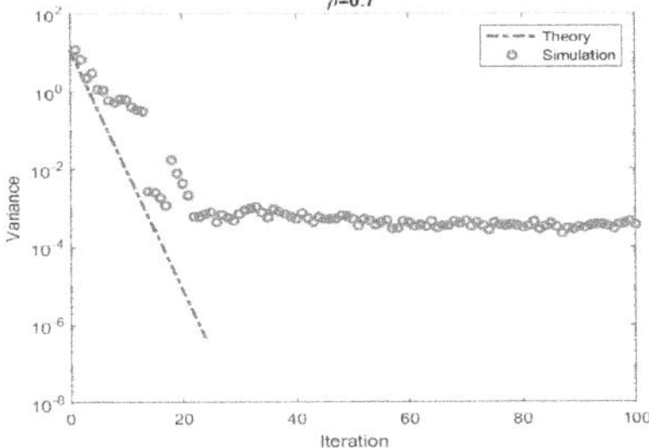

Fig. 2. Evolution of population variance at different stages of iterations for $\rho = 0.8$ (left) and $\rho = 0.7$ (right).

4.2 Rosenbrock Function

The sphere function is a convex function, and the evolution of its variances fits well to the theoretical trends for different values of ρ. Now let us test the theoretical results further using a non-convex function

$$f_2(\boldsymbol{x}) = (1 - x_1)^2 + 100 \sum_{i=2}^{D} (x_i - x_{i-1}^2)^2, \qquad -100 \le x_i \le 100. \qquad (35)$$

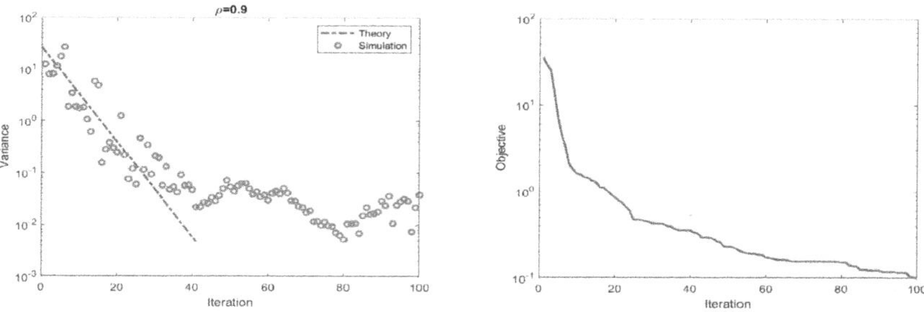

Fig. 3. The population variance for $\rho = 0.9$ for the Rosenbrock function (left) and the variations of objective values (right).

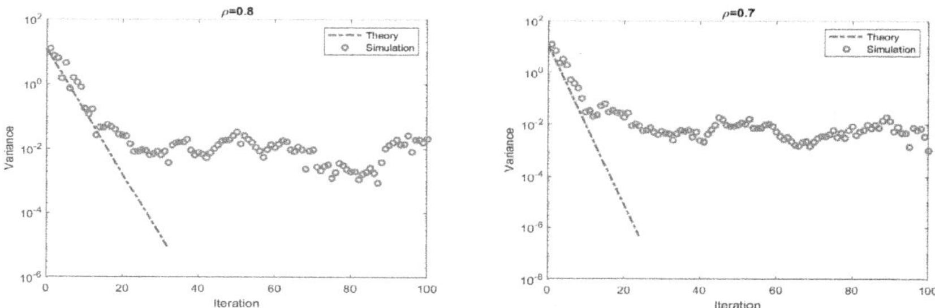

Fig. 4. The evolution of f_2 variances for $\rho = 0.8$ (left) and $\rho = 0.7$ (right).

Using the same parameter settings of the BA ($n = 20$, $t_{\max} = 100$, $D = 3$, and $\rho = 0.7, 0.8, 0.9$), the optimal solutions are found by the BA. The variations of the variances are shown in Figs. 3 and 4 where we can see that the actual variations of variances fit reasonably well to the theoretical trend on the log scale at the initial stage of the iterations. As the iteration continues, the search process becomes more focused on the local exploitation, thus the variances becomes slow varying, but objective values continue to reduce due to local refinement.

The transition from exploration to exploitation also occurs at about 22 to 44 iterations for $\rho = 0.9$. This means that the transition seems to be independent of the benchmarks in the simulation.

4.3   Spring Design

The spring design problem is to manufacture a compression and tension spring from a wire of diameter w, which will form a spring with a mean coil diameter D and the number m of active coils. The objective is to minimize the overall weight or mass

$$\min \ f(w, D, m) = (2 + m)w^2 D, \tag{36}$$

subject to four constraints

$$g_1 = 1 - \frac{mD^3}{71785w^4} \leq 0, \tag{37}$$

$$g_2 = \frac{(4D^2 - wD)}{12566(Dw^3 - w^4)} + \frac{1}{5108w^2} - 1 \leq 0, \tag{38}$$

$$g_3 = 1 - \frac{140.45w}{mD^2} \leq 0, \tag{39}$$

$$g_4 = \frac{(w + D)}{1.5} - 1 \leq 0. \tag{40}$$

These constraints are related to deflection, shear stress, frequency and physical dimension constraints. In the simple domain of

$$0.05 \leq w \leq 1.00, \quad 0.25 \leq D \leq 1.30, \quad 2 \leq m \leq 15, \tag{41}$$

the best solution in the current literature [7,13] is

$$f_{\min} = 0.01266522, \quad w = 0.05169, \quad D = 0.35673, \quad m = 11.2885. \tag{42}$$

With the same parameter settings ($t_{\max} = 100$, $n = 20$, $\rho = 0.7$), we have run the BA to find its optimal solutions. The obtained objective values and variances are plotted in Fig. 5.

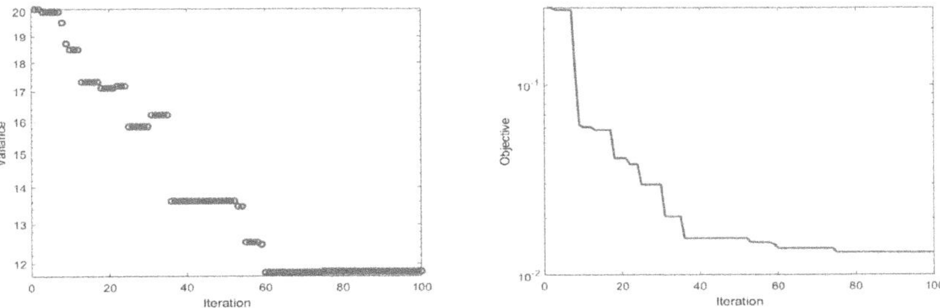

Fig. 5. The evolution of variances and spring design objective values for $\rho = 0.7$.

From Fig. 5, we can see that the variances reduce quite rapidly at the initial stage of iterations, and the transition from exploration to exploitation seems to occur between 35 to 60 iterations. Though the variances do not change much from iteration 60 onwards, the objective continues to improve/reduce gradually, which means that late iterations are mainly local exploitative moves. This characteristic is consistent with the theoretical results.

5   Probability of Acceptance

In the above analysis, we have considered only two parameters ρ and ω. In the BA, there is a switching probability between two branches based on the decision about the new solution. If a new solution is better, it will be accepted. If the solution is partially improved (i.e., not the new best solution but better than some of the old solutions in the population), it will be accepted by comparing with a random number. In essence, there is a probability p of acceptance for a given new solution.

In the rest of this paper, let us explore the possible influence of parameter settings on the effective acceptability p of new moves or solutions. For a new search move or a new solution, it will be accepted with a probability p and rejected with a probability of $1-p$. Alternatively, the solution in the new iteration will be the new solution with probability of p, while keeping the old solution x_i with a probability of $1 - p$. Thus, Eq. (10) can be rewritten as

$$z_i = (1 - p) \underbrace{x_i}_{\text{old}} + p \underbrace{[x_i + \rho v_i + (g - x_i)\omega_i]}_{\text{new solution}}$$

$$= (1 - p)x_i + px_i + \rho p v_i + pg\omega\beta - p\omega\beta x_i, \tag{43}$$

where we have used $\omega_i = \omega\beta$ with β being a uniform distribution.

In our derivations, we will need to use the properties of the variance of two uncorrelated random variables U and V with means μ_U and μ_V and variances σ_U^2 and σ_V^2, respectively. The variance of their product can be calculated by

$$\sigma_{UV}^2 = \mathrm{Var}(UV) = (\sigma_U^2 + \mu_U^2)(\sigma_V^2 + \mu_V^2) - \mu_U^2\mu_V^2, \tag{44}$$

with the standard properties

$$\mathrm{Var}(aU \pm bV) = a^2\sigma_U^2 + b^2\sigma_V^2 \pm 2ab\,\mathrm{cov}(U, V)$$

$$= a^2\sigma_U^2 + b^2\sigma_V^2, \quad a, b \in \mathbb{R}, \tag{45}$$

where we have assumed that U and V are uncorrelated. That is, $\mathrm{cov}(U, V)=0$ in the current context for the swarm population. Again as pointed out earlier, this assumption is an approximation.

Let σ_x^2 be the variance of x_i, σ_v^2 be the variance of v_i, and σ_z^2 be the variance of z_i. By taking the variance of Eq. (43), we have

$$\sigma_z^2 = (1 - p)^2\sigma_x^2 + p^2\sigma_x^2$$

$$+ p^2\rho^2\sigma_v^2 + p^2\omega^2\mathrm{Var}(g\beta) + \omega^2 p^2\mathrm{Var}(x_i\beta). \tag{46}$$

Here, we can assume that g and β are uncorrelated, and x_i and β are also uncorrelated.

The mean and variance of a uniform distribution $\beta \in [0, 1]$ are $\mu_\beta = 1/2$ and $\sigma_\beta^2 = 1/12$, respectively. The mean of g is g, and the variance of g is σ_g^2, which can be considered as the same as σ_x^2. Similarly, the mean and variance of x_i are μ_x and σ_x^2, respectively. As the current best solution is usually obtained from x_i, we can approximate it as $g = \mu_x$. Thus, we have

$$\mathrm{Var}(g\beta) = (\sigma_x^2 + g^2)\left[\frac{1}{12} + \left(\frac{1}{2}\right)^2\right] - g^2\left(\frac{1}{2}\right)^2 = \frac{\sigma_x^2}{12} + \frac{g^2}{12} + \frac{\sigma_x^2}{4}, \tag{47}$$

and

$$\mathrm{Var}(x_i\beta) = (\sigma_x^2 + \mu_x^2)\left[\frac{1}{12} + \left(\frac{1}{2}\right)^2\right] - \mu_x^2 \left(\frac{1}{2}\right)^2$$

$$= \frac{\sigma_x^2}{12} + \frac{g^2}{12} + \frac{\sigma_x^2}{4}. \tag{48}$$

Now Eq. (46) becomes

$$\sigma_z^2 = (1-p)^2\sigma_x^2 + p^2\sigma_x^2 + p^2\rho^2\sigma_v^2 + p^2\omega^2\left[\frac{2\sigma_x^2}{3} + \frac{g^2}{12}\right]. \tag{49}$$

For simplicity, we can also assume that σ_v^2 is the same as that for x_i in the previous iteration (from Eq. (3)).

With the above assumptions and notations, the preceding equation becomes

$$\sigma_z^2 = \left[(1-p)^2 + \frac{2p^2\omega^2}{3} + p^2\right]\sigma_x^2 + p^2\rho^2\sigma_x^2$$

$$= \left[(1 - 2p + 2p^2 + \frac{2p^2\omega^2}{3} + p^2\rho^2\right]\sigma_x^2 + p^2\omega^2\frac{g^2}{12}. \tag{50}$$

For many test functions or design benchmarks, the best solutions are either close to $x_* = 0$ or a known vector constant. Thus, we can consider the final term on the right-hand side of the above equation as a constant or zero in most cases.

Thus, the reduction of the variance and the convergence of the algorithm requires that

$$Q = 1 - 2p + 2p^2 + \frac{2p^2\omega^2}{3} + p^2\rho^2 \le 1, \tag{51}$$

which means that

$$p \le \frac{2}{2 + 2\omega^2/3 + \rho^2} = \frac{1}{1 + \omega^2/3 + \rho^2/2}, \tag{52}$$

where we have used the fact that $p > 0$. It is easy to see that this result implies that $0 < p \le 1$ is always true.

For the special case of $\rho = 1$ and $\omega = 4$, we have

$$\rho \le \frac{6}{41} \approx 0.146. \tag{53}$$

This is the maximum theoretical probability of accepting new solutions, but the true rate of acceptance of new moves can be lower in practice. The comparison of actual probability of acceptance is summarized in Table 1. As we can see, the theoretical values provide an upper bound for the true acceptance probability. Obviously, the true acceptance rate can depend on the ways of generating new solutions, the diversity of population, feasibility of the new solutions and the locality of the new solutions.

Table 1. Comparison of the actual acceptance probability with the theoretical limit.

Function	ρ	Maximum probability from theory	Actual Rate
f_1	0.9	0.365	0.140
	0.8	0.377	0.102
	0.7	0.388	0.091
f_2	0.9	0.365	0.307
	0.8	0.377	0.224
	0.7	0.388	0.258
Spring	0.9	0.365	0.076
	0.8	0.377	0.089
	0.7	0.388	0.115

6 Conclusion and Discussion

We have analyzed the evolution of variance for the bat algorithm in this work and have shown that the parameter ranges are consistent with the results from other theoretical analysis using dynamical system theory. In addition, the change in the variance reduction can also indicate a transition in the search mechanism from global exploration to local exploitation. The characteristics of variance evolution can be predicted well at the earlier stage of the iterations. This shows that the theoretical insights and results are correct.

We also have estimated the upper limit of the acceptance probability of new solutions in the population using variance analysis, and the results from numerical experiments are largely consistent with theoretical indications. The difference between the theoretical bounds and the actual acceptance rates means that the theory tends to over-estimate the probability. Thus, there is room for improvement to provide a tight bound. This can form a research topic for further studies.

Furthermore, the current work indicates that the transition timescale seems to be independent of the problems to be solved. In practice, there may be other factors that could affect the behaviour of a swarm population, such as population size, modality of the problem, and nonlinearity of the constraints as well as the initialization of the swarm population. This work can form the basis for further research.

Disclosure of Interests. The authors confirm that there are no relevant financial or non-financial competing interests to report. No funding was received for this research work. No datasets were received/used. All results are simulated and reproducible from the proposed method.

References

1. Aytug, H., Bhattacharrya, S., Koehler, G.J.: A Markov chain analysis of genetic algorithms with power of 2 cardinality alphabets. Eur. J. Oper. Res. **96**(1), 195–201 (1996)
2. Aytug, H., Koehler, G.J.: New stopping criterion for genetic algorithms. Eur. J. Oper. Res. **126**(2), 662–674 (2000)
3. Beltrami, E.J.: Mathematics for Dynamic Modeling, 2nd edn. Academic Press, San Diego (1998)
4. Benaroya, H., Han, S.M.: Probability Models in Engineering and Science. CRC Press, Boca Raton (2005)
5. Bergstra, J., Bengio, Y.: Random search for hyper-parameter optimization. J. Mach. Learn. Res. **13**, 281–305 (2012)
6. Boyd, S.P., Vandenberghe, L.: Convex Optimization. Cambridge University Press, Cambridge (2004)
7. Cagnina, L.C., Esquivel, S.C., Coello Coello, A.C.: Solving engineering optimization problems with the simple constrained particle swarm optimizer. Informatica **32**(2), 319–326 (2008)
8. Chatterjee, A., Siarry, P.: Nonlinear inertia variation for dynamic adaptation in particle swarm optimization. Comput. Oper. Res. **33**(3), 859–871 (2006)
9. Chen, S., Peng, G.H., He, X.S., Yang, X.S.: Global convergence analysis of the bat algorithm using a Markovian framework and dynamic system theory. Expert Syst. Appl. **114**(1), 173–182 (2018)
10. Clerc, M., Kennedy, J.: The particle swarm: explosion, stability, and convergence in a multidimensional complex space. IEEE Trans. Evol. Comput. **6**(1), 58–73 (2002)
11. Eiben, A.E., Smit, S.K.: Parameter tuning for configuring and analyzing evolutionary algorithms. Swarm Evol. Comput. **1**(1), 19–31 (2011)
12. Gandom, A.H., Yang, X.S.: Chaotic bat algorithm. J. Comput. Sci. **5**(2), 224–232 (2014)
13. Gandomi, A.H., Yang, X.S., Alavi, A.H., Talatahari, S.: Bat algorithm for constrained optimization tasks. Neural Comput. Appl. **22**(6), 1239–1255 (2013)
14. Granas, A., Dugundji, J.: Fixed Point Theory. Springer, New York (2003)
15. Grindstead, C.M., Snell, J.L.: Introduction to Probability, 2nd edn. Americal Mathematical Society, Providence (1997)
16. Hekmatinia, A., Shanghooshabad, A.M., Motevali, M.M., Almasi, M.: Tuning parameter via a new rapid, accurate and parameter-less method using meta-learning. Int. J. Data Mining Model. Manag. **11**(4), 366–390 (2019)
17. Joy, G., Huyck, C., Yang, X.S.: Parameter tuning of the firefly algorithm by three tuning methods: standard Monte Carlo, quasi-Monte Carlo and Latin hypercube sampling methods. J. Comput. Sci. **87**, Article 102588 (2025)
18. Kennedy, J., Eberhart, R.: Particle swarm optimization. In: Proceedings of the IEEE International Conference on Neural Networks, pp. 1942–1948. IEEE, Piscataway, NJ, USA (1995)
19. Khamsi, M.A., Kirk, W.A.: An Introduction to Metric Space and Fixed Point Theory. Wiley, New York (2001)
20. Oehlert, G.W.: A note on the delta method. Am. Stat. **46**(1), 27–29 (1992)
21. Osaba, E., Yang, X.S., Diaz, F., Lopez-Garcia, P., Carballedo, R.: An improved discrete bat algorithm for symmetric and assymmetric travelling salesman problems. Eng. Appl. Artif. Intell. **48**(1), 59–71 (2016)

22. Pan, F., Li, X., Zhou, Q., Li, W., Gao, Q.: Analysis of standard particle swarm optimization algorithm based on Markov chain. Acta Automatica Sinica **39**(4), 381–389 (2013)
23. Pham, D., Ghanbarzadeh, A., Koc, E., Otri, S., Rahim, S., Zaidi, M.: The bees algorithm, technical note. Technical report, Cardiff University, Manufacturing Engineering Center, Cardiff (2005)
24. Rudolph, G.: Convergence analysis of canonical genetic algorithms. IEEE Trans. Neural Networks **5**(1), 96–101 (1994)
25. Storn, R., Price, K.: Differential evolution: a simple and efficient heuristic for global optimization. J. Global Optim. **11**(4), 341–359 (1997)
26. Sudholt, D., Witt, C.: Runtime analysis of a binary particle swarm optimizer. Theoret. Comput. Sci. **411**(21), 2084–2100 (2010)
27. Trelea, I.C.: The particle swarm optimization algorithm: convergence analysis and parameter selection. Inf. Process. Lett. **85**(6), 317–325 (2003)
28. Wolter, K.M.: Introduction to Variance Estimation. Springer, New York (1985)
29. Yang, X.S.: A new metaheuristic bat-inspired algorithm. In: Cruz, C., González, J.R., Pelta, D.A., Terrazas, G. (eds.) Nature Inspired Cooperative Strategies for Optimization (NISCO 2010). Studies in Computational Intelligence, vol. 284, pp. 65–74. Springer, Berlin (2010)
30. Yang, X.S.: Nature-inspired optimization algorithms: challenges and open problems. J. Comput. Sci. **46**, 101104 (2020)
31. Yang, X.S., Gandomi, A.H.: Bat algorithm: a novel approach for global engineering optimization. Eng. Comput. **29**(5), 464–483 (2012)
32. Zaharie, D.: Influence of crossover on the behavior of the differential evolution algorithm. Appl. Soft Comput. **9**(3), 1126–1138 (2009)
33. Zaharie, D., Micota, F.: Revisting the analysis of the population variance in differential evolution algorithms. In: 2017 IEEE Congress on Evolutionary Computation (CEC), pp. 1811–1818. Donostia, Spain (2017). https://doi.org/10.1109/CEC.2017.7969521
34. Zdenek, D.: Optimal Quadratic Programming Algorithms: With Applications to Variational Inequalities. Springer, Heidelberg (2009)

Scheduled Temporal Loss Weighting for Neural Operators

Oluwaseun E. Coker[1], He Wang[1,2], Amirul Khan[1],
and Peter K. Jimack[1(✉)]

[1] University of Leeds, Leeds LS2 9JT, UK
`p.k.jimack@leeds.ac.uk`
[2] University College London, London WC1E 6BT, UK

Abstract. Neural operators offer promise for efficient solutions to time-dependent partial differential equations, but face challenges in long-term prediction due to complex dynamics, gradient accumulation, and error propagation. To address these limitations, we propose a novel curriculum learning strategy, temporal weighted loss. This method mitigates overfitting to early dynamics by dynamically adjusting the weights applied to the loss across the temporal sequence, prioritising initial time steps during early training. This approach enhances model generalisation and prediction accuracy for extended time horizons, demonstrating improved performance compared to baseline curriculum learning techniques.

Keywords: PDEs · Curriculum Learning · Neural Operator

1 Introduction

Neural operators offer a promising, computationally efficient alternative to traditional numerical methods for solving time-dependent partial differential equations (PDEs), particularly in fluid flow modelling [7]. By learning discretisation-independent mappings between functional spaces, they enable fast inference at varying resolutions, providing significant speed-ups for tasks like design optimisation [14]. Deep autoregressive neural operators have become a popular choice for modelling PDE time evolution. These **constant-timestep models** predict the next state from the previous one at a fixed interval. Unlike recurrent neural networks (RNNs), they lack internal hidden states, bypassing vanishing gradient problems and making them easier to train [17]. They are also less susceptible to **exposure bias**—the compounding error caused by discrepancies between training ground truths and testing predictions.

Despite these advantages, long-term autoregressive prediction remains challenging due to multiscale complexity, involving sophisticated spatial and temporal scales and unsteady behaviours; gradient accumulation, where "long-rollout" training can trigger numerical instability and out-of-memory (OOM) errors [12]; and exponential error propagation, where small per-step inaccuracies can compound, causing predicted trajectories to diverge from the ground truth [4,15]. To

P. Neumann et al. (Eds.): ICCS 2026, LNCS 16784, pp. 211–225, 2026.
https://doi.org/10.1007/978-3-032-29924-6_15

mitigate these model-agnostic issues, research has focused on improving training robustness through noise injection or refinement processes [10,20]. We focus on **curriculum learning**, which prioritises "easy" samples before introducing complexity [24]. In RNNs, this often involves transitioning from **teacher forcing** to **autoregressive rollout**. However, this paradigm remains under-investigated for neural operators. Our investigation into existing curricula for operators such as FNO [9] and U-NO [19] suggests that they can overfit to early dynamics, resulting in poor performance on later dynamics.

We propose **Scheduled Temporal Loss Weighting (STLW)**, a curriculum-based approach that performs only autoregressive rollout training, avoiding suboptimal teacher forcing. Unlike methods that neglect long-term gradients to avoid early-stage instability, STLW prioritises short-term accumulation without ignoring long-term gradients. We achieve this by assigning a weight to the loss at each timestep, governed by a transition function that dynamically rebalances them as training progresses. STLW initially assigns lower weights to later timesteps, reducing their loss contribution while maintaining their influence on gradient accumulation. Weights increase via a smooth schedule, converging to a uniform weighting. This facilitates a stable optimisation landscape, yielding higher accuracy and superior generalisation. Our key contributions include the **consolidation** of curriculum learning strategies for autoregressive neural operators, the **development** of STLW to bridge the gap between easy one-rollout and hard full-rollout training, the **benchmarking** of STLW against existing strategies across multiple PDE datasets, and the demonstration of the superior accuracy and robustness provided by the STLW framework.

2   Problem Statement

We formulate the learning problem by considering explicit time-stepping for a general class of time-dependent PDEs over the domain $(t, x) \in (0, T] \times D$. The governing equations, subject to boundary conditions B, are defined as:

$$\begin{aligned}
\partial_t u(t, x) &= \mathcal{F}^\dagger \left(u(t, x) \right) \qquad (t, x) \in [0, T] \times D, \\
u(0, x) &= u_0(x) \qquad x \in D, \\
u(t, x) &= B \qquad (t, x) \in (0, T] \times \partial D,
\end{aligned} \qquad (1)$$

where $u : [0, T] \times D \to \mathbb{R}^d$ is the solution function, $u_0(x)$ is the initial condition at $t = 0$ and , and $\mathcal{F}^\dagger$ denotes a spatial differential operator. Our objective is to learn a forward-explicit autoregressive neural operator, $\mathcal{F}_\theta$ with parameters $\theta \in \mathbb{R}^p$, that maps an input function $u(t)$ to the predicted solution at the subsequent timestep:

$$\tilde{u} \left(t + \Delta t \right) = \mathcal{F}_\theta \left(u(t) \right) \quad \theta \in \mathbb{R}^p. \qquad (2)$$

The learning problem seeks to identify the optimal parameters θ^* by minimising the discrepancy between the ground truth u and the prediction $\tilde{u}$. Training is performed using a finite set of time-evolution trajectories generated by a high-accuracy numerical scheme. Each trajectory is represented as an evenly spaced temporal sequence with a uniform spatial resolution. To assess performance, we use an empirical train-test split and evaluate the model on unseen test samples.

During inference, the trained model $\mathcal{F}_{\theta^*}$ is applied recursively to generate future solutions at a constant timestep Δt. We can therefore reformulate the model from Eq. 2 to define a sequence of T autoregressive rollouts, yielding the solutions $\{\tilde{u}_1, \tilde{u}_2, \ldots, \tilde{u}_T\}$:

$$\tilde{u}_t = \mathcal{F}_{\theta^*}(\tilde{u}_{t-1}), \quad 1 \leq t \leq T. \tag{3}$$

3   Related Work

Recent efforts to enhance PDE solver stability and accuracy are broadly categorised into architectural modifications, training paradigms, and inductive biases [3,18,25]. Strategies include integrating modules like PINNs for physics-based loss [25], using RNNs for temporal dynamics [16], and employing denoising or adversarial training to combat error accumulation [11,20]. Other methods utilise temporal bundling to reduce forward passes [3], latent evolution [26], or inductive biases like attention mechanisms and U-Net architectures to resolve multi-scale dynamics [8,18]. Our work aligns with the second category, focusing on enhancing training paradigms without altering underlying models.

Operator learning models, specifically the Fourier Neural Operator (FNO) [9] and U-shaped Neural Operator (U-NO) [19], have succeeded in solving various PDEs due to their resolution-independent nature [5,13]. However, research into their effectiveness for autoregressive time-stepping is limited, as standard architectures often struggle with long-term dynamics in complex PDEs. This study utilizes state-of-the-art neural operators to demonstrate a novel, robust training strategy.

Curriculum Learning (CL) improves convergence by transitioning from "easy" to "hard" samples [1], defined by a curriculum metric and a scheduler. In PDE applications, this typically involves transitioning between teacher forcing and autoregressive rollout [21,23,24]. However, teacher forcing can lead to exposure bias and suboptimal long-term performance [6]. Consequently, we avoid teacher forcing entirely, formulating our curriculum approach exclusively within the autoregressive rollout regime to ensure superior stability.

4   Baseline and Curriculum Training Strategies

Training neural operators for long-term PDE prediction is computationally demanding due to the risks of *exposure bias* and memory constraints during deep gradient accumulation. Consequently, models often train on shorter subsequences of length $\widehat{T} \ll T$. Standard static strategies include **Teacher Forcing (TF)**, a one-step rollout ($\widehat{T} = 1$) using ground-truth inputs that is efficient but prone to divergence during inference, and **Fixed-length Autoregressive Rollout (AR)**, a multi-step approach ($1 < \widehat{T} \ll T$) that better aligns training with inference (Fig. 1a). To improve robustness, Gaussian noise is often added to the inputs in the TF strategy (TF+N).

Beyond these baselines, curriculum learning (CL) improves convergence by transitioning from "easy" to "hard" tasks (Fig. 1b). **Deterministic Curricula (D-CL)** follow fixed schedules; for example, **TF–AR-D-CL** transitions from teacher forcing to autoregressive rollouts, while **AR-CL** incrementally increases the rollout length $\widehat{T}$ without employing teacher forcing. Alternatively, **Probabilistic Curricula (P-CL)** use a probability α_e to determine the training mode for each rollout. In **TF–AR-P-CL**, the model initially samples rollouts as TF, with the probability of sampling an AR rollout increasing throughout training to facilitate a stable transition to complex dynamics.

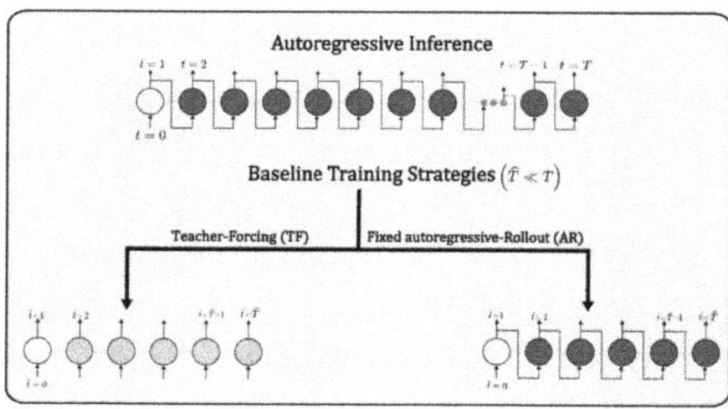

(a) Baseline training strategies of $\widehat{T}$ timestep: Teacher forcing in green (one-rollout) and autoregressive rollout in blue (multi-rollout) where T represents the total timesteps of the data and $\widehat{T}$ represent the training batch timesteps.

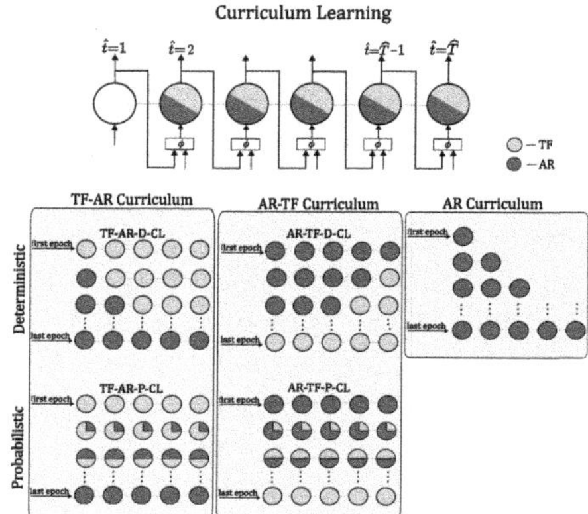

(b) Combinations of Teacher Forcing (TF) and Autoregressive Rollout (AR) across training epochs

Fig. 1. Baseline and curriculum learning strategies. Autoregressive rollout (AR) and Teacher-Forcing (TF) at each timestep are represented as blue and green, respectively. (Color figure online)

5 Scheduled Temporal Loss Weighting (STLW)

We propose Scheduled Temporal Loss Weighting (STLW), a curriculum learning strategy that treats sequence length as a continuum of difficulty. By assigning dynamic weights to each timestep, STLW enables the model to attend to the entire training batch simultaneously while prioritising "easy" early timesteps to reduce error propagation (Fig. 2). For a rollout of length $\widehat{T}$ at epoch e, the total weighted loss $\widehat{L}_t$ is:

$$\widehat{L}_t = \sum_{\hat{t}=1}^{\widehat{T}} w_{e,\,t+\hat{t}} \cdot l(u_{t+\hat{t}},\, \tilde{u}_{t+\hat{t}}), \quad w_{e,t} = \exp\left(-C_e \cdot t^2\right). \tag{4}$$

The decay parameter C_e is defined by $C_e(e) = \exp(-A \cdot e \cdot \frac{T}{E})$, where E is the total epochs and $A = \exp(5.0 \cdot T^{-0.723})$ is an empirical constant obtained by fitting a exponential curve over varying T. This Gaussian-style formulation as seen in Fig. 2b ensures a smooth transition where later timesteps begin with low weights and gradually converge to unity ($w_t \approx 1$) by the end of training.

The curriculum metric $\bar{w}_e = (1 + \sum_{t=2}^{T} w_{e,t})/T$ defines the task difficulty, transitioning from $\bar{w}_e \approx 1/T$ to full weighting ($\bar{w}_e = 1$). Unlike discrete curricula that increment the rollout length $\widehat{T}$, STLW includes all timesteps from the onset. This prevents the model from becoming "blind" to later dynamics, mitigating the risk of overfitting to early-stage temporal behaviours while maintaining numerical stability through gradient damping. STLW functions as a continuous generalisation of the discrete AR-Curriculum (see Fig. 3). While fixed AR training ($w_{e,t} = 1$) is prone to instability and discrete AR-CL ($\widehat{T}_e < T$) may overfit early dynamics, STLW balances these by applying $w_{e,t} \in (0, 1]$ across the full sequence. This approach ensures the model maintains a global view of the trajectory throughout the optimisation process, yielding superior generalisation across complex PDE benchmarks.

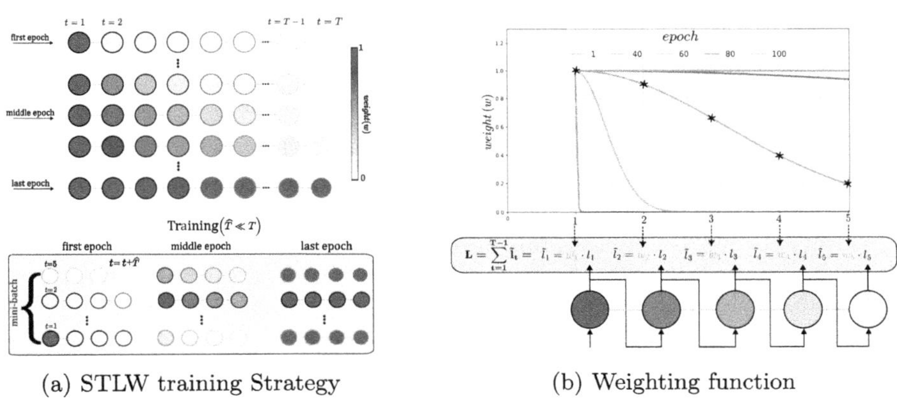

(a) STLW training Strategy   (b) Weighting function

Fig. 2. A schematic of the scheduled temporal loss Weighting (STLW) Curriculum. (a) The colour strength ranges from 0 (low) to 1 (high), indicating the weight assigned to each rollout during training. Later rollouts in the early training phase have low strength, whereas these weights gradually increase in magnitude. The weights are applied to the loss of its respective timestep and epoch. (b) For a dataset with a subsequence of length T ($T = 6$), a weight w is assigned to each timestep for $t > 0$, which controls the loss l contributed by each timestep (for example, at epoch $= 60$, the weight for each timestep is highlighted in black markers). The weighting function (curves), which determines the weight values, changes during training, and at the end of training (epoch $= 100$), the weighting function sets all weights to 1.

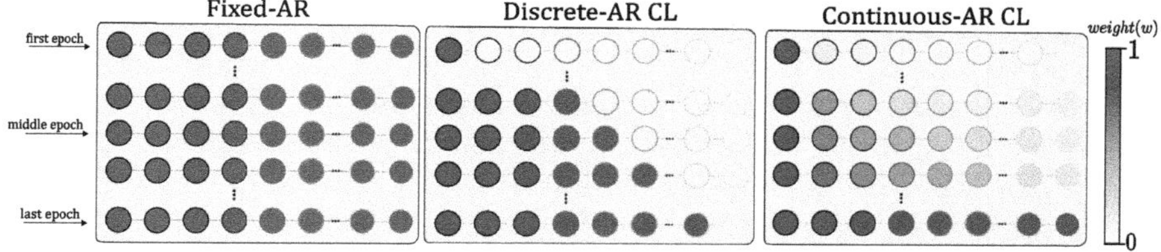

Fig. 3. Schematic comparison between the discrete AR-CL and the Scheduled Temporal Weight Loss (STWL) curriculum (right). STWL acts as a continuous variant, with a weight applied at every timestep, represented by the colour intensity of the bars.

6   STLW Gradient Propagation and Multi-dimensional Scheduling Interpretation

Under the STLW framework, the total weighted loss for a rollout of length T is $\widehat{L} = \sum_{t=1}^{T} w_{e,t} \cdot l(u_t, \tilde{u}_t) = \sum_{t=1}^{T} \hat{l}_t$. The gradient of this weighted loss at each timestep t can be derived by modifying the standard backpropagation formulation [12]:

$$\frac{\partial \hat{l}_t}{\partial \theta} = w_{e,t} \left(\sum_{tt=1}^{t} \left[\frac{\partial l_t}{\partial \tilde{u}_t} \left(\prod_{ttt=1}^{t-tt} \frac{\partial \tilde{u}_{t-ttt+1}}{\partial \tilde{u}_{t-ttt}} \right) \frac{\partial \tilde{u}_{tt}}{\partial \theta} \right] \right) = w_{e,t} \frac{\partial l_t}{\partial \theta}. \tag{5}$$

This reveals that the scheduled weights are directly backpropagated, meaning STLW acts as a scheduled gradient-weighting mechanism. In early training, earlier timesteps receive minimal damping while later steps are heavily damped, mitigating the impact of exploding gradients while the model learns fundamental dynamics.

This mechanism allows for a spatio-temporal interpretation of learning rate scheduling. By substituting the weighted gradient into the standard update rule $\theta_{e+1} = \theta_e - \eta_e \nabla_\theta l$, we obtain an effective learning rate $\widehat{\eta}_{e,t} = \eta_e \cdot w_{e,t}$. This formulation effectively adds a temporal dimension to the standard scheduler, enabling adaptive step sizes across different timesteps t. Despite this mathematical equivalence, we categorise STLW as curriculum learning because the weights w increase over time to introduce complexity, whereas standard learning rates typically decrease to facilitate late-stage convergence.

7   Experiments

To validate the **AR-STLW-CL** strategy, we evaluate it against baseline and established curriculum learning (CL) methods across four diverse PDE datasets. Our analysis addresses several research questions, including baseline stability (TF, TF+N, AR), STLW performance relative to existing CL, the impact of training rollout length $\widehat{T}$, generalisation to extended inference horizons, and sensitivity to both random initialisations and transition function parameterisation.

Evaluated strategies are categorised into three groups: **Baseline (Static)** methods, comprising Teacher Forcing (TF), TF with Gaussian noise (TF+N), and Fixed Autoregressive (AR) rollouts; **Deterministic Curricula (D-CL)**, which utilise fixed schedules like TF–AR-D-CL (transitioning from TF to AR) and AR-CL (incrementally increasing $\widehat{T}$); and **Probabilistic Curricula (P-CL)**, such as TF–AR-P-CL, which use an evolving probability α_e to shift training modes over time.

Experiments are conducted on four 1D time-dependent PDEs: **Advection (Av)**, to assess stability in linear transport [22]; two regimes of **Burgers' Equations**, including **Viscous (vB)** and **Inviscid with forcing (iB)** to test transitions between smooth and sharp features [3,22]; and the **Korteweg–De Vries (KdV)** equation, a dispersive, non-dissipative model that poses a significant challenge over long sequences of 640 timesteps [2].

8   Results

Table 1 presents the mean normalised Root Mean Squared Error (nRMSE) across four PDE datasets, evaluated over nine distinct training strategies. Each row reflects the curriculum parameter configuration that yielded the lowest nRMSE during our exploratory investigation. For each dataset, the best-performing strategy is highlighted in **bold**, and the second-best is <u>underlined</u>.

8.1   Baseline Performance Analysis

We first evaluate the static baseline strategies: TF, TF+N, and AR. Our results indicate that the AR strategy significantly outperforms TF in three out of the four datasets (Av, vB, and KdV). In contrast, TF outperforms AR on the iB dataset. To provide a rigorous comparison, we use the best-performing baseline for each dataset as the reference point to calculate the relative improvement (*rel. impro.*) of the curriculum strategies.

8.2   Comparative Effectiveness of Curriculum Learning

The empirical results demonstrate that curriculum learning strategies consistently enhance model performance. Our proposed **AR-STLW-CL** method achieved the lowest error (and consequently the greatest relative improvement) on three of the four datasets: vB, iB, and KdV, with improvements of **62.5%**, **12.0%**, and **40.3%**, respectively. The AR-CL strategy ranked second in three cases (Av, iB, and KdV), achieving relative improvements of 16.8%, 11.4%, and 36.9%, respectively.

Among the deterministic strategies, TF–AR-D-CL and TF+N–AR-D-CL showed strong performance on the viscous Burgers' (vB) dataset, ranking as the joint best and second-best strategies. Conversely, probabilistic approaches (AR–TF-P-CL and TF–AR-P-CL) generally underperformed. Notably, AR–TF-P-CL (decreasing complexity) often led to performance degradation, failing to surpass the best baseline strategies in several instances. This confirms that increasing the task difficulty over time—rather than decreasing it—is critical for training stability in autoregressive neural operators.

Table 1. Accuracy: Mean Normalised Root Mean Squared Error (nRMSE) using FNO. **Bold** and <u>underline</u> denote the best and second-best results, respectively.

Strategy	Best Curriculum $\alpha_{start} \to \alpha_{end}$	nRMSE $mean^{\pm s.d}$ ↓	rel. impro. ↑	last 10% ↓
Av				
TF	0.0	$0.0375^{\pm 1.76e-2}$	–	0.0883
TF+N	0.0	$0.0165^{\pm 5.68e-3}$	–	0.0446
AR	1.0	$0.00353^{\pm 8.70e-5}$	–	0.00536
AR-CL	1.0	$\underline{0.00293^{\pm 8.98e-5}}$	[illegible]	<u>0.00450</u>
TF–AR-D-CL	0.0 ↗ 1.0	$\mathbf{0.00272^{\pm 9.58e-5}}$	[illegible]	**0.00423**
TF+N–AR-D-CL	0.0 ↗ 1.0	$0.00296^{\pm 1.43e-4}$	[illegible]	0.00455
AR–TF-P-CL	1.0 ↘ 0.0	$0.00538^{\pm 1.18e-3}$	-52.4%	0.01460
TF–AR-P-CL	0.0 ↗ 1.0	$0.00294^{\pm 9.48e-5}$	[illegible]	0.00473
AR-STLW-CL	$1.0,\ A_c = 5.0$	$0.00303^{\pm 0.0}$	[illegible]	0.00485
vB				
TF	0.0	$0.0632^{\pm 4.23e-2}$	–	0.1040
TF+N	0.0	$0.0125^{\pm 2.39e-2}$	–	0.0154
AR	1.0	$0.00749^{\pm 1.15e-3}$	–	0.00771
AR-CL	1.0	$0.00376^{\pm 1.30e-4}$	[illegible]	0.00623
TF–AR-D-CL	0 ↗ 1	$\mathbf{0.00280^{\pm 4.83e-4}}$	[illegible]	**0.00363**
TF+N–AR-D-CL	0.0 ↗ 1.0	$\underline{0.00291^{\pm 3.59e-4}}$	[illegible]	<u>0.00422</u>
AR–TF-P-CL	1.0 ↘ 0.0	$0.0112^{\pm 8.29e-4}$	-44.9%	0.01427
TF–AR-P-CL	0.0 ↗ 1.0	$0.00413^{\pm 2.13e-4}$	[illegible]	0.00501
AR-STLW-CL	$1.0,\ A_c = 5.0$	$\mathbf{0.00280^{\pm 4.66e-4}}$	[illegible]	0.00566
iB				
TF	0.0	$0.274^{\pm 3.9e-3}$	–	0.625
TF+N	0.0	$0.278^{\pm 8.1e-3}$	–	0.628
AR	1.0	$0.306^{\pm 8.7e-3}$	–	0.683
AR-CL	1.0	$\underline{0.243^{\pm 3.4e-3}}$	[illegible]	<u>0.559</u>
TF–AR-D-CL	0.0 ↗ 1.0	$0.252^{\pm 4.4e-3}$	[illegible]	0.571
TF+N–AR-D-CL	0.0 ↗ 1.0	$0.250^{\pm 3.1e-3}$	[illegible]	0.573
AR–TF-P-CL	1.0 ↘ 0.0	$0.291^{\pm 1.4e-2}$	-6.1%	0.660
TF–AR-P-CL	0.0 ↗ 1.0	$0.266^{\pm 1.7e-3}$	[illegible]	0.603
AR-STLW-CL	$1.0,\ A_c = 5.0$	$\mathbf{0.241^{\pm 2.8e-3}}$	[illegible]	**0.558**
KdV				
TF	0.0	$0.541^{\pm 9.50e-2}$	–	0.896
TF+N	0.0	$0.347^{\pm 1.01e-1}$	–	0.623
AR	1.0	$0.189^{\pm 5.29e-3}$	–	0.311
AR-CL	1.0	$\underline{0.119^{\pm 5.24e-3}}$	[illegible]	<u>0.226</u>
TF–AR-D-CL	0.0 ↗ 1.0	$0.159^{\pm 4.13e-3}$	[illegible]	0.290
TF+N–AR-D-CL	0.0 ↗ 1.0	$0.145^{\pm 4.74e-3}$	[illegible]	0.267
AR–TF-P-CL	1.0 ↘ 0.0	$0.226^{\pm 2.0e-2}$	-19.1%	0.411
TF–AR-P-CL	0.0 ↗ 1.0	$0.189^{\pm 7.29e-3}$	0%	0.342
AR-STLW-CL	$1.0,\ A_c = 5.0$	$\mathbf{0.113^{\pm 5.02e-3}}$	[illegible]	**0.214**

8.3 Long-Term Accuracy and Stability

To assess long-term predictive performance, we computed the nRMSE over the final 10% of the temporal horizon (the "Last 10%" column in Table 1). Excluding the probabilistic variants, curriculum learning consistently enhanced accuracy at later timesteps. **AR-STLW-CL** demonstrated the lowest terminal error for two datasets (iB and KdV), while TF–AR-D-CL achieved the lowest error for Av and vB.

We also evaluated the stability of these strategies by examining the standard deviation across five independent runs per configuration. Our findings reveal that non-probabilistic curriculum strategies exhibit smaller standard deviations than static baselines, indicating greater robustness to weight initialisation. Specifically, AR-STLW-CL demonstrated the highest stability for the Av dataset, while AR-CL, TF–AR-P-CL, and TF–AR-D-CL showed the smallest variations for vB, iB, and KdV, respectively.

8.4   Error Propagation Analysis

Figure 4 illustrates the accumulation of error over time for the three top-performing curricula for each dataset. These trajectories clearly demonstrate the benefit of curriculum-based training across all physical regimes. While **AR-STLW-CL** generally achieves the lowest overall nRMSE, the plots indicate that its performance advantage over the top discrete curricula remains consistent throughout the rollout, effectively "flattening" the error growth curve compared to the best baseline.

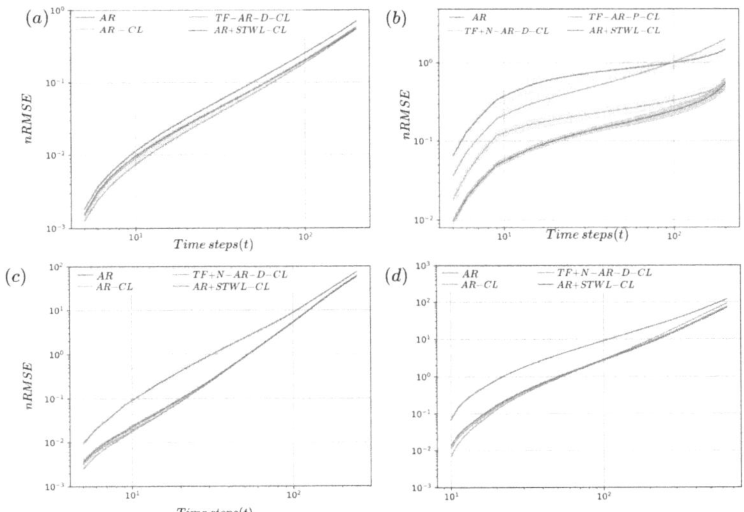

Fig. 4. Error propagation over time for the best baseline and the top two curriculum strategies for: (a) Advection (Av), (b) Viscous Burgers (vB), (c) Inviscid Burgers (iB), and (d) Korteweg–De Vries (KdV).

8.5 Impact of Training Rollout Length

As established in Sect. 5, AR-STLW-CL can be conceptualised as a continuous generalisation of the discrete AR-CL strategy. While discrete AR-CL progressively increases the number of training rollouts $\widehat{T}$, our continuous approach applies temporal weights across the entire sequence length. We investigate the impact of varying the training rollout length $\widehat{T} \in \{2, 4, 8, 16, 32\}$ on the performance of the fixed-AR, discrete AR-CL, and continuous AR-STLW-CL strategies.

Figure 5 presents the nRMSE as a function of $\widehat{T}$. Our observations indicate that **AR-STLW-CL** consistently achieves lower errors and greater stability across all rollout lengths tested. Notably:

- **Advection (Av):** AR-STLW-CL remains stable even at low $\widehat{T}$ values where other methods fluctuate.
- **Viscous Burgers (vB):** While errors generally reach a minimum at $\widehat{T} = 8$, AR-STLW-CL consistently maintains a lower error profile across the entire range.
- **iB and KdV:** Whereas the error for the fixed-AR strategy begins to diverge as $\widehat{T}$ increases beyond 8, both AR-CL and AR-STLW-CL maintain a downward trend, with AR-STLW-CL achieving the most significant reduction in error.

In summary, AR-STLW-CL demonstrates enhanced scalability and stability across different training rollouts, highlighting its effectiveness in mitigating gradient-related instabilities associated with long-horizon training.

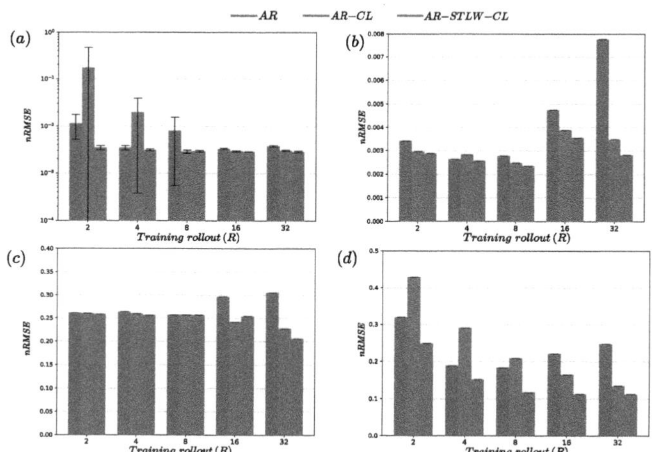

Fig. 5. Effect of increasing training rollout length $\widehat{T}$ on the nRMSE of the best baseline and the top two curriculum strategies across the four PDE datasets.

8.6   Inference Rollout Analysis

To evaluate the robustness of **AR-STLW-CL** for long-term forecasting, we analyse its performance across varying inference horizons (T). Table 2 details the mean nRMSE and standard deviation for the Advection (Av) and Korteweg–De Vries (KdV) datasets.

In this analysis, each reported value corresponds to a model trained with a specific output size (S), defined as the number of timesteps predicted per forward pass. For the Av dataset, we evaluate the configurations $(T, S) = (40, 5)$ and $(200, 1)$. For the KdV dataset, we examine increasingly long horizons: $(T, S) \in \{(128, 5), (320, 2), (640, 1)\}$.

The results indicate that AR-STLW-CL consistently outperforms alternative strategies across nearly all temporal horizons. Notably, the performance gap between our curriculum and the baselines becomes more pronounced as the rollout length T increases. While the deterministic curriculum (TF–AR-D-CL) remains competitive at shorter horizons (e.g., $T = 40$ for Av), it exhibits significant instability or divergence in long-term regimes ($T = 200$).

Strikingly, at the longest horizon for KdV ($T = 640$), most baseline and discrete-curriculum strategies either fail to converge or produce errors several orders of magnitude higher than those of our approach. In contrast, AR-STLW-CL maintains superior stability and a significantly lower error profile. This confirms that our continuous weighting strategy effectively mitigates the compounding error and gradient instabilities typically associated with extended autoregressive rollouts.

Table 2. Inference Rollout Performance: nRMSE across varying temporal horizons T. **Bold** and underline denote the best and second-best results. "NaN" and extremely high values indicate model divergence denoted with a dash).

	Strategy	Inference Rollout T		
		40		**200**
	TF	$0.0375^{\pm 1.76e-2}$		$0.486^{\pm 4.53e-2}$
	TF+N	$0.0165^{\pm 5.68e-3}$		NaN
	AR	$0.00353^{\pm 8.70e-5}$		$859.6^{\pm 1913.4}$
Av	AR-CL	$\underline{0.00293}^{\pm 8.98e-5}$		$\underline{0.0551}^{\pm 1.01e-1}$
	TF–AR-D-CL	$\mathbf{0.00272}^{\pm 9.58e-5}$		$10.9^{\pm 23.1}$
	TF+N–AR-D-CL	$0.00296^{\pm 1.43e-4}$		$1.057^{\pm 1.93}$
	AR–TF-P-CL	$0.00538^{\pm 1.18e-3}$		$0.196^{\pm 1.12e-1}$
	TF–AR-P-CL	$0.00294^{\pm 9.48e-5}$		$29.9^{\pm 65.7}$
	AR-STLW-CL	$0.00303^{\pm 0.0}$		$\mathbf{0.0135}^{\pm 8.72e-3}$

	Strategy	Inference Rollout T		
		128	**320**	**640**
	TF	$0.541^{\pm 9.50e-2}$	–	–
	TF+N	$0.347^{\pm 1.01e-1}$	$0.408^{\pm 1.14e-2}$	$0.810^{\pm 1.37e-1}$
	AR	$0.189^{\pm 5.29e-3}$	$0.298^{\pm 6.62e-2}$	$0.518^{\pm 1.94e-1}$
KdV	AR-CL	$\underline{0.119}^{\pm 5.29e-3}$	$\underline{0.196}^{\pm 6.61e-3}$	$2.49e5^{\pm 5.58e5}$
	TF–AR-D-CL	$0.159^{\pm 4.13e-3}$	$0.244^{\pm 1.42e-2}$	$\underline{0.366}^{\pm 1.29e-2}$
	TF+N–AR-D-CL	$0.145^{\pm 4.74e-3}$	–	–
	AR–TF-P-CL	$0.226^{\pm 2.00e-2}$	–	–
	TF–AR-P-CL	$0.189^{\pm 7.29e-3}$	–	–
	AR-STLW-CL	$\mathbf{0.113}^{\pm 5.02e-3}$	$\mathbf{0.170}^{\pm 1.09e-2}$	$\mathbf{0.307}^{\pm 2.85e-2}$

8.7 STLW as a Multi-dimensional Learning Rate Scheduler

The **AR-STLW-CL** curriculum can be conceptualised as a **two-dimensional learning rate scheduler**. Unlike conventional schedulers that modulate the learning rate η_e solely as a function of the epoch e, STLW introduces a temporal weighting function $w_{e,t}$ that varies across both the epoch and the prediction timestep t. This allows the model to selectively prioritise different stages of the temporal rollout throughout training. To isolate the impact of this mechanism, we evaluate variants with both fixed and variable learning rates, comparing STLW against standard AR baselines and discrete AR-CL.

As illustrated in Fig. 6 for the viscous Burgers' equation, the inclusion of our curriculum leads to a significant reduction in terminal test loss compared to fixed-η baselines, proving that scheduled weighting independently improves convergence. Furthermore, the qualitative similarity between the fixed-η STLW variants and standard variable-η approaches suggests that temporal loss weighting acts as an implicit proxy for learning rate decay, providing a comparable regularising effect. Notably, in the left figure, STLW exhibits a smoother loss trajectory than the more erratic discrete transitions of AR-CL, suggesting that continuous weighting offers a more stable and fluid optimisation strategy.

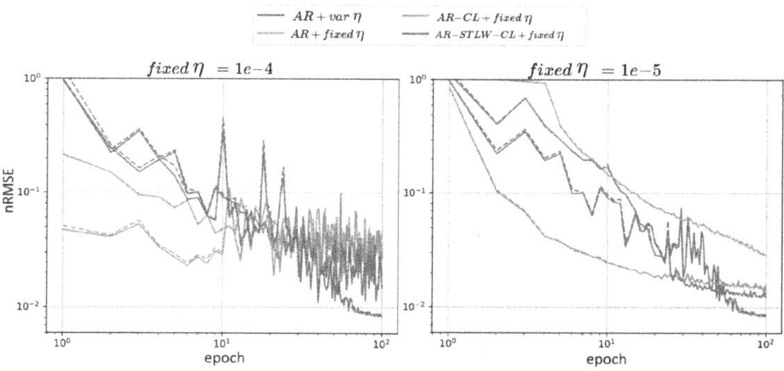

Fig. 6. Training dynamics under fixed and variable learning rates (η) across different curricula. Dashed and solid lines indicate training and validation loss, respectively.

9 Discussion

This section synthesises our empirical findings to address the six core research questions regarding scheduled temporal loss weighting.

- **Q1 Baseline Strategies:** Among non-curriculum baselines, adding Gaussian noise (TF+N) consistently improved Teacher Forcing performance. However, Autoregressive (AR) training proved superior, as it forces the model to learn error correction during rollout. This is particularly effective for the well-behaved physical structures of the PDEs investigated here [23].

– **Q2 Curriculum Effectiveness:** Consistent with [1,24], curriculum learning (CL) significantly enhanced accuracy and stability. **AR-STLW-CL** outperformed curricula that transition toward TF, which we find to be suboptimal for non-chaotic systems. This suggests that for such systems, the optimal curriculum should refine AR tasks rather than incorporate TF.
– **Q3 Training Rollout Length:** Increasing $\widehat{T}$ does not yield monotonic improvements; for the AR baseline, performance often plateaus or degrades beyond $\widehat{T} = 8$ due to error accumulation. **AR-STLW-CL** better manages the difficulty of longer rollouts, though researchers must balance marginal gains against the linear increase in computational and memory costs.
– **Q4 Inference Robustness:** STLW-trained models generalise better to extended inference horizons. While standard AR models often diverge or produce "NaN" values during extended testing in Av and KdV, **AR-STLW-CL** maintains physical plausibility and stable error profiles, effectively mitigating compounding errors.
– **Q5 Stochastic Robustness:** Across multiple independent runs, curriculum strategies exhibited lower variance than the AR baseline. This suggests CL smoothes the optimisation landscape, making models less sensitive to weight initialisation and more reliable for deployment.
– **Q6 Parameter Sensitivity:** A key advantage of **AR-STLW-CL** is its robustness to the curvature parameter A. The stability provided by the "soft" continuous weighting transition reduces the need for extensive hyperparameter tuning compared to the "hard" transitions of discrete curricula or static AR.

10   Conclusion

This work investigated the challenges of training neural operators for long-term temporal PDE forecasting, focusing on instabilities in autoregressive rollouts. We introduced **Scheduled Temporal Loss Weighting (AR-STLW-CL)**, a novel curriculum learning framework that treats training as a continuous transition from short-term to long-term temporal dependencies.

Empirical evaluation across four physical systems; Advection, Viscous Burgers', Inviscid Burgers', and Korteweg–De Vries; demonstrates that AR-STLW-CL consistently outperforms standard Teacher Forcing and discrete curricula, achieving nRMSE improvements of up to **62.5%** over the best baselines with negligible computational overhead. By providing a more smooth and continuous training through weighted loss, our approach enables more precise and reliable learning of complex physics. Future research could extend this framework to higher-dimensional chaotic dynamics and integrate physics-informed constraints to enhance conservation properties.

References

1. Bengio, Y., Louradour, J., Collobert, R., Weston, J.: Curriculum learning. In: Proceedings of the 26th Annual International Conference on Machine Learning, pp. 41–48 (2009)
2. Brandstetter, J., Welling, M., Worrall, D.E.: Lie point symmetry data augmentation for neural PDE solvers. In: International Conference on Machine Learning, pp. 2241–2256. PMLR (2022)
3. Brandstetter, J., Worrall, D., Welling, M.: Message passing neural PDE solvers. arXiv preprint arXiv:2202.03376 (2022)
4. Gonzalez, F., Demoulin, F.X., Bernard, S.: Towards long-term predictions of turbulence using neural operators. arXiv preprint arXiv:2307.13517 (2023)
5. Gupta, J.K., Brandstetter, J.: Towards multi-spatiotemporal-scale generalized PDE modeling. arXiv preprint arXiv:2209.15616 (2022)
6. Hess, F., Monfared, Z., Brenner, M., Durstewitz, D.: Generalized teacher forcing for learning chaotic dynamics. arXiv preprint arXiv:2306.04406 (2023)
7. Kovachki, N.B., Lanthaler, S., Stuart, A.M.: Operator learning: algorithms and analysis. Handb. Numer. Anal. **25**, 419–467 (2024)
8. Li, Z., Peng, W., Yuan, Z., Wang, J.: Long-term predictions of turbulence by implicit u-net enhanced fourier neural operator. Phys. Fluids **35**(7) (2023)
9. Li, Z., et al.: Fourier neural operator for parametric partial differential equations. In: International Conference on Learning Representations (2021). https://openreview.net/forum?id=c8P9NQVtmnO
10. Lippe, P., Veeling, B., Perdikaris, P., Turner, R., Brandstetter, J.: PDE-refiner: achieving accurate long rollouts with neural PDE solvers. In: Advances in Neural Information Processing Systems, vol. 36 (2024)
11. Lippe, P., Veeling, B.S., Perdikaris, P., Turner, R.E., Brandstetter, J.: PDE-refiner: achieving accurate long rollouts with neural PDE solvers. arXiv preprint arXiv:2308.05732 (2023)
12. List, B., Chen, L.W., Bali, K., Thuerey, N.: Differentiability in unrolled training of neural physics simulators on transient dynamics. Comput. Methods Appl. Mech. Eng. **433**, 117441 (2025). https://doi.org/10.1016/j.cma.2024.117441. https://www.sciencedirect.com/science/article/pii/S0045782524006960
13. Lu, L., et al.: A comprehensive and fair comparison of two neural operators (with practical extensions) based on fair data. Comput. Methods Appl. Mech. Eng. **393**, 114778 (2022)
14. Lu, L., Pestourie, R., Johnson, S.G., Romano, G.: Multifidelity deep neural operators for efficient learning of partial differential equations with application to fast inverse design of nanoscale heat transport. arXiv preprint arXiv:2204.06684 (2022)
15. McCabe, M., Harrington, P., Subramanian, S., Brown, J.: Towards stability of autoregressive neural operators. arXiv preprint arXiv:2306.10619 (2023)
16. Michałowska, K., Goswami, S., Karniadakis, G.E., Riemer-Sørensen, S.: Neural operator learning for long-time integration in dynamical systems with recurrent neural networks. In: 2024 International Joint Conference on Neural Networks (IJCNN), pp. 1–8. IEEE (2024)
17. Pascanu, R., Mikolov, T., Bengio, Y.: On the difficulty of training recurrent neural networks. In: International Conference on Machine Learning, pp. 1310–1318. PMLR (2013)
18. Peng, W., Yuan, Z., Wang, J.: Attention-enhanced neural network models for turbulence simulation. Phys. Fluids **34**(2) (2022)

19. Rahman, M.A., Ross, Z.E., Azizzadenesheli, K.: U-NO: U-shaped neural operators. Trans. Mach. Learn. Res. (2023). https://openreview.net/forum?id=j3oQF9coJd
20. Sanchez-Gonzalez, A., et al.: Learning general-purpose CNN-based simulators for astrophysical turbulence. In: ICLR 2021 SimDL Workshop (2021)
21. Takamoto, M., Alesiani, F., Niepert, M.: Learning neural PDE solvers with parameter-guided channel attention. In: International Conference on Machine Learning, pp. 33448–33467. PMLR (2023)
22. Takamoto, M., et al.: Pdebench: an extensive benchmark for scientific machine learning. Adv. Neural. Inf. Process. Syst. **35**, 1596–1611 (2022)
23. Teutsch, P., Mäder, P.: Flipped classroom: effective teaching for time series forecasting. arXiv preprint arXiv:2210.08959 (2022)
24. Vlachas, P.R., Koumoutsakos, P.: Learning on predictions: fusing training and autoregressive inference for long-term spatiotemporal forecasts. Physica D **470**, 134371 (2024)
25. Wang, S., Perdikaris, P.: Long-time integration of parametric evolution equations with physics-informed deeponets. J. Comput. Phys. **475**, 111855 (2023)
26. Wu, T., Maruyama, T., Leskovec, J.: Learning to accelerate partial differential equations via latent global evolution. Adv. Neural. Inf. Process. Syst. **35**, 2240–2253 (2022)

An Agent Based Model of Effects of Sleep Deprivation on Suicidality

Mikko Brandon[1]([✉])(iD), Valeria Krzhizhanovskaya[1,2](iD), and Johan Bollen[1](iD)

[1] University of Amsterdam, Science Park 904, 1098XH Amsterdam, The Netherlands
`mikko.brandon@student.uva.nl`, {`V.Krzhizhanovskaya,j.l.t.m.bollen`}`@uva.nl`
[2] Centre for Urban Mental Health, University of Amsterdam, Amsterdam,
The Netherlands

Abstract. The use of computational models to understand psychological phenomena, including suicidal behavior and outcomes, has become more common. Here we extend a formal computational model of suicide with social and state-dependent dynamics enabled by ABM architecture to evaluate their effects on suicidal thought and aversive internal state. The proposed model implements the General Escape Theory of Suicide [34], combined with aspects of the Interpersonal Theory of Suicide [33], particularly burdensomeness and connectedness. It is based on a system of differential equations proposed by Wang et al. [34] and extended by Engels [11]. The prevalence of suicidal thoughts and aversive internal states was compared in three conditions: a baseline model, a model that included sleep deprivation, and a model that included both state-dependent and social dynamics. We found that sleep deprivation significantly increased both outcomes, while the addition of social dynamics reduced them and increased resistance to suicidal thought. These dynamics qualitatively align with contemporary suicide research showing the protective effects of sleep and socializing. The results demonstrate the utility of ABMs in representing the interactions of internal, social, and state-dependent processes. The model may support simulation of group-level interventions, although future work is needed for quantitative validation and refinement.

Keywords: Agent Based Model · Suicide · General Escape Theory · Sleep

1 Introduction

Suicide is a major cause of death worldwide. Although global deaths from suicide have decreased over the past several decades, the rate remains high [26,30]. However, the rate of suicide attempts is much higher, ranging from 30 [31] to more than 900 [28] per death by suicide in the United States, with many attempts not recorded. Despite decades of research, there was no significant improvement in suicide prediction as assessed in 2014 [12]. Since then, smart-technology and wearables have allowed progress in the implementation of interventions and

P. Neumann et al. (Eds.): ICCS 2026, LNCS 16784, pp. 226–240, 2026.
https://doi.org/10.1007/978-3-032-29924-6_16

early identification of factors associated with suicidality [1]. However, due to the complex nature of suicidal ideation and suicide attempts, it remains difficult to determine exactly which factors are indicative of them. There are many potential paths to suicide and they vary between individuals.

Studies of complex systems increasingly involve computational modeling. The strength of the approach is that it allows for analysis of nonlinear relationships and their outcomes. There is an increasing body of work that shows that suicidal ideation and attempts can fluctuate greatly during small time frames [9,20], and be dependent on many factors [3,4], both of which are identifiers of parameters in a complex system. The field of computational psychology has begun to utilize computational models to analyze suicide as a complex system. Agent Based Models (ABMs) are known to be useful in modeling dynamic social environments with autonomous agents that have their own state-dependent interactions and exhibit varying behaviors. Despite that, the use of ABMs in suicide research remains limited. This paper attempts to answer the following research questions. 1) How does a combination of state-dependent and social effects within an ABM alter the dynamics of suicidality compared to a baseline mathematical model? 2) How do the effects of sleep alter the dynamics of suicidality within an ABM compared to a baseline mathematical model?

1.1   Related Work

The model proposed in this study is largely based on a formal theory of suicide proposed by Wang et al. [34], and extended by Engels [11]. Wang et al. proposed a mathematical model based on the General Escape Theory proposed by Millner et al., which is still in preparation. This theory, in turn, is based on Baumeister's Escape Theory [2], which frames suicidal outcomes as the result of wanting to escape an aversive internal state formed by stress, discomfort, and failure, among others. The mathematical model [34] is made up of 7 differential equations that represent the evolution of stress, aversive internal state, urge to escape, suicidal thought, escape behavior, and external and internal strategies to reduce harm. The model serves as a good foundation for simulation based on the General Escape Theory.

Engels [11] extended the model [34] with social interactions. Many other theories of suicide, such as the Interpersonal Theory of suicide (IPT) by Van Orden et al. [33] and the Integrated Motivational-Volitional model (IMV) by O'Connor and Kirtley [25], consider social effects such as burdensomeness and thwarted belongingness to be significant. Engels' key additions were a social burden parameter, a connectedness parameter, and a clustering coefficient. The relationships between parameters are maintained largely. With the model proposed in this article, we advance the extended model [11,34] by adding key features of suicidality such as memory [5,18] and time-dependent interactions.

2 Model

The agents' update rules are largely based on the formal theory of suicide [34] and Engels' extension [11], which was modified and extended based on expert opinion and literature. The ABM was developed in Python using the Mesa library [16], a standard choice for the development of ABMs. The Python libraries NumPy [15], Matplotlib [17] and Pandas [32] were used for efficient computation, plotting, and data handling, respectively. The code for the model is available at the author's github repository. The following subsections will motivate the design of the model.

2.1 Agent States

The model includes a daily routine for all agents. A high-level overview of the routine is shown in Fig. 1.

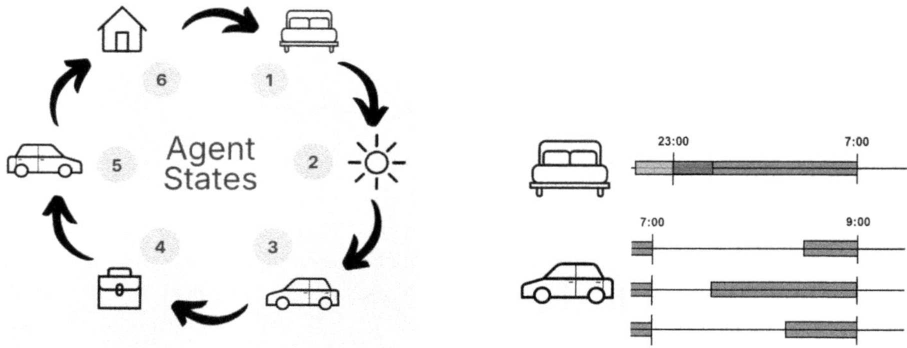

Fig. 1. Graphical representations of states and state-dependent effects in the ABM. Left: The daily schedule of an agent in the ABM. The agent sleeps (1), wakes up (2), commutes (3), works (4), commutes back (5), and is at home (6), before going to sleep again. Right: A sleep duration of less than 8 h negatively affects stress and suicidal thought. Commutes are distributed so that short commutes are more likely, but long commutes are possible.

1) Sleep: Disrupted or inconsistent sleep is believed to be detrimental to a variety of physiological processes, including mental health. Correlations have specifically been found between disrupted sleep and suicidal ideation [27]. Later sleep timing and greater variability in sleep duration are generally associated with worse health outcomes [7]. The assumption is made that sleep always ends at 7:00 in the morning and that a healthy sleep duration is 8 h. A sleep deficit is defined as the number of hours slept less than 8. Sleep longer than 8 h has no explicit negative effect.

2) Morning: After sleeping, the effects of potentially poor sleep are applied to the update equations of stress and suicidal thought during the "morning" state. The duration of this state depends on the length of the agent's commute; it ends such that it is 9:00, the start of work, after commuting.

3) Commute: Commuting is known to be a stressful event, and stress during commutes depends on various factors, including duration of commute [29]. The duration of the commute is drawn from a lognormal distribution with a mean and standard deviation specific to each agent type.

4) Work: In the "work" state, the effect of the urge to escape on other parameters increases. The workday starts at 9:00 in the morning and its duration is standardized to 8 h for all agents.

5) Home: According to expert opinion, suicidal ideation is more likely to originate and sustain at home [21,35]. Escape behavior becomes easier to engage in when the daily work schedule is completed. The duration of the home state equals the amount of time between the commute back from work and the start of the sleep state.

2.2 Social Network

Engels [11] modeled the social connections between agents according to a Newman-Watts-Strogatz small world graph [24]. In such a graph, the edges between nodes are initialized in a circle formation, after which the nodes are connected according to the mean degree of connectivity, with a probability of reassignment of edges. This effectively models a closed social network. For small numbers of nodes, such networks may be sufficiently realistic. According to Dunbar et al. [10], the average size of an individuals social network is 150 people, among which there are delimitations in closeness to the individual. One such delimitation is classified as "best friends", which consist of roughly 15 people who are either best friends or closer to the individual. A best friends network will form the basis of the analysis performed in the current project. All agents are connected to all other agents, with weights ranging between 0.99 and 1.

2.3 Parameters

A high-level overview of all parameters, coefficients, and agent states is shown in Fig. 2. In this figure, self-feedback relationships are omitted. All model parameters described in this section are functions of time. For all main parameters denoted with capital letters, the time dependency is omitted in writing for clarity, e.g. $S(t) \rightarrow S$. For visualization of a parameter's trajectory, refer to Fig. 3.

Stress. Within the field of psychology, stressors are understood to be systemic or chronic, as well as acute, with the existing literature advocating the consideration

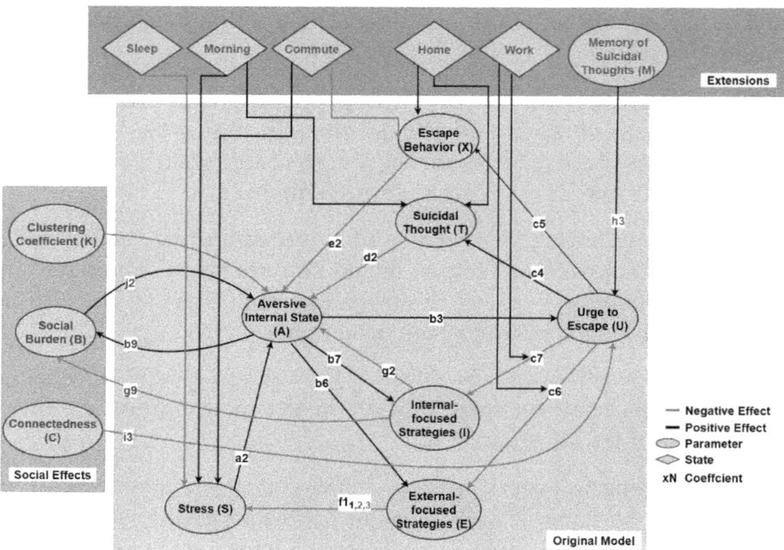

Fig. 2. Model schematic showing the relationships between parameters and states. The original model [34] is shown on the gray background. Engels' contributions [11] are shown on the blue background. New model extensions made by this paper are shown on the green background.

of both types in psychological research [14,22]. Empirical data show a high spike in cortisol levels at wake-up and a series of work-related cortisol spikes. The wake-up spike is believed to occur in preparation for stressful events later in the day [6,13].

Informed by these observations, stress is modeled as a series of spikes of uniform size, the occurrence of which is dictated by a Poisson process. A noise term is added to model minor short-term fluctuations. This allows for a baseline stress level, *i.e.*, chronic stress, with spikes that decay to the baseline at a specified rate, *i.e.*, acute stress. Stress is affected by the external strategy parameter, as was the case in model [34]. This yields the stress equation

$$S(t + dt) = L_S + e^{-\lambda_S dt}(S - L_S) + \sum P \cdot (1 - f_{1,1}E) + dW\sigma \tag{1}$$

$$L_S = L_S(0) - f_{1,2}E \tag{2}$$

$$\lambda_S = \lambda_S(0) + f_{1,3}E,$$

where L_S is the baseline stress value, λ_S is the decay rate of the cortisol spikes, P is an impulse that occurs at time t, and dW is a stochastic noise term $\sim \mathcal{N}(0, \sqrt{dt})$, which is multiplied by σ to control the strength of the stochastic fluctuations. E is the external strategy parameter at time t, $f_{1,1}$ the strength of its effect on the size of impulses, $f_{1,2}$ the strength of its effect on the baseline stress and $f_{1,3}$ the strength of its effect on the decay rate.

Impulses come from 2 different sources: morning impulses P_m, and day impulses $P_d(t)$. From the morning commute to the next sleep state, impulses P_d are determined with a Poisson process, such that the time between spikes is distributed exponentially with a given event rate r

$$P_d(t) = \alpha_P N, \tag{3}$$

with $\alpha_P = $ strength of impulse, $N(t) \sim \text{Poisson}(rdt)$. When commuting, the baseline stress increases by 0.2.

The morning impulse P_m is a single impulse after awakening at 7:00, its size being dependent on the length of sleep. The assumption is made that the increase in cortisol in the morning in anticipation of stressful situations is correlated with poor sleep, as there is evidence that poor sleep correlates with high stress [19]. The equation for the size of the spike is

$$P_m = \alpha_P \left(1 + \exp\left(\frac{\text{deficit}}{\text{healthy sleep}} \right) \right). \tag{4}$$

Urge to Escape and Past Suicidal Thought. As in model [34], urge to escape is modeled as a linear combination of itself and the aversive internal state. However, this model does not account for past suicidal ideation as a factor in escape behavior, even though there is evidence that it has an effect [5,18]. To model the effect that past suicidal behavior has on escape behavior past suicidal thought is added as a factor. This is modeled in the form of a memory component that increases with suicidal thought, and can decay more slowly than suicidal thought itself:

$$M = \begin{cases} T, & \text{if } T >= M \\ M + dt(-h_8 M), & \text{otherwise.} \end{cases} \tag{5}$$

Adding this to Engels' update equation for urge to escape with an added effect of social connectivity [11] yields

$$U(t + dt) = U + dt * (-c_3 U + b_3 A + h_3 M - i_3 C), \tag{6}$$

with Engels' additions to the model [11] highlighted in blue, and the new memory term highlighted in green.

Suicidal Thought. The update equation for suicidal thought follows [34]:

$$T(t + dt) = T + dt \left(-d_4 T + \frac{1}{1 + \exp\left(-c_{4,1}(U - c_{4,2})\right)} \right), \tag{7}$$

where $c_{4,1}$ controls the steepness of the sigmoid and $c_{4,2}$ controls the threshold. The equation includes a sigmoid function to allow for a steep increase in value when a certain threshold is reached. $c_{4,2}$ is reduced proportional to the lack of sleep in the morning state to make agents more susceptible to suicidal thought after poor sleep: $c_{4,2} = c_{4,2} - 0.1 \cdot \text{deficit}/\text{healthy sleep}$. d_4 is reduced by 0.1 in the home state, so suicidal thought decays less quickly. This reflects susceptibility to suicidal thoughts at home.

Escape Behavior. Escape behaviors other than suicidal thought, such as alcohol use and non-suicidal self-injury, are generalized as "escape behavior" in [34]. Escape behavior is modeled the same as suicidal thought, but with a lower threshold for the sigmoid function:

$$X(t + dt) = X + dt \left(-e_5 X + \frac{1}{1 + \exp\left(-c_{5,1}(U - c_{5,2})\right)} \right), \tag{8}$$

where the constants have the same meaning as in Eq. 7, but $c_{5,2}$ has a lower value than $c_{4,2}$.

External and Internal Strategies. External strategies are aimed at reducing stressors, whereas internal strategies are directly aimed at reducing aversive internal state. The update equations for external and internal strategies are adapted directly from [34]:

$$E(t + dt) = E + dt(f_6 E(K_E - E) + b_6 A - c_6 U) \tag{9}$$

$$I(t + dt) = I + dt(g_7 I(K_I - I) + b_7 A - c_7 U). \tag{10}$$

The term $\alpha_E E(K_E - E)$ models logistic growth: the strategies are naturally capped by K unless motivated by aversive internal state or discouraged by urge to escape. At work, c_6 and c_7 increase to reflect a stronger effect of existing urge to escape when spending a long time in a closed-off office space.

Social Burden. The social burden parameter is directly adapted from Engels, who describes its purpose as "captur[ing] anxiety contagion present in social networks" [11]. The parameter is governed by a weighted sum of the aversive internal states of an agent's connections, internal strategy to reduce social burden, and a feedback term:

$$B(t + dt) = \begin{cases} B + dt(-j_9 B_i - g_9 I + b_9 \sum_{n=1}^{N} w_n A_n), & \text{if } N_i > 0 \\ B + dt(P_{lonely}), & \text{if} N_i = 0. \end{cases} \tag{11}$$

Aversive Internal State. Wang et al. [34] conceptualized aversive internal state as a linear combination of suicidal thought, escape behavior, internal strategies, and stress, with an additional logistic growth term representing an individual's natural propensity towards an aversive internal state. Engels [11] added the social burden term and an effect of the agent's clustering coefficient within its social network. This yields the following update equation:

$$A(t + dt) = A + dt(b_2 A(K_A - A) + a_2 S - d_2 T - e_2 X - g_2 I + j_2 B - \kappa), \tag{12}$$

where K_A is the carrying capacity (maximum) of the logistic growth term, and κ the weighted clustering coefficient of the agent.

3   Methods and Experimental Design

For all simulations, the simulated time was 40 days in the model with no data collected for the first 20 days, which served as a warm-up period, unless specified. This warm-up period was chosen on the basis of visual inspection of the model dynamics to identify when they settled. The baseline coefficient values were chosen so that suicidal thought emerged as spikes a couple times in the defined time period, partially influenced by values suggested in section 8.1 of Engels [11]. Unless specified, these coefficient values were kept constant for all simulations, subject to potential modifications from state-dependent dynamics. The model was initially run with three different parameter settings: one with only the parameters as proposed in model [34], one where memory of suicide was introduced, and one in which all proposed extensions were included. The parameter values were tracked for each setting for high-level analysis of system dynamics.

An experiment was set up to evaluate whether the added effect of sleep deprivation on stress and suicidal thought has a significant impact on the emergence of aversive internal state and suicidal thought within the model. To compare the effect with a baseline, social effects and memory of suicidal thought were removed for this experiment, so that the only included modifications to the original model [34] were state-dependent effects.

Two types of agents were defined, the only difference being that one always sleeps 8 h (good sleep agent), and the other always sleeps 6 h (bad sleep agent). The commute duration was made the same for both types of agents. With that, the only differences in model output between agents would be due to the effects of sleep deprivation and stochasticity in the stress term. The stress term was kept heterogeneous due to the significant effect of sleep deprivation on stress [13].

The model was run 1000 times with one agent of each type, the output variable being the Area Under the Curve $\mathrm{AUC}(X) = \int_2^{20} X\,dt$ of the suicidal thought parameter T and of the aversive internal state A. Means tests were performed to assess the significance of difference. The means of both agent types were then compared to the means of a baseline agent with no state-dependent effects, $i.e.$ one with update rules as described in [34]. The type of means test chosen depended on the distribution of the data: a two-sample t-test was performed if its assumption of normality was satisfied, and a Mann-Whitney test was performed if not.

4   Results

Figure 3 shows the dynamics of a randomly chosen agent in a best friends social network subject to social burden and state-dependent effects, $i.e.$ the dynamics of the extended model, as well as the dynamics of a baseline agent with no social influences and no state-dependent effects, $i.e.$ an agent with dynamics approximately as described in [34]. Figure 4 provides a comparison between the dynamics of the baseline agent and the dynamics of an agent with an added parameter that represents memory of suicidal thought.

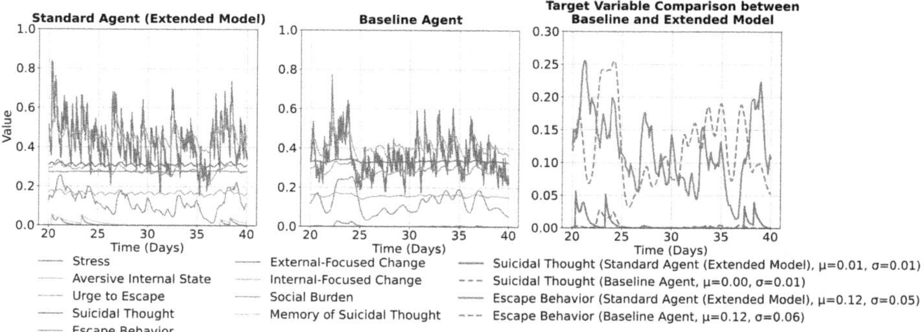

Fig. 3. Comparison of system dynamics for a random agent from the extended model (left) and an agent from the baseline model (middle). The rightmost plot shows a comparison between the suicidal thought and escape behavior parameters of each agent over time.

Figure 5 shows the dynamics of a random simulation of both the good sleep agent and the bad sleep agent, as described in Sect. 3.

Figure 6 shows the distributions of the AUC of suicidal thought and aversive internal state for each agent type over 1000 simulations. The mean AUC of the aversive internal state of the good sleep agent μ_A^{good} is 8.55. μ_T^{good} is 0.16. μ_A^{bad} is 8.98 and μ_T^{bad} is 1.05. μ_A^{base} is 8.22 and μ_T^{base} is 0.09.

Two-sample t-tests and Mann-Whitney tests were performed to compare μ_A and μ_T between the good sleep, bad sleep, and baseline groups. All tests yielded p-values much lower than $\alpha = 0.05$ (in the order of 10^{-100}), demonstrating highly significant differences between the means of the three groups.

5   Discussion

System Dynamics. In Fig. 3, the most notable differences between baseline dynamics and extended system dynamics seem to be related to escape behavior and suicidal thought. In the plot representing the baseline agent, the trajectory of escape behavior is smoother and never reaches 0. Despite that, there are only a couple of minor increases in suicidal thought. One could argue that never-ending escape behavior is unlikely, even in people with suicidal tendencies. In the extended model's dynamics, escape behavior fluctuates at a smaller amplitude but a higher frequency. Increases in suicidal thought are also higher. These dynamics most likely arise from the daily schedule the agent experiences, which causes fluctuations in parameter values by design. The short-term fluctuation of escape behavior and the sudden onset of suicidal thought resemble the dynamics of suicidal thought in real life more closely [9,20].

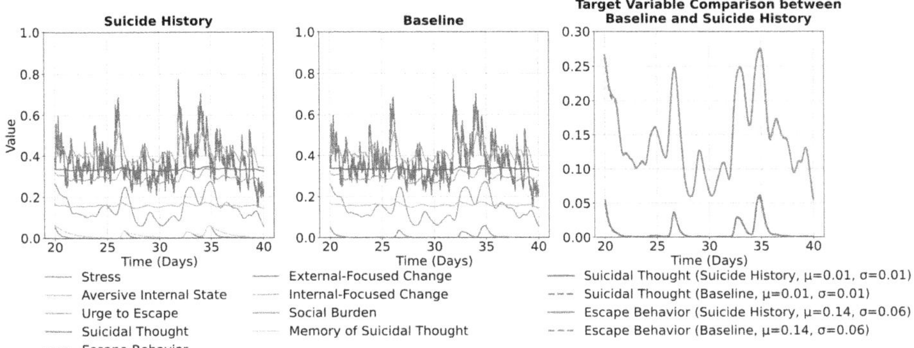

Fig. 4. Comparison of system dynamics for an agent with the memory of suicidal thought parameter added (left) and an agent from the baseline model (middle). The rightmost plot shows a comparison between the suicidal thought and escape behavior parameters of each agent.

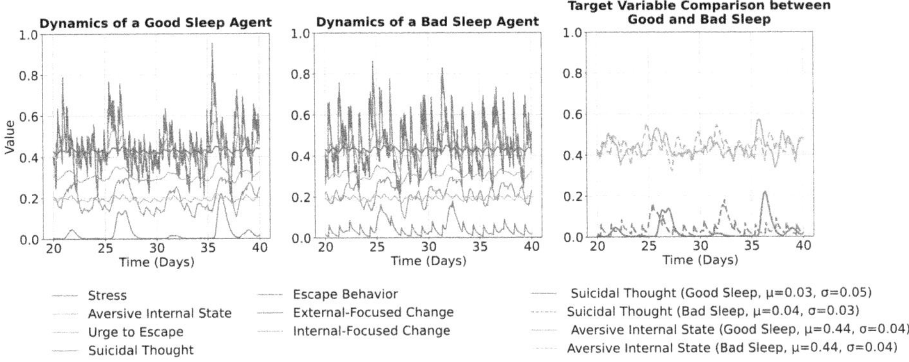

Fig. 5. Comparison of system dynamics for a good sleep agent (left) and a bad sleep agent (middle). The rightmost plot shows a comparison between the suicidal thought and aversive internal state variables of each agent.

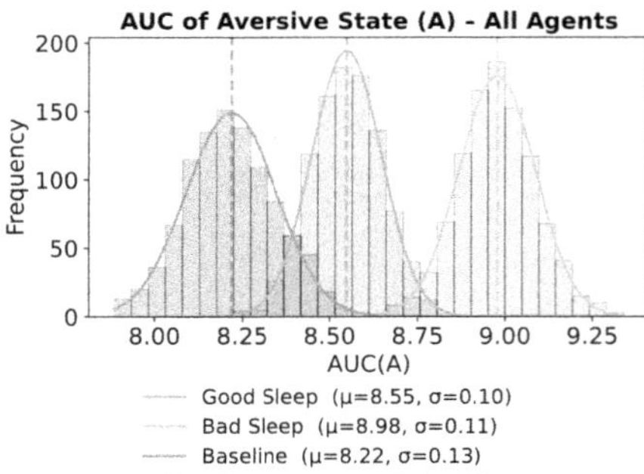

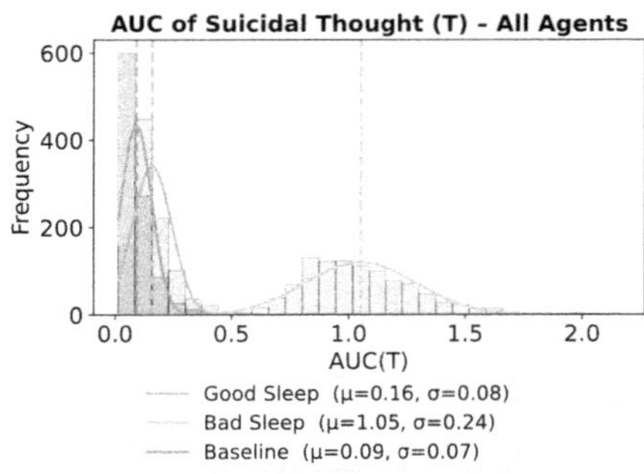

(a) All agents' AUC(A) value distributions   (b) All agents' AUC(T) value distributions

Fig. 6. Distribution of AUC values for aversive internal state A and suicidal thought T over 1000 simulations across three agent types: sufficient sleep, sleep deprived, and a baseline agent with dynamics as described in [34]. The mean is shown as a dashed line, and a fitted normal distribution is shown as a solid line.

Social burden is consistent throughout the simulation of the extension agent. The agent is connected in a best friends network, meaning social connections are strong, and agents are well-connected. This may explain a lack of suicidal thought despite social burden: connectivity reduces aversive internal state and urge to escape.

In Fig. 4, no meaningful differences can be observed between the agent with the memory of suicide parameter added and the baseline agent, apart from the presence of that parameter. The reason for this lack of effect is most likely due to the relatively low amounts of suicidal thought exhibited in the performed simulations, as well as the parameter tuning; it only slightly extends the duration of suicidal thought's effect on urge to escape. Decreasing the parameter's decay so that it persists longer could allow it to exercise its influence on the system in a more pronounced way. More research will have to be performed to justify such changes.

Sleep Deprivation. By visually inspecting the baseline dynamics in Fig. 3 and the dynamics of both agents in Fig. 5, one can already deduce that both μ_T and μ_A differ between all agent types. The good sleep agent has slightly more suicidal thoughts than both the baseline agent and the agent with all extensions applied, as shown in Fig. 3. This is in line with the observation made in Sect. 5 and in Engels [11] that a certain range of social burden is indicative of a healthy amount of social connections to other agents, which reduces suicidality.

The simulated values of $AUC(A)$ are roughly normally distributed for all agents, as shown with the overlaid normal distributions in Fig. 6. The distributions satisfy the assumption of normality of the t-test. The $AUC(T)$ distributions of the good sleep agent and the baseline agent are skewed, which is a boundary effect due to the low occurrence of suicidal thought during the simulated period.

As such, the non-parametric Mann-Whitney test was employed to means-test the $AUC(T)$ distributions. The results of the means tests support the intuition obtained in Fig. 6: the AUC means are significantly different between all agent types. Thus, the conclusion can be drawn that consistently shorter sleep, *i.e.* chronic sleep deprivation, increases aversive internal state and suicidal thought prevalence in the model. The significant difference in both aversive internal state and suicidal thought between an agent who sleeps 8 h a day and one who sleeps 6 h a day qualitatively agrees with research findings on the relationship between poor sleep quality and mental health [7,27].

Future Research. Due to the inherent complexity of suicidality, there are many avenues for future research and improvement of the model. The model has been validated qualitatively, but should still be validated quantitatively. Although many of the parameters are based on subjective metrics, such as social burden, the dynamics can be directly compared to data obtained from ecological momentary assessment studies.

The parameter update rules can be expanded to make the model more specific. Stress, for example, is known to be caused by a wide variety of events, with some having a greater impact than others [8]. Instead of the intensity of the stressors being dependent only on the local context, stressor impulses could be expanded with different types that lose intensity based on prior encounters.

Another area of improvement is agent interaction. Currently, agents have very minimal social interactions in the form of a constantly active social burden. Agents could be made to have social interactions at work dependent on their job or on cohesion within their team. The influence of social media is of great relevance as well, so any extension involving online social networks would be insightful.

Finally, the state-dependent effects could be refined and expanded. For example, social burden persists during sleep, which does not make much sense intuitively. Agents go to work every day, thus not accounting for weekends, the inclusion of which could change long-term dynamics and statistics. Work breaks could be introduced to mitigate the negative effects of being at work within the model. In future work, such additions can be introduced based on data obtained from smartphones [23] containing information about movement, location, and phone-based social interactions.

6   Conclusion

We demonstrate the utility of the ABM architecture to model interacting internal, social, and state-dependent processes in suicidality. The inclusion of social effects altered model dynamics by increasing resistance to suicidal thought through social connectivity, while sleep deprivation significantly increased both aversive internal state and suicidality compared to baseline conditions. These findings are consistent with existing literature, supporting the conclusion that such dynamics can be represented in an abstract yet meaningful way within ABMs.

The proposed model produces dynamics that are closely aligned with contemporary suicide research, including short-term fluctuations in escape behavior and the onset of suicidal thought. Its contribution to computational psychology lies in integrating internal agent dynamics with social and state-dependent effects within a unified framework. With further validation and refinement, the model could support the simulation of group-level interventions and inform policy by identifying societal factors that mediate suicidality.

Acknowledgments. This study was supported by the research priority area Urban Mental Health of the University of Amsterdam.

Disclosure of Interests. The authors have no competing interests to declare that are relevant to the content of this article.

References

1. Allen, N.B., Nelson, B.W., Brent, D., Auerbach, R.P.: Short-term prediction of suicidal thoughts and behaviors in adolescents: can recent developments in technology and computational science provide a breakthrough? J. Affect. Disord. **250**, 163–169 (2019). https://doi.org/10.1016/j.jad.2019.03.044

2. Baumeister, R.F.: Suicide as escape from self. Psychol. Rev. **97**(1), 90–113 (1990). https://doi.org/10.1037/0033-295x.97.1.90

3. de Beurs, D., et al.: A network perspective on suicidal behavior: understanding suicidality as a complex system. Suicide Life-Threat. Behav. **51**(1), 115–126 (2021). https://doi.org/10.1111/sltb.12676

4. de Beurs, D., et al.: Symptoms of a feather flock together? An exploratory secondary dynamic time warp analysis of 11 single case time series of suicidal ideation and related symptoms. Behav. Res. Ther. **178**, 104572 (2024). https://doi.org/10.1016/j.brat.2024.104572

5. Blacutt, M., O'Loughlin, C.M., Ammerman, B.A.: Bias toward escape responding during reinforcement learning among those with suicidal ideation. J. Psychiatr. Res. **181**, 586–595 (2025). https://doi.org/10.1016/j.jpsychires.2024.12.020

6. Brosschot, J.F., Pieper, S., Thayer, J.F.: Expanding stress theory: prolonged activation and perseverative cognition. Psychoneuroendocrinology **30**(10), 1043–1049 (2005). https://doi.org/10.1016/j.psyneuen.2005.04.008

7. Chaput, J.P., et al.: Sleep timing, sleep consistency, and health in adults: a systematic review. Appl. Physiol. Nutr. Metab. **45**(10 (Suppl. 2)), S232–S247 (2020). https://cdnsciencepub.com/doi/abs/10.1139/apnm-2020-0032

8. Cohodes, E.M., et al.: Development and validation of the dimensional inventory of stress and trauma across the lifespan (distal): a novel assessment tool to facilitate the dimensional study of psychobiological sequelae of exposure to adversity. Dev. Psychobiol. **65**(4), e22372 (2023). https://doi.org/10.1002/dev.22372

9. Coppersmith, D.D.L., Ryan, O., Fortgang, R.G., Millner, A.J., Kleiman, E.M., Nock, M.K.: Mapping the timescale of suicidal thinking. Proc. Natl. Acad. Sci. U.S.A. **120**(17), e2215434120 (2023). https://doi.org/10.1073/pnas.2215434120

10. Dunbar, R.I.M.: The anatomy of friendship. Trends Cogn. Sci. **22**(1), 32–51 (2018). https://doi.org/10.1016/j.tics.2017.10.004
11. Engels, S.: Social network modeling and machine learning for suicidal ideation prediction. Thesis, University of Amsterdam (2025)
12. Franklin, J.C., et al.: Risk factors for suicidal thoughts and behaviors: a meta-analysis of 50 years of research. Psychol. Bull. **143**(2), 187–232 (2017). https://doi.org/10.1037/bul0000084
13. Fries, E., Dettenborn, L., Kirschbaum, C.: The cortisol awakening response (CAR): facts and future directions. Int. J. Psychophysiol. **72**(1), 67–73 (2009). https://doi.org/10.1016/j.ijpsycho.2008.03.014
14. Hammen, C., Kim, E.Y., Eberhart, N.K., Brennan, P.A.: Chronic and acute stress and the prediction of major depression in women. Depress. Anxiety **26**(8), 718–23 (2009). https://doi.org/10.1002/da.20571
15. Harris, C.R., et al.: Array programming with NumPy. Nature **585**(7825), 357–362 (2020). https://doi.org/10.1038/s41586-020-2649-2
16. ter Hoeven, E., Kwakkel, J., Hess, V., Pike, T., Wang, B., Kazil, J.: Mesa 3: agent-based modeling with python in 2025. J. Open Source Softw. **10**(107), 7668 (2025). https://doi.org/10.21105/joss.07668
17. Hunter, J.D.: Matplotlib: a 2D graphics environment. Comput. Sci. Eng. **9**(3), 90–95 (2007). https://doi.org/10.1109/MCSE.2007.55
18. Jaroszewski, A.C., et al.: Past suicide attempt is associated with a weaker decision-making bias to actively escape from suicide-related stimuli. J. Psychopathol. Clin. Sci. **134**(5), 503–519 (2025). https://doi.org/10.1037/abn0000989
19. Kim, E.J., Dimsdale, J.E.: The effect of psychosocial stress on sleep: a review of polysomnographic evidence. Behav. Sleep Med. **5**(4), 256–278 (2007). https://doi.org/10.1080/15402000701557383
20. Kivelä, L.: Dynamics of despair: examining suicidal ideation using real-time methodologies. Ph.d. dissertation, University of Leiden (2025). https://hdl.handle.net/1887/4175271
21. Machell, K.A., Rallis, B.A., Esposito-Smythers, C.: Family environment as a moderator of the association between anxiety and suicidal ideation. J. Anxiety Disord. **40**, 1–7 (2016). https://doi.org/10.1016/j.janxdis.2016.03.002
22. McGonagle, K.A., Kessler, R.C.: Chronic stress, acute stress, and depressive symptoms. Am. J. Community Psychol. **18**(5), 681–706 (1990). https://doi.org/10.1007/bf00931237
23. National Institute for Mental Health: Brighten study (2018). https://www.synapse.org/Synapse:syn10848316
24. Newman, M., Watts, D.: Renormalization group analysis of the small-world network model. Phys. Lett. A **263**(4–6), 341–346 (1999). https://doi.org/10.1016/s0375-9601(99)00757-4
25. O'Connor, R.C., Kirtley, O.J.: The integrated motivational–volitional model of suicidal behaviour. Philos. Trans. Roy. Soc. B Biol. Sci. **373**(1754) (2018). https://doi.org/10.1098/rstb.2017.0268
26. World Health Organization: Suicide rates (2025). https://www.who.int/data/gho/data/themes/mental-health/suicide-rates
27. Pigeon, W.R., Bishop, T.M., Titus, C.E.: The relationship between sleep disturbance, suicidal ideation, suicide attempts, and suicide among adults: a systematic review. Psychiatr. Ann. **46**(3), 177–186 (2016). https://doi.org/10.3928/00485713-20160128-01

28. Singleton, M.D., Frey, L.M., Webb, A., Cerel, J.: Public health surveillance of youth suicide attempts: challenges and opportunities. Suicide Life-Threat. Behav. **50**(1), 42–55 (2020). https://doi.org/10.1111/sltb.12572
29. Sposato, R.G., Röderer, K., Cervinka, R.: The influence of control and related variables on commuting stress. Transport. Res. F: Traffic Psychol. Behav. **15**(5), 581–587 (2012). https://doi.org/10.1016/j.trf.2012.05.003
30. voor de Statistiek, C.B.: Zelfdodingen, 1970-2024 (2025). https://www.cbs.nl/nl-nl/maatwerk/2025/21/zelfdodingen-1970-2024
31. Stone, D.M., Jones, C.M., Mack, K.A.: Changes in suicide rates - united states, 2018-2019. MMWR Morbidity Mortality Weekly Report **70**(8), 261–268 (2021). https://doi.org/10.15585/mmwr.mm7008a1
32. The pandas development team: pandas-dev/pandas: Pandas (2020). https://doi.org/10.5281/zenodo.3509134
33. Van Orden, K.A., Witte, T.K., Cukrowicz, K.C., Braithwaite, S.R., Selby, E.A., Joiner, T.E., Jr.: The interpersonal theory of suicide. Psychol. Rev. **117**(2), 575–600 (2010). https://doi.org/10.1037/a0018697
34. Wang, S., Robinaugh, D., Millner, A., Fortgang, R., Nock, M.: Mathematical and Computational Modeling of Suicide as a Complex Dynamical System (2023). https://doi.org/10.31234/osf.io/b29cs
35. Yang, Q., Hu, Y.Q., Zeng, Z.H., Liu, S.J., Wu, T., Zhang, G.H.: The relationship of family functioning and suicidal ideation among adolescents: the mediating role of defeat and the moderating role of meaning in life. Int. J. Environ. Res. Public Health **19**(23) (2022). https://doi.org/10.3390/ijerph192315895

Vasculitis Outcome Prediction Using Machine Learning and Federated Learning

Kamil Woźniak[1]([✉]), Tadeusz Satława[1], Krzysztof Wójcik[2], Krystyna Milian[1], Sabina Lichołai[3,4], Tomasz Gubała[1], Grzegorz Biedroń[5], Katarzyna Wawrzycka-Adamczyk[6], Stanisława Bazan-Socha[2], Anna Masiak[7], Michał Chmielewski[7], Barbara Bułło-Piontecka[8], Alicja Dębska-Ślizień[8], Hanna Storoniak[8], Magdalena Krajewska[9], Hanna Augustyniak-Bartosik[9], Radosław Jeleniewicz[10], Maria Majdan[10], Katarzyna Jakuszko[11], Marcin Milchert[12], Marek Brzosko[12], Joanna Kur-Zalewska[13], Witold Tłustochowicz[13], Marta Madej[14], Anna Hawrot-Kawecka[15], Eugeniusz Kucharz[16], Piotr Głuszko[17], Krzysztof Bonek[18], Małgorzata Wisłowska[18], Joanna Miłkowska-Dymanowska[19], Anna Lewandowska-Polak[20], Joanna Makowska[20], Joanna Zalewska[21], Jacek Musiał[2], Jose Sousa[1], and Maciej Malawski[1]

[1] Sano - Centre for Personalised Computational Medicine, Kraków, Poland
k.wozniak@sanoscience.org
[2] Prof A. Szczeklik 2nd Chair of Internal Medicine, Department of Allergy, Autoimmunization and Hypercoagulation, Jagiellonian University Medical College, Kraków, Poland
[3] Division of Molecular Biology and Clinical Genetics, Jagiellonian University Medical College, Kraków, Poland
[4] Academic Computer Centre Cyfronet, AGH University of Science and Technology, Kraków, Poland
[5] Department of Rheumatology and Immunology, Jagiellonian University Medical College, Kraków, Poland
[6] Center for the Development of Therapies for Civilization and Age-Related Diseases, Jagiellonian University Medical College, Kraków, Poland
[7] Department of Internal Medicine, Connective Tissue Diseases and Geriatrics, Medical University of Gdansk, Gdańsk, Poland
[8] Department of Nephrology, Transplantology and Internal Diseases, Medical University of Gdansk, Gdańsk, Poland
[9] Division of Nephrology, Transplantology and Clinical Immunology at 4th Military Clinical Hospital, Department of Non-Procedural Clinical Sciences Faculty of Medicine, Wroclaw University of Science and Technology, Wrocław, Poland
[10] Department of Rheumatology and Connective Tissue Diseases, Medical University of Lublin, Lublin, Poland
[11] Department of Nephrology and Transplantation Medicine, Wroclaw Medical University, Wrocław, Poland
[12] Department of Rheumatology, Internal Medicine, Diabetology, Geriatrics and Clinical Immunology with the Gastroenterology Unit, Pomeranian Medical University in Szczecin, Szczecin, Poland
[13] Military Medical Institute, National Research Institute, Warszawa, Poland

---

Kamil Woźniak, Tadeusz Satława and Krzysztof Wójcik contributed equally with all other contributors.

P. Neumann et al. (Eds.): ICCS 2026, LNCS 16784, pp. 241–256, 2026.
https://doi.org/10.1007/978-3-032-29924-6_17

[14] Department of Rheumatology and Internal Medicine, Wroclaw Medical University, Wrocław, Poland

[15] Department of Internal Medicine and Metabolic Diseases, Medical University of Silesia, Katowice, Poland

[16] Department of Internal Medicine, Rheumatology and Clinical Immunology, Medical University of Silesia, Katowice, Poland

[17] Pratia MCM Kraków, Kraków, Poland

[18] Department of Rheumatology, National Institute of Geriatrics, Rheumatology and Rehabiitation, Warszawa, Poland

[19] Department of Pneumology, Chair of Internal Medicine, Medical University of Lodz, Łódź, Poland

[20] Department of Rheumatology, Medical University of Lodz, Łódź, Poland

[21] Department of Rheumatology and Connective Tissue Diseases, Ludwik Rydygier Collegium Medicum in Bydgoszcz of the Nicolaus Copernicus University in Torun, Bydgoszcz, Poland

Abstract. Predicting the clinical outcomes in patients with antineutrophil cytoplasmic antibody (ANCA)-associated vasculitis (AAV) remains a challenge and early identification of patients who are at risk of severe disease course is crucial. To address this, we applied machine learning (ML) and federated learning (FL) techniques to the POLVAS dataset – the largest multicenter clinical database of vasculitis cases in Poland and one of the largest AAV datasets in Europe. Our goal was to predict the key outcomes: increased risk of death and the need for renal replacement therapy (RRT), an independent risk factor of death. We also analysed the significance of individual input features for the predictive capabilities of our models. Furthermore, we compared the performance of centralized model with FL models, which allow for data privacy preservation – a key factor given the highly sensitive medical data involved. We achieved a prediction performance of 0.86 AUC for RRT prediction, and 0.81 AUC for death prediction using a centralized approach and 0.86 weighted mean AUC for RRT prediction and 0.80 for death prediction with the FL approach. The presented results show that FL can effectively predict the risk of RRT and mortality in AAV patients, addressing privacy concerns without compromising the accuracy.

Keywords: AAV · Federated Learning · Machine Learning · Vasculitis

1   Introduction

ANCA-associated vasculitides (AAV), are a group of multisystem, life-threatening rare diseases in which inflammation mainly affects small and medium-sized vessels. There are three main types of AAV, two of which are predominant, namely granulomatosis with polyangiitis (GPA) and microscopic polyangiitis (MPA). The third and the rarest form of AAV is eosinophilic granulomatosis with polyangiitis (EGPA). They are characterized by the presence of antineutrophil cytoplasmic antibodies against neutrophil cytoplasmic enzymes – proteinase 3 (PR3), usually presenting as cANCA pattern when detected by immunofluorescence technique; and myeloperoxidase (MPO), usually presenting as pANCA pattern when detected by immunofluorescence technique. GPA, the most common type of AAV, characterized mainly by granulomatous inflammation of multiple organs, is usually associated with anti- PR3. MPA, on the other hand, is in most cases associated with anti-MPO.

The course of these diseases is currently difficult to predict, posing to a clinician a problem of prediction – at the time of diagnosis – of the future progression of the disease, including its pace. The disease frequently takes an undulating course with consecutive exacerbations and remissions leading eventually to irreversible damage of various organs. Some patients present with only localized lesions involving the skin and/or single organs. In others, a systemic disease with multiorgan involvement, sometimes with a life-threatening course, develops early on. Difficulties in predicting the course of the disease are also due to incomplete understanding of its etiology. There are several hypotheses, some suggesting that genetic factors play an important role, while others assume that AAVs may be related to environmental factors such as viruses or bacterial infections. It has been shown [1] (for example), that *Staphylococcus aureus* nasal colonization is approximately three times more frequent in patients with GPA compared to healthy controls. Optimal as well as personalized treatment schemes for AAV patients are still under development.

The main objective of the presented study was, therefore, to apply a range of data analysis, machine learning (ML) and Federated Learning (FL) techniques to the Polish Vasculitis Consortium (POLVAS) cohort [2], in order to create predictive machine learning models, perform their in-depth analysis of accuracy and generalizability. These models are applied to patient's clinical data available at the time of diagnosis, in order to predict the risk of (a) developing renal impairment requiring RRT (renal replacement therapy - mainly haemodialysis and peritoneal dialysis), and (b) death. The second objective was to analyse which health-related factors increase the likelihood of death.

2 Methods

2.1 Data

Like other rare diseases, vasculitides pose problems for computational data analysis approaches due to the difficulty in involving an adequate number of patients. Fortunately, the Polish Vasculitis Consortium (POLVAS) has assembled a multi-center AAV database, forming the Polish vasculitis registry. POLVAS data is gathered from 12 centers in Poland. Adult patients diagnosed with AAV by participating centers between years 1990 and 2020 were included, with their clinical and laboratory data collected in the POLVAS registry [2–4]. We only included individuals who meet the American College of Rheumatology classification criteria for granulomatosis with polyangiitis (GPA), or microscopic polyangiitis (MPA) as well as GPA, MPA, and EGPA nomenclature proposed by the 2012 Chapel Hill Consensus Conference (CHCC 2012) [5]. Specific organ involvement, disease relapse, and disease remission were defined according to the Birmingham Vasculitis Activity Score, version 3. However, as data was collected retrospectively, the exact score for each individual patient was not available. We included patients with AAV regardless of disease severity and excluded patients with a documented diagnosis of AAV who were lost to follow-up at the time of data collection, patients younger than 18 years of age, and pregnant women.

Figure 1 depicts the distribution of data over centers and classes, i.e. renal therapy status and death status. The plots clearly indicate a high imbalance of data distribution across classes and centers. This imbalance is stronger in case of death status, where only 11% of patients have positive status, and only 8/12 centers have positive cases. In the case of renal therapy status 23% of patients have positive status and again only 8/12 centers have positive cases.

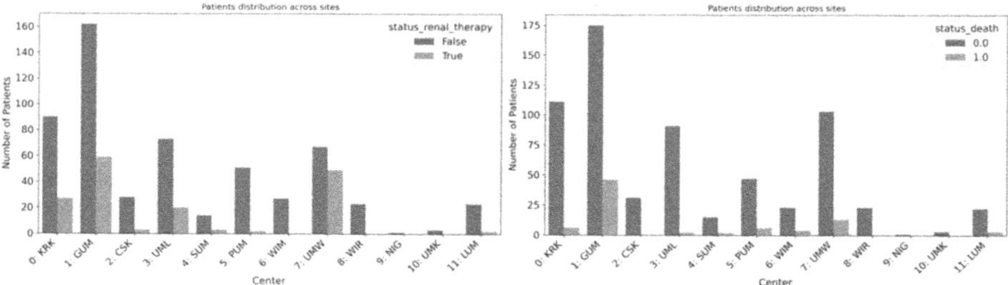

Fig. 1. Patients distribution across centers and classes.

2.2 Ethics Declaration

The data used in the presented work was collected with approval of the Bioethical Committee of the Jagiellonian University, followed by similar approvals issued by appropriate bioethical committees of all remaining POLVAS consortium participating centers. All participants have provided their written informed consent.

2.3 Pre-Processing

In such a diverse and maintained by different centers dataset it is inevitable that some values are incorrect or missing. Therefore, ensuring the quality of the dataset used for modelling was an important part of the whole process.

In total, there was data for 747 patients, however multiple checks reduced this number. Two records have been removed due to improbable relation between first symptoms date and date of death (death prior to symptoms). Additional 15 rows were removed due to date of diagnosis before date of first symptoms. Another 2 patients were removed due to missing both diagnosis and first symptoms dates. Finally, one observation which was removed had more than 43 years between onset of symptoms and diagnosis and was treated as an outlier (all other patients had no more than 28 years with vast majority less than 4 years). Finally, 727 observations have been selected for the modelling stage.

Before training the ML model, the feature engineering was applied. Few features were derived from dates of disease progression. However, there were cases when those values (periods between dates) could not be calculated due to the presence of missing values. Although selected method, LightGBM [6], automatically handles missing data, in some cases it was beneficial to impute it. Therefore, missing dates were imputed using the mean difference between diagnosis and first symptoms dates for observations having both dates (444 days). Then, for 13 rows with first symptoms but without the diagnosis date, the latter was calculated as 444 days after first symptoms. Accordingly, the date of first symptoms have been set to 444 before diagnosis for 15 patients; cases when both dates were missing have been removed as described earlier. For 10 patients there were missing value of total number of exacerbations, and these were replaced with 0 value. Twenty-one patients had information about the number of exacerbations but missing time between diagnosis to exacerbation – for these cases median value stratified by number of exacerbations was used. In the opposite case (reported time of diagnosis to exacerbation with 0 exacerbations; 11 such cases) number of exacerbations was set to 1.

Two numerical columns (CRP level in mg/l and creatinine level in mg/dl) have been first cleaned from outliers. Values less than 0 or greater than 1000 mg/l (for CRP) or 80 mg/dl (for creatinine) were treated as missing. Then those values have been set using IterativeImputer from sklearn library.

The analysis was performed on a retrospective database of 727 POLVAS patients diagnosed with AAV selected in the above manner. The demographic and clinical characteristics of the patients included in the study, organ involvement, antibody pattern as well as some laboratory data was collected and used in this study.

2.4 Developed Models and Input Selection

When designing the training procedure for the predictive models, an important factor from the clinical point of view was to discern information which could be provided to the physician performing the diagnosis. Preferably, the models should be able to communicate increased risk of RRT or death of the patient under examination, early enough for the physician to adjust therapy in order to reverse the unfavourable trajectory of the disease.

A more detailed discussion of the relative importance of specific information for prediction accuracy is provided in the Feature Significance Analysis section. The parameters used to inform predictive models included: specific organ involvement (musculoskeletal, skin, eye, ear/nose/throat, respiratory, heart, gastrointestinal tract, renal, urinary, central nervous system, neurological), detected antibody type (cANCA/anti-PR3 or pANCA/anti-MPO), CRP and creatinine levels (for risk of death prediction only), patient's age at different stages (first symptoms, diagnosis, first exacerbation), and the perceived speed of disease progression (time elapsed between selected stages). Additionally, interactions between pairs of organs (for example, eye and skin, or heart and CNS), and – based on medical expert knowledge – three- and four-organ groups, were included as well. In the RRT risk prediction model, creatinine level was explicitly excluded, since sufficiently elevated creatinine levels already call for renal replacement therapy, and the goal was to detect high-risk cases prior to that episode, when more aggressive drug treatment may still prevent the need for RRT. It is important to note that the POLVAS registry currently provides only the highest creatinine level recorded for each patient (we discuss this limitation in the Discussion section).

In the death risk prediction model application of the RRT procedure was also disregarded as a parameter – in order to base the model's predictive power only on earlier symptoms and tests.

Although data collected by the POLVAS consortium are centralized, being aware of the rarity of this scenario, in addition to the centralized models we also trained the predictive models in federated mode. Federated learning enables the development of prediction models based on data from multiple medical centers while preserving patient privacy by keeping data localized. This approach enhances predictive accuracy through diverse datasets, helps overcome data silos, and mitigates privacy concerns associated with centralized data aggregation [7]. The centralized and federated strategies were optimized independently from each other.

2.5 Centralized Models

In the model construction procedure, we employed a range of ML tools, including: Light-GBM [6], scikit-learn [8], scikit-optimize [9] and pandas [10]. We evaluated a number of different approaches to building the ML models (including logistic regression, support vector machines, random forests), obtaining the best results for the gradient boosting algorithm. We used a gradient boosting algorithm implementation called LightGBM. We performed the hyperparameter tuning procedure using the Bayesian optimization method [11, 12] and applied ten-fold cross-validation to assess generalization of models using Receiver Operating Characteristic (ROC) curve as a measure of the model's performance [13]. To prevent model overfitting [14], we used double (nested) cross-validation. We also examined the calibration of the model to assess the bias of the predicted probabilities.

2.6 Federated Models

To develop our classification models, we adapted the method and implementation presented in [15], which consists of training horizontal federated XGBoost model with a 1-layer convolutional neural network (CNN) representing local learning rates. Instead of using XGBoost, we applied LightGBM model to make the results comparable with the developed earlier centralized scenario. Additionally, we utilized W&B platform for finetuning optimal hyperparameters values and to optimize the training strategy. We trained multiple versions of the federated models and observed performance variability, with the results differing based on the specific center where they were evaluated. This observation highlighted the need for careful evaluation of the results. To assess the generalizability of the developed models, we performed training using Leave One (Center) Out (LOO) cross validation approach, using data from all but one center for training and testing on data from the remaining one. We applied stratified split with proportions: 72% of data were used for training, 13% for validation and 15% for testing, ensuring that at least one positive and negative case is reserved for validation and testing if possible.

We used the same metric, AUC, as in centralized scenario for assessing model performance. The final metrics for the federated models were calculated as a weighted mean, weighted by the test size, collected for centers with available positive samples (otherwise AUC is 0).

Based on the observation of high variability of results, in addition to preparing the globally optimized federated model, we also developed dedicated versions of the models, specifically optimized for each individual center. Besides finetuning hyperparameters (max_depth, max_bin, min_child_samples, num_leaves, learning_rate and CNN learning_rate), in this scenario we additionally allowed a selection of centers from which data were used for training. Figure 2 presents the results of optimizing training parameters for the seventh center, a plot from W&B platform, in this particular case, the model achieving the best performance was trained using data from centers: 1, 3, 4, 5, 11. The method is implemented in PyTorch using Flower framework [16].

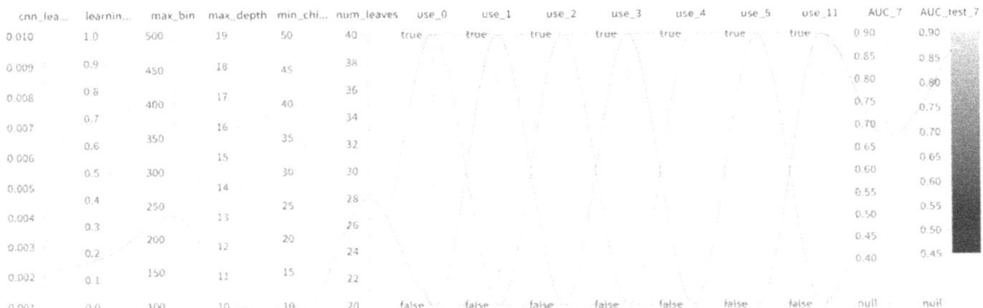

Fig. 2. Finding optimal training parameters for the federated model dedicated to the seventh center.

2.7 Rule-Based Federated Learning

Associative rules mining algorithms extract patterns from the data in the form of $F_l \wedge F_m \rightarrow C_n$ logical rules (F_l, F_m stand for specific ranges of values of the features l, m and C_n stands for class n). These algorithms, although currently somewhat overshadowed by methods based on optimization and gradient descent such as neural networks or gradient boosting, have their advantages such as high interpretability and less data needed to obtain useful results.

Among them is RIPPER [17], a robust algorithm for imbalanced datasets. It iteratively builds rules for the positive (usually minority) class and instances that do not satisfy these rules automatically default to the negative class. Algorithm runs until all positive cases are covered or the threshold number of iterations is reached. The method selects the features and their values as rule conditions that best separate positive cases from negative cases (based on FOIL's information gain [18]):

$$\text{gain} = p\left[\log\frac{p}{p+n} - \log\frac{P}{P+N}\right] \tag{1}$$

where p is the number of positive examples covered by the rule, $p + n$ is the number of all examples covered by the rule, P is the number of positive examples in the whole set, $P + N$ is the number of all examples in the set. This is followed by a pruning step, for which a separate pruning set is used from the training data, during which unnecessary conditions are removed from the rules, making the rules more compact and at the same time preventing overfitting by creating too specific rules. Each rule obtained in this way is added to the ruleset, and the cases covered by it are not taken into account when creating further rules.

Most rule-based methods emerged at a time when there was less demand for, and fewer opportunities to train, distributed models. There has been previous work attempting to train RIPPER model in a less localized way. For example, in one approach, the model was trained centrally, with RIPPER models acting as weak learners in an ensemble [19]. In another work [20], the authors presented a similar approach to the one we adopt below. This work does not explicitly position its solution as federated learning. Its authors used Hadoop framework and, as in the federated approach, they constructed local models. Then, the models in the form of rules were sent not to the central server, but to other local sites and validated there. The rules were then filtered and merged on this central server. The model demonstrated high prediction accuracy. The disadvantages of this approach, however, are the process of validating local models, the need to coordinate complex communication between local sites, high latency of server updates and increased risk when it comes to maintaining privacy. It also requires high level of trust between sites.

Here, we present a related approach as a proof of concept of the appropriateness of applying similar rule-based approach to small biomedical datasets. We chose RIPPER because it has been shown to achieve high prediction quality, often outperforming other similar methods, and is robust in handling imbalanced datasets since it prioritizes learning rules for the **minority class** first. RIPPER is also characterized by high degree of transparency, producing concise inference rules that are easy to interpret.

In this work, we trained RIPPER using a federated approach as follows: given data from multiple centers, we simulated local rule mining at each center and then sent these rules to a central server. The set of aggregated rules then created a global model. To classify a new case, each rule is checked to see if the case satisfies its conditions, and the rule applies. The matched rule determines the class to which the case belongs. If no rule covers the case, the default rule that assigns it to the majority class applies. As with the global LGBM model, here we also used the LOO approach, where each center was treated as a test set in a given iteration and the results were averaged. Again, we used Flower framework to simulate a federated environment.

2.8 Feature Significance Analysis

The second objective of our study was to gain better insight, by means of computational analysis, into which health-related factors increase the likelihood of an unfavorable course of vasculitis.

To this end, we used the optimization procedure based on ten-fold cross-validation and reapplied it to the entirety of the available data – the whole cohort of POLVAS patients. This enabled us to harness the full breadth of input data in order to gain the most accurate – given the circumstances – insight into the significance of individual features from the prediction perspective. Again, the hyperparameter tuning and the training of the best model was repeated twice: once for the prediction of the renal replacement therapy risk, and once for the prediction of the risk of death.

The measure of significance of a particular feature was computed as sum of information gained by the split on that feature for all trees in the model ensemble. It measures the amount of information that is gained (meaning how much entropy is reduced) after performing a split on feature F [21]:

$$\text{information gain}(T, F) = \text{entropy}(T) - \text{entropy}(T, F) \tag{2}$$

$$\text{entropy}(T, F) = \sum_{i}^{F_{\text{splis}}} \frac{|T_i|}{|T|} \text{entropy}(T_i) \tag{3}$$

$$\text{entropy}(T) = -p\log_2 p - (1 - p)\log_2(1 - p) \tag{4}$$

where $|T_i|$ is the number of samples in subset T_i, $|T_i|$ is the number of all samples and p is probability of a positive outcome in set T.

3 Results

3.1 Centralized Results

The model training and evaluation procedure (described in the Methods section) was performed twice: once for the RRT risk prediction model, and once for the risk of death prediction model. In both cases we obtained results which we consider promising. The outcome is a set of twenty models, ten per each clinical question – Table 1 presents the mean value and standard deviation for the ROC AUC measure across all ten trained models, with the best hyperparameters selected for each. Two ROC AUC charts in Figure 3 present the performance of all ten models in predicting each clinical event.

Table 1. Mean Area Under the ROC Curve (ROC AUC) measure, and standard deviations computed across all ten models (for each of the two clinical questions).

Model	Mean ROC AUC for 10 folds	Std deviation for ROC AUC
RRT prediction	0.86	0.04
Death prediction	0.81	0.08

As described in the Methods section, we retrained final models, using the same cross-validation scheme, on the full dataset, in order to perform feature significance analysis. The 20 most significant features per model are presented in Fig. 4.

When comparing the relevance of symptoms computed by our models (when trained on an optimal set of parameters) with clinical knowledge, it seems that inflammatory (CRP) exponents are important. For both models, this information proved to be relevant to the course of the disease. Furthermore, features related to age and progress of the disease are also important in both models. For the model which predicts the risk of RRT, features related to renal inflammation are significant, whereas the death risk prediction model takes into account involvement of other organs as well.

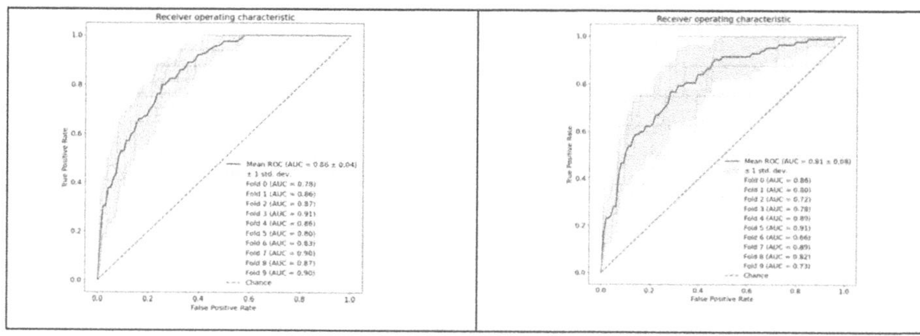

Fig. 3. ROC plot for all 10 folds (models) developed per each event prediction (need for RRT in the diagram on the left; death in the diagram on the right).

Information about the medical care unit (center) where the given patient had been treated was also significant, which is caused by slight specialization among the POLVAS centers regarding the cases which are treated at any particular center (for instance, some complex cases are transferred to a small subset of centers which have better experience in dealing with specific disease progression scenarios).

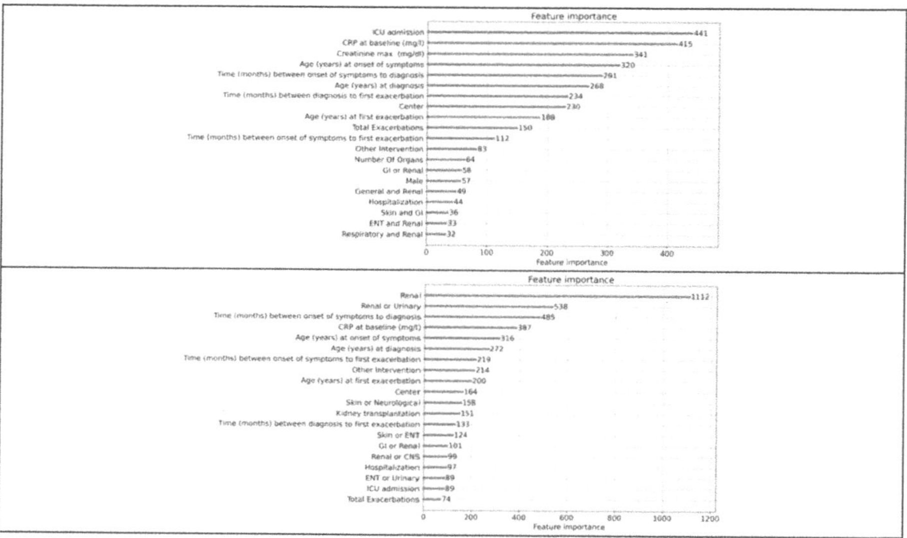

Fig. 4. Twenty features (columns in the input clinical data set used for training the models) evaluated as most significant for prediction of the risk of the clinical event in question – need for RRT in the bottom diagram and risk of death in the top diagram. Significance is computed using the sum of gained information formula (presented in Feature Significance Analysis section).

3.2 Federated Results

We optimized the global federated model and dedicated federated models for individual centers, predicting death and RRT. The obtained results are presented below.

Global Federated Models. Table 2 presents the performance achieved by the global federated models, evaluated using a LOO cross-validation approach. The mean performance metrics are derived from eight experiments, each corresponding to centers containing both positive and negative samples. The remaining 4 centers, which only contain negative cases, were excluded from the computation of the mean. The reported mean values are weighted according to the size of the test set for each individual center.

Table 2. Weighted mean test AUC and standard deviation test AUC from LOO experiments.

Model	Experiments count	Weighted mean test AUC from LOO experiments	Weighted std. test AUC from LOO experiments
RRT prediction	8 × 20	0.76	0.11
Death prediction	8 × 20	0.61	0.08

The model developed to predict the need for renal therapy obtained mean weighted AUC equal to 0.76. The model predicting death achieved 0.61 mean weighted AUC. Notably, the performance of these federated models, indicating generalizability of the model to data from external centers is substantially lower compared to the centralized versions.

Dedicated Federated Models. The observation of high variability in the performance of federated models, when evaluated on local test sets, motivated us to further investigate by training additional dedicated federated models, optimized for individual centers. Table 3 presents results of these experiments, comparing three training strategies. The first and second strategy uses entire available training data, first optimizes local validation AUC, second global validation AUC, while the third strategy uses data only from specific centers, selected during optimization processes and optimizes local validation AUC. The model predicting the need for renal therapy achieved weighted mean test AUC of 0.83 when trained with entire training data and improved to 0.86 when trained with data from the selected centers. Similarly, the model predicting mortality achieved weighted mean test AUC of 0.77/0.78 when trained on the entire dataset and increased to 0.80 when trained using the center-specific data subset.

Dedicated Rule-Based Classifier. The results obtained with the rule-based federated RIPPER using LOO cross-validation approach are shown in Table 4. The resulting average ROC AUC values from the 8 experiments are 0.71 for the need of renal therapy prediction and 0.64 for death prediction. These results are comparable to those obtained using the LGBM model in a similar manner.

Table 3. Weighted mean test AUC and standard deviation test AUC of dedicated federated model.

Model	Experiments count	Training strategy	Weighted mean test AUC of dedicated federated models	Weighted std. test AUC of dedicated models
RRT pred.	8 × 20	Using full dataset, optimizing local validation AUC	0.83	0.09
	1 × 20	Using full dataset, optimizing global validation AUC	0.83	0.11
	8 × 30	Using data only from selected centers, optimizing local validation AUC	0.86	0.12
Death pred.	8 × 20	Using full dataset, optimizing local validation AUC	0.77	0.20
	1 × 20	Using full dataset, optimizing global validation AUC	0.78	0.17
	8 × 30	Using data only from selected centers, optimizing local validation AUC	0.80	0.18

Table 4. Results obtained using federated RIPPER.

RIPPER Model	Experiments count	Training strategy	Weighted mean test AUC of dedicated federated models
RRT prediction	8	LOO-CV	0.71
Death prediction	8	LOO-CV	0.64

4 Discussion

To the best of our knowledge, this is the first analysis which applies machine learning and especially federated learning techniques to answer clinical questions using data from a multi-center vasculitis registry of this size and quality. POLVAS is currently the largest AAV registry with this much information collected for each individual in Central Europe. We posed a question as to whether, based on the available data, we could predict the course of the disease and, in particular, the risk of RRT due to end-stage renal failure, and death, in centralized and federated approach. We also identified a group of parameters that may be relevant for this outcomes analysis.

A machine learning approach in the scope of disease course prediction has been presented by Lezcano-Valverde et al. [22] among others. In their work, they presented a mortality prediction model for rheumatoid arthritis using data from two independent cohorts. Of the variables analysed, age at diagnosis, erythrocyte sedimentation rate, and number of hospital admissions exhibited the highest predictive value. This model (by the authors' own admission) appears to be overestimated but could be validated and improved with an external data set [22]. The same disease was referred to by Lin et al. [4] In their work they present a model which aims to predict the severity of the disease course using clinical data. Using a machine learning approach, they obtained $AUC = 0.758$ in the context of exacerbation of the disease [23]. A different approach was presented by Tsujitani et al. [24] In their study, they presented a bootstrapping-based neural network model to estimate the survival function. This approach is notably different from the standard Cox proportional hazards model used in this situation, and the model was tested using data from patients with primary biliary cirrhosis, with longitudinal data available [24]. When comparing our approach with the work presented above, we note, first of all, that the model is based on both clinical data and laboratory studies. We apply the machine learning approach and federated learning approach, and moreover, the disease addressed by our research has not yet been the subject of existing models. The results of experiments obtained with federated learning approach demonstrate that while generalizability of the global federated model might not be satisfactory to be implemented in medical practice, the performance of optimized models for individual centers may be sufficient. The improvement in the weighted mean AUC for both renal therapy prediction and mortality prediction suggests that tailoring the model to the specific characteristics of the data from each center can lead to more accurate predictions. This may reflect underlying heterogeneity in patient populations, clinical practices and data quality across different centers, especially in scenarios with very limited datasets. Exploratory analysis of the distribution of the most important features for both problems revealed significant variation across centers. A generalized federated model may not fully capture the nuances of individual centers. Further research, with more thorough formal statistical uncertainty measurements, is needed to investigate the generalizability of this approach across more diverse datasets and its implications for other clinical prediction tasks.

In addition, given the specifics of the problem, i.e. the size and imbalance of the data, and the domain in which the explainability of the model's decisions is extremely desirable, we conducted the experiment using the RIPPER method in a federated way. The results obtained can be considered satisfactory in comparison to those achieved by

LGBM, as shown in Table 4. RIPPER performed worse at predicting RRT, but slightly better at predicting death. We can observe the same pattern as in the case of LGM: the classification problem of renal therapy prediction proved to be easier than death prediction but in case of RIPPER, this is less evident. Although the values of the metric evaluating the predictive quality of the model obtained in this way are lower than those of the best local LGBM models, this is acceptable given the minimal complexity – and even the naivety – of the aggregation method used. Therefore, we can nevertheless positively assess the applicability of such a solution to this type of problem and medical data, where explainability and privacy preservation are top priorities and data are scarce. RIPPER results could probably have been better if a more in-depth analysis of the various parameter values had been carried out. We have not done any hyperparameter tunning which should increase the quality of predictions. Another area for improvement is the way the rules are aggregated. Nonetheless, presented approach shows promise and, since it has not yet been comprehensively explored, we leave the development of federated interpretable rule-based methods for future work.

The most important limitation of the presented study is the lack of available longitudinal data regarding when an exacerbation or adverse incident may have occurred, which would help the model take into consideration the temporal relations between laboratory tests, symptoms and exacerbation events. In the cases where the clinical parameter value refers to the worst value measured over the entire course of the disease, we abandon using such values for prediction, especially when such "worst-case" values are obtained for patients immediately prior to the predicted event. For instance, with regard to blood creatinine level, we had to remove the information as a prognostic marker for renal involvement, since the values recorded in the database for patients undergoing RRT are usually measured directly before ordering the RRT procedure. Therefore, using the worst recorded level of creatinine would reduce the trained models' predictive performance for early diagnosis scenarios. If time-series data could be collected for key laboratory test results, or indeed even more laboratory parameters were recorded in the input data (for instance: troponins, acute-phase proteins or complement factors), the models could be improved further. We are therefore considering – on the basis of results obtained thus far – a prospective study of newly recruited AAV patients in order to test whether even more precise models could be developed using a similar ML approach when finer-grained time-series characteristics are added to input data and to test against other methods, such as deep learning models.

We consider that the application of knowledge provided by the trained models, especially after further validation, definition of actionable decision thresholds and evaluation on external datasets, could be incorporated into vasculitis treatment strategies through early identification of patients with an elevated risk of exacerbation. This, in turn, might result e.g. in enrolling such individuals in a more intensive monitoring scheme of blood marker identified as most important by feature importance analysis, coupled with a more aggressive pharmacological therapy, effectively reversing the unfavourable prognosis of the disease progression.

In conclusion, we developed computational predictive models based on 727 patient records from the POLVAS registry, coming from 12-center study which is representative of the entire Polish population. These models, when supplied with clinical information describing a specific patient case, predict the risk of renal replacement therapy and death respectively. To compare the performance of different training approaches and address the common challenge of distributed datasets, we trained the models using centralized and federated learning methods. With centralized learning approach we achieved AUCs of 0.86 and 0.81 for RRT and death prediction, respectively. With federated models, we achieved weighted mean AUC of 0.86 and 0.80 for RRT and death prediction, respectively. Our findings suggest that while general federated models might not fully capture the nuances of individual centers, optimizing dedicated federated models might reflect better underlying heterogeneity in patient populations, clinical practices and other factors, leading to improved performance. Additionally, we performed feature importance analysis, which provides valuable insights into the nature and progress of AAV vasculitis and tested the utility of the highly explainable rule-based method for this type of problems, with encouraging results.

Acknowledgments. This publication is partly supported by the European Union's Horizon 2020 research and innovation programme under grant agreement "Sano" No. 857533, and by the "Sano" project, carried out within the framework of the International Research Agendas Programme of the Foundation for Polish Science No MAB PLUS/2019/13, co-financed by the European Regional Development Fund. The publication was created within the project of the Minister of Science and Higher Education "Support for the activity of Centers of Excellence established in Poland under Horizon 2020" on the basis of the contract number MEiN/2023/DIR/3796. This work was supported by a grant from Polish National Science Center UMO-2018/31/B/NZ6/03898 (to Jacek Musiał).

Author Contributions T.S., S.L., T.G., K.Woz. and K.M. were responsible for conceptual work, design of the study, and methodological development; T.S. and K.Woz. were responsible for implementing and testing the centralized machine learning models; K.M. and K.Woz. were responsible for implementing the federated models; M.Mal., J.Mus., J.S. were responsible for conceptual work and scientific leadership; K.Woj. and S.L. provided clinical consultations; K.Woj. was responsible for data curation; K.Woj., G.B, K.W.A., S.B.S., A.M., M.C., B.B.P., A.D.Ś., H.S., M.K., H.A.B., R.J., M.Maj., K.J., M.Mil., M.B., J.K.Z., W.T., M.Mad., A.H.K., E.J.K., P.G., K.B., M.Wis., J.M.D., A.L.P., J.Mak., J.Z., J.Mus. were responsible for data collection; K.M., K.Woj., K.Woz., S.L., T.G and T.S. were responsible for preparing the manuscript.

Disclosure of Interests. The authors declare no competing interests.

References

1. Salmela, A., et al.: Chronic nasal staphylococcus aureus carriage identifies a subset of newly diagnosed granulomatosis with polyangiitis patients. Rheumatol. 56(6), 965–972 (2017)
2. Musiał, J., Wójcik, K.: Polish vasculitis registry: POLVAS. Pol. Arch. Intern. Med. **127**(1), 71–72 (2017)
3. Wójcik, K., et al.: Subphenotypes of ANCA-associated vasculitis identified by latent class analysis. Clin. Exp. Rheumatol. **39**(S129), 62–68 (2021)
4. Wójcik, K., et al.: Clinical characteristics of polish patients with ANCA-associated vasculitides-retrospective analysis of POLVAS registry. Clin. Rheumatol. **38**(9), 2553–2563 (2019)
5. Jennette, J.C.: Overview of the 2012 revised international chapel hill consensus conference nomenclature of vasculitides. Clin. Exp. Nephrol. **17**(5), 603–606 (2013)

6. Ke, G., et al.: LightGBM: a highly efficient gradient boosting decision tree. In: Proc. 31st Int. Conf. Neural Inf. Process. Syst. (NIPS 2017), pp. 3149–3157 (2017)
7. Sheller, M.J., et al.: Federated learning in medicine: facilitating multi-institutional collaborations without sharing patient data. Sci. Rep. **10**, 12598 (2020)
8. Pedregosa, F., et al.: Scikit-learn: machine learning in python. J. Mach. Learn. Res. **12**, 2825–2830 (2011)
9. Head, T., et al.: scikit-optimize/scikit-optimize. Zenodo (2021)
10. McKinney, W.: Data structures for statistical computing in python. In: Proc. 9th Python Sci. Conf., pp. 56–61 (2010)
11. Turner, R., et al.: Bayesian optimization is superior to random search for machine learning hyperparameter tuning. In: Proc. NeurIPS 2020 Competition Track, PMLR, vol. 133, pp. 3–26 (2021)
12. Bergstra, J., et al.: Algorithms for hyper-parameter optimization. In: Proc. 25th Int. Conf. Neural Inf. Process. Syst. (NIPS 2011), pp. 2546–2554 (2011)
13. Mandrekar, J.N.: Receiver operating characteristic curve in diagnostic test assessment. J. Thorac. Oncol. **5**, 1315–1316 (2010)
14. Cawley, G.C., Talbot, N.L.C.: On over-fitting in model selection and subsequent selection bias in performance evaluation. J. Mach. Learn. Res. **11**, 2079–2107 (2010)
15. Ma, C., et al.: Gradient-less federated gradient boosting tree with learnable learning rates. In: Proceedings of the 3rd Workshop on Machine Learning and Systems (EuroMLSys '23), pp. 56–63. ACM, New York (2023)
16. Beutel, D.J., et al.: Flower: A friendly federated learning research framework. arXiv preprint https://arxiv.org/abs/2007.14390 (2020)
17. Cohen, W.W.: Fast effective rule induction. In: Proceedings of the Twelfth International Conference on Machine Learning (ICML '95), pp. 115–123. Morgan Kaufmann Publishers, San Francisco (1995)
18. Ali, K., Brunk, C., Pazzani, M.: On learning multiple descriptions of a concept. In: Proceedings of the International Conference on Tools with Artificial Intelligence (ICTAI 1994), pp. 476–483. IEEE, Los Alamitos (1994)
19. Khang, V.H., Anh, C.T., Thuan, N.D.: Detecting fraud transactions using RIPPER algorithm combined with ensemble learning model. Int. J. Adv. Comput. Sci. Appl. **14**, 336–345 (2023)
20. Govada, A., Thomas, V.S., Samal, I., Sahay, S.K.: Distributed multi-class rule-based classification using RIPPER. In: Proc. IEEE Int. Conf. Comput. Inf. Technol. (CIT 2016), pp. 303–309. IEEE (2017)
21. Kubat, M.: An Introduction to Machine Learning. Springer, Cham (2015)
22. Lezcano-Valverde, J.M., et al.: Development and validation of a multivariate predictive model for rheumatoid arthritis mortality. Sci. Rep. **7**, 10189 (2017)
23. Lin, C., et al.: Automatic prediction of rheumatoid arthritis disease activity from the electronic medical records. PLoS One. **8**(8), e69932 (2013)
24. Tsujitani, M., Sakon, M.: Analysis of survival data having time-dependent covariates. IEEE Trans. Neural Netw. **20**(3), 389–394 (2009)

Accelerating Nonlinear Time-History Analysis with Complex Constitutive Laws via Heterogeneous Memory Management: From 3D Seismic Simulation to Neural Network Training

Tsuyoshi Ichimura[1(✉)], Kohei Fujita[1,2], Hideaki Ito[1], Muneo Hori[3], and Maddegedara Lalith[1]

[1] Earthquake Research Institute, The University of Tokyo, Tokyo, Japan
`ichimura@eri.u-tokyo.ac.jp`
[2] RIKEN Center for Computational Science, Kobe, Japan
[3] Research Institute for Earth and Information Sciences, Japan Agency for Marine-Earth Science and Technology, Yokohama, Japan

Abstract. Nonlinear time-history evolution problems employing high-fidelity physical models are essential in numerous scientific domains. However, these problems face a critical dual bottleneck: the immense computational cost of time-stepping and the massive memory requirements for maintaining a vast array of state variables. To address these challenges, we propose a novel framework based on heterogeneous memory management for massive ensemble simulations of general nonlinear time-history problems with complex constitutive laws. Taking advantage of recent advancements in CPU-GPU interconnect bandwidth, our approach actively leverages the large capacity of host CPU memory while simultaneously maximizing the throughput of the GPU. This strategy effectively overcomes the GPU memory wall, enabling memory-intensive simulations. We evaluate the performance of the proposed method through comparisons with conventional implementations, demonstrating significant improvements in time-to-solution and energy-to-solution. Furthermore, we demonstrate the practical utility of this framework by developing a Neural Network-based surrogate model using the generated massive datasets. The results highlight the effectiveness of our approach in enabling high-fidelity 3D evaluations and its potential for broader applications in data-driven scientific discovery.

Keywords: Nonlinear Time-History Analysis · Heterogeneous Memory Management · Seismic Simulation

1 Introduction

Nonlinear time-history evolution problems play a pivotal role in the understanding and prediction of phenomena across various scientific domains. While high-fidelity physical models and finer discretization are essential for the faithful simulation of real-world phenomena, the adoption of such models not only increases computational costs but also demands an immense amount of computer memory to maintain a vast array of state variables at each time step, making the simulations highly memory-intensive. In particular, while GPU computational performance has improved dramatically, the capacity limitations of GPU memory present a severe memory wall, acting as a primary bottleneck that hinders the realization of the aforementioned large-scale, high-fidelity simulations.

To address these memory capacity constraints, conventional approaches have relied on simplifying physical models or employing multi-node parallelization using GPUs exclusively without utilizing CPU memory; however, these methods often lead to reduced accuracy of simulations or increased resource costs. On the other hand, while CPU-only approaches – leveraging the larger memory capacity of host systems – can alleviate memory shortages, they often suffer from slower processing speeds compared to GPUs, resulting in a degradation of the time-to-solution. In particular, for massive ensemble simulations – such as those required for uncertainty quantification (UQ) and dataset generation for machine learning, which have seen increasing demand – this slow computational speed and high resource cost become major drawbacks.

Meanwhile, motivated by recent increases in CPU-GPU interconnect bandwidth (e.g., [1,2]), research and development in heterogeneous computing are actively pursuing simultaneous improvements in both time-to-solution and energy-to-solution through tighter coupling of CPUs and GPUs (e.g., [3]). In light of these trends and to address the aforementioned challenges, this study proposes a novel framework based on heterogeneous memory management for massive ensemble simulations of general nonlinear time-history problems with complex constitutive laws, which effectively leverages host CPU memory while maximizing GPU throughput in a heterogeneous CPU-GPU environment. In Sect. 2, we describe the proposed method using nonlinear seismic ground response analysis as an example and evaluate its performance in terms of time-to-solution and energy-to-solution through comparisons with conventional implementations. In Sect. 3, we demonstrate the practical utility of this framework by developing a Neural Network-based surrogate model using the massive datasets generated through these ensemble simulations.

2   Method

While the proposed method is applicable to general time-history evolution problems, we describe it in detail using 3D nonlinear seismic ground response analysis with complex constitutive laws as a concrete example to provide specificity. To faithfully reproduce real-world ground responses, a detailed 3D finite element model using finer unstructured grids and high-fidelity nonlinear physical constitutive laws is indispensable, resulting in a simulation that requires both immense memory capacity and high-speed computation.

2.1   Target Problem

First, we describe the 3D nonlinear seismic ground response analysis. Following [4], taking advantage of the finite element method's superiority in modeling complex geometries and satisfying stress-free boundary conditions at the ground surface, we discretize the nonlinear wave equation – in which material properties change from moment to moment due to nonlinear soil constitutive laws – and solve the following equation discretized by the Newmark-β method at each time step to obtain the response of the nonlinear time-history problem:

$$\left(\frac{4}{dt^2}\mathbf{M} + \frac{2}{dt}\mathbf{C}^n + \mathbf{K}^n \right) \delta\mathbf{u}^n = \mathbf{f}^n - \mathbf{q}^{n-1} + \mathbf{C}^n\mathbf{v}^{n-1} + \mathbf{M}\left(\mathbf{a}^{n-1} + \frac{4}{dt}\mathbf{v}^{n-1} \right)$$

(1)

with $\mathbf{q}^n = \mathbf{q}^{n-1} + \mathbf{K}^n\delta\mathbf{u}^n$, $\mathbf{u}^n = \mathbf{u}^{n-1} + \delta\mathbf{u}^n$, $\mathbf{v}^n = -\mathbf{v}^{n-1} + \frac{2}{dt}\delta\mathbf{u}^n$, and $\mathbf{a}^n = -\mathbf{a}^{n-1} - \frac{4}{dt}\mathbf{v}^{n-1} + \frac{4}{dt^2}\delta\mathbf{u}^n$. Here, $\mathbf{M}$, $\mathbf{C}^n$, and $\mathbf{K}^n$ denote the mass matrix and the damping and stiffness matrices at the n-th time step, respectively, while $\delta\mathbf{u}^n$, $\mathbf{u}^n$, $\mathbf{v}^n$, and $\mathbf{a}^n$ represent the nodal vectors for displacement increment, displacement, velocity, and acceleration. Furthermore, dt denotes the time step interval. Rayleigh damping is employed for $\mathbf{C}^n$, which is determined using the damping h^n at the n-th time step, following the procedure in [4]. Consequently, in Eq. (1), the matrix equations including $\mathbf{K}^n$ and $\mathbf{C}^n$ must be solved while maintaining a massive number of state variables that evolve at each time step n according to the nonlinear soil constitutive laws. For the finite element discretization, second-order tetrahedral elements are used due to their excellent geometric modeling capabilities and the necessity of strain evaluation for the constitutive laws. Semi-infinite absorbing boundary conditions are applied to the bottom and side boundaries.

To achieve simulations with a higher level of fidelity than [4], this study adopts the multi-spring model [5] as a more sophisticated nonlinear constitutive law. In the finite element method, the element stiffness matrix $\mathbf{K}_e$, which constitutes $\mathbf{K}^n$ in Eq. (1), is constructed as follows:

$$\mathbf{K}_e = \sum_{j=1}^{5} w_j \mathbf{B}_{e,j}^T \mathbf{D}_{e,j} \mathbf{B}_{e,j}$$

(2)

Here, $\mathbf{B}^T e, j$ is a 6×30 matrix that converts nodal displacements into strains, $\mathbf{D}_{e,j}$ is a 6×6 elasto-plastic stiffness matrix at the integration points, and w_j represents the weights of the integration points. In the multi-spring model, $\mathbf{D}$ is determined by combining numerous empirically derived 1D nonlinear springs, which necessitates the storage of a large number of state variables. Specifically, since this study employs the modified Ramberg-Osgood model [6] and Masing rule [7] as the constitutive laws for the 1D springs, it is necessary to maintain 40 bytes of data per spring, consisting of four double-precision variables and two flags. Furthermore, with 150 1D springs per material evaluation point and four evaluation points per tetrahedral element, a total of 24 kbytes of data must be stored per element, resulting in a highly memory-intensive simulation.

2.2 Proposed Method

We propose a method that leverages the characteristics of both the large capacity of CPU memory and the high performance of GPUs for the aforementioned memory-intensive simulations. The target problem in this study consists of two types of computations: a memory-capacity-bound constitutive law calculation part and a compute-intensive linear equation solver part; while the former requires CPU memory because it exceeds GPU memory capacity, the latter is expected to achieve high-speed computation by utilizing the high-bandwidth memory and high-performance cores of the GPU. In conventional computers with limited CPU-GPU interconnect bandwidth (e.g., older PCIe), even if the compute-intensive part is executed on the GPU while keeping the memory-capacity-bound part on the CPU, the data transfer between them becomes a bottleneck, preventing overall speedup and leading to the use of CPU-only execution for both parts; however, in systems with relatively high CPU-GPU bandwidth (e.g., PCIe Gen 5 x16), GPU performance can be utilized by offloading the compute-intensive part to the GPU and performing frequent data transfers between the memory-capacity-bound part. To achieve even higher speeds, we introduce heterogeneous memory management for systems with ultra-high CPU-GPU bandwidth, such as the GH200, enabling all computations to be performed on high-performance GPUs by overlapping GPU computing with CPU-GPU data transfer in the memory-capacity-bound section while keeping massive data in CPU memory. Furthermore, the efficiency of computational performance is enhanced by employing an algorithm that manages the memory hierarchy within the GPU for the compute-intensive part. Details are described below using the target problem as an example.

The primary computations in the target problem are in solving Eq. (1) and the multi-spring calculation in Eq. (2). Since Eq. (1) involves a large number of degrees of freedom and the target matrix is a positive-definite symmetric sparse matrix, iterative solvers based on the conjugate gradient method are typically employed for its solution. Since sparse matrices are often stored in memory using compressed formats such as compressed row storage (CRS), this solver part corresponds to the compute-intensive component. Conversely, the multi-spring calculation in Eq. (2) requires a massive memory capacity to store variables for numerous 1D springs that evolve over time, corresponding to the memory-capacity-bound part. In this study, as a conventional baseline where all computations are executed on the CPU – typical for systems with limited CPU-GPU bandwidth – we utilize a preconditioned conjugate gradient method with 3×3 block Jacobi preconditioning and CRS-based sparse matrix-vector multiplication (hereafter referred to as "Baseline Method 1: CRSCPU_MSCPU"; see Algorithm 1). Additionally, as a baseline for systems with moderate CPU-GPU bandwidth, we define "Baseline Method 2: CRSGPU_MSCPU" (Algorithm 2), where the multi-spring calculation is performed on the CPU while the solver part is offloaded to the GPU, with data exchanged between them. In this method, the solver and the CRS updates in Baseline Method 1 are offloaded to the GPU.

Algorithm 1. Baseline method 1: CRSCPU_MSCPU. **D** indicate the stiffness matrix evaluated by the multispring method, while θ indicate the nonlinear spring parameters. CRS-PCG indicate 3×3 block Jacobi preconditioned conjugate gradient solver with CRS-based matrix-vector products.

1: **for** $it = 1$; $it \leq nt$; $it = it + 1$ **do**
2:      $\delta\mathbf{u}^{it} \Leftarrow$ CRS-PCG($\mathbf{A}$, $\mathbf{f}^{it}$)@CPU
3:      $\{\mathbf{D}^{it}, \theta^{it}\} \Leftarrow$ Multispring($\delta\mathbf{u}^{it}, \theta^{it-1}$)@CPU
4:      $\mathbf{A} \Leftarrow$ UpdateCRS($\mathbf{D}^{it}$)@CPU
5: **end for**

Algorithm 2. Baseline method 2: CRSGPU_MSCPU. **D** indicate the stiffness matrix evaluated by the multispring method, while θ indicate the nonlinear spring parameters. CRS-PCG indicate 3×3 block Jacobi preconditioned conjugate gradient solver with CRS-based matrix-vector products.

1: **for** $it = 1$; $it \leq nt$; $it = it + 1$ **do**
2:      $\delta\mathbf{u}^{it} \Leftarrow$ CRS-PCG($\mathbf{A}$, $\mathbf{f}^{it}$)@GPU
3:      Transfer $\delta\mathbf{u}^{it}$ from GPU to CPU
4:      $\{\mathbf{D}^{it}, \theta^{it}\} \Leftarrow$ Multispring($\delta\mathbf{u}^{it}, \theta^{it-1}$)@CPU
5:      Transfer $\mathbf{D}^{it}$ from CPU to GPU
6:      $\mathbf{A} \Leftarrow$ UpdateCRS($\mathbf{D}^{it}$)@GPU
7: **end for**

In the proposed method, we achieve high-speed computation by storing variables for the compute-intensive part in GPU memory while performing the memory-capacity-bound calculations on the GPU by accessing data in CPU memory via high-bandwidth transfers, effectively executing the entire simulation on the high-performance GPU. Here, the multi-spring calculation is divided into multiple blocks, and the time required for data transfer is hidden by overlapping the GPU computation of one block with the CPU-GPU transfer of another block, thereby circumventing GPU memory capacity constraints and reducing execution time. As shown in Algorithm 3, this method pipelines the CPU-GPU transfer of multi-spring data (θ) (Line 6) and the multi-spring calculation (Line 7). While the entire *npart* blocks must be stored on the CPU side, the GPU only needs to store two blocks at a time, allowing large-scale problems to be solved within the limited GPU memory. Hereafter, this approach is referred to as "Proposed Method 1: CRSGPU_MSGPU."

While Proposed Method 1 addresses heterogeneous memory management between CPU and GPU, even more efficient GPU computation can be achieved through effective management of the intra-GPU memory hierarchy (device memory, cache, and registers). We employ the Element-by-Element (EBE) method [8], which reduces memory footprint and transfer size at the cost of increased computational operations for the sparse matrix-vector multiplication in the solver. This converts the CRS-based sparse matrix-vector multiplication, which is typically memory-bandwidth-bound, into an atomic-add-bound operation on the L2 cache, enabling higher computational throughput. Additionally, the reduc-

---

Algorithm 3. Proposed method 1: CRSGPU_MSGPU. Data $\mathbf{D}_j$ and θ_j indicate the j-th partition of stiffness matrix and the nonlinear spring parameters, respectivey. Lines 6 and 7 are conducted simultaneously, leading to overlap of GPU-computation and CPU-GPU data transfer. While *npart* partitions of data is required in CPU memory, only 2 partitions reside on GPU memory at once; leading to using GPU computing under the low GPU-memory footprint constraint.

1: **for** $it = 1;\ it \leq nt;\ it = it + 1$ **do**
2:    $\delta\mathbf{u}^{it} \Leftarrow$ CRS-PCG($\mathbf{A}$, $\mathbf{f}^{it}$)@GPU
3:    Transfer θ_1^{it-1}, θ_2^{it-1} from CPU to GPU
4:    $\{\mathbf{D}_1^{it}, \theta_1^{it}\} \Leftarrow$ Multispring($\delta\mathbf{u}^{it}, \theta_1^{it-1}$)@GPU
5:    **for** $j = 2;\ j \leq npart - 1;\ j = j + 1$ **do**
6:       Transfer θ_{j-1}^{it} from GPU to CPU, Transfer θ_{j+1}^{it-1} from CPU to GPU
7:       $\{\mathbf{D}_j^{it}, \theta_j^{it}\} \Leftarrow$ Multispring($\delta\mathbf{u}^{it}, \theta_j^{it-1}$)@GPU
8:    **end for**
9:    $\{\mathbf{D}_{npart}^{it}, \theta_{npart}^{it}\} \Leftarrow$ Multispring($\delta\mathbf{u}^{it}, \theta_{npart}^{it-1}$)@GPU
10:    Transfer $\theta_{npart-1}^{it}$, θ_{npart}^{it} from GPU to CPU
11:    $\mathbf{A} \Leftarrow$ UpdateCRS($\mathbf{D}^{it}$)@GPU
12: **end for**

Algorithm 4. Proposed method 2: EBEGPU_MSGPU_2SET. Note that lines 2 and 3 are conducted together to reduce random memory access costs. Also, lines 4 and 5 are conducted together. Pipelined GPU computation is the same contents as in lines 3–10 in Algorithm 3. EBE-IPCG indicate an adaptive conjugate gradient solver with mixed precision multigrid-based preconditioner [9] with EBE-based matrix-vector products.

1: **for** $it = 1;\ it \leq nt;\ it = it + 1$ **do**
2:    $\delta\mathbf{u}_1^{it} \Leftarrow$ EBE-IPCG($\mathbf{D}_1^{it-1}$, $\mathbf{f}_1^{it}$)@GPU
3:    $\delta\mathbf{u}_2^{it} \Leftarrow$ EBE-IPCG($\mathbf{D}_2^{it-1}$, $\mathbf{f}_2^{it}$)@GPU
4:    Pipelined GPU computation of $\{\mathbf{D}_1^{it}, \theta_1^{it}\} \Leftarrow$ Multispring($\delta\mathbf{u}_1^{it}, \theta_1^{it-1}$)@GPU
5:    Pipelined GPU computation of $\{\mathbf{D}_2^{it}, \theta_2^{it}\} \Leftarrow$ Multispring($\delta\mathbf{u}_2^{it}, \theta_2^{it-1}$)@GPU
6: **end for**

---

tion in memory usage allows two problem sets to be loaded into GPU memory simultaneously – whereas CRS-based methods could accommodate only one – effectively doubling the degrees of freedom per node and reducing random access costs in sparse matrix-vector multiplication. The method optimized through such intra-GPU memory hierarchy management is called as "Proposed Method 2: EBEGPU_MSGPU_2SET" (Algorithm 4). Furthermore, because surplus GPU memory remains even with two problem sets loaded, we leverage this extra capacity to apply a variable-precision multi-grid preconditioner [9] to the solver for even greater efficiency.

In summary, compared to Baseline Method 1, which executes both the compute-intensive and memory-capacity-bound parts on the CPU, Baseline Method 2 offloads only the compute-intensive part to the GPU. Proposed Method 1 enables both parts to be computed on the GPU through CPU-GPU heterogeneous memory management, and Proposed Method 2 further improves GPU efficiency through memory access management within the GPU memory tiers.

2.3 Numerical Performance

We utilize a realistic ground model of a site near Tokyo, Japan, which was also employed in [4] (see Fig. 1). This site is characterized by soft sedimentary layers forming a complex 3D structure, which is known to result in significantly larger ground motions compared to neighboring areas. In other words, it is a site where body waves are converted into surface waves and trapped, leading to pronounced 3D nonlinear ground amplification, making it an ideal model for the performance measurements and application examples presented in this study. In [4], a comparison was made between observation data from the 2011 Tohoku earthquake – which caused extensive damage – and 3D nonlinear analysis results, with the model successfully validated. To analyze the primary components of seismic damage as in [4], we target a frequency range below 2.5 Hz and generate a finite element model using second-order tetrahedral elements with at least 10 elements per wavelength, following the methodology in [10]. The model features a minimum element size of approximately 4 m, with 32,502,492 degrees of freedom and 7,781,075 tetrahedral elements. We use a Cartesian coordinate system with the origin at the southwest corner of the model base, where the x, y, and z axes represent the east-west, north-south, and up-down directions, respectively. The time step increment is set to 0.005 s, consistent with [4], and the analysis is conducted for 16,000 time steps using the solution methods described in the previous section with a convergence tolerance of a relative error of 10^{-8}. The input wave for performance measurement is a random wave with frequency components above 2.5 Hz removed, featuring a uniform amplitude distribution ranging from -0.6 to 0.6 for the x, y components and -0.3 to 0.3 for the z component (one of the waveforms used for generating the neural network training dataset in the Application Example).

As an example of a system with high-speed CPU-GPU interconnects, we use the NVIDIA Grace Hopper Superchip (GH200) [2] for computational performance measurements. This system is equipped with one 72-core Grace CPU (480 GB memory, 384 GB/s) and one H100 GPU (96 GB memory, 4 TB/s) per node, with the CPU and GPU interconnected via high-speed 900 GB/s NVLink-C2C. Power consumption is measured using the `nvidia-smi -q -d POWER` command to obtain the module power (the entire board including the CPU, CPU memory, and GPU), sampled every 0.5 s and averaged over the total execution time. The power caps per module/GPU are set to the system defaults of 700 W for the GPU and 1,000 W for the module, effectively ensuring no power capping and allowing high simultaneous loads on both the GPU and CPU. The program is implemented using OpenACC for the GPU and OpenMP for the CPU multi-core parts, with 70 cores utilized for OpenMP computation per process. While performance measurements can be implementation-dependent, the implementation in this study is sufficiently optimized to a level comparable to that in [3]. To ensure the baseline methods achieve adequate performance, we employ a 3×3 Block CRS format to reduce memory access costs. Only the preconditioning part of the solver is computed in single precision, while all other calculations are performed in double precision.

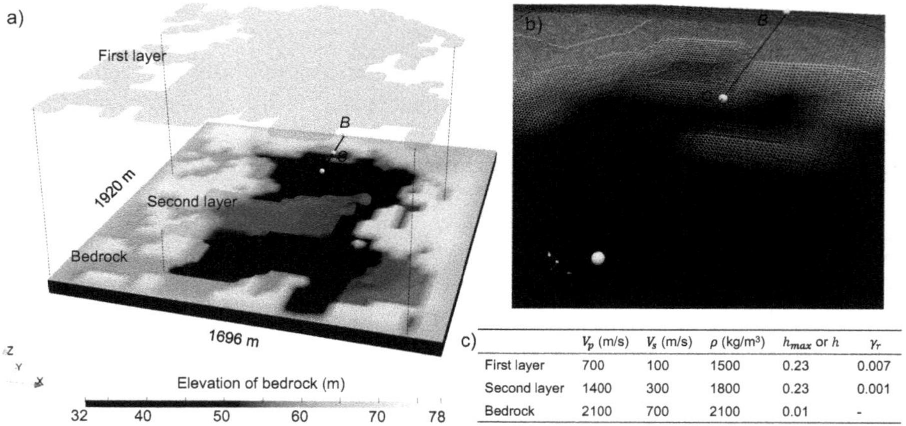

	V_p (m/s)	V_s (m/s)	ρ (kg/m³)	h_{max} or h	γ_r
First layer	700	100	1500	0.23	0.007
Second layer	1400	300	1800	0.23	0.001
Bedrock	2100	700	2100	0.01	-

Fig. 1. (a) 3D ground structure model with line A-B and point C. The x, y-coordinates of A, B, and C are (848, 1400), (848, 1900), and (848, 1648) m, respectively. (b) Close-up view of the region around line A-B. (c) Material properties of the soil structure.

Figure 2 shows the elapsed time per case when calculating with each method using one GH200 node. The figure illustrates that near the main motion where the input seismic intensity increases, the convergence deteriorates, leading to an increase in the number of solver iterations and consequently higher execution time per time step, after which convergence improves once the main motion has passed. Table 1 presents the total execution time and memory usage required for the entire simulation under these complex and practical problem settings. First, we examine the performance of the conventional baseline methods. As shown in the table, in Baseline Method 1 (CPU-only), the GPU remains idle, resulting in a low average node power of 379 W; however, due to the inability to utilize the high-throughput GPU, the execution time is as long as 182,300 s, and the energy-to-solution is high at 690 MJ. The breakdown of the execution time in Table 2 reveals that the majority of the computational time is consumed by the solver. In Baseline Method 2, where the solver is offloaded to the GPU, the solver time is significantly reduced from 9.4 s to 1.16 s, leading to a reduction in the total execution time by a factor of 4.05. Although the power consumption increases to 635 W due to the use of the high-power GPU, the reduced execution time leads to a decrease in energy consumption to 286 MJ (a factor of 2.41).

Next, we evaluate the performance of Proposed Method 1, in which the multi-spring calculations are also executed on the GPU. In this method, the entire problem of 7.7 million elements is divided into sub-regions of 0.1 million elements and executed in a pipeline, limiting the increase in GPU memory usage to only 5 GB. Consequently, the entire GPU-utilized portion of the application, including the solver's GPU memory footprint (66 GB), fits within the 96 GB GPU memory limit. The GPU computation and CPU-GPU data transfer for the multi-spring calculation part take 0.33 s and 0.38 s, respectively; as a result, the majority of

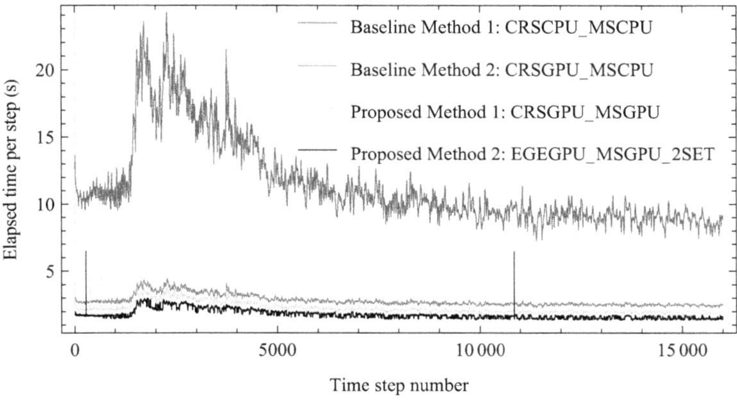

Fig. 2. Elapsed time per case.

Table 1. Performance and memory usage of each method. Note that elapsed time and energy usage is shown per case.

Method	Elapsed time	Power usage	Energy usage	CPU mem. usage	GPU mem. usage
Baseline 1: CRSCPU_MSCPU	182,300 s	379 W	690 MJ	225 GB	-
Baseline 2: CRSGPU_MSCPU	45,001 s	635 W	286 MJ	131 GB	66 GB
Proposed 1: CRSGPU_MSGPU	36,074 s	691 W	249 MJ	117 GB	71 GB
Prop. 2: EBEGPU_MSGPU_2SET	14,222 s	724 W	103 MJ	168 GB	70 GB

the computation and transfer can be overlapped, reducing the execution time of the multi-spring part from 0.94 s to 0.38 s compared to the CPU version[1]. This makes the overall application execution time 1.25 times faster than Baseline Method 2 (5.05 times faster compared to Baseline Method 1). As the GPU active time ratio is higher than in Baseline Method 2, the power consumption increases to 691 W, with a total energy consumption of 249 MJ.

Finally, we examine the performance of Proposed Method 2, which features an algorithm designed with a focus on the intra-GPU memory hierarchy. By using the EBE method to compute sparse matrix-vector multiplications on the fly, the need to store massive CRS data is eliminated, reducing GPU memory usage and allowing two problem sets to be solved simultaneously within the 96 GB memory limit. This improves memory access performance and shortens solver time; furthermore, it eliminates the need for CRS update calculations that were previously required every time material properties were updated by the multi-spring model, resulting in an execution time reduction of 1/2.54 compared to Proposed Method 1. Since the power consumption only slightly increases from Proposed Method 1, the energy consumption is reduced to 1/2.42, almost in proportion to

---

[1] Although the GH200 system supports direct access from within GPU kernels to CPU memory; using this capability increased the multi-spring computation time to 5.9 s due to the longer data-access latency in the NVLink-C2C interconnect, demonstrating the effectiveness of the proposed method.

Table 2. Breakdown of elapsed time of each method. Note that elapsed time is shown per case per time step.

Method	Total time	Solver time	CRS time	Multispring total (compute, data transfer)
Baseline 1: CRSCPU_MSCPU	11.39 s	9.40 s	0.92 s	0.92 s
Baseline 2: CRSGPU_MSCPU	2.81 s	1.16 s	0.70 s	0.94 s
Proposed 1: CRSGPU_MSGPU	2.25 s	1.16 s	0.70 s	0.38 s (0.33 s, 0.38 s)
Prop. 2: EBEGPU_MSGPU_2SET	0.89 s	0.49 s	-	0.39 s (0.34 s, 0.39 s)

the execution time. As a result, we achieve a 12.8-fold speedup (with energy consumption reduced to 1/6.70) compared to the CPU-only Baseline Method 1, and a 3.16-fold speedup (energy reduced to 1/2.78) compared to Baseline Method 2, which only uses the GPU for the solver. Note that if a widely used interconnect such as PCIe Gen 5 x16 (with 1/7 the bandwidth of NVLink-C2C) were employed, the increased data transfer time would outweigh the computational gains of our approach. We can see the usefulness of high-performance hardware combined with suitable algorithm development.

In summary, by increasing the utilization of the high-throughput and power-efficient GPU through heterogeneous memory management, performance is consistently improved across Baseline Method, Proposed Method 1, and Proposed Method 2, in terms of both time-to-solution and energy-to-solution. While these measurements were obtained using a single GH200 module, our approach is expected to scale across large-node systems as the inter-node communication involved is confined to the GPU-based iterative solver, which has already demonstrated high scalability in previous studies.

3   Application Example

Immediately after a major earthquake, rapid damage assessment is crucial, and there are high expectations for simulations utilizing urban datasets. For instance, [11] demonstrates a system that estimates input ground motion at the engineering bedrock from observed data, performs 1D nonlinear ground amplification analysis using 1D soil models constructed from urban data at each site, and then calculates the nonlinear time-history dynamic response of individual buildings using the estimated surface motion. However, soil deposits possess three-dimensional structures, which are known to cause local nonlinear ground amplification during large earthquakes – referred to as 3D dynamic nonlinear effects. To account for these 3D dynamic nonlinear effects, 3D nonlinear analysis using three-dimensional ground structures has proven effective (e.g., [4]), and various attempts have been made to reduce the required computational time. Nevertheless, such large-scale analyses still require significant computational resources and time, as detailed in the previous section, making it impractical to apply them to numerous potential damage sites immediately after an earthquake. Consequently, there is a strong demand for methods that can account for 3D dynamic nonlinear effects while enabling immediate evaluation without intensive computational overhead. In light of this, this section (1) evaluates the 3D dynamic nonlinear effects that can occur during major earthquakes using a realistic 3D ground structure, and (2) demonstrates the utility of the proposed framework by constructing and applying Neural Networks (NNs) that account for these effects using datasets generated from massive ensemble 3D simulations.

Using the ground structure model shown previously (Fig. 1), we validate the response under nonlinear behavior caused by realistic strong ground motions by inputting the Kobe wave at the bottom of the model and analyzing the ground motions obtained along line A-B and at observation point C. Line A-B corresponds to a location where local ground amplification occurs, and point C is designated as the point on line A-B where the maximum velocity of the x-component was recorded during the 3D nonlinear analysis using the Kobe wave. The Kobe wave is based on the ground motion recorded at Nakayamate, Chuo-ku, Kobe, during the 1995 Hyogo-ken Nanbu Earthquake [12], which caused catastrophic damage, and was prepared using seismic waveforms commonly utilized in Japanese seismic design. Specifically, since this is surface observed data, it was scaled by $1/2$ for conversion to an engineering bedrock input wave, and a band-pass filter (0.2-0.5-2.4-2.5 Hz) was applied to focus on the frequency band below 2.5 Hz where damage is concentrated, following [4]. To examine the application performance of NNs for nonlinear problems, we intentionally set a challenging problem where nonlinearity is clearly induced by using somewhat strong, though realistic, ground motion – achieved by not discounting the ground amplification characteristics during the surface-to-bedrock conversion. The 3D ground amplification analysis in this section employs the same time step, total steps, and convergence criteria as the performance measurements in the previous section. Furthermore, since the evaluation of the waveforms as external forces yielded similar results across the x, y, and z components, only the x-component is presented as a representative case.

3.1   3D Dynamic Nonlinear Effects

Figure 3(a) shows the maximum velocity norm distribution obtained from the 3D nonlinear dynamic analysis with the Kobe wave input. We can see that local concentrations of ground motion occurs according to the 3D ground structure. Next, Fig. 3(b) shows the maximum velocity norm distribution obtained from a 1D nonlinear dynamic analysis with the same Kobe wave input. The 1D nonlinear dynamic analysis, commonly used in ground amplification studies, approximates the soil as a horizontally layered structure, effectively reducing a 3D problem to 1D; while this significantly lowers computational costs, it fails to account for three-dimensional structural complexities. Indeed, comparing Figs. 3(a) and (b) reveals significant discrepancies near areas with three-dimensional irregularities.

To examine the differences between 3D and 1D analyses in more detail, we check the ground motions along line A-B and at point C shown in Fig. 1. The ground structure along line A-B possesses an irregularity consisting of the first layer and bedrock with a rising slope, as shown in Fig. 4(a), which raises concerns about wave concentration (this also includes 3D behavior that cannot be captured by 2D analysis due to non-uniformity in the depth direction). Figure 4(b)

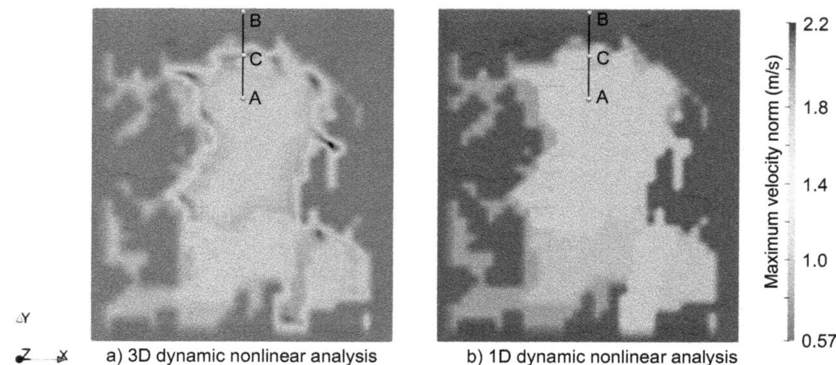

Fig. 3. Maximum velocity norm distribution at the surface for Kobe wave input.

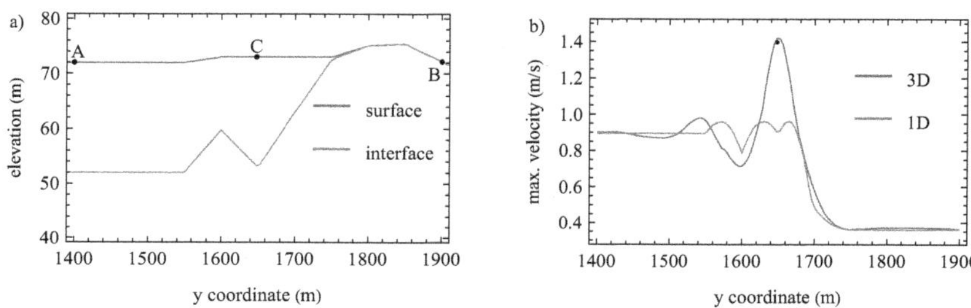

Fig. 4. (a) Cross section of ground structure at line A-B. The "surface" indicate the ground surface, while "interface" indicates the interface between the first and bedrock layers. C indicate the observation point. (b) Maximum velocity response in the x-direction along line A-B. The black dot indicates the response estimated by the NNs.

shows the maximum velocity distribution along line A-B for the Kobe wave input. In the 3D analysis, the maximum velocity increases significantly due to local amplification at the slope; however, the 1D analysis fails to capture this, resulting in a significant underestimation. For a more detailed comparison, we examine the waveforms and velocity response spectra at point C. As shown in Figs. 5(a) and (b), the 1D analysis underestimates the waveform amplitude at point C, and its potency as an external force is also markedly underestimated, as evidenced by the velocity response spectrum in Fig. 5(d). These results demonstrate that obtaining time-history waveforms provides more detailed information on external forces useful for damage assessment, and highlights the need for methods capable of accounting for 3D effects where 1D or 2D approximations are inadequate.

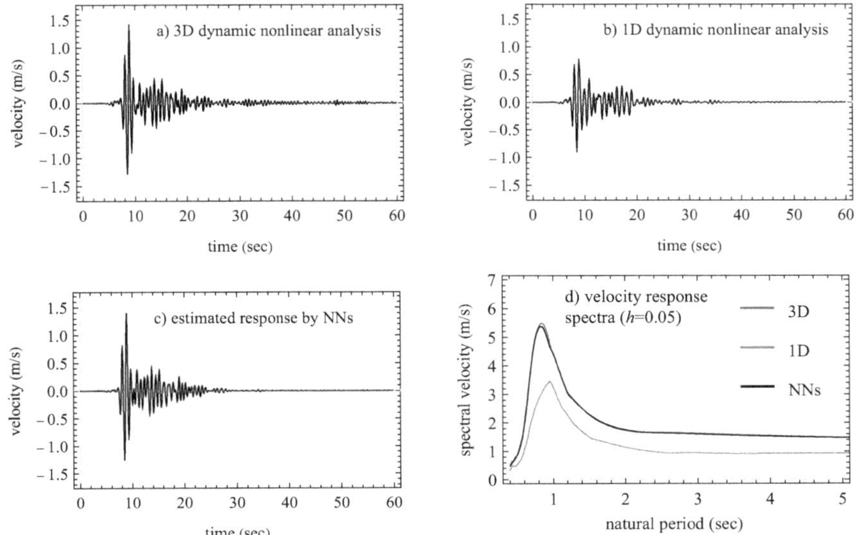

Fig. 5. Reponse at point C for Kobe wave. (a) and (b) indicate responses to 3D and 1D dynamic nonlinear analysis, while (c) shows the estimated response by NNs. (d) indicate the velocity response spectra ($h = 0.05$) for waves in (a), (b), and (c).

3.2 Effectiveness of NNs Considering 3D Dynamic Nonlinear Effects

We developed NNs capable of estimating time-history waveforms while considering the 3D nonlinear effects of the soil and the characteristics of the input waves, and demonstrate their effectiveness by estimating the waveform at point C. First, 100 random waves were generated with frequency components above 2.5 Hz removed; amplitudes followed a uniform distribution ranging from -0.6 to 0.6 for the x, y components and -0.3 to 0.3 for the z component (this setting reflects the fact that vertical components are often smaller than horizontal components in real earthquake records). Using these as input ground motions at the engineering bedrock, we conducted ensemble ground amplification simulations and observed the resulting waveforms at point C. Through this procedure, we obtained 100 sets of time-history data consisting of input random waves (x, y, z components) and the corresponding responses at point C (x, y, z components).

The developed NNs features a symmetric encoder-decoder structure using 1D-CNN and LSTM. In the encoder section (n_c layers), the three input components are temporally compressed while being expanded into a latent dimension L_{latent} to extract local waveform patterns; subsequently, LSTM layers (n_{LSTM} layers) learn temporal features such as nonlinear amplification and delays, after which the decoder section (n_c layers) then predicts the target waveforms from these latent representations. To account for varying physical characteristics among components (e.g., the weaker nonlinearity of the z-

component), the final layer of the decoder is designed to split the output into three groups for independent convolution. To suppress the excessive influence of peak amplitudes and ensure robust learning of phase and amplitude, we employed MAE loss and the Adam optimizer. Furthermore, using Optuna [13], we optimized the NNs hyperparameters and learning rate r to minimize the validation error. The search space was defined as $n_c \in \{2, 3, 4\}$, $n_{LSTM} \in \{1, 2, 3\}$, convolution kernel size $k \in \{3, 5, 9, 17, 33, 65\}$, $L_{latent} \in \{128, 256, 512, 1024\}$, and $r \in [5 \times 10^{-5}, 5 \times 10^{-4}]$. As a result of the optimization, a model with $n_c = 2, n_{LSTM} = 2, k = 9, L_{latent} = 512$, and $r = 1.75 \times 10^{-4}$ (final error: 1.41×10^{-2}) was selected. The PyTorch-based implementation was run on a single NVIDIA A100 GPU, with the entire training process including the parameter search taking approximately 87 min.

Figure 5(c) shows the time-history waveform at point C estimated by the developed NNs for the Kobe wave. It can be seen that the estimation almost perfectly matches the 3D nonlinear analysis results (Fig. 5(a)) and appropriately evaluates the amplification that was missing in the 1D analysis results (Fig. 5(b)). Furthermore, the performance of the waveform as an external force is well-estimated, as shown by the comparison of velocity response spectra (Fig. 5(d)), indicating that the waveforms predicted by the NNs serve as a high-fidelity approximation of the 3D nonlinear analysis results. The difference between the maximum velocity predicted by the NNs at point C and the result from the 3D nonlinear analysis is sufficiently small compared to the order of variation across different locations and input motions, as shown in Fig. 4(b), confirming the effectiveness of the NN-based evaluation.

4   Concluding Remarks

In this study, we proposed a novel method based on heterogeneous memory management that enables the execution of massive ensemble simulations for general nonlinear time-history problems with complex constitutive laws by effectively utilizing CPU memory while maximizing GPU computational performance in a CPU-GPU environment. In particular, Proposed Method 2 demonstrated superior performance in terms of both time-to-solution and energy-to-solution, achieving a 12.8-fold speedup (with a 1/6.7 reduction in energy consumption) compared to the CPU-only Baseline Method 1, and a 3.16-fold speedup (with a 1/2.8 reduction in energy consumption) compared to Baseline Method 2, which offloads only the solver to the GPU. In disasters such as earthquakes, highly reliable damage assessments are required immediately after the event; our application example demonstrated that surrogate models constructed using ensemble simulation data enabled by the proposed method can facilitate immediate damage estimation with significantly higher fidelity than conventional approaches. As CPU-GPU interconnect bandwidth and GPU computational speeds continue to increase, the demand for methods like the one proposed here – which achieve sophisticated simulations by cooperative use of CPU and GPU resources through heterogeneous memory management – is expected to grow.

Acknowledgments. The authors thank the Mainline Committee of the Association for the Development of Earthquake Prediction (ADEP) for providing the ground model used in this work. This work was supported by JSPS KAKENHI (25K21686, 23H00213) and supported by JST FOREST Program (JPMJFR215Q).

References

1. PCIe 5.0 specification. https://pcisig.com/. Accessed 28 Jan 2026
2. NVIDIA GH200 Grace Hopper Superchip Architecture. https://docs.nvidia.com/gh200-superchip-benchmark-guide.pdf. Accessed 28 Jan 2026
3. Ichimura, T., et al.: Heterogeneous computing in a strongly-connected CPU-GPU environment: fast multiple time-evolution equation-based modeling accelerated using data-driven approach. In: SC24-W: Workshops of the International Conference for High Performance Computing, Networking, Storage and Analysis, pp. 1967–1978 (2024). https://doi.org/10.1109/SCW63240.2024.00246
4. Ichimura, T., Fujita, K., Hori, M., Sakanoue, T., Hamanaka, R.: Three-dimensional nonlinear seismic ground response analysis of local site effects for estimating seismic behavior of buried pipelines. J. Pressure Vessel Technol. **136**(4), 041702 (8 pages) 2014. https://doi.org/10.1115/1.4026208
5. Iai, S.: Three dimensional formulation and objectivity of a strain space multiple mechanism model for sand. Soils Found. **33**(1), 192–199 (1993). https://doi.org/10.3208/sandf1972.33.192
6. Idriss, I.M., Dobry, R., Singh, R.D.: Nonlinear behavior of soft clays during cyclic loading. J. Geotech. Eng. Div. **104**, 1427–1447 (1978). https://doi.org/10.1061/AJGEB6.0000727
7. Masing, G.: Eigenspannungen und Verfestigung beim Messing. In: Proceedings of the 2nd International Congress of Applied Mechanics, pp. 332–335 (1926)
8. Winget, J.M., Hughes, T.J.R.: Solution algorithms for nonlinear transient heat conduction analysis employing element-by-element iterative strategies. Comput. Methods Appl. Mech. Eng. **52**, 711–815 (1985)
9. Ichimura, T., et al.: Physics-based urban earthquake simulation enhanced by 10.7 BlnDOF x 30 K time-step unstructured FE non-linear seismic wave simulation. In: SC 2014: Proceedings of the International Conference for High Performance Computing, Networking, Storage and Analysis, pp. 15–26 (2014)
10. Ichimura, T., Hori, M., Bielak, J.: A hybrid multiresolution meshing technique for finite element three-dimensional earthquake ground motion modeling in basins including topography. Geophys. J. Int. **177**, 1221–1232 (2009). https://doi.org/10.1111/j.1365-246X.2009.04154.x
11. Fujita, K., Ichimura, T., Hori, M., Wijerathne, M.L.L., Tanaka, S.: A quick earthquake disaster estimation system with fast urban earthquake simulation and interactive visualization. Procedia Comput. Sci. **29**, 866–876 (2014). https://doi.org/10.1016/j.procs.2014.05.078
12. Japan Meteorological Agency. https://www.data.jma.go.jp/eqev/data/kyoshin/jishin/. Accessed 28 Jan 2026
13. Akiba, T., Sano, S., Yanase, T., Ohta, T., Koyama, M.: Optuna: a next-generation hyperparameter optimization framework. In: Proceedings of the 25th ACM SIGKDD International Conference on Knowledge Discovery & Data Mining, pp. 2623–2631 (2019). https://doi.org/10.1145/3292500.3330701

Aligning and Assimilating Multi-source Data for Flood Forecasting

Kun Wang[1,2], Gabriele Bertoli[3,4], Sibo Cheng[5], Kai Schröter[6],
Enrica Caporali[3], Matthew D. Piggott[2], Yanghua Wang[1,2],
and Rossella Arcucci[2,4(✉)]

[1] Resource Geophysics Academy, Imperial College London, South Kensington, London SW7 2AZ, UK
[2] Department of Earth Science and Engineering, Imperial College London, South Kensington, London SW7 2AZ, UK
`r.arcucci@imperial.ac.uk`
[3] Department of Civil and Environmental Engineering, University of Florence, via di Santa Marta 3, Firenze, Italy
[4] Data Science Imperial, Imperial College London, London, UK
[5] CEREA, ENPC and EDF R&D, Institut Polytechnique de Paris, Île-de-France, France
[6] Leichtweiß-Institute for Hydraulic Engineering and Water Resources, Division Hydrology and River Basin Management, Technische Universität Braunschweig, Beethovenstr. 51a, 38106 Braunschweig, Germany

Abstract. Floods are among the most destructive natural hazards worldwide and frequently cause severe economic losses and significant loss of life. Therefore, reliable and timely forecasting plays a crucial role in disaster risk reduction. In recent years, approaches based on machine learning and data assimilation have attracted increasing attention for this purpose. However, a fundamental challenge remains. Predictive models generally require large volumes of high quality data, yet such data are often scarce, spatially and temporally limited, and heterogeneous in structure. This limitation substantially restricts the development of advanced flood forecasting methods. To address this problem, we elaborate three independent datasets derived from different sources, namely EFAS [27], EMO-1 [28], and LamaH-CE [15], which include meteorological, remote sensing, hydrological, and topographic information. Based on these datasets, we design two test cases consisting of a two-dimension forecasting experiment and a data assimilation experiment. Overall, the elaborated datasets and test cases provide a solid foundation for advancing flood forecasting research using machine learning and data assimilation techniques.

Keywords: Flood forecasting · Machine learning · Data assimilation

---

K. Wang and G. Bertoli—Co-first authors.

P. Neumann et al. (Eds.): ICCS 2026, LNCS 16784, pp. 272–286, 2026.
https://doi.org/10.1007/978-3-032-29924-6_20

1 Introduction

Floods, as a pervasive natural hazard, are characterized by their rapid onset and severe impacts, leading to substantial loss of life and significant economic damages worldwide each year [2,12,25]. Flood forecasting is one of the key approaches to mitigating flood impacts, placing critical emphasis on the timeliness and accuracy of predictive models [7,13,24]. In recent years, machine learning methods have been increasingly adopted for flood forecasting [4,10,24]. This growing adoption is largely due to the strong capability of machine learning models to capture complex nonlinear relationships, using a lower amount of variables (with respect to process based modelling), making them particularly suitable for flood forecasting as a nonlinear regression problem. Furthermore, with advances in computational hardware, machine learning models provide faster forecasting speeds compared to traditional hydrological models [36,37]. Consequently, machine learning-based approaches are well-positioned to meet the two essential requirements of flood forecasting: accuracy and timeliness. In addition, there is a growing trend of integrating DA techniques with machine learning methods for flood forecasting [5,14,19,20]. In this context, DA provides an effective means of combining observations from river gauging stations with predictive models, thereby enhancing forecasting accuracy. However, both machine learning and DA are inherently data-driven approaches, and their performance strongly depends on the quality and quantity of available data. In practice, flood-related datasets often face critical limitations, including restricted accessibility due to the lack of open data, inconsistencies in data formats and types, and pronounced spatio-temporal constraints. Consequently, the availability of high-quality datasets is essential for supporting the design and advancement of next-generation flood forecasting models.

1.1 Related Work and Contribution

Currently, widely used datasets for flood forecasting can generally be categorized into two types: simulated datasets and observational datasets. Simulated datasets are typically generated using hydrological models driven by meteorological, hydrological, and topographic inputs. A representative example is the Global Flood Awareness System (GloFAS) dataset [11], which provides gridded river discharge data generated by the LISFLOOD hydrological model. GloFAS offers a temporal resolution of 1 day and a spatial resolution of $0.05° \times 0.05°$, delivering acceptable spatio-temporal coverage and encompassing almost the entire globe except Antarctica, thereby serving as a valuable resource for flood forecasting studies. Nonetheless, several limitations persist. Owing to its relatively coarse spatial resolution, simulated discharges for smaller tributaries often diverge considerably from observed values, which is a common drawback of model-based datasets. Moreover, the daily temporal resolution is insufficient to capture the rapid dynamics of flood events, and the high computational cost of hydrological modeling further constrains its real-time applicability.

The second category is observational datasets derived directly from hydrological monitoring stations. For instance, the NRFA [9] provides discharge records from more than 1,000 gauging stations across the United Kingdom. While such datasets offer direct observations, they are also subject to limitations: station distribution is often sparse, and river discharge data cannot be obtained for ungauged basins, restricting their spatial representativeness. In addition, some gauging stations suffer from missing data, which further reduces the reliability and completeness of such datasets.

Furthermore, several other datasets have been proposed for more specialized purposes. For instance, FloodCastBench [35] is specifically designed for machine learning applications to capture the dynamic processes of floods, while de Bruijn et al. [6] introduces a novel Twitter-based dataset for real-time global flood detection. Although these datasets are valuable for their intended tasks, their task-specific nature limits their generalization capability and restricts their applicability to broader machine learning applications in flood forecasting.

This study elaborates three different hydrological and meteorological datasets for machine learning and data assimilation applications in flood forecasting. These datasets provide a comprehensive representation of the complex processes involved in rainfall-runoff generation. Furthermore, two test cases for flood forecasting are defined using these datasets, providing reliable data resources and a solid research foundation for research on flood forecasting and related fields. The main contributions of this work are:

- A harmonized multi-source hydrological dataset across EFAS, EMO-1, and LamaH-CE.
- A reproducible two-case benchmarking framework with a systematic evaluation under operationally relevant constraints.

2   Data

2.1   Data Sources

As introduced, flood forecasting tasks require multiple variables to describe the complex processes involved in rainfall-runoff generation. We selected three stand-alone datasets from different domains: one providing rich information on catchment characteristics through in-situ observations and geo-morphological indicators (LamaH-CE), another offering detailed meteorological variables essential for predicting rainfall-runoff patterns (EMO-1), and a third contributing historical simulations of spatially distributed runoff values to inform model calibrations and validations (EFAS). By carefully combining these datasets, we have created a rich and comprehensive resource that supports hydrological forecasting with machine learning and data assimilation techniques.

LamaH-CE. LamaH-CE (LArge-SaMple DAta for Hydrology and Environmental Sciences for Central Europe) is a large-sample catchment hydrology dataset designed for comparative hydrology and data-driven modeling in Central Europe. LamaH-CE compiles harmonized hydrometeorological time series and static descriptors for 859 gauged catchments spanning the upper Danube and all Austrian basins (including foreign upstream areas), covering 170,000 km^2 across nine countries. The domain ranges from continental lowlands to high-alpine, snow- and glacier-influenced headwaters, providing broad hydro-climatic variability that is crucial for testing the robustness of flood models under diverse forcing and response regimes. For each catchment, the dataset provides >60 attributes describing topography, climatology, hydrology, land cover/vegetation, soils and geology, alongside runoff series and meteorological forcings at both daily and hourly resolution; most series extend for >35 years, capturing multiple flood-rich periods and rare extremes. Runoff records are additionally annotated with >20 metadata attributes, including indicators of human impacts and data quality/completeness, enabling informed station selection and stratified validation. Unlike many CAMELS-style collections, LamaH-CE includes both independent basins and intermediate catchments and supplies river-network/topology information, which supports network-aware forecasting and upstream–downstream consistency checks. The long, high-frequency records, rich physiographic context, and benchmarking baseline model outputs make LamaH-CE particularly relevant for flood forecasting research, including event-based verification, regionalization/transfer learning, and comparisons between process-based and data-driven approaches.

EMO-1. We use EMO-1 (European Meteorological Observations, 1 arcmin) as the primary gridded meteorological forcing for flood forecasting experiments. EMO-1 is a pan-European, observation-based, multi-variable dataset produced within the Copernicus Emergency Management Service and distributed as 1 arcmin × 1 arcmin grids over Europe and surrounding areas, spanning 1 Jan 1990 to 31 Dec 2023 with annual updates (latest release v3.0.0). It provides daily fields of total precipitation, minimum and maximum air temperature, wind speed, solar radiation and water vapour pressure, and additionally offers 6-hourly precipitation and mean temperature, enabling both continuous simulation and event-focused analyses at sub-daily scales. The gridded fields are derived from quality-controlled station observations and generated using an Angular Distance Weighted interpolation approach, yielding spatially consistent forcing that better resolves sharp precipitation gradients in complex terrain than coarser products. Conceptually, EMO-1 is the higher-density successor to EMO-5 (5 km), which is no longer maintained, allowing direct comparison of the impact of forcing resolution on peak-flow timing and magnitude while retaining a common methodological lineage. For flood forecasting, this combination of long record length (supporting calibration on multiple extreme events), fine spatial detail (improving representation of convective and orographic rainfall hot spots), and sub-daily precipitation (supporting fast catchment response) is particularly valuable.

EFAS. EFAS (European Flood Awareness System) is the Copernicus Emergency Management Service's pan-European flood forecasting and monitoring system. It provides complementary, added-value early warnings—especially for large, transboundary river basins—by running hydrological models over the "greater European domain" independent of administrative borders, and disseminating information to national/regional hydrological services and EU civil protection actors to support preparedness before major floods. EFAS historical simulations provide a spatially continuous, model-consistent hydrological information across the EFAS domain, generated by forcing the open-source LISFLOOD hydrological model with gridded observational precipitation and temperature at 1 arcmin × 1 arcmin resolution (approximately 1.5 km at EFAS latitudes). The current dataset includes 6-hourly and daily gridded time series from 1 Jan 1992 to near real time (with a short latency for the most recent period), comprising core variables used in flood forecasting such as river discharge, surface and subsurface runoff, snow water equivalent, volumetric soil moisture (three soil layers) and a root-zone soil wetness index, complemented by static auxiliary layers (e.g., upstream area, elevation, soil depth and soil hydraulic capacities) that support catchment interpretation and feature engineering. This historical simulation archive is directly relevant because EFAS is an operational Copernicus flood forecasting and monitoring system that couples meteorological forecasts to a continental-scale hydrological model, producing probabilistic flood information and related products. EFAS historical simulations are a key reference for benchmarking forecast skill against a stable baseline, and training or calibrating data-driven models on spatially complete target fields where gauge coverage is sparse or heterogeneous.

2.2   Study Region

The study region follows the LamaH-CE domain in Central Europe. LamaH-CE covers approximately 170,000 km^2 across nine countries (mainly Austria, Germany, the Czech Republic, Switzerland). Spatially, it includes the upper Danube up to the Austrian Slovak border, as well as all Austrian catchments and their adjacent upstream areas in neighboring countries. The domain spans pronounced hydro-climatic gradients, from lowland continental settings to high-alpine environments dominated by snow and ice, and includes a large interconnected river network partitioned into multiple river regions based on major tributary systems.

2.3   Data Preprocessing

Regarding the hydrological datasets, following the preprocessing in [30], we (i) compiled the LamaH-CE gauge discharge series into a single, consistent time-indexed dataset and (ii) extracted EFAS historical simulated discharge for the corresponding region. Each catchment was then paired with a representative EFAS river-grid cell using an automated outlet/basin matching procedure with basic quality checks (and a small number of manual fixes/removals where matches were implausible). Finally, both sources were harmonized to a common

6-hourly timeline by aggregating the higher-frequency observations to the EFAS time step and restricting the analysis to the period where both datasets overlap, yielding aligned observed–simulated discharge pairs for all selected sites.

3   Methodology

3.1   CNNLSTM Forecasting Model

In flood forecasting, it is essential to predict the evolution of the river discharge field. Machine learning methods have gradually become an effective approach for modeling such spatiotemporal dynamics [23,24]. In this study, we employ a CNN-based LSTM model to forecast the spatiotemporal variations of the river discharge, named CNNLSTM [26]. CNNLSTM is a neural network architecture that integrates convolutional neural networks (CNN) and long short term memory (LSTM), and is commonly used for two-dimension spatiotemporal prediction tasks. The CNN component is responsible for extracting spatial features, which are then provided as input to the LSTM to model temporal dependencies and memory effects, as shown in Eq. 1.

$$\mathbf{X}_{t:t+3} \xrightarrow{\text{CNN}} \mathbf{z}_{t:t+3} \xrightarrow{\text{LSTM}} \mathbf{X}^{pred}_{t+4:t+7}, \tag{1}$$

where $\mathbf{X}_{t:t+3}$ denotes the input sequence of fields from time step t to $t + 3$, $\mathbf{z}_{t:t+3}$ represents the corresponding spatial feature representations extracted by the CNN, and $\mathbf{X}^{pred}_{t+4:t+7}$ denotes the predicted fields from time step $t+4$ to $t+7$.

During the training of the CNNLSTM model, the mean squared error (MSE) is adopted as the loss function. The Adam optimizer is employed with a learning rate of $1e^{-3}$. The model is trained for 200 epochs, and the model parameters corresponding to the minimum validation loss are selected as the final model.

3.2   Hybrid Data Assimilation Framework

In flood forecasting, both predictive model outputs and in situ station observations are typically available. To improve forecasting accuracy, data assimilation is employed to combine observational data with model predictions, and it is therefore widely used in flood forecasting applications [29,31–33,38]. Data assimilation methods can be classified into sequential data assimilation and variational data assimilation. Variational data assimilation can simultaneously utilize observations over a time window, resulting in better spatiotemporal consistency and satisfaction of dynamical equations. It provides improved balance in the analysis field, enables effective propagation of sparse observational information, does not rely on large ensemble sizes, and avoids sampling errors. In addition, the analysis results are smoother and more stable, and physical constraints can be incorporated. Therefore, in flood forecasting applications, variational data assimilation is commonly adopted to improve forecast accuracy and reliability [1,8,18]. Within variational data assimilation, the primary approaches are 3D-Var and 4D-Var. Compared with 4D-Var, 3D-Var requires less computational cost and provides

278   K. Wang et al.

faster execution, making it more suitable for the timeliness requirements of flood forecasting [21,22,34]. The 3D-Var method obtains the analysis field by minimizing a cost function, which effectively combines observational data with model forecasts to produce a state estimate that is closer to the true state. The cost function of 3D-Var is formulated as shown in Eq. 2,

$$\mathcal{J}(\mathbf{X}) = \|\mathbf{X} - \mathbf{X}^b\|_{\mathbf{B}^{-1}}^2 + \|\mathbf{y} - \mathcal{H}(\mathbf{X})\|_{\mathbf{R}^{-1}}^2, \tag{2}$$

where $\mathbf{X}$ denotes the state field, $\mathbf{X}^b$ represents the background field, and $\mathbf{B}$ is the background error covariance matrix. The vector $\mathbf{y}$ denotes the observations, $\mathcal{H}$ is the observation operator that maps the model state to the observation space, and $\mathbf{R}$ is the observation error covariance matrix.

However, in flood forecasting, the dimensionality of the state field is relatively high, which leads to substantial computational cost when applying 3D-Var. To address this issue, we employ a compression model that compresses the state field into a latent space. The 3D-Var procedure is then performed in this latent space, a strategy commonly referred to as latent data assimilation, thereby reducing computational cost and improving forecasting efficiency [3]. In this study, the selected compression method is truncated singular value decomposition (TSVD), as formulated in Eq. 3,

$$\tilde{\mathbf{x}} = \mathcal{E}_{TSVD}(\mathbf{X})$$
$$\hat{\mathbf{X}} = \mathcal{D}_{TSVD}(\tilde{\mathbf{x}}), \tag{3}$$

where $\tilde{\mathbf{x}}$ represents the latent state vector, $\mathcal{E}_{\mathrm{TSVD}}$ denotes the TSVD encoding operator, $\mathcal{D}_{\mathrm{TSVD}}$ is its corresponding decoding (inverse) operator, and $\hat{\mathbf{X}}$ denotes the reconstructed state field.

Within this hybrid data assimilation framework, an LSTM model is employed as the forward model in the TSVD-compressed latent space. Compared with traditional hydrological models, the LSTM does not rely on explicitly inferred internal basin states; instead, it learns catchment memory directly from data. Consequently, it often outperforms physical-based hydrological models in basins with complex or poorly understood mechanisms [16,17]. In addition, the computational speed of the LSTM is significantly higher than that of conventional hydrological models, thereby satisfying the accuracy and timeliness requirements of flood forecasting. The LSTM model used in this study is formulated as shown in Eq. 4.

$$\tilde{\mathbf{x}}_{t+4:t+7}^{pred} = \mathcal{M}_{LSTM}(\tilde{\mathbf{x}}_{t:t+3}), \tag{4}$$

where $\tilde{\mathbf{x}}_{t:t+3}$ denotes the latent state sequence from time step t to $t+3$ obtained after TSVD compression, $\mathcal{M}_{LSTM}(\cdot)$ represents the LSTM forward model, and $\tilde{\mathbf{x}}_{t+4:t+7}^{pred}$ denotes the predicted latent states from time step $t+4$ to $t+7$.

In summary, the hybrid data assimilation framework consists of TSVD as the compression model, an LSTM as the forward model, and the 3D-Var scheme.

The cost function of the hybrid data assimilation framework can be written as shown in Eq. 5,

$$\mathcal{J}(\tilde{\mathbf{x}}_{t:t+3}) = \left\|\tilde{\mathbf{x}}_{t:t+3} - \tilde{\mathbf{x}}^{b}_{t:t+3}\right\|^{2}_{\tilde{\mathbf{B}}^{-1}} + \left\|\mathbf{y}_{t:t+3} - \mathcal{H}(\tilde{\mathbf{x}}_{t:t+3})\right\|^{2}_{\mathbf{R}^{-1}}, \qquad (5)$$

where $\tilde{\mathbf{B}}$ denotes the background error covariance matrix in the latent space.

4 Case Studies and Results

We designed two case studies: (i) a 2D forecasting scenario that leverages historical river-discharge simulations together with meteorological and morphological data for the study area, and (ii) a data-assimilation framework that leverages historical simulations and observed river-discharge measurements.

4.1 Experimental Setup

All experiments are conducted on a server equipped with a NVIDIA A100 GPU running Ubuntu 22.04.5. The models are implemented in Python 3.10 using PyTorch 2.1.0. During training, the dataset is split chronologically, with the first 70% used for training, the following 15% for validation, and the final 15% for testing. After training, the model is evaluated on the test dataset. The performance is assessed using MSE, coefficient of determination R^2, structural similarity index measure (SSIM) for two-dimension forecasting, and execution time. The MSE is adopted because the squaring operation emphasizes large deviations, making it particularly sensitive to peak discharge errors that are critical in flood detection, as defined in Eq. 6,

$$\text{MSE} = \frac{1}{N} \sum_{i=1}^{N} \left(\mathbf{X}^{gt}_{i} - \mathbf{X}^{pred}_{i}\right)^{2}, \qquad (6)$$

where N denotes the total number of grid points, $\mathbf{X}^{gt}_{i}$ represents the ground truth discharge value at the i_{th} grid point, and $\mathbf{X}^{pred}_{i}$ denotes the corresponding predicted discharge value. The R^2 is used to evaluate how well the predicted discharge field reproduces the overall variability and temporal dynamics of the ground truth, as defined in Eq. 7,

$$R^2 = 1 - \frac{\sum_{i=1}^{N}(\mathbf{X}^{gt}_{i} - \mathbf{X}^{pred}_{i})^2}{\sum_{i=1}^{N}(\mathbf{X}^{gt}_{i} - \bar{\mathbf{X}}^{gt})^2}, \qquad (7)$$

where $\bar{\mathbf{X}}^{gt}$ denotes the mean of the ground truth discharge values. Values closer to 1 indicate better agreement between prediction and reference. The SSIM is adopted to assess the spatial consistency between the predicted discharge fields and ground truth, as defined in Eq. 8,

$$\text{SSIM} = \frac{(2\mu_{gt}\mu_{pred} + C_1)(2\sigma_{gt,pred} + C_2)}{(\mu_{gt}^2 + \mu_{pred}^2 + C_1)(\sigma_{gt}^2 + \sigma_{pred}^2 + C_2)}, \qquad (8)$$

where μ_{gt} and μ_{pred} denote the mean values of the ground truth and predicted fields, σ_{gt}^2 and σ_{pred}^2 denote the corresponding variances, and $\sigma_{gt,pred}$ denotes their covariance. C_1 and C_2 are small constants introduced to stabilize the division. Values closer to 1 indicate higher structural similarity.

4.2   Case Study (i): Two-Dimension Forecasting: EFAS and EMO-1

In the first case study, data from EFAS and EMO-1 are used to evaluate the performance of the proposed CNNLSTM model in two-dimension forecasting. The input variables consisted of normalized river discharge and soil wetness index from EFAS, as well as precipitation, solar radiation, temperature, water vapor pressure, wind speed, and digital elevation model (DEM) from EMO-1. The output variable is the predicted normalized river discharge field, and the ground truth is given by the river discharge from EFAS. The input sequence length is four time steps, corresponding to one day, and the model produced forecasts for the subsequent four time steps. The trained model is evaluated on the test dataset, and the performance metrics are averaged over the entire test set. The results yielded an MSE of 86.82, an R^2 of 0.99, an SSIM of 0.964, and an execution time of approximately 5 ms.

Based on the numerical metrics obtained from the test dataset, the CNNL-STM model demonstrates strong performance in the two-dimension discharge forecasting task. Specifically, the SSIM and R^2 values are both close to 1, indicating high spatial similarity and strong correlation between the predicted field and ground truth. The relatively low MSE further confirms the model's accuracy, particularly in capturing peak discharge variations. In addition, the execution time of approximately 5 ms highlights the computational efficiency of the model, meeting the timeliness requirements of flood forecasting.

To more clearly illustrate the results, we visualized the predicted fields at four consecutive time steps randomly selected from the test set, together with the corresponding ground truth fields and the absolute error between the predictions and ground truth, as shown in the Fig. 1.

As shown in Fig. 1, the absolute errors between the predicted and reference fields are generally small, indicating that the predicted discharge fields closely match the ground truth. Overall, the CNNLSTM model effectively leverages EFAS and EMO-1 data to achieve accurate and efficient two-dimension forecasting. Hydrologically, the high R^2 and SSIM suggest that the CNNLSTM reproduces the dominant spatiotemporal organization of the EFAS discharge field, consistent with coherent flood-wave propagation along the river network.

4.3   Case Study (ii): Data Assimilation: EFAS and LamaH-CE

In the second case study, data from EFAS and LamaH-CE are used to evaluate the performance of the proposed hybrid data assimilation framework. The input variable is the river discharge from EFAS, which is treated as the state field. The input sequence consisted of four consecutive time steps, and the model produced forecasts for the subsequent four time steps. After TSVD compression, the state

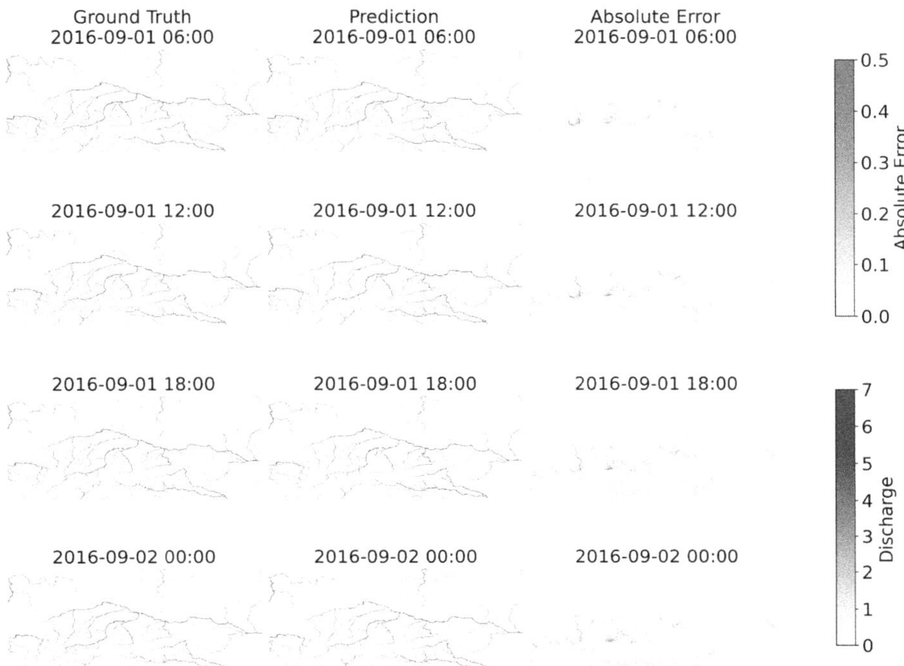

Fig. 1. Results of CNNLSTM at four consecutive time steps from 2016-09-01 06:00 to 2016-09-02 00:00. The first column shows the ground truth fields, the second column presents the corresponding predictions generated by the CNNLSTM model, and the third column illustrates the absolute error between the predictions and the ground truth.

field is transformed into a lower-dimensional state vector in the latent space and provided as input to the LSTM model. The LSTM output represented the background vector. Subsequently, river discharge observations from LamaH-CE are assimilated with the background vector to obtain the analysis vector through the data assimilation procedure. Finally, the analysis vector is reconstructed via the inverse TSVD to produce the analysis field, which constituted the final prediction, and the ground truth corresponded to the observations from the LamaH-CE dataset.

The proposed framework is evaluated on the test dataset, and the performance metrics are averaged over the entire test dataset. The numerical evaluation results are presented in Table 1.

Table 1. Averaged evaluation metrics of three methods for the data assimilation task on the test dataset. Values highlighted in red indicate the best-performing model for each metric.

Model	MSE ↓	R^2 ↑	Execution time (s) ↓
LSTM	1023.43	0.34	≈ 0.06
Hybrid data assimilation framework	356.73	0.83	≈ 20
EFAS	458.55	0.79	–

As shown in Table 1, the hybrid data assimilation framework results exhibits substantial improvements in both MSE and R^2 compared with the LSTM predictions and the original EFAS data. This indicates that hybrid data assimilation framework enhances forecasting accuracy and reliability in flood forecasting. In addition, hybrid data assimilation framework requires only approximate 20 s to complete a one-day forecast, demonstrating computational efficiency that satisfies the timeliness requirements of operational flood forecasting.

In addition, three months of results are randomly selected from the test dataset for visualization, as shown in Fig. 2.

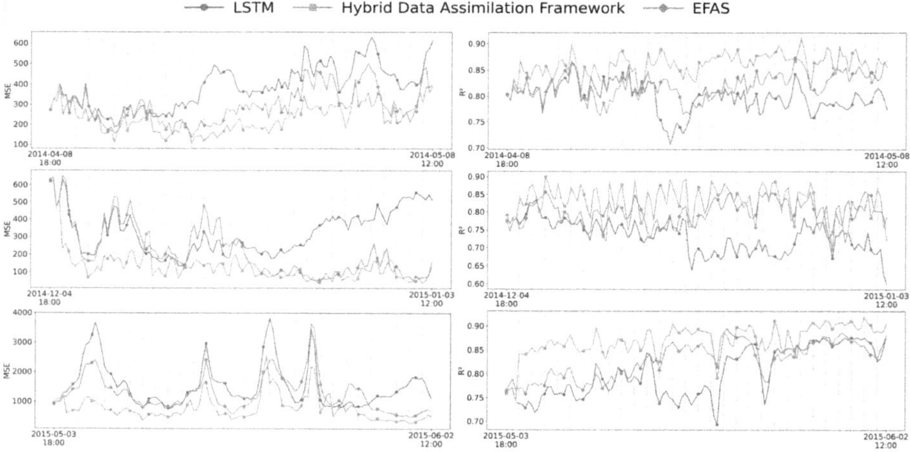

Fig. 2. Forecasting performance for three representative periods (April 2014, December 2014, and May 2015). Blue circles denote the LSTM results, orange squares denote the hybrid data assimilation framework results, and green diamonds denote the EFAS results. The left column shows MSE and the right column shows R^2. Vertical dashed lines indicate the data assimilation times. (Color figure online)

As shown in the figure, the hybrid data assimilation framework results outperform both the LSTM and EFAS in terms of MSE and R^2, which is consistent with the averaged numerical evaluation metrics obtained on the test dataset.

These results indicate that the proposed hybrid data assimilation framework achieves higher accuracy and reliability in flood forecasting by effectively integrating the river discharge field provided by EFAS with the observations from the LamaH-CE. Moreover, the behaviour of MSE and R^2 across the highlighted periods suggest that the assimilation step helps keep the forecast closer to the observed hydrograph evolution, even during high-flow dynamics. This points to a reduced sensitivity to mismatches in antecedent conditions and flow propagation when EFAS-based LSTM forecast are periodically constrained by discharge observations with data assimilation framework here provided.

5   Conclusion

This study addresses the data limitations that constrain the development of machine learning and data assimilation approaches for flood forecasting. We elaborate three independent datasets, namely EFAS, EMO-1, and LamaH-CE, which integrate meteorological, hydrological, remote sensing, and topographic data to provide long-term, multi-source data resources. Based on these datasets, two experimental test cases are designed: a two-dimension forecasting task and a data assimilation task. These experiments enable systematic evaluation of predictive performance and the benefit of integrating model forecasts with observations, while simultaneously assessing the capability of machine learning and data assimilation approaches in flood forecasting. Regarding the 2D case study, because the reference fields are taken from EFAS, the reported scores should be interpreted primarily as the model's ability to reproduce EFAS-consistent spatiotemporal discharge patterns from meteorological forcing and physiographic descriptors, rather than as a direct measure of agreement with independent observations. From a hydrological perspective, this is nevertheless a valuable result: it indicates that the CNNLSTM can act as an efficient surrogate of the EFAS discharge dynamics at the field level, preserving the large-scale organization of flow and its temporal evolution. This surrogate capability is promising for rapid scenario screening and real-time applications where computational cost is critical, and it motivates further work to assess generalization under out-of-sample events and to benchmark performance against gauge-based discharge observations (and/or alternative hydrological reanalyses) to quantify added value beyond reproducing the EFAS target. Regarding the data assimilation framework, a key limitation is that the current setup assimilates discharge only (with fixed TSVD/LSTM and error assumptions), so future work should examine sensitivity to the latent-space truncation and uncertainty specification and extend the framework to multi-source observations (e.g., soil moisture, water level, and potentially, weather forecasts) and adaptive updating to further improve robustness across regimes and events. The datasets elaborated in this study, together with the proposed test cases, indeed establish a reproducible framework for benchmarking flood forecasting methods and support future research at the intersection of hydrology and data-driven modeling.

References

1. Alvarado-Montero, R., Schwanenberg, D., Krahe, P., Helmke, P., Klein, B.: Multi-parametric variational data assimilation for hydrological forecasting. Adv. Water Resour. **110**, 182–192 (2017)
2. Apel, H., Aronica, G.T., Kreibich, H., Thieken, A.H.: Flood risk analyses–how detailed do we need to be? Nat. Hazards **49**(1), 79–98 (2009)
3. Arcucci, R., Mottet, L., Pain, C., Guo, Y.K.: Optimal reduced space for variational data assimilation. J. Comput. Phys. **379**, 51–69 (2019)
4. Bertoli, G., Schroeter, K., Arcucci, R., Caporali, E.: A hybrid machine learning framework for improved short-term peak-flow forecasting. arXiv preprint arXiv:2601.09336 (2026)
5. Boucher, M.A., Quilty, J., Adamowski, J.: Data assimilation for streamflow forecasting using extreme learning machines and multilayer perceptrons. Water Resources Res. **56**(6), e2019WR026226 (2020)
6. de Bruijn, J.A., de Moel, H., Jongman, B., de Ruiter, M.C., Wagemaker, J., Aerts, J.C.: A global database of historic and real-time flood events based on social media. Sci. Data **6**(1), 311 (2019)
7. Byaruhanga, N., Kibirige, D., Gokool, S., Mkhonta, G.: Evolution of flood prediction and forecasting models for flood early warning systems: a scoping review. Water **16**(13), 1763 (2024)
8. Ercolani, G., Castelli, F.: Variational assimilation of streamflow data in distributed flood forecasting. Water Resour. Res. **53**(1), 158–183 (2017)
9. Fry, M., Swain, O.: Hydrological data management systems within a national river flow archive (2010)
10. Ghorpade, P., et al.: Flood forecasting using machine learning: a review. In: 2021 8th International Conference on Smart Computing and Communications (ICSCC), pp. 32–36. IEEE (2021)
11. Grimaldi, S., et al.: River discharge and related historical data from the global flood awareness system, v4.0 (2022). https://doi.org/10.24381/cds.a4fdd6b9. Accessed 22 Sept 2025
12. Hirabayashi, Y., et al.: Global flood risk under climate change. Nat. Clim. Chang. **3**(9), 816–821 (2013)
13. Jain, S.K., et al.: A brief review of flood forecasting techniques and their applications. Int. J. River Basin Manag. **16**(3), 329–344 (2018)
14. Jeong, M., Kwon, M., Cha, J.H., Kim, D.H.: High flow prediction model integrating physically and deep learning based approaches with quasi real-time watershed data assimilation. J. Hydrol. **636**, 131304 (2024)
15. Klingler, C., Schulz, K., Herrnegger, M.: Lamah-ce: large-sample data for hydrology and environmental sciences for central Europe. Earth Syst. Sci. Data **13**(9), 4529–4565 (2021). https://doi.org/10.5194/essd-13-4529-2021. https://essd.copernicus.org/articles/13/4529/2021/
16. Kratzert, F., Klotz, D., Brenner, C., Schulz, K., Herrnegger, M.: Rainfall-runoff modelling using long short-term memory (LSTM) networks. Hydrol. Earth Syst. Sci. **22**(11), 6005–6022 (2018)
17. Kratzert, F., Klotz, D., Shalev, G., Klambauer, G., Hochreiter, S., Nearing, G.: Towards learning universal, regional, and local hydrological behaviors via machine learning applied to large-sample datasets. Hydrol. Earth Syst. Sci. **23**(12), 5089–5110 (2019)

18. Lai, X., Liang, Q., Yesou, H., Daillet, S.: Variational assimilation of remotely sensed flood extents using a 2-D flood model. Hydrol. Earth Syst. Sci. **18**(11), 4325–4339 (2014)
19. Lever, J., et al.: Facing & mitigating common challenges when working with real-world data: the data learning paradigm. J. Comput. Sci. **85**, 102523 (2025)
20. Li, X.L., Lü, H., Horton, R., An, T., Yu, Z.: Real-time flood forecast using the coupling support vector machine and data assimilation method. J. Hydroinf. **16**(5), 973–988 (2014)
21. Liu, Y., Liu, J., Li, C., Liu, L., Wang, Y.: A WRF/WRF-hydro coupled forecasting system with real-time precipitation-runoff updating based on 3dvar data assimilation and deep learning. Water **15**(9), 1716 (2023)
22. Liu, Y., Liu, J., Li, C., Yu, F., Wang, W.: Effect of the assimilation frequency of radar reflectivity on rain storm prediction by using WRF-3DVAR. Remote Sens. **13**(11), 2103 (2021)
23. Maspo, N.A., Bin Harun, A.N., Goto, M., Cheros, F., Haron, N.A., Mohd Nawi, M.N.: Evaluation of machine learning approach in flood prediction scenarios and its input parameters: a systematic review. In: IOP Conference Series: Earth and Environmental Science, vol. 479, p. 012038. IOP Publishing (2020)
24. Mosavi, A., Ozturk, P., Chau, K.W.: Flood prediction using machine learning models: literature review. Water **10**(11), 1536 (2018)
25. Plate, E.J.: Flood risk and flood management. J. Hydrol. **267**(1–2), 2–11 (2002)
26. SShi, X., Chen, Z., Wang, H., Yeung, D.Y., Wong, W.K., Woo, W.C.: Convolutional LSTM network: a machine learning approach for precipitation nowcasting. In: Advances in Neural Information Processing Systems, vol. 28 (2015)
27. Smith, P., et al.: On the operational implementation of the European flood awareness system (EFAS). In: Flood Forecasting, pp. 313–348. Elsevier (2016)
28. Thiemig, V., et al.: Emo-5: a high-resolution multi-variable gridded meteorological dataset for Europe. Earth Syst. Sci. Data **14**(7), 3249–3272 (2022). https://doi.org/10.5194/essd-14-3249-2022. https://essd.copernicus.org/articles/14/3249/2022/
29. Wang, K., et al.: AI-empowered latent four-dimensional variational data assimilation for river discharge forecasting. IEEE J. Sel. Top. Appl. Earth Obs. Remote Sens. (2025)
30. Wang, K., et al.: Latent three-dimensional variational data assimilation with convolutional autoencoder and LSTM for flood forecasting. In: Paszynski, M., Barnard, A.S., Zhang, Y.J. (eds.) Computational Science - ICCS 2025 Workshops, pp. 43–56. Springer, Cham (2025)
31. Wang, K., et al.: Latent three-dimensional variational data assimilation with convolutional autoencoder and LSTM for flood forecasting. In: International Conference on Computational Science, pp. 43–56. Springer (2025)
32. Wang, K., Cheng, S., Piggott, M.D., Dance, S.L., Wang, Y., Arcucci, R.: Latent data assimilation with non-explicit observation operator in hydrology. Q. J. R. Meteorol. Soc. **151**(772), e5009 (2025)
33. Wang, K., D. Piggott, M., Wang, Y., Arcucci, R.: Neural network as transformation function in data assimilation. In: International Conference on Computational Science, pp. 322–329. Springer (2024)
34. Wang, Y., Min, J., Chen, Y., Huang, X.Y., Zeng, M., Li, X.: Improving precipitation forecast with hybrid 3dvar and time-lagged ensembles in a heavy rainfall event. Atmos. Res. **183**, 1–16 (2017)
35. Xu, Q., Shi, Y., Zhao, J., Zhu, X.X.: Floodcastbench: a large-scale dataset and foundation models for flood modeling and forecasting. Sci. Data **12**(1), 431 (2025)

36. Yaseen, Z.M.: A new benchmark on machine learning methodologies for hydrological processes modelling: a comprehensive review for limitations and future research directions. Knowl.-Based Eng. Sci. **4**(3), 65–103 (2023)
37. Zhao, X., et al.: A comprehensive review of methods for hydrological forecasting based on deep learning. Water **16**(10), 1407 (2024)
38. Ziliani, M.G., Ghostine, R., Ait-El-Fquih, B., McCabe, M.F., Hoteit, I.: Enhanced flood forecasting through ensemble data assimilation and joint state-parameter estimation. J. Hydrol. **577**, 123924 (2019)

ICCS 2026 Main Track Short Papers

A Novel Tensor Resistance-Based Pore-Network Model for Pore-Scale Flow in Porous Media

Shuyu Sun[1,2]($\boxtimes$), Yushi Yang[1,2], and Tao Zhang[3]

[1] School of Mathematical Sciences, Key Laboratory of Intelligent Computing and Applications (Tongji University), Ministry of Education, Tongji University, Shanghai 200092, China
`{suns,yushiyang}@tongji.edu.cn`
[2] Shanghai Research Institute for Intelligent Autonomous Systems, Tongji University, Shanghai 200092, China
[3] The College of New Energy, China University of Petroleum (East China), Qingdao 266580, China
`tao.zhang@upc.edu.cn`

Abstract. Pore-network models (PNMs) are powerful tools for simulating fluid flow and transport in porous media, with applications spanning petroleum engineering, hydrology, and materials science. Classical PNMs simplify porous media into interconnected pore-throat networks and model flow using empirical resistance relationships. This paper introduces the Tensor Resistance-Based Pore-Network Model (TR-PNM), a high-fidelity upscaling framework designed to overcome the limitations of classical pore-network models (C-PNM) in capturing anisotropic flow within complex porous media. By utilizing a natural domain decomposition process, the TR-PNM replaces idealized scalar resistances with $n \times n$ conductivity tensors derived from solving local Stokes flow problems on the actual 3D geometry of individual pore units. This approach bridges the gap between traditional "ball-and-stick" approximations and the high accuracy of Direct Numerical Simulation (DNS), by designating interface pressures at throat centers as the primary unknowns to ensure rigorous mass conservation. By providing a scalable and physically consistent characterization of high-fidelity flow behavior, the TR-PNM offers a robust tool for industrial applications in reservoir engineering, carbon sequestration, and groundwater remediation.

Keywords: Pore-network model · Tensor resistance · Domain decomposition · Anisotropic flow · Porous media · Computational hydraulics

P. Neumann et al. (Eds.): ICCS 2026, LNCS 16784, pp. 289–297, 2026.
https://doi.org/10.1007/978-3-032-29924-6_21

1   Introduction

Porous media are ubiquitous across a vast array of natural and engineered systems, serving as the foundational structures for oil reservoirs, groundwater aquifers, fuel cells, and catalytic reactors. In these complex environments, understanding fluid flow at the pore scale is not merely a theoretical exercise but a critical necessity for accurately predicting macroscale transport behavior, effective permeability, and chemical dispersion [10,15,16,19,21]. While traditional laboratory experiments provide essential data, numerical modeling has become indispensable for gaining deeper insight into these hidden flow paths. Among these approaches, pore-network models (PNMs) [2–5,8] have emerged as a robust and highly cost-effective alternative to computationally demanding Direct Numerical Simulation (DNS) methods, such as the lattice Boltzmann method (LBM) [13,14,20], high-resolution finite volume/element methods (FVM/FEM) [1] or particle methods [9].

The **Pore-Network Model (PNM)** simplifies the pore space into a topologically equivalent graph of interconnected pore bodies (nodes) and pore throats (edges). For pore-scale incompressible single-phase flow of Newtonian fluid in porous media, the core of classical PNMs is the relationship between flow rate and pressure drop across a throat, derived from the Hagen-Poiseuille equation for laminar flow in a cylindrical tube:

$$q_{ij} = \frac{\pi r_{ij}^4}{8\mu L_{ij}}(p_i - p_j) = \frac{1}{R_{ij}}(p_i - p_j). \tag{1}$$

In this expression, r_{ij} and L_{ij} are the radius and length of throat ij, μ is the fluid viscosity, and $R_{ij} = \frac{8\mu L_{ij}}{\pi r_{ij}^4}$ defines the isotropic hydraulic resistance for that specific throat. For non-cylindrical throats (e.g., slit-shaped), the resistance is modified to: $R_{ij} = \frac{12\mu L_{ij}}{wh^3}$,
where w is the width of the slit and h is the height of the slit. We note that here, in all cases, resistance is a *scalar* (isotropic) quantity. In our new TR-PNM to be introduced shortly, resistance will become a *tensor* (anisotropic) quantity.

The Hagen-Poiseuille equation (Equation (1)) alone is not closed and cannot be used to solve for both the pressure (at all nodes) and the flux (along all throats). We need to provide one additional equation at the network scale to close the system. For an incompressible fluid, the net flow into any pore i must be sources or sinks (no mass accumulation in time):

$$\sum_{j \in \mathcal{N}(i)} q_{ij} = Q_i, \tag{2}$$

where $\mathcal{N}(i)$ is the set of neighboring nodes to i, and Q_i is the external source/sink term at node i (zero for internal nodes).

Substituting the Hagen-Poiseuille equation (Equation (1)) into the mass balance Equation (2), we obtain a linear algebraic equation for each pore. These equations together form a system of linear equations: $\sum_{j \in \mathcal{N}(i)} \frac{1}{R_{ij}}(p_i - p_j) = Q_i.$

In the matrix form, this is written as: $\mathbf{Ap} = \mathbf{Q}$. In this expression, $\mathbf{A}$ is an $N \times N$ conductance matrix with diagonal terms $A_{ii} = \sum_{j \in \mathcal{N}(i)} 1/R_{ij}$ and off-diagonal terms $A_{ij} = -1/R_{ij}$ for connected nodes, while $\mathbf{p}$ and $\mathbf{Q}$ represent the vectors of nodal pressures and source/sink terms, respectively.

Limitation of Classical PNMs: Classical PNMs represent porous media as a network of pores (nodes or cells) and throats (bonds or edges or links) with simplified geometric and hydraulic properties. These models rely on empirical correlations (e.g., Hagen-Poiseuille for laminar flow) to compute flow resistance in throats, assuming isotropic resistance and homogeneous pore geometry [17]. While classical PNMs are computationally efficient, they fail to capture anisotropic flow behaviors [12,18] in complex porous media (e.g., fractured rock or layered sediments). The classical PNMs are quite accurate for thin and small-radius pore throats, where the Hagen-Poiseuille solution is applicable, but they are not accurate for modeling thick "pore throats"; they are also satisfactory for describing a large pore body, where fluid flow resistance is negligible, but they incur pronounced modeling error for a large "pore body". In addition, the classical PNMs scale poorly for large networks ($>10^6$ pores) [6].

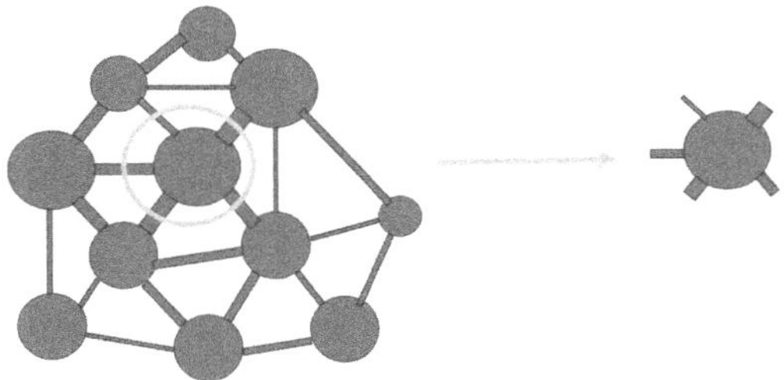

Fig. 1. The unit of TR-PNM.

2 TR-Based PNM with Domain Decomposition

The fundamental difference between the Tensor Resistance-Based Pore-Network Model (TR-PNM) and the classic PNMs lies in how they partition the void space of the porous medium. The TR-PNM approach shifts the modeling paradigm from simplified geometric conduits to high-fidelity substructures, primarily through two key innovations: the transition from scalar to tensor-based resistance to capture directional anisotropy, and the implementation of domain decomposition [11] to partition the void space into specialized "pore units".

In the TR-PNM framework, the fundamental building block is the pore unit, a composite structure that departs significantly from the discrete "ball-and-stick" components used in a classic pore-network model (C-PNM). While a C-PNM

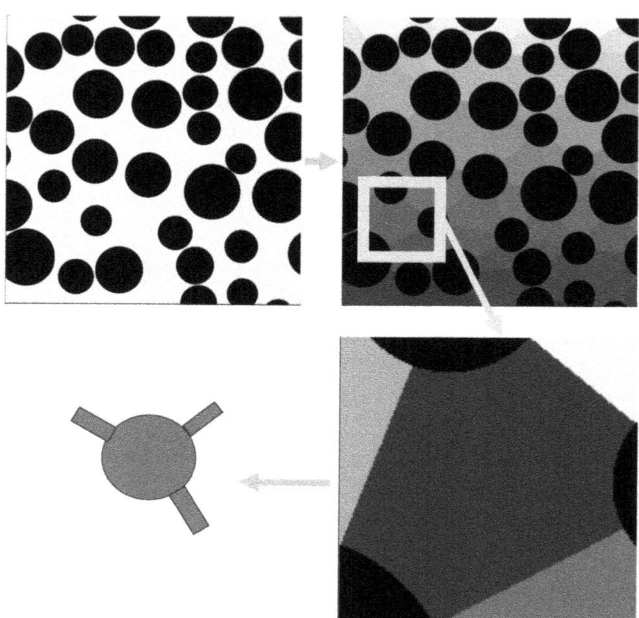

Fig. 2. From domain decomposition to the TR-PNM unit.

distinguishes between pore bodies (storage nodes) and pore throats (resistive edges), the TR-PNM utilizes a more integrated geometry. As illustrated in Fig. 1, a pore unit is created by bisecting every connected pore throat at its exact geometric center to form "half-throats". These half-throats are then aggregated with their parent pore body to form a single, self-contained entity, which we call a TR-PNM pore unit or simply a TR-PNM unit. The entire TR-PNM is built using only these pore units as the fundamental building blocks. While the classic model treats pore bodies as zero-resistance nodes and isolates flow resistance within 1D throats defined by a single real number (implicitly assuming isotropic flow), the TR-PNM recognizes the entire pore unit as a complex, potentially anisotropic resistor. This behavior is rigorously captured by an $n \times n$ conductivity tensor, where n represents the number of half-throat inlets and outlets. The extraction of the pore unit in the Tensor Resistance-Based Pore-Network Model (TR-PNM) involves a clean and natural domain decomposition process that captures the full geometric fidelity of the pore space. As shown in Fig. 2, the complex void space of the porous medium is first partitioned into subdomains by assigning a number of cutting planes. The cutting planes are located at the center of throats and are perpendicular to the orientation of throats, so that the area of cutting planes is minimized. For pore geometries that differ from pore throats in their shape, the cutting planes can still be mathematically defined using the minimization process on the area of cutting planes. For a selected sub-domain (shortly later represented by a TR-PNM pore unit), the solid-fluid interfaces are designated as no-flow boundaries, while the N interfaces where throats were bisected are assigned as inflow/outflow boundaries (see the second step of Fig. 2).

We need to assign an effective resistance or conductivity tensor for each sub-domain. This tensor is algebraically represented by a square matrix, which relates the flow rates at each half-throat to the pressures at those boundaries. For a sub-domain with n half-throats (inlets/outlets), i.e., n inflow/outflow boundaries, the tensor is an $n \times n$ matrix. To numerically determine the conductivity tensor, a local problem of Stokes flow is solved by imposing a constant unit pressure ($P = 1$) on one specific boundary while setting all other $n - 1$ boundaries to zero pressure ($P = 0$), by using a conservative numerical method, such as the cell-centered finite difference (CCFD), a finite volume method, or a conservative finite element method. This process is repeated for each boundary to populate the $n \times n$ matrix.

3 Illustration Through a Numerical Example

The transformation of a complex porous medium into a high-fidelity Tensor Resistance-Based Pore-Network Model (TR-PNM) follows a rigorous upscaling pipeline that preserves geometric realism while enabling computational efficiency. This process begins with the generation of the porous domain, as seen in the first plot of Fig. 2, where a synthetic medium is created using solid balls of varying radii and randomly generated locations. This initial 3D voxel-like representation serves as the basis for the domain decomposition, where the void space is partitioned into sub-domains through the strategic placement of cutting planes at the center of pore throats.

Once the global domain is partitioned, a specific sub-domain is isolated for detailed characterization, as illustrated in Fig. 3(left). In this example, the selected sub-domain features a central pore body connected to three neighboring half-throats. Unlike classic models that simplify this geometry into a zero-resistance sphere, the TR-PNM treats this sub-domain as a unique hydraulic unit. To prepare for numerical solving, a high-resolution mesh is applied to the unit, shown in Fig. 3(right), presenting the internal discretization that distinguishes between the fluid-occupied cells and the solid boundaries.

The core of the TR-PNM method is the solution of the local Stokes flow problem to derive a conductivity tensor. Because this sub-domain has three inlets/outlets ($N = 3$), three independent numerical experiments are performed. In each experiment, a unit pressure ($P = 1$) is applied to one half-throat interface while the others are set to $P = 0$, and the solid boundaries are treated as no-flow zones. The resulting pressure distributions across the unit for these three scenarios are captured in Fig. 4(left), Fig. 5,(left) and Fig. 6(left), showing how the pressure gradient develops specifically according to the irregular internal morphology. The corresponding fluid velocity fields, as shown in Fig. 4(right), Fig. 5,(right) and Fig. 6(right), allow for the calculation of the volumetric flow rates exiting and entering each of the three interfaces.

By integrating the flux data from these three local simulations, we construct the 3×3 conductivity tensor for the TR-PNM unit. For this specific example, the resulting tensor is: $\mathbf{C} = \begin{bmatrix} -0.0015507 & 0.0011285 & 0.00042218 \\ 0.0011276 & -0.0014306 & 0.00030297 \\ 0.00042309 & 0.00030205 & -0.00072514 \end{bmatrix}$. This matrix acts as the "fingerprint" of the pore unit, mathematically relating boundary pressures to volumetric flow rates. The off-diagonal terms represent the cross-coupling between different throats, while the diagonal terms represent the primary resistance along each path. Finally, these characterized sub-domains are reassembled into a global network. Each pore unit, represented by its central body and associated half-throats, is connected to its neighbors at the throat interfaces. By enforcing mass conservation at these interfaces, where the flux leaving one unit must equal the flux entering the next, a global sparse linear system is formed.

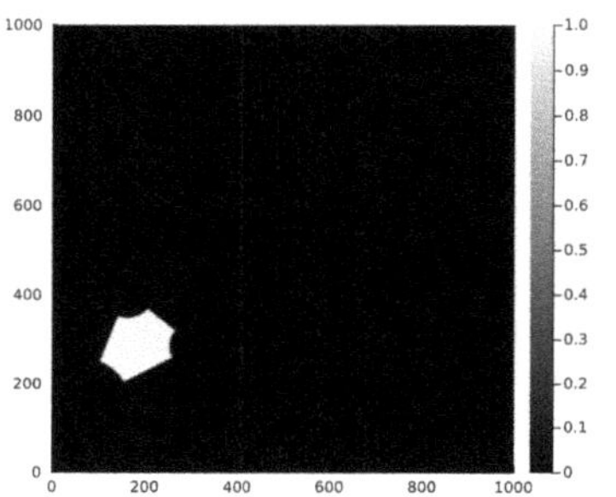

(a) Location of the selected subdomain

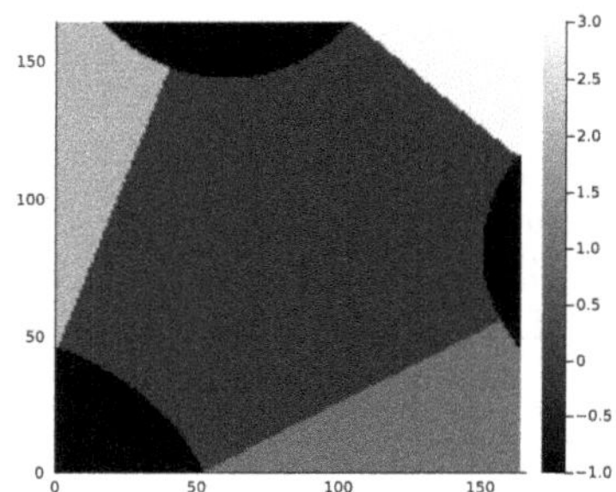

(b) Zoomed-in panel of the subdomain

Fig. 3. A selected subdomain in the domain-decomposition of the porous medium.

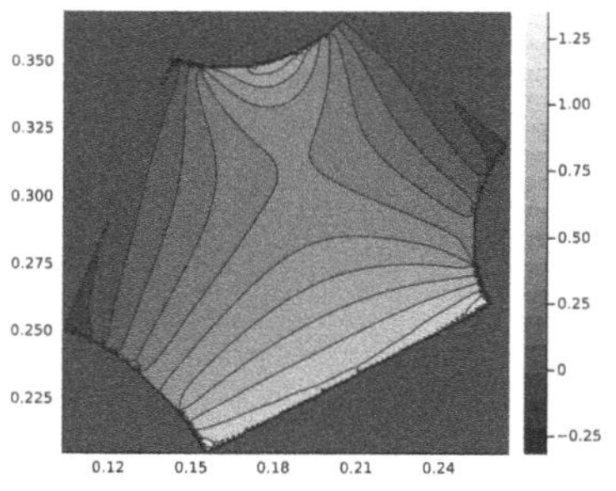

(a) The computed pressure profile

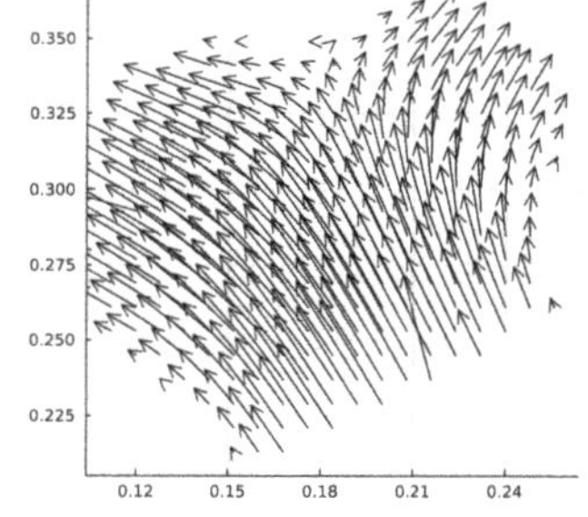

(b) The computed velocity plot

Fig. 4. CCFD solution of the first sub-problem in the selected subdomain.

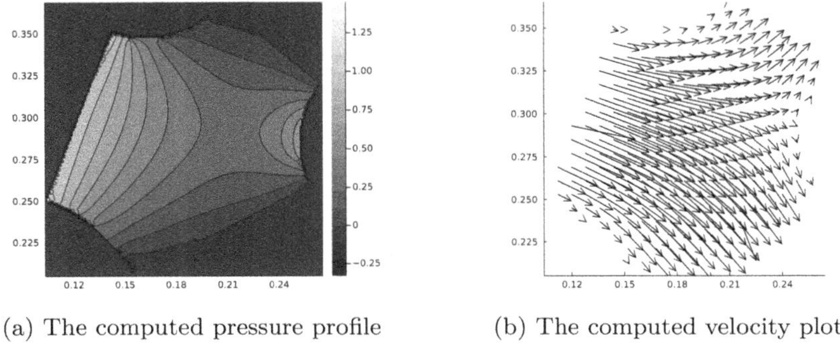

(a) The computed pressure profile   (b) The computed velocity plot

Fig. 5. CCFD solution of the second sub-problem in the selected subdomain.

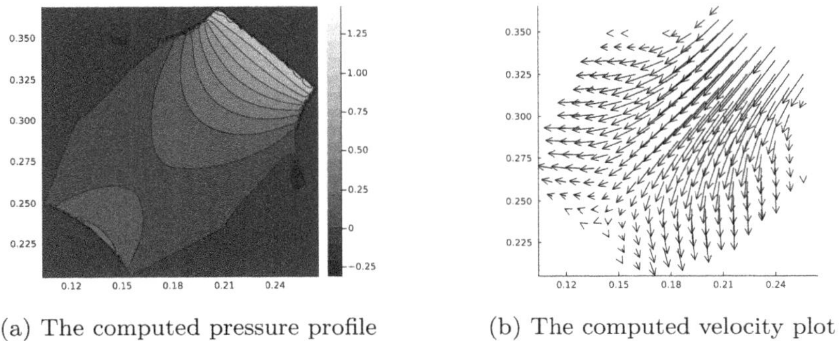

(a) The computed pressure profile   (b) The computed velocity plot

Fig. 6. CCFD solution of the third sub-problem in the selected subdomain.

4   Conclusion

We presented the Tensor Resistance-Based Pore-Network Model (TR-PNM) as a high-fidelity alternative to C-PNM, which fails to capture complex anisotropic flow in fractured/layered porous media. Using domain decomposition, it replaces scalar resistances with 3D geometry-derived conductivity tensors, balancing DNS accuracy and simulation speed, with applications in oil recovery, groundwater remediation and carbon sequestration. TR-PNM combines network efficiency and DNS rigor, scales to large systems, and supports non-linear extensions. Future work will improve interface accuracy, automate network extraction via machine learning, and extend to multiphase flow.

References

1. Chen, J., Sun, S., Wang, X.-P.: A numerical method for a model of two-phase flow in a coupled free flow and porous media system. J. Comput. Phys. **268**, 1–16 (2014)
2. Cui, R., Sun, S.: Capillary behaviors of miscible fluids in porous media: a pore-scale simulation study. In: International Conference on Computational Science, pp. 3–10. Springer, Cham (2024). https://doi.org/10.1007/978-3-031-63783-4_1
3. Cui, R., Nair, A.K.N., Ruslan, M.F.A.C., Yang, Y., Sun, S.: Interfacial properties of the hexane+ carbon dioxide+ brine system in the presence of hydrophilic silica. Ind. Eng. Chem. Res. **62**(34), 13470–13478 (2023)
4. Cui, R., Majid Hassanizadeh, S., Sun, S.: Pore-network modeling of flow in shale nanopores: network structure, flow principles, and computational algorithms. Earth-Sci. Rev. **234**, 104203 (2022)
5. Blunt, M.J.: Flow in porous media: pore-network models and multiphase flow. Curr. Opin. Colloid Interface Sci. **6**(3), 197–207 (2001)
6. Blunt, M.J.: Multiphase Flow in Permeable Media: A Pore-Scale Perspective. Cambridge University Press, Cambridge (2017)
7. Blunt, M.J., Lin, Q.: Flow in porous media in the energy transition. Engineering **14**, 10–14 (2022)
8. Liu, J.: Porous media flow modeling from molecular simulations to pore-network modeling: physics-consistent upscaling of interfacial transport parameters. Comput. Geosci. **30**(2), 15 (2026)
9. Feng, X., Qiao, Z., Sun, S., Wang, X.: An energy-stable smoothed particle hydrodynamics discretization of the Navier-Stokes-Cahn-Hilliard model for incompressible two-phase flows. J. Comput. Phys. **479**, 111997 (2023)
10. Feng, X., Liu, J., Shi, J., Ping, H., Zhang, T., Sun, S.: Phase equilibrium, thermodynamics, hydrogen-induced effects and the interplay mechanisms in underground hydrogen storage. Comput. Energy Sci. **1**(1), 46–64 (2024)
11. Griebel, M.: Parallel domain-oriented multilevel methods. SIAM J. Sci. Comput. **16**(5), 1105–1125 (1995)
12. Guo, C., Wang, Q., Ling, B.: Anisotropic lumped network model for electric properties of heterogeneous media. In: 2023 International Applied Computational Electromagnetics Society Symposium (ACES-China), pp. 01–03. IEEE (2023)
13. Ju, L., Guo, Z., Yan, B., Sun, S.: Implementation of contact line motion based on the phase-field lattice Boltzmann method. Phys. Rev. E **109**(4), 045307 (2024)
14. Raeini, A.Q., Bijeljic, B., Blunt, M.J.: Numerical modelling of sub-pore scale events in two-phase flow through porous media. Transp. Porous Media **101**(2), 191–213 (2014)
15. Sun, S., Zhang, T.: Reservoir Simulations: Machine Learning and Modeling. Gulf Professional Publishing (2020)
16. Sun, S., Firoozabadi, A., Wheeler, M.: Introduction of COMPES: finding directions in energy and computational science. Comput. Energy Sci. **1**(1), 1–2 (2024)
17. Valvatne, P.H., Blunt, M.J.: Predictive pore-scale modeling of two-phase flow in mixed wet media. Water Res. Res. **40**(7) (2004)
18. Zhang, D., Zhang, X., Guo, H., Lin, D., Meegoda, J.N., Liming, H.: An anisotropic pore-network model to estimate the shale gas permeability. Sci. Rep. **11**(1), 7902 (2021)
19. Zhang, L., Jingang, F., Dong, M., Wei, Yu., Sun, S.: A mini-review of ReaxFF molecular simulation in the heavy oil enhancing oil recovery: development, challenges and prospects. Comput. Energy Sci. **2**(2), 48–53 (2025)

20. Zhang, T., Sun, S.: A coupled Lattice Boltzmann approach to simulate gas flow and transport in shale reservoirs with dynamic sorption. Fuel **246**, 196–203 (2019)
21. Zhang, T., Sun, S., Song, H.: Flow mechanism and simulation approaches for shale gas reservoirs: a review. Transp. Porous Media **126**(3), 655–681 (2019)

Goal-Conditioned Decision Transformer for Multi-goal Offline Reinforcement Learning

Paweł Gajewski$^{(\boxtimes)}$ ⓘ, Dominik Żurek ⓘ, Marcin Pietroń ⓘ, and Kamil Faber ⓘ

Faculty of Computer Science, AGH University of Krakow, Krakow, Poland
pgajewski@agh.edu.pl

Abstract. Reinforcement learning (RL) in robotics faces significant hurdles regarding sample efficiency and generalization across varying goals. While Offline RL mitigates the need for costly online interactions, its integration with goal-conditioned policies and transformer-based architectures remains underexplored. We introduce a Goal-Conditioned Decision Transformer adapted for offline multi-goal robotics. By explicitly incorporating goal states into the sequence modeling framework, our approach efficiently solves varying tasks using only pre-collected data. We validate this method on a newly released offline dataset for the Franka Emika Panda platform. Experimental results demonstrate that our approach outperforms state-of-the-art online baselines in complex tasks and maintains robustness in sparse-reward settings, even with limited expert demonstrations.

Keywords: Data-efficient learning · decision transformer · multi-goal learning · offline reinforcement learning · reinforcement learning · robotic manipulation · robotics · transformer architectures

1 Introduction

Reinforcement learning (RL) has driven significant progress in robotics [1]. However, standard online algorithms require continuous environment interaction, making them impractical for real-world hardware due to safety concerns, wear and tear, and time constraints. While simulations offer a partial solution, they often suffer from the "sim-to-real" gap.

To address these limitations, *Offline RL* enables agents to learn optimal policies entirely from pre-collected datasets [2]. This paradigm allows for the reuse of historical data and eliminates the need for risky online exploration. However, training on a single fixed task is insufficient for general-purpose robotics. *Multi-goal RL* [3] addresses this by requiring agents to reach varying goals within the same environment structure, necessitating policies that are explicitly conditioned on the desired outcome.

Concurrently, the *Decision Transformer* (DT) [4] has reframed RL as a conditional sequence modeling problem, leveraging the Transformer architecture [5]

P. Neumann et al. (Eds.): ICCS 2026, LNCS 16784, pp. 298–306, 2026.
https://doi.org/10.1007/978-3-032-29924-6_22

to generate actions based on desired returns. While DTs have shown promise in standard tasks, their application to multi-goal offline scenarios remains under-explored.

In this work, we bridge these domains by introducing a Goal-Conditioned DT. We modify the standard DT architecture to explicitly process goal information, allowing it to solve multi-goal robotic tasks using only offline data. We validate this approach on a custom dataset generated using the Franka Emika Panda environment [6].

The contributions of this paper are threefold: (1) We extend the DT to handle multi-goal settings by incorporating explicit goal-conditioning into the input sequence; (2) We release a specialized offline RL dataset for multi-goal robotic manipulation on the Franka Emika Panda platform; and (3) We demonstrate that our approach outperforms state-of-the-art online methods (TQC+HER) and Behavioral Cloning baselines in offline settings, even under sparse reward signals.

2   Related Work

Reinforcement learning (RL) has evolved from tabular methods to Deep RL (DRL), enabling high-dimensional continuous control [7,8]. In robotic control, off-policy actor-critic methods have become the standard due to their sample efficiency. Soft Actor-Critic (SAC) [9] utilizes maximum entropy to improve stability, while Truncated Quantile Critics (TQC) [10] further alleviates overestimation bias through distributional critics and truncation. TQC currently serves as a state-of-the-art baseline for continuous control.

2.1   Multi-goal RL and HER

Standard RL typically trains for a fixed goal. To improve adaptability, Multi-Goal RL conditions the policy on a desired goal input, requiring the agent to generalize across varying targets [3]. These environments often utilize sparse, binary rewards, making exploration difficult. Hindsight Experience Replay (HER) [11]

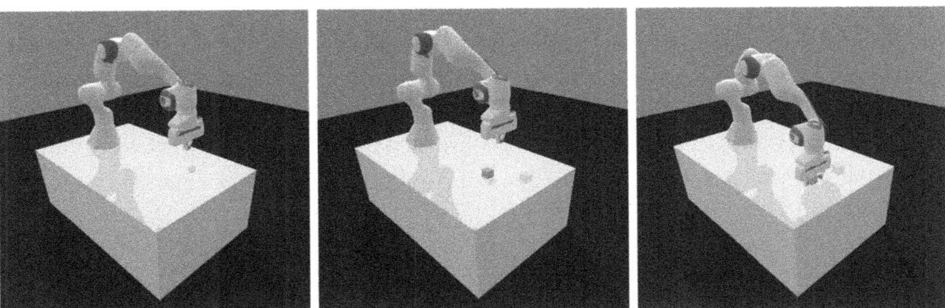

Fig. 1. Multi-goal robotic environments: Reach, Push, PickAndPlace.

overcomes this by relabeling failed trajectories as successful ones for the specific goals that were actually achieved. The combination of TQC and HER represents a robust baseline for multi-goal robotic tasks.

2.2 Transformers in RL

While Transformers [5] dominate language and vision, their application to RL is a recent development. The DT [4] reframes RL as conditional sequence modeling rather than value function approximation. By conditioning an autoregressive model on desired returns, states, and actions, DT matches or exceeds offline RL baselines on standard benchmarks. Recent extensions, such as the Multi-Objective DT [12], have applied this to multi-objective optimization, but the specific intersection of goal-conditioned, sparse-reward robotic control in an offline setting remains an active area of research that we address in this work.

3   Methodology

3.1 Decision Transformer

We employ the DT architecture, which reframes offline reinforcement learning as a conditional sequence modeling problem. Unlike methods that fit value functions or compute policy gradients, the DT outputs optimal actions using a masked Transformer [5]. This architecture allows the model to effectively model trajectories by conditioning predictions on desired future outcomes.

The input sequence consists of returns-to-go $\hat{R}_t$, states s_t, and actions a_t:

$$\tau = \{\hat{R}_1, s_1, a_1, \ldots, \hat{R}_T, s_T, a_T\} \tag{1}$$

The return-to-go at timestep t is defined as $\hat{R}_t = \sum_{t'=t}^{T} r_{t'}$, representing the cumulative future reward. This conditioning enables the generation of actions required to achieve a specific target return.

3.2 Dataset

The DT is trained entirely offline. We generated two primary dataset types using the *Panda-Gym* suite: *expert* and *random*. Expert datasets were created using converged TQC agents evaluated for 1 million timesteps. Random datasets were generated by agents sampling actions uniformly.

To evaluate data efficiency, we also created mixtures of expert and random data with varying ratios and subsets. We publicly release the dataset to support reproducibility[1].

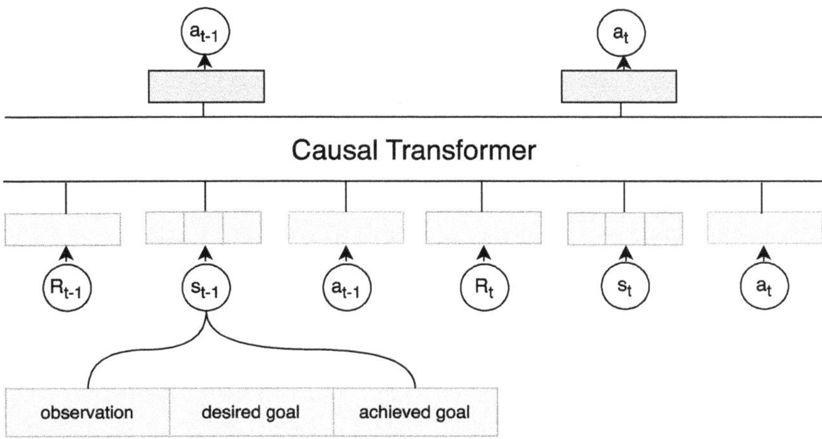

Fig. 2. Goal-conditioned Decision Transformer for multi-goal RL environments.

3.3 Goal-Conditioned Decision Transformer

We utilize multi-goal robotic environments [13] where the observation space is a dictionary comprising the current observation o_t, the desired goal g_d, and the achieved goal g_a. Consequently, the state at timestep t is a tuple $s_t = (o_t, g_d, g_a)$.

In contrast to standard DT conditioning on scalar returns, goal-conditioning provides structured, spatially meaningful supervision, which is particularly important in sparse-reward multi-goal settings where identical returns may correspond to qualitatively different objectives.

To adapt the DT to this structure, we flatten and concatenate these vectors into a single input vector:

$$s_t = [o_t^{(0)}, \ldots, o_t^{(n)}, g_d^{(0)}, \ldots, g_d^{(m)}, g_a^{(0)}, \ldots, g_a^{(m)}] \tag{2}$$

Including the achieved goal g_a allows the transformer to infer progress toward the desired goal implicitly, without requiring an explicit distance metric or reward shaping.

This modification incorporates goal-related information directly into the sequence, enabling the policy to generate actions that drive the agent toward g_d, as illustrated in Fig. 2.

Unlike standard goal-conditioned policies that treat goals as part of the state input to a reactive policy, our approach conditions an autoregressive sequence model on goal information across the entire trajectory, enabling temporally extended credit assignment with respect to goal achievement.

---

[1] https://huggingface.co/datasets/lubiluk/panda-gym-offline.

3.4   Tasks and Rewards

We evaluate the agent on a Franka Emika Panda robotic arm [6] in three tasks: *Reach* (position end-effector), *Push* (move a cube), and *PickAndPlace* (lift and move an object) illustrated by environment screenshots in Fig. 1. We test performance under two reward structures: *sparse*, where the agent receives 0 for success and -1 otherwise; and *dense*, calculated as the negative Euclidean distance between the achieved goal g_a and desired goal g_d.

A rollout is considered successful if the environment-defined success condition is met at any timestep within the evaluation horizon.

4   Experimental Setup

We compare the DT against two baselines: Behavioral Cloning (BC) and Truncated Quantile Critics with Hindsight Experience Replay (TQC+HER). Our evaluation addresses five research questions: **(RQ1)** Can DT match state-of-the-art online algorithms (TQC+HER)?; **(RQ2)** How does DT compare to BC?; **(RQ3)** How does DT handle sparse vs. dense rewards?; **(RQ4)** What is the minimum dataset size required?; and **(RQ5)** How does the expert-to-random data ratio impact performance?

Experiments are conducted using 3 random seeds, with agents evaluated over 10,000 timesteps. All results are averaged over three random seeds; while limited, we observed low variance across runs. During evaluation, we condition the DT on a target return of 0 (perfect optimality) for sparse settings and 0 (zero distance) for dense settings, prompting the model to generate the most optimal trajectory. We report average return and success rate. To address **RQ1–RQ3**, we train DT and BC on the full 1-million transition expert dataset and compare against TQC+HER trained for an equivalent number of online steps. For **RQ4**, we evaluate data efficiency by training DT on subsets ranging from 100k to 1M expert transitions. For **RQ5**, we analyze resilience to noise by fixing dataset size at 1M but varying the expert data ratio (0%, 25%, 50%, 75%, 100%) mixed with random trajectories.

Hyperparameters for TQC+HER are taken from Stable-Baselines-Zoo [14], while DT utilizes the original paper's settings. The code is publicly available[2].

While TQC+HER is trained online and thus has access to interaction during learning, we include it as a strong upper-bound baseline commonly used in robotic manipulation benchmarks.

5   Results and Discussion

We present the experimental evaluation on full (1M transitions) and subset datasets, addressing the research questions formulated previously.

---

[2] https://github.com/lubiluk/cldt.

Table 1. Performance comparison: Return/Success Rate (%)

Method	Metric	Reach	Push	PickAndPlace
		Dense Reward		
DT	Ret/Succ	−0.21/100.0	**−0.95/99.5**	**−1.30/98.9**
BC	Ret/Succ	−0.21/100.0	−1.20/95.9	−1.35/97.9
TQC+HER	Ret/Succ	−0.21/100.0	−1.04/98.7	−1.35/98.7
		Sparse Reward		
DT	Ret/Succ	**−1.72/100.0**	−8.26/95.0	**−7.63/97.8**
BC	Ret/Succ	−1.76/100.0	−8.18/94.6	−9.01/94.9
TQC+HER	Ret/Succ	−1.82/100.0	**−4.54/99.5**	−16.96/77.0

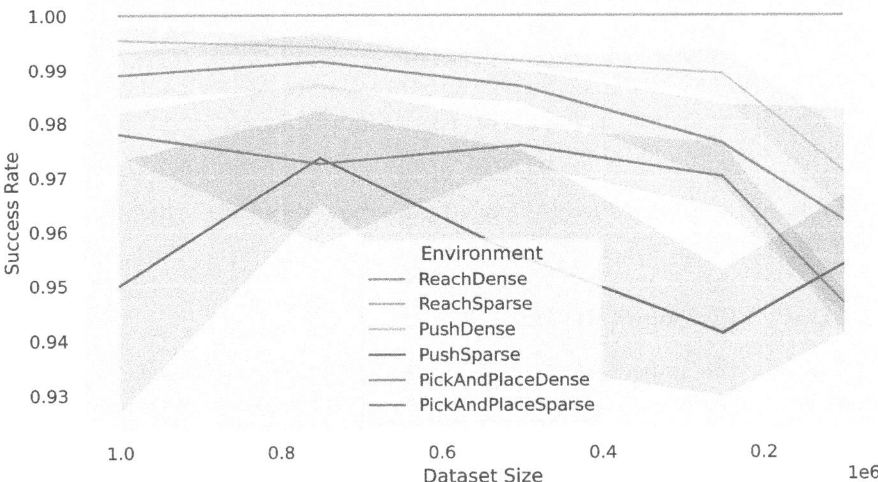

Fig. 3. Impact of dataset size on success rate.

5.1   Comparative Performance (RQ1, RQ2, RQ3)

Table 1 details the performance of DT against BC and TQC+HER. In the simplest task, *Reach*, all methods achieve near-perfect success. However, in the more complex *Push* and *PickAndPlace* environments with Dense Rewards, DT consistently outperforms both TQC+HER and BC in average return and success rate (RQ1, RQ2). Notably, DT achieves these results with significantly lower training time (80 mins) compared to the online TQC+HER baseline (240 mins).

Under Sparse Rewards, DT demonstrates superior robustness and efficiency (RQ3). In *PickAndPlace*, DT achieves a significantly higher return (−7.63 vs −16.96), indicating it solves the task in fewer steps than the baseline, while maintaining a high success rate (97.8%). In contrast, TQC+HER suffers from

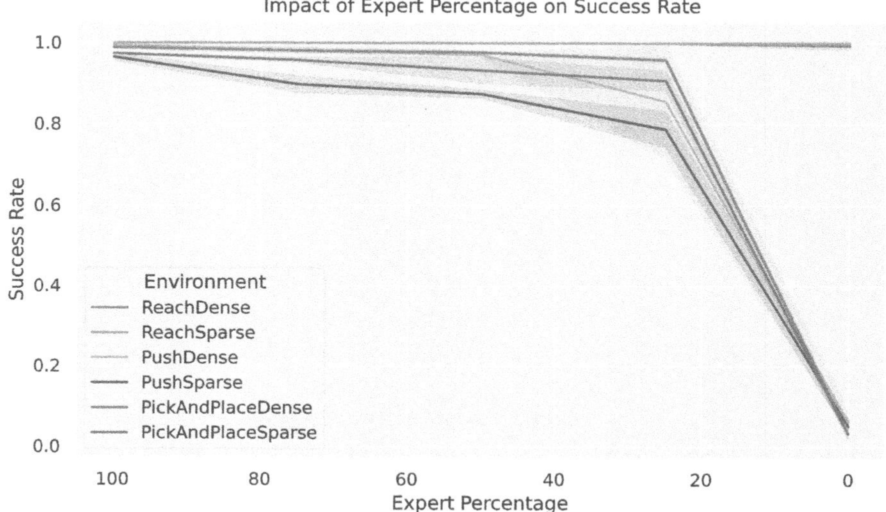

Fig. 4. Impact of expert data percentage.

instability in the sparse *PickAndPlace* task, where its success rate drops significantly to 77.0%.

5.2 Data Efficiency (RQ4)

We analyzed the impact of dataset size on performance (Fig. 3). For *Reach*, performance is invariant to size. In dense reward settings for *Push* and *PickAndPlace*, performance declines only when data falls below 250k samples; yet, even at 100k samples, DT maintains $> 96\%$ success. Sparse rewards introduce higher variance and a sharper performance drop below 250k samples.

5.3 Expert Data Ratio (RQ5)

Figure 4 illustrates DT's sensitivity to trajectory quality. Expert data, i.e. trajectories from a policy that achieves near-optimal performance, was mixed with ones from a random policy. While performance degrades as the ratio of expert data decreases, DT remains surprisingly robust, maintaining $> 80\%$ success in complex tasks even when expert data constitutes only 25% of the dataset. Below this threshold, performance drops sharply.

6 Conclusions and Future Work

We presented a goal-conditioned Decision Transformer adapted for offline multi-goal robotics by explicitly incorporating goal states into the input sequence. We also release a new offline dataset for reproducibility. We hypothesize that this robustness stems from the Transformer's ability to perform long-horizon credit assignment via self-attention, which is particularly effective in sparse-reward settings. Our results demonstrate that this approach can outperform the expert policy used to generate the training data, particularly in complex tasks like PickAndPlace. DT also exhibits robustness to suboptimal demonstrations, maintaining strong performance even when up to approximately 75% of the trajectories are random, and remains effective under sparse reward settings. Future work will extend this framework to continual learning settings and training with heterogeneous expert trajectories.

Acknowledgments. This work was supported by funds assigned by Polish Ministry of Science and Higher Education to AGH University of Krakow, and by PLGrid HPC infrastructure (ACK Cyfronet AGH, grant no. PLG/2025/018713).

Disclosure of Interests. The authors have no competing interests to declare that are relevant to the content of this article.

References

1. Dalal, M., Pathak, D., Salakhutdinov, R.: Accelerating robotic reinforcement learning via parameterized action primitives. In: NeurIPS (2021)
2. Agarwal, R., Schuurmans, D., Norouzi, M.: An optimistic perspective on offline reinforcement learning. In: Daumé III, H., Singh, A. (eds.) Proceedings of the 37th International Conference on Machine Learning, vol. 119 of Proceedings of Machine Learning Research, pp. 104–114. PMLR (2020)
3. Plappert, M., et al.: Multi-goal reinforcement learning: challenging robotics environments and request for research. arXiv (2018)
4. Chen, L., et al.: Decision transformer: reinforcement learning via sequence modeling (2022)
5. Vaswani, A., et al.: Attention is all you need. In: Advances in Neural Information Processing Systems (2017)
6. Gallouédec, Q., Cazin, N., Dellandréa, E., Chen, L.: panda-gym: open-source goal-conditioned environments for robotic learning. In: 4th Robot Learning Workshop: Self-Supervised and Lifelong Learning at NeurIPS (2021)
7. Sutton, R., Barto, A.: Reinforcement Learning: An Introduction (1979)
8. Mnih, V., et al.: Playing atari with deep reinforcement learning. In: NIPS (2013)
9. Haarnoja, T., Zhou, A., Abbeel, P., Levine, S.: Soft actor-critic: off-policy maximum entropy deep reinforcement learning with a stochastic actor. In: ICML, pp. 1856–1865 (2018)
10. Kuznetsov, A., Shvechikov, P., Grishin, A., Vetrov, D.: Controlling overestimation bias with truncated mixture of continuous distributional quantile critics. In: ICML'20: Proceedings of the 37th International Conference on Machine Learning, pp. 5556–5566 (2020)

11. Andrychowicz, M., et al.: Hindsight experience replay. In: Advances in Neural Information Processing Systems, vol. 30 (2017)
12. Ghanem, A., Ciblat, P., Ghogho, M.: Multi-objective decision transformers for offline reinforcement learning (2023)
13. Brockman, G.: Openai gym. arXiv (2016)
14. Raffin, A.: Rl baselines3 zoo (2020). https://github.com/DLR-RM/rl-baselines3-zoo

On a Class of Higher-Order Fully Decoupled Schemes for the Biot Model

Qi Zhang and Shuyu Sun(✉) ⓘD

School of Mathematical Sciences, Tongji University, Shanghai 200092, China
suns@tongji.edu.cn

Abstract. In this paper, we consider a temporally high-order, decoupled, linear and fully discrete finite element method for the Biot model. The generalized BDF method and the simplified auxiliary variable method with correction are adopted to discretize the proposed Biot model in time. Compared with the existing works for classical BDF for the Biot model, which is addressed by several novel techniques. For an arbitrary time step, we analytically prove the time-discretized energy stability. Through a series numerical experiments, we verify the stability and accuracy of the proposed scheme.

Keywords: Biot model · Generalized BDF · Energy stability

1 Introduction

The following quasi-static Biot's consolidation problem read: for a given $\Omega \subset \mathbb{R}^d (d = 2, 3)$ with bounded, connected domain with Lipschitz continuous boundary, find the displacement field $\mathbf{u} : [0, T] \times \Omega \to \mathbb{R}^d$ and pressure field $p : [0, T] \times \Omega \to \mathbb{R}$ such that

$$-\nabla \cdot \boldsymbol{\sigma}(\mathbf{u}) + \alpha \nabla p = \boldsymbol{f} \qquad \text{in } \Omega \times [0, T], \tag{1}$$

$$\frac{\partial}{\partial t}(c_0 p + \alpha \nabla \cdot \mathbf{u}) - \nabla \cdot (\kappa \nabla p) = g \qquad \text{in } \Omega \times [0, T], \tag{2}$$

$$\mathbf{u}(\boldsymbol{x}, 0) = \mathbf{u}_0, p(\boldsymbol{x}, 0) = p_0 \qquad \text{in } \Omega,$$

$$\boldsymbol{u} = \mathbf{0}, p = 0 \qquad \text{on } \partial\Omega \times [0, T],$$

where $\boldsymbol{f} : [0, T] \times \Omega \to \mathbb{R}^d$ is the body force and $g : [0, T] \times \Omega \to \mathbb{R}$ is the volumetric source/sink term. The quantity $\boldsymbol{\sigma}(\mathbf{u}) = 2\mu\boldsymbol{\varepsilon}(\mathbf{u}) + \lambda \operatorname{tr}(\boldsymbol{\varepsilon}(\mathbf{u}))\mathbf{I}$ in (1) is the elastic stress tensor and involves the displacement $\mathbf{u}$, the linearized strain tensor $\boldsymbol{\varepsilon}(\mathbf{u}) = \frac{1}{2}(\nabla\mathbf{u} + \nabla\mathbf{u}^\top)$, the $d \times d$ identity matrix $\mathbf{I}$, and the elastic moduli $\mu = E/(2(1 + \nu))$ and $\lambda = E\nu/((1 + \nu)(1 - 2\nu))$ are the two Lamé coefficients, defined in terms of Young's modulus E and Poisson's ratio ν. Moreover, $c_0 \geq 0$ is the constrained specific storage coefficient, κ is the permeability and $\alpha > 0$ is the Biot-Willis fluid-solid coupling coefficient, which is close to 1 and much smaller than the typical Lamé constants.

P. Neumann et al. (Eds.): ICCS 2026, LNCS 16784, pp. 307–315, 2026.
https://doi.org/10.1007/978-3-032-29924-6_23

This paper develops higher-order, fully decoupled, linear, and unconditionally energy-stable schemes for Biot's quasi-static poroelasticity model [1,2]. Existing finite element and decoupling methods for the Biot system [3,4] are mainly first-order accurate. To overcome the displacement–pressure coupling and parameter sensitivity, we exploit the cancellation structure in the energy law and apply the scalar auxiliary variable (SAV) approach [5]. For heterogeneous permeability, we further introduce a the explicit decomposition auxiliary variable (EDAV) strategy inspired by the corrected scalar auxiliary variable (CSAV) methods [6]. Combined with a generalized high-order backward difference formulae (BDF) framework [7] and a stabilization term, the resulting schemes are efficient, robust, and unconditionally energy stable.

The rest of the paper is organized as follows. Section 2 presents preliminary inequalities and results. Section 3 develops the fully discrete schemes and proves unconditional energy stability. Numerical experiments and conclusions are given in Sects. 4 and 5, respectively.

2 Preliminaries and Model's Equivalent Transformation

2.1 Preliminaries

As in [8], for $s \geq 0$, we denote $\|\cdot\|_s$ as the norms for the standard Sobolev spaces $H^s(\Omega)^d$. We also denote by $H_0^s(\Omega)^d$ the closure of $C_0^\infty(\Omega)^d$ with respect to the norm $\|\cdot\|_s$. In particular, $(\cdot,\cdot) := (\cdot,\cdot)_\Omega$ and $\|\cdot\|_0$ denote the inner product and norm in $L^2 := L^2(\Omega)$ or $L^2(\Omega)^d$, respectively.

As [9], we now derive the energy law at the PDE level for the Biot's includes (1)-(2).

Lemma 1. *The Biot's model (i.e., Eqs. (1)–(2)) satisfies the following energy law:*

$$\frac{d}{dt}E(\boldsymbol{u},p,\boldsymbol{f}) + \kappa\|\nabla p\|_0^2 = (g,p) - (\partial_t\boldsymbol{f},\mathbf{u}), \tag{3}$$

where $E(\boldsymbol{u},p,\boldsymbol{f}) := \frac{1}{2}\left[2\mu\|\boldsymbol{\epsilon}(\mathbf{u})\|_0^2 + \lambda\|\nabla \cdot \mathbf{u}\|_0^2 + c_0\|p(t)\|_0^2\right] - (\boldsymbol{f},\mathbf{u})$.

To apply energy techniques in our stability analysis, we recall the following lemma from Dahlquist's G-stability theory [10].

Lemma 2. *Let $\alpha(\zeta) = \alpha_k\zeta^k + \cdots + \alpha_0$ and $\mu(\zeta) = \mu_k\zeta^k + \cdots + \mu_0$ be polynomials of degree at most k, with at least one of degree k, and assume that they have no common divisor. Let $(\cdot,\cdot)$ be an inner product with associated norm $|\cdot|$. If*

$$\operatorname{Re}\frac{\alpha(\zeta)}{\mu(\zeta)} > 0 \quad for \ |\zeta| > 1, \tag{3.3}$$

then there exists a symmetric positive definite matrix $\mathbf{G} = (g_{ij}) \in \mathbb{R}^{k\times k}$ and real numbers $\delta_0,\ldots,\delta_k$ such that, for any vectors $v^0,\ldots,v^k$ in the inner product space,

$$\left(\sum_{i=0}^{k}\alpha_i v^i, \sum_{j=0}^{k}\mu_j v^j\right)^2 = \sum_{i,j=1}^{k} g_{ij}(v^i, v^j) - \sum_{i,j=1}^{k} g_{ij}(v^{i-1}, v^{j-1}) + \left|\sum_{i=0}^{k}\delta_i v^i\right|^2.$$
(3.4)

2.2   Model's Equivalent Transformation

Unlike the CSAV approach in [6], we account for heterogeneous permeability by partitioning $\Omega = \bigcup_{i=1}^{M}\Omega_i$ and introducing local auxiliary variables Q_i.

$$(Q_i^2)_t = 0, \quad Q_i|_{t=0} = 1. \tag{4}$$

Motivated by the fact that (4) admits the unique solution $Q_i \equiv 1$, we define the ODE system so that each Q_i remains close to 1. Consequently, $V(Q_i) \equiv 1$ on each Ω_i with $V(Q_i) = 1 - (1 - Q_i)^k$. Let $Q = (Q_1, \ldots, Q_M)^\top$. We further introduce a global quantity $\widetilde{V}(Q)$ with $\widetilde{V}(Q) \equiv 1$. Therefore, inserting $\widetilde{V}(Q)$ into the linear coupling terms does not alter the original Biot system (1)–(2), which can thus be reformulated equivalently as follow

$$-\nabla \cdot \boldsymbol{\sigma} + \alpha \widetilde{V}(Q)\nabla p = \boldsymbol{f} \qquad \text{in } \Omega \times [0, T], \tag{5}$$

$$\frac{\partial}{\partial t}(c_0 p + \alpha \nabla \cdot \boldsymbol{u}) - \nabla \cdot (\kappa \nabla p) + s_p \widetilde{V}(Q)(p - p) = g \qquad \text{in } \Omega \times [0, T], \tag{6}$$

$$(Q_i^2)_t + \theta_i \left(s_p(p, p)_{\Omega_i} + \alpha(p, \nabla \cdot \boldsymbol{u}_t)_{\Omega_i}\right) V(Q_i)$$
$$= \theta_i \left(s_p(p, p)_{\Omega_i} + \alpha(p, \nabla \cdot \boldsymbol{u}_t)_{\Omega_i}\right) V(Q_i) \qquad \text{in } [0, T], \tag{7}$$

where θ_i is small parameter and s_p is a stabilization parameter to be determined later. The initial conditions and the boundary conditions remain unchanged. We now clarify the role of Q_i and the ODE system (7). Since the integral terms sum to zero, $Q_i(t) \equiv 1$. To improve robustness and keep Q_i close to 1, we add the term $s_p V(Q_i)(p - p, p)_{\Omega_i}$. The roles of $\widetilde{V}(Q)$ and $V(Q_i)$ will be discussed later.

3   Numerical Scheme

This section presents temporal discretization methods for (5)–(7) based on generalized backward differentiation formula (BDF) techniques. The resulting schemes are flexible, efficient, linear, and unconditionally energy stable.

3.1   Scheme Construction

Let $\mathcal{T}_h$ be a shape-regular mesh of Ω. The finite element spaces are

$$\mathbf{X}_h = \{\mathbf{u} \in (H_0^1(\Omega))^d : \mathbf{u}|_K \in \mathcal{P}_{\ell_1}(K)\}, \quad M_h = \{p \in H_0^1(\Omega) : p|_K \in \mathcal{P}_{\ell_2}(K)\}.$$

For the temporal discretization, we use the generalized BDF-k method ($2 \leq k \leq 3$) together with a kth-order extrapolation. Let $t^n = n\Delta t$. Then

$$\frac{1}{\Delta t} \sum_{q=0}^{k} a_{k,q}(\beta)\phi(t^{n+1-k+q}) = \partial_t \phi(t^{n+\beta}) + \mathcal{O}(\Delta t^k), \tag{8}$$

$$\sum_{q=0}^{k-1} b_{k,q}(\beta)\phi(t^{n+2-k+q}) = \phi(t^{n+\beta}) + \mathcal{O}(\Delta t^k), \tag{9}$$

$$\sum_{q=0}^{k-1} c_{k,q}(\beta)\phi(t^{n+1-k+q}) = \phi(t^{n+\beta}) + \mathcal{O}(\Delta t^k). \tag{10}$$

Remark 1. For convenience, the coefficients in (8)–(10) for $k = 2, 3$ are listed below; see [7] for details.

For convenience, we introduce

$$A_k^\beta(\phi^{n+1}) = \sum_{q=0}^{k} a_{k,q}(\beta)\phi^{n+1-k+q}, \quad B_k^\beta(\phi^{n+1}) = \sum_{q=0}^{k-1} b_{k,q}(\beta)\phi^{n+2-k+q}, \tag{11}$$

$$C_k^\beta(\phi^n) = \sum_{q=0}^{k-1} c_{k,q}(\beta)\phi^{n+1-k+q}, \quad B_k^\beta(\phi^{n+1}) = \eta_k(\beta)C_k^\beta(\phi^{n+1}) + D_k^\beta(\phi^{n+1}),$$

where $\eta_2(\beta) = \frac{\beta-1}{\beta}$, $\eta_3(\beta) = \frac{\beta-1}{\beta+1}$, $\beta \geq 1$, and

$$d_{k,q}(\beta) = b_{k,q}(\beta) - \eta_k(\beta)c_{k,q}(\beta), \qquad D_k^\beta(\phi^{n+1}) = \sum_{q=0}^{k-1} d_{k,q}(\beta)\phi^{n+2-k+q}. \tag{12}$$

The numerical scheme of system (5)–(7) is formulated as follows:

Algorithm 3.1 EDAV-GBDF scheme

Step 1: Find $\mathbf{u}_h^{n+1} \in \mathbf{X}_h$ such that for all $\mathbf{v}_h \in \mathbf{X}_h$

$$2\mu\left(\epsilon(B_k^{\beta_k+1}(\mathbf{u}_h^{n+1})), \epsilon(\mathbf{v}_h)\right) + \lambda\left(\nabla \cdot B_k^{\beta_k+1}(\mathbf{u}_h^{n+1}), \nabla \cdot \mathbf{v}_h\right)$$
$$- \left(\alpha\widetilde{V}(Q^n)C_k^{\beta_k+1}(p_h^n), \nabla \cdot \mathbf{v}_h\right) = \left(\boldsymbol{f}^{n+\beta_k+1}, \mathbf{v}_h\right), \tag{13}$$

Step 2: Find p_h^{n+1} such that for all $q_h \in M_h$

$$c_0\left(\frac{A_k^{\beta_k}(p_h^{n+1})}{\Delta t}, q_h\right) + \alpha\left(\widetilde{V}(Q^n)\nabla \cdot \left(\frac{A_k^{\beta_k}(\mathbf{u}_h^{n+1})}{\Delta t}\right), q_h\right) + \left(\kappa\nabla B_k^{\beta_k}(p_h^{n+1}), \nabla q_h\right)$$

$$+ s_p\widetilde{V}(Q^n)\left(B_k^\beta(p_h^{n+1}) - C_k^\beta(p_h^n), q_h\right) = \left(g^{n+\beta_k}, q_h\right). \tag{14}$$

Step 3: Find $\widetilde{Q}_i^{n+1} \in \mathbb{R}$ such that

$$\frac{(\widetilde{Q}_i^{n+1})^2 - (Q_i^n)^2}{\Delta t} = \theta_i \alpha V(Q_i^n)\left(C_k^{\beta_k}(p_h^{n+1}) - C_k^{\beta_k+1}(p_h^n), \nabla \cdot \frac{A_k^{\beta_k}(\mathbf{u}_h^{n+1})}{\Delta t}\right)_{\Omega_i}$$

$$+ \theta_i s_p \widetilde{V}(Q^n) \left(B_k^\beta(p_h^{n+1}) - C_k^\beta(p_h^n), C_k^{\beta_k}(p_h^{n+1}) \right)_{\Omega_i}. \quad (15)$$

Step 4: To improve consistency, we further implement the following correction $\left(Q_i^{n+1}\right)^2 = \xi \left(\widetilde{Q}_i^{n+1}\right)^2 + (1 - \xi)$, where $\xi \in [0, 1]$ such that

$$\left(Q_i^{n+1}\right)^2 - \left(\widetilde{Q}_i^{n+1}\right)^2 \leq \Im \mathcal{R}_i^{n+1}, \quad 0 < \Im < 1. \quad (16)$$

with $\mathcal{R}_i^{n+1} = \frac{3\eta_k}{4}\kappa\Delta t\text{vert}\nabla C_k^\beta(p_h^{n+1})\text{vert}_{0,\Omega_i}^2$, $\quad k = 2,3$ We choose an appropriate ξ according to the following four cases:

– If $\widetilde{Q}_i^{n+1} = 1$, we set $\xi = 0$;
– If $\widetilde{Q}_i^{n+1} > 1$, we set $\xi = 0$;
– If $\widetilde{Q}_i^{n+1} < 1$ and $\left(\widetilde{Q}_i^{n+1}\right)^2 + \Im \mathcal{R}_i^{n+1} \geq 1$, we set $\xi = 0$;
– If $\widetilde{Q}_i^{n+1} < 1$ and $\left(\widetilde{Q}_i^{n+1}\right)^2 + \Im \mathcal{R}_i^{n+1} < 1$, we set $\xi = 1 - \frac{\Im \mathcal{R}_i^{n+1}}{1 - \widetilde{Q}_i^{n+1}}$.

So, Q^{n+1} can be shown to be expressed as $Q^{n+1} = Q_i^{n+1}$ in Ω_i and $\widetilde{V}(Q^{n+1}) = V(Q_i^{n+1})$ in Ω_i.

Theorem 1. *By Lemma 1 and Theorem 1 in [7], in the absence of the external force $\boldsymbol{f}$, and with the first $k - 1$ steps generated by a coupling scheme. Let λ_k^g be the smallest eigenvalue of the matrix $\mathbf{G}$, the EDAV-GBDF scheme with $k = 2,3$ and $\beta > 1$ is unconditionally stable in the sense that*

$$2\mu\lambda_k^g\|\boldsymbol{\epsilon}(\boldsymbol{u}^N)\|_0^2 + \lambda\lambda_k^g\|\nabla \cdot \boldsymbol{u}^{N+i-k}\|_0^2 + c_0\lambda_k^g\|p_h^{n+1+i-k}\|_0^2$$

$$+ \frac{3(1 - \Im)\kappa}{4}\eta_k\Delta t \sum_{k-1}^{N-1} \|\nabla C_k^\beta(p_h^{n+1})\|_0^2 + \kappa\hat{\lambda}_k^h\Delta t\|\nabla p_h^N\|_0 + \sum_{i=1}^{M} \frac{(Q_i^N)^2}{\theta_i}$$

$$\leq C\left(2\mu \sum_{i=1}^{k} \|\boldsymbol{\epsilon}(\boldsymbol{u}^{i-1})\|_0^2 + \lambda C \sum_{i=1}^{k} \|\nabla \cdot \boldsymbol{u}^{i-1}\|_0^2 + c_0 C \sum_{i=1}^{k} \|p_h^{i-1}\|_0^2\right.$$

$$\left. + \kappa C\Delta t \sum_{i}^{k} \|\nabla p_h^{i-1}\|_0^2\right) + \sum_{i=1}^{M} \frac{(Q_i^{k-1})^2}{\theta_i}. \quad (17)$$

Proof. Taking $\mathbf{v}_h = A_k^\beta(\mathbf{u}_h^{n+1})$ in (13) and $q_h = \Delta t\, C_k^\beta(p_h^{n+1})$ in (14), and then combining the resulting equations, we obtain, by Lemma 1, Theorem 1 in [7], and (11), that

$$2\mu \sum_{i,j=1}^{k} g_{ij} \left(\boldsymbol{\epsilon}(\mathbf{u}^{n+1+i-k}), \boldsymbol{\epsilon}(\mathbf{u}^{n+1+j-k})\right) - 2\mu \sum_{i,j=1}^{k} g_{ij} \left(\boldsymbol{\epsilon}(\mathbf{u}^{n+i-k}), \boldsymbol{\epsilon}(\mathbf{u}^{n+j-k})\right)$$

$$+ \lambda \sum_{i,j=1}^{k} g_{ij} \left(\nabla \cdot \mathbf{u}^{n+1+i-k}, \nabla \cdot \mathbf{u}^{n+1+j-k}\right) - \lambda \sum_{i,j=1}^{k} g_{ij} \left(\nabla \cdot \mathbf{u}^{n+i-k}, \nabla \cdot \mathbf{u}^{n+j-k}\right)$$

$$+ c_0 \sum_{i,j=1}^{k} g_{ij} \left(p^{n+1+i-k}, p^{n+1+j-k} \right) - c_0 \sum_{i,j=1}^{k} g_{ij} \left(p^{n+i-k}, p^{n+j-k} \right)$$

$$+ \kappa \Delta t \sum_{i,j=1}^{k} h_{ij} \left(\nabla p^{n+1+i-k}, \nabla p^{n+1+j-k} \right) - \kappa \Delta t \sum_{i,j=1}^{k} h_{ij} \left(\nabla p^{n+i-k}, \nabla p^{n+j-k} \right)$$

$$+ \alpha \widetilde{V}(Q^n) \left(\nabla \cdot A_k^\beta(\mathbf{u}_h^{n+1}), C_k^\beta(p_h^{n+1}) \right) - \alpha \widetilde{V}(Q^n) \left(C_k^{\beta+1}(p_h^n), \nabla \cdot A_k^\beta(\mathbf{u}_h^{n+1}) \right)$$

$$+ s_p \widetilde{V}(Q^n) \Delta t \left(B_k^\beta(p_h^{n+1}) - C_k^\beta(p_h^n), C_k^\beta(p_h^{n+1}) \right) + \eta_k \kappa \Delta t \| \nabla C_k^\beta(p_h^{n+1}) \|_0^2$$

$$\leq \frac{C_p}{\eta_k} \Delta t \| g^{n+\beta} \|_0 + \frac{\eta_k \kappa}{4} \Delta t \| \nabla C_k^\beta(p_h^{n+1}) \|_0^2 \tag{18}$$

Then, using (15), (16) and (18), and summing (18) form $k - 1 = 1$ to $N - 1$, we get

$$2\mu \lambda_k^g \| \epsilon(\mathbf{u}^N) \|_0^2 + \lambda \lambda_k^g \| \nabla \cdot \mathbf{u}^{N+i-k} \|_0^2 + c_0 \lambda_k^g \| p^{n+1+i-k} \|_0^2$$

$$+ \frac{3 \eta_k \kappa}{4} \Delta t \sum_{k-1}^{N-1} \| \nabla C_k^\beta(p_h^{n+1}) \|_0^2 + \kappa \hat{\lambda}_k^h \Delta t \| \nabla p^N \|_0 + \sum_{i=1}^{M} \frac{(Q_i^N)^2}{\theta_i}$$

$$\leq 2\mu \sum_{i,j=1}^{k} g_{ij} \left(\epsilon(\mathbf{u}^{i-1}), \epsilon(\mathbf{u}^{j-1}) \right) + \lambda \sum_{i,j=1}^{k} g_{ij} \left(\nabla \cdot \mathbf{u}^{i-1}, \nabla \cdot \mathbf{u}^{j-1} \right) \tag{19}$$

$$+ c_0 \sum_{i,j=1}^{k} g_{ij} \left(p^{i-1}, p^{j-1} \right) + \kappa \Delta t \sum_{i,j=1}^{k} h_{ij} \left(\nabla p^{i-1}, \nabla p^{j-1} \right) + \sum_{i=1}^{M} \frac{(Q_i^{k-1})^2}{\theta_i}.$$

Hence, using the above estimate, Hölder and Young's inequalities, we obtain (17). The proof is completed.

4 Numerical Experiments

Example 1. Convergence Test. In this test, we take the computational domain to be the unit square and choose the source term, boundary conditions, and initial data so that the exact solution of (1)–(2) is

$$u_1(x, y, t) = e^{-t} \left(\sin(2\pi y)(-1 + \cos(2\pi x)) + \frac{1}{\mu + \lambda} \sin(\pi x) \sin(\pi y) \right),$$

$$u_2(x, y, t) = e^{-t} \left(\sin(2\pi x)(1 - \cos(2\pi y)) + \frac{1}{\mu + \lambda} \sin(\pi x) \sin(\pi y) \right),$$

$$p(x, y, t) = e^{-t} \sin(\pi x) \sin(\pi y).$$

We set $\ell_1 = 3$, $\ell_2 = 2$ and $h = 1/150$ so that the spatial error is negligible. In this example, we choose $\theta = 10^{-4}, c_0 = 10^{-8}$, $\kappa = 1$, $\mu = 1$, $\lambda = 1$, $\alpha = 1$. Tables 1 confirm the expected convergence orders for $k = 3$. Here $\Delta t_{\text{init}} = 10^{-8}$ is chosen so that the initialization error is negligible. The results confirm the predicted spatial convergence rates.

Table 1. Errors and convergent rates of 2D with $k = 3, \beta = 6$ and $s_p = 10$.

Δt	$\|\mathbf{e}_u\|_0$	Rate	$\|\nabla \mathbf{e}_u\|_0$	Rate	$\|e_p\|_0$	Rate	$\|\nabla e_p\|_0$	Rate
$\frac{1}{8}$	3.1173e-02	-	2.2078e-01	-	6.0911e-03	-	2.7855e-02	-
$\frac{1}{16}$	8.7438e-03	1.83	6.1900e-02	1.83	1.4996e-03	2.02	6.6766e-03	2.06
$\frac{1}{32}$	9.7624e-04	3.16	6.9100e-03	3.16	1.4921e-04	3.33	6.6472e-04	3.33
$\frac{1}{64}$	1.0878e-04	3.16	7.6997e-04	3.16	1.7836e-05	3.06	8.6792e-05	2.94

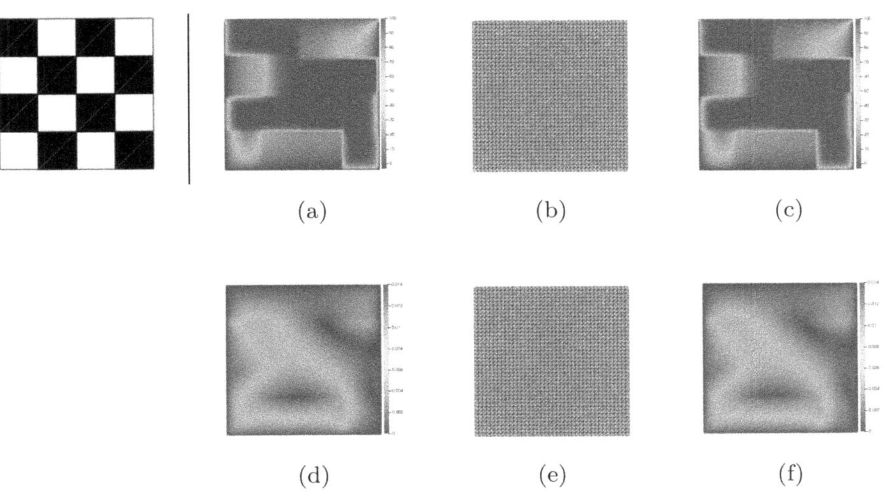

(a)   (b)   (c)

(d)   (e)   (f)

Fig. 1. Configurations of heterogeneous material properties. Panels (a)–(c) show the pressure computed by the coupling algorithm, the monolithic method, and the domain decomposition method, respectively. Panels (d)–(f) show the corresponding displacement magnitude, $|\mathbf{u}|$.

Example 2. Heterogeneous Coefficients. Following [11], we consider (1)–(2) on $\Omega = (0,1)^2$ with discontinuous, piecewise constant coefficients on a 4×4 partition; see Fig. 1. And the boundary segments are ordered as bottom, right, top, and left. We take

$$\boldsymbol{f} = \left(\tfrac{1}{2}(1 - \cos(2\pi t)), 0\right)^T, \quad g = 0, \quad \mathbf{u} = \mathbf{0} \quad \text{on } \partial\Omega \times (0,T].$$

with boundary conditions $\nabla p \cdot \boldsymbol{n} = 0$ on $\Gamma_3 \times (0,T]$, $p = 1$ on $\Gamma_j \times (0,T]$, $j = 1, 2, 4$. The parameters are set to $c_0 = 1$, $\mu = 10$, $\lambda = 10^3$, $\alpha = 1$, while the permeability κ is prescribed piecewise by

$$\kappa = \begin{bmatrix} 10^{-2} & 10^{-1} & 10^{-1} & 10^{-6} \\ 10^{-3} & 10^{-5} & 10^{-4} & 10^{-3} \\ 10^{-1} & 10^{-2} & 10^{-5} & 10^{-4} \\ 10^{-6} & 10^{-3} & 10^{-1} & 1 \end{bmatrix}.$$

For both the coupled and the EDAV-GBDF algorithms with $k = 2$, we set $h = 1/40$, $\Delta t = 0.05$, $\Delta t_{\text{init}} = 10^{-8}$, and $T = 0.5 + 10^{-8}$. For the EDAV-GBDF algorithm, we use $\beta = 2$, $s_p = 10^{-6}$, and $\theta_i = 0.5$, and compare regional partitioning ($M = 16$) with holistic treatment ($M = 1$) of the auxiliary variables. Figure 1 shows that regional partitioning gives more accurate results and performs comparably to the coupled algorithm, whereas the holistic treatment is less effective.

5   Conclusion

In summary, we propose a high-order finite element time-stepping scheme for the Biot model that is linear and fully decoupled. The scheme is unconditionally energy stable, and numerical results confirm the expected accuracy and robustness.

Acknowledgments. The authors gratefully acknowledge the financial support from the National Key Research and Development Project of China (Grant No. 2023YFA101 1701), the National Natural Science Foundation of China (Grant No. 12571466), and the Fundamental Research Funds for the Central Universities. In addition, Shuyu Sun would like to express his gratitude for the support provided by the Shanghai Magnolia Talent Fund (Innovation Talent Category) of Shanghai Municipal Human Resources and Social Security Bureau and the Chang Jiang Scholars Program of the Ministry of Education of China.

Disclosure of Interests. The authors have no competing interests to declare that are relevant to the content of this article.

References

1. Terzaghi, K.: Theoretical Soil Mechanics. Wiley, New York (1943)
2. Biot, M.A.: Theory of elasticity and consolidation for a porous anisotropic solid. J. Appl. Phys. **26**(2), 182–185 (1955)
3. Yi, S.-Y.: A study of two modes of locking in poroelasticity. SIAM J. Numer. Anal. **55**(4), 1915–1936 (2017)
4. Altmann, R., Maier, R., Unger, B.: Semi-explicit discretization schemes for weakly coupled elliptic-parabolic problems. Math. Comput. **90**(329), 1089–1118 (2021)
5. Shen, J., Xu, J., Yang, J.: The scalar auxiliary variable (SAV) approach for gradient flows. J. Comput. Phys. **353**, 407–416 (2018)
6. Yang, J., Kim, J.: On a two-phase incompressible diffuse interface fluid model with curvature-dependent mobility. J. Comput. Phys. **525**, 113764 (2025)
7. Huang, F., Shen, J.: On a new class of BDF and IMEX schemes for parabolic type equations. SIAM J. Numer. Anal. **62**(4), 1609–1637 (2024)
8. Temam, R.: Navier-Stokes Equations: Theory and Numerical Analysis. AMS Chelsea Publishing, Providence (1984)
9. Zhao, J., Chen, H., Sun, S., Li, H.: Unconditionally energy-stable and locking-free parallel splitting finite element method for the Biot model. J. Sci. Comput. **104**(3), 74 (2025)

10. Dahlquist, G.: G-stability is equivalent to A-stability. BIT Numer. Math. **18**(4), 384–401 (1978)
11. Cai, M., Pavarino, L.F., Widlund, O.B.: Overlapping Schwarz methods with a standard coarse space for almost incompressible linear elasticity. SIAM J. Sci. Comput. **37**(2), A811–A830 (2015)

How to Enhance Classification Results of the Trained Models Using Invariant Dataset Augmentation

Piotr Milczarski[1]([✉]) [iD] and Norbert Borowski[2] [iD]

[1] Faculty of Mathematics and Computer Science, University of Lodz, Łódź, Poland
`piotr.milczarski@uni.lodz.pl`
[2] Institute of Information Technology, Lodz University of Technology, Łódź, Poland
`norbert.borowski@p.lodz.pl`

Abstract. In the paper, we show how to enhance the results of the classification of the images by already trained models without retraining. We use the rotation invariance of the images and Invariant Dataset Augmentation (IDA) method instead. The results of enhancement using the IDA method are shown using the dermoscopic PH2 dataset with 200 images, the dermoscopic Derm7pt dataset with 1011 images, and the X-Ray COVID-19 dataset with 3175 images. The authors method allows us to do the test not only on the single image but also on its invariant copies. Depending on the image symmetry, there can even be an eightfold increase in the number of test images. In the presented research, we used CNN networks VGG19, XN, and Inception-ResNet-v2 for dermoscopic datasets and the three classification features of skin lesions defined by well-known dermoscopic criteria. VGG19, Xception, and Inceptionv3 networks are used for COVID-19 dataset with three classes. The confusion matrix parameters shown in the paper improved significantly comparing the tests on the original dataset versus IDA increased one and the worst case scenario. It is achieved on the original model without retraining it on the augmented dataset using IDA method. An example for dermoscopic PH2 and Derm7pt datasets resulted in precision between 98–100%, true positive rate 98–100%, false positive rate <2.3%, F1 test = 0.95 and MCC test = 0.95. The results for the COVID-19 X-ray resulted in maximum precision for 3 classes > 98.1%, F1 score almost 1.0 and MCC >0.97. The advantage of the method is that the trained model is smaller and more efficient than the new model trained on the eightfold increased dataset.

Keywords: Invariant Dataset Augmentation · Increasing classification rates · Deep learning · COVID-19 · Dermoscopic images

1 Introduction

The motivation of the paper is to enhance the classification rates provided by already trained and used models in the e.g. health-care systems. In the screening

P. Neumann et al. (Eds.): ICCS 2026, LNCS 16784, pp. 316–324, 2026.
https://doi.org/10.1007/978-3-032-29924-6_24

methods e.g. dermoscopic and X-Ray ones, we increase the efficiency by improving the confusion matrix parameters of the feature classifications that point to possible health problems. The advantage of the method is that the trained network is smaller and more efficient than the new network trained on the eightfold increased data set.

That general approach can provide better results while using CNN networks in other research disciplines, not only dermatology or pulmonology. This method is integrated during the classification stage, where the model processes both the original image and its pixel-invariant copies. Although standard CNNs do not possess inherent rotation invariance, evaluating them against a collection of pixel-invariant images improves classification performance, leading to higher metrics such as recall (TPR) and test F1 rates.

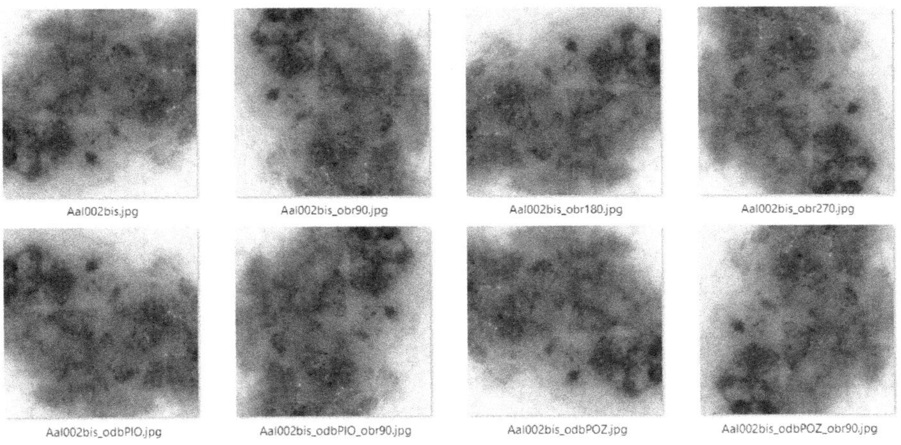

Fig. 1. The image (top-left) Aaal002.jpg from Derm7pt [1] and its invariant copies.

The second issue that the method solves is the acquisition and analysis of the data, as well as the extraction of the features. The classification of features should not depend on the orientation and position of the object in the flat 2D image (see Fig. 1). The optical sensor must exhibit rotational invariance to ensure that feature extraction remains independent of the object's spatial orientation. Consequently, we propose a methodology for CNN networks evaluation that incorporates both the primary image and its corresponding invariant representations.

As a case-study we use different medical dataset. One of them asre dermoscopic datasets of skin lesion and their assessment methodologies the three-point checklist of dermoscopy (3PCLD) [18,20] and the seven-point checklist (7PCL) [10]. The next case-study dataset contains X-ray images of the lung with their assessment methods. The problem of COVID-19 and X-Ray classification is also widely presented and several different approaches are used as in the dermoscopy case [14, 17]. The usual classification is based on X-Ray lungs images with normal lungs, with viral pneumonia, and COVID-19 ones.

Convolutional Neural Networks (CNNs) inherently lack rotational invariance, a limitation extensively documented in the literature [2,3,9,19]. To address this deficiency, various architectural enhancements and methodologies have been proposed to integrate invariant properties into deep learning frameworks [3,9]. This paper delineates a strategy that leverages geometric symmetry to optimize classification performance; comprehensive technical details and preliminary findings are further elaborated in the authors' previous works [2,12,13,15].

In the paper, we show that using Invariant Dataset Augmentation (IDA) method in a test phase provides similar results of classification the images as pretraining the models using IDA augmented models.

2   Invariant Dataset Augmentation in Trained Models

In the papers [2, 12–15], the IDA method is used to increase the number of images using invariant transformations to tackle the lack of the rotation invariant property in CNN networks. It can be explained by the properties of the convolution given by the example equation:

$$I(x,y) = \sum_{i=0}^{n} \sum_{j=0}^{m} k(i,j) I(x+i,\ y+j),$$

where the kernel of the operation is $k(I,j)$ is of size NxM. The image size is NxM, where $N \geq n$ and $M \geq m$. The classification probability of invariant images can be different for each image copy. The problem of rotation invariance is presented in, e.g. Table 1, where the classification probability of the image IMD168 from PH2 dataset [11] and its copies differs greatly for each invariant copy. The asymmetry classification (0 - no symmetry, 1 axis symmetry, 2-axis symmetry) sometimes results in opposite result.

Table 1. The classification probability of symmetry by VGG19 on image IMD168 from PH2 dataset [11]

Image IMD168 and its copies	Symmetry probability		
	0	1	2
Original	0.0131	0.9593	0.0276
90 rotation	0.5501	0.4017	0.0482
180 rotation	0.9420	0.0407	0.0173
270 rotation	0.3044	0.6713	0.0243
Vertical reflection	0.3781	0.6170	0.0050
Vert. reflection and 90 rotation	0.4937	0.4964	0.0099
Horizontal reflection	0.0543	0.9403	0.0054
Hor. reflection and 90 rotation	0.6154	0.3441	0.0405

The explanation of the IDA method and funding is provided in our other articles [2,13,15]. It is based on natural pixel invariant transformations of the images. In some cases, it is only mirroring reflection in other rotation by 90° and mirroring.

Let us briefly explain how to apply the Invariant Dataset Augmentation method for testing only after preprocessing the test image, i.e. cropping and scaling, to the CNN networks requirements in the following steps:

1. Find the image symmetry invariance features e.g. rotation, mirroring.
2. Define the number of folds of the image.
3. Create the invariant copy/-ies from the original image.
4. Classify images.
5. Use IDA's worst-case scenario to assign the class to the image.

Table 2. Classification probability of X-ray images using IDA approach for the chosen three images and their invariant copy. Where C19= COVID19(194), C19_m = COVID19(194)_mir, N = NORMAL (964), N_m = NORMAL (964)_mir, VP=Viral Pneumonia (314), VP_m = Viral Pneumonia (314)_mir.

CNN	Classification probability by CNN/True Class								
	VGG19			Xception			Inception_v3		
Img ID	C	N	V	C	N	V	C	N	V
C19	0.813	0.184	0.003	0.011	0.965	0.025	0.238	0.611	0.151
C19_m	0.007	0.993	3e-4	0.013	0.267	0.720	0.207	0.716	0.077
N	0.005	0.995	2e-4	0.285	0.641	0.074	0.856	0.135	0.009
N_m	0.001	0.999	1e-4	0.740	0.156	0.104	0.984	0.014	0.002
VP	0.000	0.000	1.000	0.0008	0.000	0.999	0.001	3e-4	0.999
VP_m	2e-4	7e-4	0.999	0.001	1e-4	0.999	0.003	2e-4	0.997

In Tables 1 and 2 detailed classification probabilities are presented to highlight the ambiguous result of the classification. Table 1 shows the classification probabilities for 3 chosen models with 8 IDA augmented images as a test. Table 2 shows the classification probabilities for 3 images and its invariant copy for each class of the X-Ray set. Table 2 shows that the classification probability for 3 classes may differ as in the dermoscopic feature case.

Rotations and mirror reflection are used for the dermoscopic images and blue-white veil feature, asymmetry, pigment network distribution. Seven new copies are achieved for each image. For X-Ray images only mirroring was applied. These transformations used by IDA do not change pixels; they are pixel invariant, mutually unambiguous, and reversible.

For the PH2 dermoscopic dataset [11], in total, 1600 images out of 200 were achieved. For Derm7pt [1,10] 8088 out of 1011 images were prepared.

Similar situation applies to X-ray lungs dataset that was built using 3175 cases from the patients with viral pneumonia (1296 images) and COVID-19

(540 images) as well as healthy ones (1339 images). A subset of the RYDLS-20 dataset [16], consisting of 1144 chest X-ray (CXR) cases, was incorporated into the analysis.

The COVID-19 dataset of 540 images was collected and chosen [14]:

- 32 from Actualmed COVID-19 chest X-ray data initiative [5].
- 162 from the North America, R. S. COVID-19 radiography database [4,17].
- 321 from Cohen, Morrison, and Dao. COVID-19 image data collection [7,8].
- 25 from COVID-19 chest X-ray data initiative [6].

3   Results

Tables 3 and 4 present a detailed comparison of the classification results obtained on the original model and the model built using the IDA augmented train set. We show for both approaches the results of testing on the original images (T1), IDA augmented images (T8), and a worst-case scenario (IDA) i.e. if one positive the case is positive. We have used several models and studied their behavior, e.g. InceptionResNetv2 (IRN2), Inception-v3, Xception, VGG19.

The research has been conducted for original and IDA augmented models with the following conditions:

- the dataset has been divided into 4 equal parts;
- the train and validation dataset consisted of 3 parts (75%) images and the test of the remaining 1 part (25%);
- the experiments are repeated 5 times for each model and dataset, resulting in 20 models for each CNN network.

In the result, different models used the same images as train and validation sets although their resolutions were different. Detailed results are shown for the blue-white feature classification because that feature can be easily lost by rotating the image at a random angle.

Table 3 shows results for the blue-white veil for models that were trained on a small PH2 dataset (case BW1), where T1 stands for test on original images, T8 - test on 8 copies independently, IDA - worst-case scenario (case BW8). Table 4 also shows the classification results of the blue-white veil for the same models as in Tab. 3 but trained on the augmented datasets. It can be derived from the research on 20 models that:

- accuracy and recall values are higher in IDA, BW1 and BW2 cases;
- VGG19 shows that in BW1 case the recall is higher by 6.7%, but FPR is also higher by 1.2%; F1 test and MCC are higher in BW1 case;
- Xception shows in BW8 case the recall higher by 2.7% with almost the same FPR as in BW1 case; F1 test and MCC are higher in BW1 case; F1 test and MCC are higher in BW1 case;
- IRN2 shows that in BW8 case the recall is higher by 2.2%, but FPR is lower by 1%; F1 test and MCC are the same in BW1 and BW8 cases;

Table 3. The classification of the blue-white veil classification using original images from PH2 as a train set. T1 - test on original images, T8 - test on 8 copies independently, IDA - worst-case scenario.

CM factor		VGG19			Xception			IRN2		
		T1	T8	IDA	T1	T8	IDA	T1	T8	IDA
w.ACC [%]	AVG	87.2	88.1	92.2	82.2	80.2	88.0	79.8	78.2	83.9
	MAX	98.8	97.5	100	87.7	85.3	94.4	88.9	86.1	93.2
TPR [%]	AVG	77.8	79.6	89.4	66.7	61.8	81.7	62.2	58.4	73.9
	VAR	11.7	10.2	8.2	7.9	7.1	9.5	13.3	16.1	10.1
	Min	55.6	66.7	77.8	55.6	51.4	66.7	33.3	23.6	55.6
	Max	100	97.2	100	77.8	73.6	88.9	77.8	76.4	88.9
FPR [%]	AVG	3.4	3.3	5.0	2.3	1.5	5.6	2.7	2.1	6.1
	VAR	2.2	2.0	2.2	1.6	1.1	3.9	1.7	1.3	2.7
	Min	0.0	0.0	0.0	0.0	0.0	0.0	0.0	0.6	2.4
	Max	7.3	7.0	7.3	4.9	3.0	14.6	4.9	5.2	12.2
Test	F1 Max	0.95	0.96	1.0	0.82	0.79	0.94	0.88	0.80	0.89
	MCC Max	0.94	0.95	1.0	0.79	0.74	0.94	0.86	0.76	0.86

Table 4. The classification of the blue-white veil classification using images from PH2 set and its 7 copies as a train set. T1 - test on original images, T8 - test on 8 copies independently, IDA - worst-case scenario.

CM factor		VGG19			Xception			IRN2		
		T1	T8	IDA	T1	T8	IDA	T1	T8	IDA
w.ACC [%]	AVG	87.4	87.7	89.5	84.9	84.1	89.5	82.9	82.9	85.5
	MAX	94.4	94.3	98.8	92.0	91.3	93.2	88.9	88.0	93.2
TPR [%]	AVG	76.7	77.6	82.7	72.2	69.9	84.4	68.3	67.8	76.1
	VAR	12.1	9.6	10.23	7.5	7.9	6.5	8.1	9.3	8.8
	Min	55.6	62.5	66.7	55.6	58.3	66.7	44.4	47.2	66.7
	Max	88.9	88.9	100	88.9	83.3	88.9	77.8	79.2	88.9
FPR [%]	AVG	2.0	2.3	3.8	2.4	1.7	5.4	2.6	1.9	5.1
	VAR	2.3	1.8	1.6	1.7	1.0	1.7	1.4	1.4	3.2
	Min	0.0	0.3	2.4	0.0	0.3	2.4	0.0	0.3	2.4
	Max	7.3	5.2	7.3	4.9	3.4	7.3	7.3	5.8	12.2
Test	F1 Max	0.94	0.93	0.95	0.84	0.90	0.89	0.88	0.81	0.89
	MCC Max	0.93	0.91	0.94	0.81	0.88	0.86	0.86	0.78	0.86

4 Conclusions

The results of the classification should not depend on the image acquisition conditions, such as angle. Retraining the models on a new augmented dataset is not often needed. The better results than on the original model and one picture test approach is also achieved while using the same model but IDA augmented images for the test taking into account their rotation importance. The results for the dermoscopic datasets show the precision between 98–100%, the true positive rate 98–100%, the false positive rate 0.0–2.3%, the F1 test 0.95 and the MCC test 0.95. The results of the COVID-19 and X-Ray image classification resulted in precision$> 97.5\%$ for the COVID-19, balanced ACC$>98.5\%$, the recall (TPR) around 97%; F1 test $= 1.0$ and MCC test>0.97 [12].

The advantage of the method is that the trained network is smaller and more efficient than the new network trained on the eightfold increased data set. We have also trained the same models using the images and their copies [2,14,15]. The results were slightly better than those presented in this paper, but the models were 8 times larger.

References

1. Argenziano, G., et al.: Interactive atlas of dermoscopy. Dermoscopy: a tutorial (Book) and CD-ROM. Edra - Medical Publishing & New Media Milan, Italy (2000)
2. Beczkowski, M., Borowski, N., Milczarski, P.: Classification of dermatological asymmetry of the skin lesions using pretrained convolutional neural networks. In: Artificial Intelligence and Soft Computing, pp. 3–14. Springer, Heidelberg (2021). https://doi.org/10.1007/978-3-030-87897-9_1
3. Cheng, G., Zhou, P., Han, J.: Learning rotation-invariant convolutional neural networks for object detection in VHR optical remote sensing images. IEEE Trans. Geosci. Remote Sens. **54**(12), 7405–7415 (2016). https://doi.org/10.1109/TGRS. 2016.2601622

4. Chowdhury, M.E.H., et al.: Can ai help in screening viral and covid-19 pneumonia? IEEE Access **8**, 132665–132676 (2020). https://doi.org/10.1109/ACCESS.2020.3010287

5. Chung, A.: Actualmed covid-19 chest x-ray dataset initiative (2020). https://github.com/agchung/Actualmed-COVID-chestxray-dataset. Accessed 28 July 2025

6. Chung, A.: Covid-19 chest x-ray dataset initiative (2020). https://github.com/agchung/Figure1-COVID-chestxray-dataset. Accessed 27 Mar 2026

7. Cohen, J.P., Morrison, P., Dao, L.: Covid-19 image data collection. arXiv:2003.11597 (2020). https://github.com/ieee8023/covid-chestxray-dataset. Accessed 27 Mar 2026

8. Cohen, J.P., Morrison, P., Dao, L., Roth, K., Duong, T.Q., Ghassemi, M.: Covid-19 image data collection: prospective predictions are the future. arXiv:2006.11988 (2020). https://github.com/ieee8023/covid-chestxray-dataset. Accessed 27 Mar 2026

9. Dieleman, S., Willett, K.W., Dambre, J.: Rotation-invariant convolutional neural networks for galaxy morphology prediction. Monthly Not. Roy. Astron. Soc. **450**(2), 1441–1459 (2015). https://doi.org/10.1093/mnras/stv632

10. Kawahara, J., Daneshvar, S., Argenziano, G., Hamarneh, G.: Seven-point checklist and skin lesion classification using multitask multimodal neural nets. IEEE J. Biomed. Health Inf. **23**(2), 538–546 (2019). https://doi.org/10.1109/JBHI.2018.2824327

11. Mendonça, T., Ferreira, P.M., Marques, J.S., Marcal, A.R., Rozeira, J.: Ph 2-a dermoscopic image database for research and benchmarking. In: 2013 35th Annual International Conference of the IEEE Engineering in Medicine and Biology Society (EMBC), pp. 5437–5440. IEEE (2013).https://doi.org/10.1109/EMBC.2013.6610779

12. Milczarski, P.: Increasing the classification rates of the trained models using invariant dataset augmentations. In: 2025 IEEE/CVF International Conference on Computer Vision (ICCV) Workshops, pp. 1083–1092 (2025). https://doi.org/10.1109/ICCVW69036.2025.00117

13. Milczarski, P., Beczkowski, M., Borowski, N.: Blue-white veil classification of dermoscopy images using convolutional neural networks and invariant dataset augmentation. In: Barolli, L., Woungang, I., Enokido, T. (eds.) Advanced Information Networking and Applications, pp. 421–432. Springer, Cham (2021). https://doi.org/10.1007/978-3-030-75075-6_34

14. Milczarski, P., Beczkowski, M., Borowski, N.: Covid-19 lungs assessment in chest x-ray images using convolutional neural networks. In: 2021 11th IEEE International Conference on Intelligent Data Acquisition and Advanced Computing Systems: Technology and Applications (IDAACS), vol. 2, pp. 1062–1067 (2021). https://doi.org/10.1109/IDAACS53288.2021.9661046

15. Milczarski, P., Beczkowski, M., Borowski, N.: Enhancing dermoscopic features classification in images using invariant dataset augmentation and convolutional neural networks. In: Neural Information Processing: 28th International Conference, ICONIP 2021, Sanur, Bali, Indonesia, 8–12 December 2021, Proceedings, Part III 28, pp. 403–417. Springer, Heidelberg (2021). https://doi.org/10.1007/978-3-030-92238-2_34

16. Pereira, R.M., Bertolini, D., Teixeira, L.O., Silla, C.N., Costa, Y.M.: Covid-19 identification in chest x-ray images on flat and hierarchical classification scenarios. Comput. Methods Prog. Biomed. **194**, 105532 (2020). https://doi.org/10.1016/j.cmpb.2020.105532

17. Rahman, T., et al.: Exploring the effect of image enhancement techniques on covid-19 detection using chest x-ray images. Comput. Biol. Med. **132**, 104319 (2021). https://doi.org/10.1016/j.compbiomed.2021.104319
18. Soyer, H.P., et al.: Three-point checklist of dermoscopy: a new screening method for early detection of melanoma. Dermatology **208**(1), 27–31 (2004). https://doi.org/10.1159/000075042
19. Tarasiuk, P., Szczepaniak, P.S.: Novel convolutional neural networks for efficient classification of rotated and scaled images. Neural Comput. Appl. **34**(13), 10519–10532 (2022)
20. Was, L., Wiak, S., Milczarski, P., Szymanski, L.: Evaluation of dermatological asymmetry measure of shape by expectation-maximization. In: Rutkowski, L., Scherer, R., Korytkowski, M., Pedrycz, W., Tadeusiewicz, R., Zurada, J.M. (eds.) Artificial Intelligence and Soft Computing, pp. 201–211. Springer, Cham (2025)

Plausible Visual Counterfactual Explanations in Latent Space with Normalizing Flows

Łukasz Lenkiewicz[(✉)] [iD], Marcel Musiałek[iD], Oleksii Furman[iD], and Maciej Zięba[iD]

Wrocław University of Science and Technology, Wybrzeże Stanisława Wyspiańskiego 27, 50-370 Wrocław, Poland
lukasz.lenkiewicz@pwr.edu.pl

Abstract. Counterfactual explanations provide interpretable insights into classifier decisions by identifying minimal input modifications that alter predictions. While extensively studied for tabular data, visual counterfactuals present unique challenges requiring semantically meaningful changes rather than imperceptible perturbations. Current approaches predominantly employ diffusion models, GANs, and VAEs, while normalizing flows remain underexplored despite offering tractable likelihood computation. We introduce PLACE (Plausible LAtent Counterfactual Explanations), a method that leverages conditional normalizing flows for explicit density estimation in counterfactual generation. Operating in the latent space of a pre-trained autoencoder, PLACE optimizes a novel composite loss function balancing validity, proximity, and plausibility. The plausibility term directly maximizes log-likelihood under the target class distribution, enabled by the flow's tractable density computation. Experiments on CelebA and MNIST demonstrate that PLACE achieves competitive performance across multiple metrics while uniquely satisfying explicit plausibility constraints through substantially improved log density scores. Our method balances computational efficiency with multi-objective optimization, validating normalizing flows as an effective approach for probabilistically constrained visual counterfactual explanations.

Keywords: Machine Learning · Counterfactual Explanations · Explainable Artificial Intelligence · Computer Vision

1 Introduction

Counterfactual explanations (CEs) [23] identify minimal perturbations to input instances that change a classifier's prediction, providing insight into learned decision boundaries. Effective CEs satisfy three properties: *minimality* (small perturbations), *realism* (plausible under the data distribution), and *actionability* (feasible to implement). While extensively studied for tabular data [5,16], generating

P. Neumann et al. (Eds.): ICCS 2026, LNCS 16784, pp. 325–332, 2026.
https://doi.org/10.1007/978-3-032-29924-6_25

visual counterfactuals poses significant challenges. Unlike adversarial examples that achieve misclassification through imperceptible pixel-level noise, counterfactual explanations require semantically meaningful changes (e.g., adding a smile to a face or changing an object's color) while preserving class-irrelevant attributes such as background, pose, and identity.

This semantic requirement has driven the adoption of generative models for visual counterfactual generation. Current approaches predominantly employ diffusion models [3,7], GANs [1,14], and VAEs [8,21]. Despite their proven effectiveness for density estimation, normalizing flows [17] remain underexplored for this task [6]. This is surprising given that flows offer a unique advantage: direct likelihood computation, allowing us to quantify the plausibility of a counterfactual as a member of the target class. This property is unavailable in other generative model families. Such probabilistic guarantees are particularly relevant in computational science applications where model interpretability must be paired with rigorous uncertainty quantification, for instance when explaining classifiers deployed in medical imaging [2], materials science [28], or computational biology [19], where stakeholders need to trust that an explanation is not only valid but also distributionally plausible.

We address this gap by introducing PLACE (**P**lausible **LA**tent **C**ounterfactual **E**xplanations), one of the first methods to utilize conditional normalizing flows for density estimation of generated counterfactuals. PLACE optimizes a novel composite loss that jointly enforces decision flipping, plausibility under the target class distribution, and proximity via L2 and LPIPS perceptual components. We evaluate on CelebA and MNIST, demonstrating competitive performance across multiple metrics against established baselines.

2   Related Works

Normalizing Flows. Normalizing flows enable exact density estimation through invertible transformations with tractable Jacobian determinants [15,17]. However, flows applied directly in pixel space may capture local correlations rather than semantic content, motivating their use in learned embedding spaces. In the counterfactual domain, PPCEF [24] optimizes explicit density functions for tabular data and CeFlow [4] uses invertible flows for mixed-type features. PluGeN [25] employs flows to disentangle attributes in pre-trained latent spaces, which we build upon for conditional density estimation.

Visual Counterfactual Explanations. Wachter et al. [23] formalized CEs as an optimization balancing classifier loss and input distance, though without plausibility constraints. REVISE [8] addresses this by optimizing in a VAE's latent space, constraining the search to the learned data manifold but suffering from a plateau effect near decision boundaries. CLARITY [21] mitigates this by training classifier ensembles directly in the latent space, producing smoother boundaries at the cost of retraining. Other notable approaches include DiVE [18] for diverse counterfactuals, prototype-guided methods [12], and GAN-based approaches [14,20]. Diffusion-based methods such as DiME [7] and DVCE [3] achieve strong results but at higher computational cost. Recent work increasingly treats plausibility as an explicit constraint [13,22], motivating our use of normalizing flows for direct density-based optimization.

3   Method

We propose PLACE, a method for generating counterfactual explanations that operates in the latent space of a pre-trained autoencoder enhanced with normalizing flows. Our approach addresses three key desiderata for visual counterfactuals: (i) *validity*, i.e., flipping the classifier's decision, (ii) *proximity*, i.e., remaining close to the original input, and (iii) *plausibility*, i.e., staying within high-probability regions of the learned data distribution.

3.1   Counterfactual Optimization

We consider a discriminative differentiable model $p_d(y|x)$ (e.g., a CNN classifier). Given an input image x with latent representation $z = E(x)$ obtained via the encoder E, current class y, and target label $\tilde{y} \neq y$, we optimize a counterfactual embedding $z' \in \mathbb{R}^d$ in the d-dimensional latent space. The counterfactual image $\tilde{x}$ is generated as $\tilde{x} = G(z')$, where G denotes the decoder. We minimize the following composite loss function:

$$\mathcal{L}(z') = \lambda_{\text{dec}}\mathcal{L}_{\text{decision}} + \lambda_{\text{dist}}\mathcal{L}_{\text{distance}} + \lambda_{\text{plaus}}\mathcal{L}_{\text{plausibility}} + \lambda_{\text{perc}}\mathcal{L}_{\text{perceptual}}, \quad (1)$$

where λ_{dec}, λ_{dist}, λ_{plaus}, and λ_{perc} control the relative importance of each term.

Decision Loss. Following Wielopolski et al. [24], we use a margin-based loss to ensure prediction flip:

$$\mathcal{L}_{\text{decision}}(\tilde{x}, \tilde{y}) = \max(0.5 + \epsilon - p_d(\tilde{y}|\tilde{x}), 0), \quad (2)$$

where $\epsilon > 0$ provides a safety margin beyond the decision boundary, ensuring robust flips that are stable under small perturbations.

Distance Loss. The distance loss penalizes large deviations from the original latent representation:

$$\mathcal{L}_{\text{distance}}(z, z') = \|z - z'\|_2, \quad (3)$$

promoting minimal-magnitude changes that preserve the original image's semantic content.

Plausibility Loss. The plausibility loss leverages the normalizing flow's exact density computation:

$$\mathcal{L}_{\text{plausibility}}(z', \tilde{y}) = -\log p_F(z'|\tilde{y}), \quad (4)$$

where $p_F(\cdot|\tilde{y})$ is the conditional normalizing flow model estimating the density for the target class $\tilde{y}$. This ensures counterfactuals lie within high-density regions of the target class distribution, preventing unrealistic examples.

Perceptual Loss. The perceptual loss preserves high-level visual features:

$$\mathcal{L}_{\text{perceptual}}(x, \tilde{x}) = \text{LPIPS}(x, \tilde{x}), \tag{5}$$

where LPIPS [27] measures distance in deep feature space. This complements $\mathcal{L}_{\text{distance}}$ by enforcing proximity at a semantic level, ensuring that texture, structure, and identity remain consistent.

3.2 Architecture

Following PluGeN [25], we combine a deterministic convolutional autoencoder (encoder $E : \mathcal{X} \to \mathcal{Z}$, decoder $G : \mathcal{Z} \to \mathcal{X}$, $\mathcal{Z} \subset \mathbb{R}^d$) with an attribute-factorized normalizing flow $F : \mathcal{Z} \to \mathbb{R}^d$ that enables tractable conditional density computation in the latent space. A separately trained classifier $p_d(y|x)$ provides the decisions we aim to explain. All components remain frozen during counterfactual generation. Figure 1 illustrates the complete pipeline.

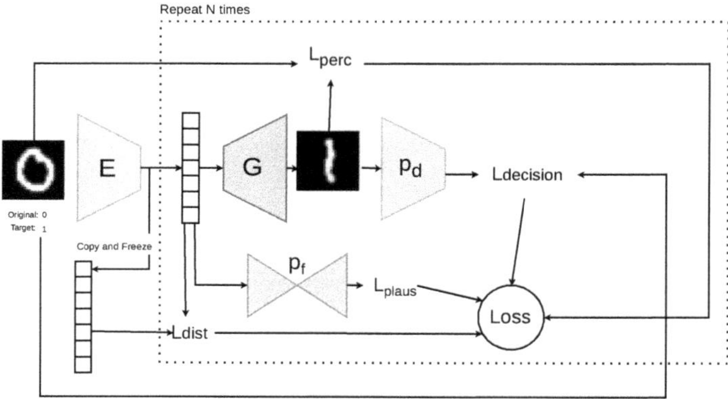

Fig. 1. Overview of the PLACE architecture. The input image is encoded into the latent space, and the embedding is iteratively optimized by minimizing a composite loss that combines decision, distance, plausibility, and perceptual terms. The decoder, classifier, and normalizing flow all remain frozen during optimization.

4   Experiments

We evaluate PLACE against established baselines on two benchmark datasets: CelebA [11] (smile classification, images resized to 256×256, standard train/test split) and MNIST [10] (digit-to-digit transformations such as $0 \to 8$ and $1 \to 5$, images resized to 32×32). We measure validity, LPIPS [27], FID [26], L2 distance, log density $\log p_F(z'|\tilde{y})$, and wall-clock time. We compare against CLARITY [21] and REVISE [8], two established latent-space counterfactual methods that share our autoencoder-based pipeline; a comparison with diffusion-based approaches [3,7], which operate under fundamentally different generative paradigms, is left to future work.

4.1 Hyperparameters

All methods use Adam [9] with early stopping. For PLACE on CelebA: learning rate 5×10^{-3}, $\lambda_{\text{dec}} = 1000$, $\lambda_{\text{dist}} = 1.0$, $\lambda_{\text{plaus}} = 2.0$, $\epsilon = 0.05$. On MNIST: learning rate 10^{-2}, $\lambda_{\text{dec}} = 10.0$, $\lambda_{\text{dist}} = 1.0$, $\lambda_{\text{plaus}} = 10.0$. REVISE and CLARITY baselines follow their original configurations. The pretrained classifier is ResNet-34 for CelebA ($>95\%$ accuracy) and a convolutional network for MNIST.

4.2 Results

Figure 2 illustrates the optimization process on CelebA, showing how PLACE progressively modifies discriminative features to achieve class change while preserving non-discriminative attributes.

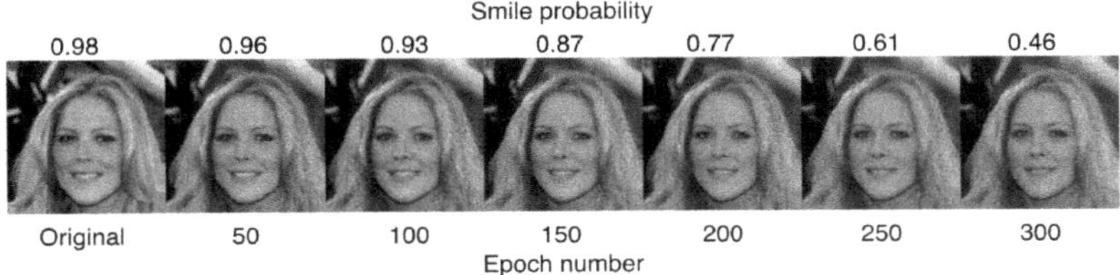

Fig. 2. Counterfactual generation on CelebA. PLACE progressively modifies smile-related features until the classifier's confidence for the original class drops below 50%, preserving identity and non-discriminative attributes.

CelebA Results. Table 1 presents results for smile classification counterfactuals. All methods achieve perfect validity. PLACE achieves the best LPIPS (0.21) and competitive log density (-1950.56), demonstrating effective balance between perceptual quality and plausibility. CLARITY achieves the best FID (105.01) and L2 (79.04) but requires the longest computation. REVISE is fastest but produces substantially worse perceptual quality (LPIPS 0.952).

Table 1. Quantitative results on CelebA dataset. All methods achieve 100% validity.

Method	Validity	LPIPS ↓	FID ↓	L2 ↓	Log Density ↑	Time (s) ↓
CLARITY	1.0	0.244	**105.01**	**79.04**	−2210.19	10424.38
REVISE	1.0	0.952	442.67	265.37	**−1909.05**	**4268.71**
Ours	1.0	**0.21**	124.27	92.69	−1950.56	7525.64

MNIST Results. Table 2 shows results on MNIST. All methods achieve perfect validity. PLACE achieves substantially better log density (-120.66) compared to CLARITY (-134.11) and REVISE (-135.67), demonstrating the effectiveness of explicit density-based plausibility constraints, with slightly higher L2 distance (15.97 vs. $\sim$13.8) as a trade-off.

Table 2. Quantitative results on MNIST dataset. All methods achieve 100% validity.

Method	Validity	L2 $\downarrow$	Log Density $\uparrow$	Time (s) $\downarrow$
CLARITY	1.0	13.87	-134.11	41.13
REVISE	1.0	**13.83**	-135.67	**0.57**
Ours	1.0	15.97	**-120.66**	14.39

Overall, PLACE uniquely satisfies explicit plausibility constraints through normalizing flows while maintaining competitive proximity and perceptual quality. The substantial log density improvement validates the advantage of tractable likelihood computation for enforcing probabilistic plausibility, a property unavailable in baseline methods.

5 Conclusions and Future Work

We presented PLACE, a method for generating visual counterfactual explanations using conditional normalizing flows for explicit plausibility estimation in the latent space of a pre-trained autoencoder. Experiments on CelebA and MNIST demonstrate that PLACE achieves competitive performance across multiple metrics while uniquely satisfying explicit plausibility constraints, as evidenced by substantially improved log density scores. Our explicit density-based optimization provides direct control over plausibility, making PLACE particularly suitable for safety-critical applications requiring trustworthy explanations.

Several directions remain for future work. First, we plan to benchmark PLACE against diffusion-based counterfactual methods [3,7] to provide a more comprehensive comparison across generative paradigms. Second, we intend to evaluate our framework on domain-specific datasets from computational science, such as medical imaging [2] and materials characterization [28], where plausibility-constrained explanations can directly support scientific discovery and clinical decision-making. Finally, scaling PLACE to higher-resolution images and exploring more expressive flow architectures may further improve the quality and applicability of the generated counterfactuals.

Acknowledgments. Oleksii Furman, Łukasz Lenkiewicz and Maciej Zięba's work was supported by the National Science Centre (Poland) Grant No. 2024/55/B/ST6/02100.

Disclosure of Interests. The authors have no competing interests to declare that are relevant to the content of this article.

References

1. Atad, M., et al.: Chexplaining in style: counterfactual explanations for chest X-rays using stylegan. arXiv preprint arXiv:2207.07553 (2022)
2. Atad, M., et al.: Counterfactual explanations for medical image classification and regression using diffusion autoencoder, vol. abs/2408.01571 (2024). https://doi.org/10.48550/ARXIV.2408.01571
3. Augustin, M., Boreiko, V., Croce, F., Hein, M.: Diffusion visual counterfactual explanations. In: Advances in Neural Information Processing Systems 35: Annual Conference on Neural Information Processing Systems 2022, NeurIPS 2022, New Orleans, LA, USA, November 28 - December 9, 2022 (2022)
4. Duong, T.D., Li, Q., Xu, G.: Ceflow: a robust and efficient counterfactual explanation framework for tabular data using normalizing flows. In: Pacific-Asia Conference on Knowledge Discovery and Data Mining, pp. 133–144. Springer (2023)
5. Furman, O., Movsum-zada, U., Marszalek, P., Zięba, M., Śmieja, M.: Dicoflex: model-agnostic diverse counterfactuals with flexible control. arXiv preprint arXiv:2505.23700 (2025)
6. Hvilshøj, F., Iosifidis, A., Assent, I.: ECINN: efficient counterfactuals from invertible neural networks. arXiv preprint arXiv:2103.13701 (2021)
7. Jeanneret, G., Simon, L., Jurie, F.: Diffusion models for counterfactual explanations. In: Computer Vision - ACCV 2022 - 16th Asian Conference on Computer Vision, Macao, China, December 4-8, 2022, Proceedings, Part VII. Lecture Notes in Computer Science, vol. 13847, pp. 219–237. Springer (2022). https://doi.org/10.1007/978-3-031-26293-7_14
8. Joshi, S., Koyejo, O., Vijitbenjaronk, W., Kim, B., Ghosh, J.: Towards realistic individual recourse and actionable explanations in black-box decision making systems. arXiv preprint arXiv:1907.09615 (2019)
9. Kingma, D.P.: Adam: a method for stochastic optimization. arXiv preprint arXiv:1412.6980 (2014)
10. LeCun, Y., Bottou, L., Bengio, Y., Haffner, P.: Gradient-based learning applied to document recognition. Proc. IEEE **86**(11), 2278–2324 (2002)
11. Liu, Z., Luo, P., Wang, X., Tang, X.: Deep learning face attributes in the wild. In: Proceedings of the IEEE International Conference on Computer Vision (ICCV), pp. 3730–3738 (2015)
12. Van Looveren, A., Klaise, J.: Interpretable counterfactual explanations guided by prototypes. In: Oliver, N., Pérez-Cruz, F., Kramer, S., Read, J., Lozano, J.A. (eds.) ECML PKDD 2021. LNCS (LNAI), vol. 12976, pp. 650–665. Springer, Cham (2021). https://doi.org/10.1007/978-3-030-86520-7_40
13. Melistas, T., et al.: Benchmarking counterfactual image generation. In: Advances in Neural Information Processing Systems 38: Annual Conference on Neural Information Processing Systems 2024, NeurIPS 2024, Vancouver, BC, Canada, 10–15 December 2024 (2024)
14. Mertes, S., Huber, T., Weitz, K., Heimerl, A., André, E.: Ganterfactual - counterfactual explanations for medical non-experts using generative adversarial learning. Frontiers Artif. Intell. **5**, 825565 (2022). https://doi.org/10.3389/FRAI.2022.825565
15. Papamakarios, G., Murray, I., Pavlakou, T.: Masked autoregressive flow for density estimation. In: Advances in Neural Information Processing Systems 30: Annual Conference on Neural Information Processing Systems 2017, 4–9 December 2017, Long Beach, CA, USA, pp. 2338–2347 (2017)

16. Pawelczyk, M., Broelemann, K., Kasneci, G.: Learning model-agnostic counterfactual explanations for tabular data. In: Proceedings of the Web Conference 2020, pp. 3126–3132 (2020)

17. Rezende, D., Mohamed, S.: Variational inference with normalizing flows. In: International Conference on Machine Learning, pp. 1530–1538. PMLR (2015)

18. Rodríguez, P., et al.: Beyond trivial counterfactual explanations with diverse valuable explanations. In: 2021 IEEE/CVF International Conference on Computer Vision, ICCV 2021, Montreal, QC, Canada, 10–17 October 2021, pp. 1036–1045. IEEE (2021). https://doi.org/10.1109/ICCV48922.2021.00109

19. Sapoval, N., et al.: Current progress and open challenges for applying deep learning across the biosciences. Nat. Commun. **13**(1), 1728 (2022)

20. Sauer, A., Geiger, A.: Counterfactual generative networks. In: 9th International Conference on Learning Representations, ICLR 2021, Virtual Event, Austria, 3–7 May 2021. OpenReview.net (2021)

21. Theobald, C., Pennerath, F., Conan-Guez, B., Couceiro, M., Napoli, A.: Clarity: an improved gradient method for producing quality visual counterfactual explanations. arXiv preprint arXiv:2211.15370 (2022)

22. Tsiourvas, A., Sun, W., Perakis, G.: Manifold-aligned counterfactual explanations for neural networks. In: International Conference on Artificial Intelligence and Statistics, pp. 3763–3771. PMLR (2024)

23. Wachter, S., Mittelstadt, B., Russell, C.: Counterfactual explanations without opening the black box: automated decisions and the GDPR. Harv. JL Tech. **31**, 841 (2017)

24. Wielopolski, P., Furman, O., Stefanowski, J., Zieba, M.: Probabilistically plausible counterfactual explanations with normalizing flows. In: ECAI 2024 - 27th European Conference on Artificial Intelligence, 19–24 October 2024, Santiago de Compostela, Spain - Including 13th Conference on Prestigious Applications of Intelligent Systems (PAIS 2024). Frontiers in Artificial Intelligence and Applications, vol. 392, pp. 954–961. IOS Press (2024)

25. Wolczyk, M., et al.: Plugen: multi-label conditional generation from pre-trained models. In: Thirty-Sixth AAAI Conference on Artificial Intelligence, AAAI 2022, Thirty-Fourth Conference on Innovative Applications of Artificial Intelligence, IAAI 2022, The Twelveth Symposium on Educational Advances in Artificial Intelligence, EAAI 2022 Virtual Event, February 22 - March 1, 2022, pp. 8647–8656. AAAI Press (2022). https://doi.org/10.1609/AAAI.V36I8.20843

26. Yu, Y., Zhang, W., Deng, Y.: Frechet inception distance (FID) for evaluating GANs. China University of Mining Technology Beijing Graduate School, vol. 3, no. 11 (2021)

27. Zhang, R., Isola, P., Efros, A.A., Shechtman, E., Wang, O.: The unreasonable effectiveness of deep features as a perceptual metric. In: Proceedings of the IEEE Conference on Computer Vision and Pattern Recognition, pp. 586–595 (2018)

28. Zhong, X., Gallagher, B., Liu, S., Kailkhura, B., Hiszpanski, A., Han, T.Y.J.: Explainable machine learning in materials science. NPJ Comput. Mater. **8**(1), 204 (2022)

Modelling Human Optimal Seeking Behaviour During Evaluation of Process Models with Subjective Complexity

Ashish Tara Shivakumar Ireddy[(✉)], Leonid A. Beloglazov, and Sergey V. Kovalchuk

ITMO University, Saint Petersburg, Russia
{ireddy,kovalchuk}@itmo.ru

Abstract. Human–Artificial Intelligence (AI) collaboration in decision support scenarios is rapidly advancing. While rigorous effort is focused on improving AI models' solutions, deriving the experts' decision-making process remains a complex task. We present an experiment to model the optimal seeking behaviour of human experts as part of the human complexity state during information perceiving from process models of four real-world medical procedures. A targeted survey captures experts' perceived complexity evaluation using subjective metrics, understandability, correctness, and usability, in a free-to-explore grid world where process models of varying complexities are traversed and an optimal one is selected. We analyse expert trajectories to define three objective feature-based metrics: state discovery rate, state visitation entropy, and exploitation score, representing optimal seeking behaviour. Using Markov Decision Processes (MDP) and Maximum entropy Inverse Reinforcement Learning (MaxEnt IRL), we model exploration–exploitation during information perceiving and derive the underlying policy–reward function that reflects experts' subjective criteria for optimal model selection. Our results provide insights into human decision behaviour during optimal information seeking and assessment as an exploration-exploitation problem.

Keywords: Human optimal seeking · exploration-exploitation · process model evaluation · information perceiving · decision support systems

1 Introduction

The induction of AI agents and large language models (LLM) into professional sectors and daily life has allowed maximisation of efficiency and expanded outreach of knowledge. Information-intensive tasks can be significantly compressed while preserving reliability and coherence that would otherwise require an experienced domain specialist. However, AI agents still lack human-level awareness and thought process to consider real-world aspects such as rationality, situational relevance and contextual states [5]. While AI agent-based decision support systems (DSS) can assist and collaborate with human users in decision-making, the inclusion of excess or reduced information gives rise to vague or ambiguous solutions that may not align with the human users' expectations [2]. The exploration–exploitation construct provides a basis to balance information gathering and reward seeking. Yet, excessive exploration can yield stringent solutions while consuming enormous computational resources, whereas excessive exploitation can result in vague or biased solutions. [1] highlights the trade-off between performance and computational cost by considering the state of internal human planning before exploration as information seeking stage. [7] simulate a nuclear power plant accident to assess information seeking, integration, and diagnosis across individuals, tasks and trials. [8] and [6] observe that exploration can emerge from exploitation of objectives provided environments have recurring structures and agents can retain past experiences. The inclusion of human perceptional state and optimal solution-seeking behaviour into AI training can improve alignment with the user's expected solution pathways. We present an experiment to derive the optimal information-seeking behaviour of human experts in a decision-making scenario. Through a targeted survey, healthcare experts were invited to evaluate process models of four medical procedures ranging from minimum to maximum complexities. Experts freely explore a grid world environment and select a model representing optimal information via subjective metrics (understandability, correctness, usability) [5]. From expert trajectories, we model optimal seeking behaviour as an exploration–exploitation problem using three feature-based metrics: state discovery rate, state visitation entropy and exploration score; that characterize user exploration. Using MDPs, we simulate imitation learning and MaxEnt IRL to recover the underlying reward function and decision policy of human optimal selection. Our results provide a collective insight into deriving optimal seeking behaviour of experts in a decision making scenario. Further, the paper is structured as follows: Sect. 2 introduces the expert evaluation and methodology of modelling. Section 3 describes the interpretation of results from imitation learning and MaxEnt IRL, Sect. 4 investigates results after simulation. Section 5 is the conclusion.

2   Evaluation of Process Model Complexity

In this section, we describe the experimental setup to collect human experts' evaluation of process model complexity via a targeted survey. We build on a prior experiment [3], where models describing four medical procedures were evaluated under limited dynamics. Here, we increase model complexity by varying *Activity rate* (AR) and *Path rate* (PR) (nodes and edges) spanning between (0, 0) to (100, 100), covering the entire state space.

Survey Setup: We use a grid world environment for exploration of the state space by assigning process model control parameters (AR, PR) to (x, y) axes. We define a 11×11 grid (121 states) with steps at $[0, 10, \ldots, 100]$, selecting the corresponding process model at each (AR, PR). This resolution allows experts to reach maximal bounds of the state space without overly precise steps while preserving crucial complexity levels. The survey was distributed via personal invitations to healthcare domain experts. On starting the survey, the experts were presented with an introduction to the evaluation task and anonymous demographic data collected. On starting the evaluation phase, (i) a 2D grid world, (ii) a control knob to select (AR, PR), (iii) a visualization of the corresponding process model, and (iv) background information on the medical process are shown. The control knob is initialized at state $(5, 5)$ to avoid bias or partial evaluation. Experts could freely explore the grid and select the process model deemed optimal. Changing the position of the control knob on the grid updates the visualized model. After optimal selection, the expert evaluated three subjective complexity metrics: **Understandability** (interpretability and legibility of the model), **Correctness** (accuracy of the presented information), and **Usability** (if information is sufficient to interpret the process). Figure 1 provides an overview of our experimental pipeline. At the time of this study, 16 responses were collected, with 10 fully usable. The survey continues to collect responses.

3   Modelling Human Optimal Seeking Behaviour

In this section, we introduce our approach to modelling human optimal seeking behaviour as part of human complexity states and notations used throughout the paper. A **grid world** environment G of dimensions $n \times n$ with grid **states** $s_i = (x_i, y_i) \in G_{n \times n}$. The **time spent** τ in each state is a state-space feature $\tau_i \in \mathbb{R}_{\geq 0}$, where each state is $\bar{s}_i = (x_i, y_i, \tau_i) \in G\, \{\mathbb{R}_{\geq 0}\}$. A set of **actions** in G is $a = \{\uparrow, \downarrow, \leftarrow, \rightarrow, \nwarrow, \nearrow, \searrow, \swarrow, stay\}$. **Displacement** is $a_i \equiv (\Delta x_i, \Delta y_i) \in \{-1, 0, 1\}^2$, where $\Delta x_i = x_i - x_{i-1}$ and $\Delta y_i = y_i - y_{i-1}$ for $i \geq 1$, with $a_0 = \{5, 5\}$ in all instances. Given a set of U **human expert responses**, the trajectory of state-transitions for an expert $u \in \{1, \ldots, U\}$ is

$$\mathcal{D}^{(u)} = \left\{ \left(s_i^{(u)}, a_i^{(u)}, \tau_i^{(u)} \right) \right\}_{i=0}^{J_u - 1} ,$$

where J_u is the trajectory length for user u. We acquired 40 trajectories (10 experts across 4 datasets), each containing fields: *(x, y) trajectory*, timestamp, and *subjective evaluation*. We compute *movement metrics* describing expert behaviour characteristics such as displacement, final state, average time per state, etc.

Exploration - Exploitation: During model evaluation, the expected behaviour of an expert is traversal across min-max areas (information seeking) and comparison of complexity between (optimal seeking). We define *exploration* as the behaviour of new knowledge discovery by moving between states and *exploitation* as the behaviour of maximizing learned knowledge to select an optimal state with maximal reward. As each expert may have varying internal states (i.e. experience, expertise level, state of mind etc.) we acknowledge the bias in users when reaching an optimal state i.e. efficiently (e.g. fewer steps, less discovery) or tediously (e.g. more interpretation). We term this as context [2], we will address this aspect in future works as it goes beyond the scope of this work.

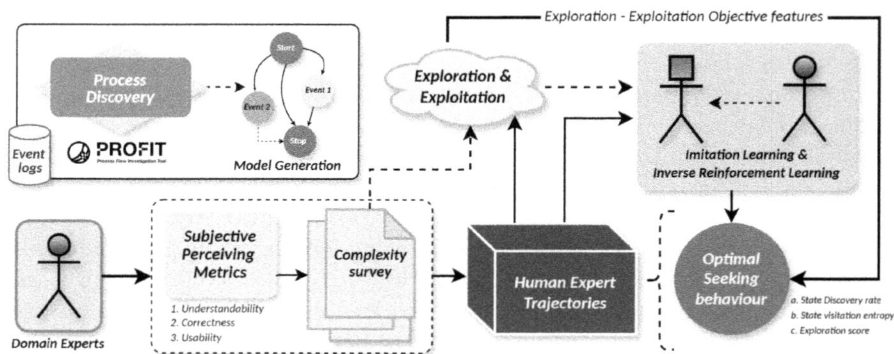

Fig. 1. Overview of our experimental setup to model human optimal seeking behaviour. Process models of varying complexities are evaluated by domain experts via a targeted survey. Exploration - exploitation behaviour during evaluation is formulated using objective feature metrics. Imitation learning and maximum entropy IRL recover underlying policy-reward function from expert trajectories.

Hence, we introduce sliding windows ω that segment the expert's trajectory into sets of length $W \in \mathbb{N}$, with effective window length $L_i = \min(W, i + 1)$ and $\omega_i = \{i - L_t + 1, \ldots, i\}$, valid for $i \geq W - 1$. Given that a user has visited states $V_{i-1} = \{s_0, s_1, \ldots, s_{i-1}\}$ before the ith step, we introduce objective feature metrics that characterize the user's behaviour in the state space.

1. State discovery rate $(S^{discovery})$ measures states visited by the user for the first time (1 for new, 0 for revisits), where $S_W^{discovery}$ is the number of new states visited within W. The state revisit rate is defined as $S_W^{revisit}(i) = 1 - S_W^{discovery}(i)$. A High $S_W^{discovery}$ and $S_W^{revisit}$ score indicates high exploration and exploitation, respectively.

2. State visitation entropy: A Shannon entropy–based metrics that quantifies state visitation frequency and interpretation time along the user trajectory as *(A) Frequency based state visitation entropy* - derived from the empirical visitation distribution $p_{i,W}^{freq}(s) = \frac{C_{i,W}^{freq}(s)}{L_i}$ of the number of visits to grid states s as $C_{i,W}^{freq}(s) = |\{k \in W_i : s_k = s\}|$ in the sliding window ω_i with k states within, normalized over maximum entropy across the complete grid space as $(H_{i,W}^{freq})^{norm} = \frac{H_{i,W}^{freq}}{\log_2(|G|)}$. *(B) Time-based state visitation entropy* $(H_{t,W}^{time})^{norm}$ follows the same principle as prior, but instead measures the time τ_k the user spends in each state s within window ω_i.

3. Exploration score: A heuristic measure of state-wise exploratory behaviour, defined as the sum of the state discovery rate and the normalized state visitation frequency over window W. This feature captures both the discovery of new states and the dispersion of exploration $E_{i,W} = S_W^{discovery}(i) + (H_{i,W}^{freq})^{norm}$.

4. Regime switch point: A metric to identify the change between exploration and exploitation regimes based on Cohen's d measure. Using expert trajectories in the grid world, we form a time series Q_i of exploration scores $E_{i,W}$ over T trajectories with i steps. We define $Q_i = E_{i,W}$ and split the series into two sections $n_1 = k+1$ and $n_2 = T-(k+1)$ where the assumed change of regime is at $k \in \{0, 1..., T-2\}$ (i.e. we aim to compute the difference in exploration score between the two sections while varying the point of regime inference between n_1 and n_2). For each k, we compute the mean exploration score $\mu(k) = \frac{1}{n}\sum_{i=0}^{k} x_i$, variance $\sigma^2(k)$, mean difference $\Delta(k) = \mu_1(k) - \mu_2(k)$ and the pooled standard deviation $s_{\text{pooled}}(k) = \sqrt{\frac{(n_1-1)\sigma_1^2(k)+(n_2-1)\sigma_2^2(k)}{n_1+n_2-2}}$ for each segment n_1 and n_2. We then compute Cohen's d as $d(k) = \frac{\Delta(k)}{s_{\text{pooled}}(k)}$ and maximize $d(k)$ for k steps $k^* = \arg\max_k d(k)$ reflecting the inferred point of change in exploration-exploitation regimes. Next, we extend this setup to select multiple points over sub-sections of the sequence, $\mathcal{K} = \{k_1, k_2, \ldots, k_m\}$ with $k_1 < k_2 < \cdots < k_m$, representing sub-interval switches over $I = [\ell, r]$ where $0 \le \ell < r \le T - 1$ and $n_1 = k - \ell + 1$, $n_2 = r - k$. We compute the mean, variance, pooled standard deviation, mean difference, and Cohen's d over these sub-intervals as in $k^*(\ell, r) = \arg\max_{k \in \{\ell, r-1\}} d(\ell, r; k)$.

Imitation Learning and Inverse Reinforcement Learning. Using experts' decision-making trajectories, and subjective evaluations we applied imitation learning (behavioural cloning) [9] to explore users' discovery paths when searching for optimal solutions, and maximum entropy inverse reinforcement learning (IRL) [10] to infer users' reward functions in the grid-world space. We define an MDP $\mathcal{M} = (S, A, T, \gamma)$ a 11×11 grid G with $|S| = 121$ states with starting state $s_0 = (5,5)$. A set A containing 9 actions with state transition function $T(s, a) = \pi_s(s + \Delta(a))$, mapping state–action pairs through policy π. Expert demonstrations trajectories as $E_{traj}^i = \{(s_0, a_0), (s_1, a_1), \ldots, (s_i, a_i)\}$ for user i, with δ_i the time the user spends in state i. We extend the exploration–exploitation metrics: state discovery rate $S^{discovery}$, state visitation entropies $H_{t,W}^{\text{time}}$ and $H_{t,W}^{\text{freq}}$, visit distribution $C_{i,W}^{freq}(s)$, and trajectory direction geometry θ, computed from the step vectors and the agent's movement orientation from Action space A. Behavioural Cloning attempts to learns a policy $\hat{\pi}(a \mid \phi(s_i))$ from state–action pairs (s_t, a_t) in a supervised manner, using feature vectors $\phi(s_i)$ $\phi(s_i) = [x_{(s_i)}, y_{(s_i)}, C_{i,W}^{freq}(s), \delta_{(s_i)}, \theta_{s_i}, H_{t,W}^{\text{norm}}, S_{s(i)}^{discovery}]$. Using a logistic regression function, we simulate agent traversal for 2000 iterations. At each iteration we infer $a_i = action(s_i, s_{i+1})$ where $s_{i+1} = T(s_i, a_i)$ and estimate parameters by maximizing entropy: $\phi^* = \arg\max_\Theta \sum_{(\phi_i, a_i) \in E_{traj}^i} \log \pi_\Theta(a_i \mid \phi_i)$; where E_{traj}^i is sampled from individual or group user trajectories. We use the grid world MDP to implement MaxEnt IRL to find an optimal policy π^* maximizing reward function R. We define a linear reward function $R_\omega(s) = \omega^\mathsf{T} f(s)$ based on exploration variables AR–PR (x, y) and descriptive QUAD metrics (replay fitness, precision, generalization, simplicity) acquired for each process model [4], where $\omega = [w_0, w_{\text{fit}}, w_{\text{prec}}, w_{\text{gen}}, w_{\text{simp}}, w_x, w_y]^\mathsf{T}$, $F \in \mathbb{R}^{121}$ is the feature matrix for transitions, and $f(s)$ is a row of F. Next, we fit the reward weights ω from $R_\omega(s)$ to obtain the assumed optimal policy π_ω^* depicting reward behaviour.

4   Case Study: Investigating Information Seeking

In this section, we investigate the results acquired from expert trajectories during optimal seeking. We compute objective feature metrics for all expert trajectories across four datasets to assess exploration-exploitation behaviour, resulting in a large set of observations. Each user had unique information-seeking and reward alignment approaches for optimal model selection (i.e. discovery of the grid space, complexity bounds, trajectory steps etc.). As our work is focused on deriving optimal seeking behaviour, we aim to address expert personalization, dataset context, descriptive metrics and trajectory behaviour in future works. To ensure a consistent scope of results, we select one expert's evaluation of process models describing a hospital billing process and collectively analyse the behaviour across all other responses with a sliding window of $\omega = 25$. Figure 2 visualizes the trajectory followed by the expert during the evaluation phase. The colour density represents the interpretation time spent in each cell. The expert discovered $\sim 60\%$ of the process complexity space while spending significant interpretation time in spaces with higher (AR, PR), i.e. more complex models. Figure 2 plots the objective feature metrics over trajectory steps. At the start of the exploration regime, the $S^{discovery}$ score is high as the state space is unexplored. With visitation to new states, the score gradually decays, while $S^{revisit}$ proportionally increases. At certain steps, we observe that discovery scores remain relatively constant or marginally increased; we identify this phase as exploitation, where the user compares already explored models to find an optimal. This behaviour is also reflected in state visitation entropy, where the expert is already in an exploitation regime. The lines n_1 and n_2 in plots Fig. 2 reflect instances of the expert switching from exploration to exploitation, where explored states are revisited and compared for optimal information. Next, we simulated the results of increasing ω from 5 to 100 in steps of 10 and observed that once ω increases over 50% of the trajectory length, the occurrence of at least one switch point is low, whereas having an extremely small window size reflects marginally small metric scores to be flagged as a change in exploration-exploitation regimes. Hence, there is also a need to select an ideal ω such that it is constrained by the trajectory length and knowledge gained. We also acknowledge that in expert trajectories, the grid area with low complexity models was left unexplored, this can be attributed to the nature of the data presented or the use case of the model, i.e. having an abstract process model is not logical to describe the medical process. This can be considered an underlying latent state as part of human perception.

Further, we acquire the results of imitation learning and MaxEnt IRL over the grid world MDP shown in Fig. 3A and 3B. We simulate the exploratory behaviour for a different expert when evaluating process models describing internal operations of a hospital. The expert here has visited both extremes of the grid space and discovered the minima and maxima models. We observe the learning agent's path to follow similar behaviour during exploitation as the expert did not visit the low complexity cells after first time exploration. The IRL reward function reflects the internal optimal reward function assumed by the user's

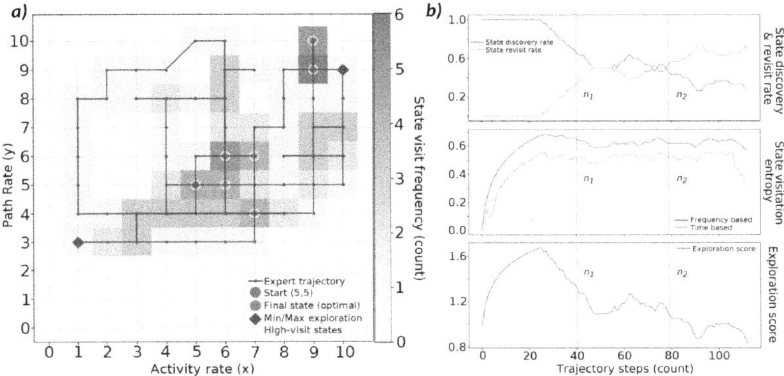

Fig. 2. Overview of exploration-exploitation behaviour of an expert evaluating process models describing a hospital billing process. (A) The expert trajectory in the grid world space where colour density represents the interpretation time spent in the cell; (B) The objective feature metrics of the expert plotted over trajectory steps at a sliding window size ($\omega = 25$), (n_1, n_2) represent the regime change from exploration to exploitation.

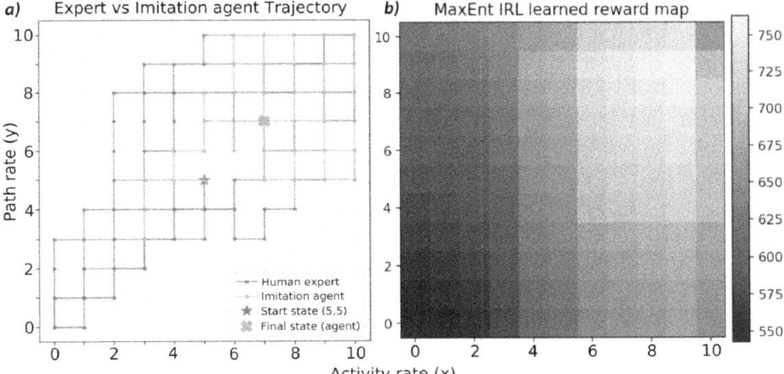

Fig. 3. (A): Expert trajectory (in blue) and imitation learning agent behaviour (in orange) when evaluating process models describing internal operations of a hospital (B): The recovered reward function from Maximum entropy IRL. (Color figure online)

exploration and exploitation. It reveals high concurrent rewards when exploiting cells with higher QUAD scores and greater process model complexity. It is worth noting that the reward at cell $(10, 10)$ is lower than the region of $(9, 9)$ to $(6, 6)$. This reflects both the user's behaviour of exploitation at the maximum complexity (high levels of information that may be deemed overcomplicated) and the descriptive metrics that indicate the model is not usable. Further, we confirm this behaviour by comparing the time spent by the expert within these states, reflecting exploitation. This trend was also observed in other datasets and experts, where the agent differentiated between the frequency of visitations and the interpretation time per state to replicate the optimal seeking behaviour of the expert during exploitation

5   Conclusion

Our work presents an approach to modelling human optimal seeking behaviour in a grid world scenario during the evaluation of process model complexity. Expert trajectories from a targeted survey were collected and exploration-exploitation behaviour was derived via three objective feature metrics State discovery rate, state visitation entropy and exploration score. Using a sliding window, we characterise information-gathering and reward-seeking regimes to identify the change from exploration to exploitation in the human user's perceptional state. We implement imitation learning and maximum entropy inverse reinforcement learning to replicate the exploration-exploitation behaviour and to recover the underlying reward function of the human expert during evaluation. Our results provide a crucial step towards modelling the human solution-seeking behaviour in decision-making scenarios. In future works, we plan to extend the study by continuing analysis with the inclusion of latent complexity states, context, personalization, descriptive and subjective metrics, to model human behaviour with online training of AI agents with feedback during interaction. More details on the background, implementation and elaboration of achieved results is available at https://github.com/maddoxx02/ICCS-2026-Modelling-Optimal-Seeking.

Acknowledgements. The research was supported by The Russian Science Foundation, agreement №24-11-00272, https://rscf.ru/project/24-11-00272/.

References

1. Callaway, F., et al.: Human planning as optimal information seeking. Manuscript in prep. (2021)
2. Ireddy, A.T.S., Kovalchuk, S.V.: Analysis of internal and external context in clinical decision scenarios with expert feedback. In: International Conference on Intelligent Information Technologies for Industry, pp. 301–313. Springer (2025)
3. Ireddy, A.T., Ionov, M.V., Beloglazov, L.A., Zatsepina, E.A., Kovalchuk, S.V.: Evaluating perceived complexity of process models from a targeted survey of healthcare domain specialists. In: International Conference on Mathematical Modeling and Supercomputer Technologies, pp. 43–58. Springer (2024)
4. Ireddy, A.T., Kovalchuk, S.V.: An experimental outlook on quality metrics for process modelling: a systematic review & meta analysis. Algorithms **16**(6), 295 (2023)
5. Kovalchuk, S., Ireddy, A.T.S.: Prediction of users perceptional state for human-centric decision support systems in complex domains through implicit cognitive state modeling. In: Proceedings of the Annual Meeting of the Cognitive Science Society, vol. 46 (2024)

6. Kulich, M., Krajník, T., et al.: To explore or to exploit? Learning humans' behaviour to maximize interactions with them. In: International Workshop on Modelling & Simulation for Autonomous Systems, pp. 48–63. Springer (2016)
7. Lyu, X., Li, Z.: Predictors for human performance in information seeking, information integration, and overall process in diagnostic tasks. Int. J. Hum.-Comput. Interact. **35**(19), 1831–1841 (2019)
8. Rentschler, M., Roberts, J.: Exploitation is all you need... for exploration. arXiv preprint arXiv:2508.01287 (2025)
9. Torabi, F., Warnell, G., Stone, P.: Behavioral cloning from observation. arXiv preprint arXiv:1805.01954 (2018)
10. Ziebart, B.D., Maas, A.L., Bagnell, J.A., et al.: Maximum entropy inverse reinforcement learning. In: AAAI, Chicago, IL, USA, vol. 8, pp. 1433–1438 (2008)

Detecting Feature Drift by Monitoring Feature-Rank Stability in Data Streams

Benjamin Mensah Dadzie[(✉)][iD] and Piotr Porwik[iD]

Institute of Computer Science, University of Silesia in Katowice, Bedzinska 39, 41-200 Sosnowiec, Poland
`{benjamin.dadzie,piotr.porwik}@us.edu.pl`

Abstract. Data stream mining requires models robust to nonstationarity. We address feature drift, defined as changes in feature-relevance rankings over time. We propose FRDD, a chunk-wise, event-driven detector that monitors feature-rank stability and raises alarms when a sufficient fraction of features violates reference intervals. The method supports supervised (LASSO) and unsupervised (Laplacian Score) ranking. Experiments on synthetic and real streams show that the supervised variant is more conservative, while the unsupervised one is more reactive.

Keywords: feature drift · drift detection · feature ranking · classification

1 Introduction

Many machine-learning systems operate on evolving data streams, where both the input distribution $p(x)$ and the predictive relationship $p(y \mid x)$ may change over time. Classical concept-drift detectors typically monitor prediction error or related statistics. Although effective, such approaches often depend on timely labels and may generate frequent alarms. An alternative is to monitor changes in feature relevance over time. In this work, feature drift is understood as instability in feature-importance rankings computed on consecutive chunks. We do not assume that feature drift is equivalent to concept drift. Instead, we investigate whether feature-rank monitoring can provide a practical alarm signal for downstream model adaptation.

Most concept drift detectors monitor prediction error or related statistics, e.g., DDM, EDDM, and ADWIN [2,4,10]. Other approaches, such as CUSUM and Page–Hinkley, rely on sequential change detection [14]. While effective, these methods typically require labeled data and may be unstable when labels are delayed. Unsupervised methods aim to detect distribution changes without labels, e.g., HDDM and RDDM [3]. However, they focus on aggregate statistics and do not explicitly model feature relevance. Recent work highlights the role of feature drift [12,13], suggesting that changes in feature importance can signal evolving concepts. At the same time, feature ranking methods such as

LASSO and Laplacian Score [8, 11] are typically used in static settings. In contrast, FRDD monitors the stability of feature rankings over time, providing a label-independent drift signal complementary to classical approaches.

1.1 Proposed Contribution

Concept drift refers to changes in the conditional distribution $p(y \mid x)$, which may degrade predictive performance and require model adaptation [1]. We further distinguish: *Data drift*: changes in the input distribution, e.g., $p_t(x) \neq p_{t+1}(x)$ and *Feature drift*: changes in the relative predictive relevance of features over time. If π_t and π_{t+1} denote feature rankings at times t and $t+1$, feature drift is observed as instability of these rankings.

We introduce **FRDD** (Feature Ranking-Based Drift Detector), a chunkwise, event-driven method that detects feature drift by monitoring violations of feature-rank stability. A reference chunk is split into N sub-chunks, feature rankings are computed, and feature-wise acceptance intervals are estimated from within-reference rank variability. An alarm is raised when the fraction of monitored features whose ranks fall outside these intervals exceeds a threshold. The reference is updated only after detected drift.

The Main Contributions are:

- A modular, interval-based detector supporting supervised and unsupervised ranking.
- An event-driven reference update policy to minimize redundant computations.
- A unified evaluation protocol with consistent adaptation.
- Empirical validation on synthetic and real streams, demonstrating the complementary nature of FRDD variants.

2 Background

Feature drift refers to changes over time in the relative predictive relevance of input features. In practice, there appears to be instability in the feature rankings computed across successive chunks. In this paper, rank instability is used as a drift signal complementary to classical error-based detectors, especially when labels are delayed, or unavailable [12].

2.1 LASSO for Supervised Feature Drift Detection

LASSO is an ℓ_1-regularized linear model widely used for sparse feature selection [8]. In FRDD, it is used only to produce a supervised feature ranking within each chunk:

$$\min_{\beta,\beta_0}\Big\{ \|\mathbf{y} - \beta_0 \mathbf{1} - \mathbf{X}\beta\|_2^2 + \lambda\|\beta\|_1 \Big\}, \tag{1}$$

where $\mathbf{X}$ is the feature matrix, $\mathbf{y}$ is the target vector, and λ controls sparsity. Features are standardized within each chunk, and importance is quantified by $|\beta_i|$. In the experiments, we use a fixed $\lambda = 0.001$.

2.2 Laplacian Score for Unsupervised Feature Drift Detection

The Laplacian Score is an unsupervised filter method that ranks features according to how well they preserve local neighborhood structure [11]. In FRDD, it provides a label-free ranking computed independently for each chunk. For feature f_r,

$$LS(f_r) = \frac{\sum_{i,j}(f_{r,i} - f_{r,j})^2 K_{i,j}}{\mathrm{Var}(\mathbf{f}_r)}, \tag{2}$$

where $K_{i,j}$ encodes instance similarity:

$$K_{i,j} = \begin{cases} \exp\left(-\frac{\|\mathbf{x}_i - \mathbf{x}_j\|^2}{2\sigma^2}\right), & \text{if } \mathbf{x}_j \text{ is among the } k \text{ nearest neighbors of } \mathbf{x}_i, \\ 0, & \text{otherwise.} \end{cases} \tag{3}$$

We set $k = 5$ and assign ranks in ascending order of LS.

2.3 Mathematical Foundations of FRDD

FRDD processes the stream in chunks of size U. Its main parameters are the number of reference sub-chunks N, the ranking procedure $R(\cdot)$, the number of monitored features m, the interval width k, and the decision threshold τ.

Let $\{(x_t, y_t)\}_{t \geq 1}$ denote a data stream, where $x_t \in \mathbb{R}^d$ and y_t is optional. The stream is processed in chunks. The l-th chunk is defined as:

$$C_l = \{(x_{l,1}, y_{l,1}), \ldots, (x_{l,U}, y_{l,U})\}. \tag{4}$$

Here, l indexes chunks, $l \in \{1, \ldots, U\}$ indexes instances within a chunk, and each $x_{l,j} \in \mathbb{R}^d$ is a d-dimensional feature vector whose components are indexed by $i \in \{1, \ldots, d\}$.

Ranking Procedure. Given a chunk C, the ranking procedure $R(\cdot)$ returns a score vector $s = R(C) \in \mathbb{R}^d$. We convert it into a rank vector $\pi = \mathrm{Rank}(s)$, where $\pi(i) \in \{1, \ldots, d\}$ and smaller values indicate higher importance. Ties are broken by feature index. We write π_t for the whole test chunk C_t and $\pi_{r,n}$ for the n-th reference sub-chunk $C_{r,n}$.

Reference Chunk Splitting. FRDD maintains a reference chunk indexed by r. Only the current reference chunk C_r is split into N non-overlapping sub-chunks of size $W = U/N$:

$$C_{r,n} = \{(x_{r,(n-1)W+1}, y_{r,(n-1)W+1}), \ldots, (x_{r,nW}, y_{r,nW})\}, \quad n \in \{1, \ldots, N\}. \tag{5}$$

For each reference sub-chunk we have, $s_{r,n} = R(C_{r,n})$, $\pi_{r,n} = \mathrm{Rank}(s_{r,n})$.

For each feature i we summarize the within-reference rank variability as

$$\mu_r(i) = \frac{1}{N} \sum_{n=1}^{N} \pi_{r,n}(i), \qquad \sigma_r(i) = \sqrt{\frac{1}{N-1} \sum_{n=1}^{N} \left(\pi_{r,n}(i) - \mu_r(i)\right)^2}. \tag{6}$$

Using the interval width parameter $\kappa > 0$, FRDD defines the acceptance interval

$$I_r(i) = \left[\mu_r(i) - \kappa\sigma_r(i),\ \mu_r(i) + \kappa\sigma_r(i)\right]. \tag{7}$$

Top-m Monitored Features. FRDD monitors only the top-m features selected from the current reference. Let

$$S_r = \{\,i:\ \mu_r(i) \text{ is among the } m \text{ smallest over } i = 1,\ldots,d\,\}. \tag{8}$$

In the experiments, we use $m = d$ to avoid additional tuning.

Test Chunk Evaluation. For each subsequent test chunk C_t $(t > r)$, FRDD computes

$$s_t = R(C_t), \qquad \pi_t = \mathrm{Rank}(s_t), \tag{9}$$

and defines the violation indicator for each monitored feature $i \in S_r$ as

$$v_t(i) = \mathbf{1}\left[\pi_t(i) \notin I_r(i)\right]. \tag{10}$$

Decision Rule. The normalized drift score is $D_t = \frac{1}{m}\sum_{i \in S_r} v_t(i)$. Feature drift is declared when $D_t \geq \tau$.

Hyperparameters. FRDD is controlled by U, N, m, κ, and τ. In the experiments, we use $N = 10$, $\kappa = 1$, $\tau = 0.5$, and choose U so that $W = U/N \geq 50$.

2.4 Evaluation Protocol

FRDD itself does not require a classifier; drift is detected solely from feature-ranking statistics. A classifier is used only to measure the downstream effect of alarms under a fixed adaptation policy. We use Random Forest (RF) [6] as a common baseline learner for all detectors.

For synthetic streams with known drift locations, alarms are evaluated using a tolerance window of size ϵ around each ground-truth drift point g. For abrupt drifts, we set $g = t_e$, where t_e denotes the drift point. For gradual and incremental drifts, we use the midpoint $g = (t_s + t_e)/2$, where t_s and t_e denote the start and end of the transition interval. For chunk-based methods such as FRDD, an alarm at chunk index t is mapped to the midpoint instance of chunk C_t.

We apply one-to-one matching between drifts and alarms: each drift can be matched to at most one alarm and each alarm to at most one drift. An alarm is counted as a true positive (TP) if it is the first unmatched alarm within the tolerance window of an unmatched drift. Remaining alarms are counted as false positives (FP), and unmatched drifts as false negatives (FN).

Algorithm 1. FRDD with event-driven reference update

Input: Stream in chunks of size U; number of reference sub-chunks N (thus $W = U/N$); ranking procedure $R(\cdot)$; top-m monitored features; interval width κ; decision threshold τ.

Output: Drift alarms at chunk indices.

Initialization

$r \leftarrow 1$; read C_r (size U) and split into $\{C_{r,n}\}_{n=1}^{N}$

for $n = 1$ **to** N **do**

  | $s_{r,n} \leftarrow R(C_{r,n})$; $\pi_{r,n} \leftarrow \mathrm{Rank}(s_{r,n})$

end

Compute $\mu_r(i)$ and $\sigma_r(i)$ for all $i = 1, \ldots, d$ from $\{\pi_{r,n}\}_{n=1}^{N}$

Compute $I_r(i) = [\mu_r(i) - \kappa\sigma_r(i), \; \mu_r(i) + \kappa\sigma_r(i)]$ for all $i = 1, \ldots, d$

Compute S_r (top-m) as the set of m smallest values of $\mu_r(i)$

for $t \leftarrow 2$ **to** ∞ **do**

  if *chunk C_t is not available* **then**

    | break

  end

  Evaluate test chunk $s_t \leftarrow R(C_t)$; $\pi_t \leftarrow \mathrm{Rank}(s_t)$

  $V \leftarrow 0$

  foreach $i \in S_r$ **do**

    if $\pi_t(i) \notin I_r(i)$ **then**

      | $V \leftarrow V + 1$

    end

  end

  $D_t \leftarrow V/m$

  if $D_t \geq \tau$ **then**

    Raise drift alarm at chunk t *Update reference* $r \leftarrow t$ Split C_r into $\{C_{r,n}\}_{n=1}^{N}$

    for $n = 1$ **to** N **do**

      | $s_{r,n} \leftarrow R(C_{r,n})$; $\pi_{r,n} \leftarrow \mathrm{Rank}(s_{r,n})$

    end

    Recompute $\mu_r(i)$, $\sigma_r(i)$, $I_r(i)$ and S_r

  end

end

---

3   Input Data Preparation

We evaluate the methods on synthetic and real data streams. Synthetic streams are generated in MOA [5] using the Hyperplane Generator under four drift regimes: abrupt, gradual, incremental, and recurring. Unless stated otherwise, each stream contains 100,000 instances, $d = 20$ features, and two balanced

Table 1. Characteristics of real datasets (#Inst/#Attrs/#Cls).

Dataset	Airlines	Ozone	Electricity	CovType
#Inst/#Attrs/#Cls	539,383/7/2	2,534/72/2	45,312/8/2	218,513/54/2

classes. For each drift type, we generate 20 independent realizations and report average results. *Abrupt*: Drift at the 50k-th instance; drift duration: 1 instance. *Gradual*: Drift at the 50k-th instance; drift duration: 20k instances. *Recurring*: Alternation between concepts every 25k instances; drift duration: 1 instance. *Incremental*: The modification weight changes by 0.001 with each instance, with a 10% probability of reversing the change direction.

Real-world streams are taken from public repositories and common stream-mining benchmarks [9,15]. Their characteristics are summarized Table 1. All experiments were conducted in Python 3.8. Code and scripts are publicly available.[1]

4   Experimental Evaluation: Synthetic Datasets

FRDD operates on chunks of size U. For synthetic streams, we set $U = 5,000$ and average results over 20 runs. We report ACC, complemented by TP/FP statistics (Table 2). Statistical significance is evaluated following the Demšar protocol [7], using the Friedman test and the Nemenyi post-hoc test. The corresponding critical difference diagrams for ACC are presented in Fig. 1.

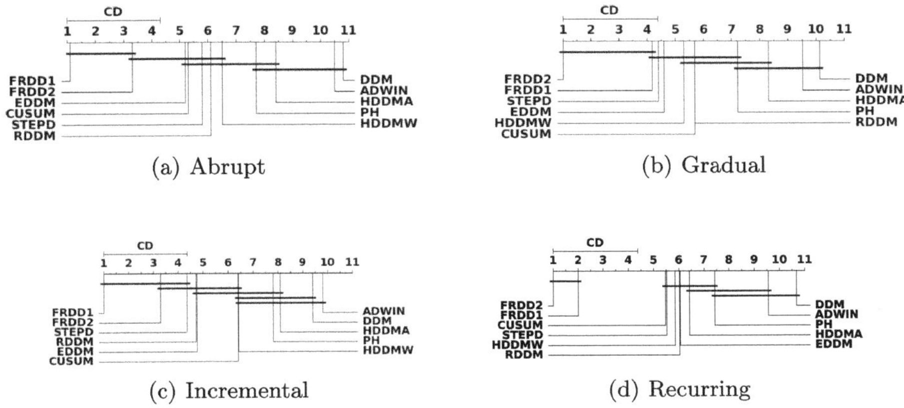

Fig. 1. Critical difference diagrams for ACC obtained with the Nemenyi post-hoc test on synthetic data with known drift points.

Table 2 shows mean TP/FP over 20 runs. FRDD1 is more conservative (lower FP), while FRDD2 is more sensitive (more alarms), especially for gradual and incremental drifts; thus, FRDD1 favors precision and FRDD2 sensitivity.

Table 2. Detection results (TP/FP) for different drift types.

Detector	Abrupt		Gradual		Incremental		Recurring	
	TP	FP	TP	FP	TP	FP	TP	FP
Oracle	1.0	0.0	1.0	0.0	1.0	0.0	3.0	0.0
FRDD1	0.80	**0.60**	0.30	**1.45**	0.20	**1.70**	0.60	**0.90**
FRDD2	0.85	**0.60**	0.20	3.00	0.20	**4.00**	0.60	5.20
CUSUM	1.00	2.80	0.55	3.95	0.30	7.70	2.80	10.00
PH	1.00	1.80	0.10	3.20	0.30	6.25	3.00	1.05
HDDM-A	1.00	1.95	0.15	3.10	0.20	6.00	2.85	2.15
HDDM-W	1.00	3.75	0.55	5.20	0.30	9.05	2.50	5.50
RDDM	1.00	10.35	0.60	10.55	0.45	12.30	2.40	7.60
DDM	0.07	8.45	0.65	6.20	0.35	4.60	0.95	2.60
EDDM	1.00	17.10	0.55	16.05	0.75	18.10	2.05	13.85
ADWIN	0.90	9.10	0.90	2.55	0.35	4.65	1.90	1.10
STEPD	1.00	13.05	0.75	13.65	0.70	13.95	2.60	11.65

Table 3. Wilcoxon signed-rank test based on the two-tailed W^+ statistic for average ACC values on synthetic data. Table entries are p-values.

FRDD1 vs.	CUSUM	PH	DDM	EDDM	HDDM$_A$	HDDM$_W$	RDDM	ADWIN	STEPD
Abrupt	= 0.001	< 0.001	< 0.001	= 0.004	< 0.001	= 0.002	< 0.001	< 0.001	= 0.001
Gradual	= 0.016	= 0.004	< 0.001	=**0.059**	= 0.002	= 0.001	= 0.018	= 0.001	=**0.052**
Incremental	=**0.330**	=**0.227**	= 0.048	=**0.784**	=**0.185**	=**0.374**	=**0.538**	=**0.131**	=**0.627**
Recurring	< 0.001	< 0.001	< 0.001	< 0.001	< 0.001	< 0.001	< 0.001	< 0.001	< 0.001
FRDD2 vs.	CUSUM	PH	DDM	EDDM	HDDM$_A$	HDDM$_W$	RDDM	ADWIN	STEPD
Abrupt	< 0.001	< 0.001	< 0.001	< 0.001	< 0.001	< 0.001	< 0.001	< 0.001	< 0.001
Gradual	< 0.001	< 0.001	< 0.001	< 0.001	< 0.001	= 0.001	< 0.001	= 0.001	= 0.001
Incremental	< 0.001	< 0.001	< 0.001	< 0.001	< 0.001	< 0.001	< 0.001	< 0.002	= 0.004
Recurring	< 0.001	< 0.001	< 0.001	< 0.001	< 0.001	< 0.001	< 0.001	< 0.001	< 0.001

5 Experimental Evaluation: Real Datasets

We evaluate FRDD on the real-world streams listed in Table 3. As true drift locations are unknown, methods are compared within the same RF-based adaptation pipeline. Figure 2 reports ACC and the number of detections.

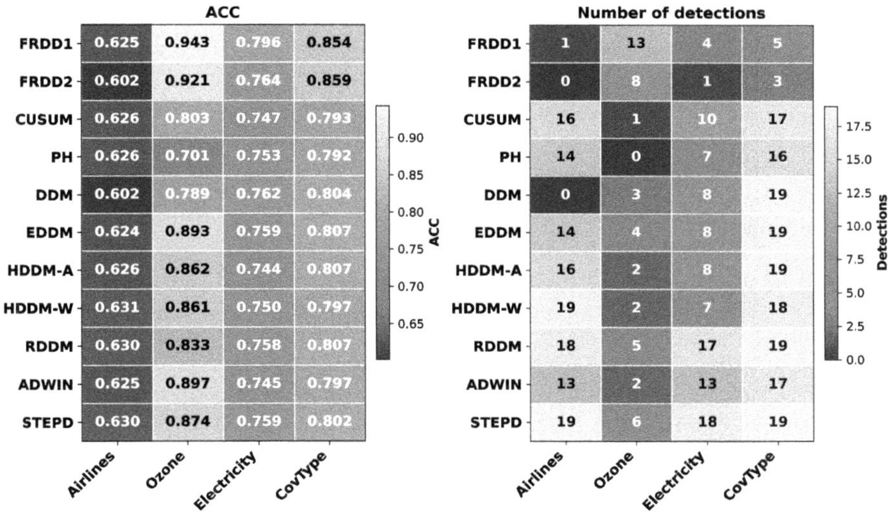

Fig. 2. Heatmaps of real-world performance under detector-triggered adaptation. Left: classification accuracy (ACC). Right: number of detected drifts. Rows correspond to detectors and columns to datasets.

6 Solution Complexity

Assume a stream of L_c chunks, each of size U. FRDD computes one ranking per chunk at cost $A(U, d)$. After each detected drift, it rebuilds the reference from N sub-chunks of size $W = U/N$, giving an additional cost $N\,A(W, d)$. Therefore,

$$\mathcal{O}(L_c\,A(U, d) + L_d\,N\,A(W, d)). \tag{11}$$

Since N is constant and $L_d \leq L_c$, the total complexity is $\mathcal{O}(L_c\,A(U, d))$.

Ranking Cost. LASSO (coordinate descent): $A(U, d) = \mathcal{O}(TUd)$, $A(W, d) = \mathcal{O}(TWd)$. Laplacian Score (k-NN graph): $A(U, d) = \mathcal{O}(U^2d)$, $A(W, d) = \mathcal{O}(W^2d)$.

7 Conclusion

We introduced FRDD, a chunk-based event-driven detector that identifies feature drift by monitoring feature-rank stability. The method supports both supervised (FRDD1, LASSO) and unsupervised (FRDD2, Laplacian Score) rankings. Experiments on synthetic and real-world streams show that rank-based monitoring provides a useful alarm signal under a unified adaptation policy. The study is primarily empirical. Hyperparameter sensitivity analysis, and real-world evaluation with drift annotations remain future work. *Reproducibility.* All data and source code used in this study, including the scripts for running the experiments and generating the reported tables and figures, are publicly available at https://github.com/ZSKPP/drift.

References

1. Agrahari, S., Singh, A.K.: Concept drift detection in data stream miningâĂŕ: a literature review. J. King Saud Univ. Comput. Inf. Sci. **34**(10), 9523–9540 (2022). Part B
2. Baena-Garcia, M., Campo-Avila, J., Bifet, A., Gavald, R., Morales-Bueno, R.: Early drift detection. In: Advances in Artificial Intelligence. Lecture Notes Artificial Intelligence, vol. 3171, pp. 286–295 (2006)
3. Barros, R.S., Cabral, D.R., Gonçalves, P.M., Santos, S.G.: RDDM: reactive drift detection method. Expert Syst. Appl. **90**, 344–355 (2017)
4. Bifet, A., Gavaldà, R.: Learning from time-changing data with adaptive windowing. In: Proceedings of the 7th SIAM International Conference on Data Mining, pp. 443–448 (2007)
5. Bifet, A., Holmes, G., Kirkby, R., Pfahringer, B.: MOA: massive online analysis. J. Mach. Learn. Res. **11**, 1601–1604 (2010)
6. Breiman, L.: Random forests. Mach. Learn. **45**(1), 5–32 (2001)
7. Demšar, J.: Statistical comparisons of classifiers over multiple data sets. J. Mach. Learn. Res. **7**(1), 1–30 (2006)
8. Efron, B., Hastie, T., Johnstone, I., Tibshirani, R.: Least angle regression. Ann. Stat. **32**(2) (2004)
9. Frank, A., Asuncion, A.: UCI machine learning repository (2010). http://archive.ics.uci.edu/ml
10. Gama, J., Medas, P., Castillo, G., Rodrigues, P.: Learning with drift detection. In: Advances in Artificial Intelligence - SBIA 2004, pp. 286–295 (2004)
11. He, X., Cai, D., Niyogi, P.: Laplacian score for feature selection. In: Proceedings of the 18th International Conference on Neural Information Processing Systems, pp. 507–514 (2005)
12. Hinder, F., Vaquet, V., Hammer, B.: Feature-based analyses of concept drift. Neurocomputing **600**, 127968 (2024)
13. Nguyen, H.L., Woon, Y.K., Ng, W.K., Wan, L.: Heterogeneous ensemble for feature drifts in data streams. In: Advances in Knowledge Discovery and Data Mining, pp. 1–12 (2012)
14. Page, E.S.: Continuous inspection schemes. Biometrika **41**(1/2), 100–115 (1954)
15. Souza, V.M.A., dos Reis, D.M., Maletzke, A.G., Batista, G.E.A.P.A.: Challenges in benchmarking stream learning algorithms with real-world data. Data Min. Knowl. Discov. **34**(6), 1805–1858 (2020)

Financial Management System for SMEs: Real-World Deployment of Accounts Receivable and Cash Flow Prediction

Bartłomiej Małkus[1]([☒]), Szymon Bobek[2], and Grzegorz J. Nalepa[2]

[1] Doctoral School of Exact and Natural Sciences, Jagiellonian University,
Kraków, Poland
`bartlomiej.malkus@doctoral.uj.edu.pl`
[2] Department of Human-Centered Artificial Intelligence, Institute of Applied
Computer Science, Faculty of Physics, Astronomy and Applied Computer Science,
Jagiellonian University, Kraków, Poland
`{szymon.bobek,grzegorz.j.nalepa}@uj.edu.pl`

Abstract. Small and Medium Enterprises (SMEs), particularly free-lancers and early-stage businesses, face financial management challenges due to limited data, small customer bases, and irregular cash flows. We present a deployed financial prediction system that combines accounts receivable prediction with cash flow forecasting for SME settings. The system integrates a binary classifier for invoice payment delays with a modular cash flow forecasting model designed to operate under incomplete historical data. A prototype was implemented and integrated into Cluee's platform, demonstrating practical feasibility for real-world SME financial management.

Keywords: accounts receivable · cash flow prediction · financial modeling · SME · freelancers · deployed systems

1 Introduction

Small and Medium Enterprises (SMEs), particularly early-stage businesses, micro-enterprises, and freelancers, face financial management challenges that differ significantly from those of large corporations. With limited customer bases and smaller operational scales, these businesses are particularly vulnerable to cash flow disruptions and payment delays [1,9,11]. A single delayed invoice can represent a substantial portion of monthly revenue, making financial prediction not just beneficial but critical for survival.

Traditional financial forecasting tools are designed for large enterprises with extensive historical data, dedicated finance teams, and complex enterprise systems. SMEs operate under fundamentally different constraints: limited historical data, basic invoicing systems, incomplete record-keeping, and minimal resources for financial analysis [12]. In practice, this means sparse customer histories, heterogeneous income sources, and irregular cash flow patterns. These constraints

P. Neumann et al. (Eds.): ICCS 2026, LNCS 16784, pp. 351–358, 2026.
https://doi.org/10.1007/978-3-032-29924-6_28

also limit the use of feature-rich methods commonly assumed in the literature, since many SMEs cannot provide long customer histories or detailed operational data. At the same time, prediction outputs must remain understandable and actionable enough to support direct financial decisions, for example by indicating which invoices are risky or which cash-flow components drive the forecast.

To address this challenge, we developed and deployed a financial management system in collaboration with Cluee[1], a startup providing self-organization and smart-budgeting tools for freelancers. Our system combines two components: accounts receivable prediction to anticipate payment delays, and cash flow forecasting to estimate future financial positions. These tasks are closely linked in SME workflows, since delayed receivables directly affect short-term liquidity and therefore influence broader cash flow planning. The system supports both standalone accounts receivable prediction for individual invoice management and integrated cash flow forecasting that incorporates payment delay estimates for more comprehensive financial planning.

This paper presents the real-world deployment of the system, focusing on practical challenges, architectural decisions, and business-oriented design rather than purely algorithmic contributions. We demonstrate how to build useful financial prediction systems under realistic SME constraints, including limited data availability, incomplete information, heterogeneous financial flows, and the need for transparent outputs.

Key contributions of this work include:

1. a deployed integrated system combining accounts receivable prediction and cash flow forecasting for SME constraints;
2. practical solutions for handling limited, incomplete, and heterogeneous financial data in real business environments;
3. deployment-based validation and lessons learned from building financial prediction systems for resource-constrained businesses.

2   Related Work

Financial prediction for businesses has been extensively studied, but most existing work focuses on large enterprises or settings with substantially richer data than those available in SMEs. Research in accounts receivable prediction typically examines large datasets and feature-rich customer histories [3, 10, 15], while cash flow forecasting studies commonly use data from power companies, construction projects, or other larger-scale operations [5–7].

Accounts receivable prediction approaches employ machine learning methods such as gradient boosted trees, random forests, and neural networks on feature-rich datasets [2, 3]. Zeng et al. [15] highlighted the importance of customer- and history-based features, while Hu [10] analyzed prediction settings with extensive customer cooperation histories. Such feature requirements exceed what typical

---

[1] See https://www.cluee.app for the company webpage.

SMEs can provide, where invoicing records are often limited to basic transactional information and short customer histories.

Cash flow forecasting methods include ARIMA, Prophet [13], and neural networks such as LSTM and GRU [5,14]. Cheng et al. proposed adaptive support vector regression [6] and evolutionary fuzzy decision models [7] for construction projects. These approaches generally assume longer financial histories and more regular patterns than those observed in small businesses and freelance work.

Limited research addresses SME-specific constraints directly. Weytjens et al. [14] compared machine learning to traditional methods, but still relied on relatively large datasets. The gap between enterprise-oriented methods and SME needs remains substantial, particularly for deployed systems that must jointly handle accounts receivable prediction and cash flow forecasting under sparse, incomplete, and heterogeneous data. Our work addresses this gap with a practical integrated solution designed for resource-constrained environments.

3   Deployed Solution

3.1   System Architecture

Our deployed system consists of two interconnected prediction modules integrated through a unified data processing pipeline. The architecture prioritizes modularity and transparency to accommodate the diverse data patterns and understandability requirements identified in SME workflows.

The accounts receivable prediction module operates as a binary classifier, determining whether invoices will be paid within a grace period (7 days past due date) or experience significant delays. The cash flow forecasting module employs a multi-component approach, with separate sub-models for different income and expense categories that are then aggregated into unified predictions.

As illustrated in Fig. 1, the system supports standalone accounts receivable prediction and integrated cash flow forecasting that incorporates payment delay predictions. Raw invoice and project data is preprocessed and enriched with historical features, processed by the accounts receivable module, and then integrated into the cash flow forecasting pipeline, where payment delay predictions inform future cash flow estimates.

3.2   Accounts Receivable Prediction Module

The accounts receivable module addresses the challenge of predicting payment delays under limited customer history, which is common in SME settings. To maximize information extraction from sparse data, we designed a feature engineering approach combining basic invoice information (amount, payment terms, customer ID) with historical cooperation metrics derived from past interactions.

The engineered features include payment ratios (late payments versus total payments), average delay times, outstanding invoice counts, and monetary aggregations of past payment behavior. To capture changes in customer payment behavior over time, we also use moving-average-based trend features computed

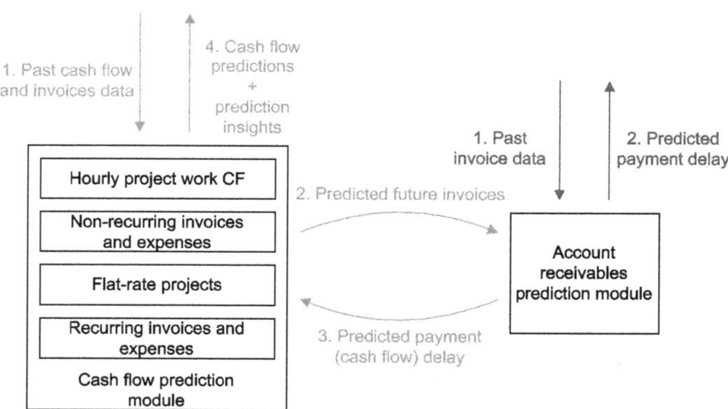

Fig. 1. System architecture supporting standalone accounts receivable prediction and integrated cash flow forecasting. The cash flow module consists of four sub-modules handling different income and expense categories.

from recent payment delays and payment outcomes. Short-window averages capture recent changes, while longer-window averages reflect more stable historical patterns.

The module employs Support Vector Machines (SVM) [8] as the primary classification algorithm, selected for their effectiveness on small datasets and clear decision boundaries. The model is trained separately for each business to account for differences in payment patterns across industries and customer relationships.

3.3   Cash Flow Forecasting Module

The cash flow forecasting module handles the heterogeneous nature of SME income and expense streams through a modular architecture with four specialized sub-modules. Each sub-module addresses a specific category of financial data, allowing the system to operate even when some data categories are missing or incomplete.

The hourly project work module calculates cash flows from ongoing projects based on recorded work sessions, hourly rates, and project timelines. Daily cash flows are computed as:

$$CF(d) = \sum_{p \in P} \sum_{t \in T_p} \frac{h_t}{d^{(w)}} \cdot w_t \tag{1}$$

where $CF(d)$ is the predicted cash flow for one day, P is the set of variable-rate projects, T_p is the set of tasks in project p, h_t is hours spent on task t, w_t is the hourly wage, and $d^{(w)}$ is the number of working days in the historical period.

The non-recurring invoices and expenses module handles irregular payments using a conservative prediction approach:

$$CF(m_k) = \begin{cases} \max(i, i_k) & \text{if } i > 0 \text{ and } i_k > 0 \\ i + i_k & \text{otherwise} \end{cases} \tag{2}$$

where $CF(m_k)$ is predicted cash flow for month k, i is mean income from the last 6 months, and i_k is planned income for month k. This conservative approach helps SMEs avoid overcommitting resources based on overly optimistic forecasts.

The flat-rate projects module manages fixed-fee projects by associating payment amounts with project completion dates, while the recurring invoices and expenses module handles subscription-based income and regular expenses with known schedules and amounts.

3.4 Integration and Deployment

The system operates in two modes to provide coherent financial projections. For standalone accounts receivable prediction, the system processes individual invoices to estimate payment delay likelihood. For integrated cash flow forecasting, the cash flow module directly calls the accounts receivable module to obtain payment delay predictions, which adjust timing assumptions in cash flow forecasts and improve short-term liquidity projections.

The system is implemented as a REST API using Flask and deployed on Google App Engine. This architecture supports integration with existing SME financial management tools while minimizing infrastructure requirements for the startup partner.

The API returns both compact summaries and component-level prediction details. For cash flow forecasting, the response includes contributions from each of the four sub-modules together with invoices flagged as potentially delayed. For accounts receivable prediction, the response includes the predicted delay outcome and recent customer payment-trend information.

4 Real-World Performance and Impact

4.1 Evaluation Setup and Datasets

Our evaluation focused on system effectiveness under realistic SME constraints. We used three datasets representing different scales of business operation: a startup-provided dataset from Cluee (297 invoices, 60 customers), and two public datasets filtered to match SME characteristics - IBM Late Payment Histories [16] (2,466 invoices) and Payment Date Dataset [17] (12,071 invoices).

To better reflect typical SME customer relationships, we limited customer cooperation history to a maximum of 50 invoices per customer. We also applied a 7-day grace period for payment delay classification to account for payment processing delays common in small business transactions.

Because real cash flow data was limited, we developed a synthetic data generator producing realistic project-based work patterns for 1,000 simulated users over one year (422,306 work sessions). The generator incorporates variable working hours, multiple concurrent projects, and wage dynamics typical of freelance environments.

4.2   Accounts Receivable Prediction Performance

The accounts receivable module demonstrated consistent performance across datasets, with the startup dataset representing the most challenging scenario due to limited training data. We evaluated multiple classification algorithms using 5-fold cross-validation, with balanced accuracy [4] as the primary metric to account for class imbalance.

Table 1 shows comparative performance across methods. Additional evaluation using F1-score showed consistent trends with balanced accuracy. Based on these results, we selected SVM as the primary algorithm due to its consistent performance across datasets. While gradient boosting methods such as XGBoost are commonly used for tabular data, our focus was on models that remain interpretable and robust under very limited customer histories, which motivated the use of simpler models in this setting. On the startup dataset, a balanced accuracy of 0.56, while modest, is meaningful given the severe data constraints, with 50% of customers having only 1–2 invoices.

Table 1. Balanced accuracy of accounts receivable prediction across datasets.

Method	Startup	IBM	Kaggle
Decision Tree	0.54	0.68	**0.70**
Random Forest	0.52	0.69	0.67
SVM	**0.56**	**0.72**	0.68
kNN	**0.56**	0.68	0.66
Naive Bayes	0.54	**0.72**	0.62

Moving average features improved performance across datasets by 3–5% points. The system also remained applicable in settings with very limited history, even with as few as two previous customer interactions.

4.3   Cash Flow Forecasting Results

Cash flow forecasting evaluation highlighted the importance of model simplicity and transparency in resource-constrained environments. Our custom modular approach consistently outperformed traditional time series methods (ARIMA, Prophet, SVR) when training data was limited.

In the most challenging scenario, predicting 11 months based on only 1 month of historical data, our approach achieved 11.85% mean absolute percentage error (MAPE), compared to 159.40% for Prophet and 166.24% for SVR. This result illustrates the difficulty of applying standard time series approaches in SME cold-start settings.

Table 2 summarizes performance across representative evaluation scenarios, showing consistent advantages of the proposed approach under SME-typical data constraints.

Table 2. MAPE (%) across representative cash flow forecasting scenarios. CF (X/Y months) denotes forecasting Y months ahead using X months of training data.

Method	CF (9/3 months)	CF (6/6 mo)	CF (1/11 mo)
SVM/SVR	14.19	19.11	166.24
Prophet	14.29	19.01	159.40
ARIMA	19.61	10.72	-[a]
Our Method	**13.06**	**9.41**	**11.85**

[a] ARIMA is missing, as there is not enough data in one month for AutoARIMA to determine the order. ARIMA is performed on weekly aggregated data as it performed much better than on the daily one.

The modular architecture was important for handling incomplete data categories. Unlike monolithic approaches that fail when data is missing, the system maintained useful predictions when only a subset of data sources was available.

5 Discussion and Future Directions

This work presented the design, implementation, and deployment of an integrated financial prediction system for SMEs operating under severe data and resource constraints. The system combines accounts receivable prediction with cash flow forecasting in a unified architecture, enabling short-term liquidity management and medium-term planning. The results indicate that useful prediction is possible even under sparse and incomplete data, provided that the methods are designed around SME constraints. The modular architecture was also important operationally, as it allowed the system to remain useful under heterogeneous data availability and partial financial information.

In practice, predictions were integrated into the platform as lightweight decision-support signals rather than prescriptive recommendations. Accounts receivable predictions identified invoices with elevated delay risk, while cash flow forecasts emphasized near-term liquidity trajectories adjusted for expected payment delays. This reflected feedback from the startup team that users preferred conservative, short-term insights and outputs whose reasoning could be inspected, such as which invoices were flagged as risky and which cash-flow components contributed most to the forecast.

The study remains limited by the small startup dataset and the use of synthetic data for part of the cash flow evaluation. Future work will focus on broader validation in more diverse SME settings, richer integration of receivable risk into forecasting, and extension of the system as more deployment data becomes available.

References

1. Afrifa, G.A., Tingbani, I.: Working capital management, cash flow and SMEs' performance. Int. J. Bank. Account. Financ. **9**(1), 19–43 (2018)
2. Appel, A.P., Malfatti, G.L., Cunha, R.L.D.F., Lima, B., de Paula, R.: Predicting account receivables with machine learning. arXiv preprint arXiv:2008.07363 (2020)
3. Appel, A.P., Oliveira, V., Lima, B., Malfatti, G.L., de Santana, V.F., de Paula, R.: Optimize cash collection: use machine learning to predicting invoice payment. arXiv preprint arXiv:1912.10828 (2019)
4. Brodersen, K.H., Ong, C.S., Stephan, K.E., Buhmann, J.M.: The balanced accuracy and its posterior distribution. In: 2010 20th International Conference on Pattern Recognition, pp. 3121–3124. IEEE (2010)
5. Chen, S., et al.: Cash flow forecasting model for electricity sale based on deep recurrent neural network. In: 2019 IEEE International Conference on Power Data Science (ICPDS), pp. 67–70. IEEE (2019)
6. Cheng, M.Y., Hoang, N.D., Wu, Y.W.: Cash flow prediction for construction project using a novel adaptive time-dependent least squares support vector machine inference model. J. Civ. Eng. Manag. **21**(6), 679–688 (2015)
7. Cheng, M.Y., Roy, A.F.: Evolutionary fuzzy decision model for cash flow prediction using time-dependent support vector machines. Int. J. Project Manage. **29**(1), 56–65 (2011)
8. Cortes, C., Vapnik, V.: Support-vector networks. Mach. Learn. **20**, 273–297 (1995)
9. Farrell, D., Wheat, C.: Cash is king: flows, balances, and buffer days. Technical report, JPMorgan Chase Institute (2016)
10. Hu, P.: Predicting and improving invoice-to-cash collection through machine learning. Ph.D. thesis, Massachusetts Institute of Technology (2015)
11. Shamsudin, A., Kamaluddin, A.: Impending bankruptcy: examining cash flow pattern of distress and healthy firms. Procedia Econ. Finan. **31**, 766–774 (2015)
12. Tawil, A.R.H., Mohamed, M., Schmoor, X., Vlachos, K., Haidar, D.: Trends and challenges towards effective data-driven decision making in UK small and medium-sized enterprises: case studies and lessons learnt from the analysis of 85 small and medium-sized enterprises. Big Data Cogn. Comput. **8**(7) (2024)
13. Taylor, S.J., Letham, B.: Forecasting at scale. Am. Stat. **72**(1), 37–45 (2018)
14. Weytjens, H., Lohmann, E., Kleinsteuber, M.: Cash flow prediction: MLP and LSTM compared to ARIMA and prophet. Electron. Commer. Res. **21**(2), 371–391 (2021)
15. Zeng, S., Melville, P., Lang, C.A., Boier-Martin, I., Murphy, C.: Using predictive analysis to improve invoice-to-cash collection. In: Proceedings of the 14th ACM SIGKDD International Conference on Knowledge Discovery and Data Mining, pp. 1043–1050 (2008)
16. Account Receivables Dataset on Kaggle (IBM Late Payment Histories). https://www.kaggle.com/hhenry/finance-factoring-ibm-late-payment-histories. Accessed 10 May 2023
17. Payment Date Dataset on Kaggle. https://www.kaggle.com/datasets/rajattomar132/payment-date-dataset. Accessed 10 May 2023

GenPlanner: From Noise to Plans - Emergent Reasoning in Flow Matching and Diffusion Models

Agnieszka Polowczyk[(✉)] [iD], Alicja Polowczyk[iD], and Michał Wieczorek[iD]

Faculty of Applied Mathematics, Silesian University of Technology,
44-100 Gliwice, Poland
agnieszkapolowczyk11@gmail.com

Abstract. Path planning is a fundamental component of agent-based systems, where individual agents must navigate complex environments while satisfying spatial constraints. This makes the problem relevant not only in classical navigation tasks but also in broader settings such as multi-agent simulations and decision-making systems. In this paper, we explore the potential of using generative models as planning and reasoning mechanisms. We propose GenPlanner, an approach based on diffusion models and flow matching, along with two variants: DiffPlanner and FlowPlanner. We demonstrate the application of generative models to find and generate correct paths in mazes. A multi-channel condition describing the structure of the environment, including an obstacle map and information about the starting and destination points, is used to condition trajectory generation. Unlike standard methods, our models generate trajectories iteratively, starting with random noise and gradually transforming it into a correct solution. Experiments conducted show that the proposed approach significantly outperforms the baseline CNN model.

Keywords: Generative planning · Diffusion Models · Flow Matching · Visual reasoning · Maze navigation

1 Introduction

Recent years have seen a rapid development of generative models and large language models (LLMs), which demonstrate significant capabilities in many domains. Despite these successes, tasks requiring logical reasoning and spatial planning still pose significant challenges [2]. Standard Vision-Language Models (VLMs) often hallucinate, failing to maintain logical consistency over long planning horizons [10]. There are comprehensive machine learning-based planning approaches that avoid sequential methods [8]. Additionally, diffusion-based solutions have been proposed that utilize computationally expensive inference-time optimizations [7]. In navigation tasks, global trajectory modeling using additional guidance mechanisms is crucial [9].

© The Author(s), under exclusive license to Springer Nature Switzerland AG 2026
P. Neumann et al. (Eds.): ICCS 2026, LNCS 16784, pp. 359–367, 2026.
https://doi.org/10.1007/978-3-032-29924-6_29

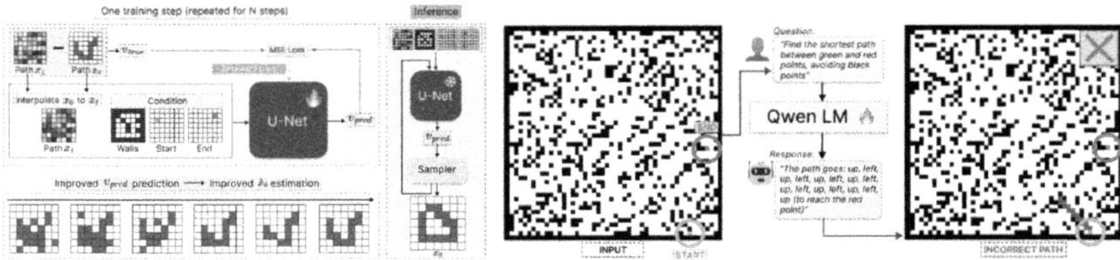

Fig. 1. Comparison of approaches. Left: **Overview of FlowPlanner training and inference.** Right: **Failure case of logical and spatial reasoning in a vision–language model.** Given a maze image with start and goal locations, the VLM (Qwen) generates a plausible sequence of directional moves, yet the resulting path is invalid.

In this work, we interpret reasoning as the ability to generate globally consistent trajectories that satisfy spatial constraints, such as obstacle avoidance and connectivity between start and goal, without explicit search. We propose a novel approach GenPlanner that solves the problem of planning in a maze with varying mesh sizes by formulating it as an image generation task. Instead of using expensive optimization during inference, we developed the FlowPlanner and DiffPlanner algorithms based on generative models: Flow Matching and Diffusion. Our model takes as input a noisy mesh and a conditioning tensor, whose individual channels encode the starting position, goal, and wall layout. Experiments show that our method achieves a path generation efficiency of 89% for solving 48 × 48 mazes. In summary, our principal contributions are as follows:

- We introduce a new representation of the planning problem in the form of a multi-channel conditional tensor (start, end, and walls), which allows the generative model to learn obstacle avoidance.
- We introduce GenPlanner in two variants: DiffPlanner and FlowPlanner, for planning and reasoning tasks.
- We experimentally demonstrate that our model effectively handles the growing solution space for larger meshes.

2   Related Works

Contemporary research confirms that, despite great advances in vision tasks, VLM models encounter fundamental difficulties in tasks requiring reasoning, see Fig. 1. These models struggle to abstract rules and perform worse than humans even on real-world images [8,10]. Furthermore, benchmarks such as VisuLogic [13] and ENIGMATA [2] reveal that models often generate semantically correct but logically inconsistent solutions. Recent studies based on the DynaMath [14] and PARTNR [1] benchmarks confirm VLM's sensitivity to small visual variances in mathematical tasks and its shortcomings in long-term spatial planning. The application of diffusion models to planning is a rapidly developing area, employing global attention mechanisms [9] or costly constrained optimization to enforce collision-free behavior [7]. In the context of robotics, datasets such as RoboCerebra [4] and WOMB [6] emphasize the need to integrate navigation with the physics of the environment. Unlike methods based on decomposition [11], our model solves the problem through a denoising process. Furthermore, we are also inspired by the observations from the work [10], which shows that longer reasoning correlates with correctness on difficult tasks. In our case, this role is played by an iterative diffusion process.

3   GenPlanner

This section introduces our GenPlanner method, a generative approach to planning based on conditional models, see Fig. 1. It includes two variants: DiffPlanner, which utilizes a diffusion model, and FlowPlanner, which is based on flow matching.

Input Data Representation. The input to the model comprises two components: a noisy path map and a condition that describes the maze structure. The binary path map $x_0 \in \{0,1\}^{H \times W}$ is initially mapped to the range of $[-1, 1]$ and then noisy by linear interpolation with a random noise sample $\epsilon \sim \mathcal{N}(0, I)$. For the diffusion model, the noised sample is constructed for a timestep $t \in \{0, \ldots, T-1\}$ as follows:

$$x_t = \sqrt{\alpha_t}x_0 + \sqrt{1 - \alpha_t}\epsilon. \tag{1}$$

where $T = 1000$ in all experiments and $\alpha_t \in [0,1]$ is a timestep-dependent coefficient controlling the balance between the clean signal and the injected noise. For the flow model, a sample is created for a randomly selected t in the range $[0, 1]$:

$$x_t = (1 - t)x_0 + tx_1 \tag{2}$$

where in the flow matching formulation, the noise variable is denoted by x_1 instead of ϵ. The condition $c \in \{0,1\}^{3 \times H \times W}$ is the concatenation of three binary masks: the walls map, the starting point mask, and the destination point mask. The final input to the network is obtained by concatenating x_t and c along the channel dimension, resulting on a four-channel input tensor. In the inference phase, pure noise ϵ is supplied instead of x_t, and the model generates a path map conditioned solely on the maze structure.

DiffPlanner Training. During training, a forward diffusion process is simulated, in which Gaussian noise ϵ is gradually added to the binary path map x_0 for a specified timestep t, according to Eq. 1. The model, conditioned on the maze representation c, learns to predict noise based on the triplet (x_t, c, t), i.e., it estimates the noise $\epsilon_\theta(x_t, c, t)$. Training is accomplished by minimizing the mean square error:

$$\mathcal{L}_{\text{DiffPlanner}} = \mathbb{E}_{x_0, t, \epsilon}\left[\|\epsilon - \epsilon_\theta(x_t, c, t)\|_2^2\right]. \tag{3}$$

FlowPlanner Training. FlowPlanner instead of iteratively adding and removing noise, as in diffusion, a flow matching approach is used, in which the model directly learns the vector field that controls this transformation. For each sample, a noise map $x_1 \sim \mathcal{N}(0, I)$ is sampled, and the ground-truth path mask x_0 is used. For a randomly sampled scalar t, an intermediate point is computed according to Eq. 2. The target vector field is defined as the time derivative of the interpolation trajectory (x_t is defined in Eq. 2):

$$\frac{dx_t}{dt} = x_1 - x_0 \tag{4}$$

The model, conditioned on the maze representation c, estimates the function $v_\theta(x_t, c, t)$, which describes the local direction and rate of this transformation. The network parameters are optimized by minimizing the mean square error between the predicted and target velocities.

$$\mathcal{L}_{\text{FlowPlanner}} = \mathbb{E}_{x_0, x_1, t} \left[\|(x_1 - x_0) - v_\theta(x_t, c, t)\|_2^2 \right] \tag{5}$$

FlowPlanner Inference. Path generation is formulated as a solution to an ordinary differential equation describing continuous dynamics transforming random noise into a solution. In the inference phase, FlowPlanner starts generation with a random noise sample $x_1 \sim \mathcal{N}(0, I)$. Then, the model, conditional on the maze structure c, estimates the vector field $v_\theta(x_t, c, t)$ describing the instantaneous evolution rate of the sample. Based on this velocity, the Sampler (see Fig. 1) updates the state using the explicit Euler schema:

$$x_{t+\Delta t} = x_t + \Delta t \, v_\theta(x_t, c, t) \tag{6}$$

where $\Delta t < 0$ corresponds to backward integration in time from $t = 1$ to $t = 0$, with the interval $[0, 1]$ discretized into T uniform integration steps. This process is repeated iteratively until a final state is obtained corresponding to the path map.

DiffPlanner Inference. Path generation is implemented via an inverse diffusion process, in which random noise is gradually transformed into a solution map. The process begins with a Gaussian random noise sample $x_T \sim \mathcal{N}(0, I)$. For the subsequent time steps $t = T - 1 \ldots, 0$, the model, conditioned on the maze structure c, predicts the additional noise $\epsilon_\theta(x_t, c, t)$ and then updates the state. During inference, a deterministic DDIM-sampler [12] is used instead of the stochastic DDPM sampler [5]. First, the clean sample is estimated as:

$$\hat{x}_{0,t} = \frac{x_t - \sqrt{1 - \alpha_t} \, \epsilon_\theta(x_t, c, t)}{\sqrt{\alpha_t}}. \tag{7}$$

Next, the transition to the subsequent timestep is performed according to:

$$x_{t-1} = \sqrt{\alpha_{t-1}} \, \hat{x}_{0,t} + \sqrt{1 - \alpha_{t-1}} \, \epsilon_\theta(x_t, c, t). \tag{8}$$

In our work, the DDIM sampler was adopted due to the possibility of selecting a smaller number of steps in the inference process. The effect of choosing the number of steps is shown in the Table 3.

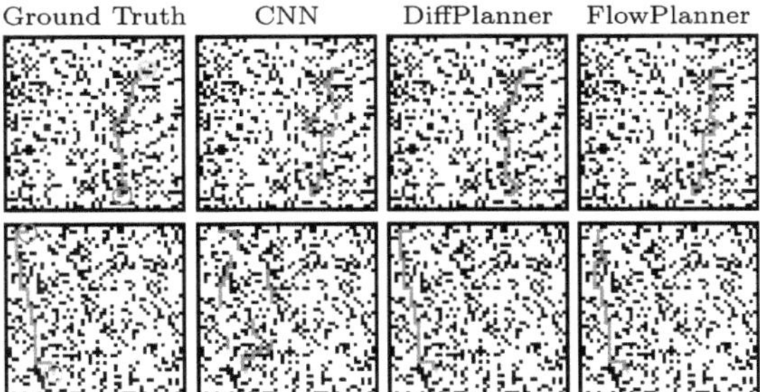

Fig. 2. Qualitative comparison of paths generated by CNN, DiffPlanner, and Flow-Planner on 48 × 48 mazes.

4   Experiments

In this section, we present both visual and quantitative experimental results and compare them with those obtained by other methods.

Dataset. The dataset consists of randomly generated grid mazes with varying sizes and obstacle densities, where start and goal positions are sampled from free cells. Ground-truth paths are computed using the A* algorithm [3], and samples without valid solutions are discarded. While A* is efficient in this setting, we use 2D mazes as a testbed to evaluate whether generative models can learn spatial reasoning and generalize to more complex planning problems. For each valid sample, four binary masks (obstacles, start, goal, and solution path) are stored, and datasets are generated across multiple grid sizes (8 × 8 to 48 × 48), with 5,000/250 samples for 8 × 8, 10,000/500 for 16 × 16, and 20,000/1,000 for both 32 × 32 and 48 × 48 (train/test splits), and corresponding minimum path lengths of 1, 5, 10, and 20.

Metrics. Four metrics assess the quality of the generated paths. *Validity* checks whether the generated path forms a continuous connection between the starting point and the goal. *Single-Path* metric assesses whether the generated trajectory forms a single, unbranched path. *Single-Path* equals 1 only if *Validity* = 1, the path has no branches (*Branch-Rate* = 0), and exactly two endpoints. *Branch-Rate* measures the percentage of the cells in the path with at least three neighbors (i.e., branching) with lower values indicating more regular trajectories. *Length Ratio* is the ratio of the length of the generated path to the length of the shortest path determined by the A* algorithm.

5   Results

Table 1. Quantitative comparison of CNN, DiffPlanner, and FlowPlanner across different grid sizes. The best results are achieved by FlowPlanner, which leverages a learned vector field to guide the sample along a continuous trajectory toward the solution.

Maze Size	Model	Validity (%) ↑	Single-Path (%) ↑	Length Ratio ↓	Branch-Rate (%) ↓
8 × 8	CNN	92.80	89.20	**1.00**	0.29
	FlowPlanner	**94.00**	**92.40**	**1.00**	**0.26**
	DiffPlanner	90.40	77.20	1.02	1.95
16 × 16	CNN	74.00	65.20	**1.00**	0.82
	FlowPlanner	**88.60**	**86.20**	1.01	**0.19**
	DiffPlanner	84.60	67.60	1.03	2.15
32 × 32	CNN	49.60	45.20	**1.00**	0.42
	FlowPlanner	82.20	81.60	1.01	**0.05**
	DiffPlanner	**88.60**	**82.80**	1.03	0.44
48 × 48	CNN	38.70	28.40	**1.00**	0.95
	FlowPlanner	88.00	**86.10**	1.02	**0.09**
	DiffPlanner	**89.00**	76.10	1.04	0.47

Table 2. Quantitative ablation results for FlowPlanner different conditioning channel combinations on 48 × 48 mazes. Each condition channel is crucial for accurately generating the trajectory.

Config	Conditioning		Metrics			
	Start,End	Walls	Validity (%) ↑	Single-Path (%) ↑	Length Ratio ↓	Branch-Rate (%) ↓
1	✗	✗	0.00	33.70	N/A	0.18
2	✓	✗	6.40	6.30	1.06	**0.03**
3	✗	✓	0.10	73.30	**1.00**	0.22
Ours	✓	✓	**88.00**	**86.10**	1.02	0.09

We compare three models: a CNN (U-Net), DiffPlanner, and FlowPlanner, see (Fig. 2). Preliminary experiments with VLMs show that their outputs are inconsistent and frequently fail to produce valid or coherent paths, which aligns with the qualitative failure case presented in Fig. 1. The CNN directly predicts the path, while DiffPlanner and FlowPlanner iteratively construct a solution, starting with random noise and gradually transforming it into a valid trajectory using a diffusion process and a trained vector field, respectively. Results in Table 1 demonstrate a clear advantage of generative methods, with FlowPlanner consistently outperforming the other methods. All models achieve *Length*

Table 3. Impact of the number of sampling steps on the performance of FlowPlanner and DiffPlanner for 48 × 48 mazes. FlowPlanner is characterized by high stability regardless of the number of generation steps.

Model	Steps T	Validity ↑	Single-Path ↑	Length Ratio ↓	Branch-Rate ↓
FlowPlanner	50	**88.00**	**86.10**	1.02	**0.09**
	30	87.70	85.50	1.02	0.10
	20	86.40	84.60	1.02	0.10
	10	85.80	83.00	1.02	0.15
	5	79.10	75.90	1.01	0.14
	1	23.70	20.40	**1.00**	0.65
DiffPlanner	50	89.00	**76.10**	1.04	**0.47**
	30	88.00	71.10	1.04	0.62
	20	85.50	65.60	1.03	0.71
	10	81.30	52.00	1.03	1.27
	5	65.70	10.70	1.03	3.91
	1	**98.90**	0.00	**1.00**	71.05

Ratio values close to one, indicating near-optimal path lengths, but only generative methods combine this with high correctness and structural regularity. FlowPlanner achieves the highest *Single-Path* and the lowest *Branch Rate*, producing clean, unbranched trajectories.

We conduct an ablation study on 48 × 48 mazes to assess the impact of conditioning components, comparing models with no condition, start-goal only, obstacles only, and the full conditioning, see Table 2. Removing any component lead to a significant drop in trajectory quality. The *N/A* value of the *Length Ratio* metric for the configuration without any conditioning results from the lack of valid trajectories generated (*Validity* = 0).

Table 3 shows that reducing the number of generation steps degrades performance in both methods, but FlowPlanner remains significantly more stable, maintaining high *Validity* and *Single-Path* with low *Branch-Rate* even at 10 steps. In contrast, DiffPlanner is highly sensitive to step reduction, producing fragmented and branched trajectories and failing to generate meaningful paths at very low step counts, highlighting the efficiency advantage of FlowPlanner.

6   Conclusion

We presented GenPlanner, an approach to path planning with two variants: DiffPlanner and FlowPlanner. Diffusion and flow-based models can act as planning mechanisms, progressively refining solutions while maintaining global consistency and respecting constraints. Experiments showed that the proposed methods significantly outperform the baseline CNN model in terms of the correctness of generated trajectories, their regularity, and structural stability. In particular,

FlowPlanner achieves the best results in all key metrics, maintaining high quality even when the number of generation steps is severely limited.

In future work, we plan to extend the framework with mechanisms for refining generated paths, especially in uncertain cases, and to explore applications in continuous and dynamic environments.

Acknowledgments. The authors acknowledge the contribution to this research from the Polish Ministry of Education and Science under grant No. PN/02/0084/2023.

Disclosure of Interests. The authors have no competing interests to declare that are relevant to the content of this article.

References

1. Chang, M., et al.: PARTNR: a benchmark for planning and reasoning in embodied multi-agent tasks. In: The Thirteenth International Conference on Learning Representations (2025)
2. Chen, J., et al.: Enigmata: scaling logical reasoning in large language models with synthetic verifiable puzzles. In: The Thirty-Ninth Annual Conference on Neural Information Processing Systems (2025)
3. Futuhi, E., Sturtevant, N.R.: Learning admissible heuristics for a*: theory and practice. In: The Fourteenth International Conference on Learning Representations (2026)
4. Han, S., et al.: Robocerebra: a large-scale benchmark for long-horizon robotic manipulation evaluation. In: The Thirty-Ninth Annual Conference on Neural Information Processing Systems Datasets and Benchmarks Track (2025)
5. Ho, J., Jain, A., Abbeel, P.: Denoising diffusion probabilistic models. In: Proceedings of the 34th International Conference on Neural Information Processing Systems, NIPS '20. Curran Associates Inc., Red Hook, NY, USA (2020)
6. Li, Y., et al.: WOMD-reasoning: a large-scale dataset for interaction reasoning in driving. In: Singh, A., et al. (eds.) Proceedings of the 42nd International Conference on Machine Learning. Proceedings of Machine Learning Research, vol. 267, pp. 34288–34311. PMLR (2025). https://proceedings.mlr.press/v267/li25l.html
7. Liang, J., Christopher, J.K., Koenig, S., Fioretto, F.: Simultaneous multi-robot motion planning with projected diffusion models. In: Forty-Second International Conference on Machine Learning (2025)
8. Lin, B.Y., et al.: Zebralogic: on the scaling limits of LLMs for logical reasoning. In: Forty-Second International Conference on Machine Learning (2025)
9. Lu, H., Han, D., Shen, Y., Li, D.: What makes a good diffusion planner for decision making? In: The Thirteenth International Conference on Learning Representations (2025)
10. Małkiński, M., Pawlonka, S., Mańdziuk, J.: Reasoning limitations of multimodal large language models. a case study of bongard problems. In: Forty-Second International Conference on Machine Learning (2025)
11. Ryu, H., Kim, G., Lee, H.S., Yang, E.: Divide and translate: compositional first-order logic translation and verification for complex logical reasoning. In: The Thirteenth International Conference on Learning Representations (2025)
12. Song, J., Meng, C., Ermon, S.: Denoising diffusion implicit models. In: International Conference on Learning Representations (2021)

13. Xu, W., et al.: Visulogic: a benchmark for evaluating visual reasoning in multi-modal large language models. In: The Fourteenth International Conference on Learning Representations (2026)
14. Zou, C., Guo, X., Yang, R., Zhang, J., Hu, B., Zhang, H.: Dynamath: a dynamic visual benchmark for evaluating mathematical reasoning robustness of vision language models. In: The Thirteenth International Conference on Learning Representations (2025)

BVH-Accelerated Ray Tracing
for High-Frequency Electromagnetic
Backscattering

Marco Pasquale$^{(\boxtimes)}$, Andong Hu, Luca Pennati, Ivy Peng, and Stefano Markidis

KTH Royal Institute of Technology, Stockholm, Sweden
{marcopas,andonghu,pennati,bopeng,markidis}@kth.se

Abstract. As computational complexity in electromagnetics increases with frequency, full-wave solvers become computationally infeasible for electrically large problems. A shooting and bouncing rays (SBR) method for modeling electromagnetic backscattering from large metallic objects is presented, coupling multi-reflection geometrical optics with a physical optics discretized surface integral. To handle the massive intersection search space, we implement a bounding volume hierarchy (BVH) in a trace-integrate pipeline. Numerical accuracy is controlled through an incident-ray sampling rule to mitigate spatial aliasing. The method is validated against Mie solutions for a perfectly electrically conducting sphere, and applied to a complex aircraft for monostatic radar cross-section prediction, exhibiting robust parallel scaling on NVIDIA and AMD GPUs.

Keywords: Shooting and bouncing rays · Bounding volume hierarchy · Electromagnetic scattering · Radar cross section · GPU acceleration

1 Introduction

Computational electromagnetics (CEM) comprises numerical and asymptotic methods for predicting electromagnetic fields across applications such as antenna design, radar, and channel modeling [1,2]. Full-wave methods are preferred when resonance or strong coupling dominate. However, when a structure is electrically large, meaning its characteristic dimension D spans many wavelengths λ ($D/\lambda \gg 1$), full-wave discretizations require exceptionally fine meshes that push memory and runtime beyond practical limits. This scaling pressure is increasingly prominent in emerging radar and 6G scenarios extending toward sub-terahertz frequencies [3]. In the high-frequency (HF) asymptotic limit (often mathematically denoted as $\lambda \to 0$), wave propagation behaves locally like plane waves and can be accurately approximated by ray optics. This motivates asymptotic methods that replace global field solves with a transport-and-accumulation procedure: tracing ensembles of rays through the geometry and coherently accumulating the scattered field produced at the surface [4]. Shooting and bouncing rays (SBR) is a representative Geometrical Optics plus Physical Optics (GO+PO) method introduced to enable radar cross-section (RCS) predictions for complex geometries [5,6].

P. Neumann et al. (Eds.): ICCS 2026, LNCS 16784, pp. 368–376, 2026.
https://doi.org/10.1007/978-3-032-29924-6_30

While recent work has leveraged GPU-accelerated ray tracing for channel modeling [7,8], the application of these techniques to high-fidelity, multi-bounce RCS prediction requires careful treatment of the PO accumulation step to avoid phase aliasing. The primary novelty and contribution of this work is the development of a computationally efficient SBR algorithm tailored explicitly for CEM precision. Specifically, we: (i) formulate a ray-tube discretization driven by a strict sampling rule to guarantee phase accuracy; (ii) map the SBR procedure to a parallel traceÃ¢Ć̌ñâĂIJintegrate pipeline that minimizes GPU thread divergence; and (iii) provide a comprehensive performance and scaling analysis across differing architectures (NVIDIA A100 vs. AMD MI250X), highlighting trade-offs between single (FP32) and double (FP64) precision arithmetic. The method is implemented in the open-source code `SagittaSBR` [9].

2 Problem Formulation

To bypass the memory constraints of global field solvers, we employ the SBR method. In the following equations, ε and μ are the permittivity and permeability of the medium, and the subscript "r" indicates the relative values compared to a vacuum. Time-harmonic fields in the high-frequency limit admit an eikonal formulation [10]:

$$\mathbf{E}(\mathbf{r}) = \mathbf{e}(\mathbf{r})e^{-jk_0 L(\mathbf{r})}, \qquad \mathbf{H}(\mathbf{r}) = \mathbf{h}(\mathbf{r})e^{-jk_0 L(\mathbf{r})},$$

where $L(\mathbf{r})$ is the optical path length and $k_0 = 2\pi/\lambda_0$ is the free-space wavenumber. The phase is $\Phi(\mathbf{r}) = k_0 L(\mathbf{r})$. Substituting this ansatz into Maxwell's equations and extracting the leading order terms under the HF assumption yields the eikonal equation:

$$|\nabla L(\mathbf{r})|^2 = n^2(\mathbf{r}), \qquad n(\mathbf{r}) = \sqrt{\mu_r(\mathbf{r})\,\varepsilon_r(\mathbf{r})}.$$

Rays are curves $\mathbf{r}(s)$ normal to the wavefronts. In homogeneous media ($\nabla n = 0$), these rays propagate as straight lines and undergo specular reflection at boundaries. Geometrical optics provides these trajectories, but the scattered field is obtained by accumulating contributions over the illuminated surface using physical optics (PO). For a perfect electric conductor (PEC), the induced surface current is approximated as:

$$\mathbf{J}_s \approx \begin{cases} 2\hat{n} \times \mathbf{H}_{\text{inc}}, & \text{illuminated region,} \\ 0, & \text{shadowed region,} \end{cases}$$

where $\hat{n}$ is the unit outward surface normal. In the far-field, the scattered electric field follows the Stratton–Chu formulation [11]:

$$\mathbf{E}_s(\mathbf{r}) \approx \frac{-j\omega\mu_0}{4\pi r}e^{-jk_0 r}\int_S \left[\mathbf{J}_s(\mathbf{r}') - (\mathbf{J}_s(\mathbf{r}') \cdot \hat{r})\hat{r}\right] e^{jk_0 \mathbf{r}' \cdot \hat{r}}\, dS'.$$

From a computational perspective, this continuous integral is discretized using ray tubes: each ray represents an area element ΔA on the launch grid. It should be noted that it is not strictly necessary for the mesh triangles to be larger than the ray tube cross-section ΔA; ray tubes serve as discrete sample points of the surface fields, and as long as the surface is adequately sampled, the validity of the discrete integral holds. For the monostatic case, the total far-field amplitude is the coherent sum over the valid rays:

$$A = \sum_{i=1}^{N_{\text{rays}}} \frac{jk\Delta A}{4\pi} 2\left(\hat{n}_i \cdot -\hat{k}_{\text{inc}}\right) \Gamma^{N_i} e^{-j2kR_i},\tag{1}$$

where $\hat{n}_i$ is the surface normal at the first interaction, $\hat{k}_{\text{inc}}$ is the incident direction, R_i is the accumulated optical path length including reflections, N_i is the number of reflections, and Γ is the reflection coefficient. The monostatic RCS is $\sigma = 4\pi|A|^2$.

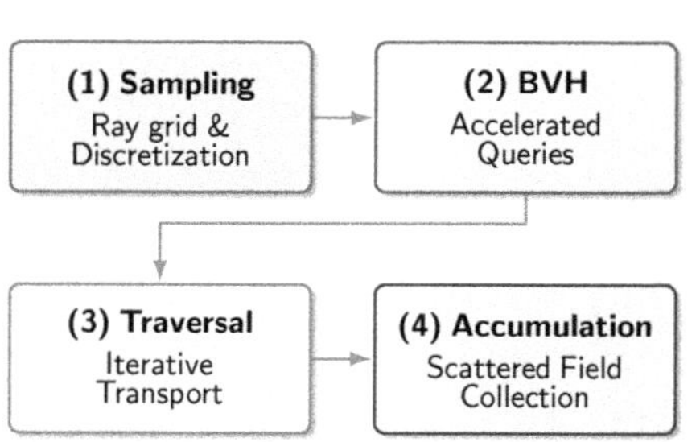

Fig. 1. SagittaSBR pipeline. Rays are launched from an orthographic grid. BVH accelerates traversal, and scattered field is accumulated from valid hits.

Fig. 2. Independent multi-bounce transport. At the final valid hit, path length, first-hit normal, and reflection count are recorded for the PO integral.

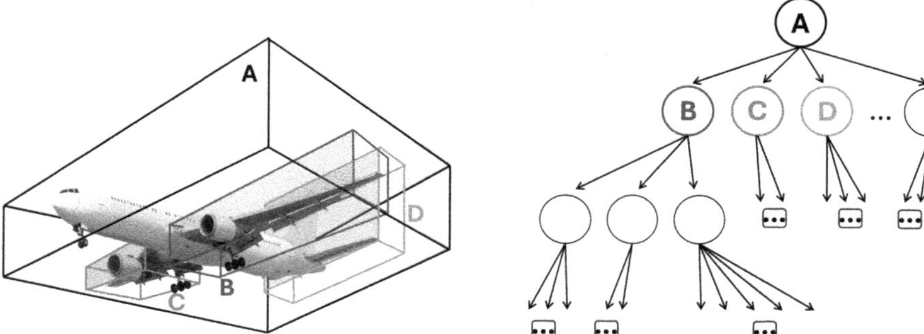

Fig. 3. Illustration of a BVH built with the binned SAH method. Bounding volumes are subdivided recursively, partitioning geometry into increasingly tight AABBs that reduce the number of intersection tests during traversal, accelerating the SBR pipeline.

3   Methodology and Architecture

The SBR evaluation is organized into a *trace-integrate* pipeline (Fig. 1). For each incident direction, we approximate the incident field using an orthographic bundle of rays originating from a virtual aperture spanning the target's bounding box.

Ray Grid Resolution.   The PO integral (Eq. 1) is evaluated as a discrete sum. If the ray spacing Δs is too large, the sum undersamples the phase variation across the surface, producing spatial aliasing that manifests as nonphysical oscillations in the RCS pattern. To enforce numerical stability and act as a Nyquist-like criterion for the electromagnetic phase, we enforce a strict sampling rule: $\Delta s \leq \lambda/5$. This dictates that as frequency increases, computational workload scales *quadratically*.

BVH Acceleration.   In complex geometries, an exhaustive ray-triangle intersection search is computationally prohibitive. We mitigate this by constructing a Bounding Volume Hierarchy (BVH) over the mesh. While a BVH does not reduce the intrinsic arithmetic cost of a ray-triangle intersection test, it drastically reduces the *search space* by choosing large portions of the geometry using Axis-Aligned Bounding Boxes (AABBs). To optimize tree traversal, we implement two partitioning options: a fast *median split*, which halves the volume along its longest axis, and a binned *Surface Area Heuristic* (SAH). The SAH estimates the expected cost of splitting a parent node P into children L and R. In Eq. 2, $SA(\cdot)$ denotes the surface area of the bounding box, N_L and N_R are the triangle counts in the respective children, and C_T and C_I are the constant computational costs of traversing a node and intersecting a triangle. Algorithm 1 outlines this recursive construction process represented in Fig. 3.

$$C_{\mathrm{SAH}}(P \to L, R) = C_T + C_I \left(\frac{SA(L)}{SA(P)} N_L + \frac{SA(R)}{SA(P)} N_R \right) \tag{2}$$

3.1   GPU Optimizations and Pipeline

Adapting the SBR pipeline for high-throughput GPU execution requires carefully balancing memory locality and warp divergence, diverging from standard graphics ray tracing. We address these computational bottlenecks through different design choices.

Trace-Integrate Decomposition.   To mitigate thread divergence, the workload is decoupled into two GPU kernels. The *trace* kernel (Algorithm 2, Fig. 2) iteratively traverses the BVH, processing up to $B_{\max}$ reflections per ray. To prevent self-intersection from floating-point inaccuracies, secondary ray origins are shifted by a normal-aligned ε-offset [12]. Instead of accumulating the physical optics integral in-flight, which would severely unbalance warp execution times, the trace kernel writes a state record (first-hit normal, path length, bounce count, and validity flag). Rays failing to return to the monostatic receiver are marked invalid. Next, the *integrate* kernel performs the parallel reduction strictly over valid records. This separates the divergent memory-gather operations of ray transport from the arithmetic-heavy PO summation.

Algorithm 1. BVH construction (selectable split)	**Algorithm 2.** Multi-reflection SBR traversal
Require: Triangles T, threshold N_{leaf}, split rule (MEDIAN/SAH) **Ensure:** Linearized arrays `nodes`, `tris` 1: Compute centroids and global AABB; initialize root with T 2: BUILD(root) 3: Linearize nodes (preorder); store triangle ranges 4: **function** BUILD(n) 5: **if** $|T(n)| \le N_{\text{leaf}}$ **then** 6: Mark n as leaf; **return** 7: **end if** 8: Choose split axis/position; partition $T \to T_L, T_R$ 9: Create children L, R with AABBs 10: Parallel: BUILD(L), BUILD(R) 11: **end function**	**Require:** BVH `nodes`, `tris`, ray $(\mathbf{o}, \hat{d})$, max bounces $B_{\max}$ **Ensure:** Valid flag, $\hat{n}_0$, path length R, bounces N 1: $R \leftarrow 0, N \leftarrow 0$; `valid` $\leftarrow$ **false** 2: **for** $b = 1$ to $B_{\max}$ **do** 3: $(\texttt{hit}, t, \hat{n}) \leftarrow$ INTERSECT$(\mathbf{o}, \hat{d}, \texttt{nodes}, \texttt{tris})$ 4: **if** $\neg$`hit` **then** 5: **break** 6: **end if** 7: $\mathbf{x} \leftarrow \mathbf{o} + t\hat{d}$ 8: $R \leftarrow R + t, N \leftarrow N + 1$ 9: **if** $N = 1$ **then** 10: $\hat{n}_0 \leftarrow \hat{n}$; `valid` $\leftarrow$ **true** 11: **end if** 12: $\hat{d} \leftarrow \hat{d} - 2(\hat{d} \cdot \hat{n})\hat{n}$ 13: $\mathbf{o} \leftarrow \mathbf{x} + \varepsilon \hat{n}$ 14: **end for** 15: **return** (`valid`, $\hat{n}_0$, R, N)

State Management and Occupancy. Although orthographic rays initially provide excellent spatial locality and L1 cache utilization, post-reflection rays rapidly diverge. To robustly handle deep, multi-bounce BVH traversal without recursion, we utilize a carefully sized explicit memory stack. By keeping this local state bounded, we minimize per-thread register pressure, which prevents register spilling and maximizes active warps per Streaming Multiprocessor (SM).

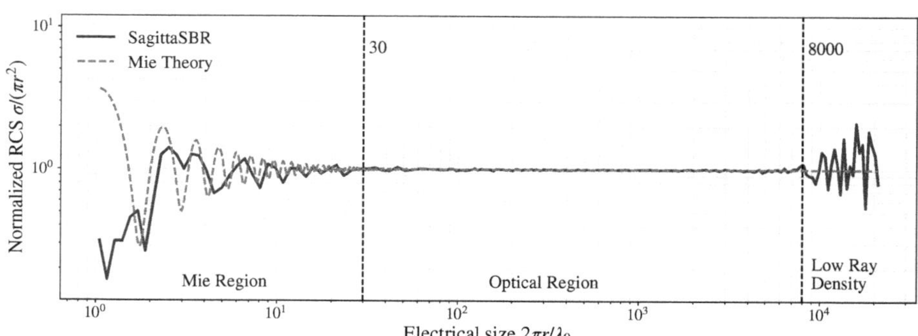

Fig. 4. Frequency scan of monostatic RCS for a triangulated PEC sphere. Here, the ray grid was held constant. The method achieves excellent agreement in the optical region until the shrinking wavelength violates the spatial sampling criterion, causing aliasing.

MPI Distribution. Because a monostatic angular sweep is intrinsically decoupled, we distribute the incident angles across MPI ranks. This coarse-grained parallelization allows each GPU to autonomously compute a subset of the full spherical sweep, reducing communication to zero during the trace-integrate execution.

4   Numerical Results and Performance

4.1   Validation with PEC Sphere

To validate the physical accuracy of the solver, we computed the RCS of a PEC sphere against analytical Mie scattering theory (Fig. 4). Electrical size is defined as $kr = 2\pi r/\lambda$. At $kr < 30$ (the Mie resonance region), ray-based GO+PO approximations are fundamentally inapplicable. However, entering the optical region ($kr \geq 30$), our method accurately captures the scattering physics with a standard deviation of $\sim 2.5\%$. It is important to clarify the breakdown at extreme frequencies ($kr \approx 8,000$). To isolate the effect of frequency across this sweep, the simulation utilized a *constant* launch grid of $22,000 \times 22,000$ rays. Consequently, as the frequency increased (and λ decreased), the fixed grid eventually violated the $\Delta s \leq \lambda/5$ criterion. The undersampling of the wavelength causes the aliasing seen at the far right of the plot.

4.2   Radar Cross Section of Complex Geometries

To evaluate solver performance on electrically large, complex geometries, an A380 aircraft ($80 \times 73 \times 21$ m) was modeled as a PEC object at $10\,\text{GHz}$ ($\lambda \approx 3$ cm). Ensuring the $\lambda/5$ criterion required a dense $30,000 \times 30,000$ launch grid. The full spherical monostatic scan ($125,000$ observation points, max 100 reflections per ray) processed 1.12×10^{14} rays in $\sim 27\,\text{min}$ using 8 nodes of the LUMI supercomputer (32 AMD MI250X GPUs). The resulting heatmap (Fig. 5) clearly identifies high-intensity broadside specular reflections from the fuselage and wings.

Table 1. Kernel-time breakdown for A380 scattering simulations ($18,000 \times 18,000$ rays) using one MPI process. Statistics evaluated over 10 independent trials.

Device	Kernel	time FP32, ms	time FP64, ms	Δ-time
NVIDIA A100 (Full)	Ray Launch	98.96 ± 1.18	151.30 ± 1.75	$+52.9\%$
	PO Integral	6.43 ± 0.09	6.01 ± 0.06	-7.0%
AMD MI250X (1 GCD)	Ray Launch	249.81 ± 0.52	198.70 ± 0.31	-20.5%
	PO Integral	4.83 ± 0.01	7.41 ± 0.01	$+53.4\%$

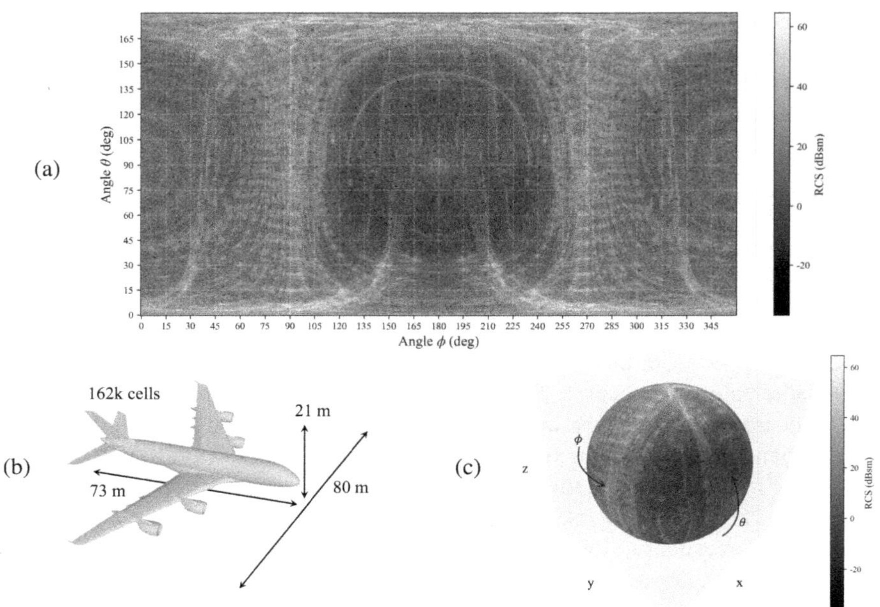

Fig. 5. RCS calculation and geometry for an A380 aircraft. (a) Full angular RCS scan (500 samples in ϕ, 250 in θ at 10 GHz) generated via a 30,000 × 30,000 ray grid. (b) Simulated aircraft model (80 × 73 × 21 m, 162k triangular elements). (c) Visualization of the RCS mapped onto a bounding spherical surface.

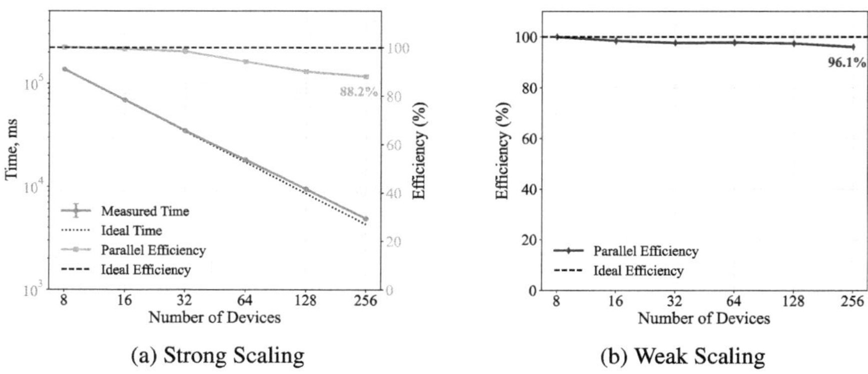

Fig. 6. Scaling performance on LUMI using FP32. The x-axis shows the total number of GCDs utilized on AMD MI250X GPUs. Strong scaling maintains an efficiency of $\sim 88\%$ at 256 GCDs, while weak scaling retains $\sim 96\%$ efficiency.

4.3   Performance, Precision, and Scaling Analysis

The ray generation and intersection kernel dominates the computational workload, accounting for the vast majority of execution time relative to the PO integral reduction. Depending on the incident angle relative to the object's profile, the percentage of rays that actually intersect the target can be as low as 5–10%, meaning standard SBR performs significant intersection searches on invalid rays. This raises an interest for potential early filtering strategies, which could speed-up the process, but would require a simplified hit-detection mechanism, potentially disturbing final accuracy. Table 1 compares this kernel performance across NVIDIA A100 and AMD MI250X architectures. Unlike FP64, in FP32 a slight accumulation error ($\sim 3\%$ deviation) was observed after 100 reflections due to the microscopic phase terms (kR_i). While the NVIDIA A100 shows the expected massive penalty ($\sim 53\%$ slower) when switching to FP64, the AMD MI250X executed the ray launch kernel $\sim 20\%$ *faster* in FP64. This indicates that optimal precision choices in modern SBR solvers must be strictly architecture-aware. Parallel scalability was assessed on the LUMI supercomputer by distributing angular sweeps across MPI ranks (Fig. 6). Strong scaling maintained an excellent efficiency of $\sim 88\%$ at 256 GCDs. Weak scaling, where the base angular workload was scaled proportionally with the number of nodes, retained $\sim 96\%$ efficiency, proving that MPI communication overhead is negligible compared to multi-bounce ray tracing computations.

5   Discussion and Conclusion

We presented an efficient SBR method for evaluating the monostatic RCS of electrically large objects, implemented in the open-source `SagittaSBR`. By enforcing an incident-ray sampling rule, we mitigated the phase aliasing common in discretized PO integrals. The method demonstrated robust scalability across heterogeneous GPU architectures. Future extensions will focus on adding diffraction corrections (e.g., GTD/UTD/PTD) [13,14] to improve fidelity. These extensions introduce additional interaction pathways (e.g., ray spawning) and increase variability in per-ray work, requiring dynamic scheduling and careful memory management. Moreover, because hit-misses constitute a major portion of the workload, future work will explore early filtering heuristics (e.g., rasterizing a bounding silhouette before launch) and directional BVH optimizations, such as angle-specific subtrees, to reduce unnecessary intersection queries.

Acknowledgments. This work has received funding from the Swedish Research Council's Research Environment grant (SEE-6GIA 2024-06482).

References

1. Taygur, M.M., Sukharevsky, I.O., Eibert, T.F.: Computation of antenna transfer functions with a bidirectional ray-tracing algorithm utilizing antenna reciprocity. In: 2018 2nd URSI Atlantic Radio Science Meeting (AT-RASC), Gran Canaria, pp. 1–4. IEEE (2018). https://doi.org/10.23919/URSI-AT-RASC.2018.8471651, https://ieeexplore.ieee.org/document/8471651/

2. Yun, Z., Iskander, M.F.: Ray tracing for radio propagation modeling: principles and applications. IEEE Access **3**, 1089–1100 (2015). https://doi.org/10.1109/ACCESS.2015.2453991, http://ieeexplore.ieee.org/document/7152831/

3. Li, P., Fan, J., Wu, J.: Exploring the key technologies and applications of 6G wireless communication network. iScience **28**(5), 112281 (2025). https://doi.org/10.1016/j.isci.2025.112281, https://linkinghub.elsevier.com/retrieve/pii/S2589004225005425

4. Mittra, R. (ed.): Computational Electromagnetics: Recent Advances and Engineering Applications (2014). https://doi.org/10.1007/978-1-4614-4382-7.

5. Ling, H., Chou, R., Lee, S.: Shooting and bouncing rays: calculating RCS of an arbitrary cavity. In: 1986 Antennas and Propagation Society International Symposium, vol. 24, pp. 293–296 (1986). https://doi.org/10.1109/APS.1986.1149823, https://ieeexplore.ieee.org/document/1149823

6. Sefi, S.: Computational electromagnetics: software development and high frequency modelling of surface currents on perfect conductors. Ph. D. thesis, KTH Royal Institute of Technology, Stockholm (2005). DiVA portal

7. Schiller, M., Knoll, A., Mocker, M., Eibert, T.: GPU accelerated ray launching for high-fidelity virtual test drives of VANET applications. In: 2015 International Conference on High Performance Computing & Simulation (HPCS), Amsterdam, Netherlands, pp. 262–268. IEEE (2015). https://doi.org/10.1109/HPCSim.2015.7237048, http://ieeexplore.ieee.org/document/7237048/

8. Gómez, J., Tayebi, A., Hellín, C.J., Valledor, A., Barranquero, M., Cuadrado-Gallego, J.J.: Accelerated ray launching method for efficient field coverage studies in wide urban areas. Sensors **23**(14), 6412 (2023). https://doi.org/10.3390/s23146412, https://www.mdpi.com/1424-8220/23/14/6412

9. Pasquale, M.: Sagittasbr

10. Balanis, C.A.: Balanis' Advanced Engineering Electromagnetics, 1 edn. Wiley (2023). https://doi.org/10.1002/9781394180042, https://onlinelibrary.wiley.com/doi/book/10.1002/9781394180042

11. Stratton, J.A.: Electromagnetic Theory. McGraw-Hill, New York (1941). https://doi.org/10.1002/9781119134640

12. Kwon, S.J., Im, J., Joo, H.G.: Resolution of self-intersection issue in monte Carlo simulations employing graphics ray tracing technology. Korean Nuclear Society (2023)

13. Kouyoumjian, R.G., Pathak, P.H.: A uniform geometrical theory of diffraction for an edge in a perfectly conducting surface. Proc. IEEE **62**(11), 1448–1461 (1974). https://doi.org/10.1109/PROC.1974.9651, https://ieeexplore.ieee.org/document/1451581

14. Ya, P.: Ufimtsev. Fundamentals of the Physical Theory of Diffraction. Wiley, Hoboken, NJ (2007). https://doi.org/10.1002/0470109017

Interpretable Gravitation-Based Outlier Detection via Density-Guided Mass Adaptation

Agnieszka Duraj[1]([envelope])[iD], Piotr S. Szczepaniak[1][iD], and Daria Rogowska[2]

[1] Institute of Information Technology, Lodz University of Technology, al. Politechniki 8, 93-590 Łódź, Poland
{agnieszka.duraj,piort.szczepaniak}@p.lodz.pl
[2] Accenture Poland, University Business Park, Wólczańska 178, 90-530 Lodz, Poland

Abstract. Centroid-based classifiers are attractive due to their interpretability and low computational cost, yet their performance degrades in the presence of class imbalance, irregular decision boundaries, and local density variations. This paper introduces DG-MA (Density-Guided Mass Adaptation), a gravitation-based model that incorporates local density information into the global structure of the Gravitation Model. The method applies a single batch adaptation of class masses derived from density-based structural statistics, avoiding iterative coupling between clustering and classification. As a result, DG-MA preserves the simplicity of gravitational decision rules while improving robustness to non-uniform data distributions in supervised outlier detection. Experimental results on multiple benchmark datasets show that DG-MA consistently improves over the classical Gravitation Model and remains competitive with density-based methods, while maintaining favourable computational efficiency.

Keywords: gravitation model · outlier detection · local density

1 Introduction

Outlier detection in high-dimensional and imbalanced data remains challenging due to local density variation, irregular class geometry, and the need for computationally efficient decision models. In this study, we consider supervised outlier detection formulated as a binary classification task, where normal observations form the negative class and outliers form the positive class.

Centroid-based models are commonly used due to their simplicity and low computational cost [1]. In particular, the Gravitation Model (GM) represents each class by a centroid and a mass parameter controlling class influence [2–4].

To address this limitation, we propose Density-Guided Mass Adaptation (DG-MA), a hybrid extension of GM in which DBSCAN [5] is used only during training to extract density-based structural statistics. These statistics are

© The Author(s), under exclusive license to Springer Nature Switzerland AG 2026
P. Neumann et al. (Eds.): ICCS 2026, LNCS 16784, pp. 377–385, 2026.
https://doi.org/10.1007/978-3-032-29924-6_31

then aggregated into a single batch correction of class masses, after which inference remains purely centroid-based. As a result, the method combines local density information with a transparent gravitational decision rule while preserving linear-time prediction complexity. Unlike existing Gravitation Model extensions based on iterative learning or misclassification-driven updates, DG-MA introduces a non-iterative density-guided mass adaptation mechanism. This approach preserves analytical interpretability while incorporating local structural information into the model.

The main contributions of this paper are as follows:

- we introduce a density-guided extension of the Gravitation Model for supervised outlier detection;
- we show how density-induced structural errors translate into global mass-ratio adjustments and decision-boundary shifts;
- we experimentally demonstrate that DG-MA improves over GM on several benchmark datasets while maintaining low inference complexity.

The remainder of this paper is organised as follows. Section 2 reviews related work on outlier detection and gravity-based classification models. Section 3 introduces the proposed DG-MA framework and analyses its theoretical properties. The experimental setup and evaluation protocol are described in Sect. 4, while the obtained results are discussed in Sect. 5. Finally, Sect. 6 concludes the paper and outlines directions for future research.

2   Related Work

Outlier detection aims to identify observations that deviate from the underlying data distribution and correspond to rare events [6]. A wide range of approaches has been developed, differing in modelling assumptions, scalability, and interpretability [7,8].

Statistical methods identify outliers as low-probability samples [9], but are sensitive to model mismatch and high dimensionality. Distance-based approaches (e.g., k-NN [10]) rely on neighbourhood dispersion, yet degrade in high-dimensional spaces.

Density-based methods such as LOF, COF, and DBSCAN [5,11,12] detect outliers in low-density regions and capture complex cluster shapes, but are parameter-sensitive and computationally demanding. Machine learning approaches, including one-class SVMs, autoencoders, and ensembles [13–15], model complex patterns but often lack interpretability.

Importantly, methods such as LOF, Isolation Forest, and one-class SVM operate at the instance level, focusing on local deviations rather than explicitly shaping global decision boundaries. Consequently, they do not address geometrically interpretable boundary recalibration in centroid-based models.

In contrast, gravity-based classifiers provide a global and interpretable framework. The Gravitation Model (GM) represents each class by a centroid and mass [2,3], with extensions addressing imbalance and feature weighting [16,17].

However, these approaches remain inherently global and rely on misclassification-driven updates.

Relatively few methods combine global class representations with local density information while preserving interpretability and low inference cost. Existing hybrid approaches often rely on iterative clustering–classification coupling, increasing complexity.

The proposed DG-MA addresses this gap by performing a single density-guided mass correction using DBSCAN, followed by purely centroid-based inference. Unlike prior GM extensions, it uses density-induced structural discrepancies instead of classification errors, preserving interpretability and linear-time prediction.

3 Methods

3.1 Gravitation Model

The Gravitation Model (GM), proposed in [4], is a centroid-based classification method inspired by the law of gravitation. Each class C_j is represented by its centroid c_j and an associated mass M_j, which controls the influence of the class in the feature space. This formulation allows the model to account for class asymmetry and partially compensate for class imbalance.

For an object x, the attraction of class C_j is defined as

$$F(x, c_j) = M_j \cdot sim(x, c_j), \tag{1}$$

where $sim(\cdot, \cdot)$ denotes a similarity function. In this work, we use the regularised inverse Euclidean similarity

$$sim(x, c_j) = \frac{1}{\|x - c_j\|_2 + \varepsilon_{\text{sim}}}, \tag{2}$$

where $\varepsilon_{\text{sim}} > 0$ ensures numerical stability. The predicted label is assigned to the class with the largest attraction force.

Unlike the standard nearest-centroid rule, GM introduces class-specific masses, which provide a more flexible global decision mechanism.

3.2 Density-Guided Mass Adaptation (DG-MA)

DG-MA extends the Gravitation Model by incorporating local density information extracted using DBSCAN. Unlike classical GM learning, class masses are not updated iteratively but determined via a single density-guided correction step.

Let $D_{tr} \subset \mathbb{R}^d$ denote the training set with K classes. Each class C_j is represented by centroid c_j and mass M_j, and prediction follows the standard gravitational rule:

$$\hat{y}(x) = \arg \max_{1 \leq j \leq K} F(x, c_j). \tag{3}$$

DBSCAN assigns cluster labels $L(x)$, with $L(x) = -1$ denoting noise. Each cluster ℓ is mapped to a class via majority voting:

$$\mathrm{map}(\ell) = \arg\max_j |\{x : \; L(x) = \ell \wedge y(x) = C_j\}| . \tag{4}$$

Two class-level structural errors are then defined:

$$\beta_{j1} = |\{x : \; y(x) = C_j, \; (L(x) = -1 \vee \mathrm{map}(L(x)) \neq C_j)\}| , \tag{5}$$

$$\beta_{j2} = |\{x : \; y(x) \neq C_j, \; L(x) \neq -1, \; \mathrm{map}(L(x)) = C_j\}| . \tag{6}$$

These quantify lack of support and contamination. A normalised error is given by

$$\tilde{\beta}_j = \frac{\beta_{j1} + \lambda \beta_{j2}}{|C_j|}, \tag{7}$$

and class masses are adapted as

$$M_j = \max\left(M_{\min}, \; 1 - \alpha\,\tilde{\beta}_j\right). \tag{8}$$

After this single update, DG-MA applies the standard GM decision rule, preserving interpretability and linear-time inference. Since DBSCAN is used only to extract aggregated statistics, the method is less sensitive to parameter variations than instance-level density models.

However, the hard majority mapping may over-penalise minority samples in heterogeneous clusters, potentially leading to over-correction.

3.3   Influence of the Mass Ratio on Decision Boundaries

For two classes C_p and C_q with centroids c_p, c_q and masses M_p, M_q, the decision boundary is defined by

$$M_p\, sim(x, c_p) = M_q\, sim(x, c_q). \tag{9}$$

Using the regularised inverse Euclidean similarity, this yields

$$\frac{\|x - c_p\|_2 + \varepsilon_{\mathrm{sim}}}{\|x - c_q\|_2 + \varepsilon_{\mathrm{sim}}} = \frac{M_p}{M_q}. \tag{10}$$

In the limit $\varepsilon_{\mathrm{sim}} \to 0^+$,

$$\frac{\|x - c_p\|_2}{\|x - c_q\|_2} = \frac{M_p}{M_q}, \tag{11}$$

which defines an Apollonius surface. Thus, the boundary geometry is fully determined by the mass ratio $\frac{M_p}{M_q}$.

In DG-MA, where $M_j = 1 - \alpha\tilde{\beta}_j$, density-induced structural errors directly control boundary shifts: higher $\tilde{\beta}_j$ reduces M_j and contracts the decision region, while lower values expand it.

Hence, DG-MA preserves the analytical form of the classifier while globally adjusting boundaries via mass adaptation.

3.4   Computational Complexity Analysis

In GM, classification requires $O(K \cdot d)$ per instance, yielding $O(n \cdot d)$ for fixed K. DG-MA adds a single DBSCAN execution during training, with complexity ranging from $O(n \cdot d + n \log n)$ to $O(n \cdot d + n^2)$ [18]. Thus, training cost increases, but inference remains $O(K \cdot d)$. Although DG-MA reduces sensitivity to DBSCAN parameters through class-level aggregation, strongly suboptimal configurations may still affect mass estimation.

4   Experiments

The evaluation was conducted on five benchmark datasets reformulated as binary outlier detection tasks: Cardio [19], Vowels [20,21], Musk [22], Chemical [23], and Synthetic [24]. Cardio contains 1831 instances with 21 features (9.6% outliers), Vowels 1456 instances with 12 features (3.4%), Musk 3062 instances with 166 features (3.2%), Chemical 3251 instances with 34 features (6.2%), and Synthetic 1000 instances with 10 features (5.0%).

We compared DBSCAN, the Gravitation Model (GM), and the proposed DG-MA. DBSCAN parameters (ε, $minPts$) were tuned on the training set via grid search maximising $F_{1,\mathrm{out}}$, using an inner validation split within the training data. The same protocol was applied when DBSCAN was used within DG-MA.

All experiments used a 70:30 train–test split with 10 repeated stratified runs. Features were standardised using training-set statistics, and all parameter tuning, including DBSCAN parameters (ε, $minPts$) and DG-MA parameters (α, λ), was performed exclusively on the training data. Performance was evaluated using ROC-AUC, PR-AUC, $F_{1,\mathrm{out}}$, TPR_{out}, and MCC, which together reflect ranking quality and rare-class detection under class imbalance. The same data splits were used for all compared methods to ensure a fair and consistent evaluation.

Although DBSCAN parameters depend on data density, in DG-MA they are used only to extract aggregated structural statistics from the training set. These statistics are computed at the class level and do not rely on precise cluster assignments in the test data. As a result, the method is less sensitive to density variations between training and test sets compared to standard density-based classifiers. Moreover, the use of repeated stratified splits reduces the impact of sampling variability on parameter estimation.

All evaluation metrics are maximised, i.e., values closer to 1 indicate better performance. In particular, $F_{1,\mathrm{out}}$, PR-AUC, and ROC-AUC jointly reflect detection quality under class imbalance. All experiments were implemented in Python using scikit-learn, and code together with parameter settings will be made publicly available upon acceptance.

5   Results

All results are reported on the test set following the protocol described in Sect. 4. A comparison of DBSCAN, GM, and DG-MA is presented in Table 1. All evaluation metrics are maximised (values closer to 1 indicate better performance).

Table 1. Comparison of outlier detection performance for DBSCAN, GM, and DG-MA.

Metric	Dataset/Algorithm														
	Cardio			Vowels			Musk			Chemical			Synthetic		
	DBSCAN	GM	DG-MA	DBSCAN	GM	DG-MA	DBSCAN	GM	DG-MA	DBSCAN	GM	DG-MA	DBSCAN	GM	DG-MA
$F_{1,\text{out}}$	0.52	0.61	0.66	0.62	0.49	0.55	1.00	1.00	1.00	1.00	0.76	0.86	0.84	0.10	0.22
PR–AUC	0.56	0.63	0.64	0.64	0.50	0.55	1.00	1.00	1.00	1.00	0.78	0.88	0.86	0.16	0.38
ROC-AUC	0.71	0.77	0.78	0.77	0.72	0.74	1.00	1.00	1.00	1.00	0.78	0.88	0.88	0.47	0.59

As shown in Table 1, DBSCAN achieves near-perfect performance on Musk and Chemical (all metrics close to 1.0), but degrades under weak separability (Cardio), reflecting limitations of purely local density modelling. GM provides a stable and interpretable global model, performing well on separable datasets but degrading for heterogeneous structures (Vowels, Synthetic).

DG-MA consistently improves over GM in datasets with non-uniform density. The largest gains are observed for Cardio and Vowels, where higher $F_{1,\text{out}}$, PR-AUC, and ROC-AUC indicate improved rare-class detection. On Chemical, DG-MA significantly outperforms GM and approaches DBSCAN. For Musk, all methods achieve near-perfect results, while for Synthetic both GM and DG-MA remain limited.

Results correspond to mean values over 10 repeated splits, with standard deviations below 0.03 for all configurations. The analysis focuses on $F_{1,\text{out}}$, PR-AUC, and ROC-AUC as robust metrics under class imbalance. Additional comparison with classical methods is shown in Table 2.

On Cardio, One-Class SVM achieves the highest ranking performance, while DG-MA remains competitive with LOF. On Vowels, LOF dominates in ranking metrics, whereas DG-MA provides a more balanced precision–recall trade-off. Isolation Forest exhibits high recall but low precision. On Musk, DG-MA achieves near-perfect separation on this dataset. These results confirm that incorporating density information into centroid-based models improves robustness to heterogeneous data distributions while preserving interpretability.

DG-MA differs from instance-level methods by aggregating density information at the class level, enabling a transparent decision mechanism with linear-time inference. Its effectiveness depends on data structure: it is most beneficial for heterogeneous density and moderate overlap, while density-based methods remain preferable for well-separated data and performance remains limited for highly irregular distributions.

The additional computational cost arises from a single DBSCAN execution during training, whereas inference remains identical to GM ($O(K \cdot d)$). All baseline methods were evaluated using the same data splits and evaluation protocol for consistency.

Table 2. Comparison of DG-MA with classical outlier detection methods.

Datasets	Algorithm	ROC-AUC	PR-AUC	$F_{1,\text{out}}$	TPR_{out}
Cardio	LOF	0.9437	0.6268	0.6000	0.6000
	Isolation Forest	0.8021	0.2110	0.1176	0.2000
	One-Class SVM	0.9803	0.8002	0.6804	0.9429
	DG-MA	0.78	0.64	0.66	0.65
Vowels	LOF	0.9897	0.7796	0.7000	0.7000
	Isolation Forest	0.9872	0.7215	0.1301	1.0000
	One-Class SVM	0.8670	0.5460	0.3444	0.5000
	DG-MA	0.74	0.55	0.55	0.51
Musk	LOF	1.0000	1.0000	0.9744	1.0000
	Isolation Forest	0.9553	0.4836	0.2375	1.0000
	One-Class SVM	1.0000	1.0000	0.5846	1.0000
	DG-MA	1.00	1.00	1.00	1.00

6   Conclusions

This paper investigated the Gravitation Model (GM) and its density-guided extension (DG-MA) for binary outlier detection. The proposed method integrates global centroid-based classification with local density information through a single mass adaptation step. The results show that DG-MA improves over GM in datasets with heterogeneous local structure, while preserving interpretability and linear-time inference complexity. At the same time, both models remain effective in well-separated settings, whereas purely density-based methods may be preferable for highly irregular data distributions. Overall, DG-MA provides a favourable trade-off between detection performance, transparency, and computational efficiency by translating local structural inconsistencies into global mass adjustments. These findings suggest that DG-MA is particularly suitable for data with non-uniform density structure and moderate separability, where neither purely global nor purely local methods are sufficient.

The main limitation of the proposed method is its dependence on DBSCAN parameterisation during training, as suboptimal choices of ε and $minPts$ may affect the quality of the extracted structural statistics and the resulting mass adaptation. While DG-MA reduces sensitivity through class-level aggregation, performance may degrade for highly irregular or poorly separable data distributions.

Future work will include a systematic empirical analysis of execution time, the trade-off between computational cost and detection performance, sensitivity to DBSCAN parameter choices, and soft cluster-to-class weighting strategies for heterogeneous clusters.

References

1. Han, J., Kamber, M., Pei, J.: Data Mining: Concepts and Techniques, 3 edn. Morgan Kaufmann (2011)
2. Peng, L., Yang, B., Chen, Y., Abraham, A.: Data gravitation based classification. Inf. Sci. **179**(6), 809–819 (2009)
3. Shafigh, P., Hadi, S.Y., Sohrab, E.: Gravitation based classification. Inf. Sci. **220**, 319–330 (2013)
4. Liu, C., Wang, W., Tu, G., Xiang, Y., Wang, S., Lv, F.: A new centroid-based classification model for text categorization. Knowl.-Based Syst. **136**, 15–26 (2017)
5. Ester, M., Kriegel, H.P., Sander, J., Xu, X.: Density-based spatial clustering of applications with noise. In: International Conference Knowledge Discovery and Data Mining, vol. 240 (1996)
6. Hawkins, D.M.: Identification of Outliers, vol. 11. Springer (1980). https://doi.org/10.1007/978-94-015-3994-4
7. Aggarwal, C.C.: Outlier Analysis, 2nd edn. Springer (2017). https://doi.org/10.1007/978-3-319-47578-3
8. Chandola, V., Banerjee, A., Kumar, V.: Anomaly detection: a survey. ACM Comput. Surv. (CSUR) **41**(3), 1–58 (2009)
9. Barnett, V., Lewis, T.: Outliers in Statistical Data, 3rd edn. Wiley (1994)
10. Ramaswamy, S., Rastogi, R., Shim, K.: Efficient algorithms for mining outliers from large data sets. In: Proceedings of the 2000 ACM SIGMOD International Conference on Management of Data, pp. 427–438 (2000)
11. Breunig, M.M., Kriegel, H.P., Ng, R.T., Sander, J.: LOF: identifying density-based local outliers. In: Proceedings of the 2000 ACM SIGMOD International Conference on Management of Data, pp. 93–104 (2000)
12. Tang, C., He, Z., Kao, B.K.: Enhancing effectiveness of outlier detections for low density patterns. In: Advances in Knowledge Discovery and Data Mining, pp. 535–548. PAKDD (2002)
13. Schölkopf, B., Platt, J.C., Shawe-Taylor, J., Smola, A.J., Williamson, R.C.: Estimating the support of a high-dimensional distribution. Neural Comput. **13**(7), 1443–1471 (2001)
14. Sakurada, M., Yairi, T.: Anomaly detection using autoencoders with nonlinear dimensionality reduction. In: Proceedings of the MLSDA 2014 2nd Workshop on Machine Learning for Sensory Data Analysis, pp. 4–11 (2014)
15. Zimek, A., Schubert, E., Kriegel, H.P.: Ensembles for unsupervised outlier detection: challenges and research questions a position paper. ACM SIGKDD Explor. Newsl. **15**(1), 11–22 (2014)
16. Peng, L., Zhang, H., Yang, B., Chen, Y.: A new approach for imbalanced data classification based on data gravitation. Inf. Sci. **288**, 347–373 (2014)
17. Peng, L., Zhang, H., Zhang, H., Yang, B.: A fast feature weighting algorithm of data gravitation classification. Inf. Sci. **375**, 54–78 (2017)
18. Schubert, E., Sander, J., Ester, M., Kriegel, H.P., Xu, X.: DBSCAN revisited, revisited: why and how you should (still) use DBSCAN. ACM Trans. Database Syst. (TODS) **42**(3), 1–21 (2017)
19. Rayana, S.: Cardiotocography dataset (2016). http://odds.cs.stonybrook.edu/cardiotocography-dataset/
20. Rayana, S.: Japanese vowels dataset (2016). http://odds.cs.stonybrook.edu/japanese-vowels-data/

21. Kudo, M., Toyama, J., Shimbo, M.: Japanese vowels data set. In: UCI Machine Learning Repository (1999)
22. Rayana, S.: Musk dataset (2016). http://odds.cs.stonybrook.edu/musk-dataset/
23. Rayana, S.: Odds library (2016)
24. Koncar, P.: Synthetic dataset for outlier detection (2018)

MeshSplats: Mesh-Based Rendering
with Gaussian Splatting Initialization

Rafał Tobiasz[1,2,4]([✉]) [iD], Grzegorz Wilczyński[1,2,4] [iD], Marcin Mazur[1] [iD],
Sławomir Tadeja[3] [iD], Weronika Smolak-Dyżewska[1,2] [iD],
and Przemysław Spurek[1,4] [iD]

[1] Faculty of Mathematics and Computer Science, Jagiellonian University,
Kraków, Poland
[2] Doctoral School of Exact and Natural Sciences, Jagiellonian University,
Kraków, Poland
`rafal.tobiasz@doctoral.uj.edu.pl`
[3] Department of Engineering, University of Cambridge, Cambridge, UK
[4] IDEAS Research Institute, Warsaw, Poland

Abstract. Gaussian Splatting (GS) is an emerging, pivotal technique in 3D computer graphics. Most GS-based algorithms exclude the use of classical methods such as ray tracing, which offer numerous inherent advantages in rendering. For example, ray tracing can handle incoherent rays for advanced lighting effects, including shadows and reflections. To address this issue, we introduce MeshSplats, a method which converts GS to a mesh-like format. Following the completion of training, MeshSplats transforms Gaussian elements into mesh faces, enabling rendering using ray tracing methods with all their associated benefits. Our model can be used immediately after transformation, yielding a mesh without additional training, with only a slight reduction in reconstruction quality. We can enhance the quality by applying a dedicated optimization algorithm that operates on mesh faces rather than Gaussian components. Importantly, MeshSplats acts as a wrapper, converting pre-trained GS models into a ray-traceable format. The efficacy of our method is substantiated by experimental results, underscoring its extensive applications in computer graphics and image processing.

Keywords: Gaussian Splatting · Ray Tracing · Mesh Generation ·
Novel View Synthesis · 3D Computer Graphics

1 Introduction

Classical meshes enable rapid rendering [2], which can be coupled with ray tracing to handle incoherent rays for secondary lighting effects, such as shadows and reflections [13]. Unfortunately, training meshes directly on 2D images is challenging. In contrast, Gaussian Splatting (GS) [8] offers high-quality, real-time

R. Tobiasz and G. Wilczyński—Equal contribution.

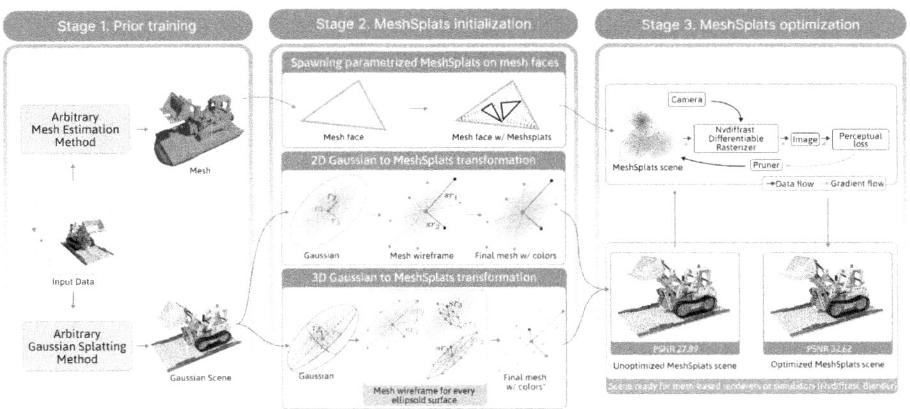

Fig. 1. MeshSplats features two modes: (1) a GS prior, converting trained GS ellipses into fan-type meshes (with optional fine-tuning), and (2) a Mesh prior, training triangles directly on external meshes [14,17].

3D reconstruction, but its reliance on rasterization complicates the addition of lighting or reflections [8,10]. Consequently, recent methods combine GS with ray tracing to achieve such effects [1,9,10], but they require dedicated renderers.

We address these limitations with MeshSplats, which converts GS into a disjoint mesh-like representation natively renderable in standard pipelines like Blender[1] or Nvdiffrast[2]. Rather than approximating macro-geometry, Mesh-Splats acts as a wrapper, transforming individual Gaussians into independent, semi-transparent colored polygons. This enables out-of-the-box ray tracing with complex lighting. We then fine-tune these meshes to mitigate artifacts from ellipse-to-polygon conversion.

While applicable to all GS models (Fig. 1), MeshSplats is particularly effective for flat Gaussians, as their planar morphology simplifies conversion into mesh faces compared to volumetric 3D Gaussians. MeshSplats supports two scenarios (Fig. 1). Using a *GS prior*, it wraps models into disjoint fan-type meshes with minimal tuning, prioritizing render quality over editability. Alternatively, using a *mesh prior* from external tools [14,17], MeshSplats overlays semi-transparent triangle faces onto a classical geometry mesh. This two-level setup requires more fine-tuning but permits direct manual shape editing. Both seamlessly integrate complex lighting in standard pipelines.

Our contributions are as follows:

- MeshSplats, a novel method converting flat Gaussians into mesh-based formats for direct integration with classical 3D tools;
- native support for traditional rendering environments, eliminating the need for specialized GS renderers;

---

[1] https://www.blender.org.
[2] https://nvlabs.github.io/nvdiffrast.

(a) Qualitative comparison

(b) Classical rendering tools

Fig. 2. (a) Qualitative results: GT, MeshSplats, and 3DGS (w/o SH). Rows 1-2: Mip-NeRF360 (res 4). Row 3: "Truck" scene. **(b)** MeshSplats supports simulations and rendering in classical tools (e.g., Blender, Nvdiffrast).

– an optimization pipeline that reduces conversion artifacts, refining geometric details for photorealistic rendering.

2   Related Works

3D Gaussian Splatting (3DGS) [8] represented scenes as anisotropic Gaussians optimized by differentiable rasterization. Extensions like Mip-Splatting [20] reduced aliasing, while 2DGS [6] improved surface alignment. However, these methods rely on spherical harmonics to approximate view-dependent effects, resulting in blurry reflections under complex lighting. Works like GaussianShader [7] and 3DGS-DR [19] incorporated environment maps for distant reflections. 3iGS [15] introduced illumination fields via tensorial factorization, but bounded scene assumptions limit real-world use. Crucially, all these methods rely on rasterization, which struggles with incoherent rays needed for effects like shadows and interreflections.

Various works sought to overcome rasterization issues by integrating GS with ray tracing. 3D Gaussian Ray Tracing (3DGRT) [10] yields excellent visual effects by encompassing each Gaussian in bounding primitives for efficient ray tracing. Similarly, RaySplats [1] used ellipses as an approximation instead of bounding primitives, and LinPrim [9] employed linear primitives (e.g., octahedra and tetrahedra) for differentiable volumetric rendering. Other methods, such as EnvGS [18], introduced environment Gaussians to model reflections, while IRGS [4] proposed differentiable 2D Gaussian ray tracing for inverse rendering.

While these methods highlight the massive potential of ray tracing and enable advanced lighting effects, they all inherit the structural limitations of GS: they require complex Monte Carlo sampling or necessitate highly specialized, custom environments for both training and rendering. In contrast, our approach directly outputs universally compatible meshes.

3   MeshSplats with Gaussian Splatting Prior

The core of our approach consists of three straightforward steps. First, we use classical GS to create a collection of Gaussians. Next, we apply MeshSplats to transform Gaussian elements into separate mesh faces that approximate their shapes while preserving color and opacity. This step results in a high-quality reconstruction (Fig. 2), although minor artifacts may still be visible. Finally, we refine this representation as in GS, using separate mesh faces instead of Gaussians. Figure 1 demonstrates the scheme of MeshSplats transformation.

Gaussian Splatting. The GS reconstructs a 3D scene using 3D Gaussians, each defined as $(\mathcal{N}(\mathbf{m}, \Sigma), \sigma, c)$, where $\mathbf{m}$ is the mean (position), Σ is the covariance matrix, σ is the opacity, and c is the color. Colors are typically represented with Spherical Harmonics (SH) [3,11], but can be replaced with standard RGB at a slight cost to view-dependent quality. In MeshSplats, we use RGB colors for mesh compatibility, enabling external lighting with a minor loss in quality.

MeshSplats Transformation for Flat Gaussians. While several approaches use flat Gaussians [5,6,16], we adopt the GaMeS representation [16], defined as $\mathcal{N}(\mathbf{m}, R, S)$, where $S = \mathrm{diag}(\varepsilon, s_2, s_3)$ enforces flatness and $R = [\mathbf{r}_1, \mathbf{r}_2, \mathbf{r}_3]$. Discarding the negligible s_1 dimension, we approximate each 2D Gaussian as a triangle fan inscribed in an ellipse (Fig. 1).

This mapping uses three hyperparameters: $scale\_mul = 2.7$, no_triag, and $opac\_mul$. The ellipse axes are defined as scaled$_$rot$_k = scale_mul \cdot \exp(s_{k+1}) \cdot \mathbf{r}_{k+1}$ for $k \in \{1, 2\}$. We construct the triangle fan by sampling no_triag boundary vertices $\mathbf{v}_i$ via evenly distributed angles $\theta_i \in [-\pi, \pi]$:

$$\mathbf{v}_i = \mathbf{m} + \cos(\theta_i) \cdot \text{scaled\_rot}_1 + \sin(\theta_i) \cdot \text{scaled\_rot}_2. \tag{1}$$

Vertices inherit the Gaussian's RGB color. To simulate the Gaussian fall-off, opacity is linearly interpolated: the center ($\mathbf{m}$) keeps the exact opacity, while boundary vertices ($\mathbf{v}_i$) are scaled by $opac\_mul$.

MeshSplats Transformation for 3D Gaussians. The 3D Gaussians transformation into meshes builds upon the 2D methodology but extends it to three dimensions. Instead of discarding the smallest scale, all three scale constants (s_1, s_2, s_3) and rotation vectors $(\mathbf{r}_1, \mathbf{r}_2, \mathbf{r}_3)$ are retained to compute three orthogonal principal axes. Using the same hyperparameters, no_triag points are generated along the boundaries of the three orthogonal surfaces spanned by these axes. Shared points at surface intersections are merged to avoid redundant vertices and ensure a seamless mesh. Triangle fans are assigned to each of the three

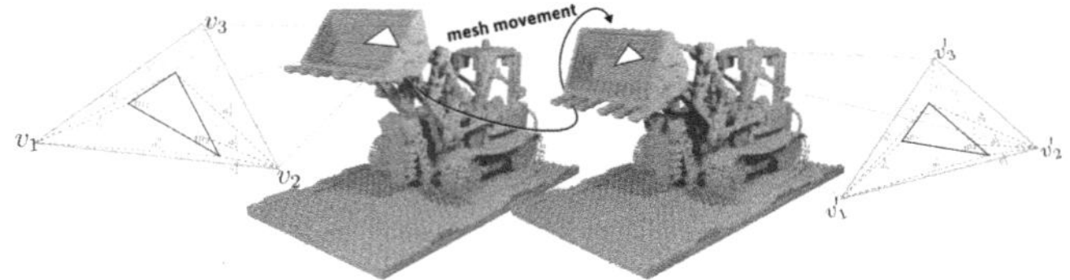

Fig. 3. Using an external mesh prior, MeshSplats employs a base geometry mesh for shape and a parameterized MeshSplats-generated mesh of disjoint triangles, allowing manual editing.

Before optimization   After optimization

Fig. 4. Before (left) and after (right) MeshSplats optimization in Nvdiffrast. The optimized result eliminates floaters and reconstructs missing fine structures (red), like bicycle spokes. (Color figure online)

surfaces, resulting in $3 \cdot no\_triag$ triangles per Gaussian. Color and opacity are assigned exactly as in the 2D case. While this captures the full 3D spatial extent, it results in higher vertex counts, increasing memory usage and rendering time (Fig. 4).

MeshSplats Rendering and Fine-tuning. To refine the mesh soup and eliminate conversion artifacts, we fine-tune the vertices against ground-truth target scenes. The mesh is rasterized using Nvdiffrast [12], which employs a standard model-view-projection (MVP) matrix and depth-peeling to accurately composite overlapping transparent geometry. We optimize the vertex colors and opacities (learning rate lr_{color}) as well as their positions ($lr_{\text{verts}} = \exp(-3) \cdot lr_{\text{color}}$) using a loss function that blends L_1 and structural similarity: $\mathcal{L} = \lambda \cdot L_1(\hat{y}, y) + (1 - \lambda) \cdot \text{SSIM}(\hat{y}, y)$, where $\lambda = 0.6$. To ensure efficiency, a pruning step is executed every 10 epochs. Faces are deleted if all their vertices fall below an opacity threshold of $\exp(-4)$, and orphaned vertices are subsequently removed.

4   MeshSplats with Mesh Prior

When using MeshSplats with a GS prior, we achieve high-quality renderings via a simple, efficient transformation. However, the resulting mesh is optimized solely for rendering and lacks precise geometric accuracy, making it unsuitable for detailed shape approximation. Editing these meshes in Blender resembles manipulating point clouds, akin to GaMeS [16]. To overcome this, we integrate external mesh estimation tools as priors [5]. MeshSplats utilizes the estimated geometry mesh as a base, and constructs a secondary layer composed of disjoint, colored triangles with associated opacity attributes directly on top of it. This approach uses standard triangular elements instead of the fan-type meshes typical of the GS prior, significantly reducing the total face count and enabling precise control over rendering quality and manual editing (Fig. 3). Training is efficiently constrained to the geometry mesh surface, and the initialization of secondary triangles is directly based on the faces of this mesh.

Consider a single triangular face of the geometry mesh with vertices: $M = \{\mathbf{m}_1, \mathbf{m}_2, \mathbf{m}_3\} \subset \mathbb{R}^3$. Each vertex $\mathbf{v}_i$ of a new triangle $V = \{\mathbf{v}_1, \mathbf{v}_2, \mathbf{v}_3\}$ is expressed as a convex combination of the geometry face vertices: $\mathbf{v}_i(\alpha_1, \alpha_2, \alpha_3) = \alpha_1 \mathbf{m}_1 + \alpha_2 \mathbf{m}_2 + \alpha_3 \mathbf{m}_3$, where the trainable parameters $\alpha_1, \alpha_2, \alpha_3$ satisfy $\alpha_1 + \alpha_2 + \alpha_3 = 1$ and $\alpha_1, \alpha_2, \alpha_3 \geq 0$, see Fig. 3. This ensures that all generated triangles remain within the bounds of the original geometry mesh and are therefore optimally positioned for rendering.

To maintain consistency and efficiency, MeshSplats employs a fixed number of triangles per mesh face. MeshSplats is fine-tuned using Nvdiffrast, following a process analogous to that used for the GS prior. This hierarchical and parameterized structure facilitates seamless integration with standard graphics pipelines and manual mesh-editing workflows, enabling advanced editing capabilities.

5   Experiments

In this section, we present the outcomes of our experimental study. For all quantitative comparisons (Table 1), we employed MeshSplats with a GS prior to achieve optimal visual quality, as our mesh-prior mode prioritizes editability and geometric control.

Furthermore, we elucidate the behavior of our algorithm after parametrization and training.

Quantitative Results. We evaluated the performance of MeshSplats across three benchmark datasets (Table 1). On the Mip-NeRF360 and Tanks and Temples datasets, results were highly comparable to existing methods, aligning closely with state-of-the-art approaches like 3DGS [8] and RaySplats [1]. Despite its mesh-based representation, our method achieved scores matching standard rasterization-based techniques. Noteworthy is MeshSplats's superior performance on the Deep Blending dataset among RGB-based methods, suggesting high efficacy in managing intricate indoor geometries and transparency.

Table 1. Quantitative comparison. Despite being mesh-based, MeshSplats matches rasterization methods on Mip-NeRF360 and Tanks and Temples, and excels on Deep Blending (indoor scenes). Dashes indicate that baseline results are unavailable for specific datasets.

		Mip-NeRF360			Tanks and Temples			Deep Blending		
		SSIM ↑	PSNR ↑	LPIPS ↓	SSIM ↑	PSNR ↑	LPIPS ↓	SSIM ↑	PSNR ↑	LPIPS ↓
Spherical Harmonics	MobileNeRF	0.527	23.06	0.430	–	–	–	–	–	–
	NeRF2Mesh	0.523	22.74	0.460	–	–	–	–	–	–
	Plenoxels	0.670	23.63	0.440	0.379	21.08	0.795	0.510	23.06	0.510
	INGP-Base	0.725	26.43	–	0.723	21.72	0.330	0.797	23.62	0.423
	INGP-Big	0.751	26.75	0.300	0.745	21.92	0.305	0.817	24.96	0.390
	M-NeRF360	0.844	**29.23**	–	0.759	22.22	0.257	0.901	29.40	0.245
	3DGS-30K	**0.87**	28.69	0.220	**0.841**	23.14	**0.183**	**0.903**	**29.41**	**0.243**
	3DGRT	0.854	28.71	0.250	0.830	**23.20**	0.222	0.900	29.23	0.315
	GS-IR	0.812	26.57	0.238	–	–	–	–	–	–
	LinPrim	0.803	26.63	0.221	–	–	–	–	–	–
	RadiantFoam	0.830	28.47	**0.210**	–	–	–	0.890	28.95	0.260
RGB	RaySplats	**0.846**	27.31	0.237	**0.829**	**22.20**	**0.202**	**0.900**	**29.57**	0.320
	MeshSplats (our)	0.817	**28.08**	**0.229**	0.766	21.71	0.248	0.890	29.50	**0.254**

Qualitative Results. Nvdiffrast renders of MeshSplats visually match 3DGS without spherical harmonics (Fig. 2). Both methods exhibit similar artifacts when approximating reflections on transparent surfaces like glass. Although MeshSplats yields marginally coarser reconstructions in high-frequency regions (e.g., dense grass), its overall fidelity remains comparable to 3DGS. Furthermore, Blender's EEVEE engine (Fig. 2) seamlessly renders MeshSplats with coherent geometry, accurate colors, and functional physical light interactions.

6 Conclusions

In this paper, we present MeshSplats, a method that addresses the limitations of GS by transforming it into a mesh-like structure compatible with ray tracing. This enables enhanced rendering with improved lighting, shadows, and reflections. MeshSplats provides an efficient and practical solution that can be further refined through our optimization algorithm. Extensive experiments confirm its effectiveness and versatility across diverse datasets. Despite using a mesh-based representation, MeshSplats achieves photorealistic quality that is comparable to or better than GS, eliminating floaters and refining structural details. These results highlight MeshSplats as a strong alternative for high-quality rendering in computer graphics.

The main limitation of MeshSplats is that artifacts such as fragmented geometry and inconsistent opacity can appear in large, low-texture areas because mesh-based interpolation struggles to mimic the smooth falloff of Gaussians.

Acknowledgments. The project "Effective rendering of 3D objects using Gaussian Splatting in an Augmented Reality environment" (FENG.02.02-IP.05-0114/23) is carried out within the First Team programme of the Foundation for Polish Science cofinanced by the European Union under the European Funds for Smart Economy 2021-2027 (FENG).

References

1. Byrski, K., et al.: Raysplats: ray tracing based gaussian splatting. arXiv preprint arXiv:2501.19196 (2025)
2. Foley, J.D., Van Dam, A., Feiner, S.K., Hughes, J.F., Phillips, R.L.: Introduction to Computer Graphics, vol. 55. Addison-Wesley Reading (1994)
3. Fridovich-Keil, S., Yu, A., Tancik, M., Chen, Q., Recht, B., Kanazawa, A.: Plenoxels: radiance fields without neural networks. In: CVPR, pp. 5501–5510 (2022)
4. Gu, C., Wei, X., Zeng, Z., Yao, Y., Zhang, L.: IRGS: inter-reflective gaussian splatting with 2D gaussian ray tracing. arXiv preprint arXiv:2412.15867 (2024)
5. Guédon, A., Lepetit, V.: Sugar: surface-aligned gaussian splatting for efficient 3D mesh reconstruction and high-quality mesh rendering. In: CVPR (2024)
6. Huang, B., Yu, Z., Chen, A., Geiger, A., Gao, S.: 2D gaussian splatting for geometrically accurate radiance fields. In: ACM SIGGRAPH 2024 Conference Papers, pp. 1–11 (2024)
7. Jiang, Y., et al.: Gaussianshader: 3D gaussian splatting with shading functions for reflective surfaces. In: Proceedings of the IEEE/CVF Conference on Computer Vision and Pattern Recognition, pp. 5322–5332 (2024)
8. Kerbl, B., Kopanas, G., Leimkühler, T., Drettakis, G.: 3D gaussian splatting for real-time radiance field rendering. ACM Trans. Graph. **42**(4), 139–1 (2023)
9. von Lützow, N., Nießner, M.: Linprim: linear primitives for differentiable volumetric rendering. arXiv preprint arXiv:2501.16312 (2025)
10. Moenne-Loccoz, N., et al.: 3D gaussian ray tracing: fast tracing of particle scenes. ACM Trans. Graph. (TOG) **43**(6), 1–19 (2024)
11. Müller, T., Evans, A., Schied, C., Keller, A.: Instant neural graphics primitives with a multiresolution hash encoding. ACM Trans. Graph. (ToG) **41**(4), 1–15 (2022)
12. Munkberg, J., et al.: Extracting triangular 3D models, materials, and lighting from images. In: Proceedings of the IEEE/CVF Conference on Computer Vision and Pattern Recognition, pp. 8280–8290 (2022)
13. Peddie, J.: Ray Tracing: A Tool for All, 1st edn. Springer Publishing Company, Incorporated (2019). https://doi.org/10.1007/978-3-030-17490-3
14. Rosu, R.A., Behnke, S.: PermutoSDF: fast multi-view reconstruction with implicit surfaces using permutohedral lattices. In: Proceedings of the IEEE/CVF Conference on Computer Vision and Pattern Recognition, pp. 8466–8475 (2023)
15. Tang, Z.J., Cham, T.J.: 3iGS: factorised tensorial illumination for 3D gaussian splatting. In: European Conference on Computer Vision, pp. 143–159. Springer, Cham (2025). https://doi.org/10.1007/978-3-031-72630-9_9
16. Waczyńska, J., Borycki, P., Tadeja, S., Tabor, J., Spurek, P.: Games: mesh-based adapting and modification of gaussian splatting. arXiv preprint arXiv:2402.01459 (2024)
17. Wang, P., Liu, L., Liu, Y., Theobalt, C., Komura, T., Wang, W.: NeuS: learning neural implicit surfaces by volume rendering for multi-view reconstruction. arXiv preprint arXiv:2106.10689 (2021)
18. Xie, T., et al.: EnvGS: modeling view-dependent appearance with environment gaussian. arXiv preprint arXiv:2412.15215 (2024)

19. Ye, K., Hou, Q., Zhou, K.: 3D gaussian splatting with deferred reflection. In: ACM SIGGRAPH 2024 Conference Papers, pp. 1–10 (2024)
20. Yu, Z., Chen, A., Huang, B., Sattler, T., Geiger, A.: Mip-splatting: alias-free 3D gaussian splatting. In: Proceedings of the IEEE/CVF Conference on Computer Vision and Pattern Recognition, pp. 19447–19456 (2024)

A New Concept of Partial Domination and Algorithms for the Directed Feedback Vertex Set Problem

Sylwester Swat[(✉)] and Marta Kasprzak

Poznan University of Technology, Institute of Computing Science, Piotrowo 2, 61-138 Poznań, Poland
`sylwester.swat@put.poznan.pl`

Abstract. In the Directed Feedback Vertex Set problem (DFVS) one seeks a minimum-size set of vertices whose removal makes a given directed graph acyclic. The problem is known to be NP-complete. It is therefore natural to address it using heuristic methods and preprocessing techniques. In contrast to many other combinatorial optimization problems, however, a limited number of data reduction rules are known for the DFVS. Here we introduce a new concept of partial domination and develop data reduction rules derived from this notion. Moreover, we present a linear-time algorithm for identifying cycle-dominators, a problem of considerable importance in various areas of computational science, most notably in control-flow graph analysis. We provide a thorough analysis of the proposed algorithms, along with results from computational experiments that demonstrate their practical effectiveness.

Keywords: Induced acyclic graph · Data reduction rules · Domination

1 Introduction

One of the classical NP-complete problems in graph theory is the Directed Feedback Vertex Set problem (DFVS). Given a directed graph, the goal is to determine a minimum-size set of vertices whose removal renders the graph acyclic. The problem arises in numerous practical applications. It plays an important role, e.g., in argumentation frameworks [6] and is relevant in the design of very-large-scale integration (VLSI) circuits [11]. Due to its theoretical and practical relevance, the DFVS was selected as the focus problem of the 7th Parameterized Algorithms and Computational Experiments Challenge (PACE 2022), an international algorithm engineering competition organized annually since 2016.

It is well known that the DFVS is NP-hard [7] and fixed-parameter tractable (FPT) with respect to the solution size. Determining its parameterized tractability was posed as an open question in early foundational works on fixed-parameter algorithms [5], and it took considerable time before an FPT algorithm was finally discovered. In a breakthrough result [3], an algorithm with running time $O(4^k k! k^4 n^4)$ was presented, establishing the FPT status of the DFVS. Although

P. Neumann et al. (Eds.): ICCS 2026, LNCS 16784, pp. 395–403, 2026.
https://doi.org/10.1007/978-3-032-29924-6_33

subsequent improvements refined the polynomial factors (e.g., [15] gives an $O(4^k k! k^5 (n+m))$ algorithm) and an improvement of the algorithm, with a running time $O(k! k^5 2^{o(k)}(n+m))$, has been presented [18], the dependence on k remains prohibitive for practical purposes. Despite the close relationship to the Vertex Cover problem, the two problems differ significantly in practical difficulty.

Data reduction techniques play a crucial role in accelerating solution methods. Several reduction rules have been known for years [13,14], and many new rules have been introduced recently, often as byproducts of submissions to the PACE 2022 challenge [1,2,4,12,16]. Nevertheless, compared to the extensive body of kernelization results and reduction techniques for the Vertex Cover, the repertoire of preprocessing methods for the DFVS remains relatively limited.

In this work we propose data reduction rules for the DFVS based on a new concept of partial domination. We also present a surprisingly simple linear-time algorithm for finding cycle-dominators in directed graphs and incorporate it to improve performance of designed rules. Although several algorithms for finding dominators in directed graphs exist (which can be used to find cycle-dominators) [8,10,17], the only known linear-time algorithm for the problem is highly complex. In the end, we provide results and analysis of a conducted computational experiment and evaluate the impact of designed algorithms on preprocessing.

2   Notions and Definitions

We begin by introducing terminology and notation used throughout the paper. Let $G = (V, A)$ be a directed graph. An arc $(u, v) \in A$ is called a *pi-arc* if $(v, u) \in A$, otherwise (u, v) is referred to as a *nonpi-arc*. Let $A_{pi} \subseteq A$ be the set of all pi-arcs. The *pi-graph* G_{pi} is the subgraph of G induced by A_{pi}, that is, $G_{pi} = G[A_{pi}]$. Analogously, let A_{npi} denote the set of all nonpi-arcs, and define the *nonpi-graph* $G_{npi} = G[A_{npi}]$. A vertex $v \in V$ is called a *pi-node* if every arc incident to v is a pi-arc. Otherwise, v is called a *nonpi-node*. For a vertex $v \in V$, we denote by $N^+(v)$ its out-neighborhood and by $N^-(v)$ its in-neighborhood. We define $N^{pi}(v) = N^-(v) \cap N^+(v)$. Furthermore, we write $N^-_{npi}(v) = N^-_{G_{npi}}(v)$ and $N^+_{npi}(v) = N^+_{G_{npi}}(v)$ for the in- and out-neighborhoods of v in the nonpi-graph G_{npi}. The closed neighborhood of v is denoted by $N[v] = N(v) \cup \{v\}$, and analogously for N^-, N^+, and N^{pi}. A *chordless cycle* is a cycle C such that the induced graph $G[C]$ is a cycle. The *contraction* of a vertex $v \in V$ consists of adding all missing arcs from $(N^-(v) \times N^+(v)) \setminus A$ to the graph, and subsequently removing the vertex v together with all arcs incident to it. For a given pair of distinct nodes $s, t \in V$ and node $u \in V$, we say that node u dominates node s with respect to node t if every path from s to t contains node u. We also say that a vertex u *cycle-dominates* a vertex v if u belongs to every directed cycle that contains v.

3   Partial Domination Concept and New Reduction Rules

Before we proceed to the description of new data reduction rules, let us mention the following easy observation, which is a basis for many data reduction rules:

Lemma 1. *A set $S \subset V$ hits the set of all cycles in a directed graph G if and only if it hits the set of all chordless cycles in G.*

Let us now describe the new concept of domination, we called *partial domination*. By *partial contraction* of node $v \in V$ we mean the procedure of adding to the graph all arcs from the set $(N_{npi}^-(v) \times N_{npi}^+(v)) \setminus A$ and removing from the graph all nonpi-arcs incident to v. By partially contracting a node, it is effectively removed from any oriented cycle of length greater than two, and this significantly reduces the graph's structure and increases chances of applying other rules.

Reduction 1 (partial-domination-1). Let $v \in V$ and let $U \subseteq V$ be such that $G_{npi}[U]$ is a path or a cycle that contains v. Denote the path or cycle by $P = (u_0, u_1, \dots, u_p)$ and let k be such an index that $u_k = v$. If $|N_{npi}^-(u_i)| = 1$ for all $0 < i \leq k$, $|N_{npi}^+(u_i)| = 1$ for all $k \leq i < p$, and $N^{pi}(v) \subseteq \bigcup_{u \in U} N^{pi}(u)$, then node v can be partially contracted.

Theorem 1. *Reduction rule 1 is safe. Existence of a partially contractable node $v \in V$ can be checked in total time $O(|A|)$.*

Proof. Let S be an optimal solution for G and let S' be an optimal solution for G after partially contracting v (G'). From a previous remark if follows that a solution for G' is also a solution for G, hence we have $|S'| \geq |S|$. We now prove that $|S'| \leq |S|$. If S is a solution for G', then the condition holds, and we are done. Assume then that S is not a feedback vertex set of G'. This can only be the case if $v \in S$, as otherwise all cycles in G' are hit by S. If $N^{pi}(v) \subseteq S$, then the set $S^* = S \setminus \{v\} \cup \{u_0\}$ is a solution for G' and we have $|S'| \leq |S^*| = |S|$, and we are done. Suppose now that there exists $w \in N^{pi}(v)$ such that $w \notin S$. From condition $N^{pi}(v) \subseteq \bigcup_{u \in U} N^{pi}(u)$ it follows that there exists $u \in U$ such that $u \in S$. Hence S is also a feedback vertex set of G', because the in-degree and out-degree conditions imply that all chordless cycles of length larger than three in G that contain v are hit by u. A contradiction to the assumption that S is not a feedback vertex set of G'. This completes the proof of safeness.

To determine the existence of a partially contractable node in linear time, it is enough to see that all nodes v and corresponding best candidate paths (or cycles) P can be considered by starting a DFS traversal only from nodes u_1 for which $N^-(u_1) = \{u_0\}$ and $deg^+(u_0) > 1$ (or any node in P if it is an isolated cycle in G_{npi}) and counting, by dynamically updating array entries, for each node $w \in V$ the number $|N^{pi}(w) \cap P|$. Traversing over P a second time, we check for each $v \in P \setminus \{u_0, u_p\}$ whether $|N^{pi}(w) \cap P| > 1$ for each $w \in N^{pi}(v)$, which is equivalent to the condition $N^{pi}(v) \subseteq \bigcup_{u \in U} N^{pi}(u)$.

The first partial domination rule is particularly useful for graphs for which G_{npi} contains long, trivially induced paths, as it significantly simplifies the graph's structure by bringing it somewhat "closer" to the vertex cover problem. Even if the structure of G_{npi} does not contain long induced paths, it might still be possible to apply a similar approach. Instead of considering paths ending in a node v, we consider a set of all cycle-dominators of node v in G_{npi}.

Reduction 2 (partial-domination-2). Let U be a set of all cycle-dominators of a node v in G_{npi}. If $N^{pi}(v) \subseteq \bigcup_{u \in U} N^{pi}(u)$, then v can be partially contracted.

Theorem 2. *Reduction rule 2 is safe. Checking a single node $v \in V$ can be done in time $O(|A|)$.*

Proof. The proof of safeness of this reduction rule is analogous to the proof of rule 1. The difference is that, instead of finding a set U corresponding to a path P in G_{npi}, we need to find a set of all cycle-dominators in G_{npi}.

Algorithm 1. Finding s-t dominators

```
 1: P ← (s, u₁, ..., u_{p-1}, t)                              ▷ any path from s to t
 2: Create 0-filled bitvector was and vector largest_j filled with values −1
 3:
 4: function DFS(ind, v)
 5:     was[v] ← True
 6:     for all w ∈ N⁺_{npi}(v) do
 7:         if w lies on path P then
 8:             j ← index of w on path P                              ▷ u_j = w
 9:             largest_j[v] ← max(largest_j[v], j)
10:         else if was[w] then                        ▷ w was considered earlier
11:             largest_j[v] ← max(largest_j[v], largest_j[w])
12:     for all w ∈ N⁺_{npi}(v) do
13:         if not was[w] and w does not lie on path P then
14:             DFS(ind, w)
15:             largest_j[v] ← max(largest_j[v], largest_j[w])
16:     return                                                      ▷ backtrack
17:
18: dominators ← ∅
19: for all 1 ≤ i < p do
20:     Run search by calling DFS(i, u_{i-1})
21:     if largest_j[u_{i-1}] ≤ i then
22:         add u_i to dominators
23:     largest_j[u_i] ← max(i, largest_j[u_{i-1}])
24: return dominators
```

To find a set of cycle-dominators of node v, let us consider a more general algorithm given by Algorithm 1, which finds, for given $s, t \in V$, all nodes that dominate s with respect to t. By adding to G_{npi} two new nodes v_+ and v_-, where $N^+(v_+) = N^+_{npi}(v)$ and $N^-(v_-) = N^-_{npi}(v)$, and running the algorithm for $s = v_+$ and $t = v_-$, we find all cycle-dominators of v. At the beginning, an arbitrary path $P \leftarrow (u_0, \ldots, u_p,)$ from $u_0 = s$ to $u_p = t$ is found, then we start iterating over nodes on the path. We want to find for each node $u_i \in P$ the largest index j such that u_j is reachable from nodes $\{u_0, \ldots, u_i\}$ in graph $G[A \setminus (A' \cup \{(u_i, u_{i+1})\})]$, where $A' = \{(x, y) : x \in \{u_{i+1}, \ldots, u_p\}, y \in N^+(x)\}$.

The crucial point is to observe that this can be done by running the DFS using only nodes that were not visited in previous DFS calls. To achieve that, we store for each node $u \in V$ the value $largest\_j[u]$ (written briefly $lj[u]$ from now on) equal to the largest j as described earlier. When considering node v in the DFS call, we find the value $lj[v] = \max(X, Y)$, where X is the largest of values $lj[w]$ among visited earlier neighbors w of node v, and Y is the largest index j such that $u_j \in N^+(v)$ (or -1 if such index does not exist). It remains to be seen that each node $u_i \in P$ for which $lj[u_{i-1}] \leq i$ dominates node s with respect to t, that is every path from s to t contains u_i. If u_i would not be a dominator, then there would exist a path P' from s to t that did not contain u_i. But then, for some node u_k with $k < i$ (as an index k we can take, e.g., the largest integer smaller than i for which $u_k \in P'$) we would have to get $lj[u_k] > i$. This is impossible, as $lj[u_i] \geq lj[u_j]$ for any $j < i$. Since every node in the graph is visited only once during all calls to DFS for subsequent nodes on path P, and we need to iterate only once over neighbors of each node, the complexity of the algorithm is $O(\sum_{v \in V} |N^+(v)|) = O(|A|)$.

Reduction rule 2 is a generalization of rule 1, but cannot be checked as efficiently. The linear-time algorithm for finding all cycle-dominators constitutes also an improvement of an algorithm proposed in work [4]. Using our approach, the complexity of the rule "Rule DFVS 2" from that paper can be improved from $O(n^2(n + m))$ to $O(nm)$, which makes it feasible for much larger graphs.

Rules 1 and 2 required to find a subset or the full set of cycle-dominators of a given node. Both rules would remain valid if we considered as dominators of node u not nodes that belong to every cycle containing u, but nodes that belong to every chordless cycle containing u. Finding chordless cycles, however, is computationally difficult. We therefore consider the following algorithm:

Reduction 3 (partial-domination-3). Let L be a fixed integer. For a given node $u \in V$ run a depth-first search with backtracking to find the intersection U of all cycles that do not contain a chord among its first L (at most) nodes. Apply rule 2 to the set U (in rule 2 set U contains all cycle-dominators for a given node, here it is a subset of all chordless-cycles-dominators).

We omit the proof of safeness of this reduction, as it is very easy, for the reduction is conceptually a straightforward realization of the brute-force search for all chordless cycles containing a given node, restricted to at most L initial nodes on a cycle. By applying several software-engineering optimizations we are able to run the rule for $L = 12$ on most graphs, as for graphs that do not contain chordless-cycle-dominators, it can be usually quickly determined that the intersection U is empty, and the search can be terminated. There are graphs, however, where the search for such a large value of L takes too long and we terminate the search after a fixed time period.

4   Experiment

In this section we provide results of the conducted computational experiment. For evaluation we used all 400 graph instances from the PACE 2022 contest [9].

This set contains, among others, real-world instances representing web graphs, social networks, and autonomous system graphs, as well as many random graphs generated according to various models. Used graphs contained up to $5 \cdot 10^6$ arcs.

We implemented three preprocessing procedures, called Set 1, Set 2, and Set 3, each based on a different collection of data reduction rules. Set 1 comprised only basic reduction rules: loop removal, parallel arc elimination, and the single-node neighborhood rule. Set 2 additionally incorporated several previously known reduction rules: core, dome, pie, and in-out-clique, as well as the folding, twin, desk and domination rule, the last four restricted to subgraphs in which the required vertices and their neighbors are pi-nodes (see [1,2,4,12–14,16] for more details). This configuration was used to produce instances suitable for evaluating the impact of partial-domination-based reductions on already preprocessed graphs. Since such graphs underwent substantial initial simplification, they are expected to be considerably less susceptible to further reductions than the unprocessed structures. Set 3 extended Set 2 by including partial-domination-based reduction rules introduced and described in this paper. It is necessary to mention that rule 2 was used only when the number of arcs in a graph did not exceed $5 \cdot 10^4$, as its complexity $O(|V| \cdot |A|)$ makes it inefficient for larger graphs. To assess effectiveness of the sets of reduction rules we use the reduction ratio measure, defined as the value $1 - \frac{|V_{G'}|}{|V_G|}$, where G' is the graph obtained by preprocessing G. A summary of obtained results is shown in Table 1.

Table 1. Comparison of results obtained by application of three sets of reduction rules to all 400 used graph instances.

	Set 1	Set 2	Set 3
Fully solved instances	2	84	94
Instances improved	356	385	385
Average reduction ratio	0.271	0.589	0.597
Median reduction ratio	0.092	0.700	0.724
Average reduction time	0.18 s	5.14 s	66.86 s
Median reduction time	0.01 s	0.26 s	3.41 s

By applying rules from the three sets, we were able to improve 356, 385, and 385 instances, respectively, out of the 400 test instances used. Among these, 2, 84, and 94 instances were fully solved, meaning that an optimal solution was obtained using only data reduction rules. Thus, for Set 3 we notice a significant 12% increase in the number of fully solved instances over Set 2. This comes at a cost of a longer average computational time, 66.86 vs. 5.14 s. We observe, however, that such a large difference is mainly caused by a few outliers, and the median time remains feasible for both sets, 3.41 and 0.26 s. The average reduction ratio values are almost identical (0.597 vs. 0.589). This might be, at first glance, misleading. If, e.g., Set 2 reduced a graph with million nodes to a graph with

1000 nodes, and Set 3 reduced it further to 500 nodes - thus achieving a huge 50% improvement over Set 2 - the reduction ratios for the two sets would equal 0.999 and 0.9995, respectively. If the impact of the sets of rules is measured only for the 316 graphs for which Set 2 did not fully solve the instance and compared relative to graph sizes obtained for Set 2, we observe that the reduction rules proposed in this paper yielded ca. 8.1% increase in the reduction ratio - a fairly reasonable result, since the improved graphs have already been subjected to a strong preprocessing.

To measure the sole influence of each rules 1–3, we preprocessed graphs using Set 2 extended by a single rule, for which the impact we wanted to measure. For this comparison we considered only graphs where Set 2 yielded better results than Set 1. Such a procedure allows for a clearer comparison, as it effectively removes graphs with highly complex structures, for which one could expect that no reduction rule would be applicable. The largest improvement was obtained for rule 2 with the average reduction ratio approximately 0.220, over two times the value than for the other two rules (0.099 for rule 3 and 0.092 for rule 1). The smallest impact on the average computation time can be observed for rule 1, roughly 92% larger for rule 2, and 2.15 times larger for rule 3. Median values are roughly 7x smaller than the average times, which indicates that there are outliers (notably, the two largest average times equalled 1497.02 and 669.28 s), for which application of our rules remains very time-consuming (Table 2).

Table 2. Comparison of the impact of particular reduction rules on the graph reduction ratio. Only 255 graphs that were not fully solved by Set 2 were considered and subjected to further preprocessing. Obtained reduction ratio values are relative to sizes of the graphs preprocessed using Set 2. Median reduction ratios are not presented, as they were very small and did not exceed 0.005.

	Set 2 + rule 1	Set 2 + rule 2	Set 2 + rule 3
Instances improved	142	155	145
Average reduction ratio	0.092	0.220	0.099
Average reduction time	78.06 s	150.40 s	168.73 s
Median reduction time	12.40 s	23.69 s	22.37 s

5   Conclusions

In the paper we introduced a new concept related to domination, called partial domination. Based on this concept, we provided data reduction rules for the Directed Feedback Vertex Set problem, which can significantly simplify a graph's structure. They also require less locality to be applicable than typical domination-based rules. We also provided an efficient linear-time algorithm for finding, for a given pair of nodes s, t, all dominators of s with respect to t.

This deceptively simple algorithm constitutes an improvement of an algorithm for finding cycle-dominators, used in other works, reducing the complexity by an order of magnitude, from $O(nm)$ to $O(m)$. Finally, we provided results of a computational experiment for evaluating the designed reduction rules on a wide variety of graph classes, demonstrating their practicality.

Funding. This research received funding from the National Science Centre, Poland (grant No. 2023/49/N/ST6/02506, PI: Sylwester Swat).

References

1. Angrick, S., et al.: Solving directed feedback vertex set by iterative reduction to vertex cover. In: Proceedings of SEA 2023, pp. 10:1–10:14 (2023). https://doi.org/10.4230/LIPIcs.SEA.2023.10
2. Behr, T., Storandt, S.: Lossy reduction rules for the directed feedback vertex set problem. In: Proceedings of ALENEX 2023, pp. 53–64 (2023). https://doi.org/10.1137/1.9781611977561.ch5
3. Chen, J., Liu, Y., Lu, S., O'Sullivan, B., Razgon, I.: A fixed-parameter algorithm for the directed feedback vertex set problem. J. ACM **55**, 21:1–21:19 (2008)
4. Dirks, J., Gerhard, E., Grobler, M., Mouawad, A., Siebertz, S.: Data reduction for directed feedback vertex set on graphs without long induced cycles. In: Proceedings of SOFSEM 2024, pp. 183–197 (2024). https://doi.org/10.1007/978-3-031-52113-3_13
5. Downey, R., Fellows, M.: Fixed-parameter intractability. In: Proceedings of SCT 1992, pp. 36–49 (1992).https://doi.org/10.1109/SCT.1992.215379
6. Dvořák, W., Ordyniak, S., Szeider, S.: Augmenting tractable fragments of abstract argumentation. Artif. Intell. **186**, 157–173 (2012)
7. Garey, M., Johnson, D.: Computers and Intractability. A Guide to the Theory of NP-Completeness. W.H. Freeman and Company, San Francisco (1979)
8. Georgiadis, L., Tarjan, R., Werneck, R.: Finding dominators in practice. J. Graph Algorithms Appl. **10**, 69–94 (2006)
9. Großmann, E., Heuer, T., Schulz, C., Strash, D.: The PACE 2022 parameterized algorithms and computational experiments challenge: directed feedback vertex Set. In: Proceedings of IPEC 2022, pp. 26:1–26:18 (2022). https://doi.org/10.4230/LIPIcs.IPEC.2022.26
10. Harel, D.: A linear algorithm for finding dominators in flow graphs and related problems. In: Proceedings of STOC 1985, pp. 185–194 (1985). https://doi.org/10.1145/22145.22166
11. Hudli, A., Hudli, R.: Finding small feedback vertex sets for VLSI circuits. Microprocess. Microsyst. **18**, 393–400 (1994)
12. Kiesel, R., Schidler, A.: A dynamic MaxSAT-based approach to directed feedback vertex sets. In: Proceedings of ALENEX 2023, pp. 39–52 (2023). https://doi.org/10.1137/1.9781611977561.ch4
13. Levy, H., Low, D.: A contraction algorithm for finding small cycle cutsets. J. Algorithms **9**, 470–493 (1988)
14. Lin, H., Jou, J.: On computing the minimum feedback vertex set of a directed graph by contraction operations. IEEE Trans. Comput. Aided Des. Integr. Circuits Syst. **19**, 295–307 (2000)

15. Lokshtanov, D., Ramanujan, M., Saurabh, S.: When recursion is better than iteration: a linear-time algorithm for acyclicity with few error vertices. In: Proceedings of SODA 2018, pp. 1916–1933 (2018). https://doi.org/10.1137/1.9781611975031.125
16. Meiburg, A.: Reduction rules and ILP are all you need: minimal directed feedback vertex set. arXiv:2208.01119 (2022)
17. Parotsidis, N., Georgiadis, L.: Dominators in directed graphs: a survey of recent results, applications, and open problems. In: Proceedings of ISCIM 2013, pp. 15–20 (2013). https://dspace.epoka.edu.al/handle/1/836
18. Xiong, Z., Xiao, M.: A simplified parameterized algorithm for directed feedback vertex set. In: Proceedings of SOSA 2025, pp. 378–384 (2025). https://doi.org/10.1137/1.9781611978315.29

A Two-Stream CNN Framework for Spatiotemporally Resolved NO_2 Estimates Using TEMPO and Sentinel-2 Satellite Data

Adam Bloom[1], Zhen Qu[2], and Ranga Raju Vatsavai[1,3](✉)

[1] Center for Geospatial Analytics, Raleigh, NC, USA
abloom@ncsu.edu
[2] Department of Marine, Earth and Atmospheric Sciences, Raleigh, NC, USA
zqu5@ncsu.edu
[3] Department of Computer Science, North Carolina State University,
Raleigh, NC, USA
rrvatsav@ncsu.edu

Abstract. A comprehensive understanding of ground-level air pollutants is essential for developing policies and strategies that effectively reduce associated human health, environmental, and economic risks. Nitrogen dioxide is a key air pollutant that poses its own risks to human health and is also essential to the formation of secondary air pollutants, including ozone and particulate matter. Air quality monitoring technologies enable concentration measurements at high temporal frequencies but are spatially constrained by site locations. In contrast, remote sensing satellites expand spatial coverage, yet accurately capturing short-term exposure variability remains challenging. In 2023, NASA successfully launched the TEMPO (Tropospheric Emissions: Monitoring of Pollution) geostationary satellite, which enables high spatial resolution retrievals at hourly intervals. Advancements in deep learning and computer vision effectively leverage spatial context to more accurately estimate ground-level pollution. Our research integrates these technological advancements within a deep learning framework capable of estimating hourly ground-level NO_2 concentrations at spatial scales as fine as $10\,\text{m}$ across the continental United States. This methodology can expand knowledge of sources driving diurnal variation of ground-level NO_2, inform emissions control policy and technologies, and deepen understanding of drivers of atmospheric chemical processes. Our thorough experimental evaluation offers several useful insights. Code (https://zenodo.org/records/19474505.) and data (Scripts used to obtain the data are included in the code, and a tarball of the data can be made available upon request.) are publicly available.

Keywords: Air pollution · deep learning · diurnal NO_2 · remote sensing

P. Neumann et al. (Eds.): ICCS 2026, LNCS 16784, pp. 404–411, 2026.
https://doi.org/10.1007/978-3-032-29924-6_34

1   Introduction

Air pollution is a major challenge to global public health and the environment. Nitrogen dioxide (NO_2) is designated by the EPA as a criteria air pollutant with distinct environmental and public health impacts [1,7]. Exposure to NO_2 increases the risk of respiratory infections, asthma, and lung cancer, and it plays a key role in acid rain formation [1,7]. Moreover, NO_2 is an important precursor to other criteria pollutants, including ozone (O_3) and atmospheric aerosols that form secondary particulate matter [7]. Monitoring sites effectively measure air pollutants but are spatially limited [4]. Remote sensing data offer a means to expand spatial coverage by combining vertical column density retrievals with land use analysis. Existing statistical, machine learning, and physics-based methods can estimate ground-level NO_2 effectively, but they are largely constrained to coarser temporal resolutions [4,5]. Understanding short-term (hourly) ground-level NO_2 concentrations is crucial for assessing its role as a precursor to secondary pollutants, identifying pollution sources, and characterizing cycles that influence community exposures [5]. A new generation of geostationary satellites, such as NASAs Tropospheric Emissions: Monitoring of Pollution (TEMPO), provides hourly vertical column densities (VCDs) for NO_2, ozone, and formaldehyde at a $0.02° \times 0.02°$ spatial resolution [5]. These retrievals present a novel opportunity to model hourly NO_2 concentrations across the United States using remote sensing.

Computer vision and convolutional neural networks (CNNs) have proven effective for quantifying ground-level air pollution using Sentinel-2 imagery and pollutant-specific retrieval products [4,10]. These networks require minimal effort to set up, yield highly accurate predictions, and generalize well to new areas. Employing multiple convolutional backbones to extract features from different remote sensing inputs enhances accuracy and generalizability for ground-level NO_2 predictions [10]. Although CNNs provide flexible and efficient pathways to accurate spatial estimations, they have historically been constrained by the daily revisit rates of sun-synchronous satellites, limiting their ability to capture short-term variability [4,10]. New geostationary satellites address this gap by providing estimates at higher temporal resolution [6].

In this work, we propose a two-stream network with a late fusion module to effectively exploit multisource data. Our specific contributions are:

1. A flexible CNN framework that can effectively exploit multisource data.
2. More accurate monthly NO_2 concentration estimates compared to prior work, achieved using higher-temporal-resolution retrievals.
3. High-resolution ground-level NO_2 estimates at both high temporal (hourly) and spatial resolution.

2   Related Work

Statistical Methods and Traditional Machine Learning: Land-use regression (LUR) and kriging are commonly used to model ground-level NO_2 concentrations at monitoring sites [7,10]. LUR estimates long-term exposures using geospatial variables but cannot capture short-term variability and requires extensive GIS data [7,10]. Kriging interpolates spatially, treating NO_2 as a random variable with the best linear unbiased estimator, and provides variance estimates and confidence intervals [10]. While remote sensing mitigates traditional data limitations, high-dimensional satellite data has shifted the field toward ML algorithms. Tree-based and ensemble models successfully leverage remote sensing products [7], but they typically require manual feature engineering for spatiotemporal context. Consequently, Deep Learning has become the state of the art for generalizable NO_2 estimation.

Deep Learning: Convolutional neural networks (CNNs) have been shown to extract spatial features from remote sensing data for ground-level pollution modeling [4,10], while LSTMs can further improve forecasting by encoding temporal dependencies [8]. Our work is motivated by two-stream architectures [3,10], where Sentinel-2 imagery and satellite NO_2 retrievals modeled ground-level NO_2 at high spatial but coarse temporal scales (monthly to multi-year) with robust out-of-domain generalizability [10]. However, Sentinel-5P's near-daily revisit is limited to a short-term context. We retain the two-stream structure, replace the Sentinel-5P backbone with hourly TEMPO Level-3 NO_2 retrievals, and incorporate temporal, demographic, and land-use predictors to improve spatiotemporal estimation.

Regionally Limited Hourly Estimation Studies: High-temporal-resolution NO_2 estimation using remote sensing has historically been limited by the low revisit rates of available satellite products. Several hourly ground-level NO_2 approaches have been developed using the geostationary GEMS satellite, which covers East Asia and the Asian Pacific [6]. Launched in 2020, three years before NASA's TEMPO satellite, GEMS has enabled multiple hourly estimation efforts. The most successful models ($R^2 = 0.72$) incorporate region-specific features and are not generalizable to other locations [6]. A similar local approach for the Netherlands modeled hourly PM2.5 and NO_2 with strong performance ($R^2 = 0.35 - 0.78$), but relied on physical chemical transport models [9]. These approaches demonstrate the promise of machine learning for high-resolution estimation but remain largely limited to small geographic regions.

Chemical Transport Modeling: Chemical transport models simulate four-dimensional atmospheric chemistry processes and can model the distribution of chemicals over time and space. These models achieve high performance in ground-level pollution monitoring by leveraging emissions inventories to estimate exposures [9]. Remote sensing observations can constrain these physical models to reduce simulation errors [9]. However, physical models remain computationally intensive and may introduce simulation errors into machine learning estimates. For these reasons, this study focuses on a purely data-driven approach to ground-level NO_2 estimation.

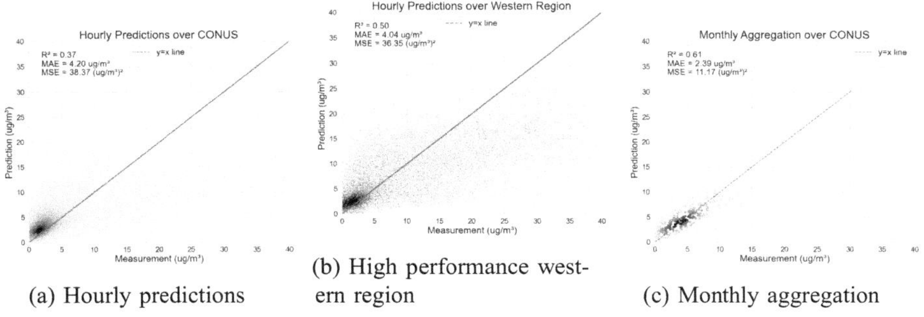

(a) Hourly predictions   (b) High performance western region   (c) Monthly aggregation

Fig. 1. Model performance for hourly predictions across the continental United States and a high-performing western region, along with monthly aggregated results over the continental United States.

3   Methods

We now present technical details of our two-stream CNN architecture.

3.1   Two-Stream CNN Architecture

Two-stream (or multi-stream) architectures [3,10] are a popular approach for modeling multi-source (multi-resolution) data. Individual networks are designed specifically for each input type to extract discriminative features, which are then fused with any additional sources before the prediction head. Our base model extends the two-stream neural network presented in [10] by introducing an hourly TEMPO retrieval backbone. This backbone comprises two convolutional layers with 10 and 15 channels, respectively, each followed by a rectified linear unit (ReLU) activation layer, along with two max pooling layers and a final linear layer. The output is a 128-dimensional feature vector. This shallow architecture is sufficient to model the low spatial resolution (2 km (north-south) by 4.75 km (east-west)) of the TEMPO satellite image.

To extract land use features from multi-spectral Sentinel-2 images (10 m resolution), we employ a ResNet50 model fine-tuned on land use classification with the BigEarthNet dataset [11]. This feature extraction knowledge is directly transferable to identifying features that drive short- and long-term variations in NO_2. Given the number of input bands, the resulting vector (2048 dimensions) is substantially larger than the TEMPO backbone output.

The feature vectors from both backbones are fused and concatenated with encoded temporal variables, population density, and degree of urbanization, before the regression head. Although various fusion strategies (e.g., addition or multiplication) could be used, concatenation was chosen due to differing feature vector lengths. The regression head comprises two fully connected layers separated by a ReLU activation, and the full network is trained with the Adam optimizer to minimize MSE loss.

3.2 Evaluation

We evaluate our model using R^2, MSE, MAE, and mean bias (MB) to identify regional trends. Data are split by station (not by individual sample) to prevent memorization. Metrics are computed for raw hourly predictions and for daily/monthly aggregates, enabling direct benchmarking against prior studies [10]. Since high-frequency estimates at this large scale are largely unexplored, we compare against the deep learning satellite models (Sentinel-2/Sentinel-5P at monthly, quarterly, and two-year spans) and the land use regression OSM-only model from [10] to assess whether our algorithm achieves comparable accuracy at higher temporal frequencies. We also highlight strong performance across six western U.S. states (Colorado, California, Utah, Arizona, Washington, and Nevada), defining this group as the "Western Region" and including its statistics in our analysis.

4 Experiments

4.1 Data and Preprocessing

Ground Truth: We use hourly NO_2 measurements from the EPA Air Quality System (AQS) as training targets. Samples were collected over five months in 2024 at 432 stations, totaling 185,323 hourly measurements. Measurements flagged for data quality issues are excluded.

Sentinel-2: We retrieve Sentinel-2 [2] images centered on each AQS site, with dimensions of $12 \times 120 \times 120$. All bands are resampled to a consistent 10 m spatial resolution. A single image is used per site, as significant land use changes are not anticipated within a single year, and this backbone is not expected to capture short-term NO_2 variability. The image with the lowest cloud cover in 2024 is selected to ensure optimal quality.

TEMPO: We use Level 3 TEMPO [5] NO_2 vertical column densities, as their consistent gridding reduces preprocessing. These images have a pixel resolution of approximately $0.02° \times 0.02°$. For each AQS station and hour with a recorded measurement, we retrieve a 10×10 grid of NO_2 retrievals centered on the station and resample it to 120×120 to match Sentinel-2 dimensions. Observations with data-quality flags are excluded, as are retrievals with large gaps caused by cloud cover or reflective surfaces.

Temporal Variables: Diurnal and weekly cycles in NO_2 concentrations arise from anthropogenic sources. To help the model learn these patterns, we encode time of day, day of week, and month of year using cyclical encoding:

$$\text{hour}_{\text{sin}} = \sin\left(\tfrac{2\pi\,\text{hour}}{24}\right) \qquad \text{hour}_{\text{cos}} = \cos\left(\tfrac{2\pi\,\text{hour}}{24}\right)$$

$$\text{month}_{\text{sin}} = \sin\left(\tfrac{2\pi\,\text{month}}{12}\right) \qquad \text{month}_{\text{cos}} = \cos\left(\tfrac{2\pi\,\text{month}}{12}\right)$$

$$\text{day}_{\text{sin}} = \sin\left(\tfrac{2\pi\,\text{day\_of\_week}}{7}\right) \qquad \text{day}_{\text{cos}} = \cos\left(\tfrac{2\pi\,\text{day\_of\_week}}{7}\right)$$

Population Density and Degree of Urbanization: From the 2022 American Community Survey, we extracted population density within a three-mile radius of each AQS site. Additional contextual information came from AQS data in the form of a categorical degree of urbanization, specifically rural, suburban, or urban, which is based on U.S. Census block groups and therefore supports inference at unmonitored locations. We applied one-hot encoding to this categorical variable.

4.2   Experimental Set Up

We trained the model on 185,323 hourly observations from 432 monitoring stations, using a station-level split of 60% for training, 20% for validation, and 20% for testing to prevent spatial leakage. Training was conducted on a single NVIDIA A10 GPU (24 GB memory) with two CPU cores and 40 GB of system memory. The model was implemented in PyTorch and trained with a batch size of 50 using the Adam optimizer, a learning rate of 5×10^{-5}, and a mean squared error (MSE) loss function. Dropout with a probability of 0.05 was applied to the final two fully connected layers. Each model was trained for up to 30 epochs with early stopping based on validation loss.

Table 1. Comparison of Prior Studies and Our Model

Input	Span	R^2	MAE	MSE
Prior Studies				
Sen.-2/5P (Monthly)	18–20	0.51	6.54	78.96
Sen.-2/5P (Quarterly)	18–20	0.53	6.05	72.53
Sen.-2/5P	18–20	0.57	5.50	58.47
OSM Only	18–20	0.34	7.22	88.29
Our Model				
Hourly	2024	0.37	4.20	38.37
Western Region	2024	0.50	4.04	36.35
Daily Aggregation	2024	0.40	3.84	29.27
Monthly Aggregation	2024	0.61	2.39	11.17

Note: Prior studies did not include mean bias, so we only compare R^2, MAE, and MSE in this table.

5   Results and Discussion

Monthly, Daily, and Hourly Performance: We iteratively optimized our architecture by adding features to the two-backbone baseline from [10]. Initial results showed over-prediction of low NO_2 and under-prediction of high NO_2; adding cyclical temporal variables, population density, and urbanization progressively improved performance. The final model achieves hourly $R^2 = 0.37$, MAE=4.20 $\mu g/m^3$, and MSE=38.37 $(\mu g/m^3)^2$ across the continental US (Fig. 1a). While R^2 is lower than Sentinel-2/Sentinel-5P models [10] (expected due to higher temporal resolution and variance), it exceeds the OSM-only baseline for long-term exposures, and MSE/MAE are consistently lower than all Sentinel-2/Sentinel-5P models (Table 1). Aggregating hourly estimates to daily and monthly averages yields further gains: monthly aggregation achieves $R^2 = 0.61$, MAE=2.39 $\mu g/m^3$, MSE=11.17 $(\mu g/m^3)^2$ (Fig. 1c), significantly outperforming the monthly results in [10]. This demonstrates that higher-resolution estimates better represent long-term exposures than directly predicting averages from lower-frequency products.

Regional Trends: The spatial analysis of station-level mean prediction bias indicates systematic under-prediction in the Mid-Atlantic and slight over-prediction in the Northeast. The largest over-predictions occur in Oklahoma, Wyoming, and western Kentucky—stations with belowaverage NO_2—reflecting "regression to the mean", common in large spatial models. At the Kentucky site, bias may arise from land features outside the 1.2×1.2 km Sentinel-2 patch: although the patch appears urban, the broader region is rural with extensive forest cover, highlighting spatial context limitations. Stations in Michigan, Illinois, and Ohio show significant underestimation, likely due to few training examples near major highways and pretraining on European imagery (BigEarthNet) [11], which may not encode North American highway interchanges and low-density sprawl as distinctly. Conversely, high performance is observed across six western states: Colorado, California, Utah, Arizona, Washington, and Nevada (Fig. 1b).

6 Conclusion

In this study, we develop a deep learning architecture that estimates hourly NO_2 concentrations across the continental United States. Expanding spatial coverage of hourly air pollution is critical for evaluating public exposures and advancing understanding of atmospheric chemistry. We leverage NASA's geostationary TEMPO satellite, which provides hourly NO_2 retrievals covering the entire continental U.S. By incorporating these retrievals into a two-backbone CNN architecture, we generate efficient and accurate NO_2 estimates nationwide. Compared to prior approaches using similar architectures at coarser temporal resolutions, we achieve lower MSE and MAE, despite a slightly lower R^2. This lower R^2 reflects regional variability in hourly NO_2 and the diversity of environments across the U.S. We identify regions where the model performs particularly well, including six western states where hourly estimates achieve an R^2 of 0.50—nearly identical to monthly aggregated R^2 in prior studies [10]. These findings highlight strong regional performance and opportunities for future enhancement.

While our model demonstrates significant promise, particularly in specific regions, several limitations and future directions remain. Progressive performance gains from added features suggest that incorporating 3D spatiotemporal retrievals, meteorological variables, or traffic data could further enhance accuracy. Regional fine-tuning may also better capture localized NO_2 dynamics.

Acknowledgments.. Vatsavai is supported in part by the "AI Institute for Land, Economy, Agriculture and Forestry (AI-LEAF)," which is supported by USDA National Institute of Food and Agriculture (NIFA) and the National Science Foundation (NSF) National AI Research Institutes Competitive Award no. 2023-67021-39829. Project website: https://cse.umn.edu/aileaf.

Generative AI Usage Disclosure:. The authors used Generative AI tools exclusively for language editing to improve readability. No AI tools were used to generate any new content in this paper.

Disclosure of Interests. The authors have no competing interests to declare that are relevant to the content of this article.

References

1. Chen, T.M., Kuschner, W.G., Gokhale, J., Shofer, S.: Outdoor air pollution: nitrogen dioxide, sulfur dioxide, and carbon monoxide health effects. Am. J. Med. Sci. **333**(4), 249–256 (2007)
2. Drusch, M., et al.: Sentinel-2: ESA's optical high-resolution mission for GMEs operational services. Remote Sens. Environ. **120**, 25–36 (2012). https://doi.org/10.1016/j.rse.2011.11.026
3. Gadiraju, K.K., Ramachandra, B., Chen, Z., Vatsavai, R.R.: Multimodal deep learning based crop classification using multispectral and multitemporal satellite imagery. In: Rajesh Gupta, E.A. (ed.) KDD '20: The 26th ACM SIGKDD Conference on Knowledge Discovery and Data Mining, Virtual Event, CA, USA, August 23-27, 2020, pp. 3234–3242. ACM (2020). https://doi.org/10.1145/3394486.3403375
4. Hong, K.Y., Pinheiro, P.O., Weichenthal, S.: Predicting global variations in outdoor PM2.5 concentrations using satellite images and deep convolutional neural networks (2019). arxiv:1906.03975
5. Jin, X., Yang, Y., Gonzalez Abad, G., Nowlan, C., Liu, X.: Observing the diurnal variations of OZONE-NOX-VOC chemistry over the U.S. from the geostationary tempo instrument. Geophys. Res. Lett. **52**(14) (2025)
6. Lee, H.J., Kim, N.R., Shin, M.Y.: Capabilities of satellite geostationary environment monitoring spectrometer (gems) no2 data for hourly ambient no2 exposure modeling. Environ. Res. **261**, 119633 (2024)
7. Liu, J., Chen, W.: First satellite-based regional hourly no2 estimations using a space-time ensemble learning model: a case study for Beijing-Tianjin-Hebei region, China. Sci. Total Environ. **820**, 153289 (2022). https://doi.org/10.1016/j.scitotenv.2022.153289
8. Mahmudimanesh, M., Mirzaee, M., Dehghan, A., Bahrampour, A.: Forecasts of cardiac and respiratory mortality in Tehran, Iran, using Arimax and CNN-LSTM models. Environ. Sci. Pollut. Res. **29**(19), 28469–28479 (2022)
9. Ndiaye, A., et al.: Hourly land-use regression modeling for no2 and PM2. 5 in the Netherlands. Environ. Res. **256**, 119233 (2024)
10. Scheibenreif, L., Mommert, M., Borth, D.: Toward global estimation of ground-level no2 pollution with deep learning and remote sensing. IEEE Trans. Geosci. Remote Sens. **60**, 1–14 (2022)
11. Sumbul, G., Charfuelan, M., Demir, B., Markl, V.: BigEarthNet: a large-scale benchmark archive for remote sensing image understanding. In: IEEE International Geoscience and Remote Sensing Symposium, pp. 5901–5904. IEEE (2019)

Think Like a Researcher: A Dataset for Scientific Ideation with Large Language Models

Julia Moska[(✉)] [iD], Maciej Piasecki [iD], and Arkadiusz Janz [iD]

Wrocław University of Science and Technology, Wrocław, Poland
`julia.moska@pwr.edu.pl`

Abstract. Research hypothesis generation using Large Language Models (LLMs) remains largely prompt-based, with limited work on model alignment. We present one of the few systematic reviews of existing datasets for hypothesis generation, analyzing their structure and suitability for alignment. Based on this analysis, we introduce a dataset designed for training and aligning LLMs that encodes literature-derived background knowledge as structured concept connections, along with evaluation metrics grounded in references and their content. Using this dataset, we study how alignment with structured knowledge affects the novelty and grounding of generated hypotheses.

Keywords: scientific ideation · hypothesis generation · LLMs · preference dataset · alignment · LLM fine-tuning

1 Introduction

Advances in LLMs enabled new NLP applications including creative generation, mathematical proof synthesis, and drug discovery. However, autonomous research, focused on LLM-based scientific hypothesis generation, designing experiments, and supporting publishable research is still challenging due to the challenges of literature review, identification of knowledge gaps, ideation and planning, and execution of experiments. *Idea generation* remains underexplored in several aspects. Existing solutions [6] often rely on API access, which limits reproducibility and adaptation. The field still lacks robust datasets and benchmarks. Scientific ideas must be novel, grounded in prior work, and methodologically feasible. Current evaluation methods, such as semantic similarity or LLM-as-a-judge [7], only partially address this challenge, often oversimplifying novelty and ignoring the motivational and structural context of idea generation. Moreover, existing datasets often represent references as flat collections of related papers [17], rather than as structured and evolving knowledge.

Following [6,17,22] we introduce a dataset for scientific ideation built from structured, pre-processed background knowledge. It pairs ground-truth work with semantically labeled citation graphs and structured summaries (Fig. 1),

© The Author(s), under exclusive license to Springer Nature Switzerland AG 2026
P. Neumann et al. (Eds.): ICCS 2026, LNCS 16784, pp. 412–420, 2026.
https://doi.org/10.1007/978-3-032-29924-6_35

enabling fine-tuning, alignment, and evaluation for scientific ideation. Compared with [6], we construct an offline semantically filtered multi-hop citation graph, preserving fine-grained relations between articles. Unlike [17], our approach retains a broader citation context and represents each paper with structured summaries of its ideas, methods, limitations, and future directions. In contrast to [22], our representations are deterministic, reusable, and independent of a specific inference-time pipeline. Valid research ideas may diverge from the ground truth while still addressing meaningful gaps. We introduce metrics beyond surface-level semantic similarity to assess conceptual relevance and logical coherence with the citation context. We use them to compare preference-aligned models against base models and reasoning models evaluated under the same conditions.

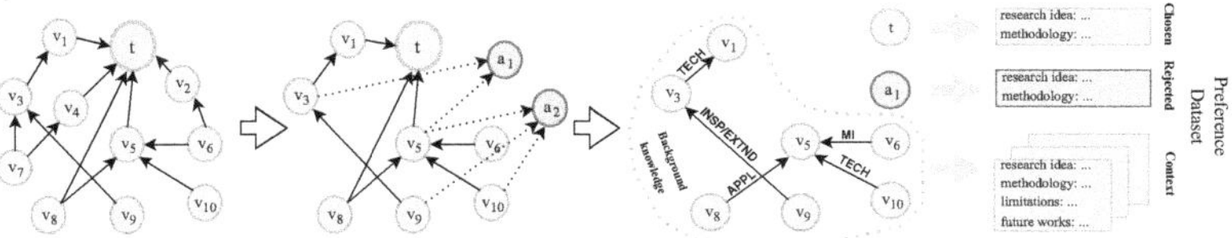

Fig. 1. A citation network is mined and processed to create chosen-rejected research ideamethod pairs, forming DPO preference samples (**(author?)** 18).

2   Related Work

Scientific idea generation is framed as inference-time retrieval over scientific knowledge. Systems start from a seed paper or query and traverse citation graphs to collect context for generation [6,19], typically through public APIs such as arXiv[1] or Semantic Scholar[2]. Training-based alternatives use SFT [5,15] apply preference learning over topic-aligned abstracts, and [8] explore reinforcement learning in a domain-specific multi-agent setting. Such approaches may overlook prior problems with correct grounding essential for relevant idea generation. Most prior work relies on inference-time API access, limiting task-specific fine-tuning, and controlled experimentation. Although resources such as ArXiv Dataset [4], Open Academic Graph [20], SciPIP [22], and BigSurvey [12] provide metadata and citations, but often reduced to titles and abstracts. Additional structures may come from IE [15,21], but such methods lack validation (Table 1).

The evaluation of scientific ideas, a non-trivial task for humans, is a challenge to automate, leading to proxy-based metrics. The novelty assessment is carried out by cosine similarity to existing work [7,19], embedding-based distance [5], and comparing similarity to both historical and contemporary literature [17].

---

[1] https://arxiv.org/help/api/.
[2] https://api.semanticscholar.org/.

Table 1. Existing datasets for scientific ideation along key dimensions: domain, data format, availability of k-hop citation graph (K-REF), readiness for SFT (SFT-R) and alignment training (AL-R), validation of the paper summaries and extracted metadata (HV), availability of the data in open access (OA).

Dataset	Domain	Data format	K-REF	SFT-R	AL-R	OA	HV
[4]	multi-domain	abstracts/full texts	✗/ ✓	✗	✗	✗/ ✓	N/A
[12]	multi-domain	abstracts	✗	✗	✓	✓	N/A
[7]	LLMs	abstracts	✗	✗	✗	✗	N/A
[20]	multi-domain	abstracts	✓	✗	✗	✓	N/A
[5]	multi-domain	abstracts	✗	✓	✓	✗	N/A
[17, 21]	biomedical	abstracts	✗	✓	✗	✓	N/A
[10]	AI	full text*	✗	✓	✗	✗	N/A
[1]	biomedical	knowledge graph	✗	✗	✗	✓	N/A
[15, 16]	biomedical	summaries	✗	✓	✗	✗	✗
[13]	computer-science	summaries	✗	✓	✗	✓	✗
[22]	AI	summaries	✗	✗	✗	✓	✗
ours	NLP/AI	summaries	✓	✓	✓	✓	✓

Although novelty remains a central focus, other dimensions such as feasibility, diversity, clarity, and potential impact [6,7,9,19] are considered in a holistic assessment. The use of the LLM-as-a-Judge framework is widespread [11,17], but the evaluation of scientific ideation remains a challenge due to the lack of sufficient human annotation. Sections such as future work and limitations are only rarely used as explicit signals in the evaluation process.

3　Alignment Data for Scientific Ideation

We propose a scientific idea generation dataset for both training and evaluation. It combines structured knowledge with textual summaries of key paper content[3], and represents the literature as a semantically annotated graph (Fig. 1), enabling a richer view of the research context evolution. To avoid potential data leakage, the dataset construction began with the test set. The research papers were retrieved via Semantic Scholar, using keywords covering several NLP terms within the core area of expertise of the authors. 223 target articles T were identified, which form the basis of the evaluation. The publication cut-off date was chosen to ensure that the content was not seen by the selected open-source models. Full-text content was extracted using the OLMOCR[4].

For each target article $t \in T$, citation data was retrieved up to three hops from the global citation graph G to build a local literature subgraph $G_t = (V_t, E_t)$,

---

[3] Dataset: https://github.com/mskaa3/think-like-a-researcher.
[4] https://olmocr.allenai.org.

where V_t are articles and E_t citation edges. We applied the personalised PageRank algorithm [14] to identify the most relevant nodes in G_t. Using QWEN2 1.5B GTE[5], each node $v_j \in V_t$ received a relevance score $w_j = \text{cos-sim}(v_j, t)$, capturing semantic similarity to t. After normalizing these scores into a valid personalization vector, we pruned nodes below the dynamic threshold $\mu + \sigma$, resulting in a reduced and semantically focused subgraph $\tilde{G}_t \subseteq G_t$. Additionally, we define proximate articles as those with substantial structural overlap with the target articles local citation subgraph G_t. For each node $v_j \in V_t$, we searched the global citation graph G for external articles $a_j \notin V_t$ that cite v_j, producing candidate neighbours that reference a subset of nodes in V_t (see Fig. 1). For each a_j, we defined its reference set V_{a_j} and measured overlap with V_t using Jaccard set similarity $Jaccard(V_{a_j}, V_t) = \frac{|V_{a_j} \cap V_t|}{|V_{a_j} \cup V_t|}$. Articles with scores exceeding experimentally established thresholds $\Theta = \langle 0.3, 0.4, 0.5 \rangle$ were retained in neighbourhood sets $\mathcal{A}_t(\Theta)$, encoding increasing levels of structural similarity.

Inter-paper Relation Recognition. Building on [6], we expand the typology of inter-paper relations (see Fig. 1), by annotating each citation edge $(v_j, v_k) \in \tilde{G}_t$ with a semantic citation label $\ell_{jk} \in \mathcal{L}$ using LLaMA 3 70B[6]. Given that the semantic similarity used to filter the initial graph does not capture nuanced dependencies, these labels aim to capture how one work relates conceptually or methodologically. Relation types include Inspiration, Extension, Critique, Foundation, Replication, Comparison, Application, Supplement, Historical background, Technical, and Marginal Influence. We developed detailed annotation guidelines and had a subset of citation links manually annotated by two domain experts. Agreement was measured using Gwets AC1 (Table 2), chosen for its robustness against the high-agreementlow-kappa problem [3], particularly relevant in imbalanced data. To evaluate relation recognition, we computed the agreement score between domain experts and LLaMA 3 70B (Table 2).

Table 2. Inter-annotator agreement (IAA) and modelannotator agreement (AIhuman) scores per citation category, measured using Gwets AC1.

	FOUND	EXTND	SUPPL	REPL	INSP	CRIT	COMPR	APPL	MENT
AC1 Human-AI	0.747	0.413	0.241	0.842	0.906	0.837	0.368	0.820	0.928
AC1 IAA	0.714	0.631	0.453	0.964	0.926	0.855	0.309	0.850	0.947

Paper Summary Extraction. To obtain concise but informative article representations, we used GPT-4o mini[7] to generate structured summaries covering four dimensions: *research idea*, *methodology*, *limitations*, and *future directions*. They serve both as elements of learning examples and as an evaluation basis. A

---

[5] https://huggingface.co/Alibaba-NLP/gte-Qwen2-1.5B-instruct.
[6] https://huggingface.co/meta-llama/Llama-3.3-70B-Instruct.
[7] https://openai.com.

domain expert assessed summary quality by comparing the extracted descriptions with the original papers on a five-point scale. The results indicate good extraction quality, with average scores of 3.95±0.47 for research idea, 3.36±0.63 for method details, 3.54±0.85 for limitations, and 3.40±0.77 for future work. We retrieved an additional 1,000 articles published before Oct. 2024 using the same keyword set as training set, following the same processing pipeline, with any overlap with the test set removed. Each data instance is a tuple $(\tilde{G}_t, t, A_t)$, where $\tilde{G}_t$ is a directed citation graph, with each node $v_j \in \tilde{G}_t$ represented as $v_j = (r_j, m_j, l_j, f_j)$, and each edge (v_j, v_k) annotated with semantic label $\ell_{jk} \in \mathcal{L}$. The target article t is abstracted as $t = (r_t, m_t)$. Proximate article sets $\mathcal{A}_t(\theta)$ for thresholds $\theta \in \{0.3, 0.4, 0.5\}$ where $a_j \in \mathcal{A}_t(\theta)$ represented as $a_j = (r_{a_j}, m_{a_j})$.

4   Evaluation of Model-Driven Scientific Ideas

Scientifically valid ideas may diverge from the gold outputs by extending, reinterpreting, or building on prior work. To capture contextual grounding, we introduce measures based on limitations and future directions identified in prior works, revealing scientific motivations and constraints. Let $(\tilde{G}_t, t, \mathcal{A}_t)$ denote the representation of a test instance as defined in Sect. 3. The k generated ideas for t are embedded as vectors $\mathbf{g}_1, \ldots, \mathbf{g}_k$, using QWEN2 1.5B GTE, while the target idea is represented by $\mathbf{t}$. The context embeddings set is $\mathcal{V} = \{\mathbf{v}_1, \ldots, \mathbf{v}_n\}$, where each $\mathbf{v}_j$ corresponds to a referenced article $v_j \in \tilde{G}_{t_i}$. The proximate article embeddings is $\mathcal{A} = \{\mathbf{a}_1, \ldots, \mathbf{a}_m\}$, where $\mathbf{a}_j$ corresponds to $a_j \in \mathcal{A}_t$.

(1) Inter-Generation Dissimilarity. To assess idea diversity, we compute pairwise cosine distances among the k generations for each test example. The diversity score is $D = \frac{2}{k(k-1)} \sum_{1 \leq i < j \leq k} (1 - \cos(\mathbf{g}_i, \mathbf{g}_j))$, where $\cos(\mathbf{g}_i, \mathbf{g}_j)$ is the cosine similarity. The final score is the average D over all test examples.

(2) Gold Similarity. We compute the cosine similarity between the embeddings of each generated idea $\mathbf{g}_i$ and the reference answer $\mathbf{t}$ as $GoldSim. = \frac{1}{k} \sum_{i=1}^{k} \cos(\mathbf{g}_i, \mathbf{t})$. Scores are averaged across all examples to provide a clear measure of how closely the model adheres to the target response, as in [7,19].

(3) Relative Novelty. Inspired by [17], we define a relative novelty score as the ratio of an ideas semantic similarity to proximate articles ($\mathcal{A}$) to its similarity to background references ($\mathcal{V}$): $N = \frac{1+s(\mathcal{A})}{1+s(\mathcal{V})}$. Our approach utilizes references as historical context and all existing proximate articles as current context. The normalized cosine similarity between the generated ideas and the reference set $\mathcal{X}$ is $s(\mathcal{X}) = \frac{1}{k|\mathcal{X}|} \sum_{i=1}^{k} \sum_{\mathbf{x} \in \mathcal{X}} \frac{\cos(\mathbf{g}_i, \mathbf{x}) + 1}{2}$.

(4) Limitations and Future Directions Alignment Scores. For each test article, we extract limitations $L = \{l_1, \ldots, l_n\}$ and future directions $F = \{f_1, \ldots, f_n\}$ from reference papers in V. To assess whether a generated idea addresses a limitation or aligns with a future direction, we use an LLM-as-a-judge function $M(g_i, s_j)$, where $s_j \in L$ or $s_j \in F$, returning 1 if the relation holds. For $S \in \{L, F\}$, where $S = \{s_1, \ldots, s_{|S|}\}$, we define

$$A_{\max}(S) = \max_{i=1}^{k} \left(\frac{1}{|S|} \sum_{j=1}^{|S|} M(g_i, s_j) \right), A_{\mathrm{avg}}(S) = \frac{1}{k} \sum_{i=1}^{k} \left(\frac{1}{|S|} \sum_{j=1}^{|S|} M(g_i, s_j) \right) \quad (1)$$

where $M(g_i, s_j) = 1$ if generated idea g_i addresses s_j, and 0 otherwise. For $S = L$, this yields $LA_{\max}$ and LA_{avg}; for $S = F$, $FDA_{\max}$ and FDA_{avg}.

(5) Topic Consistency Score. It extends the thematic coherence of generated ideas [5] and idea-to-topic matching [17] by measuring the alignment of generated ideas with keyword-based topics derived from the set of reference papers (V).

5   Results and Conclusions

We fine-tuned QWEN 7B INSTRUCT[8] with DPO [18]. The prompting-only base model serves as the main baseline, and DEEPSEEK-R1-DISTILL-QWEN-7B[9] as an additional reasoning baseline. Rejected samples are drawn either from proximate articles $\mathcal{A}_t$ or randomly from the corpus, defining proximate and unrelated negative settings. Inputs follow [2] and consist of an instruction with a textual citation-graph representation with node summaries and semantic edge labels (Fig. 1); MI, TECH, and HIST edges are removed. We compare full summaries (research idea, methodology, limitations, future directions) with reduced summaries (research idea, methodology only). Training uses AdamW for 10 epochs with learning rate 10^{-6}, weight decay 0.001, 5% warm-up, linear scheduling, and $\beta = 0.01$. The evaluation is performed at $T \in \{0.1, 0.5\}$ with 10 generations per instance. Table 3 demonstrates the impact of alignment strategies and contextual information on the quality of generated research ideas.

Effect of DPO Alignment. The alignment improves core semantic metrics but reduces inter-generation diversity. The drop in limitations alignment suggests that increased consistency comes at the cost of overfitting to surface-level patterns rather than engaging with the reference literature. Compared with the base model, which draws on a broader range of background material and addresses limitations more variably, fine-tuning narrows behavior toward a smaller set of preferred patterns, reducing perspective and creativity in a manner reminiscent of catastrophic forgetting.

Influence of Rejected Answer Sampling Strategy. Models trained with unrelated rejected samples consistently outperform those trained with adjacent rejected samples in semantic similarity and topic consistency. This suggests that more diverse chosen-rejected pairs guide the model more effectively toward the ground truth. However, this also reduces output diversity and weakens alignment with intended limitations, indicating a shift toward topical relevance over the specific methodological or conceptual gaps emphasized in the reference context.

---

[8] https://huggingface.co/Qwen/Qwen2.5-7B-Instruct.

[9] https://huggingface.co/deepseek-ai/DeepSeek-R1-Distill-Qwen-7B.

Table 3. Evaluation results of baseline and DPO-aligned models under different contextual configurations, reported at temperatures (T) 0.1 and 0.5. Baselines are evaluated in a prompting-only setup, while aligned models are fine-tuned with different rejected-sample strategies and context keys derived from structured summaries.

Model	Gold Sim.	Rel. Nov.	Dissim.	LA_{avg}	LA_{max}	FDA_{avg}	FDA_{max}	TCS	T
keys in context: research idea, methodology, limitations, future works									
Q_{base}	0.585	0.878	6.386	**0.239**	0.472	0.277	0.459	0.177	0.1
$Q_{prox.}$	0.591	**0.891**	5.155	0.184	0.275	0.219	0.374	0.203	
$Q_{unrel.}$	**0.602**	**0.892**	4.432	0.096	0.171	0.204	0.371	**0.217**	
$Q_{reason.}$	0.554	0.884	13.621	0.228	**0.482**	**0.322**	**0.577**	0.168	
Q_{base}	0.584	0.879	10.687	0.207	**0.461**	0.288	0.515	0.176	0.5
$Q_{prox.}$	0.586	**0.891**	9.426	0.132	0.323	0.216	0.393	0.202	
$Q_{unrel.}$	**0.597**	**0.893**	8.406	0.106	0.284	0.201	0.374	**0.219**	
$Q_{reason.}$	0.559	0.880	13.002	**0.214**	0.429	**0.311**	**0.565**	0.168	
keys in context: research idea, methodology									
Q_{base}	0.587	0.878	6.231	**0.236**	**0.497**	0.296	0.460	0.177	0.1
$Q_{prox.}$	**0.599**	0.881	4.733	0.123	0.282	0.198	0.343	0.203	
$Q_{unrel.}$	**0.601**	**0.892**	4.180	0.095	0.272	0.194	0.354	**0.222**	
$Q_{reason.}$	0.565	0.885	13.726	**0.236**	0.490	**0.334**	**0.573**	0.167	
Q_{base}	0.593	0.878	10.443	0.201	0.438	0.291	0.468	0.179	0.5
$Q_{prox.}$	**0.597**	0.881	9.348	0.120	0.310	0.212	0.379	0.202	
$Q_{unrel.}$	**0.597**	**0.893**	7.646	0.094	0.253	0.204	0.366	**0.220**	
$Q_{reason.}$	0.572	0.882	13.083	**0.247**	**0.469**	**0.322**	**0.577**	0.167	

The Impact of Structured Summary Content. Across aligned models, differences in LA and FDA are small, suggesting that fine-tuning mainly increases semantic similarity to the ground truth rather than explicit use of limitations or future work. In contrast, restricting the context to only research ideas and methodology consistently reduces output diversity, indicating that access to limitations and future directions supports more exploratory ideation. Reasoning models tend to utilize contextual information more effectively, suggesting that their fine-tuning is a promising direction for exploiting structured summaries.

Influence of Decoding Temperature. Higher decoding temperature increases inter-generation dissimilarity, indicating greater output diversity. This increase does not reduce topic relevance or semantic similarity, which remain relatively stable across decoding conditions. Therefore, higher temperature provides a viable mechanism for encouraging idea variation without sacrificing quality. Reasoning models show lower sensitivity to decoding temperature without alignment, suggesting that their diversity is less driven by sampling effects.

LA and FDA Metrics. These metrics are demanding yet informative measures of conceptual grounding and relevance. Ground-truth ideas achieve modest scores, which is expected, as citation subgraphs capture diverse problems and multi-hop relations, while individual contributions derive from a subset of closely related works. Even so, LA and FDA provide a more discriminative signal than surface-level semantic metrics. Reasoning models achieve higher scores, indicating a stronger tendency to ground their ideas in limitations and future directions of the literature. This suggests that they leverage background knowledge more explicitly, though at the cost of dissimilarity, reflecting broader exploration rather than tight semantic alignment.

Our results highlight both the promise and the limits of alignment for scientific ideation. Fine-tuning improves consistency and semantic alignment, but reduces diversity and weakens grounding in limitations and future directions, indicating that semantic alignment alone is insufficient to capture deeper reasoning and creativity. Citation graphs and extracted key summaries provide rich context within practical length constraints, while access to limitations and future directions supports more diverse and exploratory ideation. Reasoning models emerge as a promising direction for balancing broader exploration with stronger grounding in prior work. Future work may benefit from citation-graph based reasoning, fine-tuning reasoning models and designing objectives that jointly optimize relevance and explanatory depth.

Acknowledgements. Financed by: CLARIN-PL project financed as part of the investment: "CLARIN ERIC – European Research Infrastructure Consortium: Common Language Resources and Technology Infrastructure (2024-2026), funded by the Polish Ministry of Science and Higher Education (2024/WK/01).

Disclosure of Interests. The authors declare that they have no competing interests.

References

1. Buehler, M.J.: Accelerating scientific discovery with generative knowledge extraction, graph-based representation, and multimodal intelligent graph reasoning. Mach. Learn.: Sci. Technol. 5 (2024)
2. Chen, N., Li, Y., Tang, J., Li, J.: GraphWiz: an instruction-following language model for graph computational problems. In: Proceedings of KDD, pp. 353–364 (2024)
3. Cicchetti, D.V., Feinstein, A.R.: High agreement but low kappa: II. Resolving the paradoxes. J. Clin. Epidemiol. **43**(6), 551–558 (1990)
4. Clement, C.B., Bierbaum, M., O'Keeffe, K.P., Alemi, A.A.: On the use of ArXiv as a dataset (2019). arXiv:1905.00075
5. Dasgupta, D., Mondal, A., Chakrabarti, P.P.: Empowering AI as autonomous researchers: evaluating LLMs in generating novel research ideas through automated metrics. In: AI for Research and Scalable, Efficient Systems, pp. 108–141 (2025)
6. Gao, X., Zhang, Z., Xie, M., Liu, T., Fu, Y.: Graph of AI ideas: leveraging knowledge graphs and LLMs for AI research idea generation (2025). arXiv:2503.08549

7. Hu, X., et al.: Nova: an iterative planning and search approach to enhance novelty and diversity of LLM generated ideas (2024). arXiv:2410.14255

8. Hu, X., Liu, G., Zhao, Y., Zhang, H.: De novo drug design using reinforcement learning with multiple GPT agents. In: Proceedings of the 37th NeurIPS (2023)

9. Li, L., et al.: Chain of ideas: revolutionizing research via novel idea development with LLM agents (2024). arXiv:2410.13185

10. Li, R., Jing, L., Han, C., Zhou, J., Du, X.: LDC: learning to generate research idea with dynamic control (2025). arXiv:2412.14626

11. Lin, E., Peng, Z., Fang, Y.: Evaluating and enhancing Large Language Models for novelty assessment in scholarly publications. In: AISD 2025, pp. 46–57 (2025)

12. Liu, S., Cao, J., Yang, R., Wen, Z.: Generating a structured summary of numerous academic papers: dataset and method. In: Proceedings of IJCAI, pp. 4259–4265 (2022)

13. O'Neill, C., et al.: Sparks of science: hypothesis generation using structured paper data (2025). arXiv:2504.12976

14. Page, L., Brin, S., Motwani, R., Winograd, T.: The PageRank citation ranking: bringing order to the web. Tech. Rep. 1999-66, Stanford InfoLab (1999)

15. Qi, B., Zhang, K., Li, H., Tian, K., Zeng, S., Chen, Z.R., Zhou, B.: Large language models are zero shot hypothesis proposers (2023). arXiv:2311.05965

16. Qi, B., et al.: Large language models as biomedical hypothesis generators: a comprehensive evaluation (2024). arXiv:2407.08940

17. Qiu, Y., et al.: AI idea bench 2025: AI research idea generation benchmark (2025). arXiv:2504.14191

18. Rafailov, R., Sharma, A., Mitchell, E., Ermon, S., Manning, C.D., Finn, C.: Direct preference optimization: your language model is secretly a reward model. In: Proceedings of NeurIPS, p. 2023 (2023)

19. Si, C., Yang, D., Hashimoto, T.: Can LLMs generate novel research ideas? A large-scale human study with 100+ NLP researchers. In: ICLR 2025 (2025)

20. Tang, J., Zhang, J., Yao, L., Li, J., Zhang, L., Su, Z.: ArnetMiner: extraction and mining of academic social networks. In: ACM SIGKDD 2008, pp. 990–998 (2008)

21. Wang, Q., Downey, D., Ji, H., Hope, T.: SciMON: scientific inspiration machines optimized for novelty. In: Proceedings of the ACL 2024, pp. 279–299 (2024)

22. Wang, W., et al.: SciPIP: an LLM-based scientific paper idea proposer (2025). arXiv:2410.23166

The Spatial and Temporal Resolution of Motor Intention in Multi-target Prediction

Marie D. Schmidt[1,2](✉) and Ioannis Iossifidis[1]

[1] Institute of Computer Science, University of Applied Science Ruhr West,
Mülheim an der Ruhr, Germany
[2] Institute for Neural Computation, Ruhr-University Bochum, Bochum, Germany
`marie.schmidt@ruhr-uni-bochum.de`

Abstract. Reaching, grasping, and object manipulation are essential motor functions in everyday life. This study predicts movement direction and target location from multichannel electromyography (EMG) signals, examining how spatially and temporally accurate intentions can be detected relative to movement onset. A computational pipeline combining data-driven temporal segmentation with Random Forest model is applied to EMG data across planning, execution, and contact phases of a reaching task.

Early prediction can improve device responsiveness and support motor recovery with up to 80% accuracy across classification of 25 spatial targets. Results further show that motor intentions can be reliably decoded with reduced data, highlighting the potential for efficient, anticipatory control in adaptive rehabilitation systems.

Keywords: Motor Control · Random Forest · HMI · EMG

1 Introduction

Reaching, grasping, and manipulating objects are fundamental components of human daily activity. These motor functions rely critically on the upper limb, highlighting the importance of preserving arm function for independence and interaction with the environment. While the neural decision-making and motor control are complex [14], in this study, we focus specifically on intention prediction, the ability to infer the direction and target of a movement from the electromyography (EMG) signal.

A key question in this context is how precisely movement intentions can be decoded from EMG signals in both spatial and temporal resolution, that is, how accurately the intended target can be identified and how early it can be predicted relative to movement onset. Previous studies suggest that neural signals recorded via EEG may reflect a general "go" signal, but provide limited information about the specific movement direction. Previous work has demonstrated that measurable EMG activity emerges as early as approximately 50 ms prior to movement

P. Neumann et al. (Eds.): ICCS 2026, LNCS 16784, pp. 421–428, 2026.
https://doi.org/10.1007/978-3-032-29924-6_36

onset, indicating early activation of motor commands [3] (Fig. 1c). It remains an open question whether such pre-movement EMG activity also encodes spatial aspects of the upcoming movement, such as reach direction or endpoint position. Understanding these limits is essential not only for basic neuroscience, but also for practical applications in rehabilitation and humanmachine interfaces (HMI), such as prosthetic control and assistive robotics. An early prediction of movement intention enables HMI to anticipate actions rather than react and can assist patients when they intend to move, encouraging active participation. This reduces delays and promotes more effective and intuitive motor recovery.

To demonstrate this, we use a delayed reaching task with 5×5 spatial targets distributed by $14°$ azimuth/altitude to investigate upper-limb movement. In this task, the spatial goal of the reach is revealed to the participant in advance, while the initiation of the movement is withheld until a go cue (Fig. 1e). This setup ensures that EMG activity observed before movement onset can be attributed to motor planning and preparatory processes rather than to actual movement execution. This allows us to examine if the preparatory phase contains sufficient information not only to predict the imminent onset of movement, but also to infer the intended movement direction or target location before execution begins.

We start with assessing the classification performance to determine how accurately EMG can resolve different movement directions based on the EMG signal. To achieve this, we employ a Random Forest (RF), suited for these tasks [10]. We then systematically evaluate channel selection and feature reduction, determining how the number of EMG channels and temporal features affects predictive performance. Furthermore, we analyze predictive accuracy across temporal windows, spanning pre-motion, early motion, late motion, and holding to determine how intention-related information evolves over time.

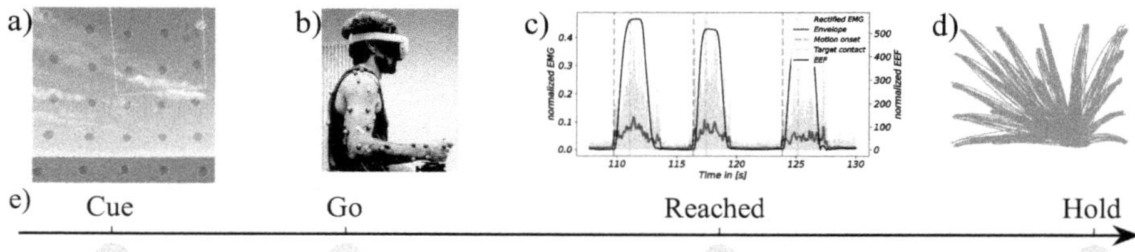

Fig. 1. Experimental setup and task: a) VR environment from the participant's perspective. b) placement of motion capture markers and EMG electrodes. c) EMG and End-EFfector trajectory, and task events. d) EEF trajectory. e) Task event timeline.

2   Method

The delayed reaching task is implemented in Unity and presented via an Oculus Quest 2 headset. Participants reach toward targets arranged in a 5×5 spherical grid ($14°$ spacing) with a radius adapted to individual arm length (500650 mm), enabling reaching without trunk movement (Fig. 1a,d). The experiment consists of 3 sessions with 6 repetitions each; target order is randomized, resulting in 18 reaches per target. The study is approved by the Ethics Committee of Ruhr-University Bochum, and all participants provided written informed consent. EMG and positional data are recorded simultaneously. EMG is acquired at 2000 Hz using a Delsys Trigno system with 10 electrodes placed (triceps and biceps brachii, wrist and extensor, deltoid posterior/lateral/anterior, pectoralis, trapezius, latissimus dorsi), and processing is according to SENIAM [9]. Motion capture is performed at 100 Hz using a Vicon system with 6 cameras and 20 markers based on a modified Southampton Upper Limb model [16] (Fig. 1b,d).

3   Results

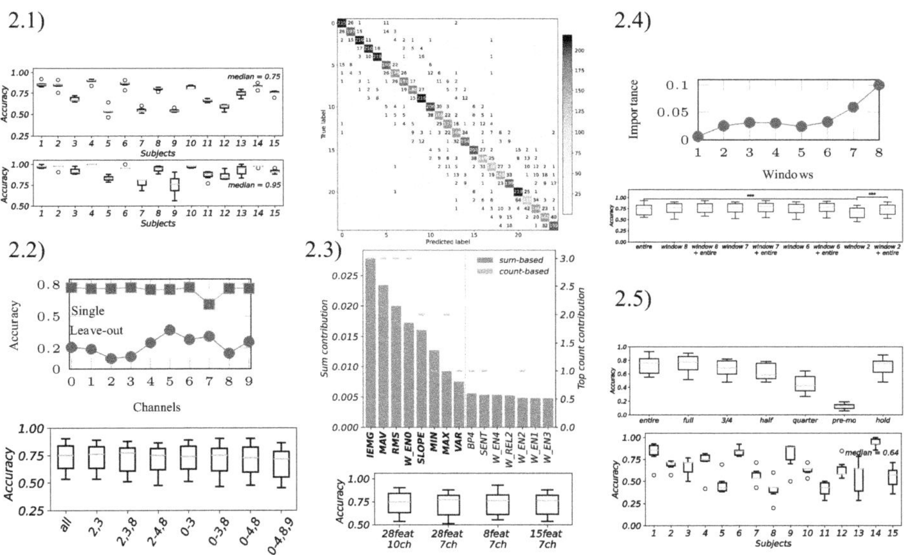

Fig. 2. Comprehensive Random Forest analysis combining baseline classification performance (2.1), channel importance (2.2), feature importance (2.3), temporal segmentation (2.4), and early intention decoding (2.5).

3.1   Spatial Resolution Baseline Classification

Random Forest (RF) is commonly used as a baseline model due to its strong performance on high-dimensional, heterogeneous data and robustness to noise [6]. EMG features often exhibit correlation and redundancy due to muscle synergies and co-contraction patterns, which RF handles effectively through feature subsampling and ensemble averaging, reducing overfitting while preserving discriminative power.

To optimize model performance, hyperparameters are tuned using Optuna with a Tree-structured Parzen Estimator sampler. The optimized hyperparameters include 500 estimators, a maximum tree depth of 10, a minimum of 2 samples for splitting, 3 samples per leaf, and a maximum feature selection of the square root of number of features.

We evaluate the RF classifier using 5-fold cross-validation with an 80/20 traintest split in each fold. To account for inter-subject variability, separate models are trained for each participant. As an initial benchmark, a baseline configuration is assessed to provide an overall measure of classification performance. This baseline uses all available EMG channels, a single temporal window covering the entire reaching movement, and the full set of 28 extracted features. Under this configuration, the median classification accuracy across subjects was 75%, corresponding to a spatial resolution of up to 14°. Individual subject accuracies range from 50% to 90% (Fig. 2.1), with lower-performing subjects (50% − 60%: subjects 5, 7, 9, 11, and 12) showing similar trends across other classification approaches.

The confusion matrix (Fig. 2.1) illustrates the relationship between predicted and true class labels. As expected, given the high overall accuracy, the diagonal elements dominate, indicating a high rate of correct predictions. Misclassifications primarily occur between spatially adjacent targets left, right, above, or below the true location suggesting that errors are confined to nearby classes and reflecting a graded spatial encoding of movement direction in the EMG signals.

To explore the impact of task difficulty, we compare the full 5×5 target grid (each target 14° apart with 75% accuracy) with a reduced number of targets (every second target omitted, leaving 12 or 13 classes). Classification accuracy substantially improves, with median accuracy across participants reaching 95% (Fig. 2.1). Most subjects even approach 100% accuracy, though lower-performing subjects remain below this ceiling. Misclassifications continues to occur primarily between neighboring classes.

These results highlight that baseline performance is robust, while classification errors are localized to nearby targets. The next step is to systematically reduce data dimensionality to identify the most informative EMG channels and feature subsets for movement prediction.

3.2 EMG Channel Importance

EMG signals are recorded from ten muscles involved in reaching movements. Some muscles may carry redundant information due to co-contraction or antagonistic patterns. To assess their contribution, we evaluate each muscle individually and via a leave-one-out approach (Fig. 2.2).

This analysis identifies the wrist flexor, wrist extensor, and trapezius as the least informative channels. Excluding these three, the RF model maintains a median accuracy of 75% (Fig. 2.2). Further channel reduction leads to decreased accuracy, indicating that most recorded muscles provide relevant information for the prediction task, despite limited redundancy.

3.3 Feature Importance

To characterize EMG signals for upper-limb intention decoding, we extract features from the time, frequency, and timefrequency domains [2,12].

Time-domain features include mean absolute value, root mean square, waveform length, variance, integrated EMG, slope, as well as minimum and maximum values. Frequency-domain features comprise mean frequency, median frequency, peak frequency, spectral entropy, total power, and relative band power. Time-frequency features are obtained using a discrete wavelet transform, from which wavelet energy, relative energy, and wavelet entropy are computed.

All features are calculated independently for each EMG channel and concatenated into a single feature vector, yielding 28 features in total. While many time-domain features are highly correlated, RF classifiers are robust to such redundancy. To refine the feature set, we analyze each feature's contribution to prediction accuracy (Fig. 2.3) and select 8 features that preserve maximal performance. This subset retains all time-domain features except waveform length, includes wavelet entropy, and excludes most frequency- and timefrequency features. Using this reduced feature set and fewer channels, the median classification accuracy slightly improves to 76%, with a substantial reduction in data dimensionality from 280 to 56.

3.4 Temporal Resolution

So far, all features are computed over the entire movement from go cue to target contact. To identify which temporal segments contribute most to classification, the reach is divided into eight non-overlapping windows of ~ 200 ms each, recommended by [8], with 8 features computed for 7 channels per window. This preserves the chronological structure of muscle activation patterns. Window-wise permutation importance (Fig. 2.4) reveals that late segments dominate, with windows 7 and 8 (final ~ 400 ms before target contact) contributing most to classification. Evaluating accuracy across different window selections (Fig. 2.4) shows peak performance when excluding only the first window and further improves when the full-movement window is included, reaching 80%. Removing additional windows reduces accuracy, indicating that while late segments are most informative, early windows provide complementary cues. Overall, these results demonstrate that discriminative information is temporally concentrated toward the end of the reach, but that aggregating information across multiple time scales, including an entire window, yields the most robust classification.

3.5 Early Intention Decoding

We have demonstrated that 25 different movement classes can be reliably predicted from EMG signals. Beyond identifying configurations that maximize classification performance, it is also clinically relevant to determine how early in time the intended movement direction can be inferred and what trade-offs in accuracy arise when predictions are made from partial temporal information. To this end, we systematically evaluate classification performance using progressively longer temporal segments, including the first quarter, first half, first three quarters, and full reach duration, as well as the post-contact hold phase. Additionally, we analyze pre-motion conditions in which the target is known, but actual movement is constrained (Fig. 2.5).

Prediction performance decreases systematically when the analysis is restricted to earlier temporal segments. Using only the first quarter of the reach results in an accuracy of 42%, reflecting lower discriminative information during early movement execution. Notably, the median classification accuracy during the pre-motion interval is 13% across participants, despite the absence of observable movement, which is still three times better than a random selection of 4 options.

We further aim to determine the resolution limit of our approach, specifically the minimum number of classes to which the problem must be reduced in order to achieve reliable classification performance. By reducing the number of classes to 4, i.e. only considering the corner targets, the median classification accuracy across subjects in the pre-motion interval increases to 64% (Fig. 2.4). However, substantial inter-subject variability persisted, with some participants achieving considerably higher performance than others. This finding suggests that preparatory muscle activation already encodes information about the intended target before movement onset, which has important implications for rehabilitation, as it enables anticipatory, intention-driven assistance rather than purely reactive control, thereby supporting more natural and effective motor recovery and daily-life interaction.

4   Discussion

Classification performance exhibits substantial inter-subject variability. While several participants achieve high accuracies, others show reduced performance. This high variability of EMG signal derives from differences in anatomy, electrode placement, and subcutaneous tissue properties [5,15], [1,4,7,11,13]. Also, the trajectory of the arm movement varies more. Such inter-subject differences are well known in EMG-based classification studies and highlight the challenges of developing subject-independent and universally robust decoding models.

Channel selection reveals physiologically meaningful patterns: proximal muscles dominate target discrimination, while wrist muscles and trapezius contribute little. In contrast, biceps, triceps, anterior deltoid, and pectoralis major are most informative, consistent with their role in arm transport. This aligns with the biomechanics of reaching movements performed in front of the body. Overall selecting 7 of 10 channels provides strong discriminative power.

The feature selection results are consistent with previous EMG classification studies [12], [2]. Time-domain features exhibit high discriminative power, reflecting their sensitivity to muscle activation amplitude and temporal structure. In addition, wavelet entropy emerge as a highly informative feature, capturing the complexity and non-stationary characteristics of EMG signals.

Optimizing the number of channels, features, and temporal windows results in a substantial reduction of the input data dimensionality while maintaining classification performance. The best-performing configuration consists of seven EMG channels, eight features, and a combination of seven temporal windows plus an entire window spanning the whole reach, achieving a median accuracy of 80%. Which is high compared to other reaching predictions [8] for 8 targets with around 70%.

Furthermore, we investigate the earliest point in time at which movement intention can be reliably decoded. As expected, prediction performance is highest when using the full reach. However, meaningful classification is already possible before initial target contact. During the pre-motion interval, when the target is known but movement execution has not yet started, classification accuracy reaches 13%, averaged for all 25 targets, and 64% in the simplified four-class scenario. This finding indicates that preparatory muscle activity encodes target-specific information well before actual movement begins. The ability to decode movement intention during pre-motion and early execution phases is particularly relevant for assistive robotics, exoskeleton control, and neurorehabilitation. Early intention detection could enable more responsive and anticipatory assistance, improving user comfort and task performance. Moreover, the demonstrated reduction in required sensors and features supports the feasibility of deploying such systems in practical, wearable settings.

5   Conclusion

This study shows that intended reaching targets can be reliably decoded from upper-limb EMG using a compact and physiologically meaningful representation. A reduced setup of 7 channels, 8 features, and several temporal windows achieves up to 80% accuracy with minimal loss in performance. Proximal muscles dominate target discrimination, while wrist muscles contribute little, and time-domain and wavelet features are most informative. Importantly, movement intention can be predicted also before movement onset, with performance well above chance in the pre-motion phase. This highlights the potential of EMG-based decoding for anticipatory control in assistive and rehabilitation systems.

Acknowledgment. This work is supported by grants GE-2-2-023A (REXO) and IT-2-2-023 (VAFES), and grant 163V9070 (RooWalk-HRW).

Disclosure of Interest. The authors declare that they have neither a financial nor a non-financial competing interest.

References

1. Araujo, R.C., Duarte, M., Amadio, A.C.: On the inter-and intra-subject variability of the electromyographic signal in isometric contractions. Electromyogr. Clin. Neurophysiol. **40**(4), 225–230 (2000)

2. Corvini, G., de Nobile, A., Del Grossi, T., De Marchis, C., Gandolla, M., Ambrosini, E., Schmid, M.: EMG-based reaching prediction for upper limb rehabilitation: a systematic analysis of factors affecting the classification accuracy. Res. Square (2025)
3. Deecke, L., Scheid, P., Kornhuber, H.H.: Distribution of readiness potential, premotion positivity, and motor potential of the human cerebral cortex preceding voluntary finger movements. Exp. Brain Res. **7**(2), 158–168 (1969)
4. Farina, D., Cescon, C., Merletti, R.: Influence of anatomical, physical, and detection-system parameters on surface EMG. Biol. Cybern. **86**(6), 445–456 (2002)
5. Farina, D., Jiang, N., Rehbaum, H., Holobar, A., Graimann, B., Dietl, H., Aszmann, O.C.: The extraction of neural information from the surface EMG for the control of upper-limb prostheses: emerging avenues and challenges. IEEE Trans. Neural Syst. Rehabil. Eng. **22**(4), 797–809 (2014)
6. Fernández-Delgado, M., Cernadas, E., Barro, S., Amorim, D.: Do we need hundreds of classifiers to solve real world classification problems? J. Mach. Learn. Res. **15**(1), 3133–3181 (2014)
7. Hogrel, J.Y., Duchêne, J., Marini, J.F.: Variability of some SEMG parameter estimates with electrode location. J. Electromyogr. Kinesiol. **8**(5), 305–315 (1998)
8. Irastorza-Landa, N., et al.: Design of continuous EMG classification approaches towards the control of a robotic exoskeleton in reaching movements. In: 2017 International Conference on Rehabilitation Robotics (ICORR), pp. 128–133. IEEE (2017)
9. Konrad, P.: Emg-Fibel. Eine Praxisorientierte Einführung in die Kinesiologische Elektromyographie (2005)
10. Mora-Rubio, A., et al.: Multi-subject identification of hand movements using machine learning. In: Sustainable Smart Cities and Territories International Conference, pp. 117–128. Springer (2021)
11. Nordander, C., et al.: Influence of the subcutaneous fat layer, as measured by ultrasound, skinfold calipers and BMI, on the EMG amplitude. Eur. J. Appl. Physiol. **89**(6), 514–519 (2003)
12. Phinyomark, A., Khushaba, N., Scheme, R., E.: Feature extraction and selection for myoelectric control based on wearable EMG sensors. Sensors **18**(5), 1615 (2018)
13. Schmidt, M.D., Glasmachers, T., Iossifidis, I.: The concepts of muscle activity generation driven by upper limb kinematics. Biomed. Eng. Online **22**(1), 1–29 (2023)
14. Schmidt, M.D., Glasmachers, T., Iossifidis, I.: Insights into motor control: predict muscle activity from upper limb kinematics with LSTM networks. Sci. Rep. , (2026)
15. Sheng, X., Lv, B., Guo, W., Zhu, X.: Common spatial-spectral analysis of EMG signals for multiday and multiuser myoelectric interface. Biomed. Signal Process. Control **53**, 101572 (2019)
16. Warner, M.: Instructions for ProCalc Implementation of Upper Limb Model, Southampton, UK (2023). technical documentation

A Three-Stage Neuro-Symbolic Recommendation Pipeline for Cultural Heritage Knowledge Graphs

Krzysztof Kutt[✉][iD], Elżbieta Sroka[iD], Oleksandra Ishchuk, and Luiz do Valle Miranda[iD]

Department of Human-Centered Artificial Intelligence, Institute of Applied Computer Science, Faculty of Physics, Astronomy and Applied Computer Science, Jagiellonian University, prof. Stanisława Łojasiewicza 11, 30-348 Kraków, Poland
{krzysztof.kutt,elzbieta.sroka,luiz.miranda}@uj.edu.pl

Abstract. The growing volume of digital cultural heritage resources highlights the need for advanced recommendation methods capable of interpreting semantic relationships between heterogeneous data entities. This paper presents a complete methodology for implementing a hybrid recommendation pipeline integrating knowledge graph embeddings, approximate nearest-neighbour search, and SPARQL-driven semantic filtering. The work is evaluated on the JUHMP (Jagiellonian University Heritage Metadata Portal) knowledge graph developed within the CHExRISH project, which at the time of experimentation contained ≈3.2M RDF triples describing people, events, objects, and historical relations affiliated with the Jagiellonian University (Kraków, PL). Despite sparse and heterogeneous metadata, the approach produces useful and explainable recommendations, which were also proven with expert evaluation.

Keywords: Cultural heritage · Recommendations · Hybrid recommender · Knowledge graphs · Knowledge graph embedding · RDF · HNSW

1 Introduction and Motivation

Cultural heritage (CH), including museum, library, and archival collections as well as the achievements of cultural, scientific, and political figures, is an invaluable source of knowledge about a community's art, history, and identity. Mass digitization has rapidly expanded the volume of digital CH resources , shifting research from scarcity to an era of "abundance," where inconsistent cataloging and metadata reduce search quality and overload researchers [22]. In practice, scholars must navigate multiple, disconnected search interfaces and iteratively refine queries, often obtaining large sets of irrelevant or low-quality results [12] that cannot be filtered due to missing or coarse metadata [9].

© The Author(s), under exclusive license to Springer Nature Switzerland AG 2026
P. Neumann et al. (Eds.): ICCS 2026, LNCS 16784, pp. 429–437, 2026.
https://doi.org/10.1007/978-3-032-29924-6_37

These challenges stem from the distinctive nature of CH metadata: (1) *VISU complexity*—vagueness, incompleteness, subjectivity, and uncertainty [13]—makes digital representation of historical narratives inherently difficult [11], (2) *Fragmented and low-quality metadata*, often limited to basic catalog descriptions [4], (3) *Heterogeneous metadata schemas* across institutions, particularly visible in large aggregators like Europeana [7], and (4) *Lack of user history*.

Addressing these issues requires multiple perspectives. First, semantic data modeling—using technologies such as RDF and SPARQL [16]—enables representing CH information as knowledge graphs (KGs) that capture complex relationships among objects, creators, dates, functions, and places [4,18]. This approach is increasingly adopted by cultural institutions [16,18]. Second, automated and semi-automated metadata enrichment leverages machine learning to extract semantic features and map them to structured ontologies [6]. Expert validation complements these methods, correcting errors and adding contextual interpretation that automated tools cannot yet provide [12]. However, these efforts primarily expand and refine metadata rather than support researchers in navigating vast CH collections [10]. Although KGs have enabled semantic search [3] and query/document expansion [1], they still extend traditional keyword-based search without fundamentally improving user interaction.

We argue that recommendation systems (RS) offer a promising direction. Although widely used in domains like entertainment and e-commerce [14], RSs remain uncommon in CH and typically provide only simple thematic suggestions [2,10,15]. This work evaluates the feasibility of applying modern RS techniques to CH data. We introduce a three-stage recommendation pipeline (Sect. 2) and test it on a heterogeneous KG representing the cultural heritage of Jagiellonian University, developed within the CHExRISH project (Sect. 3). The method is generic and applicable to diverse CH datasets.

2   Methods

2.1   Three-Stage Recommendation Pipeline

Guided by the challenges outlined in Sect. 1, we designed a recommendation pipeline grounded in four assumptions:

1. RDF KGs as data backbone, ensuring interoperability and reusability [18].
2. Graph embedding-based recommendations are required [23], as traditional content-based or collaborative filtering is unsuitable in CH due to VISU properties, metadata heterogeneity, and lack of user history.
3. An approximate nearest-neighbor (ANN) search is necessary for scalable candidate generation; HNSW or FAISS can be chosen depending on scale-latency-memory constraints [17].
4. Symbolic filtering must complement pipeline to enforce logical consistency, remove low-quality candidates, and incorporate domain constraints, following evidence that rule-based refinement improves accuracy and novelty [19].

Following these assumptions, we implemented a three-stage neuro-symbolic pipeline tailored to CH data summarized in Fig. 1 [8].

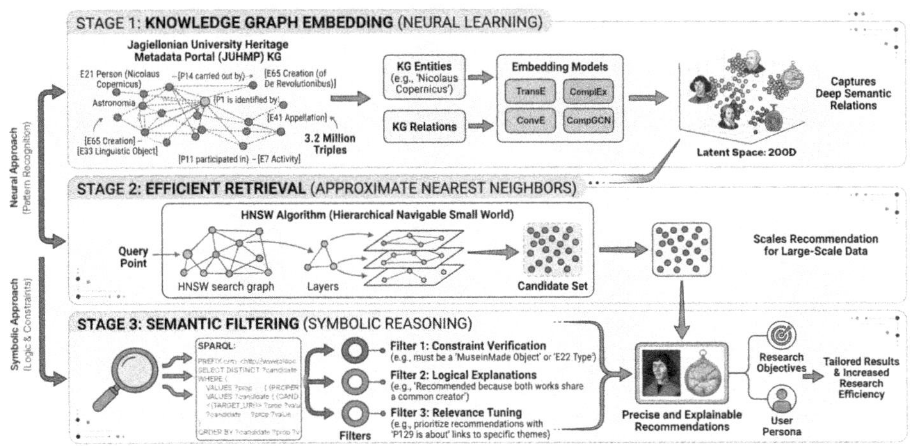

Fig. 1. Three-stage recommendation pipeline overview.

2.2 CHExRISH Use Case

The pipeline was developed within the CHExRISH project (https://chexrish.id.
uj.edu.pl/), which creates the JUHMP (Jagiellonian University Heritage Metadata Portal). It integrates heterogeneous archival (AUJ), museum (MUJ), and
library (JL) datasets into a CIDOC-CRM-based KG capturing people, events,
places, and objects associated with Jagiellonian University since the 14th cen-
tury [20]. Cross-institution alignment in the second JUHMP prototype is based
on a semi-automatically generated authority file with 824 verified matches [21].

Because the graph is person-centric, the primary scenario was defined
as: *given a historical individual, identify other people who are similar or
meaningfully connected.* Similarity deliberately remains open-ended to support
exploratory research, i.e., scenarios not well served by keyword-based search.

With this in mind, two versions of the graph were used as the basis for the
reported work: *Prototype2* with only cross-institution matches (402,948 triples)
and *FullCAC_260128* extended with all AUJ persons (3,202,711 triples; the
largest possible graph at the time of writing).

2.3 Pipeline Implementation for CHExRISH Use Case

A preliminary benchmark on *Prototype2* compared four embedding models[1]:
TransE, ComplEx, ConvE, and CompGCN. ComplEx achieved the best bal-
ance of quality, runtime ($\approx$46 min for 10 epochs), and memory use (+64
MB). Although CompGCN achieved slightly higher accuracy, its training time

---

[1] For detailed results and a description of the experimental setup, see
ICCS2026_Supplement.pdf in the repository linked in *Code and Data Availability.*

```
 1  PREFIX crm: <http://www.cidoc-crm.org/cidoc-crm/>
 2
 3  SELECT DISTINCT ?candidate ?prop ?value
 4  WHERE {
 5      VALUES ?prop      { {PROPERTIES_URIS} }
 6      VALUES ?candidate { {CANDIDATES_URIS} }
 7      <{TARGET_URI}> ?prop ?value .
 8      ?candidate      ?prop ?value .
 9  }
10  ORDER BY ?candidate ?prop ?value
```

Listing 1.1. SPARQL query used to check whether the target and candidates share the same value in given set of properties.

($\approx$13.3h) made it impractical. ConvE showed consistently poor results. Hyperparameter tuning showed that $lr = 0.01$ (learning rate) and $dim = 200$ (embedding dimensionality) offered the best trade-off between predictive quality (MRR, $Hits@k$) and resource consumption for ComplEx. For ANN search, ComplEx embeddings were indexed with HNSWLib Python package. A grid search yielded the following configuration: $M = 16$ (graph connectivity), $efConstruction = 400$ (build-time search breadth), $efSearch = 50$ (query-time search breadth). Because indexing is a one-time operation, selection criteria focused on retrieval quality ($Recall@k$) and query latency rather than build-time cost.

At query time, based on the target node, the pipeline first retrieves the nearest neighbors from the HNSW index. These candidates are then refined using a set of SPARQL queries that ensure semantic validity and contextual relevance. The semantic filtering stage is a general concept but is highly dependent on the KG used as input and covered scenarios. In evaluated scenario, candidates are restricted to instances of *crm:E39_Actor* or *crm:E21_Person*, after which a predefined set of SPARQL tests checks for shared relations with the target node. Allowed connection types include same objects connection, same events, close death dates, same place of birth, etc. For example, the "same events" filter identifies candidates linked to the same event via *crm:P11i_participated_in*, *crm:P12i_was_present_at*, or *crm:P14i_performed* (see Listing 1.1). A candidate is retained only if there is at least one such exact link. The pipeline also records the specific shared predicates, enabling for explainability.

2.4   Evaluation Approach

After selecting the best model configuration , the full pipeline was applied to both KGs (Sect. 2.2). The evaluation focused on nine historically significant figures from Jagiellonian University (e.g., Nicolaus Copernicus; see Table 1). This approach, focusing on well-known individuals, facilitated the expert evaluation.

Quantitative evaluation focused on verifying the basic performance of the embedding and ANN stages. The experts then assessed whether the top 10 recommendations for each target were meaningful and historically grounded. They received an online questionnaire and rated each candidate on a scale: *2 – close connection*, a user reading information about X will be interested in person Y; *1 – distant connection*, the user may be interested in such a suggestion; *0 –*

very distant connection (incorrect), the user will not be interested in such a suggestion; *-1 – I do not know this person*. Optional comments could also be provided.

The expert study group included people from AUJ, MUJ and JL. These are people with extensive experience in the field of history and heritage of Jagiellonian University. Four experts were involved in the evaluation of *Prototype2*. The larger model (*FullCAC_260128*) was evaluated by 10 experts.

3 Results and Discussion

3.1 Quantitative Evaluation

For *Prototype2*, the final 120-epoch ComplEx model achieved $MRR = 0.2207$, indicating that the correct entity typically appeared within the top 4–5 ranked positions, although not consistently at rank 1. $Hits@1 = 0.1659$ confirms limited ability to place the correct entity first, while $Hits@3 = 0.2421$ and $Hits@10 = 0.3288$ show that the model retrieved the correct entity within the top 10 in roughly one-third of the queries. Overall, the model reliably surfaced relevant candidates but struggled to prioritize the correct one at the very top. Training required ≈ 22 h on a CPU-only node.

For *FullCAC_260128*, training was completed in 108 h (GPU node) with $MRR = 0.1393$, $Hits@1 = 0.1057$, $Hits@3 = 0.1572$ and $Hits@10 = 0.2098$. Lower metrics were expected due to the graph's characteristics: it is both sparser (many individuals with few connections) and denser in population (contains all persons linked to the University between the 14th and 18th centuries), making the embedding task more difficult. Despite this, the larger model produced semantically closer recommendations. The similarity of the top recommendation ranged from 0.40 to 0.85, compared to $[-0.41; 0.21]$ for *Prototype2* (cosine similarity ranging from -1 to 1). Its greater historical coverage also enabled the pipeline to recommend a wider and more accurate set of relevant individuals. Therefore, we expected stronger expert evaluation results for the larger graph despite the lower quantitative metrics.

3.2 Expert Evaluation

Experts assessed the top 10 recommendations for each of the nine targets (historical figures), rating connections as close or distant (Table 1). Despite the *Prototype2* graph's limited size, experts validated at least one meaningful connection per target. When relevant links existed in the graph, the model typically surfaced them, and experts confirmed their correctness. However, the small graph inherently restricted the number of plausible connections, limiting the frequency of close matches. The larger model (*FullCAC_260128*) produced more close and distant connections, as expected from its higher population density and broader temporal coverage. Experts confirmed that the pipeline successfully identified historically grounded relationships, reflecting the advantages of training on a more complete graph.

Table 1. Number of close and distant recommendations as indicated by experts for both models. Target labels are abbreviated for clarity.

Target	Prototype2		FullCAC_260128	
	Close	Distant	Close	Distant
Benedykt z Koźmina ...	1	5	2	1
Sebastian Sierakowski (hrabia)	0	7	1	9
Stanisław Reszka z Buku ...	0	2	2	1
Jan III Sobieski (król Polski ; ...)	0	1	0	6
Maciej Karpiga z Miechowa ...	0	5	2	10
Mikołaj Kopernik (Copernicus) ...	0	3	0	6
Jakub Górski (młodszy) ...	0	2	3	6
Andrzej z Buku (starszy)	0	1	2	6
Jan Brożek (Broscius) ...	0	2	2	6

In the free comment fields, experts noted several factors that affected their ability to assess the recommendations. In some cases, individuals shared identical names and places of origin, making it difficult to determine whether a suggested connection was historically valid. The experts therefore suggested including identifiers from the AUJ database to avoid ambiguity. They also emphasized the need for greater explainability, expressing interest in seeing why the algorithm selected each recommendation, such as shared events or locations. Finally, they observed that the distinction between "close" and "distant" connections remained subjective, even with provided definitions, since evaluating the strength of historical relationships often depends on contextual knowledge and interpretation.

4   Conclusions

We presented an end-to-end three stage (embedding, HNSW candidate generation, SPARQL-based semantic filtering) recommendation pipeline for cultural heritage data. It exemplifies a neuro-symbolic recommender: vector neighborhoods provide recall, while ontological/SPARQL constraints supply correctness and explanations. This approach is aligned with current practice in heritage KGs and with sector needs for transparency [19].

The evaluation demonstrates both the feasibility and usefulness of the approach, while also highlighting the importance of ongoing collaboration with domain experts. Future development must include a dedicated user interface closely coupled with the KG exploration environment, allowing users to access stable identifiers and clear explanations for each recommendation. Experts also noted that the definitions of "close" and "distant" connections require refinement. Therefore, we plan to conduct workshops to co-design appropriate recommendation scenarios, evaluation criteria, and corresponding filters.

This hybrid framework addresses directly the overload of irrelevant or low-quality results that motivated the work by combining the predictive capabilities of neural models with the precision of symbolic constraints. With continued data curation and hybrid modeling, the method can generalize beyond persons to places, events, and artworks. Finally, text-to-SPARQL techniques [5] offer a promising path toward personalized recommendations without requiring users to manually define semantic filters.

Acknowledgment. We would like to express our sincere gratitude to the experts from the JU Archives, the JU Museum, and the Jagiellonian Library for their time spent evaluating the pipeline. This publication was funded by a flagship project "CHExRISH: Cultural Heritage Exploration and Retrieval with Intelligent Systems at Jagiellonian University" under the Strategic Programme Excellence Initiative at Jagiellonian University. The research for this publication has been supported by a grant from the Priority Research Area DigiWorld under the Strategic Programme Excellence Initiative at Jagiellonian University. We gratefully acknowledge Polish high-performance computing infrastructure PLGrid (HPC Center: ACK Cyfronet AGH) for providing computer facilities and support within computational grant no. PLG/2025/018037. During the preparation of this work the authors used MS Copilot and Writefully in order to improve the readability and language of the manuscript. The initial version of the pipeline diagram (Fig. 1) was generated with Google Gemini. After using these tools, the authors reviewed and edited the content as needed and take full responsibility for the content of the published article.

Code and Data Availability. All code is publicly available in the repository: https://gitlab.geist.re/pro/chex-recs. Input KGs and intermediate files (e.g., embeddings) are available upon request.

Disclosure of Interests. The authors have no competing interests to declare that are relevant to the content of this article.

References

1. Alma'aitah, W.Z., Talib, A.Z., Osman, M.A.: Opportunities and challenges in enhancing access to metadata of cultural heritage collections: a survey. Artif. Intell. Rev. **53**(5), 3621–3646 (2020). https://doi.org/10.1007/s10462-019-09773-w
2. Casillo, M., Colace, F., Conte, D., Lombardi, M., Santaniello, D., Valentino, C.: Context-aware recommender systems and cultural heritage: a survey. J. Amb. Intell. Hum. Comput. **14**, 3109–3127 (2023). https://doi.org/10.1007/s12652-021-03438-9
3. Chansanam, W., et al.: Cultural heritage preservation through ontology-based semantic search systems. Conserv. Sci. Cult. Herit. **23**(1), 183–196 (2023). https://doi.org/10.6092/issn.1973-9494/20048
4. Dangerfield, M.C., Kalshoven, L.: Report and recommendations from the task force on metadata quality. Tech. rep., Europeana (2015). https://pro.europeana.eu/files/Europeana_Professional/Europeana_Network/metadata-quality-report.pdf
5. Hansali, A., Hocine, K.B., Zemmouchi-Ghomari, L., Ghomari, A.R.: Translation from natural language questions to SPARQL: a survey. In: 4th Edition of the National Study Days on Research on Computer Sciences, JERI'2020 (2020)

6. Ignatowicz, J., Kutt, K., Nalepa, G.J.: Position paper: metadata enrichment model: Integrating neural networks and semantic knowledge graphs for cultural heritage applications. In: 2025 International Joint Conference on Neural Networks (IJCNN), pp. 1–8 (2025). https://doi.org/10.1109/IJCNN64981.2025.11228881

7. Isaac, A.: Case study: Enriching and sharing cultural heritage data in Europeana. Tech. rep., W3C (2012). https://www.w3.org/2001/sw/sweo/public/UseCases/Europeana/

8. Ishchuk, O.: Search and recommendation methods in graph knowledge bases describing cultural heritage, Jagiellonian University (2025). supervisor: K. Kutt Master's thesis

9. Kamal, A.M., Golub, K.: Subject matters: metadata standards and subject access for library and museum catalogues. In: Hanssen, J.M., Furuseth, S. (eds.) The Hermeneutics of Bibliographic Data and Cultural Metadata, pp. 204–239. National Library of Norway (2025)

10. Li, J., Bikakis, A.: Towards a semantics-based recommendation system for cultural heritage collections. Appl. Sci. **13**, 8907 (2023). https://doi.org/10.3390/app13158907

11. Lian, Y., Xie, J.: The evolution of digital cultural heritage research: identifying key trends, hotspots, and challenges through bibliometric analysis. Sustainability **16**(16), 7125 (2024). https://doi.org/10.3390/su16167125

12. Lorenzini, M., Rospocher, M., Tonelli, S.: On assessing metadata completeness in digital cultural heritage repositories. Digit. Scholarship Human. **36**(Supplement_2), ii182–ii188 (2021). https://doi.org/10.1093/llc/fqab036

13. Mariani, F.: Introducing VISU: vagueness, incompleteness, subjectivity, and uncertainty in art provenance data. In: Rochat, Y., Métrailler, C., Piotrowski, M. (eds.) Proceedings of COMHUM 2022, pp. 63–84. CEUR Workshop Proceedings, CEUR-WS.org (2022). https://ceur-ws.org/Vol-3602/paper5.pdf

14. Raza, S., et al.: A comprehensive review of recommender systems: transitioning from theory to practice. Comput. Sci. Rev. **59**, 100849 (2026). https://doi.org/10.1016/j.cosrev.2025.100849

15. Ruotsalo, T., et al.: SMARTMUSEUM: a mobile recommender system for the web of data. J. Web Semant. **20**, 50–67 (2013). https://doi.org/10.1016/J.WEBSEM.2013.03.001

16. Schreur, P.E.: The use of linked data and artificial intelligence as key elements in the transformation of technical services. Catalog. Classif. Quart. **58**, 473–485 (2020). https://doi.org/10.1080/01639374.2020.1772434

17. Shah, H.: A comparative study of HNSW implementations for scalable approximate nearest neighbor search (2025). https://doi.org/10.36227/techrxiv.175321947.71782908/v1

18. Silva, A.L., Terra, A.L.: Cultural heritage on the semantic web: the Europeana data model. IFLA J. **50**, 93–107 (2024). https://doi.org/10.1177/03400352231202506

19. Spillo, G., Musto, C., de Gemmis, M., Lops, P., Semeraro, G.: Recommender systems based on neuro-symbolic knowledge graph embeddings encoding first-order logic rules. User Model. User Adapt. Interact. **34**(5), 2039–2083 (2024). https://doi.org/10.1007/S11257-024-09417-X

20. do Valle Miranda, L., Kutt, K., Nalepa, G.J.: CIDOC-CRM and the first prototype of a semantic portal for the Chexrish project. In: Bruns, O., Graciotti, A., Sartini, B., Tietz, T. (eds.) Proceedings of SemDH 2025. CEUR Workshop Proceedings, vol. 4009. CEUR-WS.org (2025). https://ceur-ws.org/Vol-4009/paper_14.pdf

21. do Valle Miranda, L., Mozolewski, M., Kutt, K., Nalepa, G.J.: A Wikidata-based workflow for entity reconciliation strategies evaluation: a study on early modern polish personal names. In: Proceedings of ESWC 2026 (2026). accepted for publication (to appear)
22. Zaagsma, G.: Digital history and the politics of digitization. Digital Scholarship i Human. **38**(2), 830–851 (2022). https://doi.org/10.1093/llc/fqac050
23. Zhao, X., et al.: Embedding in recommender systems: a survey. CoRR abs/2310.18608 (2023). https://doi.org/10.48550/ARXIV.2310.18608

Modelling Traffic Policy with Drivers and Government Behavior Using Evolutionary Game Theory

Ilia Beregovenko$^{(\boxtimes)}$, Maxim Kashcheev, Yixin Wang, and Sergey Kovalchuk

ITMO University, Saint Petersburg, Russia
283091@niuitmo.ru

Abstract. The article proposes a model describing the dynamics of offenses in terms of non-compliance with safety regulations and speeding, taking into account the established rules and national specifics. The method suggested in the article is a combination of game theory methods and evolutionary algorithms, where "Mild" and "Strict" government policies compete with each other in a population of governments, and law-abiding and law-breaking drivers compete in a population of motorists. The study examines the impact of penalties on driver behavior within the model.

Keywords: Evolutionary game theory · government regulation · traffic policy · speeding rate · government spendings · seatbelt wearing rate

1 Introduction

Over the past hundred years road safety has become one of the main tasks for the governments. The key factors in increasing the importance of traffic control were the growing number of drivers, both advances and limitations in technologies, as well as involvement of road policy developers.

European countries provide an example of a positive trend in road safety, manifested in a significant reduction in the number of fatal accidents [2]. However, implementing policies that would reduce the frequency of accidents is still pressing for all governments due to the cumulative economic damage [3] summarizing the cost of repairing the damaged vehicles, losses caused by transport downtime, the expenditures for reconstructing and repairing the damaged roads and road structures and of investigating a traffic accident by police officers, to name a few.

To minimize losses and expenditures, modeling road safety as a system that takes into account various forms of regulation and the social context is highly relevant.

The current study suggests an environment model, which describes the dynamics of offenses in terms of non-compliance with the speed limit and wearing a seat belt, taking into account the socio-psychological and regulatory specifics of the national environment (within, a community or a county).

Using Germany as an example, we conducted a numerical modeling of the general dynamics of law enforcement for regulating the road sector. The model refers to the government policy in terms of the original state of the road infrastructure, fixed fines for violations of the speed limit and unbuckled seat belts and fixed parameters of national specifics and driver behavior patterns.

The study considers the impact of certain system parameters on the frequency of offenses and overall government spending, and explore the importance of penalty policies on changing the dynamics of offenses among drivers.

2 Related Work

Currently, legal regulation modeling within the socio-psychological context does not appear to be amply researched. Most of the studies focus either on strategies for organizing police to minimize accidents [4], or on modeling the driver's decision-making function [5], otherwise specific traffic situations are studied using the example of games [6]. Very few studies link the forms of regulation with their impact on the dynamics of offenses. The authors in [7] discussed agent-based transportation modeling using government control standards. However, their research is mainly aimed at studying the issue of regulation of commercial transportation rather than private transport. Our work was also based on a review study [6, 8] which analyzed using game theory elements to model various traffic situations, for example, the confrontation between drivers exceeding the speed limit and the police. In addition, we referred to the studies on the driver's satisfaction with the trip [9], which revealed that one of the main factors is the duration of the latter. The reports of the European commission and public organizations [10, 11, 14, 15] and the report from the international transport forum [1], initialized the model parameters, playing a key role in the study.

3 Traffic Policy Modeling with Evolutionary Game Theory

A model of the dynamics of law enforcement in the road sector (see Fig. 1) was based on the assumption that all drivers in the system drive identical cars, the police are always called to the scene in case of an accident, and drivers wait for their arrival. Based on the results of our literature review, we built a model based on the assumption that the key factor in driver satisfaction with the road is the subjective time spent on the trip [9], whereas the government is trying to decrease the average spendings per epoch including regulation enforcement and accident cost [3]. The condition of the road appears to affect the frequency of accidents [13]. Within the framework of the model, we assumed that the country we are considering has a federal structure, which makes it possible to implement different regulatory measures in different regions. During the initialization stage we generated an independent set of agents with "Driver" and "Government" types (further referred to as "D" and "G" agents, respectively).

Each "G" type agent is independently assigned with equal probability one of two policies ("Mild" or "Strict"). This implies a random belt penalty $feeB_s$ ($feeB_m$) from a uniform distribution with boundaries between $feeB^s_{min}$ ($feeB^m_{min}$) and $feeB^s_{max}$ ($feeB^m_{max}$) for "Strict" ("Mild") belt policy in EUR, a random speeding penalty $feeS_s$ ($feeS_m$) from a uniform distribution with boundaries between $feeS^s_{min}$ ($feeS^m_{min}$) and $feeS^s_{max}$ ($feeS^m_{max}$) for "Strict" ("Mild") speeding policy in EUR. The following parameters are set for all agents

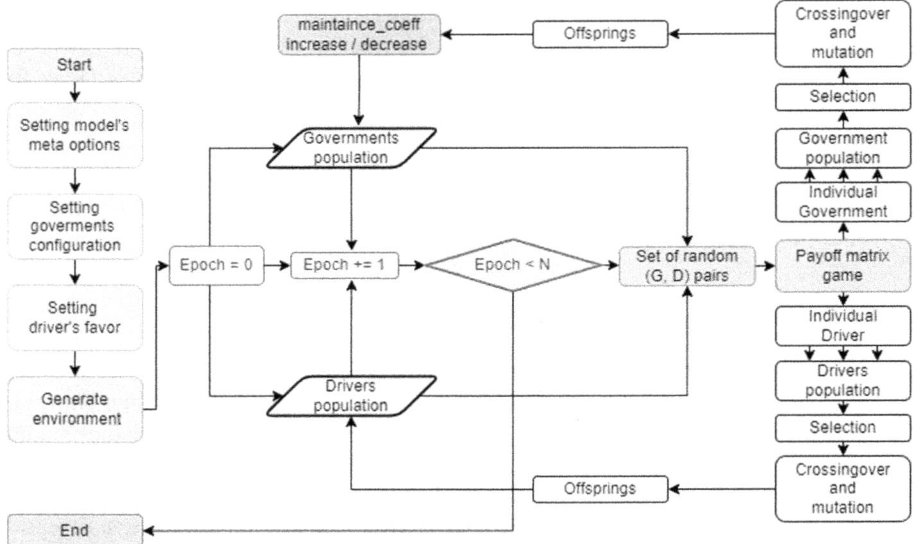

Fig. 1. Algorithm of the system for conducting a single experiment.

Table 1. Payoff matrix for games

| Government's | Driver's speed strategy | |
Regulation strategy	Obeying speed limit	Speeding
Strict regulation	GSO, DSO	GSS, DSS
Mild regulation	GMO, DMO	GMS, DMS

in environment: average accident cost c, EUR; the rate of infrastructure degradation Δ_{ma} ($\Delta_{ma} \in [0; 1]$); length of the road trip len, km; the coefficient of reduction of fatal outcome for belt users f_{min}. Each policy is characterized by the following parameters: car crash chance $crash_s$ ($crash_m$); chance of the fatal outcome $fatal_s$ ($fatal_m$); chance to be stopped for verification by the police $check_s$ ($check_m$); check duration d_s (d_m), hrs; initial value of the coefficient of the infrastructure of the government θ_{ma} set between 0.4 and 1; average policy spendings per driver tr_s (tr_m), EUR; mean μ_s (μ_m), standard deviation σ_s (σ_m) of police arrival time (hrs) in counties with "Strict" ("Mild") regulation policy.

Each "D" type agent can be independently and with equal probability assigned one of the two speed strategies (observing or violating the speed limit) and belt status (fastened or not), a random value of the expected travel time and a random speed $speed$ from the range between $speed^o_{min}$ and $speed^o_{max}$ in km/h, if the driver adheres to the speed limit, and from the range between $speed^s_{min}$ between $speed^s_{max}$ in km/h, if they do not. Also, during the initialization stage the driver receives a random normal distributed value of the subjective ride duration set by mean μ_{exp} and standard deviation σ^2_{exp} of the driver's ride time later defined as d_{exp} in hours.

Finally, we set the national specific parameters: decreasing coefficient of subjective speeder's road duration θ_d; increasing coefficient of fatal outcome for speeder θ_{fc};

increasing coefficient of crash accident for speeder θ_{cr}; coefficient of subjective perception of policy expenses θ_{sp}; coefficient of fees conversion θ_{fee} and coefficient of subjective perception of the check duration θ_{ch}.

To conduct a series of games, each element from the set of agents of the "D" type was randomly assigned an element from the set of agents of the "G" type. Each pair of "D"-"G" agents participates in the game described by the payoff matrix (see Table 1). Note that all random components drop out once per pair.

Notice that payoff for "G" agents was expressed in terms of average policy expenses per driver within a single game (see Table 2), whereas payoff for the "D" agents was expressed in terms of subjective time spent for the ride (see Table 3).

Table 2. Government's payoff

Name	Unit	Formula
GSO	EUR	$(-c \cdot \mathrm{Bern}(\mathrm{crash}_s) - tr_s) + \theta_{sp}$ $+ (\textit{belted} \cdot \mathrm{feeB}_s)\,\mathrm{Bern}(\mathrm{check}_s)$
GSS	EUR	$(-c \cdot Bern(crash_s \cdot \theta_{cr}) - tr_s) + \theta_{sp}$ $+$ $(\textit{belted} \cdot \mathrm{feeB}_s + \mathrm{feeS}_s)\mathrm{Bern}(\mathrm{check}_s)$
GMO	EUR	$(-c \cdot \mathrm{Bern}(\mathrm{crash}_m) - \mathrm{tr}_m) + \theta_{sp}$ $+$ $(\textit{belted} \cdot \mathrm{feeB}_m) \cdot \theta_{fee} \cdot \mathrm{Bern}(\mathrm{check}_m)$
GMS	EUR	$(-c \cdot \mathrm{Bern}(\mathrm{crash}_m \cdot \theta_{cr}) - tr_m) + \theta_{sp}$ $+ (\textit{belted} \cdot \mathrm{feeB}_m + \mathrm{feeS}_m)\mathrm{Bern}(\mathrm{check}_m)$

In a series of $N_{drivers}$ games, each agent of the sets of "G" and "D" received a reward. The system then generated subsets for each of the agent types, consisting of half of the initial elements with the highest reward rates, after which it transmitted the received arrays to the crossing over.

Then the resulting set of drivers was duplicated and "D"-"D" pairs were randomly formed, each of them having an equal probability of either an exchange of the "belted" feature, or a proportional exchange of speeds, or both an exchange of the "belted" feature and a proportional exchange of speeds. A new unified population was then formed from the two subsets, which was transmitted by mutation. Simultaneously, the resulting set of policies was duplicated and "G"-"G" pairs are randomly formed, each of which was equally likely to have either an exchange of the θ_{ma} feature, or a proportional exchange of penalty policies for belts, or a proportional exchange of penalty policies for exceeding the speed limit. A new single population was then formed from the two subsets, which was transmitted by mutation.

For each element of the "D" set, with a chance equal to that of mutation m_d a new speed for the current behavior strategy can be generated, the "belted" feature can be replaced with the opposite and a new agent cab be created to replace the previous one from the opposite strategy class, but with the same "belted" feature. This resulted in a new population sample and the end of the driver era. For each element of the G set for the current implemented policy with a chance equal to that of mutation m_g a new penalty for violating the safety rules for the current behavior strategy can be generated, a new penalty for speeding for the current behavior strategy can be generated, the attribute can be replaced with a random value from 0.4 to 1, and a new agent can be created to replace the previous strategy from the opposite class with a random set of characteristics. After mutation, for all agents with a "Strict" management policy, the θ_{ma} indicator increases by the rate of degradation Δ_{ma}, if it does not exceed the threshold of 1, for agents with a "Mild" regulation policy, the θ_{ma} indicator drops by Δ_{ma} to at least 0.4.

After that, a new population sample was formed and the epoch for repeated states ended. The experiment finished when the epoch variable reached the parameter value N_epochs. After that, the system completed the experiment.

Table 3. Driver's payoff

Name	Unit	Formula
DSO	hrs	$d_{exp} - \dfrac{len}{speed \cdot \theta_{ma}} - \text{Bern}(check_s) \cdot d_s \cdot \theta_{ch} -$ $- \text{Bern}\big(fatal_s \cdot (1 - belted \cdot (1 - f_{min}))\big) \cdot 10^6$ $- \text{Bern}()\, crash_s \cdot \big(N(\mu_s,\sigma_s^2) + d_s \cdot \theta_{ch}\big)$
DMO	hrs	$d_{exp} - \dfrac{len}{speed \cdot \theta_{ma}} - \text{Bern}(check_m) \cdot d_m \cdot \theta_{ch} -$ $- \text{Bern}\big(fatal_m \cdot (1 - belted \cdot (1 - f_{min}))\big) \cdot 10^6 -$ $- \text{Bern}(crash_m) \cdot \big(N(\mu_m,\sigma_m^2) + d_m \cdot \theta_{ch}\big) -$
DSS	hrs	$d_{exp} - \dfrac{len}{speed \cdot \theta_{ma}} \cdot \theta_d -$ Bern Bern $- - (fatal_s \cdot \theta_{fc} \cdot (1 - belted \cdot (1 - f_{min}))) \cdot 10^6 - -$ $(crash_s \cdot \theta_{cr}) \cdot \big(N(\mu_s,\sigma_s^2) + d_s \cdot \theta_{ch}\big)$
DMS	hrs	$d_{exp} - \dfrac{len}{speed \cdot \theta_{ma}} \cdot \theta_d -$ Bern $\text{Bern} - - (fatal_m \cdot \theta_{fc} \cdot (1 - belted \cdot (1 - f_{min}))) \cdot 10^6 - -$ $(crash_m \cdot \theta_{cr}) \cdot \big(N(\mu_m,\sigma_m^2) + d_m \cdot \theta_{ch}\big)$

4   Case Study: Modeling of Traffic Policy Environment in Germany

As part of the study, we defined Norway and Germany traffic regulation policies as "Strict" and "Mild" respectively, as Norway has the highest fees for speeding and unbelted driving and is leading among all EU countries in road safety rating [1, 2]. The chances of accidents and fatalities were calculated as the ratio of the number of accidents to the number of registered cars [1, 14]. For Norway, the chance of an accident was calculated from the chance of fatal outcomes [11] in proportion to the German data. Pairs of $\mu_s - \mu_m$, $d_s - d_m$, $\sigma_s - \sigma_m$ are equal for all policies and taken from American research [12].

The boundaries of penalty policies for exceeding the speed limit were defined as a minimum fine for exceeding the limit by 5 km/h and a maximum fine for exceeding the limit by 50 km/h for the current traffic policy in Germany and Norway. As part of the experiment, we modelled the case of driving in rural areas where speed limits in Germany and Norway allow acceleration to 100 km/h. Then experiment set speed initialization limits between 70 km/h and 100 km/h for the drivers who follow the speed limit, and between 100 km/h and 150 km/h for those who do not. We do not consider higher speeds, because for exceeding the speed limit above 50 km/h, their license is withdrawn. The ride length is set at 100 km, the average expected travel time is 1 h with an average deviation of 0.1 h. The average spending on policy implementation for each country was calculated as the sum of government expenditures on Police services and R&D Public order and safety in EUR divided by the total number of the population of the country in 2023 [15]. Finally, assuming that the average cost of an accident is the same for all countries and only cases with severe and mild injuries are included (without fatal outcomes, since they are quite rare), the cost of an accident was amounted to 1.539.328 NOK or 137.008 EUR [11]. Since the model has a pronounced stochastic nature, we set 10 launches with 300 epochs per launch in one experiment. The Δ_m was determined to be 0.05. We set the m_d and m_g equal to 0.09. The f_{min} indicator will be 0.6. The parameters of Germany's national specifics were selected through a series of launches with an attempt to approximate the values of indicators expressed in the percentage of drivers who do not use a seat belt, which is 98%, and in the percentage of drivers who exceed the speed limit, which is 74% [10]. With the current parameters for an average of 300 epochs with trajectories averaged over 10 launches 90.4% of drivers fasten seat belts (with an average deviation of 4.9%), and 74.6% of drivers exceed the speed limit (with an average deviation of 4.9%).

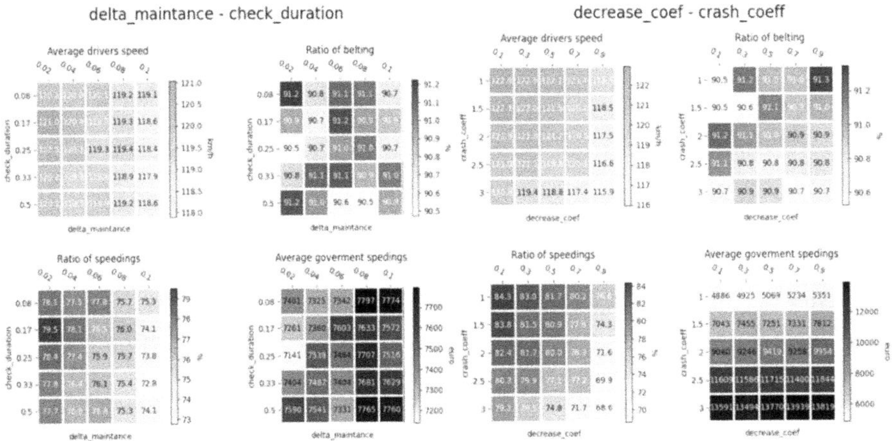

Fig. 2. Mapped effects

5 Conclusion and Future Work

As part of the experiments, we considered the impact of the right-hand boundaries of penalty policies on the dynamics of law violations in terms of the speed limit and respecting the seat belt rules and conducted a series of two Two-Way ANOVA tests. For one case, we fixed all the parameters except for pairs of values $feeB_{max}^s - feeB_{max}^m$ (set between 600 and 2200 with step 400 and between 200 and 600 with step 100, respectively). In the other case we fixed all the parameters except the pair $feeS_{max}^s - feeS_{max}^m$ (set between 200 and 400 with step 50 and between 50 and 200 with step 50, respectively). All other parameters remained fixed. After that 2 series of experiments were launched, each of them with 25 independent experiments on a grid of 5 for each of the modifiable parameters, fixing the average values of the percent of belted and speeding drivers in each of the 10 iterations of the experiment. Based on the collected data, a two-way ANOVA showed that the factors $feeB_{max}^s$, $feeB_{max}^m$ and their combination did not affect the frequency of violations. However, factor $feeS_{max}^m$ effects speeding with p-value of 5%, but its combination with the $feeS_{max}^s$ factor did not produce any effects, which partially confirms the early studies [6]; showing that amount of penalties has no effect on speed limit violation (Table 4).

Table 4. Two-way ANOVA tests results.

Factor name	P(>F) Influence on ratio of belt usage	Influence on ratio of speeding
$C(feeB_{max}^m)$	0.467	0.8985
$C(feeB_{max}^s)$	0.84043	0.6211
$C(feeB_{max}^m){:}C(feeB_{max}^s)$	0.6738	0.1159
$C(feeS_{max}^m)$	0.1917	**0.011** *
$C(feeS_{max}^s)$	0.7595	0.521
$C(feeS_{max}^m){:}C(feeS_{max}^s)$	0.1093	0.674

* p<0.05

As shown in Fig. 2, a decrease in the rate of degradation Δ_{ma} does not reduce the frequency of speeding or the average driver's speed. On the other hand, the national specific factors, namely the accident probability coefficients θ_{cr} and the decreasing coefficient θ_d, had the greatest effect on reducing the frequency of speeding. Noteworthily, an increase in the reduction coefficient leads to a gradual but significant increase in the average driver expenses. Additionally, an increase in the accident probability coefficient resulted in a significant increase in the average expenses.

Further work would include testing the approach in other countries. The quality of the model can also be improved by increasing the number of factors affecting the driver's speed, which in turn will lead to additional balancing indicators. Also, in the future, it would be interesting to consider the impact of the cost of an accident on the dynamics of key parameters. To strengthen the validation claims we will run the model for Norway. To increase the descriptive accuracy of the model, we will refer to additional information to select the optimal parameters. Also, it would be important to consider generalizing the model, which allows for the transition between different driving zones (city, highways, and rural areas) and introducing a public opinion component that would allow drivers to explicitly influence regulatory policy.

Acknowledgements. The research was supported by The Russian Science Foundation, agreement №24-11-00272, https://rscf.ru/project/24-11-00272/.

References

1. International Transport Forum: Germany: Road Safety report 2021. https://www.itf-oecd.org/sites/default/files/germany-road-safety.pdf (2021). Accessed Feb 2026
2. Nikolaoua, P., Dimitrioub, L.: Evaluation of road safety policies performance across Europe: results from benchmark analysis for a decade. Transp. Res. A. **116**, 232–246 (2018)
3. Pukalskas, S., Pečeliūnas, R., Sadauskas, V., Kilikevičienė, K., Bogdevičius, M.: The methodology for calculation of road accident costs. Transport. **30**(1), 33–42 (2015)
4. Lloyd, D.J.B., Santitissadeekorn, N., Short, M.B.: Exploring data assimilation and forecasting issues for an urban crime model. Eur. J. Appl. Math. **27**, 451–478 (2016)
5. Liu, Y., Ozguner, U.: Human driver model and driver decision making for intersection driving. In: 2007 IEEE Intelligent Vehicles Symposium Istanbul (2007)
6. Bjornskau, T., Elvik, R.: Can road traffic law enforcement permanently reduce the number of accidents? Accid. Anal. Prev. **24**(5), 507–520 (1992)
7. Liu, Z., Huang, N., Hu, B., Zhao, Y., Kown, I.S.: An evolutionary game study of traffic safety risk regulation considering public participation behavior. Sci. Rep. **14**, 30069 (2024)
8. Elvik, R.: A review of game-theoretic models of road user behaviour. Accid. Anal. Prev. **62**, 388–396 (2014)
9. Morris, E.A., Guerra, E.: Are we there yet? Trip duration and mood during travel. Transp. Res. Part F. **33**, 38–47 (2015)
10. European Road Safety Observatory: National Road Safety Profile—Germany. https://road-safety.transport.ec.europa.eu/document/download/adbd19af-b384-4fb7-a7dc-2ae199aa8453_en?filename=erso-country-overview-2023-germany_0.pdf (2023). Accessed Feb 2026
11. European Road Safety Observatory: National Road Safety Profile—Norway. https://road-safety.transport.ec.europa.eu/document/download/bf91675a-3f89-461a-97cf-b451d0de61d8_en (2023)
12. Liu, C.: Exploration of the police response time to motor-vehicle crashes in Pennsylvania, USA. J. Safety Res. **80**, 243–253 (2025)
13. Navarro-Moreno, J., Calvo-Poyo, F., de Oña, J.: Influence of road investment and maintenance expenses on injured traffic crashes in European roads. Int. J. Sustain. Transp. **17** (2023). https://doi.org/10.1080/15568318.2022.2082344
14. Destatis: Statistisches Bundesamt. Traffic accidents. https://www.destatis.de/EN/Themes/Society-Environment/Traffic-Accidents/_node.html (2023). Accessed Feb 2026
15. Eurostat: Government expenditure by COFOG. https://ec.europa.eu/eurostat/statistics-explained/index.php?title=Government_expenditure_by_function_–_COFOG (2023). Accessed Feb 2026

MultiHedge: Adaptive Coordination via Retrieval-Augmented Control

Feliks Bańka$^{(\boxtimes)}$ and Jarosław A. Chudziak

The Faculty of Electronics and Information Technology, Warsaw University of
Technology, Warsaw, Poland
{feliks.banka.stud,jaroslaw.chudziak}@pw.edu.pl

Abstract. Decision-making under changing conditions remains a fundamental challenge in many real-world systems. Existing approaches often fail to generalize across shifting regimes and exhibit unstable behavior under uncertainty. This raises the research question: can retrieval-augmented LLM coordination improve the robustness of modular decision pipelines? We propose MultiHedge, a hybrid architecture where an LLM produces structured allocation decisions conditioned on retrieved historical precedents, and execution is grounded in canonical option strategies. In a controlled evaluation using U.S. equities, we compare MultiHedge to rule-based and learning-based baselines. The key result is that memory-augmented retrieval confers greater robustness and stability than increasing model scale alone. Our paper contributes a controlled computational study showing that memory and architectural design play a central role in robustness in modular decision systems.

Keywords: Computational experiments · Retrieval-augmented systems · Large language models · Risk management

1 Introduction

Financial markets are characterized by frequent regime shifts and volatility bursts, complicating risk management and making risk management unstable [13]. Even established option strategies such as collars and straddles provide only partial protection if not coordinated over time [2]. Selecting and adjusting these hedges under changing market conditions is a sequential control problem involving both discrete and continuous decisions [12].

Recent advances in large language models (LLMs) have enabled structured workflows that integrate heterogeneous signals and produce auditable rationales [6]. Retrieval-based memory mechanisms offer a lightweight way to condition decisions on similar past states, improving robustness under distribution shift [1]. However, most hedging frameworks focus on end-to-end learning or static overlays, rarely studying retrieval-conditioned coordination over modular, interpretable decision primitives [11].

This raises a central research question: can retrieval-augmented coordination enhance the robustness of modular decision pipelines under distributional shift

P. Neumann et al. (Eds.): ICCS 2026, LNCS 16784, pp. 446–454, 2026.
https://doi.org/10.1007/978-3-032-29924-6_39

and regime instability? We address this by introducing *MultiHedge* (Sect. 3.1), a hybrid computational architecture in which the LLM serves as a bounded heuristic approximator within a constrained optimization loop. Allocation decisions are strictly conditioned on retrieved historical analogues, while execution is handled by formally defined option-hedging modules. This design dynamically coordinates canonical strategies, separating stochastic reasoning from symbolic execution to align language-model inference with constrained portfolio control [7]. Code and experimental configuration files are publicly available at: https:// github.com/latent-systems-lab/MultiHedge.

The main contributions of this work are as follows. First, we formulate retrieval-conditioned coordination as a structured sequential decision problem. Second, we introduce a modular hybrid architecture that separates reasoning, action generation, and execution within a reproducible workflow. Third, we present a controlled computational study—including limited robustness checks—that isolates the role of memory and coordination in improving robustness beyond model scale.

2   Related Work

Large language models (LLMs) and retrieval-augmented generation (RAG) workflows have been integrated into structured decision systems to ground outputs in external evidence and improve interpretability [5,7]. In finance, such systems support sentiment extraction, event interpretation, and tool-augmented trading components [16]. Retrieved episodes provide precedents that align model reasoning with historical cases [1]. Conditioning decisions on retrieved experiences improves robustness under distribution shift and non-stationarity [15], with episodic memory acting as a non-parametric prior that grounds inference in observed trajectories rather than purely parametric knowledge. In structured decision architectures, LLMs increasingly operate as bounded reasoning modules over constrained action spaces, where outputs are parsed and executed by deterministic components [5,10]. In *MultiHedge*, episodic recall informs allocation decisions over option-level primitives, coupling regime inference with historical outcome alignment [16].

From a computational-science perspective, modular control architectures are standard mechanisms for robustness under non-stationarity and partial observability [8,12]. Specialist modules capture complementary behaviours, while a coordinator performs context-dependent selection under explicit constraints. Learning-based hedging and risk-control frameworks demonstrate that such policies can operate under frictions when embedded into a well-defined execution model [4], and classical parameterised primitives remain widely used due to predictable cost–benefit trade-offs [10]. Existing financial LLM systems such as FinAgent primarily emphasize signal interpretation and tool use [16]. Ensemble and mixing approaches improve downside stability [3,14], yet they rarely formalise retrieval-conditioned coordination over fixed interpretable primitives within a constrained sequential control and backtesting framework. Our work addresses this gap by explicitly separating retrieval, allocation synthesis, and symbolic execution in a reproducible computational workflow.

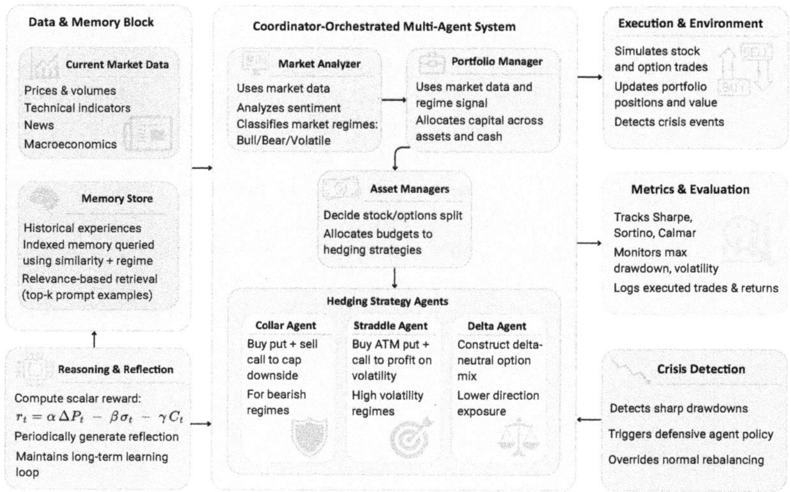

Fig. 1. MultiHedge system architecture: modular components, episodic memory, and hybrid control pipeline.

3 MultiHedge: Hybrid Architecture, Episodic Memory, and Modular Coordination

This section details the MultiHedge architecture, which integrates episodic memory, modular coordination, and a hybrid control pipeline. Figure 1 illustrates the system's main components and their interactions.

We formulate dynamic hedging as a constrained sequential control problem under partial observability, where portfolio allocation must remain bounded under regime shifts and transaction frictions. Partial observability arises because regime and volatility states are latent.

Formally, the problem is represented as a Partially Observable Markov Decision Process (POMDP) [12]:

$$\langle \mathcal{S}, \mathcal{A}, \mathcal{O}, \mathcal{T}, \mathcal{R} \rangle,$$

where $\mathcal{S}$ is the latent market–portfolio state space, $\mathcal{A}$ is a mixed discrete–continuous action space, $\mathcal{O}$ are observable signals (prices, volatility, news features), $\mathcal{T}$ denotes transition dynamics, and $\mathcal{R}$ is a risk-adjusted reward functional. *MultiHedge* implements a hybrid computational architecture that combines symbolic option-hedging structures, retrieval-augmented memory, and language-model-based reasoning within this decision process.

3.1 System Overview

As shown in Fig. 1, MultiHedge consists of several interacting modules: an LLM-based inference layer, a portfolio and allocation layer, symbolic hedging agents, and a deterministic safety layer. The figure provides a visual summary of how these components coordinate to produce memory-augmented decisions.

The LLM processes multimodal signals and outputs regime classification and structured allocation candidates. The portfolio layer implements a risk-adjusted objective, while hedging agents execute canonical option strategies. The safety layer enforces stability constraints by overriding actions during drawdown events, ensuring bounded risk and robust system behavior.

3.2 Decision Process and Action Formulation

We model hedging as a constrained decision process where, at each trading day t, the system observes a partially informative state and produces structured allocation and hedging actions subject to feasibility and stability constraints. Formally:

$$w_t = \pi_{\text{alloc}}(s_t, R_t, E_t), \tag{1}$$

$$a_{i,t}^{H} = \pi_{\text{agent}}^{H}(s_t, w_t), \quad \forall H \in \{\text{collar, straddle, delta-neutral}\}. \tag{2}$$

Under this formulation, the LLM acts as a constrained reasoning engine. It produces structured outputs that are grounded via retrieval and executed through interpretable primitives. These outputs are parsed and validated against explicit financial constraints, including budget, liquidity, and risk limits. This ensures that all actions remain feasible, interpretable, and bounded by the system's operational parameters at every step.

To mitigate hallucinations and enforce stability, a deterministic safety layer overrides the LLM's outputs when drawdown thresholds are breached. Deterministic inference (temperature zero) further reduces stochasticity, ensuring predictable behavior under stress.
The retrieval-augmented policy update is given by:

$$\pi^* \leftarrow \arg\max_{\pi} \ \mathbb{E}_{(s,a)\sim\mathcal{M}} \left[\text{sim}(\phi(s,a), \phi(s',a')) - \lambda\,\mathcal{L}(\pi) \right]$$

where $\text{sim}(\cdot,\cdot)$ denotes embedding similarity, ϕ is the embedding function, λ controls retrieval strength, and $\mathcal{L}(\pi)$ is a regularization term. Under this formulation, retrieval constrains policy updates toward historically aligned trajectories, acting as a non-parametric regularizer under distributional shift.

3.3 Memory-Augmented Reasoning via Metric Retrieval

As illustrated in Fig. 2, the system follows a retrieval–reason–act–update loop driven by a non-parametric episodic memory buffer $\mathcal{M}$. Past decision episodes

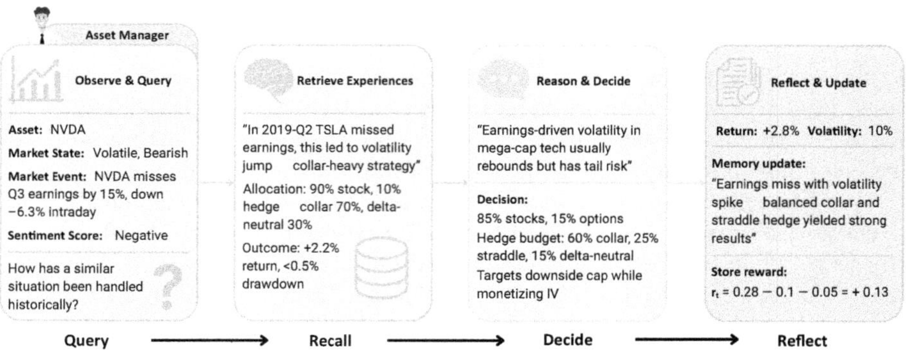

Fig. 2. Episodic memory loop in MultiHedge: past state–action–outcome tuples are retrieved via similarity search, used to condition current allocation decisions, and then stored for future reuse.

are stored within this buffer as state–action–outcome tuples, establishing a continuous cycle where historical trajectories are retrieved to condition current actions and then updated for future reuse.

During the decision phase, the controller retrieves the top-k most similar episodes using cosine similarity and anchors its allocation logic to their realized outcomes. By explicitly conditioning on these retrieved precedents, the system reuses empirically validated strategies in analogous contexts rather than relying solely on parametric generalization.

4　Experimental Evaluation Under Changing Market Conditions

We evaluate MultiHedge in a setting where market conditions vary over time. The system is compared against classical and learning-based baselines, and we perform targeted ablations to isolate the effects of memory, coordination, and model scale.

4.1　Experimental Setup and Robustness Metrics

We use daily historical market data for large-cap equities (AAPL, TSLA, NVDA) from January 2021 to December 2023, with memory index calibration on 2016–2020. Trading costs and liquidity constraints are enforced, and the LLM controller GPT-4.1 operates deterministically ($T = 0.0$).

Evaluation relies on core performance and tail-risk metrics: Total Return (TR), Sharpe Ratio (SR; return per unit of total volatility), Maximum Drawdown (MD; largest peak-to-trough drop), and Conditional Value at Risk (CVaR). We additionally track auxiliary stability indicators: Sortino (SoR) and Calmar (CaR) ratios for downside-adjusted returns, Value at Risk (VaR), worst-month return (WM), downside deviation (DDv; volatility of negative returns), time spent in severe drawdown (TDD > 10%), and maximum consecutive loss days (MCL). These metrics exhibit consistent trends and reinforce the observed improvements in risk-adjusted performance. Auxiliary robustness checks, including broad-market stress and synthetic regime-switching tests, further confirm the stability.

Table 1. Performance Comparison: Core Metrics and Downside Risk

Strategy	SR	TR (%)	MD (%)	CVaR (%)	WM (%)	DDv (%)
Buy & Hold	0.81	107.08	53.08	5.36	−21.96	25.34
Equal Weight	0.77	95.34	53.53	5.41	−21.29	25.73
PPO	0.74	66.46	39.72	3.95	−15.59	18.68
FinAgent	0.63	69.74	54.60	5.99	−21.92	28.69
FinRL	0.56	57.08	61.51	6.48	−25.19	30.78
MultiHedge	**1.69**	**152.08**	**16.22**	**2.29**	**-4.58**	**10.93**

4.2 Benchmark Results

Table 1 shows that MultiHedge consistently improves both performance and risk characteristics relative to all baselines. The Sharpe ratio increases substantially compared to classical strategies, while total return improves without a corresponding increase in risk. The most pronounced gains appear in downside risk. Maximum drawdown is reduced by over 70% relative to Buy & Hold (53.08% → 16.22%), and CVaR is more than halved. The worst-month loss improves from approximately −22% to −4.6%, indicating strong mitigation of extreme negative events. Similarly, downside deviation is reduced by more than 50%, suggesting that improvements are not limited to isolated tail events but reflect a broader compression of downside volatility.

These effects indicate that MultiHedge not only improves average performance but systematically reshapes the loss distribution, reducing both the magnitude and persistence of adverse regimes. Consistent improvements across additional monitored metrics (SoR, CaR, VaR, TDD, MCL) further support this interpretation. Auxiliary tests under stress and regime-switching scenarios confirm that these gains remain stable across perturbations, validating retrieval-conditioned coordination as a robust mechanism for non-stationary environments.

4.3 Architectural Ablation Studies

We conduct ablation studies to isolate the effects of memory, stochasticity, and model scale. GPT-4o Mini is used as a reduced-capacity baseline to assess the effect of model scale under fixed architecture. Table 2 shows that memory is the dominant factor driving robustness. Removing memory leads to a near tripling of drawdown (16.22% → 46.18%) and a substantial deterioration in tail risk (CVaR: 2.29 → 4.78). The degradation is also visible in worst-month losses and downside deviation, indicating both more frequent and more severe adverse outcomes.

Introducing stochasticity further degrades performance, suggesting that deterministic, constrained inference is important for stability in sequential decision settings. In contrast, reducing model capacity results in a comparatively smaller performance drop across all metrics. While we consider a limited comparison of model scales, these results indicate that architectural components—particularly memory—have a stronger impact on robustness than model size in this setting.

Table 2. Ablation of Control Architecture: Core and Downside Risk Metrics

Configuration	SR	TR (%)	MD (%)	CVaR (%)	WM (%)	DDv (%)
MultiHedge (GPT-4.1)	1.69	152.08	16.22	2.29	−4.58	10.93
GPT-4o Mini	1.14	97.44	20.41	2.87	−9.26	13.77
Stochastic ($T = 0.7$)	0.96	84.58	28.28	3.28	−12.27	15.86
No Memory	0.80	93.94	46.18	4.78	−19.95	22.89

5 Discussion and Future Work

The empirical outperformance of MultiHedge over reinforcement learning baselines highlights a broader shift in designing computational financial agents. Deep RL approaches, such as PPO or FinRL [9], often struggle with sudden regime shifts because they optimize over historically stationary reward landscapes [4]. Conversely, purely LLM-based trading systems [16] risk unstable, unconstrained execution. By restricting the LLM to a coordinating role and offloading execution to deterministic primitives, our architecture achieves robust downside protection without requiring end-to-end retraining. This suggests that grounding modular components via episodic memory can provide a more stable path to robustness than relying solely on parametric scale [5,7].

Despite these advantages, limitations remain. Restricting evaluation to large-cap equities limits generalisation to asset classes with different microstructures. Furthermore, while deterministic inference reduces instability, the system remains sensitive to retrieval quality, prompt specification, and inherent LLM training biases or data leakage.

Future work will explore three directions: incorporating term-structure and volatility surface features to improve regime sensitivity; integrating risk-sensitive objectives to stabilise extreme-event performance [11]; and generalising the architecture to structured multi-agent settings where specialised controllers interact via explicit coordination protocols [10].

6 Conclusion

Financial decision-making under market regime shifts often suffers from instability and increased downside risk. While recent approaches leverage large language models or end-to-end learning, it remains unclear whether their success stems from raw model scale or structural design. This raises a key question: can conditioning decisions on retrieved historical precedents systematically improve system robustness?

To address this, we introduced *MultiHedge*, a hybrid architecture that combines structured decision rules with LLM-based reasoning guided by retrieved historical examples. Our results show consistent improvements in performance and substantial reductions in downside risk compared to both rule-based and learning-based baselines. Ablation studies indicate that memory and system design play a larger role than model size in driving these gains. Overall, this paper contributes to the field of robust decision systems by showing that combining memory with modular decision structures can improve performance under changing conditions.

References

1. Aamodt, A., Plaza, E.: Case-based reasoning: foundational issues, methodological variations, and system approaches. AI Commun. **7**(1), 39–59 (1994)
2. Bańka, F., Chudziak, J.A.: Options pricing platform with neural networks, LLMs and reinforcement learning. In: Recent Challenges in Intelligent Information and Database Systems, pp. 202–216. Springer Nature Singapore (2025)
3. Bańka, F., Chudziak, J.A.: Deltahedge: a multi-agent framework for portfolio options optimization. In: PACIS 2025 Proceedings. No. 25 (2025)
4. Buehler, H., Gonon, L., Teichmann, J., Wood, B.: Deep hedging. Quant. Finance **19**(8), 1271–1291 (2019)
5. Guo, T., et al.: Large language model based multi-agents: a survey of progress and challenges (2024)
6. Kirtac, K., Germano, G.: Sentiment trading with large language models. Financ. Res. Lett. **62**, 105227 (2024)
7. Lewis, P., et al.: Retrieval-augmented generation for knowledge-intensive NLP tasks. In: Advances in Neural Information Processing Systems (NeurIPS) (2020)
8. Liberzon, D.: Switching in Systems and Control. Birkhäuser (2003)
9. Liu, X.Y., Xiong, Z., Zhong, S., Yang, H., Walid, A.: Practical deep reinforcement learning approach for stock trading (2022)
10. Macal, C.M., North, M.J.: Tutorial on agent-based modelling and simulation. J. Simul. **4**(3), 151–162 (2010)
11. Malekzadeh, P., Poulos, Z., Chen, J., Wang, Z., Plataniotis, K.N.: Ex-DRL: hedging against heavy losses with extreme distributional reinforcement learning (2024)
12. Puterman, M.L.: Markov Decision Processes: Discrete Stochastic Dynamic Programming. Wiley (1994)
13. Shu, Y., Yu, C., Mulvey, J.M.: Dynamic asset allocation with asset-specific regime forecasts (2024)

14. Szydlowski, K.L., Chudziak, J.A.: Toward predictive stock trading with hidformer integrated into reinforcement learning strategy. In: Proceedings of the 36th International Conference on Tools for Artificial Intelligence (ICTAI 2024) (2024)
15. Xiao, M., et al.: Retrieval-augmented large language models for financial time series forecasting (2025)
16. Zhang, W.: A multimodal foundation agent for financial trading: tool-augmented, diversified, and generalist (2024)

Fourier Neural Operators
for Rayleigh–Bénard Convection

Chelsea Maria John[1,2](✉) [ID], Thibaut Lunet[2] [ID], Sebastian Götschel[2] [ID],
Andreas Herten[1] [ID], Stefan Kesselheim[1] [ID], and Daniel Ruprecht[2] [ID]

[1] Jülich Supercomputing Centre, Jülich, Germany
{c.john,a.herten,s.kesselheim}@fz-juelich.de
[2] Hamburg University of Technology, Hamburg, Germany
{thibaut.lunet,sebastian.goetschel,ruprecht}@tuhh.de

Abstract. We propose an improved Fourier Neural Operator (FNO)
for modeling two-dimensional Rayleigh–Bénard convection by predicting time increments instead of full solutions, achieving higher accuracy
than a standard FNO baseline. The resulting model is compact (314k
parameters, 1.26 MB) and fast (7 ms inference), while maintaining similar accuracy as demonstrated in previous benchmarks. We show that
although FNOs generalize to finer meshes, accuracy remains limited by
the resolution of the training data.

Keywords: Fourier Neural Operator · Rayleigh–Bénard convection

1 Introduction

Modeling turbulent convection is challenging and has applications from atmospheric flows [11] to industrial processes such as silicon wafer production [10].
A standard benchmark is Rayleigh–Bénard convection (RBC), where a fluid
heated from below develops an overturning circulation [6] with the strength of
turbulence governed by the Rayleigh number (Ra). At high Ra the flow becomes
strongly turbulent, making high-resolution numerical simulations computationally expensive. Recent machine learning approaches, particularly Fourier Neural
Operators (FNOs) [7], provide an alternative to mesh-based solvers by learning
solution operators that, unlike PINNs [2], generalize across resolutions. In this
work, we apply FNOs to 2D RBC using Dedalus [1] as ground truth, focusing
on stable small-step predictions that preserve turbulent statistics and align with
time-stepping solvers. We propose a lean FNO design suitable for use in iterative
methods such as Parareal [4,8].

Related Work. Hammoud et al. [3] show that PINNs reconstruct previous RBC
states with relative L_2-errors on the order of 10^{-1} at Ra $= 10^7$, while Almeida
et al. [12] achieve less than 10% reconstruction error using an encoder–decoder
DeepONet-based approach [9]. Wu et al. [14] introduce COAST, a causal operator framework with adaptive time stepping, reporting a VRMSE of 0.23 for

P. Neumann et al. (Eds.): ICCS 2026, LNCS 16784, pp. 455–462, 2026.
https://doi.org/10.1007/978-3-032-29924-6_40

$Ra = 10^7$ over a 5-step rollout. Straat et al. [13] apply FNO to 2D RBC at multiple Rayleigh numbers and obtain an average relative L_2-error of 0.021 on a 96×64 grid. In contrast, our 2D lean FNO model learns to predict increments rather than solutions and achieves significantly higher accuracy when predicting future solution states. It has fewer parameters and faster inference, which is beneficial when coupled with iterative numerical algorithms. However, it exhibits faster error accumulation under longer auto-regressive rollouts or larger time steps compared to 3D FNOs.

Contributions. We propose a lean FNO architecture that learns the *increment* from the state at time t to a state at time $t + \Delta t$, similar to a time-stepping algorithm in a mesh-based simulation. We perform an ablation study which reveals that using multi-layer 1D convolutional scaling operators delivers better accuracy than linear layers. The performance of our lean FNO architecture in terms of accuracy, memory footprint and inference times is compared against the model by [13]. Finally, we analyze how FNO generalizes across spatial and temporal resolutions and show that it interpolates to new meshes, but that accuracy remains limited by the resolution of the training data.

2   Rayleigh-Bénard Convection

Rayleigh-Bénard convection occurs when a fluid within a confined channel is subjected to a temperature difference. In our setup, the lower plate is heated to a temperature θ_H while the upper plate is cooled to θ_C with a vertical distance (d) between the plates. This causes the cooler, denser fluid to sink and the warmer, lighter fluid to rise, generating convective rolls whose patterns are influenced by the aspect ratio of the channel and the physical properties of the fluid. The non-dimensional momentum conservation equations governing the dynamics of RBC are

$$\frac{\partial \mathbf{u}}{\partial t} + (\mathbf{u} \cdot \nabla)\mathbf{u} = -\nabla p + \theta \hat{\mathbf{z}} + \sqrt{\frac{\mathrm{Pr}}{\mathrm{Ra}}}\nabla^2 \mathbf{u}. \tag{1}$$

Here, $\mathbf{u} = (u, w)$ denotes the velocity vector with horizontal component u and vertical component w, p is the pressure, θ is buoyancy, and the Prandtl number Pr is the ratio of kinematic viscosity μ and thermal diffusivity κ. The Rayleigh number Ra, which characterizes the convective motion, is defined as

$$\mathrm{Ra} = \frac{\alpha \mathrm{g}(\theta_H - \theta_C)d^3}{\mu \kappa} \tag{2}$$

with α being the thermal expansion coefficient and g the acceleration due to gravity. The continuity equation for incompressible flow that ensures mass conservation is

$$\nabla \cdot \mathbf{u} = 0 \tag{3}$$

Conservation of energy provides the following equation for the temperature

$$\frac{\partial \theta}{\partial t} + (\mathbf{u} \cdot \nabla)\theta = \frac{1}{\sqrt{\mathrm{Ra}\ \mathrm{Pr}}} \nabla^2 \theta. \tag{4}$$

3   Fourier Neural Operator

Fourier Neural Operators (FNOs) solve PDEs by learning mappings between function spaces using spectral representations [7]. The architecture consists of an input lifting layer $\mathcal{P}$ that maps the input function a from channel dimension d_a to a higher-dimensional representation v of dimension d_v, followed by multiple Fourier layers and a final projection $\mathcal{Q}$ that maps to the output u with channel dimension d_u. Each Fourier layer applies a Fourier transform $\mathcal{F}$, performs spectral convolution on a fixed set of low-frequency modes R, and transforms back via the inverse transform $\mathcal{F}^{-1}$. A local linear term Wv and a nonlinear activation σ are added to capture local and higher-frequency features beyond the truncated spectrum.

3.1   Generation of Training Data

Training and evaluation data were generated using Dedalus [1] on a 256×64 grid with a $RK443$ time stepper and $\Delta t = 10^{-3}$, with $\theta_H = 1$ and $\theta_C = 0$. Simulations start from random perturbations, run to $T_{init} = 100$ to reach a pseudo-steady turbulent state. Data is collected from $T_{init} = 100$ to $T_{sim} = 200$ for $\mathrm{Pr} = 1$ and $\mathrm{Ra} = 10^7$, with spectral analysis confirming adequate resolution. Ten simulations with different random seeds are used to record $\mathcal{U}(t) = [\mathbf{u}(t), \theta(t), p(t)]$ at each time step, forming 200 input–output pairs $(\mathcal{U}(t), \mathcal{U}(t + \Delta t))$ over $[100, 200]$. From 2000 samples, 80% are used for training and 20% for validation.

3.2   Learning Objective

FNOs are typically trained to predict the full solution of a PDE, but learning updates to the state can be more effective. We therefore compare two objectives: a **solution objective**, where the model directly predicts $\mathcal{U}(t + \Delta t)$ from $\mathcal{U}(t)$, and an **increment objective**, where it predicts the scaled update $\Delta\mathcal{U} = \Delta t^{-1}(\mathcal{U}(t + \Delta t) - \mathcal{U}(t))$. In the latter case, the solution is recovered via $\mathcal{U}(t + \Delta t) = \mathcal{U}(t) + \Delta t\, \mathcal{O}(\mathcal{U}(t))$, where $\mathcal{O}(\mathcal{U}(t))$ is the model increment prediction, making the FNO analogous to a one-step time integrator.

Both objectives are trained using a relative L_2 loss, applied either to the solution or the increment. For evaluation, we measure the relative error in the reconstructed solution. Note that loss and error coincide only for the solution objective. Since small Δt leads to nearly identical states, trivial predictions can yield low loss; therefore, we compare against an identity baseline that propagates $\mathcal{U}(t)$ unchanged (or predicts zero increment) to ensure meaningful learning beyond this naive predictor.

4 Results

Training was conducted on a single NVIDIA A100 (40 GB) GPU of the JURECA-DC supercomputer, using a custom codebase [5] and data[1]. Our ablation study on $\mathcal{P}$ and $\mathcal{Q}$ (linear vs. 1D convolutional layers with $d_v = 16$) shows that increasing both depth and width improves performance and using cosine LR scheduler leads to better learning. The improved model is further evaluated to test the temporal and spatial generalization, and extended to compare against existing work.

4.1 Training

The baseline model is trained using both the solution and increment objectives for $\Delta t = 10^{-3}$. Table 1 compares the relative error for both objectives across the four components of the solution, that is velocity in the horizontal (u) and vertical (w) directions, buoyancy(θ), and pressure (p), averaged over 200 samples. Furthermore, the training loss is lower than the identity loss for increment objective but not for the solution objective.

The average relative error for the increment objective is two orders of magnitude smaller than for the solution objective. The noise introduced by the FNO when predicting the solution leads to an increase in error by about a factor of ten compared to when the FNO predicts the increment for buoyancy contours. Predicting increments substantially improves the quality of the generated solutions.

Table 1. Relative error computed for increment and solution objective.

Variable	Increment	Solution	IdError
u	5.7e–05	1.6e–03	2.0e–04
w	9.3e–05	1.7e–03	1.9e–04
θ	6.0e–05	1.0e–03	1.1e–04
p	2.4e–05	1.4e–03	7.2e–05
Average	**5.8e–05**	1.4e–03	1.4e–04

4.2 Improved Model

Based on the results above, we propose the model configuration described in Table 2 as improvement over the baseline FNO. We train both for 11 500 epochs to predict increments $\Delta t = 10^{-3}$ using data generated as mentioned in Sect. 3.1 which takes 11h on a single NVIDIA A100 GPU. Table 2 also shows the relative error in the four variables in (1) and (4) against the Dedalus reference on 256 $\times$ 64 grid for 200 samples from the validation dataset when predicting a single increment $\Delta t = 10^{-3}$.

---

[1] https://huggingface.co/datasets/chelseajohn/FNO-RBC2D_paper_artefacts.

Table 2. Comparison of the improved and baseline FNO configuration

Component	Improved Model	Baseline Model
Objective	Increment	Solution
Kernel	FNO	FNO
Activation Function (σ)	GELU	GELU
Optimizer	Adam	Adam
LR Scheduler	Cosine	StepLR
Fourier Layers	2	2
Fourier Modes	12	12
Scaling Layer ($\mathcal{P},\mathcal{Q}$)	$4\times$1D Conv (width=$4d_v$)	$1\times$Linear (width=d_v)
Input Channels (d_a)	4	4
Projection Channels (d_v)	16	16
Output Channels (d_u)	4	4
Total Parameters	314772	295552
Model Size (MB)	1.26	1.18
Inference time for batchsize = 1 (ms)	7	5
Relative Error in u	2.4e-05	1.6e-03
Relative Error in w	3.2e-05	1.7e-03
Relative Error in θ	1.8e-05	1.0e-03
Relative Error in p	8.5e-06	1.4e-03
Average error	**2.1e-05**	1.4e-03

4.3 Impact of Model Time Step and Autoregressive FNO Application

To evaluate the impact of different time steps, the model is retrained for $\Delta t = 1$, 10^{-1}, 10^{-2}, in addition to 10^{-3} using the same architecture (Table 2) on 2000 samples for 11 500 epochs. Models are evaluated over time horizons of 1, 0.1, 0.01, and 0.001 starting from $t = 100$, using autoregressive rollout when the model time step is smaller than the target horizon. As shown in Table 3, shorter horizons yield lower validation errors due to reduced solution change, while autoregressive inference introduces mild error accumulation, leading to slightly higher errors than single-step predictions at matching time steps.

4.4 Resolution Invariance

To evaluate generalization across mesh resolutions, the FNO trained on $\Delta t = 10^{-3}$ increments is tested on a 512×128 grid, twice the training resolution of 256×64 used for $Ra = 10^7$. Errors are computed against reference Dedalus solutions and are found to be of the same order as those on the 256×64 grid (Table 4). Errors change very little if the reference solution on a 512×128 is restricted to a 256×64 mesh and this data used as input to the FNO. Evaluating the FNO

Table 3. Relative error under temporal generalization.

Data Timestep	Model Timestep	Model Steps	u	w	θ	p	Average Error
1	0.001	1000	8.7e–02	9.8e–02	5.0e–02	4.0e–02	6.9e–02
0.1	0.001	100	8.5e–03	1.2e–02	7.4e–03	3.7e–03	8.0e–03
0.01	0.001	10	8.6e–04	1.3e–03	7.7e–04	3.6e–04	8.1e–04
0.001	0.001	1	8.6e–05	1.3e–05	7.8e–05	3.7e–05	8.2e–05

Table 4. Relative error against the $(256, 64)$ Dedalus reference when evaluating the FNO trained on $(256, 64)$ across different meshes; the $(512, 128)$ case is compared to its own Dedalus reference. The interpolation column shows the error when $(256, 64)$ FNO outputs are upsampled to $(512, 128)$ via FFT.

Variable	(64, 64)	(256, 32)	(64, 32)	(256, 64)	(512, 128)	Interpolation
u	7.9e–04	4.9e–04	5.3e–04	2.4e–05	1.0e–04	1.1e–4
w	4.7e–04	6.2e–04	4.6e–04	3.2e–05	1.4e–04	2.3e–4
θ	2.4e–04	2.6e–04	2.7e–04	1.8e–05	9.2e–05	2.0e–4
p	2.4e–04	3.9e–04	6.1e–04	8.5e–06	4.0e–05	4.0e–5
Average	4.4e–04	4.4e–04	4.7e–04	**2.1e–05**	9.4e–05	1.5e–4

on the trained resolution (256×64) and interpolating the output to the finer grid via FFT delivers very similar errors as evaluating the FNO directly on the finer mesh. This demonstrates that the FNO shows mesh invariance by interpolating to unseen resolutions without significant additional error. However, unlike numerical solvers, increasing inference resolution does not improve accuracy, which is instead determined by the resolution of the training data.

4.5   Comparison with Straat et al.

To evaluate the performance of our improved FNO architecture, we compare it against the model of Straat et al. [13] for $Ra = 5 \times 10^6$ with $Pr = 0.7$ on a 96×64 grid and boundary temperatures $\theta_H = 2$ and $\theta_C = 1$. We adopt their setup but use an architecture with 8 Fourier layers, 64 projection channels, and 16 Fourier modes to better capture the turbulent dynamics and larger time step. The model is trained on 44 940 samples from 15 Dedalus simulations and validated on 14 980 samples from 5 simulations, each run for 300 s with data sampled at $\Delta t = 0.1$ after a 200 s warm-up, and trained on JURECA-DC using 8 NVIDIA A100 GPUs for 500 epochs in 3.5 h, reaching a training and validation loss of 0.03.

For evaluation, predictions are generated over a 30 s window via 60 recursive steps with a model time step of 0.5 s. Averaged over 50 samples from 10 random starting points across 5 validation runs, our model achieves an average loss of 0.11 (Table 5), compared to 0.04 reported by Straat et al. Direct component comparison is not possible due to lack of data in Straat et al. While their FNO3D accumulates error more slowly, our model attains comparable initial accuracy despite its much smaller architecture, requiring only 132 MB (33 million, FP32 parameters) versus 3037 MB, and achieves faster inference times of 10 ms (batch size 10) and 30 ms (batch size 50) per prediction window, compared to 0.45 s on an NVIDIA A40 for Straat et al.

Table 5. Relative error solving the Straat et al. benchmark.

Variable	$t = 0.5$		$t = 30\,\mathrm{s}$	
	Error	IdError	Error	IdError
u	4.6e–02	1.8e–01	2.0e–01	2.1e–01
w	4.9e–02	1.4e–01	1.8e–01	2.0e–01
θ	2.1e–02	3.4e–02	3.1e–02	3.6e–02
p	1.3e–02	3.0e–02	3.5e–02	3.7e–02
Average	**3.2e–02**	9.8e–02	**1.1e–01**	1.2e–01

5   Conclusion

In this work, we systematically evaluate Fourier Neural Operators for two-dimensional Rayleigh–Bénard convection in the turbulent regime. We find that predicting increments rather than full states significantly improves accuracy and stability, reducing errors by up to two orders of magnitude for small time steps and mitigating noise, effectively turning the FNO into a data-driven one-step integrator. Architectural choices such as deeper 1D convolutional lifting/projection layers and a cosine learning rate scheduler further improve accuracy, yielding a compact and efficient model.

Our results show that FNOs are resolution-invariant in the sense that they interpolate to unseen meshes, but their accuracy is ultimately limited by the training data resolution rather than improved by finer inference grids. Compared to the much larger 3D FNO by Straat et al., our lean model achieves a trade-off between accuracy, memory, and inference speed, with substantially smaller footprint and faster runtime but stronger long-horizon error accumulation. These properties highlight the potential of FNOs as efficient surrogate models and as coarse propagators in space–time parallel methods such as Parareal.

Acknowledgments. This project received funding from the European High-Performance Computing Joint Undertaking (JU) under grant No. 101118139 (Horizon Europe), with compute time on the GCS Supercomputer JURECA at JSC provided by the Gauss Centre for Supercomputing e.V.

References

1. Burns, K.J., Vasil, G.M., Oishi, J.S., Lecoanet, D., Brown, B.P.: Dedalus: a flexible framework for numerical simulations with spectral methods. Phys. Rev. Res. **2**(2), 023068 (2020)
2. Cai, S., Mao, Z., Wang, Z., Yin, M., Karniadakis, G.E.: Physics-informed neural networks (PINNS) for fluid mechanics: a review (2021)
3. Hammoud, M.A., Alwassel, H., Ghanem, B., Knio, O., Hoteit, I.: Physics-informed deep neural network for backward-in-time prediction: application to Rayleigh-Bénard convection. Artif. Intell. Earth Syst. **2**(1) (2023)
4. Ibrahim, A.Q., Götschel, S., Ruprecht, D.: Space-time parallel scaling of pareal with a physics-informed fourier neural operator coarse propagator applied to the Black-Scholes equation. In: Proceedings of the Platform for Advanced Scientific Computing Conference, pp. 1–11 (2025)
5. John, C.M., Lunet, T., Götschel, S.: CFNO: chebyshev fourier neural operators (software) (2024). https://github.com/Parallel-in-Time/cfno. bSD-2-Clause license
6. Kadanoff, L.P.: Turbulent heat flow: structures and scaling. Phys. Today **54**(8), 34–39 (2001)
7. Li, Z., et al.: Fourier neural operator for parametric partial differential equations (2021)
8. Lions, J.L., Maday, Y., Turinici, G.: A"parareal" in time discretization of pde's. Comptes Rendus de l'Académie des Sciences. Série I. Mathématique **332**(1) (2001)
9. Lu, L., Jin, P., Pang, G., Zhang, Z., Karniadakis, G.E.: Learning nonlinear operators via deeponet based on the universal approximation theorem of operators. Nat. Mach. Intell. **3**(3), 218–229 (2021)
10. Oyama, H., Nieman, K., Tran, A., Keville, B., Wu, Y., Durand, H.: Computational fluid dynamics modeling of a wafer etch temperature control system. Digit. Chemic. Eng. **8**, 100102 (2023)
11. Shipley, D., Weller, H., Clark, P., McIntyre, W.: Two-fluid single-column modelling of Rayleigh-Bénard convection as a step towards multi-fluid modelling of atmospheric convection (2021)
12. de Sousa Almeida, J.L., Rocha, P.R.B., de Carvalho, A.M., Jr, A.C.N.: A coupled variational encoder-decoder - deepONet surrogate model for the Rayleigh-bénard convection problem. In: When Machine Learning meets Dynamical Systems: Theory and Applications (2023)
13. Straat, M., Markmann, T., Hammer, B.: Solving turbulent Rayleigh-Bénard convection using fourier neural operators (2025)
14. Wu, Z., et al.: Tante: time-adaptive operator learning via neural Taylor expansion (2025)

Employing Neo-psychometric Natural Language Processing in Classification of Anti-trans Social Media Posts

Sofia Przyłuska[1]([envelope]) and Mikołaj Biesaga[2](iD)

[1] College of Inter-faculty Individual Studies in Mathematics and Natural Sciences,
University of Warsaw, Warsaw, Poland
`s.przyluska@student.uw.edu.pl`
[2] Robert Zajonc Institute for Social Studies, University of Warsaw, Warsaw, Poland
`m.biesaga@uw.edu.pl`

Abstract. While significant progress has been made in the area of prejudice detection, most contemporary attempts at hate speech classification lack theoretical backing, which is especially pronounced on the levels of feature extraction and classifier architecture. This limitation becomes problematic considering the limited size (or quality) of most datasets used, and is well illustrated in anti-transgender hate speech detection. In the present paper, we introduce the Neo-Psychometric Machine Learning approach. We define it as the use of Psychometric measures and domain knowledge for the broader purpose of addressing Machine Learning tasks. We propose a theory-driven classifier architecture using similarity metrics to questionnaire items from a psychometric operationalization of Transmisogyny theory. Our results show that the Neo-Psychometric NLP approach can be successfully applied to the task of classifying anti-trans social media posts from the TIDEs dataset, while reducing the risk of overfitting on construct-unrelated features and providing potential for theory-driven explanations. We show that anti-trans prejudice can be accurately classified even using similarity metrics to questionnaire items that do not include explicit statements about transgender people, but are rooted in the theoretical operationalization of the predictors of transphobia. While the Neo-Psychometric approach would, in our view, not be best suited in applications where the aim is to maximize accuracy, profit, or other performance metrics, we believe it can be applied in situations where theoretical backing, explainability and reducing construct-unrelated model bias is crucial—with good results.

Keywords: Neo-Psychometric Machine Learning · Psychometric Machine Learning · Natural Language Processing · Hate Speech · Explainable Machine Learning · Prejudice · Transgender · Transphobia · Transmisogyny · Sexism · Gender Essentialism

P. Neumann et al. (Eds.): ICCS 2026, LNCS 16784, pp. 463–471, 2026.
https://doi.org/10.1007/978-3-032-29924-6_41

1   Introduction

Machine learning models can aid content moderation and make big data analysis possible. However, the quality of their performance depends on the datasets they are trained on, which very often are prepared with the help of human annotators. In the context of prejudice detection, this poses ethical concerns related to exposing humans to large volumes of hate speech, which comes with psychological burden and mental health risks. To address this issue, the machine learning community has come up with two possible solutions. One approach is the manual labelling of the dataset by the researchers themselves and therefore mitigating the risk for unprepared annotators [e.g., 5,10]. The other solution focuses on practices grounded in care for the mental wellbeing of annotators at every stage of the construction of a dataset [7].

One limitation of those approaches is the high cost and effort needed for the creation of datasets, which currently means that – in the context of hate speech classification – high quality and, especially, ethically produced datasets are not large, and large datasets are, in turn, often not high quality or not ethically sourced. This, consequently, increases the risk of classifier overfitting, inability to infer hate speech qualities adequately and, finally, misclassification.

To address this issue, we propose the Neo-Psychometric Machine Learning approach. Broadly speaking, this approach uses psychometric measures and domain knowledge for the broader purpose of addressing Machine Learning tasks. In the present study, we propose a theory-driven classifier architecture. We utilize Contextualized Construct Representations [1] – similarity metrics of the classified text and relevant psychometric scale item embeddings from a sentence transformer model – as intermediate features for traditional classification models. We demonstrate this approach on the task of classifying anti-trans social media posts from TIDEs dataset (Transgender and Nonbinary Community-Labeled Dataset for Transphobia Identification in Digital Environments).

Anti-Trans Hate Speech Classification. A number of strategies have been employed to classify anti-transgender hate-speech in social media posts.

In a study employing a Retrieval-Augmented Generation pipeline to classify sentiment towards transgender people Leitner et al. (2025) [10] examine the network structure of anti-trans actors on Tik-Tok. They analyze transcribed video content, descriptions, hashtags, usernames and tagged users from 59,860 videos. Their findings suggest that, while pro-trans users tend to either be very isolated or found in tight knit clusters, the anti-trans actors are deeply embedded with the neutral users and prevalent throughout the network. Notably, the classification pipeline they employ (Overall Accuracy = 0.67, F1 Anti-Trans = 0.48, F1 Pro-Trans = 0.83, F1 Neutral = 0.56), which uses RAG samples and taxonomy, can be described as theory driven. Nevertheless, the Llama3 model they utilize, even in the smallest variants, uses billions of parameters, which in some contexts (like CPU constrained computation or big data analysis) can be unfeasible.

Lameiro et al. (2025) [7] introduce the TIDEs dataset. It contains 3,509 annotated posts and comments (42.7% of them labelled as Transphobic) from

YouTube, Tumblr, Truth Social, and Reddit. The authors compare a number of classification approaches, including metrics from Perspective API [9], a Logistic Regression model, and a state of the art DeBERTa classifier trained on their dataset. Because the TIDEs dataset was used in the present study, the performance metrics of the models can be found in Table 1 as a comparison for the model architectures proposed herein.

While these approaches are promising, they lack theoretical structure, which is especially pronounced on the levels of feature extraction and classifier architecture. This limitation becomes problematic considering the limited size (or quality) of most datasets used in the field.

Psychometric Machine Learning. Psychometric Machine Learning leverages classical ML and Deep Learning methods to indirectly study human behavior, characteristics and psychological states. This can include top-down (i.e., theory driven) and bottom up approaches, analyzing both multi-modal and semi-modal (e.g. textual) data [see 4].

Notably, theory-driven Psychometric NLP can employ textual embedding based methods, which allow for operationalizing psychological constructs in vector spaces – akin to traditional Psychometric methods [see 13]. One of those methods – Contextualized Construct Representations (CCR) [1] – focuses on utilizing similarity scores of sentence transformer embeddings between questionnaire scale items and the examined text. The method outperforms traditional text vectorization methods (i.e., Distributed Dictionary Representations and word-counting) in predicting psychological constructs and has the ability to capture nuanced context, while retaining the theoretically meaningful structure of the resulting vector space.

2 Neo-psychometric Machine Learning

In the present paper, we introduce the Neo-Psychometric Machine Learning approach. We define it as the use of Psychometric measures and domain knowledge for the broader purpose of addressing Machine Learning tasks. In the case of NLP, we focus solely on analyzing text itself, which we treat as stimuli that can reflect a theoretical construct. We do this regardless of the authors intention. In contrast to Psychometric NLP, we are explicitly not interested in the psychological state, or characteristics, of the authors of the text. We posit that this framing is very well aligned with the goal of hate speech classification.

Herein, we utilize CCR – similarity metrics of the classified text and relevant psychometric scale item embeddings produced by a sentence transformer model – as intermediate features for such traditional classification models as logistic regression, Support Vector Machine and XGBoost. We test two theoretical approaches using our operationalization of the transmisogyny theory – Gender Essentialism, Social Determinism, and Ambivalent Sexism – one including the explicit transphobia scales (ATTM and ATTW) and one based solely on the constructs stemming from Transfeminist Theory.

3   Methods

The proposed Anti-Trans Hate Speech Classifier architecture assumes trans-related posts as inputs. We utilize the pre-trained all-MiniLM-L12-v2 model (33.4M parameters, 384-dim output vector) [11], and the associated tokenizer to produce the text embeddings. We then calculate the CCR – dot product to the questionnaire items and use one of the three classifiers: Logistic Regression, XGBoost and Support Vector Machine.

Because all-MiniLM-L12-v2 normalizes the embedding vectors, in the present paper, we use dot product as the similarity metric, as, for normalized vectors, dot product is equivalent to cosine similarity. Higher scores in dot product reflect higher similarity of the post to a particular questionnaire item. Because, traditionally, in psychometric scales some items are inverted, we multiply the dot product by -1 for those items during feature calculation. This should not significantly impact model training, but it streamlines scale-wise interpretations of the similarity metrics – both in the case of dataset exploration and possibly in model-level and decision-level explainability.

Theory – Transmisogyny, Used Questionnaires. We used two operationalizations of the Transmisogyny theory [12]. We chose this theory, because of its potential to capture intersectional prejudice towards transgender women, comprehensive explanation of anti-trans prejudice and a number of empirical studies that align with it [e.g., 2,8].

Serano [12] posits that prejudice towards trans people, especially trans women, is rooted in Oppositional Sexism (a construct well mirrored by the psychological construct of Gender Essentialism), Traditional Sexism, Cissexism – the belief that the gender identity of cis people is more valid or real than the gender identity of trans people, and Transphobia – an irrational fear, aversion to, or discrimination against people, whose gender identities or expression deviates from societal norms. We operationalize those constructs using scales grounded in Psychological literature:

1. Gender Essentialism scale (18 items) [8] (used subscales: Inductive Potential, Biological Determinism, Immutability) to operationalize Oppositional Sexism.
2. Social Determinism scale (6 items) [8], as an additional dimension connected to Gender Essentialism, which is in line with contemporary feminist discourse.
3. Ambivalent Sexism Questionnaire (22 items) [6] – capturing Hostile and Benevolent aspects of sexist beliefs and narratives.
4. Attitudes Towards Transgender Men and Women Questionnaire (24 items) [3] as a direct measures of transphobia directed at binary trans people.

Dataset. In the present paper, we used the TIDEs dataset as it reflects the wide array of transphobic narratives, multi-platform sourcing and high quality of annotation. Therefore, we posit that the dataset is suitable for the examination of the proposed architecture, as well as for the training and, especially, evaluation of anti-trans hate speech models.

Figure 1 presents the distributions of total scale scores (CCR sum, not standardized). Note that the relationships seen in the TIDEs dataset plots are pronounced and align with the chosen theory.

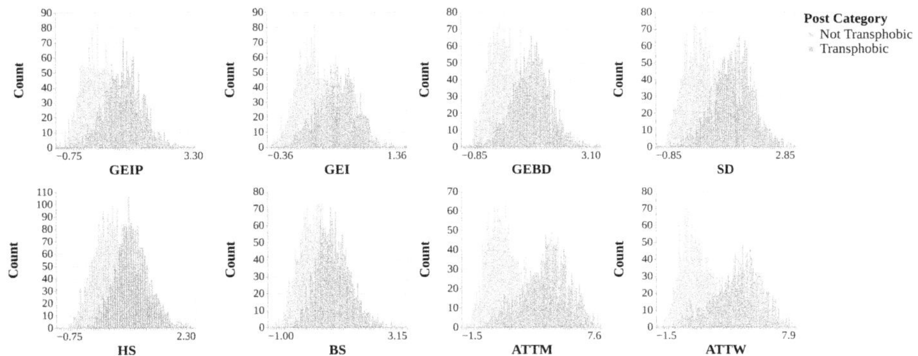

Fig. 1. Distributions of total scale scores by post category. GEIP : Gender Essentialism – Inductive Potential; GEI : Gender Essentialism – Immutability; GEBD : Gender Essentialism – Biological Determinism; SD : Social Determinism; HS : Hostile Sexism; BS : Benevolent Sexism; ATTM : Attitudes Towards Transgender Men; ATTW : Attitudes Towards Transgender Women.

4   Results

All classifier variants performed well in the task of classifying transphobic posts. The SVM classifier achieved an F1 score of 0.79 (Accuracy = 0.81, Precision = 0.81, Recall = 0.76) over one run with a train-test split of 80:20. The XGBoost classifier achieved an F1 score of 0.78 (Accuracy = 0.81, Precision = 0.80, Recall = 0.76) over one run with a train-validation-test split with 80:10:10 ratio and early stopping. Logistic Regression achieved an F1 score of 0.75 (Accuracy = 0.79, Precision = 0.77, Recall = 0.74) over one run with a test-train split of 80:20. Table 1 shows comparisons to the models trained by Laimeiro et al. [7]. We argue that those results are comparable to the performance of a DeBERTa black box classifier [7] (Accuracy = 0.82, F1 = 0.81), while reducing the risk of overfitting on construct-unrelated features and providing potential for theory-driven explanations.

Alternative operationalization. An alternative operationalization stemming solely from the theoretical predictors of transmisogyny was tested in order to validate the approach and reduce potential construct-related bias. In the TIDEs dataset, the word "transgender" is more common in the Transphobic ($n = 895$), than in the Non-Transphobic ($n = 152$) category and has the highest mutual information with post category. Moreover, the discrepancy is also seen for words

Table 1. Comparison of the Neo-Psychometric Model (NPM) to other classifiers.

Model	Accuracy	Precision	Recall	F1	Source
Perspective API (toxicity)	0.63	0.91	0.59	0.72	TIDEs
Perspective API (identity attack)	0.71	0.80	0.68	0.74	TIDEs
Logistic Regression	0.79	0.87	0.70	0.77	TIDEs
DeBERTa	**0.82**	0.89	0.74	**0.81**	TIDEs
NPM – Logistic Regression	0.79	0.77	0.74	0.75	Herein
NPM – XGBoost	0.81	0.80	0.76	0.78	Herein
NPM – SVM[a]	**0.81**	0.81	0.76	**0.79**	Herein

[a] Support Vector Machine.

referring to men and women. While this can plausibly reflect real world differences in frequency distributions of these words, it can also introduce construct-related bias to any model trained on this dataset (i.e., classifying posts mentioning transgender people or gender as Transphobic). This is problematic in black box models and – in our approach – with the use of the ATTMW scales, because all items from both scales contain the phrases "transgender men" and "transgender women". This could potentially result in higher similarity of posts containing these words to all ATTMW scale items. Our approach allowed for reducing the risk of this bias by excluding the ATTM and ATTW scales. Even after this change, the models retained high performance metrics (see Table 2).

Table 2. Neo-Psychometric Model Performance over 100 runs with random 80:20 train-test splits.

Model	Accuracy	Precision	Recall	F1	ATTMW[a]
NPM – Logistic Regression	0.79	0.75	0.75	0.75	Yes
NPM – XGBoost[b]	0.79	0.75	0.76	0.75	Yes
NPM – SVM[c]	0.79	0.75	0.77	0.76	Yes
NPM – Logistic Regression	0.78	0.75	0.74	0.74	No
NPM – XGBoost[b]	0.78	0.74	0.75	0.75	No
NPM – SVM[c]	0.79	0.74	0.77	0.76	No

[a] ATTM and ATTW scales.
[b] No early stopping.
[c] Support Vector Machine.

5   Discussion

The present study introduced the notion of Neo-Psychometric Machine Learning. We showed that this approach can be successfully applied in an NLP task – classification of anti-trans hate speech. Utilizing CCR of psychometric scale items, we have represented unstructured textual data in a vector space with theoretically meaningful dimensions. Because the feature space becomes theoretically meaningful, we posit that this is more than simple dimensionality reduction.

Moreover, this approach does not require heavy compute power, as it does not involve fine-tuning of the sentence transformer model. All of the computations reported in the present paper were run on CPU (11th Gen Intel Core i5-1135G7 (8), 4.2GHz). Furthermore, because the scales used were already psychometrically validated, we could avoid the process of stimuli labelling.

Explainability. A notable advantage of the proposed approach is its potential for improving explainability on every stage of a classifiers life cycle. As shown in Fig. 1 the intermediate features can be used for dataset exploration in a theoretically structured manner. For instance, it is informative, that transphobic posts score higher on the Social Determinism scale than other trans-related posts in a particular dataset. Notably, this can be used to evaluate theoretical fit of a dataset prepared for a specific purpose. In our case, we would argue that the TIDEs dataset reflects the theoretical aspects of anti-trans prejudice very well.

Moreover, we argue that the Neo-Psychometric approach is very well suited for model-level and decision-level explainability. Using this approach, researchers can define the conceptual structure of the analyzed construct (e.g., anti-trans prejudice) themselves – instead of delegating the theoretical work to a machine learning model. This further allows for reducing the hard problem of explaining how transformers represent a complex construct to two simpler ones – sentence similarity, and explaining statistical relationships between the Neo-Psychometric dimensions and the predicted class label.

In other words, using this approach we take the conceptual work of defining what Transphobia is away from the model, giving the control over representing the construct in question back to the researcher and leaving the computation to the machine learning implementation.

Limitations. While the Neo-Psychometric Classification approach can, in our view, help reduce both construct-unrelated and construct-related bias, this requires robust dataset evaluation and theoretical examination. Moreover, it is still too early to tell how effective it is at reducing bias overall, and especially in real-world applications. A notable limitation of using psychometric scale items as references for theory-driven dimensionality reduction is the fact that similarity to questionnaire items might overall reflect not only the intended construct, but also the "questionnaire-ness" of the classified texts. This has been mentioned by [13] who propose the use of Correlational Anchored Vectors to ameliorate this problem in the context of Psychometric NLP.

Furthermore, as seen in Table 1, our approach reduced the classifiers performance metrics, however not drastically. We propose that future research should employ fine tuning alongside Neo-Psychometric feature extraction in order to maximize model performance and improve usability.

Conclusions. While the Neo-Psychometric approach would, in our view, not be best suited in applications where the aim is to maximize accuracy, profit, or other performance metrics, we believe it can be applied in situations where theoretical backing, explainability and reducing construct-unrelated model bias is crucial – with good results.

Acknowledgments. We thank Adam Zadrożny, Wojciech Przytuła, Joanna Rączaszek-Leonardi, Wiktor Rorot, and Szymon Rynkun for making it possible for Sofia to write significant portions of the code used in the current project during their seminars, as well as for their valuable insights.

Disclosure of Interests. The authors declare no competing interests.

References

1. Atari, M., Omrani, A., Dehghani, M.: Contextualized Construct Representation: Leveraging Psychometric Scales to Advance Theory-Driven Text Analysis (2023)
2. Atwood, S., Morgenroth, T., Olson, K.R.: Gender essentialism and benevolent sexism in anti-trans rhetoric. Soc. Issues Policy Rev. **18**(1), 171–193 (2024)
3. Billard, T.J.: Attitudes Toward Transgender Men and Women: Development and Validation of a New Measure. Front. Psychol. **9** (2018)
4. Celli, F., et al.: Twenty years of personality computing: threats, challenges and future directions. ACM Comput. Surv. 3806009 (2026)
5. Channon, L., Mathieson, N.: Automated Detection of Mainstreamed Transphobic Content on YouTube (2025). https://doi.org/10.57814/49JZ-0663
6. Glick, P., Fiske, S.T.: Hostile and benevolent sexism: measuring ambivalent sexist attitudes toward women. Psychol. Women Q. **21**(1), 119–135 (1997)
7. Lameiro, F., Dunagan, L., Card, D., Gilbert, E., Haimson, O.: TIDEs: a Transgender and nonbinary community-labeled dataset and model for transphobia identification in digital environments. In: Proceedings of the 2025 ACM Conference on Fairness, Accountability, and Transparency, pp. 1411–1423 (2025)
8. Lee, K.Y., Reis, H.T., Rogge, R.D.: Seeing the world in pink and blue: developing and exploring a new measure of essentialistic thinking about gender. Sex Roles , 685–705 (2020). https://doi.org/10.1007/s11199-020-01141-1
9. Lees, A., et al.: A New Generation of Perspective API: Efficient Multilingual Character-level Transformers. In: Proceedings of the 28th ACM SIGKDD Conference on Knowledge Discovery and Data Mining, pp. 3197–3207 (2022)
10. Leitner, M., Dorn, R., Morstatter, F., Lerman, K.: Characterizing Network Structure of Anti-Trans Actors on TikTok (2025)
11. Reimers, N., Gurevych, I.: Sentence-BERT: sentence embeddings using Siamese BERT-networks. In: Proceedings of the 2019 Conference on Empirical Methods in Natural Language Processing and the 9th International Joint Conference on Natural Language Processing, pp. 3982–3992. Association for Computational Linguistics (2019)
12. Serano, J.: Whipping girl: a transsexual woman on sexism and the scapegoating of femininity (2007)
13. Teitelbaum, L., Simchon, A.: Neural text embeddings in psychological research: a guide with examples in R. Psychol. Methods (2025)

Containers Are (Almost) Free: Energy and Performance Analysis of AI Workloads Under CPU Virtualization and GPU Power Capping

Michał Kościowski[1]([envelope]) [iD], Jerzy Proficz[2]([envelope]) [iD], and Paweł Czarnul[1]([envelope]) [iD]

[1] Gdansk University of Technology, Faculty of Electronics, Telecommunications and Informatics, Narutowicza 11/12, 80-233 Gdansk, Poland
{michal.kosciowski,pawel.czarnul}@pg.edu.pl
[2] Gdansk University of Technology, Centre of Informatics—Tricity Academic Supercomputer and networK (CI TASK), Narutowicza 11/12, 80-233 Gdansk, Poland
j.proficz@task.gda.pl

Abstract. In contemporary computing, we can observe simultaneous: adoption of virtualization that has become mainstream, popularity of AI workloads, as well as very considerable increase of energy costs. The latter result from high prices and huge requirements of the aforementioned workloads. In this context, we present a performance- and energy-aware comparison of virtual machines and containers against bare metal using three modern AI workloads: Single Shot Detector (SSD) from MLPerf Inference, and two PyTorch benchmarks – ResNet50 training and hf_BERT inference – both in 32-bit floating-point precision. Compared to the state-of-the-art, we contribute by: using a multi(8)-GPU environment, considering another variable being a power cap imposed on each of the GPUs, and assessment of not only resulting execution times and energy consumption but also the Energy Delay Product (EDP) metric. We found that Docker has a negligible impact on performance (0.03% on average), while KVM causes a performance drop of 21.22% on average compared to bare metal. For energy consumption overheads for Docker and KVM are -0.03% and 1.63%, while for EDP 0% and 23.14%, respectively. We have also determined that power caps that minimize EDP are different for KVM and Docker/bare metal, which is an important observation for optimization of that essential performance-energy trade-off.

Keywords: Energy-aware computing · Virtual machines · Containers · Power capping · AI workloads

1 Introduction

Modern AI workloads require computationally intensive GPU processing. Such computations are performed on servers in data centers, which can have power

P. Neumann et al. (Eds.): ICCS 2026, LNCS 16784, pp. 472–479, 2026.
https://doi.org/10.1007/978-3-032-29924-6_42

demands reaching hundreds of megawatts. Reducing energy consumption can lead to significant savings.

The main motivation of this work is to provide a performance and energy-aware comparison of virtual machine (VM) and container based environments against a bare metal system for contemporary AI workloads. Furthermore, compared to the existing works on comparative assessment of such environments, we contribute by providing comparison for:

1. a parallel workload running in a multi-GPU environment, specifically run on a machine with eight NVIDIA QUADRO RTX6000 GPUs,
2. various power caps imposed on the GPUs,
3. not only execution time but also energy and EDP metrics [6], for power caps in the available range.

The results indicate that KVM introduces average overheads of 1.63% in energy consumption (up to 2.71%) and 21.22% in execution time (up to 36.49%), while container-based systems remain at a very low overhead level, with average and maximum values of −0.03% and 0.26% for energy, and 0.03% and 0.31% for execution time, respectively.

The following section reviews related work. Next, we present the motivation and main contributions of the paper, followed by a description of the measurement methodology, the experimental setup and results. The paper is concluded with final remarks and directions for future work.

2 Related Work

In the following articles, the authors examine the impact of virtualization on GPU and CPU performance in HPC, rack server, desktop, SoC, grid, and cloud environments, as well as research findings and state-of-the-art tools that improve energy efficiency and execution time.

In work [8], MPI applications are evaluated on CPUs using Docker and bare metal. Experiments show Docker overheads of 7.59%, 13.29%, and 15.3%, for 64, 128 and 256 application processes respectively.

Authors of paper [4] compare the performance of Docker containers and KVM VMs using bare metal as reference. Benchmarks covering CPU, memory, storage, and network performance on Linux show that Docker incurs up to 2% overhead, while KVM overhead reaches up to 40% in I/O workloads.

In paper [13], Docker containers are compared with bare metal. CPU overhead for HPL is below 1% while for HPCG it is 0.244% and 0.556%, for desktop and server-grade, respectively. GPU tests report a performance difference of 0.61% and 1.72%, respectively. Sequential I/O tests show differences of 0.636% and 3.448%, random I/O performance is up to 100% higher on container thanks to use of Multi-Tier Cache Technology.

Authors of work [2] evaluate ease of deployment and performance of KVM- and VirtualBox-based VMs and Docker containers against bare metal. The start-up time ranges from 49–59 s and 39–41 ms; CPU performance shows 27% degradation and no difference for VMs and containers, respectively. I/O and network bandwidth overheads are highest for VMs, while container shows moderate overhead.

In paper [5], authors evaluate VMs (Xen, KVM, VirtualBox, VMware) and containers (Docker, Podman) against bare metal and OpenStack bare metal on an OpenStack-managed cluster. A Linux kernel compilation test shows overheads of 2.0–2.3% for containers, synthetic benchmarks 0.1–3.0% and while I/O tests are up to 8.7% better than bare metal. For VMs, CPU performance and network bandwidth is reduced by 0.2–9.3% and 0.4–24.8%, respectively. Synthetic memory tests for Xen and KVM exceed bare metal by 0.4% and 5.5%.

In work [11], authors evaluate virtualization overhead on an ARM-based Cubieboard2 SoC, comparing Docker containers vs KVM VMs against bare metal. The results demonstrate CPU overheads of 0.1% vs 4.27% (NBench), 0.25% vs 1.17% (Sysbench) and 34.77% vs 991.65% (Linpack); storage I/O overheads of 3.1% vs 66.6% (Bonnie++) and 1.4% vs 81.15% (dd); memory overheads of 0.28% vs 2.54% (STREAM); and network overheads of 2.8% vs 22.9% (TCP) and 0.6% vs 18% (UDP) for containers vs VMs.

In paper [1], authors review optimization metrics and methods for controlling energy consumption in systems based on single devices, grids, clusters and cloud solutions. They analyze possibilities offered by CPUs and GPUs and provide a comprehensive analysis of methods for optimizing power and energy consumption using schedulers, DVFS/DFS/DCT and power capping using APIs provided by hardware manufacturers such as Intel RAPL, NVIDIA NVML, AMD APM, and IBM EnergyScale.

In work [10], authors propose an automatic GPU energy profiling approach based on the NVIDIA NVML API and introduce the EnergyProfiler tool, which measures energy consumption, execution time, and average power. By evaluating multiple power limits, the authors managed to save up to 30% of energy with a 12% drop in performance.

In paper [9], authors analyze the performance-energy trade-off in training of Deep Convolutional Neural Networks for image recognition on NVIDIA Quadro RTX6000 and V100 GPUs. Using the NVIDIA NVML API for power monitoring and power capping, they minimize Energy, EDP, and EDS. Energy savings reach 28.5–32.5% and 24–33%, EDP 25–28% and 23–27%, and EDS 22–27% and 23.5–27.3%, with performance losses of 4.5–15.4% and 4.5–21% for RTX6000 and V100, respectively.

3   Experiments and Testbed Environment

In this work, we used the StEP (Static Energy Profiler) tool from the SPLiT[1] package setup for NVIDIA GPUs. The StEP tool was presented and discussed in more detail in paper [9]. For each test, a power cap was set separately before execution using the StEP tool. Power monitoring was also performed using StEP. Preliminary tests showed that the overhead of such monitoring is well below 1%, amounting to 0.18% of CPU utilization.

---

[1] https://projects.task.gda.pl/akrz/split.

We used three different benchmarks. Single Shot Detector (SSD)[2] used in MLPerf Inference Benchmarks from the MLCommons reference implementation, based on ResNeXt50_32x4d [12] and subset of OpenImagesV7[3] reduced to 12 classes. Two benchmarks from PyTorch benchmark suite[4]: image recognition network ResNet50 [7] training benchmark and pretrained transformer from Hugging Face – hf_Bert [3] inference benchmark, 32-bit floating point precision. We selected benchmarks so that the GPU load would be as high as possible throughout the entire duration of the tests.

We test the impact of the virtualization environment in the form of Docker and VM running in KVM vs bare metal using power capping thanks to the StEP tool. Docker tests include 8 parallel containers, KVM tests include 8 parallel virtual machines. Each environment has its own GPU. Bare metal tests are run as 8 parallel processes. We compare training time, energy and EDP at GPU power set to $P_{cap} = 100 + 8 \times n, \forall n \in \{1, \cdots, 20\}$ on each GPU. Each test for every configuration was run 10 times.

We conducted the tests on a rack server machine equipped with 2 Intel Xeon Silver 4210 CPUs, 384 GB RAM and 8 NVIDIA Turing QUADRO RTX6000 GPUs. The operating system used during testing on bare metal and as host system was Ubuntu 22.04.3 LTS with CUDA Toolkit 12.2, Python 3.10 and PyTorch 2.7.1. The software versions are the standard versions available in the OS being used. The selected LTS version of the operating system is a stable and proven distribution widely used in commercial solutions, thanks to its 5-year support period, which can be extended to 10–15 years with the Pro version. The same software configuration was used in VMs and containers. For the VMs, we allocated 32 GB of RAM and 8 CPU cores to each machine, the driver used to communicate with the GPU was vfio-pci.

4 Results and Analysis

The results can be divided into three sets, all presented in the context of power limits imposed by power-capping mechanisms. The first set concerns workload performance, where execution times (T) were measured. The second set enables direct comparison of energy consumption (E). The third set represents a trade-off between these two aspects and is expressed using the Energy-Delay Product, $EDP = E \cdot T$. These metrics were averaged over individual workloads running on the different GPUs; each workload was executed 10 times and the results were averaged, and such values are presented next for various power constraints.

The observed execution times differ across the compared configurations; however, the container-based approach is only marginally slower than bare metal execution, with average and maximum overheads of 0.19% and 0.31%, respectively. For the SSD benchmark, the VM configuration performs significantly worse,

---

[2] https://github.com/mlcommons/training/tree/master/retired_benchmarks/ssd-v1/ssd.

[3] https://storage.googleapis.com/openimages/web/download_v7.html.

[4] https://github.com/pytorch/benchmark.

exhibiting average and maximum overheads of 3.84% and 4.64%, respectively. As for the results related to the energy consumption, similarly to the performance data, the container-based configuration exhibits only a marginal increase in energy usage compared to bare metal execution, with average and maximum overheads of 0.12% and 0.26%, respectively. In contrast, the VM-based execution performs noticeably worse, showing average and maximum energy overheads of 1.78% and 2.51%, respectively. Concerning EDP, we observe that the container-based configuration continues to exhibit very low overheads, with average and maximum values of 0.31% and 0.45%, respectively. In contrast, the VM-based configurations perform significantly worse, showing average and maximum overheads of 5.67% and 7.25%, respectively. In the case of the hf_Bert benchmark, the overheads observed for the container-based configuration are practically imperceptible. Workload execution times are on average 0.02% faster and at most 0.1% slower than bare metal. Average energy consumption was 0.08% lower for container-based, while the maximum was 0.07% higher than bare metal. VM-based configurations are significantly worse. The execution time overhead averages at 28.9%, with a maximum of 36.47%, compared to bare metal. The energy consumption is not significantly higher, averaging at 1.45% and reaching a maximum of 2.06%. The EDP, calculated in the same way as in the previous test, also shows an average decrease of 0.1% and a maximum increase of 0.15% for container-based configuration compared to bare metal. In the case of VM, EDP is significantly higher due to the long duration of individual workloads, averaging 30.74% and a maximum of 38.91% compared to bare metal. A very similar situation can also be observed for the resnet50 benchmark. The duration of the container-based workload is on average 0.08% shorter and at a maximum 0.27% longer, while the energy consumption is on average 0.14% smaller and at a maximum 0.21% higher than for bare metal. EDP, calculated in the same way as in the previous tests, is on average 0.22% lower and up to 0.5% higher compared to bare metal. The VM also performs worse in this test. The workload duration has an overhead of 30.91% on average and 36.49% at a maximum. Energy consumption is 1.65% higher on average and 2.71% at a maximum. EDP is 33.02% higher on average and 39.42% at a maximum compared to bare metal. In all cases, we noticed that the time required for IO operations had a significant impact on the execution time, which confirms the observations noted in work [4]. Detailed results and charts are available in the repository[5].

Charts in Fig. 1 present the aforementioned results in a chart-based representation. The plots confirm that the overhead introduced by the container-based configuration is negligible overall. In contrast, the VM-based execution results in significantly higher overheads for both energy and performance.

Moreover, the gap observed for EDP is clearly larger than for its individual components considered separately. We can also observe that execution under lower power caps tends to be more unstable, and that the performance and energy differences between the VM and the bare metal/container configurations are smaller when lower power limits are imposed.

---

[5] https://kask.eti.pg.gda.pl/gitlab/mickosc2/iccs2026.

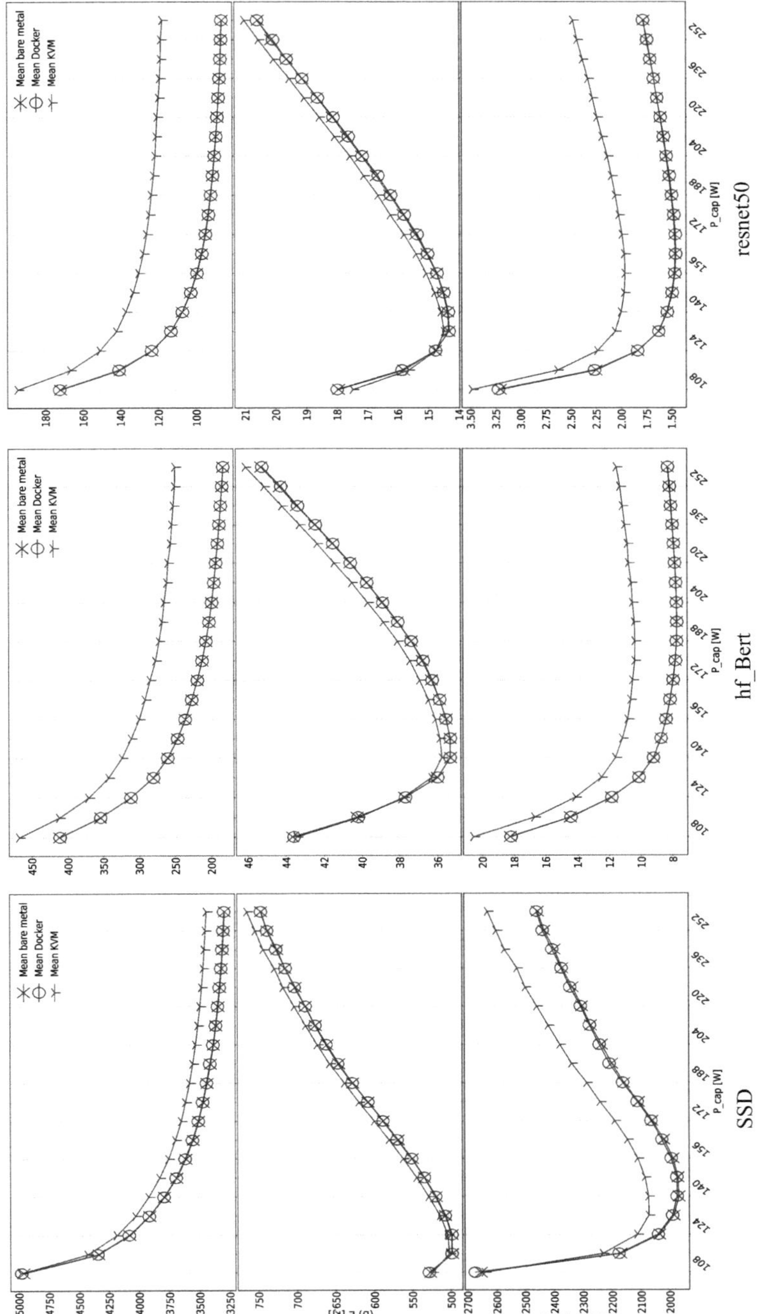

Fig. 1. Experimental results for SSD, hf_Bert and resnet50 benchmarks, (a): execution time [s], (b): energy consumption [kJ], (c) Energy–Delay Product (EDP) [MJs] under different power caps.

Concluding the above results, we can note that the influence of containerization on GPU-based AI workloads is negligible, in contrast to the VM-based configuration, where the performance and energy penalties are significant, although they decrease under more aggressive power caps. This demonstrates that CPU-side virtualization overhead remains visible even for highly GPU-dominated AI workloads.

Therefore, we strongly recommend using container-based configurations deployed directly on bare metal, without an additional VM layer, wherever such an approach is feasible and does not conflict with higher-priority constraints, such as security policies.

5 Summary and Future Work

In this paper, we provided a comparison of execution of AI workloads in Virtual Machine (KVM) and containerized (Docker) environments against a bare metal system, analyzing metrics such as execution time, energy consumption and Energy-Delay Product (EDP). Furthermore, we performed comparative assessment in a multi 8 GPU system for a range of power caps imposed on the GPUs, starting from the default value of 260 W per GPU down to 108 W per GPU. We conclude that the overhead of Docker versus bare metal is virtually negligible – with average and maximum values across power caps tested: 0.03% and 0.31% for the execution time, -0.03% and 0.26% for energy and 0% and 0.5% for EDP. For KVM, we observe visibly larger penalties of 21.22% and 36.49% for the execution time, 1.63% and 2.71% for the energy consumption and 23.14% and 39.42% for EDP. An interesting observation is that these penalties become smaller for more restrictive (smaller) power caps.

Within future work, we plan to extend this research by testing additional virtualization solutions – both VM-based and container-based ones – such as Xen, VMware, and Podman, Singularity, across a broader range of systems and workloads. We will also explore the impact of software and hardware configurations, including different versions of components from the compiler and CUDA to AI frameworks, as well as diverse computing platforms and GPUs such as NVIDIA A100, H100, and AMD GPUs.

Acknowledgments. The research was supported in part by project "Cloud Artificial Intelligence Service Engineering (CAISE) platform to create universal and smart services for various application areas", No. KPOD.05.10-IW.10-0005/24, as part of the European IPCEI-CIS program, financed by NRRP (National Recovery and Resilience Plan) funds. The computations were performed at the Department of Computer Architecture, Faculty of Electronics, Telecommunications and Informatics, Gdansk University of Technology. During the preparation of this work, the authors used LLM to improve the language, grammar, and general text flow of the manuscript. Following the use of this tool, the authors reviewed and edited the content as needed and take full responsibility for the final content of the publication.

References

1. Czarnul, P., Proficz, J., Krzywaniak, A.: Energy-aware high-performance computing: survey of state-of-the-art tools, techniques, and environments. Sci. Program. 1–19 (2019). https://doi.org/10.1155/2019/8348791
2. Deochake, S., Maheshwari, S., De, R., Grover, A.: Comparative Study of Virtual Machines and Containers for DevOps Developers (2023). https://doi.org/10.48550/arXiv.1808.08192
3. Devlin, J., Chang, M.W., Lee, K., Toutanova, K.: Bert: pre-training of deep bidirectional transformers for language understanding (2019). https://doi.org/10.48550/arXiv.1810.04805
4. Felter, W., Ferreira, A., Rajamony, R., Rubio, J.: An updated performance comparison of virtual machines and Linux containers. In: 2015 IEEE International Symposium on Performance Analysis of Systems and Software (ISPASS), pp. 171–172. IEEE (2015). https://doi.org/10.1109/ISPASS.2015.7095802
5. Giallorenzo, S., Mauro, J., Poulsen, M.G., Siroky, F.: Virtualization costs: benchmarking containers and virtual machines against bare-metal. SN Comput. Sci. $2(5)$, 1–20 (2021). https://doi.org/10.1007/s42979-021-00781-8
6. Gonzalez, R., Horowitz, M.: Energy dissipation in general purpose microprocessors. IEEE J. Solid-State Circ. 1277–1284 (1996). https://doi.org/10.1109/4.535411
7. He, K., Zhang, X., Ren, S., Sun, J.: Deep residual learning for image recognition (2015). https://doi.org/10.48550/arXiv.1512.03385
8. Kononowicz, T., Czarnul, P.: Performance assessment of using docker for selected MPI applications in a parallel environment based on commodity hardware. Appl. Sci. 8305 (2022). https://doi.org/10.3390/app12168305
9. Krzywaniak, A., Czarnul, P., Proficz, J.: GPU power capping for energy-performance trade-offs in training of deep convolutional neural networks for image recognition. In: Computational Science – ICCS 2022, pp. 667–681. Springer International Publishing (2022). https://doi.org/10.1007/978-3-031-08751-6_48
10. Krzywaniak, A., Czarnul, P.: Performance/Energy Aware Optimization of Parallel Applications on GPUs Under Power Capping. In: Parallel Processing and Applied Mathematics, pp. 123–133. Springer International Publishing (2020). https://doi.org/10.1007/978-3-030-43222-5_11
11. Ramalho, F., Neto, A.: Virtualization at the network edge: A performance comparison. In: 2016 IEEE 17th International Symposium on A World of Wireless, Mobile and Multimedia Networks (WoWMoM), pp. 1–6. IEEE (2016). https://doi.org/10.1109/WoWMoM.2016.7523584
12. Xie, S., Girshick, R., Dollár, P., Tu, Z., He, K.: Aggregated Residual Transformations for Deep Neural Networks (2017). https://doi.org/10.48550/arXiv.1611.05431
13. Xu, P., Shi, S., Chu, X.: Performance Evaluation of Deep Learning Tools in Docker Containers (2017). https://doi.org/10.48550/arXiv.1711.03386

When One Becomes n: Realising Distributed Concurrency with ARBOC

Y. Samarth Bhat[(✉)], Varun Shenoy, Vibhav Tiwari, Samar Garg, and Gowri Srinivasa

PES Center for Pattern Recognition, Department of Computer Science and Engineering, PES University, Bengaluru, India
`samarthbhaty@gmail.com`, `shenoy.varun@protonmail.com`, `gsrinivasa@pes.edu`

Abstract. Parallel programming remains notoriously difficult, primarily due to the cognitive load of managing synchronisation and non-deterministic state across distributed nodes. While Behaviour-Oriented Concurrency (BoC) simplifies this on single-system architectures by unifying parallelism and coordination, its reliance on shared memory limits its horizontal scalability. This paper presents ARBOC (Arbitrated Runtime for Behaviour Oriented Concurrency), a distributed runtime that extends BoC across multiple systems while preserving its core semantic guarantees. ARBOC separates coordination from execution through centralised arbitration, scheduling behaviours via a dependency-aware directed acyclic graph and executing them on distributed workers without exposing programmers to message passing, distributed locks, or explicit synchronisation. We describe the execution semantics, architecture, and implementation of ARBOC, and evaluate it on a range of parallel and coordination-intensive benchmarks. Results show that ARBOC scales effectively for parallelisable compute-heavy workloads while retaining predictable behaviour under contention, demonstrating that BoC's abstraction naturally generalises to distributed environments.

Keywords: Parallel Programming · Distributed Systems · Behaviour Oriented Concurrency · Concurrency

1 Introduction

Parallel programming is inherently complex, particularly when it requires expressing the coordination of concurrent, atomic tasks. BoC addresses this complexity by unifying parallelism and coordination into a single abstraction. This enables asynchronous, atomic, and ordered work units over independent resources. However, the current single-system design limits scalability and precludes the performance benefits of distributed environments.

This paper presents ARBOC (Arbitrated Runtime for Behaviour Oriented Concurrency)[1], which extends Behaviour-Oriented Concurrency [4,5] to support

---

Y. Samarth Bhat, V. Shenoy, V. Tiwari and S. Garg—All authors have equal contributions.

[1] The source code for ARBOC: https://github.com/CPR-research/ARBOC.

P. Neumann et al. (Eds.): ICCS 2026, LNCS 16784, pp. 480–487, 2026.
https://doi.org/10.1007/978-3-032-29924-6_43

execution across multiple systems. The original guarantees of exclusive access, atomicity, and ordering are preserved while facilitating the coordination of shared dependencies for isolated data objects. It is demonstrated that the model naturally generalises to distributed settings without exposing programming complexities such as explicit message passing, distributed locking, or conflict resolution. The extended model is presented herein to address distribution challenges and outline how simplicity and expressiveness are retained at scale.

Prior work approaches parts of this problem but makes different trade-offs. Ownership-based languages such as Rust [7] and capability-based runtimes like Pony [6] enforce safety via type systems, but push synchronisation concerns onto the programmer and do not directly address distributed execution. Actor-based systems [1,9] like Erlang [2] scale well across nodes, but inherently expose non-determinism in message ordering and state evolution. DAG-based schedulers provide deterministic execution for dataflow and batch workloads, but are not designed for fine-grained, contended mutable state with exclusive access requirements. Related concurrency models include isolation-typed actors [10], capability-based type systems [8], and composable integration of actors with other paradigms [11].

ARBOC occupies a distinct point in this design space. By retaining BoC's cown-based exclusivity and deterministic scheduling, while introducing centralised arbitration and distributed execution, ARBOC preserves the simplicity and reasoning model of BoC even when scaled across a cluster.

2   Background

2.1   Scope and Assumptions

(1) **Reliable network:** the cluster networking must guarantee reliable and in-order data delivery. (2) **Fail-stop processes:** processes may fail by stopping execution but do not exhibit Byzantine behaviour. (3) **Closed-world resource definition:** the complete set of resource objects and tasks constituting a workload must be statically defined in advance. These assumptions allow us to focus on the core challenge addressed in this work—extending BoC's coordination semantics to distributed systems while preserving the simplicity of its programming model. Fault tolerance, failure detection, and network partition handling, while important, are prospects of future work.

2.2   Core Concepts

ARBOC defines its fundamental primitives and execution semantics based on the principles of Project Verona [3], extending its concepts of concurrent ownership and ordered execution of discrete work units to a distributed environment. The following concepts, defined by BoC serve as guidelines for the execution model. A *cown (concurrent owner)* serves as an abstraction used to manage an isolated piece of data involved in concurrent tasks and provides the only point of entry to mutate and read the resource. This ensures mutual exclusion across concurrent behaviours. A cown may exist either in the *available* or *acquired* state. The *behaviour* forms a unit of concurrent execution, and is defined by the `When()` construct, which takes cowns as parameters.

Execution Semantics. Two primary semantics are enforced to ensure safe concurrent operation. **(i) Atomicity of Ownership:** A behaviour begins execution only after it has acquired exclusive access to its complete set of required cowns. This ensures that the behaviour's operations are isolated and data-race free, and **(ii) The Happens-Before Relation:** ARBOC maintains deterministic execution through the *happens-before* relationship - *a behaviour b will happen before another behaviour b' iff b and b' require overlapping sets of cowns, and b is spawned before b'.*

2.3   Overview

The system follows a centralised-scheduling, distributed-execution pattern and is organised into four primary stages:

1. **Definition Phase:** An ARBOC program defines all behaviours and cowns prior to the top-level `When()` call which schedules the initial behaviour. At this stage, behaviours are added to a node-local registry and each cown is statically assigned a home node.
2. **Scheduling Phase:** When execution encounters a `When()` call, the corresponding behaviour is submitted to the centralised Dispatcher that maintains a Directed Acyclic Graph (DAG) which tracks cown dependencies. The DAG ensures that a behaviour gets dispatched with exclusive access to its required set of cowns. Resource contention is thus converted into a well-defined execution order.
3. **Distribution Phase:** When a behaviour becomes unblocked in the DAG, i.e., it reaches the root position for all cown dependencies, it is dispatched to a message broker. The broker delivers the behaviour to one of the available Executors in the distributed cluster.
4. **Resolution Phase:** The assigned Executor executes the behaviour and returns the updated state of the associated cowns to the master process. Upon completion, the Dispatcher updates the DAG, unblocking and triggering subsequent behaviours waiting on the same cowns. (see Fig. 1).

3   System Architecture

3.1   The Dispatcher

Script Execution and Behaviour Capture. The Dispatcher handles workload scheduling throughout the system. The user script runs on the Dispatcher, which creates behaviour instances upon encountering a `When()` call and enqueues it into the DAG. **The DAG** Scheduling in ARBOC is built around a DAG where behaviours are represented as nodes, and edges encode dependencies on required

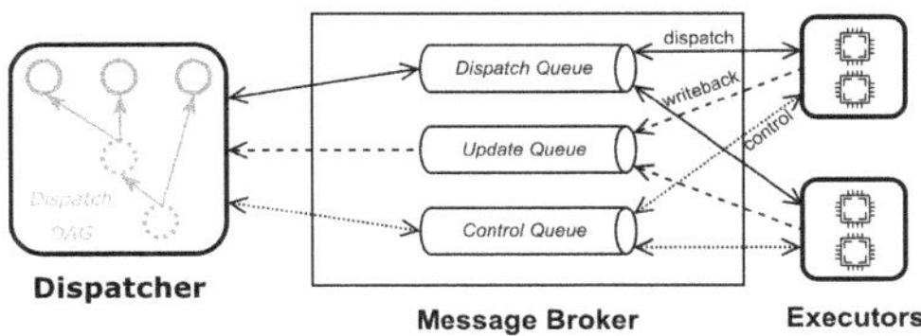

Fig. 1. ARBOC architecture showing a single Dispatcher with a message broker and multiple Executors (each Executor can receive a dispatch, control and write-back message).

cowns. When a new behaviour is scheduled, it is added to the DAG with edges pointing either to the cown itself or to the terminal node of that cown's current dependency chain, ensuring that required access ordering is preserved. Figure 2 shows a bank transfer behaviour using nested `When()` constructs. The Dispatcher translates this code into the dependency graph visualised in Fig. 2. A behaviour becomes ready for execution on reaching the root level of all its cown dependencies, i.e. when no other behaviours requiring the same cown precede it. At this point, the behaviour and its required cowns are sent to the message broker. For this proof of concept, ARBOC utilises Neural Autonomic Transport System (NATS) [12] – a lightweight, high-performance publish-subscribe messaging system. No explicit load-balancing algorithm was implemented, as NATS defaults to a native random selection approach for message distribution.

Post-Execution Resolution Once the execution is complete, the Dispatcher updates the modified cown values to reflect the changes in its local records. The behaviour is then purged from the DAG, potentially triggering a cascading effect where newly freed up resources allow a behaviour to be immediately dispatched.

Behaviour Registry To avoid the overhead of serialising function bytecode to send across the network, ARBOC initialises a node-local *Behaviour Registry* that maps behaviour names to their function definitions. During the initialisation phase, this registry is populated with the complete set of behaviour definitions required for the computation. This architecture enables the Dispatcher to transmit a lightweight execution payload that only consists of the behaviour name and the cowns.

3.2   The Executor

Distributed Execution and Behaviour. An instance of ARBOC can host multiple Executors. It is limited only by the capacity of the underlying message broker and network topology. The Executor is responsible for the life-cycle of behaviour execution. Upon receiving a set of cowns and a behaviour identifier, the Executor instantiates a local copy of the behaviour from the Behaviour Registry. It then spawns a dedicated worker thread on which the behaviour runs.

Result Transmission and Modular Deployment. Upon completion, the Executor constructs a mapping of the updated cown values which is then sent to

```
type Acc struct {bal int32}
func transfer(src Cown[Acc], dst Cown[Acc], amt Cown[int32]) {
    When(src, amt) { // check
    amount = amt.val
        if src.val.bal >= amt.val {
            When(src) { src.val.bal -= amount } // debit
            When(dst) { dst.val.bal += amount } // credit
        }
    }
}
```

Fig. 2. Bank transfer using nested behaviours and its associated DAG

the Master via the message queue to synchronize state across the system. The separation between the Master and Executor enables a modular architecture that supports heterogeneous deployments, allowing Executors to operate across diverse hardware platforms and execution environments.

3.3 Communication Infrastructure

The interaction between the Dispatcher and the Executors is mediated by a message broker, which serves as an asynchronous transport layer. This decouples task scheduling from task execution. When a behaviour is ready for execution, its metadata is serialised into a message and published to a work queue. This infrastructure facilitates two critical system properties:

1. **Dynamic Work Distribution:** The broker can act as a load balancer, ensuring that dispatched behaviours are distributed among available Executors. This prevents the Dispatcher from needing to maintain the state or health of individual worker nodes.
2. **Backpressure and Buffering:** By using a queue-based model, the system can handle bursts in behaviour spawns. The broker buffers pending behaviours, allowing Executors to pull work at varying processing rates.

4   Results and Evaluation

ARBOC is evaluated across a suite of six benchmarks **shared by BoC–** representing diverse computational patterns: Parallelisable tasks (*Monte Carlo Pi*, *MatMul*, *Convolution*), recursive workloads (*Fib*), and coordination-heavy scenarios (*Bank*, *Dining Phil*). All benchmarks were executed on dedicated CPU Linode instances (AMD EPYC 7713, 2 core 4GB RAM / 4 core 8GB RAM) within a Virtual Private Cloud. To establish the baseline (BoC), we executed the workloads[2] on two standalone configurations: a 2-core instance and a 4-core instance. For the ARBOC benchmarks, a 4-core dedicated node served as the

---

[2] Scale: MCPI $\sim 10^{11}$ samples; MatMul/Conv $\sim 4K \times 4K$; Bank used thousands of transactions; Dining Phil/Fib used small fixed setups.

centralised Dispatcher, managing a cluster of 2-core worker nodes. Performance is measured in total execution time (seconds).

Table 1 presents the execution times for both the single-system baseline (BoC within the ARBOC framework) and the distributed cluster (ARBOC) across various core and worker configurations.

Table 1. Benchmark Execution Times (seconds): Comparing Single-Node Baseline (BoC) vs. Distributed Scalability (ARBOC)

Benchmark	Single-Node Baseline		Distributed ARBOC (Cluster)			
Configuration	2 Cores (Local)	4 Cores (Local)	2 Cores (1 Worker)	4 Cores (2 Workers)	6 Cores (3 Workers)	8 Cores (4 Workers)
Monte Carlo Pi	342.343	301.212	608.490	340.917	225.333	**179.439**
MatMul	100.246	82.926	196.617	111.643	81.349	**68.951**
Fib	**1.325**	1.376	3.221	3.153	3.025	3.227
Bank	**6.340**	5.970	42.025	35.240	33.230	32.080
Dining Phil	27.543	**26.501**	149.008	137.886	133.276	133.175
Convolution	12.743	11.739	22.444	14.722	10.468	**8.206**

4.1 Baseline and Comparative Analysis

The single-node results establish the performance floor for our architecture. When comparing BoC and ARBOC at the 4-core mark, we observe a performance delta where single-system execution is generally faster (e.g., *MatMul* at 82.9 s vs 111.6 s). This overhead is attributed to communication costs (Fig. 3). However, for compute-heavy workloads like *Monte Carlo Pi*, *Convolution* and *MatMul*, ARBOC begins to outperform the single-node baseline as the cluster scales to 6 and 8 cores. Despite the distribution overhead, the system scales horizontally. Conversely, in highly sequential or small-scale computations like *Dining Phil*, *Fib* and *Bank*, the distribution overhead is more pronounced, since the behaviours are too small to offset the communication overhead.

4.2 Scalability in a Distributed Environment

The distributed results demonstrate varying degrees of speedup tied to the compute-to-coordination ratio of the workload:

1. **Performance Leads:** *Monte Carlo Pi* showed the largest speedup, running **67.9% faster** than the best local single-node result, *Convolution* and, *MatMul* achieved a speed up of **43.1%** and **20.3%** respectively.

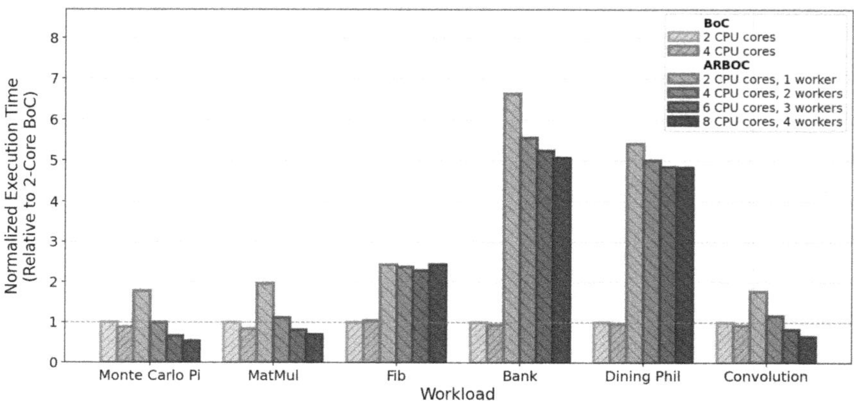

Fig. 3. Normalised execution time relative to 2-core BoC baseline (lower is better) across all configurations.

2. **Coordination Bottlenecks:** Workloads with high resource contention, such as *Bank*, showed minimal improvement. Performance suffers when many behaviours contend over the same cowns, because the Dispatcher only permits exclusive access.

3. **Overhead Analysis:** Small, rapid-fire and inherently sequential workloads (*Fib*) show nearly flat performance across core counts. *Dining Phil* ran slower on our system, an expected result given the sequential nature of the problem; the latency introduced by the message broker and DAG scheduling logic outweighs the benefits of parallel execution. As for *Bank*, its nested behaviour spawning pattern means the Dispatcher repeatedly serialises and re-dispatches behaviours across the cluster, making serialisation and dispatch overhead the dominant cost.

5   Conclusion

This paper introduced ARBOC, a distributed runtime for the Behaviour-Oriented Concurrency (BoC) model implemented in Go. By utilising a centralised arbitrator and distributed executors, the system achieves a total decoupling of coordination from execution. It proves that BoC abstractions can be preserved in a distributed setting without resorting to manual locking. Further, ARBOC shows near-linear scaling on compute-bound, highly parallel workloads, maintaining efficiency as the system scales and demonstrating the practicality of the approach for large deployments. While ARBOC successfully extends BoC, there are still several areas for improvement. The centralised Dispatcher poses as a single point of failure and a possible bottleneck for behaviour spawning at scale. Fault tolerance for node failures during atomic behaviour execution remains a requirement for production systems. ARBOC demonstrates that

Behaviour-Oriented Concurrency can scale to distributed settings without losing its simplicity, enabling safe and powerful parallel programming.

Disclosure of Interests. The authors have no competing interests to declare that are relevant to the content of this article.

References

1. Agha, G.A.: Actors: a model of concurrent computation in distributed systems (parallel processing, semantics, open, programming languages, artificial intelligence). University of Michigan (1985)
2. Armstrong, J.: A history of erlang. In: Proceedings of the third ACM SIGPLAN Conference on History of Programming Languages, pp. 6–1 (2007)
3. Arvidsson, E., et al.: Reference capabilities for flexible memory management. Proc. ACM Program. Languages **7**(OOPSLA2), 1363–1393 (2023)
4. Cheeseman, L., Castegren, E., Drossopoulou, S., Wrigstad, T., Clebsch, S., Parkinson, M.: Decoupling isolation and concurrency: an actor-centric view of behaviouroriented concurrency. In: Concurrent Programming, Open Systems and Formal Methods: Essays Dedicated to Gul Agha to Celebrate His Scientific Career, pp.165–186. Springer (2025)
5. Cheeseman, L., et al.: When concurrency matters: behaviour-oriented concurrency. Proc. ACM Program. Languages **7**(OOPSLA2), 1531–1560 (2023)
6. Clebsch, S., Franco, J., Drossopoulou, S., Yang, A.M., Wrigstad, T., Vitek, J.: Orca: Gc and type system co-design for actor languages. Proc. ACM Program. Languages **1**(OOPSLA), 1–28 (2017)
7. Crichton, W., Gray, G., Krishnamurthi, S.: A grounded conceptual model for ownership types in rust. Proc. ACM Program. Languages **7**(OOPSLA2), 1224–1252 (2023)
8. Haller, P., Loiko, A.: Lacasa: lightweight affinity and object capabilities in scala. In: Proceedings of the 2016 ACM SIGPLAN International Conference on Object Oriented Programming, Systems, Languages, and Applications, pp. 272–291 (2016)
9. Hewitt, C., Bishop, P., Steiger, R.: Session 8 formalisms for artificial intelligence a universal modular actor formalism for artificial intelligence. In: Advance papers of the conference. vol. 3, p. 235. Stanford Research Institute Menlo Park, CA (1973)
10. Srinivasan, S., Mycroft, A.: Kilim: Isolation-typed actors for java: (a million actors, safe zero-copy communication). In: European Conference on Object-Oriented Programming, pp. 104–128. Springer (2008)
11. Swalens, J., De Koster, J., De Meuter, W.: Chocola: integrating futures, actors, and transactions. In: Proceedings of the 8th ACM SIGPLAN International Workshop on Programming Based on Actors, Agents, and Decentralized Control, pp. 33–43 (2018)
12. Synadia Communications: NATS: The cloud native messaging system (2024). https://nats.io. Accessed: 2025

An Empirical Evaluation of HPC Processors for a Coupled Scientific Simulation

Jelle van Dijk[1]([🖂])(iD), Okba Hamitou[2], Gabor Zavodszky[1](iD),
Ana-Lucia Varbanescu[1,3](iD), Andy D. Pimentel[1](iD), and Alfons Hoekstra[1](iD)

[1] Informatics Institute, FNWI, University of Amsterdam,
Amsterdam, The Netherlands
`Jelle.van.dijk@uva.nl`
[2] Eviden, Bezons, France
[3] EEMCS Faculty, University of Twente, Enschede, The Netherlands

Abstract. Scientific simulations grow increasingly complex, and require massive compute and energy resources. To address these requirements, new HPC processors emerge regularly. Quantifying the performance and energy-efficiency impact of new HPC processors is non-trivial, yet critical for next generation (super)computers development. In this work, we demonstrate how comprehensive benchmarking contributes to quantifying the performance and energy efficiency impact of five different processors on HemoCell, a complex coupled scientific simulation. We constructed representative benchmarks and ran hundreds of benchmarks to provide both coarse-grained data, focusing on metrics such as utilization and speed-up, and fine-grained data, based on hardware performance counters. Our detailed data analysis provides insights into the impact of higher memory bandwidth, the need for higher cache capacity, the relevance of high core-density, and the effect of low-power designs. Our results show that cache capacity is the *highest-impact* feature for both the performance increase and energy consumption reduction of HemoCell.

Keywords: Energy Efficiency · Performance · Coupled Scientific Simulation · Benchmarking · Performance Analysis

1 Introduction

Scientific computing applications are increasingly complex. In turn, they require substantial computational power and energy; these developments lead to increasing concerns regarding supercomputing's energy bill [9]. To address this, new processors deliver higher peak compute throughput (FLOP/s), memory bandwidth (GB/s), and energy efficiency (FLOPs/Watt). Processors achieve these improvements with features such as higher core counts, larger caches [8], and power optimizations, all of which *should* help improve the performance and efficiency of high-performance computing (HPC).

© The Author(s), under exclusive license to Springer Nature Switzerland AG 2026
P. Neumann et al. (Eds.): ICCS 2026, LNCS 16784, pp. 488–496, 2026.
https://doi.org/10.1007/978-3-032-29924-6_44

In this work, we show that improvement is not guaranteed, as we investigate the impact of different HPC processors on a coupled scientific simulation. Specifically we show the methodology and results of a benchmarking campaign to characterize the performance and energy efficiency impact of five HPC processors on a coupled scientific simulation. We analyze five processors spanning high-bandwidth memory (*Intel SPR $\pm$ HBM*), high core density (*AMD Bergamo*), low-power ARM design (*Ampere Altra*), and two AMD Zen architectures (*Rome, Genoa*).

Our representative scientific application is HemoCell [12], a coupled large-scale scientific framework that simulates cell-resolved blood flow. In prior work, performance predictive and descriptive models have been built for Hemocell. [1,11] However, none of these models are suitable for the evaluation of new processors, as these require calibration and are not designed for cross-processor evaluation.

Thus, we propose the first benchmarking strategy that enables performance and energy impact assessment of new processors on HemoCell. To understand the processors' impact on the performance and energy efficiency of HemoCell, we propose a three-step strategy: (1) peak-performance benchmarking, (2) application benchmarking, (3) fine-grained application benchmarking. Combining this data shows how these processors have different impact on HemoCell, and highlights the large cache per core of *AMD Genoa* as the highest-impact feature.

2   Methodology

Benchmarking. The goal of benchmarking is to collect data to characterize the impact of the processor for the application of interest. In this work, we propose two types of benchmarks: (1) hardware-specific, to validate the processors' peak performance, and (2) application-specific, to determine the ability of the application to utilize this peak. Peak performance is the highest achievable FLOP/s and memory bandwidth of a hardware configuration. For the application-specific data we run a set of single-node HemoCell benchmarks. Here we collect high-level performance metrics and detailed performance data in the form of hardware events, such as the number of cycles, instructions, and cache misses.

Performance Analysis. We propose two levels of performance analysis: (a) a high-level performance comparison, and (b) a fine-grained performance-pattern identification. With high-level analysis we compare the main performance metrics, e.g., runtime and energy consumption. These metrics enable objective performance comparisons between workloads and/or systems. However they are insufficient to explain the observed performance because of their lack of detail. For fine-grained analysis, we use the hardware event data, which improves our understanding of the performance. Hardware performance counters keep track of metrics related to code execution and hardware behavior, e.g., cache hits/misses, number of cycles, and number of retired instructions.

3 Experimental Setup

This section describes the application, hardware, and tools we used for data collection and analysis. In Table 1 we describe all processors used in this study.

3.1 Application Under Test: Hemocell

HemoCell couples separately modeled blood plasma and red-blood cells (RBCs) [12]. The domain is decomposed into N equally sized subdomains (one MPI process per CPU core). During the simulation neighboring processes exchange the outer fluid layer and RBCs crossing subdomain boundaries. Domain size is expressed in lattice units (LU).[1] Each benchmarks is a cubic domain, with 18% of the volume occupied by RBCs. We benchmark two domain sizes, S1 ($200 \times 200 \times 100$ LU, 20,000 iterations) and S2 ($200 \times 200 \times 200$ LU, 10,000 iterations), chosen to provide equivalent computational workloads across processors , while respecting the $25 \times 25 \times 25$ LU minimum subdomain constraint, imposed by HemoCell, for the highest-core-count processor (AMD Bergamo, 256 cores).

Table 1. The processors under study, characterized by Lithography (L), Thermal design power (TDP), Frequency, Number of cores, Sockets per Node (S), Cache sizes (L1 and L2 per core, L3 shared), Channels per socket (C), memory technology (DIMMs), throughput, and size.

Processor	TDP [W]	Base/Max Freq. [GHz]	Cores (Sockets)	L1/L2/L3 Cache size	C DRAM	Size [GB]
AMD Epyc Bergamo 9754	400	2.25/3.1	128 (2)	32 kB / 1 MB 256 MB	12 DDR5 4800 MT/s	384
AMD Genoa 9654	360	2.4/3.55	96 (2)	32 kB / 1 MB 384 MB	12 DDR5 4800 MT/s	384
AMD Rome 7H12	280	2.65/3.3	64 (2)	32 kB / 512 kB 256 MB	8 DDR4 3200 MT/s	256
Ampere Altra Q8030	210	3.0	80 (1)	64 kB / 1 MB 32 MB	8 DDR4 3200 MT/s	256
Intel Sapphire Rapids 9480	350	1.9/3.5	56 (2)	48 kB / 2 MB 112.5 MB	8 DDR5 4800 MT/s	512
Intel Sapphire Rapids HBM 9480 (Cache mode)	350	1.9/3.5	56 (2)	48 kB / 2 MB 112.5 MB	8 HBM2e 3200 MT/s	128

3.2 Compilers and Monitoring Tools

For all experiments, we use the gcc compiler (versions between 11.3 and 13.2 for all AMD and Intel CPUs, and version 8.5.0 for the Ampere CPU), and OpenMPI 4.1.5. Hemocell is compiled with *-O3,-march=native*, and *-std=c++11* flags. For each runtime or energy data point, we run 3 repetitions and report the average. For hardware events measurements, two repetitions are performed.

---

[1] 1 LU = 0.5 µm.

Runtime and Performance Counters. Execution time is captured by internal HemoCell timers. For detailed measurements we use Score-P [5], an automatic code instrumentation and profiling tool. Hardware counters are read using `perf`.

Peak Performance. For the *AMD Bergamo*, *Intel SPR*, and *Ampere Altra* processors we use Stream [7] for memory bandwidth and HPL, an implementation of the LINPACK [3], for FLOP/s. On the other processors we collect the peak performance results through the empirical roofline model toolkit (ERT) [6].

Energy Consumption. For the *AMD Bergamo*, *Intel SPR*, and *Ampere Altra* processors, we measure the power consumption of the node at a frequency of 0.7 Hz, using processor-specific tools. For the *AMD Rome* and *AMD Genoa* processors, we measure the total energy consumption using EAR [2].

4   Evaluation

The benchmarking results are analyzed in the following five sections[2].

4.1   Peak Performance

Fig. 1 shows the peak performance for all processors. The results reveal the significant influence of the *AMD Bergamo* and *Intel SPR* processor features. Firstly, the high number of cores on the *AMD Bergamo* processors provides peak FLOP/s. Secondly, the *HBM* has a significant impact on the peak memory bandwidth. Enabling *HBM* increases the peak memory bandwidth to 1400 GB/s.

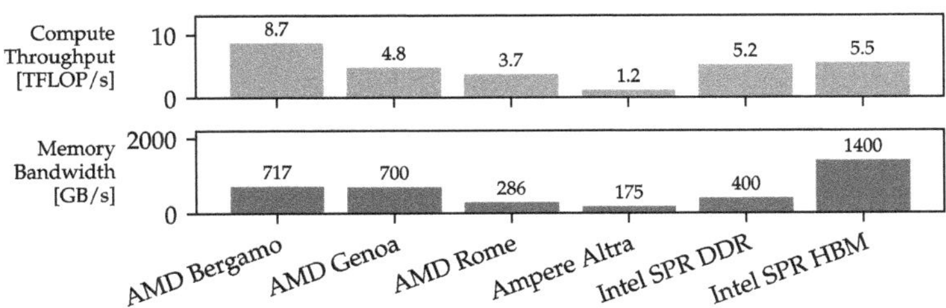

Fig. 1. Performance results for main memory bandwidth and double-precision FLOP/s.

---

[2] Benchmarks, results and plot generation scripts are available at, https://doi.org/10.5281/zenodo.15003101 and https://doi.org/10.5281/zenodo.18701790.

4.2 Runtime and Energy

In Fig. 2, we show time, energy, and power results for the S1 benchmark. We observe the best performance on the *AMD Genoa* processor, with both the shortest time per iteration, 14 ms, and the highest energy efficiency, 11 J/iteration. Even though it does not have the highest peak performance or bandwidth. This confirms that the performance of a complex application is hard to predict based only on peak performance measurements.

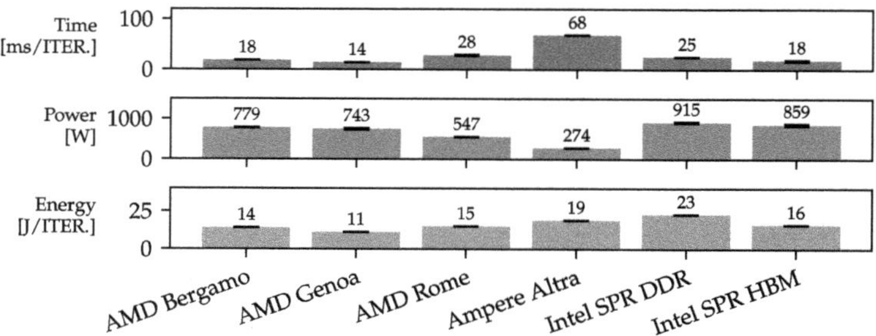

Fig. 2. Time, power, and energy per iteration for S1 (mean and Std. dev. from 3 runs).

Figure 2 confirms the advertised low power consumption of the *Ampere Altra*. However, because of the low peak performance the energy efficiency is worse than all other processors except for the *Intel SPR DDR*.

On the *Intel SPR*, enabling *HBM* leads to a speedup of around 1.4, and improves the energy efficiency. The effect of *HBM* indicates a memory bottleneck. However, the improvement is not as high as the peak memory bandwidth improvement, which is 3.5 times higher than *DDR*. This suggests that HemoCell is unable to utilize all the available memory bandwidth.

In Fig. 3 we show time and energy consumption per iteration for a varying number of MPI processes. On a two socket node, using half the cores only utilizes a single socket. For all but one of the processors, we observe a reduction in runtime and energy consumption with a decrease in MPI processes. However, on the *Ampere Altra* processor, there is no performance loss if we do not utilize all cores. Due to this and a higher power consumption when using more cores, increasing the number of MPI processes above 32 decreases energy efficiency. This result indicates a memory bottleneck, because adding more compute power does not reduce the runtime - we investigate this further in Sect. 4.4.

4.3 Cycles and Instructions

Table 2 presents the number of instructions, cycles, cycles per instruction (CPI), and data requests per instruction (MOPI), as indicators of how the processors handle the instruction mix of the application. Strikingly, there is a large deviation in the instruction count, both between processors and when changing the

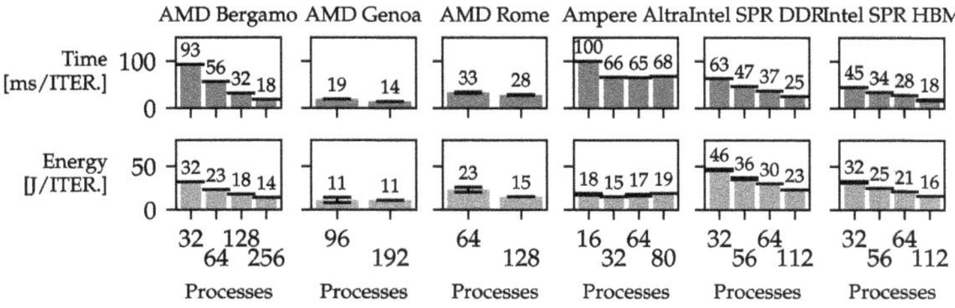

Fig. 3. Time and energy per iteration for S1, for a varying number of processes.

number of processes. The difference in the instruction count likely stems from the differences in ISAs, compilers, and even different levels of auto vectorization.

Table 2. Number of instructions (# Inst.), cycles (# Cycles), cycles and memory operations per instruction per processor (CPI and MOPI), when running S1 with a varying number of processes (NP) per processor. CPI = (Cycles/Instructions) × processes, MOPI = L1 accesses/Instructions.

Processor	NP	# Inst. $\times 10^{12}$	# Cycles $\times 10^{12}$	CPI	MOPI	NP	# Inst. $\times 10^{12}$	# Cycles $\times 10^{12}$	CPI	MOPI
AMD Bergamo	128	278	1.56	0.72	0.51	256	358	0.86	0.61	0.52
AMD Genoa	96	188	0.78	0.40	0.51	192	309	0.67	0.42	0.51
AMD Rome 7H12	64	211	2.27	0.69	0.50	128	303	1.34	0.57	0.51
Ampere Altra	64	199	3.15	1.01	0.37	80	178	3.25	1.46	0.37
Intel SPR DDR	56	192	1.85	0.54[a]	0.35	112	204	0.95	0.52[a]	0.35
Intel SPR HBM	56	174	1.31	0.42[a]	0.36	112	185	0.69	0.42[a]	0.35

[a]For the *Intel SPR* processor we can only measure the L1 loads.

Both the *AMD Genoa* and *Intel SPR* with *HBM* processors have a CPI of 0.42. However, their performance and energy efficiency differ significantly. The *Ampere Altra* shows a noticeably high CPI of 1.46. But, due to the completely different instruction set architecture (ISA), this comparison does not necessarily translate into a corresponding performance drop.

On all *AMD* processors, we observe that the number of L1 requests per executed instruction is between 0.50 and 0.52. On the *Ampere Altra* processors this ratio is lower, at 0.35. This higher ratio can be explained by difference in ISA: the *ARM*-based *Ampere Altra* favors simple instructions and uses a load-store architecture, resulting in fewer L1 accesses per instruction.

4.4 Cache and Memory Bandwidth Utilization

The observed L1 miss-rate across all processes is between 1.1% and 2.4%. In Table 3 we show last-level-cache (LLC) requests and misses. We note that, due to restricted access, we only have this data for the *Intel SPR* and *Ampere Altra* processors. Table 3 reveals a clear difference in the number of LLC requests between the two processors. Specifically, there are approximately 8× and 4× more LLC misses on *Ampere Altra* than on *Intel SPR*. We expect the larger L2 cache of the *Intel SPR* to cause this difference. Furthermore, this difference translates to memory bandwidth utilization, which we show in Table 4.

Table 3. Total requests (req.), request misses and miss rate (MR) for Last-level cache (LLC) per processor, for the S1 benchmark with a varying numbers of processes (NP)

Platform	NP	# LLC req. $\times 10^{12}$	# LLC misses $\times 10^{12}$	MR	NP	# LLC req. $\times 10^{12}$	# LLC misses $\times 10^{12}$	MR
Ampere Altra	64	4.12	2.07	0.50	80	4.03	2.03	0.50
Intel SPR DDR	56	0.45	0.41	0.91	112	0.47	0.41	0.87
Intel SPR HBM	56	0.49	0.43	0.88	112	0.53	0.45	0.84

Table 4. Memory bandwidth utilization for the S1 and S2 benchmarks (B), for varying numbers of processes (NP) and two different processors. Data $=$ L3 misses $\times 64\,B$, Bandwidth $=$ Data/Runtime.

Platform	NP	B	Time [s]	Data [GB]	Bandwidth [GB/s]	NP	B	Time [s]	Data [GB]	Bandwidth [GB/s]
Ampere Altra	64	S1	1315	132421	102	64	S2	1180	116921	100
	80	S1	1358	130136	96	80	S2	1392	135757	98
Intel SPR DDR	56	S1	962	26276	28	56	S2	983	30752	32
	112	S1	505	26229	53	112	S2	527	30943	60
Intel SPR HBM	56	S1	684	27779	41	56	S2	689	31915	47
	112	S1	365	28775	79	112	S2	365	32960	92

On the *Intel SPR*, we notice an increase in memory bandwidth utilization with the increase in either the number of processes or the problem size. This is explained by cache availability. Increasing the number of processes reduces the cache per process, while an increase in problem size increases the demands on the memory bandwidth. Even this higher demand on memory bandwidth is only 6% or 15% of the peak bandwidth. Based on this, we conclude that the cache size is large enough that the main memory bandwidth is not the bottleneck.

On the *Ampere Altra*, the behavior is different. Here we observe a consistent bandwidth utilization across all experiments. This is around 58% of the peak memory bandwidth. We do not observe a similar increase in memory bandwidth utilization as on the *Intel SPR* processor, which suggests that the memory bandwidth is a bottleneck. In Sect. 4.2, we observed a lack of scaling when using more cores on the *Ampere Altra*. The results in Table 4 indicate that this poor scaling emerges because performance is limited by the main memory bandwidth.

4.5   Roofline Analysis

To explore the observed memory bottleneck we construct a Roofline plot on the best performing processor, i.e., *AMD Genoa*, in Fig. 4. A Roofline model is designed to analyze if an application is compute or memory bound, and, if the latter, at which memory level. This is done by exploring the relation between memory bandwidth, at each memory level, and the peak performance of the processor [4]. We capture the operational intensity (OI) of HemoCell in GB/sec and the memory requests per numerical method, i.e., fluid and particle computation. We show the OI in relation to L1 and L2 requests.

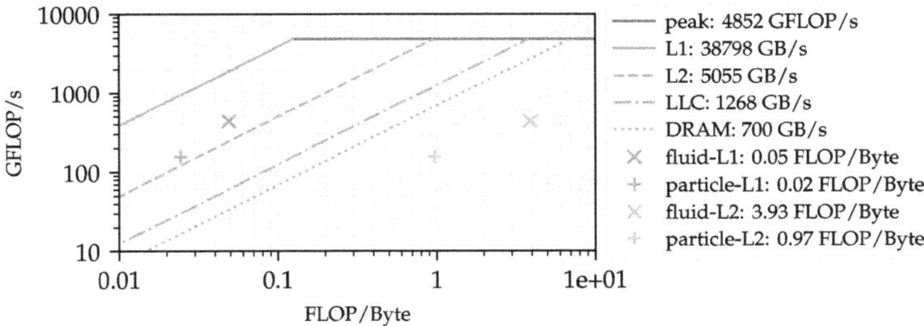

Fig. 4. Roofline model for S1 on AMD Genoa. Data is collected with ERT [6] and LIKWID [10]. Bytes processed is calculated as L1 requests $\times$ 8.

Figure 4 shows that HemoCell has a low OI, i.e., a high number of memory operations per FLOP, for both of the numerical methods. The model clearly shows that both kernels should be bound by the bandwidth of L2, LLC and main memory. However, due to the efficient utilization of L1, shown in Sect. 4.4, only 2.5% of the memory requests are serviced by L2, LLC, or main memory. This is confirmed by the higher OI in relation to the L2 requests. For these kernels, the OI is the number of FLOPs divided by the number of bytes requested from L2. We observe that these kernels are not bound by the L2 bandwidth anymore. However, depending on the miss rate on L2, performance can still be limited by LLC or main memory bandwidth. Thus, a small cache will cause the performance of HemoCell to be limited by the main memory bandwidth. This reaffirms that cache-size per process is the most influential feature. However, since the two numerical methods react differently to features, no single feature is sufficient to predict the ranking of the tested processors.

5   Conclusion

This work investigated the impact of different HPC processors on the performance of HemoCell. We found that our analysis can capture the diverse impact these processors' features have on performance. Based on the results, we conclude that (1) the CPU with the best performance and energy efficiency for HemoCell is the *AMD Genoa*, (2) the feature with the highest impact on HemoCell performance is the cache size per core, and (3) since energy use closely tracks runtime, cutting runtime remains key to reducing energy.

Beyond HemoCell. Even with built-in instrumentation, and highly configurable setups, this study still required 869 benchmarks, over 116 h, using six profiling tools producing data in ten file formats. The lack of a unified benchmarking framework remains a significant barrier for large benchmarking studies.

Acknowledgment. We thank Eviden for providing access to HPC resources on their BullSequana supercomputer.

References

1. Alowayyed, S., et al.: Load balancing of parallel cell-based blood flow simulations. J. Comput. Sci. **24** (2018). https://doi.org/10.1016/j.jocs.2017.11.008
2. Corbalan, J., et al.: Energy optimization and analysis with EAR. In: Cluster'20 (2020). https://doi.org/10.1109/CLUSTER49012.2020.00067
3. Dongarra, J.J., Luszczek, P., Petitet, A.: The LINPACK benchmark: past, present and future. CCPE **15**(9) (2003). https://doi.org/10.1002/cpe.728
4. Ilic, A., Pratas, F., Sousa, L.: Cache-aware Roofline model: upgrading the loft. IEEE Comput. Archit. Lett. **13** (2014). https://doi.org/10.1109/L-CA.2013.6
5. Knüpfer, A., et al.: Score-P: A joint performance measurement run-time infrastructure for periscope,Scalasca, TAU, and Vampir. In: Tools High Perform. Comput. 2011. Springer (2012). https://doi.org/10.1007/978-3-642-31476-6_7
6. Lo, Y.J., et al.: Roofline Model Toolkit: a practical tool for architectural and program analysis. In: High Perform. Comput. Syst. Perform. Model. Benchmarking Simul. LNCS, Springer International Publishing, Cham (2015). https://doi.org/10.1007/978-3-319-17248-4_7
7. McCalpin, J.: Memory bandwidth and machine balance in high performance computers. In: IEEE Technical Committee on Computer Architecture Newsletter (1995)
8. McCalpin, J.D.: Bandwidth limits in the intel xeon max (Sapphire Rapids with HBM) processors. In: High Performance Computer LNCS, Springer Nature Switzerland, Cham (2023). https://doi.org/10.1007/978-3-031-40843-4_30
9. Patel, T., et al.: What does power consumption behavior of HPC Jobs reveal? In: IPDPS'20 (2020). https://doi.org/10.1109/IPDPS47924.2020.00087
10. Treibig, J., et al.: LIKWID: lightweight performance tools. In: Competence in High Performance Computing 2010. Springer Berlin Heidelberg, Berlin, Heidelberg (2011). https://doi.org/10.1007/978-3-642-24025-6_14
11. van Dijk, J., et al.: Building a fine-grained analytical performance model for complex scientific simulations. In: PPAM'23. LNCS, Springer International Publishing (2023). https://doi.org/10.1007/978-3-031-30442-2_14
12. Zavodszky, G., et al.: HemoCell: a high-performance microscopic cellular library. Proc. Comput. Sci. **108** (2017). https://doi.org/10.1016/j.procs.2017.05.084

Accurate Image-Based Reconstruction of Non-Parametric Antenna EM-Simulation Models

Adrian Bekasiewicz[(✉)] [iD] and Remigiusz Martyniak [iD]

Faculty of Electronics, Telecommunications and Informatics, Gdansk University of Technology, Narutowicza 11/12, 80-233, Gdansk, Poland
`adrian.bekasiewicz@pg.edu.pl`

Abstract. Development of new antennas is an inherently cognitive task that often involves re-use of structures from the literature, or their responses (e.g., for performance comparisons). The process might also be associated with reconstruction of their electromagnetic (EM) simulation models which—when performed manually—is both time-consuming and prone to errors. In this work, a proof-of-concept framework for image-based, non-parametric reconstruction of antenna EM models has been proposed. The method boils down to extraction of shape-related coordinates from photograph of a structure, followed by their processing and incorporation to a script that enables reconstruction and simulation of EM model. The approach has been demonstrated using two antennas.

Keywords: antenna reconstruction · computer-aided design · cost-efficient development · EM simulations · image-based processing

1 Introduction

Design of modern antennas is an inherently cognitive process. It involves a mix of experience-driven topology development and its iterative tuning (preferably, using robust numerical algorithms). A fundamental challenge associated to identification of suitable topology w.r.t. specifications is lack of analytical, or empirical formulas that can govern the process. Instead, the development is an engineer in-the-loop procedure where geometry is iteratively altered and evaluated based on electromagnetic (EM) simulations [1]. In practice, new topologies are often derived through (more or less fundamental) modifications of baseline structures from the literature [2, 3]. Performance figures of literature-based antennas are also useful for benchmarks purposes [3]. Unfortunately, the required metrics might not always be accessible in the references [3, 4]. Furthermore, the reported ones are affected by the specifics of measurement, and/or simulation setups used for their determination, hindering unequivocal interpretation of data. The outlined difficulties can be alleviated by reconstructing the EM models of antennas from the literature.

© The Author(s), under exclusive license to Springer Nature Switzerland AG 2026
P. Neumann et al. (Eds.): ICCS 2026, LNCS 16784, pp. 497–505, 2026.
https://doi.org/10.1007/978-3-032-29924-6_45

Re-design of antenna from the literature is a time-consuming process. It typically involves identification of relevant parameters followed by reconstruction of all topological features of the radiator. The task can be hindered by inconsistencies between descriptions and visualizations of structures, as well as missing, or incorrect data on their dimensions. A counter-measure involves reverse-engineering of geometry based on analysis of available schematic illustrations and/or photographs [5]. Unfortunately, the process is not only tedious but also prone to errors.

Reconstruction of antennas from the literature can be performed using image processing techniques. For planar structures, the problem boils down to identification of geometry-specific coordinates from the image and their use to restore the EM model. The latter can be automated using appropriate scripts (supported by commercially available EM software) [5–8]. Image-based generation of antennas can be performed using machine learning (ML) techniques [7, 8]. In [7], a combination of convolutional neural network (CNN) and long-short-term memory (LSTM) models has been used for generation of parametric antenna models. A related concept, where processing of structures with complex antennas is realized using CNN-LTSM that maps a binary lattice onto the given topology has been proposed in [8]. Main limitation of the mentioned methods is that they require a large amount of labeled data for training of ML models. Furthermore, the predictive capabilities of ML models are limited to geometries that resemble reference data [7]. Given versatility of antennas from the literature (even when only variants of the given structure are considered [9]) the limitations of ML-based reconstruction are difficult to overcome. From this perspective, restoration of antenna EM models based on their images remains an open problem.

In this work, recreation of non-parametric EM models based on photographs of antenna prototypes has been proposed. The method does not rely on ML. Instead, it involves extraction of topology-specific coordinates based on identification of edges within a single photograph. The points also undergo de-noising, stratification (i.e., separation of individual polygons from the points), and reduction. The processed coordinates are fed to the script that automatically reconstructs EM model of the image-based radiator. The presented proof-of-concept framework has been demonstrated using two planar antennas. Discrepancy between frequency responses of the image-derived and reference EM models (in terms of resonance shift) does not exceed 2%.

2 Methodology

2.1 Problem Formulation

Let I be a grayscale image (M px $\times$ N px) of the antenna at hand. Also, let $I(x, y)$ be an element of I at x, y ($1 \leq x \leq M$, $1 \leq y \leq N$). EM model reconstruction involves three stages. First, a set $P = \{p_1, ..., p_d\}$, $d = 1, ..., D$, of points $p_d = [x_d, y_d]$ that represent edges from I is to be extracted. Next, a sequence of shapes (polygons) $S = \{S_1, ..., S_o\}$, $o = 1, ..., O$, is to be sought, where each $S_o \subset P$ is the antenna building block. Note that $p_{o.r} = [x_{o.r}\ y_{o.r}]$ ($x_{o.r} \leq N$; $y_{o.r} \leq M$) elements of each $S_o = \{p_{o.1}, p_{o.2}, ..., p_{o.r}\}$ are ordered to ensure that the extracted polygons do not self-intersect ($r < d$). Also, the points that constitute each S_o sequence are unique (i.e., they do not repeat between the extracted polygons). The last stage involves automatic generation of the script (a so-called macro) that describes the antenna to be restored, as well as reconstruction of the EM model and its simulation. The details concerning each step are given below.

2.2 Image-Based Extraction of Antenna Coordinates

Extraction of edge coordinates based on image processing is a key component of the proposed framework. The algorithm is as follows [10]. Let $G(\sigma)$ be an $\lambda \times \lambda$ matrix containing Gaussian kernel. Its $G(x, y, \sigma)$, $x, y \leq \lambda$, components are given as [10]:

$$G(x, y, \sigma) = \left(2\pi\sigma^2\right)^{-1} \exp\left(-\frac{x^2 + y^2}{2\sigma^2}\right) \tag{1}$$

where σ is user-defined; $\lambda = \lceil 6\sigma \rceil$ ("$\lceil \cdot \rceil$" denotes round-up to integer). Also, let $M = (G_x^2 + G_y^2)^{0.5}$ and $\alpha = \tan^{-1}(G_y/G_x)$ be a magnitude and direction of estimated edges (both $M \times N$) given gradients $G_x = I_G * S_x$ and $G_y = I_G * S_y$ ("$*$" is a convolution operator); $I_G = I * G(\sigma)$ is a blurred input image, whereas S_x and S_y are Sobel filters [10]:

$$S_x = \begin{bmatrix} -1 & 0 & 1 \\ -2 & 0 & 2 \\ -1 & 0 & 1 \end{bmatrix}, S_y = \begin{bmatrix} -1 & -2 & -1 \\ 0 & 0 & 0 \\ 1 & 2 & 1 \end{bmatrix} \tag{2}$$

Edges within the image are found using non-maxima suppression [10]. Let d_k ($k = 1, \ldots, 4$) be basic directions (angular orientations of edges w.r.t. x-axis in a Cartesian system). Also, let α_1 and K_1 be 3×3 matrices extracted from α and M around x_s, y_s ($x_s \leq M$, $y_s \leq N$ point). The values of nearest neighbors to $K_0 = M(x_s, y_s)$ are selected from K_1 along $d_{min} = d_k$ (i.e., an orientation with the smallest distance to α_1). The elements of non-maxima suppressed image E are set to $E(x_s, y_s) = 0$ when K_0 is smaller than the values for any of its neighbors; otherwise $E(x_s, y_s) = K_0$. Finally, matrices comprising so-called strong (true) and weak edges E_s, E_w are identified. Their components are found as $E_s(x, y) = E(x, y) \geq t_h$, $E_w(x, y) = E(x, y) \geq t_l$ (t_l, t_h are user-defined); weak edge matrix is derived as $E_w = E_w - E_s$. The weak edges are labeled as true provided their 8-connection to the strong ones, i.e., existence of a continuous path that connects weak-to-strong edge [10]. The elements of final matrix E^* are $E^*(x, y) = 1$ for each x, y pair corresponding to true edges; otherwise $E^*(x, y) = 0$. The set of extracted points P—that correspond to indices of pixels from E^* for which $E^*(x, y) = 1$—undergoes further processing.

2.3 Coordinate-Based Polygons Extraction

A set of coordinates P is processed in multiple steps in order to identify non-intersecting polygons that constitute the antenna to be reconstructed. First the points are sorted. Let $p^{(0)} \in P^{(0)}$ be a left-lower corner from $P^{(0)} = P$. The sequence of points is initialized as $P_S = p^{(0)}$. At each step i ($i = 1, \ldots$) the method identifies $p^{(i+1)} = \operatorname{argmin}(\|p^{(i)} - p_j\|)$, where $p_j \in P^{(i)}$ ($j = 1, \ldots, D-i$) and $P^{(i)} = P^{(i-1)}\backslash\{p^{(i)}\}$. Next, the point $p^{(i+1)}$ is included at the end of sequence $P_S = [p^{(0)} \ldots p^{(i)} \, p^{(i+1)}]^T$ and the iteration index is increased as $i = i + 1$. The algorithm is terminated when $|P^{(i)}| = 0$. Next, P_S is rotated to ensure its alignment with x-axis of the coordinate system. Let $P_{R\text{tmp}}(\theta) = P_S R(\theta)$ represent coordinates rotated according to:

$$R(\theta) = \begin{bmatrix} \cos(\theta) & -\sin(\theta) \\ \sin(\theta) & \cos(\theta) \end{bmatrix}^T \tag{3}$$

Now, given that $P_{R\text{tmp}}$ is an $D \times 2$ matrix of rotated x, y coordinates, i.e., $P_{R\text{tmp}} = [X_R{}^T\ Y_R{}^T]$, let $p_l = [\min(X_R)\min(Y_R)]$ and $p_u = [\max(X_R), \max(Y_R)]$ be the corners that bound P_R. The rotated coordinates are obtained by solving $P_R = \text{argmin}(A(P_{R\text{tmp}}(\theta)))$, where $A(P_{R\text{tmp}}(\theta))$ is the area of the rectangle that bounds $P_{R\text{tmp}}$ according to p_l and p_u. Next, P_N is obtained after unity-based normalization of P_R. The sequence $P_N = [p_{N.1} \dots p_{N.D}]^T$ is then processed to remove noise (e.g., small groups of points separated from the remaining coordinates). Let $\delta = [\delta_1\ \delta_2 \dots \delta_{D-1}]^T$ be the vector of distances between the consecutive points from P_N. Also, let e_D and σ_D be the average and standard deviation of δ; $k = [k_1 \dots k_{l1} \dots k_{l2} \dots k_L]^T$ $(l_1 < l_2 < L < D - 1)$ is a vector with indices of points for which $\delta > e_D + \sigma_D$. In other words, elements of k are indices that represent abnormal separation between points (i.e., indicate disjoint shapes). Now, let $\Delta k = [\Delta k_1 \dots \Delta k_{l1} \dots \Delta k_{l2} \dots \Delta k_{L-1}]$, where $\Delta k_l = k_{l+1} - k_l$ are lengths of separated groups of points $P_{kl1} = [p_{kl1+1}\ p_{kl1+2} \cdots p_{kl2-1}\ p_{kl2}]^T$ (note that $|P_{kl1}| = \Delta k_{l1}-1$) between consecutive indices from k and $t_L = \beta(D-1)$ be threshold for minimum acceptable number of points in such groups (β is user-defined). The de-noised vector P_U comprises only P_{kl} groups for which the cardinality satisfies $|P_{kl}| > t_L$ inequality. Next, P_U is separated into a set of sequences comprising individual shapes. The procedure is largely the same as the one outlined above. It involves calculation of δ and identification of outlier indices $k_0 = [k_{0.0}\ k_{0.1} \dots k_{0.o-1}\ k_{0.o}]$, where $k_{0.0} = 1$ and $k_{0.o} = |P_U|$. The oth shape separated from P_U is given as $S_o = \{p_{v1}, p_{v2}, \dots, p_{vt-1}, p_{vt}\}$, where $v_1 = k_{0.(o-1)} + 1$, $v_2 = k_{0.(o-1)} + 1$, $v_{t-1} = k_{0.o}-1$, and $v_t = k_{0.o}$, respectively. The set comprising all sequences is given as $S = \{S_1, \dots, S_o\}$.

Finally, lengths of S_o sequences are reduced while preserving the retained shape. The goal here it to scale down irregularities resulting from image-based edge detection in order to ensure manageable simulation cost (discretization of uneven edges is subject to increased mesh density, which negatively affects the cost of EM simulations). To simplify the notation, let $Q = S_o$ be an ordered sequence of points that represent oth polygon such that $Q = \{q_1, \dots q_K\}$, where $K = |Q|$. Then, let Ψ be a set that contains selected subsequences of Q. The algorithm is as follows [11]:

1. Set $\Psi = \{Q\}$, $I = |\Psi|$, $i = 1$, $P_{\text{out}} = \{q_1, q_K\}$, and $\Psi_{\text{tmp}} = \{\}$;
2. Select $Q_i \subset \Psi$ and set $K = |Q_i|$;
3. Calculate δ_i, i.e., a vector of perpendicular distances of $q_{i.k} \in Q_i$ points ($k = 2, \dots, K-1$) to a line segment defined by $\{q_{i.1}, q_{i.K}\} \subset Q_i$ pair;
4. Calculate $\delta_{\max} = \max(\delta_i)$; If $\delta_{\max} < \varepsilon$ go to 6; otherwise set $k_{\max}$ as index of $\delta_{\max}$ in δ_i and go to Step 5;
5. Set $P_{\text{out}} = P_{\text{out}} \cup q_{i.k\max}$, $Q_{i1} = \{q_{i.1}, \dots, q_{i.k\max}\}$, $Q_{i2} = \{q_{i.k\max}, \dots, q_{i.K}\}$, $\Psi_{\text{tmp}} = \Psi_{\text{tmp}} \cup \{Q_{i1}, Q_{i2}\}$;
6. If $i = I$, go to Step 7; otherwise, set $i = i + 1$ and go to step 2;

7. If $\boldsymbol{\Psi} = \{\}$, set $\boldsymbol{S}^* = \boldsymbol{P}_{\text{out}}$ and END; otherwise reorder sequences from $\boldsymbol{\Psi}_{\text{tmp}}$ by their descending lengths, set $\boldsymbol{\Psi} = \boldsymbol{\Psi}_{\text{tmp}}$, $i = 1$, $I = |\boldsymbol{\Psi}|$ and go to Step 2.

Upon termination $\boldsymbol{S}_o = \boldsymbol{S}^*$ is set. The tolerance threshold ε is user-defined. Sequence for which all $\boldsymbol{\delta}_i$ distances are below the threshold are not considered for further processing, hence $\boldsymbol{\Psi} = \{\}$ is equivalent to reduction of all sequences. The routine is executed for all $\boldsymbol{S}_o \subset \boldsymbol{S}$ polygons.

The coordinate-based polygons extraction procedure described above can be summarized as follows:

1. Extract $\boldsymbol{P}_S$, i.e., a sorted matrix of coordinates from $\boldsymbol{P}$;
2. Generate $\boldsymbol{P}_R$ through rotation of $\boldsymbol{P}_S$; normalize $\boldsymbol{P}_R$ obtain $\boldsymbol{P}_N$;
3. Obtain $\boldsymbol{P}_U$ by distance-based de-noising of $\boldsymbol{P}_N$;
4. Separate $\boldsymbol{P}_U$ into $\boldsymbol{S}_1, \boldsymbol{S}_2, \ldots, \boldsymbol{S}_o$ and perform reduction of polygons.

Upon processing, the set $\boldsymbol{S}$ can be used to reconstruct the antenna structure.

2.4   Reconstruction of Antenna EM Model

Feasibility of the antenna EM model is subject to availability of substrate with straight edge. The latter is necessary to accommodate a reference point for excitation of the driven element (i.e., the radiator) through a waveguide port while maintaining consistency of mesh [12]. Unfortunately, polygons $\boldsymbol{S}_o \subset \boldsymbol{S}$ might not fulfill the mentioned requirement. This is due to the noise associated with determination of edges using algorithm of Sect. 2.2, as well as challenges related to separation of antenna feed from the outline (substrate) based on evaluation of outliers as explained in Sect. 2.3. In this work, the problem is addressed using a bounding box $\boldsymbol{P}_B$ generated w.r.t. $\boldsymbol{S}_o$ with the largest area. The procedure involves uniform scaling of the box to $\boldsymbol{P}_{BS} = \gamma \boldsymbol{P}_B$ (here, $\gamma = 0.995$ is used) followed by generation of $\boldsymbol{S}_{B.o} = \boldsymbol{S}_o \setminus \boldsymbol{P}_{BS}$ for all o shapes; if $\boldsymbol{S}_{B.o} = \{\}$, then $\boldsymbol{S}_{B.o} = \boldsymbol{P}_{BS}$ is used which defines the substrate for antenna generation (see Fig. 1 for conceptual illustration). Next, the modified shapes are scaled according to measured dimensions of the prototype $x_{\max}$, $y_{\max}$ (both user-defined) to obtain the final set $\boldsymbol{S}_F = \{\boldsymbol{S}_{F.1}, \ldots, \boldsymbol{S}_{F.o}\}$ that represents individual layers of the antenna geometry. Finally, each of $\boldsymbol{S}_{F.o}$ shapes is labeled according to its function (i.e., substrate, metal, cutout; the list of ordered labels is given as $\boldsymbol{L} = \{L_1, L_2, \ldots\}$) and position w.r.t. the substrate side $\boldsymbol{Z} = \{Z_1, Z_2, \ldots\}$. Note that the parameters can be set either to 0 or h, *i.e.,* bottom or top. Moreover, a coordinate point $\boldsymbol{p}_f = [x_f \ y_f]$ that represents location of the port for structure excitation is obtained based on analysis of coordinates from $\boldsymbol{S}_{F.o}$ that are located on the edge of shape labeled as substrate.

Once $\boldsymbol{S}_F$ and $\boldsymbol{p}_f$ are obtained, the antenna EM model can be reconstructed using automatically generated script. Inputs for the latter include substrate properties, i.e., permittivity ε_r, thickness h, loss tangent $\tan(\delta)$, as well as metal thickness T, and frequency range [6]. EM model generation involves iterative processing of $\boldsymbol{S}_{F.o} \subset \boldsymbol{S}_F$ shapes followed by determination of appropriate operations between them (e.g., subtraction) based on appropriately ordered lists of labels $\boldsymbol{L}$ and substrate-related orientations $\boldsymbol{T}$. The routine can be summarized as follows:

1. Generate EM solver configuration and substrate properties based on provided list of input parameters;
2. Define substrate brick based on $S_{F.1}$ and thickness h; set $l = 2$;
3. If $l \leq O$ and L_l indicates "metal", go to Step 4; if $l \leq O$ and L_l indicates "cutout", go to Step 5; otherwise, go to Step 7;
4. Generate a polygon brick defined by $S_{F.l}$ at Z_l plane on the substrate and set $l = l + 1$ and go to Step 3;
5. Generate a polygon brick defined by $S_{F.l}$ at Z_l plane on the substrate;
6. Find index $1 < l_1 < l$ that identifies "metal" polygon $S_{F.l1}$ which overlaps with $S_{F.l}$ shape; define subtraction operation, set $l = l + 1$ and go to Step 3;
7. Generate microwave port according to the given p_f point and END.

It should be noted that generation of macros that support configuration of solver, definition of substrate, frequency range, shapes (polygons), as well as operations between the shapes are well explained in the documentation of EM simulation packages (here, CST Studio [12]). Having that in mind, discussion of specific functions and their syntax are beyond the scope of this work. It is worth mentioning, however, that the above outlined routine is configured to generate macros in Basic programming language which is supported by CST Studio package [12].

Finally, the generated macro can be used to generate the EM model of the image-based antenna and execute its simulation to obtain $R(S)$ response. All of the outlined routines have been implemented in Python. Conceptual illustration of the proposed framework is shown in Fig. 2. It should be reiterated that the presented method involves an end-to-end processing of only one image, which is fundamentally different when compared against ML-based techniques of [7, 8].

3 Results

The proposed framework has been validated based on two manufactured planar antennas. Upon reconstruction, performance figures of the radiators are evaluated using the same simulation settings as for the models used for fabrication of prototypes.

Consider a rectangular patch implemented on AD255C substrate (cf. Fig. 3; $h = 1.5$ mm). The image (868 px $\times$ 1205 px) processing is performed using the algorithm of Sect. 2. The user-defined parameters are $\{\sigma, t_h, t_l, \beta, \varepsilon, x_{max}, y_{max}\} = \{0.5, 1.2, 0.4, 0.01, 0.003, 46.95, 33.77\}$; x_{max}, y_{max} (in mm) are measured using a caliper. The number of points that represent the extracted structure is only 21 (from initial 4584). The antenna EM model comprises 79,000 mesh cells (vs. 62,800 for the reference design). Reflection responses for the reference and regenerated models are compared in Fig. 4. The discrepancy between shapes—here, a median distance between points from image-based and reference geometries—is just 0.1 mm. The resonance shift of the reconstructed response is 20 MHz, or just 0.5% w.r.t. the 4.1 GHz center frequency for the reference model, which also emphasizes high similarity between the geometries.

The second image (1163 px $\times$ 931 px) comprises a tri-band dipole on a RO4358B substrate ($h = 0.76$ mm; cf. Fig. 3) [2]. The radiator is excited through a coplanar line (with narrow gaps between the feed and ground plane) which makes its reconstruction challenging. Except for the substrate size (here, $x_{max} = 51.17$ mm, $y_{max} = 33.55$ mm), the algorithm settings are the same as for the patch. The initial number of coordinates is reduced from 10743 to 381. Nonetheless, the recreated model features 2.5-fold denser mesh (325,600 cells) w.r.t. the reference one (124,600). As shown in Fig. 4, reflection responses obtained for both EM models are similar. Maximum shift of resonances is 100 MHz, or just 1.8% relative to 5.3 GHz (the third frequency of operation). A distance between geometries (shape-wise) is around 0.4 mm.

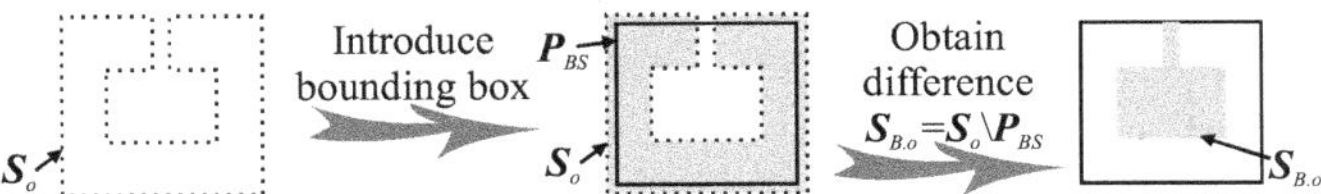

Fig. 1. The use of scaled-down bounding box (—) and difference operation to refine a point-based (···) polygon (gray) that incorrectly blends the substrate and outline of the radiator.

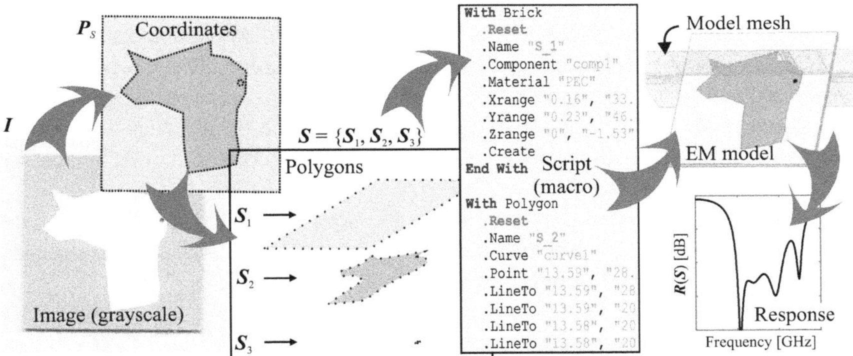

Fig. 2. Image-based reconstruction of antenna EM model: conceptual illustration of the proposed framework with highlight on the key post-processing steps.

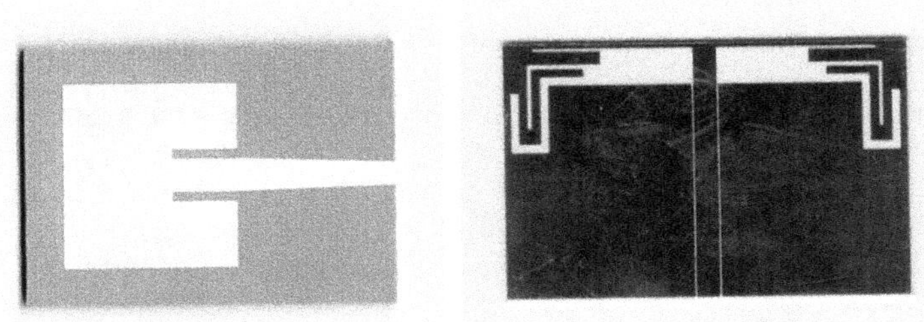

Fig. 3. Photographs of the example antennas: microstrip patch (left) and tri-band dipole (right).

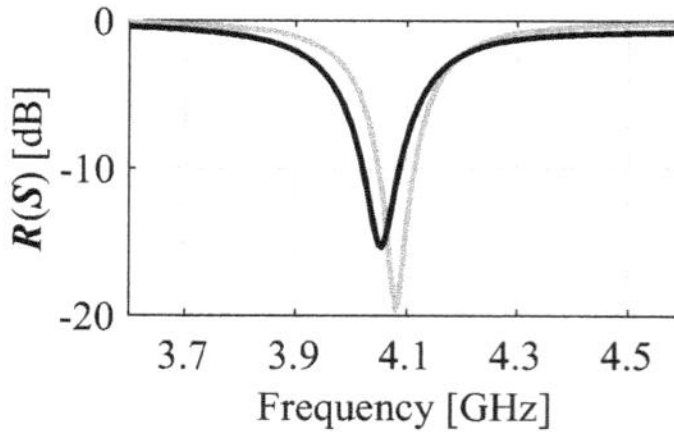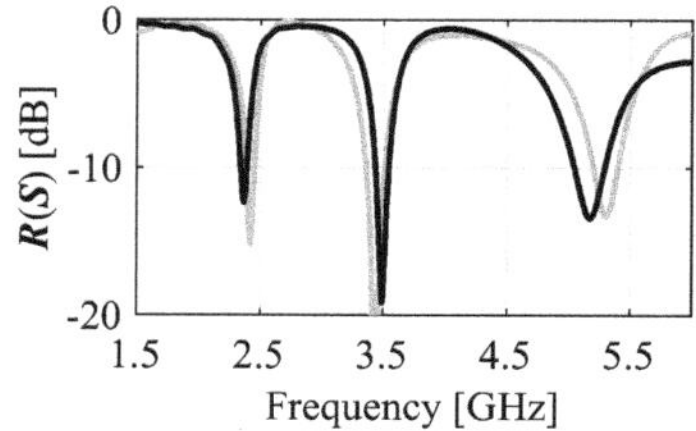

Fig. 4. Reflection responses obtained for the original (gray) and reconstructed from images (black) antenna EM models for: patch radiator (left) and tri-band dipole (right).

4   Conclusion

In this work, a proof-of-concept framework for non-parametric reconstruction of antenna EM simulation models based on images of their manufactured prototypes has been proposed. The method involves several processing steps that include identification and conversion of edges to coordinates, as well as their de-noising, stratification, reduction and scaling. The obtained points are fed to automatically generated scripts that reconstruct the EM model of antenna at hand and enable its simulation. The approach has been demonstrated using two planar radiators. High resemblance between the reference and reconstructed models has been achieved. The performance discrepancy (expressed in terms of resonances shift) does not exceed 2%. Dissimilarity of geometries (shape-wise) is also maintained below 0.5 mm.

Future work will focus on streamlining the geometry extraction procedure, as well as its extension to handle more complex microwave geometries and dual-layer components. Parametric reconstruction of topologies will also be considered.

Acknowledgments. This work was supported in part by the National Science Center of Poland Grant 2021/43/B/ST7/01856.

Disclosure of Interests. The author declares no conflicts of interests.

References

1. Koziel, S., Ogurtsov, S.: Antenna Design by Simulation-Driven Optimization. Springer, Cham (2014)
2. Bekasiewicz, A., Koziel, S.: Miniaturized uniplanar triple-band slot dipole antenna with folded radiator. Microwave Opt. Technol. Lett. **60**(2), 386–389 (2018)
3. Khan, M.S., et al.: A compact CSRR-enabled UWB diversity antenna. IEEE Antennas Wireless Propagat. Lett. **16**, 808–812 (2017)
4. Haq, T., Koziel, S.: Novel complementary multiple concentric split ring resonator for reliable characterization of dielectric substrates with high sensitivity. IEEE Sensors J. **24**(10), 16233–16241 (2024)
5. Jacobs, J.P.: Accurate modeling by CNN regression of resonant frequencies of dual-band pixelated microstrip antenna. IEEE Antennas Wireless Propagat. Lett. **20**(12), 2417–2421 (2021)

6. Bekasiewicz, A., et al.: Strategies for feature-assisted development of topology agnostic planar antennas using variable-fidelity models. J. Comput. Sci. **85**, 102521 (2025)
7. Wei, Z., et al.: Fast and automatic parametric model construction of antenna structures using CNN–LSTM networks. IEEE Trans. Antennas Propagat. **72**(2), 1319–1328 (2024)
8. Zhu, Z., Tian, Y., Sun, J.: Antenna modeling based on image-CNN-LSTM. IEEE Antennas Wireless Propagat. Lett. **23**(9), 2738–2742 (2024)
9. Bekasiewicz, A., Koziel, S.: Structure and computationally efficient simulation-driven design of compact UWB monopole antenna. IEEE Antennas Wireless Propagat. Lett. **14**, 1282–1285 (2015)
10. Gonzalez, R.C., Woods, R.E.: Digital Image Processing, 4th edn. Pearson, New York (2018)
11. Shi, W., Cheung, C.K.: Performance evaluation of line simplification algorithms for vector generalization. Cartogr. J. **43**(1), 27–44 (2006)
12. Dassault Systems: CST Microwave Studio, 10 rue Marcel Dassault, CS 40501. Vélizy-Villacoublay Cedex, France (2019)

Estimating Data Split Error for Training Knowledge Graph Embeddings

Aleksander Suchorab[(✉)] [iD], Igor Wojnicki [iD], and Andrzej Bielecki [iD]

AGH University of Krakow, al. Mickiewicza 30, 30-059 Kraków, Poland
{asuchorab,wojnicki,bielecki}@agh.edu.pl

Abstract. When graph data is divided into a train-test split, which is common in machine learning, it alters the graph structure. In particular, some splits may result in a training set that is unable to distinguish certain groups of vertices as a consequence of graph topology. It can lead to an increased number of errors in evaluation when the test set requires a distinction between those groups but the training set provides none. We propose methods to identify, explain, and estimate the split error of a graph dataset with a particular assignment of triples into splits. The method uses graph entropy differences, based on automorphism of labeled graphs. We examine the approach on a variety of knowledge graph embedding models and datasets. Various datasets were found to have differing potential for split errors, depending on their structure.

Keywords: Knowledge Graph Embedding · Information theory · Structural information · Network analysis · Training-test split

1 Introduction and Motivation

Knowledge graphs use vertices to represent conceptual entities, while the edges define the relationships between them. However, graph structures are unfit for processing using many machine learning algorithms which operate on tensors. In order to resolve that issue, Knowledge Graph Embedding (KGE) techniques can be used, which transform graph relationships into fixed-length, lower-dimensional vectors, aiming to preserve structural information and properties.

There are many surveys [4] and benchmarks [8] of various KGE algorithms, although a fair comparison is difficult [8]. KGE methods are often evaluated on dense, curated datasets that do not represent real-world graphs, and sparsity has been shown to degrade performance [11].

For most machine learning tasks, including KGE, a dataset is divided into at least two subsets: training and testing. The naive approach to dividing a dataset involves random sampling. Such sampling might lead to bias, which has been investigated for non-graph machine learning tasks [5, 12].

Due to the nature of graph data, some vertices may not be distinguishable in the graph topology. Redundant vertices have been shown to degrade machine learning performance [10]. Graph entropy [6] can be used, among other things,

P. Neumann et al. (Eds.): ICCS 2026, LNCS 16784, pp. 506–514, 2026.
https://doi.org/10.1007/978-3-032-29924-6_46

to quantitatively describe topologically indistinguishable vertices and has been extensively investigated with many applications to machine learning [3,7,13].

We posit that these vertices introduce topological bias in train-test splits. We propose an approach that uses graph entropy to describe the information difference between the data subsets that leads to increased evaluation error, which is the main contribution of this paper. Our framework includes a method of detecting and explaining this class of error, which we call split error, and a method of estimating its effect on evaluation error in a particular train-test split, which is also able to determine which test triples contribute to this error.

The proposed approach is tested on several KGE models and datasets by evaluating the models on the provided data splits, and then on test sets without triples that contribute to split error. Then, we compare the performance of the models with error estimates described by our framework.

2   Formulation of Split Error in Graph Data

A graph dataset G is understood as a set of vertices or entities V and a set of labelled edges or triples E. The isomorphism of edge-labeled graphs, similarly as in [9], is one that preserves not only the graph structure but also edge labels. In particular, we will consider automorphism of this kind. A pair of nodes $x, y \in V$ is said to be indistinguishable if they belong to one automorphism orbit.

One way to measure degree to which the graph contains indistinguishable vertices, used in [10], is to use the proportion of vertices with singleton orbits, to all vertices, which will be denoted as p_s. This method does not take into account the distribution of nodes into orbits of varying sizes greater than 1. To better describe this, graph entropy [6] can be used:

$$H = -\sum_{i=1}^{k} \frac{n_i}{n} log_2 \frac{n_i}{n}, \tag{1}$$

where k is the number of automorphism orbits and n_i is the size of the i-th orbit. The maximum possible entropy for a graph with n nodes is $log_2 n$ and this value could be used to normalize the entropy to the range $[0, 1]$, written as H_{norm}.

We examined various graph datasets available in the PyKEEN library [2]. The datasets exhibit varying amounts of indistinguishable vertex pairs. H_{norm} ranges from 0.8729 for DBpedia50, through 0.9670 for WN18, to values near 1 like 0.9994 for PharmKG8k, while p_s ranges from low 0.5224 for DBpedia50, through 0.7674 for WN18 to 0.9928 for PharmKG8k. Another commonly used benchmarking set, FB15k, is also characterized by values near 1. Similar findings were made by [10] on a different selection of datasets.

We examined the structural patterns that characterize indistinguishable vertices. The findings are summarized in Table 1. They are concentrated in sparse parts of the graphs, as illustrated by mean and median amount of incident edges. Another insight is that the orbits typically consist of vertices within 2 hops. This corresponds to a pattern where they are connected to one or a few hub vertices.

This and similar patterns that involve common connections should result in embedding vectors in one orbit to converge, as they experience identical influence from neighbors. Therefore, they should be rated similarly in head or tail completion. There are factors that may cause them to not converge, such as insufficient training or regularization. Any significant deviations of embeddings in one orbit are likely to be noise, rather than informed in any way.

Table 1. Properties of vertices that are in non-singleton orbits in the training parts of datasets, p_s is the proportion of singleton orbit vertices, and n_{ns} is the number of vertices in non-singleton orbits. The "incident" columns describe the mean and median amount of edges incident to these vertices vertex with "expect" describing expected edges per vertex as estimated by $\frac{2|E|}{|V|}$ for the whole graph. The "compactness" columns describe the proportion of classes of which all elements are within d distance or hops.

Dataset	p_s	n_{ns}	incident			compactness	
			expect	mean	median	d=1	d=2
PharmKG8k	0.9928	14	106.7	2.43	3	0.0	1.0
FB15k237	0.9739	347	37.52	4.12	1	0.0	0.977
FB15k	0.9651	101	64.63	3.35	2	0.036	1.0
OpenEA	0.8306	3056	4.08	1.44	1	0.003	0.935
CoDExMedium	0.9987	6	21.8	9.67	10	0.0	1.0
DBpedia50	0.5224	12470	2.62	1.30	1	0.010	0.773
WD50KT	0.8348	7897	8.21	1.38	1	0.0	0.993
WN18RR	0.7723	8823	4.28	1.67	2	0.003	0.976
WN18	0.7674	6906	6.91	3.15	2	0.003	0.987
AristoV4	0.7262	11615	11.55	1.19	1	0.0	0.993
CoDExLarge	0.9713	1625	14.14	5.16	5	0.017	1.0
DB100K	0.8823	8954	12.00	2.82	3	0.002	0.980

When KGE models are trained on data with a training-test split, the model learns embeddings on just the triples present in the training set. This set, when interpreted as a graph, has a different topology than the initial set. In particular, distinguishability of a pair of nodes can change between those sets, and this discrepancy is the cause of the split error.

We consider transductive [1] link prediction, often used to evaluate KGE models, although these considerations apply to any task in which vertices are chosen or rated. The transductive setup also requires that the test set only contains entities and triples present in the training set, which is ensured by default in PyKEEN, and it is assumed in further considerations.

Let (V_{train}, E_{train}) be the training set and (V_{test}, E_{test}) be the test set, $V_{test} \subseteq V_{train}$, $E_{train} \cap E_{test} = \emptyset$. Also, $E_{full} = E_{train} \cup E_{test}$, which is the totality of data available at the point of evaluation. We compute the automorphism orbits of E_{train} and E_{full}, and interpret them as partitions of V_{train}

and filter them, so they only contain vertices from V_{test}, and denote them P_{train} and P_{full}. Finally, let us compute the intersection of these partitions $P_{inter} = \{x : x = a \cap b, x \neq \emptyset, a \in P_{train}, b \in P_{full}\}$.

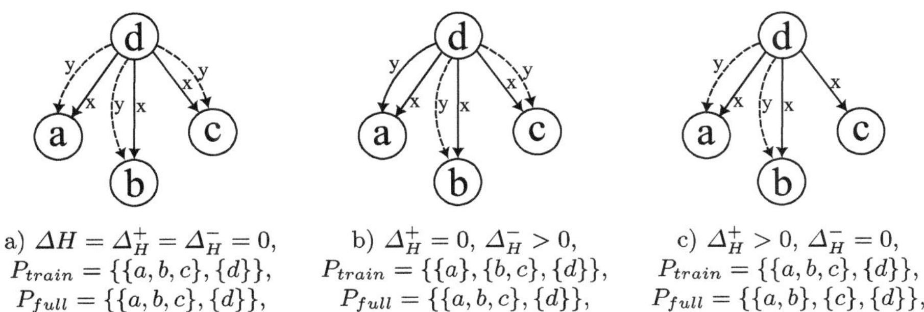

a) $\Delta H = \Delta_H^+ = \Delta_H^- = 0$,
$P_{train} = \{\{a, b, c\}, \{d\}\}$,
$P_{full} = \{\{a, b, c\}, \{d\}\}$,

b) $\Delta_H^+ = 0$, $\Delta_H^- > 0$,
$P_{train} = \{\{a\}, \{b, c\}, \{d\}\}$,
$P_{full} = \{\{a, b, c\}, \{d\}\}$,

c) $\Delta_H^+ > 0$, $\Delta_H^- = 0$,
$P_{train} = \{\{a, b, c\}, \{d\}\}$,
$P_{full} = \{\{a, b\}, \{c\}, \{d\}\}$,

Fig. 1. Example cases of edge patterns present in training and test sets. The solid and dashed lines represent the training and test sets respectively, and "x" and "y" are distinct relations. The examples should be understood as parts of a larger graph, where a model should be able to infer some relationships. In case c), the model has no information that could differentiate a or b from c, leading to split error.

Finally, the entropy of partitions P_{train}, P_{inter} and P_{full}, denoted as H_{train}, H_{inter} and H_{full}, can be computed using Eq. 1, where $n = |V_{test}|$ and n_i are filtered to exclude vertices outside of V_{test}. Then, $\Delta H = H_{full} - H_{train}$ describes the gain or loss of vertex distinguishability in evaluation compared to training. However, it is insensitive to gain in one part of the graph and loss in another. Since P_{inter} always contains the more granular divisions out of both P_{train} and P_{full}, $H_{inter} \geq \max(H_{train}, H_{full})$. We define $\Delta_H^+ = H_{inter} - H_{train}$ and $\Delta_H^- = H_{inter} - H_{full}$, which can be used to measure only the gain and loss of distinguishability information respectively.

We posit that any gain in this information, that is, an increase in the ability to distinguish vertices compared to the training data, is detrimental in evaluation, so $\Delta_H^+ > 0$ is an indication of the split error. This can be illustrated using Fig. 1, where case c) displays such scenario. The influence of Δ_H^- is uncertain.

The difference in distinguishability information measured by Δ_H^+ indicates the presence of the split error but does not make a prediction of the error. We propose a procedure for estimating the split error from the perspective of each triple in the test set, suited for link prediction. A vertex that belongs to a smaller orbit in E_{inter} than in E_{train}, as discussed above, will be called ambiguous.

The procedure assigns a score from 0 to 1 for each vertex match, head and tail separately, where 1 is the score in absence of split error, and lower values otherwise,. This assumes that the model is able to correctly predict any triple without ambiguous vertices, in other words there are no other sources of error.

For each triple, head and tail predictions are performed, and their expected scores depend on the ambiguity of the head and tail vertices, so the score for vertex x is defined as

$$s_v(x) = \frac{|\text{orb}_{inter}(x)|}{|\text{orb}_{train}(x)|}, \tag{2}$$

where orb_{inter} and orb_{train} are the orbits of a vertex in the respective partitions. The estimated split error factor using scores for the head and tail vertices for each edge can be calculated as

$$s = \frac{1}{|E_{test}|} \sum_{(h,r,t)\in E_{test}} \left(1 - \frac{s_v(h) + s_v(t)}{2}\right). \tag{3}$$

This estimation is not derived from any scoring metric, such as Mean Reciprocal Rank (MRR) or Hit Rate at k (hits@k), but instead summarizes the effect of ambiguous vertices weighted by the occurrence of triples that contain them.

This estimate was further adjusted experimentally to improve its ability to predict evaluation differences. One considered technique was using squares of s_v:

$$s_v(x)' = \frac{|\text{orb}_{inter}(x)|^2}{|\text{orb}_{train}(x)|^2}. \tag{4}$$

The split error factor can also be adjusted with the computed metric m such as MRR or hits@10, with scores in range $[0, 1]$. This is not fully explained, but can be motivated by the fact that for lower scores, noisy predictions from ambiguous vertices will not lower the score by much.

$$s' = ms \tag{5}$$

3   Comparison of Split Error Estimation and Embedding Evaluation

We conducted KGE training using the PyKEEN [2] library. We considered KGE models RESCAL, TransE, DistMult, ComplEx, MuRE, RotatE, CrossE, TuckER, TorusE, SimplE, BoxE and AutoSF. We used datasets AristoV4, CoDExLarge, DB100K, DBpedia50, FB15k237, OpenEA, PharmKG8k, WD50KT, and WN18RR, as provided by PyKEEN. Some datasets from Tab. 1, that is CoDExMedium and FB15k, are not examined further, as they do not contain ambiguous vertices. When loading the datasets with PyKEEN, filtering is performed by default, removing entities and relations not appearing in the training set. All computations were performed on those filtered datasets.

Each combination of model and dataset has been run with a grid hyperparameter search, as influenced by some publications on KGE models [14]. For all, stochastic Local Closed World Assumption (sLCWA) training loop available in PyKEEN was used, with batch size 512, Adagrad optimizer with learning rate in $\{0.002, 0.1, 0.5\}$, "basic" negative sampler with ratio of 10, L2 regularizer with weight in $\{0, 0.0001, 0.01\}$. The embedding dimensions were chosen depending on size of the dataset, with $\{50, 100\}$ if $|E| < 10000$ else $\{100, 150\}$ if $|E| < 50000$

Table 2. Results of KGE evaluation averaged across all models, before and after the processing to reduce split error.

Dataset	hits@10		MRR	
	baseline	change	baseline	change
PharmKG8k	0.28321	$8.9 \cdot 10^{-6}$	0.14657	$5.2 \cdot 10^{-6}$
FB15k237	0.36719	0.00028	0.21305	0.00016
OpenEA	0.31560	0.00939	0.21844	0.00686
DBpedia50	0.32182	0.02907	0.24445	0.02193
WD50KT	0.24431	0.00410	0.13723	0.00245
WN18RR	0.42778	0.02161	0.35027	0.01910
WN18	0.91208	0.00279	0.76966	0.00237
AristoV4	0.24131	0.00092	0.13696	0.00038
CoDExLarge	0.23860	0.00034	0.13870	0.00017
DB100K	0.31281	0.00106	0.18134	0.00043

Table 3. Sizes of the test sets, amount of removed test triples during processing, entropy differences and error estimates. The error estimates use Eq. 3, although e uses Eq. 2 for vertex scores while e_{sqr} uses Eq. 4.

Dataset	$|E_{test}|$	removed	ΔH	Δ_H^+	e	e_{sqr}
PharmKG8k	49764	2	0.0000	$3.0 \cdot 10^{-4}$	$2.2 \cdot 10^{-5}$	$3.2 \cdot 10^{-5}$
FB15k237	20438	23	0.0017	0.0034	$7.5 \cdot 10^{-4}$	$9.1 \cdot 10^{-4}$
OpenEA	3826	242	0.0645	0.0670	0.0445	0.0588
DBpedia50	2095	521	0.1220	0.2545	0.1693	0.1996
WD50KT	45284	1998	0.0755	0.1205	0.0200	0.0259
WN18RR	2924	174	0.0411	0.0571	0.0426	0.0538
WN18	5000	18	-0.0375	0.0018	0.0077	0.0112
AristoV4	18414	116	0.0043	0.0173	0.0100	0.0125
CoDExLarge	30622	159	-0.0052	0.0054	0.0030	0.0042
DB100K	50000	672	-0.0117	0.0205	0.0091	0.0119

else $\{150, 200\}$. If a model supports different relation and embedding dimensions, the relation dimension was set to the same value. An early stopper was used, evaluating once every 10 epochs with patience 4 and relative delta 0.002, with max epochs set to 1000.

We evaluated the models on link prediction using RankBasedEvaluator in PyKEEN, on the test set with filtered evaluation. We calculated MRR and hits@10 metrics. The full data can be provided upon request and the averages can be seen in Tab. 2 in the "baseline" columns.

To determine the effect of the split error, we processed the test sets so that they do not contain any ambiguous vertices, to force $\Delta_H^+ = 0$. This was done by removing all edges incident to them. The summary of the process and error estimates can be seen in Tab. 3. We evaluated the models again on the processed test sets. The results can be provided upon request and the effect on averages across models can be seen in Tab. 2 in the "change" columns.

We compared Δ_H^+ with the changes in evaluation. The entropy difference does not predict the change well, although the datasets with larger evaluation differences are generally not close to $\Delta_H^+ = 0$. Additionally, datasets with high entropy differences are concentrated among datasets that do not perform well.

We tested the ability our error estimation methods to predict changes in evaluation. The estimate from Eq. 3 shows the ability to predict the evaluation difference using linear regression. We tested some variations of the estimate, including adjustments from Eq. 4 and Eq. 5. The estimation with both adjustments performs best, although the unadjusted estimate still displays prediction capability. Fitting $f(x) = mx$, the best estimate achieves $MAE = 1.80 \cdot 10^{-3}$ and $MRE = 0.42$ with $m = 0.506$ for hits@10 and $MAE = 1.68 \cdot 10^{-3}$ and $MRE = 0.56$ with $m = 0.520$ for MRR. Therefore, a recommendation for roughly estimating the error could be to multiply the adjusted estimate by 0.5.

4 Discussion

The variety of datasets and models should show wide applicability of our framework. We tried to balance equal treatment of all models and datasets, with adjustment or search for each combination, and also time and hardware limitations. We acknowledge that these results do not represent the best performance, and some models or datasets may have been put at a disadvantage.

The method used to eliminate the split error was to remove all triples that contain an ambiguous vertex. It could be possible to remove just enough triples to achieve appropriate automorphism orbits. We made an attempt to isolate the edges causing the error, but all approaches resulted in retaining very few additional edges, as the test sets are already sparse.

The evaluation results on the unprocessed and processed test sets may not be directly comparable. The removal of some triples may introduce a new source of bias. However, removal of the ambiguous vertices did improve the metrics by a predictable magnitude in all cases, which shows the efficacy of our framework.

5 Conclusion

We proposed a framework for explaining and estimating a class of evaluation errors in KGE training that arise due to differences in topology in the training-test split. The split error estimate uses differences of vertex distinguishability based on automorphism orbits. We have demonstrated the ability to predict differences in link prediction scores using KGE models.

The proposed concepts can be applied to perform a more informed KGE evaluation, either by removing ambiguous vertices from test data, finding a better data split, or accounting for effects of split error. It is especially important when comparing multiple datasets, where each can have different characteristics.

To further explore this topic, more thorough testing could be performed on various datasets and KGE models. The proposed method could also be applicable to Graph Neural Networks. The effect of split error on validation sets could be evaluated. We also expect to develop a method of creating better train-test splits without removing parts of the data.

References

1. Ali, M., et al.: Improving inductive link prediction using hyper-relational facts (2021). https://arxiv.org/abs/2107.04894
2. Ali, M., Berrendorf, M., Hoyt, C.T., Vermue, L., Sharifzadeh, S., Tresp, V., Lehmann, J.: PyKEEN 1.0: a Python library for training and evaluating knowledge graph embeddings. J. Mach. Learn. Res. **22**(82), 1–6 (2021). http://jmlr.org/papers/v22/20-825.html
3. Bielecki, A., Stocki, R.: The concept of structural information and possible applications. Philosoph. Problems Sci. (Zagadnienia Filozoficzne w Nauce) (75), 157–183 (2023). https://doi.org/10.59203/zfn.75.654, https://zfn.edu.pl/index.php/zfn/article/view/654
4. Cai, H., Zheng, V.W., Chang, K.C.C.: A Comprehensive Survey of Graph Embedding: Problems, Techniques and Applications (2018)
5. Cervellera, C., Macciò, D.: Distribution-preserving stratified sampling for learning problems. IEEE Trans. Neural Netw. Learn. Syst. **29**(7), 2886–2895 (2018). https://doi.org/10.1109/TNNLS.2017.2706964, https://ieeexplore.ieee.org/document/7945296
6. Dehmer, M., Mowshowitz, A.: A history of graph entropy measures. Info. Sci. **181**(1), 57–78 (2011). https://doi.org/10.1016/j.ins.2010.08.041, https://www.sciencedirect.com/science/article/pii/S0020025510004147
7. Duan, L., Chen, X., Liu, W., Liu, D., Yue, K., Li, A.: Structural Entropy Based Graph Structure Learning for Node Classification. Proc. AAAI Conf. Artif. Intell. **38**(8), 8372–8379 (2024). https://doi.org/10.1609/aaai.v38i8.28679, https://ojs.aaai.org/index.php/AAAI/article/view/28679
8. Goyal, P., Huang, D., Goswami, A., Chhetri, S.R., Canedo, A., Ferrara, E.: Benchmarks for graph embedding evaluation (2019). https://doi.org/10.48550/arXiv.1908.06543
9. Hsieh, S.-M., Hsu, C.-C., Hsu, L.-F.: Efficient method to perform isomorphism testing of labeled graphs. In: Gavrilova, M.L., et al. (eds.) ICCSA 2006. LNCS, vol. 3984, pp. 422–431. Springer, Heidelberg (2006). https://doi.org/10.1007/11751649_46
10. Ivanov, S., Sviridov, S., Burnaev, E.: Rethinking graph classification problem in presence of isomorphism. Dokl. Math. **110**, 312-S331 (2024). https://doi.org/10.1134/S1064562424602385
11. Pujara, J., Augustine, E., Getoor, L.: Sparsity and Noise: where knowledge graph embeddings fall short. In: Proceedings of the 2017 Conference on Empirical Methods in Natural Language Processing, pp. 1751–1756. Association for Computational Linguistics, Copenhagen, Denmark (2017). https://doi.org/10.18653/v1/D17-1184

12. Singh, V., Pencina, M., Einstein, A.J., Liang, J.X., Berman, D.S., Slomka, P.: Impact of train/test sample regimen on performance estimate stability of machine learning in cardiovascular imaging. Sci. Rep. **11**(1), 14490 (2021). https://doi.org/10.1038/s41598-021-93651-5, https://www.nature.com/articles/s41598-021-93651-5
13. Sun, Z., Wang, X., Ding, C., Fan, J.: Learning graph representation via graph entropy maximization. In: Proceedings of the 41st International Conference on Machine Learning. ICML'24, vol. 235, pp. 47133–47158. JMLR.org, Vienna, Austria (2024)
14. Trouillon, T., Welbl, J., Riedel, S., Éric Gaussier, Bouchard, G.: Complex embeddings for simple link prediction (2016). https://arxiv.org/abs/1606.06357

Prediction and Causality of Functional MRI and Synthetic Signal Using a Zero-Shot Time-Series Foundation Model

Alessandro Crimi[1]([✉])[iD] and Andrea Brovelli[2][iD]

[1] AGH University of Krakow, Krakow, Poland
`alecrimi@agh.edu.pl`
[2] Institut de Neurosciences de la Timone UMR 7289, Aix Marseille Université, CNRS, 13005 Marseille, France
`andrea.brovelli@univ-amu.fr`

Abstract. Time-series forecasting and causal discovery are key tools for studying brain dynamics and disease. With the rise of foundation models, it remains unclear how they compare to classical methods and whether they generalize in zero-shot settings.

Here, we compared a foundation model to classical methods for inferring directional interactions from human data. More specifically, we evaluated forecasting in zero-shot and fine-tuned settings, and compared its Granger-like estimates with standard Granger causality. We validated results about forecast on real time series from stroke patients from functional magnetic resonance imaging, and causality on synthetic time series from ground-truth models (logistic map coupling and Ornstein–Uhlenbeck processes). The foundation model achieved competitive zero-shot forecasting (mean absolute percentage error of 0.55 in controls and 0.27 in patients) and competitive result on the effective connectivity experiments. Overall, these findings suggest that foundation models offer versatility, strong zero-shot performance, and potential utility for forecasting and causal discovery in time-series data.

Keywords: ARIMA · Granger causality · fMRI · Foundation models

1 Introduction

Time-series analysis in neuroscience is of considerable importance, as it enables the characterization of dynamic brain processes and the inference of underlying mechanisms; however, it remains challenging due to the high dimensionality, noise, and intrinsic complexity of neural signals [2]. Time series are also the basis for network-level analyses of brain activity and inference of effective and functional connectivity [11], quantifying relationships that can ultimately be exploited as biomarkers. Recent advances in foundation models for time series, such as TimesFM [8], Time-MOE [16], and Llama-lag [14], promise zero-shot forecasting capabilities that could benefit brain science. Analogous to

P. Neumann et al. (Eds.): ICCS 2026, LNCS 16784, pp. 515–522, 2026.
https://doi.org/10.1007/978-3-032-29924-6_47

large language models, these models encode time series into latent embeddings and predict future trajectories without task-specific training. Domain-specific transformers trained on EEG [4,5], fMRI [17], or combined EEG–fMRI data [1] face recurring challenges from data heterogeneity and inter-subject variability, suggesting that general-purpose foundation models may provide a more viable solution. Among traditional approaches, ARIMA [3] remains widely used and has demonstrated robust performance in neuroimaging, often outperforming neural network–based methods [12]; we therefore use it as a primary baseline. To date, most studies have focused exclusively on forecasting, while extensions to causality and effective connectivity remain unexplored. Here we investigate whether a foundation model can be adapted for causal inference in analogy to Granger causality, the most widely used method for estimating directional interactions from neural time series. Since ground-truth causality is absent in real data, we validate our approach on two synthetic systems with known causal structure: coupled logistic maps and multivariate Ornstein–Uhlenbeck processes, which additionally allow testing of excitatory versus inhibitory interactions. We selected TimesFM for this purpose as it natively supports time-varying covariates, a requirement not fulfilled by other foundation models.

2 Methods

2.1 Dataset and Pre-processing

We used three datasets in this study. The first two dataset are synthetic datasets designed to test causal discovery: one with causal relationships defined by coupled logistic maps, and the other based on multivariate Ornstein–Uhlenbeck processes. The third dataset is a real-world dataset comprising both healthy and patient participants, used to evaluate differences in the prediction of healthy versus pathological fMRI time series (Fig. 1).

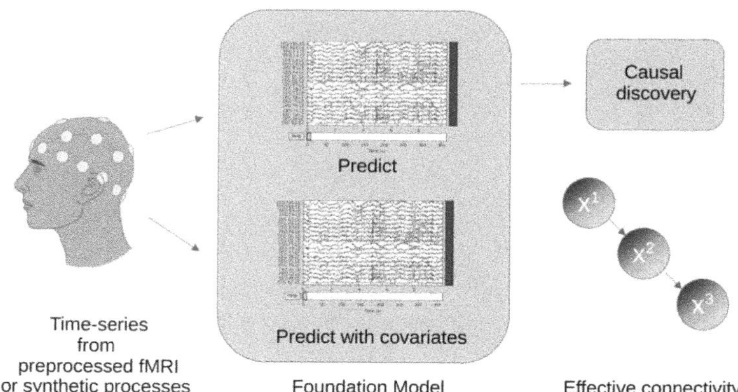

Fig. 1. Overview of the experiments: first we investigate the predictive power of the TimeSeries foundation model with brain signals, and then we evaluate if the time series predicted with it, can also be used for causal discovery.

Synthetic Data. We generate synthetic data sets with known ground-truth causality: **Logistic Map Coupling.** Three unidirectionally coupled discrete-time processes $\{X_t^{(1)}\}$, $\{X_t^{(2)}\}$, and $\{X_t^{(3)}\}$ were generated for $t = 1, \ldots, n$ with $n = 100$ time points. The initial conditions were defined as $X_0^{(j)} = c_j + \epsilon_j$, $\quad j \in \{1, 2, 3\}$, where $c_1 = 0.1$, $c_2 = 0.2$, and $c_3 = 0.3$, and $\epsilon_j \sim \mathcal{U}(-0.01, 0.01)$ represents small random perturbations. In this way the dynamics evolve according to the following coupled logistic map recurrences:

$$X_t^{(1)} = rX_{t-1}^{(1)}(1 - X_{t-1}^{(1)}),$$
$$X_t^{(2)} = rX_{t-1}^{(2)}(1 - X_{t-1}^{(2)}) + \alpha X_{t-1}^{(1)},$$
$$X_t^{(3)} = rX_{t-1}^{(3)}(1 - X_{t-1}^{(3)}) + \alpha X_{t-1}^{(2)},$$

where r and α are coupling coefficients. We generated 10 simulations with α ranging from 0.1 to 0.9, and kept r=3.9 from previous literature. **Multivariate Ornstein–Uhlenbeck (MOU):** We simulated $N = 10$-node MOU processes $d\mathbf{X}_t = C\mathbf{X}_t\,dt + \Sigma^{1/2}\,d\mathbf{W}_t$, where $\mathbf{W}_t$ is an N-dimensional Wiener process with $d\mathbf{W}_t \sim \mathcal{N}(0, I_N\,dt)$. The connectivity matrix $C \in \mathbb{R}^{N \times N}$ was random with density $d \in (0, 1)$ and nonzero entries drawn uniformly from $\left[-\frac{1}{Nd}, \frac{1}{Nd}\right]$ and rescaled for stability. Simulation used the Euler–Maruyama scheme. . Noise was implemented as $\sigma\sqrt{dt}\,\epsilon_t$, with $\epsilon_t \sim \mathcal{N}(0, I_N)$ and $\sigma = 0.01$, yielding $\Sigma = \sigma^2 I_N = 10^{-4}I_N$. For each $d \in \{0.1, \ldots, 0.9\}$, we generated 10 independent realizations with different random seeds and varying time-step dt between 0.1 and 0.2.

Human fMRI Data. The neuroimaging data were previously acquired by the School of Medicine at Washington University in St. Louis, with full acquisition and clinical procedures described in [6]. Briefly, the dataset includes 26 healthy control participants and 104 stroke patients who underwent fMRI scanning in the acute post-stroke phase. For the present study, we selected 26 control subjects and randomly sampled 26 stroke patients to obtain a balanced cohort. Preprocessing of the fMRI data was performed using fMRIPrep 23.1.3 [9]. The pipeline included skull stripping, spatial normalization to a standard brain template, and nuisance regression with 36 confounding parameters. The voxel-wise 4D signal was then parcellated into 117 regions of interest (ROIs) using the Schaefer atlas [15], yielding 117 regional time series per subject. Series were also MinMax scaled [0,1] prior to analysis. For each subject, 600 time points (20 min) were extracted and split into training (first 540 time points) and testing (remaining 60 time points) sets, corresponding to a 90%–10% split.

2.2 Forecasting Models

We compared TimesFM—a 200M-parameter pre-trained model, evaluated with default hyperparameters (batch size=32) against several baselines:

- naive forecasters (mean strategy $\hat{y}_{t+1} = \frac{1}{T}\sum i = 1^T y_i$ and last-value strategy $\hat{y}_{t+1} = y_t$);

- linear regression (LR) (window length=60);
- ARIMA(p,d,q=5; no seasonality);
- Error, Trend, and Seasonality (ETS) with automated trend and damping selection.

All models were evaluated using the mean absolute percentage error (MAPE), defined as $= \frac{100\%}{n} \sum_{i=1}^{n} |(y_i - \hat{y}_i)/y_i|$.

2.3 Causality Analysis

Traditional approaches rely on the Wiener–Granger causality principle, which is based on predictability: if past values of one time series improve the prediction of another (beyond the latter's past values alone), the first is said to Granger-cause the second [7]. Granger causality can be computed by comparing a restricted autoregressive (AR) model of Y against a full model that also includes lagged values of X. The significance of the improvement is tested using an F-test on the residual variances. To expand this reasoning to time series modeled with a foundation model, we consider additional time series as covariates to build a full model and inspect the residuals. Here, the foundation model also generates predictions $\hat{Y}_t$ based on historical data $\hat{Y}_t = \text{TimesFM}(Y_{t-w:t-1})$, where w is the window size (context length) and $Y_{t-w:t-1} = \{Y_{t-w}, Y_{t-w+1}, \ldots, Y_{t-1}\}$. The residuals between the observed and predicted data of the foundation model are: $r_t = Y_t - \hat{Y}_t$. To computed Granger causality from the foundation model, we tested whether lagged covariates explain the residuals that the foundation model cannot capture. In the reported synthetic experiments, we fixed the total length of the MOU time series to 100 time points. Thus, the context window for TimesFM was set to $w = 30$, which represents one third of the total length of the series, constituting a sufficiently long interval. We fit a linear regression $r_{t+\ell} = \delta + \theta_\ell X_t + \eta_t$ and computed both the Pearson correlation ρ_ℓ and the coefficient of determination R^2. The best lag $\ell \in [1, 5]$ was selected after Benjamini–Hochberg false discovery rate correction. In summary, for the **classical Granger test**, X is said to Granger-cause Y if the F-statistic is significant, indicating that including lagged values of X significantly improves the prediction of Y. In contrast, under the **TimesFM residual method**, X is considered to have a causal influence on Y if lagged values of X are significantly correlated with, or explain a significant portion of, the residuals r_t—i.e., the component of Y not captured by the foundation model. This indicates that X contains predictive information about Y beyond what TimesFM could account for. In practice, directionality is deemed significant at a threshold of $\alpha = 0.05$, correcting for multiple testing if we choose among many lags. The intuition behind the residual-based approach is as follows. TimesFM models the autoregressive component of a signal using a large pretrained context encoder; its residuals therefore represent variance not explained by the signal's own history. If a second time series X systematically predicts those residuals at some lag, this is analogous to the Granger criterion— X contains information about Y beyond Y's past alone. The key difference from classical Granger causality is that the autoregressive component is captured by a nonlinear, attention-based model rather than a linear autoregressor, potentially allowing the method to detect interactions that linear models miss. The residual regression then serves as a lightweight linear probe on top of this nonlinear baseline. The causal discovery was evaluated by computing the mismatch in directionality, whether a true causality was detected or not, and whether it was for example $X^{(1)} \rightarrow X^{(2)}$ or vice-versa. We tested mostly the synthetic data, as even if reported the average total causality for the fMRI data, we cannot evaluate it against a ground-truth. For the logistic coupling accuracy, precision and recall are sufficient. For the MOU, we need to take into account the sign of causality (excitatory or inhibitory). The foundation model used was TimesFM 1.2.0 accessed using Python 3.11 and PyMOU to generate the MOU processes [13]. The code is accessible at URL https://github.com/alecrimi/timesFM_stroke.

3 Results

Table 1 summarizes the precision of the forecast between the methods and the subject groups. TimesFM produced lower MAPE. However, Treating measurements across brain regions as unpaired observations, we found non-significant the results for the control subjects, and only significant ($pval < 0.05$) the results for the patient dataset. Fine-tuning the TimesFM model led to an improvement 8% for control subjects and 14% for stroke patients, quantified as 0.50 ± 0.17 for control and 0.23 ± 0.01 for stroke patients. Causality detection performance for the 3-node synthetic data is reported in Table 2. Qualitatively, it was observed that the mismatch using Granger causality was very often caused by not detecting the causality, while for the foundation model approach, the mismatch was given by introducing a spurious causality between $X_t^{(1)}$ and $X_t^{(3)}$. For MOU-based networks, the results are shown in Fig. 2, where this behavior was even more pronounced, with qualitatively the mismatch given for Granger due to miss causality, and by TimesFM-based causality having more false positive. The metrics are calculated by varying the density of causality as described in Sect. 2.1. While TimesFM does not require training time (zero-shot), its inference time is nearly 10× higher than ARIMA. Memory usage follows a similar pattern, with TimesFM requiring 2.1 GB versus ARIMA's 350 MB. On the human fMRI data, TimesFM detected a mean of 4,650 causal relationships compared to 3,390 with classical Granger causality. Without ground truth, it is not possible to determine whether the additional connections reflect genuine causal influences or false positives. This is consistent with the precision–recall trade-off observed in the synthetic experiments, where TimesFM showed higher recall but also more false positives than classical Granger causality.

Table 1. Forecasting performance (MAPE $\pm$ variance).

	TimesFM(zero-shot)	LR	Mean	Last	ARIMA	ETS
Ctrl	0.55 ± 0.42	0.59 ± 0.51	0.57 ± 0.46	0.59 ± 0.37	0.61 ± 0.64	0.63 ± 0.51
Pat	0.27 ± 0.01	0.39 ± 0.01	0.32 ± 0.01	0.32 ± 0.02	0.35 ± 0.04	0.32 ± 0.02

Table 2. Performance comparison for 3-node networks. Mean ± Variance

Method	Accuracy	Precision	Recall
TimesFM (zero-shot)	0.875 ± 0.0016	1.000 ± 0.0000	0.750 ± 0.0064
Granger	0.875 ± 0.0016	0.8033 ± 0.0026	1.000 ± 0.0000

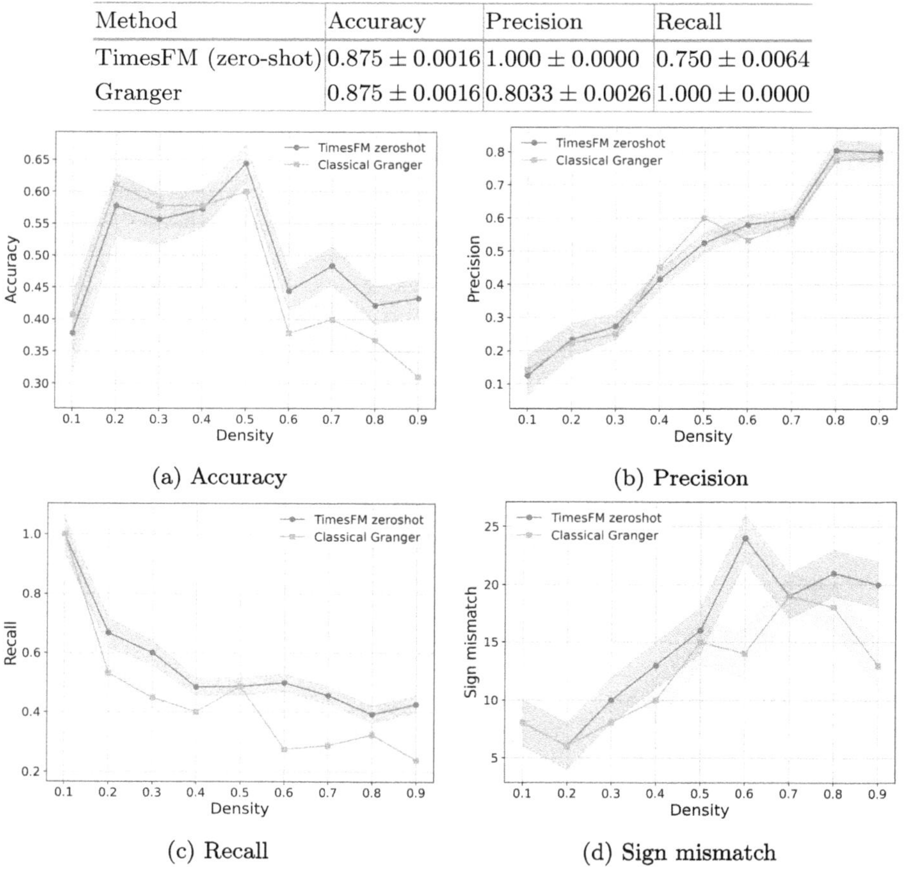

(a) Accuracy

(b) Precision

(c) Recall

(d) Sign mismatch

Fig. 2. Accuracy, precision, recall, and causality sign mismatch for both methods, varying causal density in 10-node MOU networks.

4 Discussion

TimesFM in a zero-shot setting consistently achieved the lowest reconstruction error across both groups, suggesting that large foundation models trained on diverse time-series corpora can generalize to domains not explicitly represented during pretraining. The non-significant difference in controls likely reflects the relatively stationary, near-linear characteristics of healthy fMRI signals, which limit the discriminative power of any single method. Conversely, patient time series exhibit stronger nonlinear patterns—irregular fluctuations and abrupt shifts driven by pathological mechanisms [10]—that violate linear model assumptions, potentially explaining the observed degradation in LR performance in this group. Fine-tuning TimesFM further improved performance, particularly in patients, although our primary focus here is on zero-shot capability. For causal discovery, no meaningful differences between methods were observed in the simple 3-node case. As shown in the results, in the logistic coupling experiments the TimesFM-based Granger-like approach exhibited high precision and low recall, whereas classical Granger causality showed higher recall and lower precision, leading to comparable overall accuracy. Advantages of the foundation model became more apparent in MOU experiments at higher causal densities. Classical Granger causality, constrained by its reliance on linear vector autoregressions, tends to miss true causal relationships (false negatives). In contrast, TimesFM, by leveraging attention and sequence modeling, is able to capture nonlinear and long-range dependencies, yielding higher recall at the cost of increased false positives and occasional sign mismatches—a trade-off that becomes more pronounced as network density increases. This sensitivity–specificity trade-off has practical implications. Classical Granger causality may be preferable when specificity is paramount, such as in small-n clinical hypothesis testing. The TimesFM residual-based method may instead be better suited as a first-pass screening tool in exploratory analyses, particularly when nonlinear dynamics are suspected, with identified connections subsequently validated through complementary approaches. To improve specificity, future work could explore L_1-regularization during residual regression to enforce sparsity, as well as permutation-based null distributions to yield better-calibrated significance thresholds. Finally, increasing noise levels (higher σ) in the MOU setting were associated with an overall deterioration in performance.

5 Conclusion

Our study suggests that even without fine-tuning, foundation models applied to time series can achieve reasonable performance in early event prediction, even for clinically relevant cases. However, causal discovery remains challenging. Our experiments do not provide clear or consistent evidence of advantages for using the investigated foundation model over traditional Granger causality. Nevertheless, future work may explore incorporating sparsity-inducing approaches to mitigate false positives and improve the reliability of causal relationships.

Acknowledgments. The research presented in this article received partial funding from the Polish Ministry of Science and Higher Education assigned to the AGH University of Science and Technology in Krakow. We thank the School of Medicine at Washington University in St. Louis for providing the data.

References

1. Bayazi, M.J.D.: General-purpose brain foundation models for time-series neuroimaging data. In: NeurIPS Workshop on Time Series in the Age of Large Models, (2024)
2. Biswal, B.B., et al.: Toward discovery science of human brain function. Proc. Natl. Acad. Sci. **107**(10), 4734–4739 (2010)
3. Box, G.E., Jenkins, G.M., Reinsel, G.C., Ljung, G.M.: Time Series Analysis: Forecasting and Control. John Wiley & Sons (2015)
4. Chen, C.S., Chen, Y.J., Tsai, A.H.W.: Large cognition model: towards pretrained EEG foundation model. arXiv preprint arXiv:2502.17464 (2025)
5. Chen, Y., et al.: EEGFormer: towards transferable and interpretable large-scale EEG foundation model. arXiv preprint arXiv:2401.10278 (2024)
6. Corbetta, M., et al.: Common behavioral clusters and subcortical anatomy in stroke. Neuron **85**(5), 927–941 (2015)
7. Crimi, A., Dodero, L., Sambataro, F., Murino, V., Sona, D.: Structurally constrained effective brain connectivity. Neuroimage **239**, 118288 (2021)
8. Das, A., Kong, W., Sen, R., Zhou, Y.: A decoder-only foundation model for time-series forecasting. In: Forty-first International Conference on Machine Learning (2024)
9. Esteban, O., et al.: fMRIPrep: a robust preprocessing pipeline for functional MRI. Nat. Methods **16**(1), 111–116 (2019)
10. Falcó-Roget, J., Cacciola, A., Sambataro, F., Crimi, A.: Functional and structural reorganization in brain tumors: a machine learning approach using desynchronized functional oscillations. Commun. Biol. **7**(1), 419 (2024)
11. Friston, K.J.: Functional and effective connectivity: a review. Brain Connect. **1**(1), 13–36 (2011)
12. Ganesan, A., Paul, A., Nagabushnam, G., Gul, M.: Human-in-the-loop predictive analytics using statistical learning. J. Healthcare Eng. (1) (2021)
13. Gilson, M., Moreno-Bote, R., Ponce-Alvarez, A., Ritter, P., Deco, G.: Estimation of directed effective connectivity from fMRI functional connectivity hints at asymmetries of cortical connectome. PLoS Comp Bio **12**(3), e1004762 (2016)
14. Rasul, K., et al.: Lag-llama: Towards foundation models for time series forecasting. In: R0-FoMo: Robustness of Few-shot and Zero-shot Learning in Large Foundation Models (2023)
15. Schaefer, A., Kong, R., Gordon, E.M., Laumann, T.O., Zuo, X.N., Holmes, A.J., et al.: Local-global parcellation of the human cerebral cortex from intrinsic functional connectivity MRI. Cereb. Cortex **28**(9), 3095–3114 (2018)
16. Shi, X., et al.: Time-MOE: billion-scale time series foundation models with mixture of experts. arXiv:2409.16040 (2024)
17. Wang, C., et al.: Towards a general-purpose foundation model for fMRI analysis. arXiv preprint arXiv:2506.11167 (2025)

Simulation-Based Structural Optimization for Neural Networks

Szymon Świderski[1] and Agnieszka Jastrzębska[1,2]([✉])

[1] Warsaw University of Technology, Warsaw, Poland
A.Jastrzebska@mini.pw.edu.pl
[2] The John Paul II Catholic University of Lublin, Lublin, Poland

Abstract. Optimizing already trained neural networks is one of the core problems in the domain of Artificial Intelligence. In this paper, we present a new approach capable of optimizing the structure of an already trained neural network. We present a new way of removing neurons from layers that is based on matrix scaling, which truly decreases the number of parameters in a model rather than zeroing weights. We present a simulation-based approach for optimizing the structure of a neural network that can select the best change to the network without causing data loss. A suite of empirical experiments demonstrated that the proposed approach can optimize already-trained neural networks, achieving up to 89% parameter reduction in the best case (OrganMNIST) with less than 0.05 decrease in performance. On average (excluding KMNIST), the method reduces parameters by 37% with minimal degradation (0.02). The resulting models use less than 2% of the parameters of ResNet-18 while maintaining comparable performance, supported by a neuron removal method based on matrix rescaling.

Keywords: neural network compression · post-training optimization · model size reduction · neuron pruning · simulation-based optimization

1 Introduction

The demand for efficient neural networks is increasing. Although there are many methods for training neural networks, there are very few tools to optimize them. Therefore, in this paper, we propose a novel method for optimizing the neural network structure while preserving its previously learned knowledge.

The method presented in this paper is general and can be applied to any existing neural network structure. Starting from a given model, the algorithm iteratively modifies the structure, gradually transforming it into a more optimized version. The term "optimization" in this context refers to reducing the number of parameters. Each structural modification is designed to preserve previously learned knowledge. However, small losses in learned information may

The research was funded by the National Science Centre, Poland, grant number 2024/53/B/ST6/00021.

P. Neumann et al. (Eds.): ICCS 2026, LNCS 16784, pp. 523–531, 2026.
https://doi.org/10.1007/978-3-032-29924-6_48

still occur. For this reason, access to the original training dataset is required to effectively optimize the network structure.

During optimization, the simulation may apply an unusual and complex sequence of actions to reduce the size of the model. For example, this can include removing large layers and replacing them with several smaller ones, or gradually reducing the number of neurons in selected layers. If the simulation is configured correctly, the resulting action tree can become highly complex. However, it is guided by the score function, which prioritizes maintaining accuracy while reducing the number of parameters.

To support reproducibility, we have released our implementation as an open-source package named `growingnn`. The package is available on PyPi at https://pypi.org/project/growingnn/, where all relevant links, including the GitHub repository with the source code and documentation, can be found. This tool is implemented entirely from scratch using only the NumPy library. As a result, migrating it to larger frameworks such as PyTorch or TensorFlow may be challenging, but it is still possible and is planned as future work.

2   Literature Survey

Currently, one of the most well-known approaches capable of stable structural changes is the method proposed by Evci *et al.*, called GradMax, grows a network neuron-by-neuron by leveraging gradient information to decide where adding capacity will most reduce loss function [4]. GradMax demonstrated faster convergence and better final performance than static networks of equivalent size, and was validated on image classification benchmarks. Another recent paper by Yoon *et al.* proposed Dynamically Expandable Networks (DEN) for lifelong learning, which dynamically expands network capacity by performing selective retraining [14].

In addition to the aforementioned methods, which we consider most relevant to our work, there exist several other approaches. A comparative description of the approaches available in the field of dynamic neural networks can be found in two survey papers. In the first survey by Han *et al.* [7], the authors offer a clear categorization of different types of dynamic neural networks. The first family discussed is sample-wise dynamic networks. These networks can be seen as multiple subnetworks combined together. This approach was, for example, implemented in BranchyNet [13], which introduces multiple intermediate "exit" classifiers along a deep network. During inference, if an early classifier is sufficiently confident, the prediction is produced immediately, skipping subsequent layers. Bolukbasi *et al.* [1] proposed a similar idea by training an adaptive cascade of models of increasing depth.

The second interesting survey that summarizes and categorizes algorithms in the dynamic neural networks domain is titled "Dynamic Neural Network Structure: A Review of Its Theories and Applications" [5]. It proposes a completely different set of categories that better fit the idea of growing and shrinking neural networks. The first notable category is named "Dynamic architectures". These methods allow a network's topology (neurons, layers, or sub-networks) to evolve during training which also includes pruning or structure reduction for eliminating features[1].

In addition to manual growth/pruning heuristics, another major branch of dynamic network construction methods was listed under the name "Neural Architecture Search" (NAS). A pioneering work by Zoph and Le [15] framed architecture search as a reinforcement learning problem, by training a controller RNN to generate optimal convolutional network architectures. Many subsequent NAS methods introduced alternative search strategies.

3 The Method

From a high-level point of view, the proposed method aims to modify the structure of the neural network to improve the accuracy that takes place while the network is training. An essential use-case scenario for the proposed method is to take an already-trained neural network or a pre-trained neural network and use our method as a fine-tuning tool.

3.1 Simulation Description

The decision-making process for choosing the best action uses a variant of Monte Carlo Tree Search (MCTS) [11], adapted for neural network structure optimization. Training is divided into generations. In each generation, the simulation starts from the current model M and expands it by considering all possible actions $a \in \mathcal{A}(M)$. Each action produces a new candidate model M_a. We then evaluate M_a using a short training step and assign it a score $S(M_a)$ based on the weighted sum. In the expansion phase, every action a is applied to the current model M, producing a new child node with model $M_a = a(M)$. From each model M_a, we simulate random actions up to depth d, briefly training and evaluating intermediate models. We use UCB1 to balance exploration and exploitation: $\text{UCB1}(n) = v(n) + c \cdot \sqrt{\frac{\ln N}{n}}$ [3]. The score of M_a is a weighted combination of accuracy and parameter count:

$$S(M_a) = \frac{w_{\text{acc}} \cdot S_{\text{acc}}(M_a) + w_{\text{params}} \cdot \frac{1}{1 + \beta \cdot p_a}}{w_{\text{acc}} + w_{\text{params}}}, \tag{1}$$

where $S_{\text{acc}}(M_a)$ denotes the short-run training accuracy of the model. The coefficient w_{acc} is fixed at 1.0 in all experiments, serving as a reference since accuracy is the main optimization objective. The variable p_a represents the total number of parameters in M_a, including weights, biases, and filter parameters across all layers. The meta-parameter β (currently set to 0.001) adjusts how the grade for the number of parameters is computed.

---

[1] Interestingly, pruning and structure reduction methods for eliminating features date back to optimal brain damage analysis (see the work of LeCun *et al.* [9]) and optimal brain surgeon concept (see the work of Hassibi *et al.* [8]).

The parameter w_{params} controls how strictly parameter count affects the simulation score and is a key focus of our experiments. Since models are compared from the same initial structure, those with similar accuracy are preferred when they have fewer parameters.

3.2 Removing Neurons

The contribution presented in this paper addresses a more challenging optimization task requiring a broader set of actions. We introduce operations to **add or remove neurons**, along with a **novel mathematical formulation** for neuron removal. Unlike prior approaches [6], neurons are fully removed rather than zeroed, reducing weight matrix size while aiming to **preserve learned information** through controlled scaling.

The neuron removal action in some layer ℓ reduces the number of neurons from n to n' by scaling the weight matrix $W_\ell \in \mathbb{R}^{n \times d}$ and bias vector $b_\ell \in \mathbb{R}^n$ using a quasi-identity matrix $Q \in \mathbb{R}^{n' \times n}$:

$$W_\ell' = Q_I W_\ell, \quad b_\ell' = Q_I b_\ell \tag{2}$$

A quasi-identity matrix Q is constructed by resizing an identity matrix, preserving information through optimal linear projection rather than truncation or averaging. This approach is very beneficial because if the reduction ratio is small, for example $r = 0.1$, the matrix Q_I is almost identical to the identity matrix. From the formulas above, we can then assume that $W_\ell' \approx W_\ell$.

4 Empirical Analysis

4.1 Dataset and Empirical Setup

Experiments were conducted on multiple datasets, including BreastMNIST, EMNIST Letters, FMNIST, MNIST, KMNIST, OrganMNIST, PneumoniaMNIST, and RetinaMNIST. For simplicity in tables and figures, we use abbreviated names (e.g., OrganMNIST as OrganM), while MNIST retains its original name. We focus on optimizing pre-trained neural networks. After selecting metaparameters, the algorithm is applied to fully trained models. We evaluate changes in accuracy and parameter count, aiming to reduce model size while maintaining performance. These effects are summarized by the **optimization score**.

The algorithm is implemented from scratch and follows a two-step procedure. First, the network is grown with early stopping to reach over 90% accuracy with minimal size. Second, the model is optimized, stopping if accuracy drops by less than 10% while parameters decrease by at least 20%, or when the maximum number of generations is reached.

4.2 Classification Quality of the New Approach

The experiments carried out aimed to empirically validate two hypotheses concerning the proposed algorithm for structure optimization.

RH1 Reducing the number of neurons via matrix rescaling has a minimal impact on the model's predictive performance during the optimization process.

RH2 The growingNN algorithm for dynamic network structure modification can reduce the number of trainable parameters while preserving its predictive performance.

To verify the first hypothesis (RH1), we analyze how often neuron removal actions were applied during optimization and their effect on model accuracy. Table 1 summarizes the frequency of actions in all datasets.

Table 1. Frequency of actions selected by the simulation across datasets.

Action	BreastM	EMDigits	EMLetters	FMNIST	KMNIST	MNIST	OrganAM	PneumoniaM	RetinaM	Sum
Add Neurons	1	1	0	0	1	0	0	0	0	3
Add Res. Conv Layer	2	0	1	1	1	1	0	0	2	8
Add Res. Layer	0	1	0	6	3	3	2	1	1	17
Add Seq. Conv Layer	2	0	0	1	0	0	0	0	1	4
Add Seq. Layer	0	0	0	3	3	0	0	1	0	7
Del Layer	1	0	1	2	3	1	1	0	1	10
Del Neurons (0.1)	0	1	0	0	2	0	0	1	2	6
Del Neurons (0.5)	0	0	0	0	4	0	0	1	1	6
Del Neurons (0.9)	0	0	0	0	2	0	0	0	0	2
Total	6	3	2	13	19	5	3	4	8	**63**

Table 1 shows that neuron removal was applied 14 times (6+6+2), more often than layer deletion. Since training stops after achieving 20% parameter reduction with less than 10% accuracy loss, the total number of actions is limited. Growth actions were generally more frequent, typically adding small layers before removing a larger one. Despite this, neuron removal was common and largely preserved accuracy (Table 2). In the original growingNN paper [10], we describe how new layers are added. To preserve performance, they must be properly initialized. Sequential layers use quasi-identity mappings, while residual layers allow more flexibility, making them more frequently used.

Figure 1 shows training histories from the optimization phase, with green lines indicating neuron removal actions. Accuracy remains stable overall, with

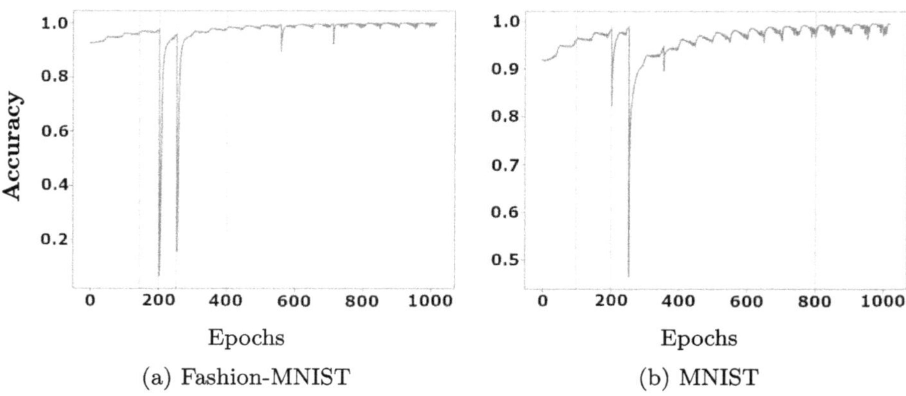

(a) Fashion-MNIST   (b) MNIST

Fig. 1. Training history during the second optimization phase with optimization weight set to 2, training was set to 20 generation each 50 epoch Green lines mark the execution of neuron removal actions, while red lines indicate layer removal actions. In the MNIST example, the largest accuracy drop is caused by adding a residual layer. (Color figure online)

only small, temporary drops that quickly recover, while larger drops are linked to other modifications. These results confirm that neuron removal via matrix rescaling preserves learned knowledge and is a stable, safe operation, supporting RH1.

The second hypothesis (RH2) was verified by analyzing changes in accuracy and parameter count in the evaluated datasets. To illustrate the optimization capacity of the proposed method, Table 2 compares the results obtained by ResNet-18 models in the same datasets [2] [12] with approximately 11 million parameters. Table 2 shows training accuracy and parameter count before and after optimization. The results demonstrate significant parameter reduction with only minor accuracy changes. Although initial models are already compact, the optimization phase further reduces their size, indicating effective action selection. Excluding the outlying result for KMNIST, the average parameter reduction is 37%, with an average performance decrease of 0.02. The method achieves up to 89% parameter reduction for OrganMNIST, with less than 0.05 decrease in performance. Even for the largest resulting models, the number of parameters remains below 2% of that of ResNet-18. Plots in Fig. 2 illustrate how structural changes impact model architecture. Early generations add small layers around a larger one, which is later removed, reducing parameters while maintaining accuracy. The process stops once parameters are reduced by over 20% without significant accuracy loss, as intended.

Table 2. Comparison of accuracy and parameter count before and after optimization across datasets.

Metric	BreastM	EM	FashionM	MNIST	KMNIST	OrganM	PneumoniaM	RetinaM
Acc. (Before)	0.91	0.91	0.92	0.98	0.90	0.91	0.91	0.83
Params (Before)	129077	144601	13629	6869	20589	20619	20349	131319
Acc. (After)	0.86	0.86	0.97	0.94	0.99	0.80	0.90	0.83
Params (After)	26853	125908	8450	7059	147059	2139	12200	118041
Param Change [%]	-79	-12	-37	2.7	614	-89	-40.0	-10
Acc. Change	-0.049	-0.048	0.049	-0.003	0.095	-0.108	-0.003	0.002
ResNet-18 Acc.	0.863	0.96	0.93	0.99	0.97	0.935	0.854	0.524
Relative Size	0.0024	0.0114	0.0008	9.0×10^{-8}	0.0134	0.0002	0.0011	0.0107

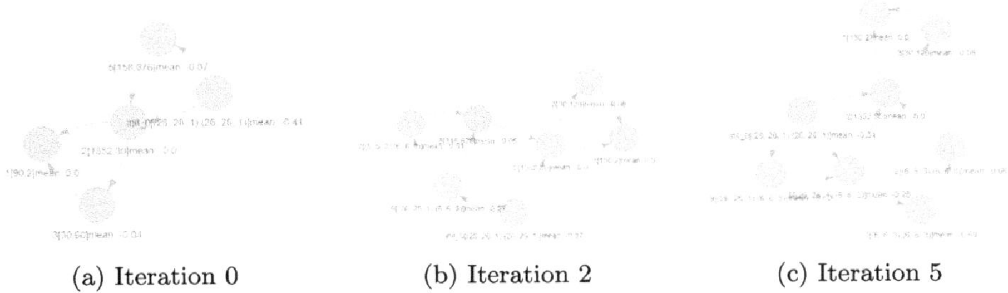

(a) Iteration 0   (b) Iteration 2   (c) Iteration 5

Fig. 2. Evolution of the neural network structure: (a) initial architecture, (b) architecture in 2nd iteration, (c) architecture in 5th (and last) iteration.

5 Conclusion

In this paper, we delivered a novel dynamic neural network training scheme that can be used to train a network from scratch and, importantly, can be used to fine-tune an already-trained neural model. The method is guided by a parameter w_{params}, which influences the optimization process. Higher values lead to smaller network size but may cause larger accuracy drops. The properly chosen value of w_{params} allows a good balance between reducing network size and preserving accuracy. Each experiment was divided into a training phase and an optimization phase, simulating a practical scenario in which an already trained model is structurally optimized. The results indicate that this approach is effective in reducing model size while preserving most of the learned knowledge. A common strategy observed during the simulations was to add several small layers followed by the removal of a larger one, leading to a significant reduction in model size. This sequence of actions was selected most frequently, as also illustrated in Fig. 2. This resulted in parameter reductions of up to 89% on OrganMNIST, with only a minimal decrease in performance (below 0.05). On average (excluding KMNIST), the method achieved a 37% reduction in parameters with negligible performance degradation (0.02). Even for the largest resulting models, the number of parameters remained below 2% of those of architectures such as ResNet-18.

References

1. Bolukbasi, T., Wang, J., Dekel, O., Saligrama, V.: Adaptive neural networks for efficient inference. In: Precup, D., Teh, Y.W. (eds.) Proceedings of the 34th International Conference on Machine Learning. Proceedings of Machine Learning Research, vol. 70, pp. 527–536. PMLR (2017)
2. Clanuwat, T., Bober-Irizar, M., Kitamoto, A., Lamb, A., Kazuaki, Y., Ha, D.: Deep learning for classical japanese literature (2018). https://doi.org/10.20676/00000341
3. Coquelin, P., Munos, R.: Bandit algorithms for tree search. CoRR **abs/cs/0703062** (2007). http://arxiv.org/abs/cs/0703062
4. Evci, U., Drozdzal, M., Unterthiner, T., Lamblin, P., Bacon, P.L.: Gradmax: Growing neural networks using gradient information. In: International Conference on Learning Representations (ICLR) (2022)
5. Guo, J., Chen, C.L.P., Liu, Z., Yang, X.: Dynamic neural network structure: a review for its theories and applications. IEEE Trans. Neural Netw. Learn. Syst. **36**(3), 4246–4266 (2025)
6. Han, S., Pool, J., Tran, J., Dally, W.J.: Learning both weights and connections for efficient neural networks. In: Proceedings of the 29th International Conference on Neural Information Processing Systems, pp. 1135–1143. NIPS'15, MIT Press (2015)
7. Han, Y., Huang, G., Song, S., Yang, L., Wang, H., Wang, Y.: Dynamic neural networks: a survey. IEEE Trans. Pattern Anal. Mach. Intell. **44**(11), 7436–7456 (2022)
8. Hassibi, B., Stork, D., Wolff, G.: Optimal brain surgeon and general network pruning. In: IEEE International Conference on Neural Networks, vol. 1, pp. 293–299 (1993)
9. LeCun, Y., Denker, J., Solla, S.: Optimal brain damage. In: Touretzky, D. (ed.) Advances in Neural Information Processing Systems, vol. 2. Morgan-Kaufmann (1989)
10. Świderski, S., Jastrzębska, A.: Dynamic growing and shrinking of neural networks with monte carlo tree search. In: Franco, L., de Mulatier, C., Paszynski, M., Krzhizhanovskaya, V.V., Dongarra, J.J., Sloot, P.M.A. (eds.) Computational Science – ICCS 2024, pp. 362–377. Springer Nature Switzerland (2024)
11. Swiechowski, M., Godlewski, K., Sawicki, B., Mandziuk, J.: Monte Carlo tree search: a review of recent modifications and applications. Artif. Intell. Rev. **56**(3), 2497–2562 (2023)
12. Tareen, S.A.K., Khan Tareen, F.: Optimally deep networks - adapting model depth to datasets for superior efficiency. In: 2025 5th International Conference on Digital Futures and Transformative Technologies (2025)

13. Teerapittayanon, S., McDanel, B., Kung, H.: Branchynet: Fast inference via early exiting from deep neural networks. In: 2016 23rd International Conference on Pattern Recognition (ICPR) pp. 2464–2469 (2016)
14. Yoon, J., Yang, E., Lee, J., Hwang, S.: Lifelong learning with dynamically expandable networks (2017)
15. Zoph, B., Le, Q.V.: Neural architecture search with reinforcement learning. CoRR **abs/1611.01578** (2016). http://arxiv.org/abs/1611.01578

Viability of Parallelization of Saturation and Extraction Algorithms for E-Graphs

Szymon Zyguła$^{(\boxtimes)}$ and Krzysztof Kaczmarski

Warsaw University of Technology, Faculty of Mathematics and Information Science, Warsaw, Poland
{szymon.zygula,krzysztof.kaczmarski}@pw.edu.pl

Abstract. Equivalence graphs (e-graphs) are data structures used in rewriting systems for representing expressions from a language, e.g. a programming language. An algorithm called *equality saturation* expands an e-graph representing a single expression to an e-graph representing all expressions equivalent to the starting one in accordance with a set of rewriting rules. Although effective, this process is computationally expensive, and parallelization remains largely unexplored. We evaluate parallel strategies for saturation and extraction, demonstrating significant speedups in matching and extraction phases, while highlighting fundamental limitations in parallelizing rule application within current architectures. Additionally, we introduce a general-purpose parallel Union-Find data structure featuring efficient lock-free path compression.

Keywords: E-Graphs · Equality Saturation · Rewriting · Parallel Union Find

1 Introduction and Related Work

Equivalence graphs (e-graphs) are data structures that represent multiple equivalent expressions, making them useful for program optimization, algebraic simplification, computer algebra [6], and numerical accuracy optimization [12].

E-graphs are used to represent expressions from some language, e.g. a programming language or the language of algebraic expressions. In contrast to traditional expression representation using trees, e-graphs can compactly represent multiple equivalent expressions. This makes e-graphs useful for optimization, where the goal is to find an equivalent expression minimizing a cost function. Such optimizations are done through a procedure called *term rewriting*: having a set of rewrite rules we apply them to the optimized expression until we achieve the desired result [2]. These rules can be, e.g. in the case of a programming language, loop unrolling or constant folding. A basic optimization algorithm applies a given rule set to the given expression until no rules can be applied anymore. The problem with this process is that it is *destructive*, i.e. application of one rule modifies the existing expression. This can lead to situations in which application of one rewrite rule prevents application of other rules.

P. Neumann et al. (Eds.): ICCS 2026, LNCS 16784, pp. 532–539, 2026.
https://doi.org/10.1007/978-3-032-29924-6_49

Let us consider a classical example of rewriting in computer program optimization: rules replacing $x * 2$ with $x << 1$ and $(x * y)/y$ with x yield different results on $(x * 2)/2$ depending on order—$(x << 1)/2$ if shifting first, or optimal x if simplifying first. This *phase-ordering problem* [15] is often solved by heuristics or backtracking, but these are time- and memory-intensive. E-graphs solve this by representing multiple equivalent expressions non-destructively, applying rewrites until saturation, then extracting the optimal form via a cost function.

Despite their simplicity and better performance than backtracking, e-graphs are still vastly slower than traditional term rewriting systems with heuristics and rarely achieve saturation because explosive growth can make them too large to fit in memory [7]. Although slow saturation is a well-known problem, no known literature describes any attempts at tackling the problem by using multiple parallel threads. Parallelizing their operations introduces challenges such as managing dependencies in rule application, avoiding excessive synchronization overhead, and handling dynamic structural updates.

E-graphs, introduced by Nelson [10] for congruence closure in Automated Theorem Provers (ATP), can be seen as an extension of the Union-Find (UF) data structure [3, 14]. Tate et al. introduced *Equality saturation* [15] for program optimization to mitigate the phase-ordering problem. Nieuwenhuis and Oliveras presented efficient, human-readable *explanations* for expression provenance [11].

The popular *egg* library [16] is a flexible and extensible implementation of e-graphs and equality saturation. It introduced features like analysis data and deferred rebuilding, which improve performance by separating read and write operations; however, it is single-threaded by default, leaving parallelization unexplored. Our work improves egg in this dimension. De Moura and Bjørner developed an efficient e-matching algorithm for SMT solvers [5], which egg uses.

In our research we found out that in our parallel algorithms it is particularly useful to have a work-stealing scheduler, which is provided by the *Rayon* library [13] alongside *Crossbeam* [4].

Jayanti and Tarjan proposed concurrent Union-Find algorithms using atomic operations like Double Compare and Swap and Compare and Swap [8]. Alistarh et al. evaluated several concurrent UF algorithms [1], but they are not well suited for our needs. We designed a new lock-free parallel UF data structure. Although it was designed for the specific access patterns of e-graphs, it can be employed in other applications as well.

2   Parallel Saturation and Extraction Algorithms

We denote an e-graph by $G = (V, C)$, where V are the e-nodes, and C are the e-classes. Expressions and e-nodes are denoted by $S(c_1, c_2, \ldots, c_n)$, where S is the root symbol, and $c_1, c_2, \ldots, c_n$ are either subexpressions or e-classes. The cost of an expression $S(c_1, c_2, \ldots, c_n)$ is written as $k_S(k_1, k_2, \ldots, k_n)$, where k is a cost function and k_i is the cost of c_i.

2.1 Parallel Saturation

The saturation algorithm's main loop [16] is split into 3 parts:

1. finding expressions to which each rule can be applied (FINDMATCHESPAR),
2. applying the rewrite rules to the e-graph (APPLYMATCHESPAR),
3. rebuilding the e-graph.

Deferred rebuilding proves useful in parallelization, as it allows us to easily postpone some work requiring modification of the e-graph to when all threads have completed tasks which can be done in parallel without locking and data races. Given that the matching phase does not modify the e-graph structure, it is well-suited for parallelization. The parallel matching algorithm differs from the sequential algorithm in two respects: both the iteration over rewrite rules and, for each rule, the scan of candidate e-classes are performed in parallel, and the algorithm uses the parallel UF structure. When matching of expressions is performed, the UF is searched for e-classes of nodes, and so parallel path compression is performed.

The parallel application algorithm modifies the e-graph, which prevents effective parallelization of this part of saturation.

Our algorithm performs some work in parallel and defers other tasks to a later stage, where they are executed sequentially. The rule application algorithm begins by spawning an *applier thread* and a *manager thread*. The applier thread (Fig. 1a) then spawns additional threads, each of which takes care of a different match from the matching step. They do so by creating e-nodes, which need to be added to the e-graph, and generating identifiers (IDs) for each of them. This is done using the parallel Union-Find data structure, described in detail in Sect. 2.3. When all nodes and IDs are created, they are sent to the applier thread through a multi-producer single-consumer (MPSC) channel, together with information on which e-classes unions need to be performed.

The manager thread (Fig. 1b) receives e-nodes which need to be added to the e-graph and IDs of e-classes to merge. When applier threads exit, the manager thread adds all nodes to the e-graph and performs necessary unions. This work consists almost exclusively of sequentially dependent writes to the e-graph, and thus cannot be easily parallelized.

Also, the parallel Union-Find developed in Sect. 2.3 is used for parallel set ID creation (Fig. 1a) and parallel path compression for node searching.

2.2 Parallel Extraction

The parallel cost calculation algorithm, which is the main part of extraction, is presented in Fig. 1c. The main difference in comparison to the sequential algorithm is the parallelization of the *for* loop with some synchronizations.

The variable b must be atomic, and assignments to it in parallel threads use relaxed memory ordering [9], denoted here by $\leftarrow_A$. Relaxed ordering provides the least amount of guarantees of all ordering types. In return, it works with the least amount of overhead and in some architectures its synchronization overhead

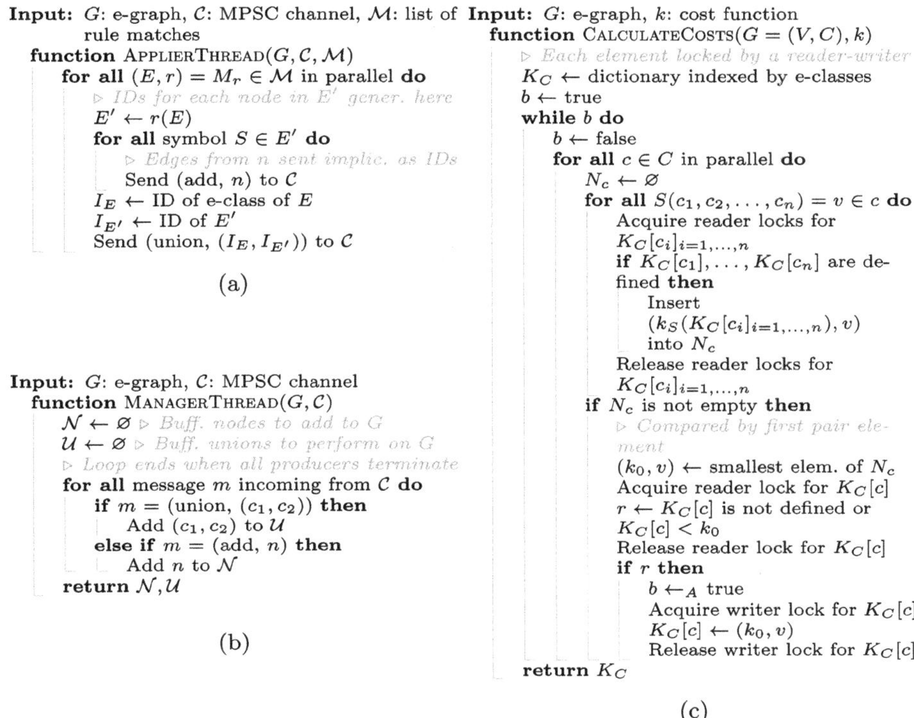

Fig. 1. Parallel rewrite rule application: applier thread (a), manager thread (b) and expression cost calculation in parallel extraction (c)

is zero [9]. Relaxed memory ordering is sufficient here because the variable b is not read when multiple threads operate on it, and implicit joining of the threads at the end of the parallel loop constitutes a memory barrier, making all threads see the same changes. Another necessary change is protecting each element of K_C with a separate *reader-writer* lock.

2.3 Parallel Lock-Free Union-Find

The UF in egg is a dynamic array where indices serve as node IDs. Parent pointers form trees for each e-class, where the root ID defines the e-class identifier.

Parallelizing the application phase is challenged by the Union-Find's dynamic growth. Sequentially, adding elements is a simple append, but capacity limits trigger reallocation. Concurrently, this is hazardous: if one thread triggers a memory move, others holding references face dangling pointers, memory corruption, or use-after-free errors. While a global lock ensures safety, it serializes access, negating parallelism benefits.

Our solution decouples ID reservation from array modification via a two-phase deferred update. First, PROMISESET uses a relaxed atomic fetch-and-add on SET_COUNT [9] to reserve unique IDs lock-free. This is extremely efficient, typically requiring a single instruction. After parallel tasks finish, a single call to MAKEPROMISEDSETS performs an uncontended batch update, resizing the UF array once for all reserved IDs. This mechanism ensures safety by separating high-performance parallel reservation from sequential structure modification.

Path compression flattens UF trees during `find` operations, reducing amortized costs [3]. In classical settings, this creates data races. For example, if a thread traverses a path from node A to B to C while another concurrently changes B's parent to D, the first thread might read an inconsistent pointer. While locks prevent this, they serialize operations and eliminate parallelism benefits. Our solution uses atomic variables for each parent pointer. Atomic reads and writes ensure threads always see valid pointers within the UF structure. Crucially, relaxed memory ordering is sufficient: the fundamental invariant is that `find` must terminate at the canonical representative. The exact path taken or the visibility order of intermediate tree states does not affect correctness. This lock-free path compression avoids expensive synchronization like acquire-release semantics and is nearly overhead-free on architectures like x86 [9].

3 Results of the Parallel Method Evaluation

In the experiments we used: egg v.0.9.5 [16]; Rayon v.1.10.0 [13]; rustc v.1.79; Ubuntu Linux Kernel 5.4.0; AMD Rome 7742 CPUs with quota of 34 cores and 200GB of RAM allocated.

Evaluation Methodology. We evaluated 60 randomly generated expressions from egg's real-calculus and propositional-calculus test languages. Five expressions were generated for sizes from 10^2 to 10^6. Real calculus uses more symbols and floating-point constants, yielding less sharing and larger e-graphs; propositional calculus is more compact.

Saturation was benchmarked for the original single-threaded egg implementation and for our parallel algorithm with 1–32 physical cores. Rules relating to commutativity, associativity, and distributivity were omitted in the evaluation to avoid unbounded growth of e-graphs.

Execution Time. The resulting total running time as a function of the number of threads is shown in Fig. 2a, together with the running time of the sequential algorithm.

Scaling depends primarily on work granularity. Propositional calculus exhibits high subexpression sharing, so even large ASTs produce relatively small e-graphs; for small inputs, this leaves too little work to amortize parallel overhead, and even large inputs scale only modestly. Real calculus produces less sharing and therefore larger e-graphs, so large instances provide enough parallel work for strong scaling. For expressions of size 10^6, real calculus approaches inverse scaling with thread count, close to the best achievable under Amdahl's law.

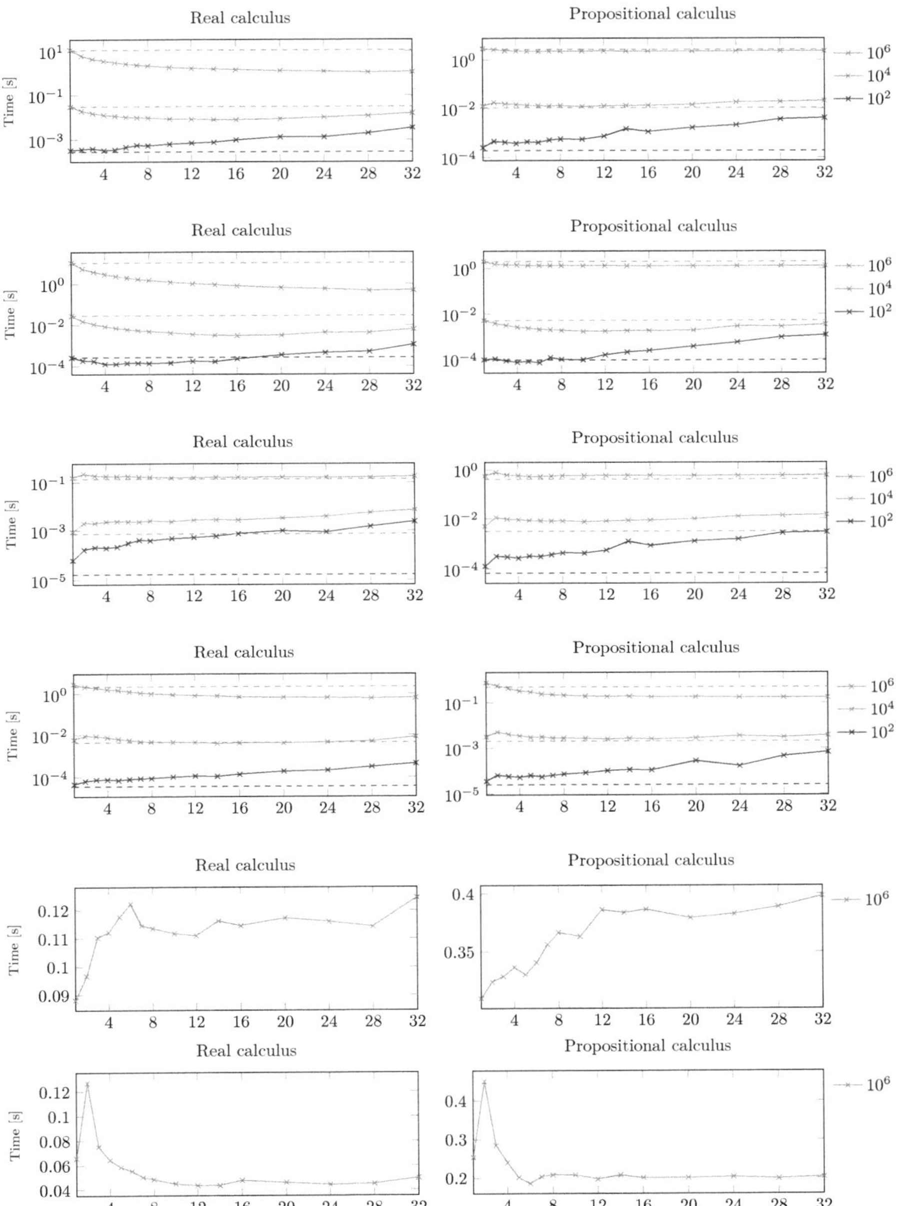

Fig. 2. Running times versus thread count: total saturation (a), matching (b), application (c), extraction (d), deferred work (e), and multithreaded work (f). Panels (a)–(d) are logarithmic; panels (e) and (f) are linear and show expressions of size 10^6. Solid lines show parallel runs by expression size; dashed lines show the sequential algorithm.

Figure 2b and Fig. 2c show that matching benefits substantially from parallelism, whereas application does not outperform the sequential baseline. Figure 2f and Fig. 2e explain this: most time is spent in the deferred, effectively single-threaded part dominated by e-graph updates. This suggests that substantially faster rule application would require a different e-graph architecture rather than a local optimization of the current one.

In our experiments, most of the saturation time lies in matching, which scales well and is practically worthwhile to parallelize. Instances where this is not true tend to exhibit explosive e-graph growth, making saturation unattractive regardless.

The extraction phase was evaluated on the same expressions as saturation. Figure 2d shows that parallel extraction becomes beneficial mainly for large instances. The speedup is smaller than for matching but still substantial, and again depends on both input size and language.

4   Conclusions

This paper presents a systematic evaluation of intra-process parallelization for the core algorithms of equality saturation. Our findings reveal a sharp dichotomy in the potential for speedup: while read-intensive phases (matching and extraction) are highly amenable to parallelism, the write-intensive rule application phase is fundamentally constrained. The matching algorithm parallelizes the search over e-classes, achieving near-linear speedups for large, complex problems. The extraction algorithm, in turn, uses a combination of reader-writer locks and atomic operations to concurrently compute optimal expressions. Foundational to these successes is our development of a novel, lock-free parallel Union-Find data structure. This contribution provides two key techniques: efficient, concurrent path compression using relaxed-ordering atomics, and a deferred-update mechanism for concurrent set creation. These techniques yield a general-purpose primitive for high-performance disjoint-set operations with low overhead on common architectures like x86.

A key finding of our work concerns the rule application phase. Our analysis demonstrates that this phase, which is bottlenecked by the overall volume of sequentially dependent writes to the e-graph's core data structures, fails to achieve a significant speedup from parallelization. This suggests that achieving fully parallel saturation may be infeasible without a foundational redesign of the underlying data structure to better support concurrent writes.

Therefore, our findings suggest that future research in high-performance equality saturation should focus on searching for a new e-graph architecture with parallel processing model as a first-order design principle. This could involve exploring batch-based e-class merging, alternative approaches to maintaining analysis data, or fundamentally different expression representations that avoid the sequential bottlenecks we have identified. Our work highlights the value of this research direction.

References

1. Alistarh, D., Fedorov, A., Koval, N.: In Search of the Fastest Concurrent Union-Find Algorithm. In: 23rd International Conference on Principles of Distributed Systems (OPODIS 2019). Schloss Dagstuhl – Leibniz-Zentrum für Informatik (2019)
2. Baader, F., Nipkow, T.: Term Rewriting and All That, Cambridge University Press (1998)
3. Cormen, T.H., Leiserson, C.E., Rivest, R.L., Stein, C.: Introduction to Algorithms, Fourth Edition, MIT Press (2022)
4. Crichton, A., Kang, J., Turon, A., Endo, T., et al.: Crossbeam. https://crates.io/crates/crossbeam (2024). https://crates.io/crates/crossbeam. Accessed 07 June 2024
5. de Moura, L., Bjørner, N.: Efficient E-matching for SMT solvers. In: Pfenning, F. (ed.) CADE 2007. LNCS (LNAI), vol. 4603, pp. 183–198. Springer, Heidelberg (2007). https://doi.org/10.1007/978-3-540-73595-3_13
6. Gowda, S.: High-performance symbolic-numerics via multiple dispatch. ACM Commun. Comput. Algebra **55**(3), 92–96 (2022)
7. He, G., Singh, Z., Yoneki, E.: MCTS-GEB: Monte Carlo Tree Search is a Good E-graph Builder. In: Proceedings of the 3rd Workshop on Machine Learning and Systems, pp. 26–33. EuroMLSys '23, Association for Computing Machinery (2023)
8. Jayanti, S.V., Tarjan, R.E.: Concurrent disjoint set union. Distrib. Comput. **34**(6), 413–436 (2021)
9. Moiseenko, E., Podkopaev, A., Koznov, D.: A survey of programming language memory models. Program. Comput. Softw. **47**(6), 439–456 (2021). https://doi.org/10.1134/S0361768821060050
10. Nelson, C.G.: Techniques for Program Verification, Stanford University (1980). Ph.D. thesis
11. Nieuwenhuis, R., Oliveras, A.: Proof-producing congruence closure. In: Giesl, J. (ed.) RTA 2005. LNCS, vol. 3467, pp. 453–468. Springer, Heidelberg (2005). https://doi.org/10.1007/978-3-540-32033-3_33
12. Panchekha, P., Sanchez-Stern, A., Wilcox, J.R., Tatlock, Z.: Automatically improving accuracy for floating point expressions. ACM SIGPLAN Notices **50**(6), 1–11 (2015)
13. Stone, J., Matsakis, N.: Rayon. https://crates.io/crates/rayon (2024). https://crates.io/crates/rayon. Accessed 07 June 2024
14. Tarjan, R.E.: Efficiency of a good but not linear set union algorithm. J. ACM **22**(2), 215–225 (1975)
15. Tate, R., Stepp, M., Tatlock, Z., Lerner, S.: Equality saturation: a new approach to optimization. In: Proceedings of the 36th Annual ACM SIGPLAN-SIGACT Symposium on Principles of Programming Languages, pp. 264–276. Association for Computing Machinery (2009)
16. Willsey, M., Nandi, C., Wang, Y.R., Flatt, O., Tatlock, Z., Panchekha, P.: Egg: fast and extensible equality saturation. Proc. ACM Programm. Lang. **5**, 1–29 (2021) POPL

Topology-Agnostic Antennas: Surrogate-Assisted Optimization of Fabrication Yield in a Distributed Setup

Adrian Bekasiewicz[1]([✉]) [iD], Slawomir Koziel[1,2] [iD], Khadijeh Askaripour[1] [iD], and Yingsong Li[3] [iD]

[1] Faculty of Electronics, Telecommunications and Informatics, Gdansk University of Technology, Narutowicza 11/12, 80-233, Gdansk, Poland
adrian.bekasiewicz@pg.edu.pl
[2] Department of Engineering, Reykjavik University, Menntavegur 1, 102, Reykjavik, Iceland
[3] Key Laboratory of Intelligent Computing and Signal Processing Ministry of Education, Anhui University, Jiulong Rd. 111, 230601 Hefei, China

Abstract. Maximization of yield is essential for reducing the cost of *en masse* manufactured antennas. Conventional approaches to the problem, based on Monte Carlo (MC) analysis, are impractical due to overwhelming cost associated with simulations of modern structures. In this work, a surrogate-assisted optimization of yield for multi-dimensional antennas is considered. The method shifts expensive MC to an approximation surrogate that is iteratively re-set in the course of optimization. The algorithm embeds a mechanism for automatic tuning of yield for nominal designs that violate the specifications. The method has been demonstrated using two topology-agnostic radiators represented using 22 and 52 parameters, respectively. To ensure low optimization cost (time-wise) training designs for surrogate identification are evaluated using an in-house distributed computing system. The maximized yields for both considered antenna designs amount to 97% and 79%, respectively. Validation of the results against yield estimated based on direct EM simulations is also provided.

Keywords: topology-agnostic antennas · distributed computing · yield optimization · surrogate-based methods · Monte Carlo

1 Introduction

Antenna design is a challenging task that involves determination of topology and its tuning in order to fulfill the performance requirements. An additional step of the process—crucial for *en masse* manufacturing—involves evaluation of sensitivity to tolerances, i.e., small, random deviations of the optimized (also referred to as nominal) structure dimensions that stem from the fabrication processes [1]. Sensitivity of nominal design to tolerances might result in violation of specifications. The undesirable outcome is reduced yield and increased production cost (due to waste of resources used for fabrication of components that violate requirements and thus are rejected).

P. Neumann et al. (Eds.): ICCS 2026, LNCS 16784, pp. 540–548, 2026.
https://doi.org/10.1007/978-3-032-29924-6_50

Yield can be estimated using geometrical methods, or approaches based on Monte Carlo (MC) simulations [2–5]. The latter boil down to performance evaluation for a large set of random perturbations w.r.t. the nominal design. Yield represents a ratio of designs that fulfill specifications to all samples [3]. Geometrical methods generate convex approximations to a feasible region of the search space (i.e., where specifications are met) [4]. Shifting the nominal design to the center of such region maximizes yield [5]. Unfortunately, these approaches require thousands of simulations for accuracy. which is impractical for modern antennas that can be evaluated only using numerically expensive electromagnetic (EM) simulations [4]. Cost-acceptable alternative involves worst-case analysis which, however, is overly pessimistic [6].

The cost of yield optimization can be reduced using surrogate methods [3, 4, 7, 8]. The latter shift the burden associated with antenna EM simulations to cheap, iteratively updated models [3, 7]. Surrogate-based optimization coupled with geometric and/or MC-based techniques proved to be useful for maximization of yield at a manageable cost. In [4], a cost-efficient design centering based on space mapping enhanced data-driven model has been proposed. In [3], yield optimization has been performed by shifting MC analyses to iteratively re-set feature-based models. Owing to less non-linear mapping between geometry and structure performance, feature models can be constructed using a low number of samples. A variant of the technique, where the surrogate is derived from low-fidelity simulations, has been presented in [9]. Despite proved usefulness, all the considered techniques have been validated using structures with well-defined, low-dimensional topologies.

Recently, an increased effort towards generation of antennas without engineering inference can be observed [10]. In such a setup, topology development is formulated as a specification-oriented optimization problem, which represents a significant departure from cognitive, experience-driven approaches. It has been demonstrated that the approach is useful for generation of high-performance radiators with non-intuitive geometries [10]. Evaluation of the effects of manufacturing tolerances on performance of topology-agnostic structures is difficult. The main problem is representation of geometries using dozens of parameters, as well as unknown relations between them. From this perspective, the problem associated with yield optimization for such structures remains open.

In this work, a cost-aware optimization of topology-agnostic antennas for maximization of fabrication yield is considered. The method involves a series of local optimizations where MC analyses are shifted to feature-based data-driven models. The latter are re-set after each iteration around the best nominal design. To enable optimization from infeasible nominal designs (i.e., the ones for which none of the perturbed solutions fulfills the defined specifications), the algorithm embeds a mechanism that adjusts the threshold for calculation of yield. The framework has been demonstrated using two topology-agnostic radiators with 22 and 52 design parameters, respectively. The computational cost (time-wise) associated with evaluation of the samples required for feature models identification has been reduced using distributed EM simulations. The method has been compared in terms of cost and accuracy against direct EM-based MC performed at the optimized nominal designs. Overall, nearly 21000 EM simulations (associated with ~10 days of CPU-time) have been performed to generate the results. Error for the estimated yield obtained using the discussed surrogate method is below 4% of the direct estimation based on EM simulations.

2 Methodology

2.1 Problem Formulation

Let $R(x_0)$ be the reflection response obtained (over the frequency f) from EM simulation of the topology-agnostic antenna model at the nominal design x_0. Then, let $X = \delta_0\{x_1, x_2, ..., x_m\}$ and $U(x) = U(R(x))$ be a set of $m = 1, ..., M$ random designs generated according to the assumed probability distribution and scaled w.r.t. δ_0 and the objective function. The manufacturing yield is a ratio of designs that met the specifications to all perturbations around x_0. It is given as follows [3]:

$$Y(x_0, X) = \frac{1}{M} \sum_{m=1}^{M} H(U(\mathbf{x}_0 + \delta\mathbf{x}_m)) \tag{1}$$

Note that $H(x) = H(U(x)) = 1$ when $U(x) \leq U_0$ (i.e., when $U_0 = 0$, the specifications are fulfilled); otherwise, $H(x) = 0$. Note that the accuracy of MC-based yield depends on the number M of evaluated random designs (preferably, hundreds or thousands), which is impractical when EM antenna models are used.

The problem pertinent to unacceptable computational cost can be mitigated by shifting the burden associated with MC to a cheap data-driven surrogate constructed around x_0 using a limited number of EM-based training samples.

2.2 Representation of Antenna Characteristics Using Response Features

The accuracy of surrogate-assisted yield estimation is subject to fidelity of data-driven model used for MC simulations. For topology-agnostic antennas, the frequency responses are highly non-linear functions of geometry [10]. Given that the considered structures are characterized by dozens of parameters, a large number of training samples would be needed for construction of accurate frequency-based models. Instead, the antenna behavior can be represented in the form of carefully selected features. In such a setup, the properties are first extracted from the frequency responses of training designs and then used for identification of auxiliary data-driven surrogate.

Let $F = F(x) = P(R(x))$ be the feature-based antenna response extracted using function P. The matrix $F = [\omega\ L]^T$ comprises $q = 1, ..., Q$ pairs of frequency- and level-related points $\omega = [\omega_1 ... \omega_q]^T$ and $L = [L_1 ... L_q]^T$. Each pair can be extracted either w.r.t. selected frequency point, or reflection level. Compared to $R(x)$, $F(x)$ is much less non-linear function of design parameters. Hence, response features are useful for construction of a simple, yet accurate approximation models (see Fig. 1). For more detailed discussion on the concept, see [1, 9, 11].

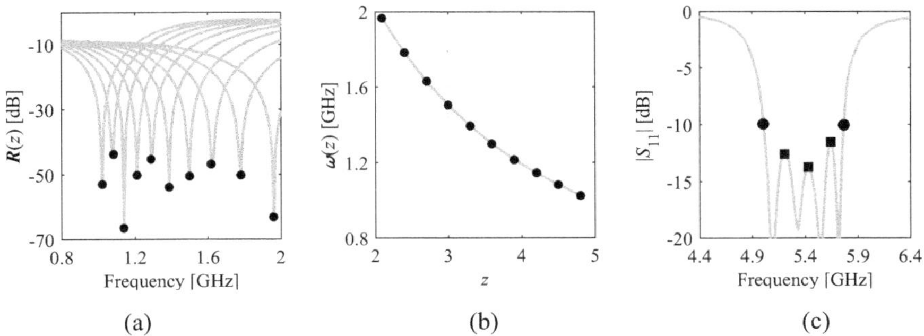

Fig. 1. Feature-assisted design: (a) frequency and (b) feature responses as a function of some parameter z [10], as well as (c) features ($Q = 5$) extracted from the frequency data (—) that represent response levels (■) at local maxima and frequencies in GHz (●) at bandwidth edges (defined at -10 dB level). Note that changes of $\omega(z)$ are much less non-linear compared to $R(z)$.

2.3   Distributed Framework for Feature-Assisted Yield Estimation

To ensure cost-efficient evaluation of yield, MC analyses are executed using a second order polynomial model. Let $X_t = [x_{t.0} \; x_{t.1} \; \ldots \; x_{t.n}]$, $n = 0, 1, \ldots, 2D$, be a $D \times N$ matrix of training designs ($N = 2D + 1$, where D is the number of antenna geometry parameters). When $n = 2d$ ($d = 1, \ldots, D$), the vector $x_{t.n} = x_0 - \delta_d$, whereas for $n = 2d - 1, x_{t.n} = x_0 + \delta_d$; $x_{t.0} = x_0$. The elements of δ_d are zero for all but dth parameter, i.e., $\delta_d = [\delta_1 \ldots \delta_d \ldots \delta_D]^T = [0 \ldots \delta \ldots 0]^T$ (δ is the user-defined) [3, 9]. The surrogate is a composition of models defined according to frequency and level features: $G = [G_\omega \; G_L] = [G_\omega(x) \; G_L(x)]$. Let A_ω be the matrix of polynomial model $G_\omega(x)$ coefficients given as:

$$A_\omega = \begin{bmatrix} \mathbf{a}_0 \; \mathbf{a}_1 & \cdots & \mathbf{a}_n \end{bmatrix} = \begin{bmatrix} \alpha_{1.0} & \cdots & \alpha_{1.n} \\ \vdots & \ddots & \vdots \\ \alpha_{q.0} & \cdots & \alpha_{q.n} \end{bmatrix} \tag{2}$$

Also, let $\alpha_q = [\alpha_{q.0} \; \alpha_{q.1} \ldots \alpha_{q.n}]$ be a vector that represents qth row of A_ω obtained as $\alpha_q = \beta\omega_q$, where $\omega_q = [\omega_{q.0} \; \omega_{q.1} \ldots \omega_{q.n}]^T = [\omega_q(x_{t.0}) \; \omega_q(x_{t.1}) \ldots \omega_q(x_{t.n})]^T$ is a vector containing qth feature points extracted from EM-based responses of training designs from X_t; $\beta = (V^T V)^{\dagger} V^T$ and V is a Vandermonde matrix constructed from X_t (note that "$\dagger$" is a pseudo-inverse). The surrogate response at x (constrained to the $l_b = -\mathbf{1}^T\delta$, $u_b = \mathbf{1}^T\delta$ bounds, where $\mathbf{1}^T$ is a D-dimensional vector of ones) is given as:

$$G_\omega(x) = \mathbf{a}_{\omega.1} + x^T \mathbf{a}_{\omega.2} + (x \circ x)^T \mathbf{a}_{\omega.3} \tag{3}$$

The coefficients in (3) are extracted from columns of A_ω as $\mathbf{a}_{\omega.1} = \mathbf{a}_0 = [\alpha_{1.0} \ldots \alpha_{q.0}]^T$, $\mathbf{a}_{\omega.2} = [\mathbf{a}_1 \ldots \mathbf{a}_{n1}]$, and $\mathbf{a}_{\omega.0} = [\mathbf{a}_{n1+1} \ldots \mathbf{a}_{n2}]$, respectively. Note that $n_1 = D$, $n_2 = 2D$, whereas the symbol "$\circ$" in (3) is a Hadamard product. The model $G_L(x)$ is derived accordingly. Finally, the surrogate is used to obtain $G(x_0 + \delta_0 x_m)$ response features for all $x_m \in X$ designs (cf. Sect. 2.1). The responses are then evaluated using (1)—with $U(x) = U(G(x))$—to provide approximated yield at x_0 design.

As indicated above, identification of polynomial model coefficients A_ω (and A_L) involves EM simulations of the antenna at nominal design x_0 and $2D$ perturbations around it. For multi-dimensional structures (as in this work), the cost associated with sequential evaluation of X_t can be inacceptable. Here, the problem is mitigated through parallelization of EM simulations using an in-house developed distributed computing system that comprises a few heterogenic nodes (machines) with EM simulation software. The system implements a client-server architecture. For construction of model G, the server generates a set of N simulation packages (one for each $x_{t.n} \in X_t$ design) and uploads them to a shared repository. The latter is accessed by the clients which download data, evaluate the design and send the responses back to the repository. Finally, the server aggregates the designs and EM responses within a common database. The computational speed-up resulting from the use of the outlined distributed system is proportional to the number of nodes. In practice, it is bounded from above by the number of available licenses for the EM-simulation software.

2.4   Yield Optimization Algorithm

Let $Y_S(x_0, X) = Y_S(x_0, X, U_0)$ be the yield obtained using the feature-based surrogate model of Sect. 2.3. Now, let $U_X = [U(G^{(i)}(x^{(i)} + \delta_0 x_1)) \ldots U(G^{(i)}(x^{(i)} + \delta_0 x_m))]$ be a vector of objective function responses obtained for all X perturbations around $x^{(i)}$; $U_{X.l} = \min(U_X)$ and $U_{X.u} = \max(U_X)$. The optimization involves iterative ($i = 0, 1, \ldots$) tuning of the nominal design to maximize the yield by solving [3]:

$$x^{(i+1)} = \arg\min_x \left(-Y_S{}^{(i)}\left(x^{(i)}, X\right) \right) \tag{4}$$

where $Y_S{}^{(i)}$ is obtained from the $G^{(i)}$ responses. The algorithm is as follows:

1. Set $i = 0$, $x^{(i)} = x_0$, $\delta = 2\delta_0$, $U_0 = 0$ and generate X;
2. Generate $G^{(i)}$ model around $x^{(i)}$ design as explained in Sect. 2.3;
3. Set $E^{(i)} = -Y_S(x^{(i)}, X)$; If $E^{(i)} = 0$, go to Step 4; otherwise go to Step 5;
4. Calculate $U_{X.l}{}^{(i)}$, $U_{X.u}{}^{(i)}$, and find $U_0 = U_0(\gamma)$ that shifts yield according to Y_0;
5. If $i > 0$, $E^{(i)} < 0$, $E^{(i-1)} \leq E^{(i)}$, set $x_0{}^* = x^{(i-1)}$ and END; otherwise go to Step 6;
6. Generate $x^{(i+1)}$ by solving (4), set $U_0 = 0$, $i = i + 1$, and go to Step 2.

It should be reiterated that $U_0(\gamma) = \gamma U_{X.u}{}^{(i)} + (1 - \gamma)U_{X.l}{}^{(i)}$ in Step 4 is identified only if $E^{(i)} = 0$, i.e., when all perturbations around currently best design $x^{(i)}$ violate the performance specifications. The coefficient γ is obtained by solving:

$$\gamma^* = \arg\min_\gamma \left(\left| Y_S\left(x^{(i)}, X, U_0(\gamma)\right) - Y_0 \right| \right) \tag{5}$$

Here, $Y_0 = 0.3$ is selected as target value. The consequence of adjusting U_0 using (5) is that yield can be minimized using (4) even from the nominal designs that violate the specifications. The latter might be the case, e.g., for structures with highly selective responses. The method, however, should not be considered as a generic yield-oriented optimization from poor starting points as it does not embed mechanisms for adjusting X_t perturbations used for construction of $G^{(i)}$ surrogate. At each iteration, nominal design is tuned within $l_{b0} = -\mathbf{1}^T \delta_0$, $u_{b0} = \mathbf{1}^T \delta_0$ bounds. Also, given that $G^{(i)}$ is constrained to a $\delta = 2\delta_0$ range around $x^{(i)}$, evaluation of $x^{(i)} + X$ does not involve extrapolation. For conceptual illustration of yield optimization, see Fig. 2.

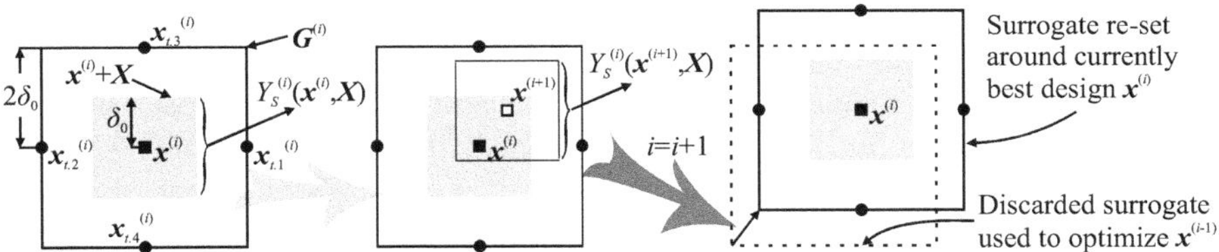

Fig. 2. Surrogate-based yield optimization at ith algorithm iteration: a conceptual illustration.

3 Results

The considered yield optimization methodology is demonstrated using two topology-agnostic antennas represented using 22 and 52 independent design parameters, respectively. For each antenna, the numerical experiments are performed using a total of $M = 10000$ random designs with Gaussian distribution ($\sigma = 0.03$). The scale for perturbations is set to $\delta_0 = 3\sigma$ [3, 9]. A comparison of manufacturing yield calculated, for the optimized nominal designs, using surrogate model and directly from EM simulations is also provided. A total of five nodes have been used to perform distributed computations. Note that the number is limited by availability of licenses for EM simulation software.

3.1 Antenna Model

Consider a topology-agnostic planar antenna of Fig. 3a [10]. It is implemented on a Rogers AD255C substrate ($\varepsilon_r = 2.55$, $h = 1.52$ mm). The radiator is in the form of a polygon fed through a concentric probe. The antenna is defined by a D-dimensional vector $x = [x_{c.1}\ y_{c.1}\ x_{c.2} \cdots x_{c.D/2}\ y_{c.2} \cdots y_{c.D/2}]^T$ comprising xy coordinates of points defined in a Cartesian system (here, D is set to 22 and 52 for the first and second test case, respectively). Parameters: $o = 5, r_1 = 1.27$, and $r_2 = 2.84$ are fixed (all dimensions are in mm); $B = 2(\max(|x|) + o)$. The antenna is implemented in CST Microwave Studio. The EM model R is discretized using ~400,000 cells and computational cost (averaged across the available distributed nodes) amounts to 200 s. The objective function is defined as $U = \max(\{U_1, U_2, U_3\})$, where $U_1 = \max([L_2 \cdots L_{Q-1}]) - L_{\text{thd}}$, $U_2 = \omega_1 - f_L$, $U_3 = f_H - \omega_Q$ (cf. Sect. 2.2). The feature coordinates used to represent the structure performance are specified w.r.t. levels at local maxima located between corner frequencies specified at the target level of $L_{\text{thd}} = -10$ dB (see Fig. 1c for illustration).

3.2 Topology-Agnostic WiFi Antenna

Consider a WiFi antenna (cf. Fig. 3b) defined using a 22-parameter nominal design $x_0 = [-0.17-1.88\ 6.89\ 13.18-4.22\ -4.34\ -22.75\ -12.31\ -3.31\ 7.83\ 22.75\ 6.89-0.67\ 14.08\ 19.45\ 7.92\ 0.74-15.99\ -7.30\ -19.45\ -7.25\ -0.67]^T$. The corner frequencies are $f_L = 5.25$ GHz and $f_H = 5.85$ GHz. The initial design violates the requirements (see Fig. 3b), hence $Y_S(x_0, X) = 0$. The optimized nominal design $x_0^* = [-0.28-1.74\ 6.76\ 12.96-3.73\ -4.25\ -22.43\ -12.61\ -3.62\ 7.16\ 22.43\ 6.76-0.61\ 14.07\ 19.32\ 7.80\ 1.15-15.4\ -7.21\ -19.32\ -8.03\ -0.61]^T$ is obtained after 8 iterations of the algorithm (cf. Sect. 2.4). Note that the first 3 steps are associated with shifting the design w.r.t.

the specifications. The final yield is $Y_S(x_0{}^*, X) = 0.966$. The computational cost of optimization corresponds to 344 EM simulation (~3.8 h of CPU-time using all available nodes). For the sake of comparison, EM-based evaluations of all X perturbations around $x_0{}^*$ are also performed for direct estimation of yield. The final response is $Y(x_0{}^*, X) = 0.989$, which represents a 2.3% discrepancy w.r.t. $Y_S(x_0{}^*, X)$. Note that direct yield evaluation required 10000 EM simulations (~111.1 h of CPU-time, or over 4.6 days for all nodes). Given that EM-driven minimization of (4) is infeasible as it would require evaluations of (1) per iteration, the algorithm of Sect. 2.4 offers acceptable accuracy. Responses at x_0, $x_0{}^*$, and selected perturbations around $x_0{}^*$ (feature- and frequency-based) are shown in Fig. 3b.

3.3 Topology-Agnostic UWB Antenna

Consider ultra-wideband antenna (cf. Fig. 3c) design: $x_0 = [-0.06-10.06\ 11.81\ 14.77$ $17.36\ 11.01\ 4.11-1.92\ -6.66\ -9.14\ -7.51\ -11.09\ -13.72\ -12.47\ -10.4\ -10.87$ $-15.57\ -17.36\ -13.03\ -6.32\ -0.96\ 4.79\ 10.27\ 15.04\ 16.36\ 14.93\ 11.81\ 0.36\ 4.71$ $7.12\ 11.13\ 11.42\ 11.58\ 14.77\ 17.52\ 9.71\ 11.14\ 12.61\ 8.37\ 1.93-2.63\ -5.4\ -8.7\ -$ $13.38\ -13.24\ -13.45\ -17.52\ -17.38\ -16.84\ -10.87\ -5.02\ 0.36]^T$. The yield is to be maximized within $f_L = 5.95$ GHz to $f_H = 7.05$ GHz, hence x_0 violates specifications. The design $x_0{}^* = [-0.14-9.98\ 11.80\ 14.93\ 17.47\ 11.27\ 4.25-1.78\ -6.46\ -8.88\ -$ $7.54\ -10.92\ -13.68\ -12.43\ -10.28\ -10.72\ -15.65\ -17.47\ -13.12\ -6.27\ -0.83\ 4.95$ $10.43\ 15.26\ 16.48\ 15.19\ 11.8\ 0.4\ 4.47\ 7.1\ 11.17\ 11.44\ 11.5\ 14.89\ 17.5\ 9.8\ 11.35\ 12.83$ $8.4\ 2.06-2.69\ -5.31\ -8.75\ -13.47\ -13.09\ -13.45\ -17.51\ -17.44\ -16.9\ -10.82\ -$ $4.96\ 0.4]^T$ is obtained after just 4 iterations (420 EM simulations, ~4.7 h of CPU-time). The obtained yield is $Y_S(x_0{}^*, X) = 0.793$ which represents 3.6% discrepancy w.r.t. $Y(x_0{}^*, X) = 0.829$ (obtained based on 10000 EM simulations). Responses at $x_0, x_0{}^*$ and perturbations around $x_0{}^*$ are shown in Fig. 3c.

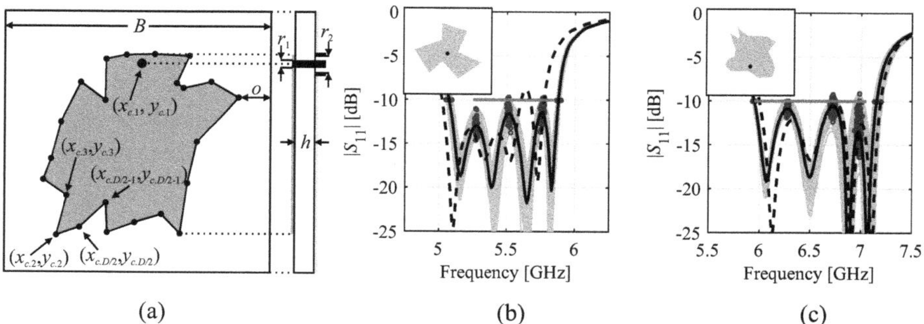

Fig. 3. Topology-agnostic radiator: (a) geometry with highlight on coordinates (●), as well as responses at x_0 (− −), $x_0{}^*$ (—), EM-based (gray), and feature-based (○) MC perturbations around $x_0{}^*$ obtained for antennas with: (b) 22 (Sect. 3.2), and (b) 55 parameters (Sect. 3.3).

4 Conclusion

In this work, a surrogate-assisted yield optimization of topology-agnostic antennas has been considered. The algorithm sequentially generates feature-based data-driven surrogate that are used for local maximization of yield through a series of MC analyses that involve evaluations of random designs with the assumed probability distribution. To ensure acceptable cost of optimization for multi-parameter designs, generation of training designs for feature-based surrogates is handled by a distributed computing system. To enable optimization from designs that violate specifications, the algorithm embeds the mechanism that adjusts the threshold for yield evaluation. The method has been demonstrated based on two topology-agnostic patch antennas represented using 22 and 52 parameters, respectively. For the considered structures, the optimized yields of around 97% and 79% have been obtained, which represents up to 3.6% (more pessimistic) deviation from direct estimation. The cost of surrogate-assisted yield optimization is less than 5 h of CPU-time per structure (two-fold lower compared to EM-based yield estimation around just a single nominal design).

Acknowledgments. This work was supported in part by the National Science Center of Poland Grant 2021/43/B/ST7/01856 and Gdansk University of Technology (Excellence Initiative – Research University) Grant 13/2025/IDUB/I.2/EINSTEINIUM.

Disclosure of Interests. The authors declare no conflicts of interest.

References

1. Olsson, T., Koptioug, A.: Statistical analysis of antenna robustness. IEEE Trans. Antennas Propagat. **53**(1), 566–570 (2005)
2. Zhang, J.C., Styblinski, M.A.: Yield and Variability Optimization of Integrated Circuits. Kluwer Academic Publishers, New York (1995)
3. Koziel, S., Bandler, J.: Rapid yield estimation and optimization of microwave structures exploiting feature-based analysis. IEEE Trans. Microwave Theory Techn. **63**(1), 107–114 (2015)
4. Abdel-Malek, H., et al.: The ellipsoidal technique for design centering of microwave circuits exploiting space-mapping interpolating surrogates. IEEE Trans. Microwave Theory Techn. **54**(10), 3731–3738 (2006)
5. Abdel-Malek, H., Hassan, A., Bakr, M.: A boundary gradient search technique and its application in design centering. IEEE Trans. Comput.-Aided Design Integrated Circuits Syst. **18**(11), 1654–1661 (1999)
6. Li, D., Chen, R.: Circuit tolerance analysis and yield maximization using SPICE with parallel processing techniques. Int Conf Circuits Syst., pp. 761–764, Shenzhen (1991)
7. Bandler, J., et al.: Space mapping: the state of the art. IEEE Trans. Microwave Theory Techn. **52**(1), 337–361 (2004)
8. Zhang, J., et al.: Polynomial chaos-based approach to yield-driven EM optimization. IEEE Trans. Microwave Theory Techn. **66**(7), 3186–3199 (2018)
9. Koziel, S., Bekasiewicz, A.: Variable-fidelity response feature surrogates for accelerated statistical analysis and yield estimation of compact microwave components. IET Microwaves Antennas Propagat. **13**(14), 2539–2543 (2019)

10. Bekasiewicz, A., et al.: Strategies for feature-assisted development of topology agnostic planar antennas using variable-fidelity models. J. Comput. Sci. **85**, 102521 (2025)
11. Pietrenko-Dabrowska, A., Koziel, S.: Response Feature Technology for High-Frequency Electronics. Optimization, Modeling, and Design Automation. Springer, New York (2024)

Constrained Graph Generation: Preserving Diameter and Clustering Coefficient Simultaneously

Dávid Ferenczi[(✉)] and Alexander Grigoriev

Maastricht University, Maastricht 6211LM, Netherlands
`{d.ferenczi,a.grigoriev}@maastrichtuniversity.nl`

Abstract. Generating graphs subject to strict structural constraints is a fundamental computational challenge in network science. Simultaneously preserving interacting properties, e.g., the diameter and the clustering coefficient, is particularly demanding. Simple constructive algorithms often fail to locate vanishingly small sets of feasible graphs, while traditional Markov-Chain Monte Carlo (MCMC) samplers suffer from severe ergodicity breaking. In this paper, we propose a two-step hybrid framework combining Ant Colony Optimization (ACO) and MCMC sampling to overcome the aforementioned limitations.

Keywords: Graph generation · ACO · MCMC

1 Introduction

Generating graphs with prescribed properties is a well-known problem at the intersection of random graph theory [4,12] and network science [11,14]. From a theoretical perspective, inquiry focuses on constructive existence: Can a member of a graph family $\mathcal{G}$ be generated in polynomial time?

For properties that can be checked in polynomial time, Markov-Chain Monte Carlo (MCMC) methods can be used [15], but these methods often fail due to the lack of ergodicity [5]. To overcome this limitation, we turn to using Ant Colony Optimization (ACO) algorithms [3,6] for their ability to explore $\mathcal{G}$ efficiently by constructing graphs one edge at a time. We utilize ACO-generated graphs as diverse seeds for MCMC. In the nutshell, our two step framework combines ACO to explore $\mathcal{G}$ by finding various seed graphs, and then using MCMC for sampling, yet preserving the desired properties of generated graphs.

In this paper we want to sample graphs with a given number of nodes and edges maintaining the diameter and clustering coefficient within parametrized bounds. Notice, these parameters strongly interact with each other: increasing clustering coefficient creates structural redundancy decreasing the diameter of the graph [13,17]. In applied network analysis, generating ensembles of such strictly constrained graphs is essential for creating rigorous null models allowing researchers to test the statistical significance of complex phenomena observed

P. Neumann et al. (Eds.): ICCS 2026, LNCS 16784, pp. 549–557, 2026.
https://doi.org/10.1007/978-3-032-29924-6_51

in real-world systems against baselines that preserve both local transitivity and global path lengths.

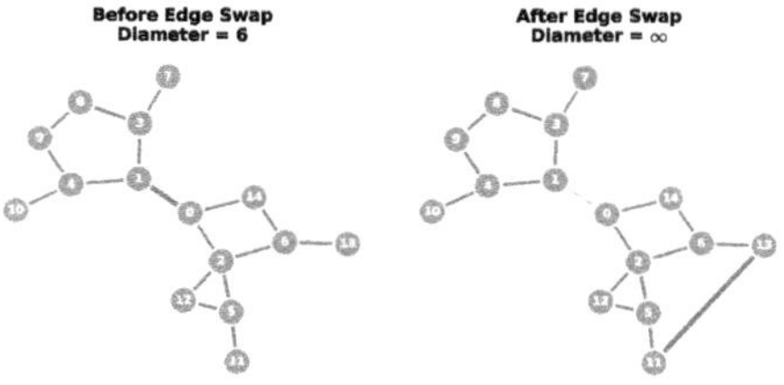

Fig. 1. Impact of an edge swap on diameter. Moving a single red edge from a central position (Left) to a boundary position (Right) fundamentally alters the diameter. (Color figure online)

2 Problem Statement and Preliminaries

Let $G = (V, E)$ be a simple graph on n nodes and m edges. A *triplet* in a graph is 3 nodes connected by two edges, and a *closed triplet* is a graph on 3 nodes, that forms a triangle. If there is at least one triplet in the graph, we refer to $\mathrm{gcc}(G) = \frac{\text{number of closed triplets}}{\text{number of all triplets}}$ as the *global clustering coefficient* and we let $\mathrm{gcc}(G) = 0$ if there are no triplets in the graph. In the literature, this quantity is also referred as *transitivity* or *global clustering coefficient*. The number of closed triplets is 3 times the number of triangles [9]. We will use the notation Δ_G and Λ_G for the number of triangles and triplets, respectively.

The *diameter* of G is defined as $\mathrm{diam}(G) = \max_{u,v \in V} d(u,v)$ and the *eccentricity* of a node $u \in V$ is $\mathrm{ecc}(u) = \max_{v \in V \setminus \{u\}} d(u,v)$, where $d(u,v)$ is the length of the shortest path connecting u and v. Using the eccentricity we can state the following well-known bound for the diameter [9]: $\mathrm{ecc}(v) \leq \mathrm{diam}(G) \leq 2 \cdot \mathrm{ecc}(v)$ for any node $v \in V$.

Now we formally state the problem. Given the number of nodes n, the number of edges m, and intervals $[\mathrm{gcc}_{\min}, \mathrm{gcc}_{\max}]$, $[\mathrm{diam}_{\min}, \mathrm{diam}_{\max}]$, we want to generate a set of graphs $(G_i)_{i=1}^{\ell}$, such that $\mathrm{gcc}(G_i) \in [\mathrm{gcc}_{\min}, \mathrm{gcc}_{\max}]$ and $\mathrm{diam}(G_i) \in [\mathrm{diam}_{\min}, \mathrm{diam}_{\max}]$.

2.1 Simple Edge Swaps

An *edge swap* is simultaneous deletion of an edge between two connected nodes u and v, and insertion of an edge between two disconnected nodes x and y. Such an operation is often used in graph rewiring algorithms [2]. We can see in Fig. 1, that the diameter can behave erratically under simple edge swaps.

For an arbitrary node $x \in V$, we call the set of nodes $N_x = \{u | (u,x) \in E\}$ the neighborhood of x. For the degree of node x, we use the notation δ_x. Note that a naive calculation of $\mathrm{gcc}(G)$ would take $\mathcal{O}(n\langle\delta\rangle^2)$ time, where $\langle\delta\rangle$ is the expected degree in the graph. However, for every swap operation in a graph, we can update the value $\mathrm{gcc}(G)$ in $\mathcal{O}(\delta_{max})$ time as the changes to the triangle count are strictly local.

Incremental Update Rule for gcc. An edge swap between u, v and x, y alters the triangle count Δ_G and triplet count Λ_G locally. Specifically, $\Delta_{\mathrm{new}}(G) = \Delta(G) - |N_u \cap N_v| + |N_x \cap N_y|$, and $\Lambda_{\mathrm{new}} = \Lambda(G) + \delta_x + \delta_y - (\delta_u + \delta_v - 2)$. The updated clustering coefficient is then: $\mathrm{gcc}(G') = 3\Delta_{new}/\Lambda_{new}$.

Effect on the Diameter. Due to the global nature of the diameter, there are no guaranteed bounds for the change of the diameter under edge swaps. Recalculation of the diameter after each attempted edge swap requires an All-Pair-Shortest-Path algorithm, with runtime $\mathcal{O}(n(n + m))$. We can approximate the diameter using the Double-Sweep BFS heuristic [1], that runs in linear time, and outputs an estimator $\hat{D}$, which often coincides with the real diameter [10]. Combining $\hat{D}$ with the eccentricity inequality yields a strict range for the true diameter.

3   Algorithm Overview

We continue by providing an overview of our algorithm.

First, we describe a Metropolis-Hastings algorithm in Subsect. 3.1, that takes a graph as an input and rewires its edges, keeping n and m fixed, while diam and gcc within bounds. This is not a proper graph generation method, as it does not generate graphs from scratch, but it can rewire a given seed graph, and therefore it can serve for sampling.

To generate seeds, we introduce an ACO algorithm in Subsect. 3.2, which can construct graphs given a list of desired parameters. We combine the algorithms by running ACO first to get a set of graphs that can be used as an input for the MCMC to reshuffle, and therefore get uniformly distributed samples.

3.1   Metropolis-Hastings Algorithm

By proposing edge swaps and accepting the new graphs if the new clustering coefficient and diameter are within an acceptable range, we define a rewiring algorithm that keeps both properties within required bounds.

This simple mechanism is in fact a Metropolis-Hastings algorithm, which can be used to sample graphs uniformly at random [5,7,16]. The steps of the procedure are detailed in Algorithm 1.

It can be shown that not every graph can be constructed by MCMC from a given seed graph by rewiring when using only simple edge swaps. This means that the Markov-chain is not ergodic, which is essential for our sample to be truly uniformly distributed. We overcome this limitation by using an ACO algorithm, that generates a set of different starting graphs, that will serve as different seeds for the MCMC.

Algorithm 1. Metropolis-Hastings Step

Require: $(G_t, \Delta_t, \Lambda_t, C_{bounds}, D_{bounds})$
1: $(u, v) \leftarrow \text{rand}(E(G_t)); \quad (x, y) \leftarrow \text{rand}(V^2 \setminus E(G_t))$
2: $G' \leftarrow (G_t \setminus \{(u, v)\}) \cup \{(x, y)\}$
3: Update Δ', Λ', C' via Eq. 1 $\hspace{4cm}$ ▷ Local check
4: **if** $C' \in [C_{\min}, C_{\max}]$ **and** $\text{DOUBLESWEEPBFS}(G') \in [D_{\min}, D_{\max}]$ **then**
5: $\quad$ **return** (G', Δ', Λ') $\hspace{5cm}$ ▷ Accept
6: **else**
7: $\quad$ **return** $(G_t, \Delta_t, \Lambda_t)$ $\hspace{5cm}$ ▷ Reject
8: **end if**

3.2   ACO for Graph Construction

To resolve the ergodicity issue practically, we propose a hybrid framework, where ACO serves as a *constructive* global searcher [3,6]. Using this approach, we can generate a broader variety of structurally different graphs, while keeping our constrained parameters in control.

ACO starts as a random search and governs itself in the direction of feasible solutions by learning from the mistakes and good choices it made while searching. In order to guarantee that the diameter remains within bounds, and exploit the constructive nature of ACO, we are using a layered constructing heuristic.

Layered Construction. In order to guarantee a lower bound $\text{diam}_{\min}$ for the diameter, we split the set of nodes n into $\text{diam}_{min} + 1$ groups $L_1, L_2, \ldots L_{\text{diam}_{\min+1}}$. A layer of nodes is a subset of vertices that constraints the edge formation in order to preserve the diameter. Edges are only allowed to be formed within layers and between neighboring layers. Formally, we create a set $\mathcal{E}_{\text{available}}$, consisting of allowed edges in the graph: $(u, v) \in \mathcal{E}_{\text{available}} \iff |\text{layer}(u) - \text{layer}(v)| \leq 1$.

Pheromones and Edge Probabilities. To continue building our ACO algorithm we need to specify how the pheromone scores affect ants preferences towards certain edges. Let τ_e be the pheromones corresponding to the edge $e = (i, j)$. The probability for an edge being chosen by an ant is given by

$$p_e = \frac{\tau_e}{\sum_{o \in \mathcal{E}_{available}} \tau_o}. \tag{1}$$

Notice, ACO is a repetitive process. In the beginning, the pheromones are assumed to be uniformly distributed, i.e., $\tau_e = 1$ if $e \in \mathcal{E}_{\text{available}}$, and 0 otherwise. At each step of the ACO algorithm, k ants try to construct a valid graph by picking M distinct edges from $\mathcal{E}_{\text{available}}$, where every edge is chosen according to the distribution described by Eq. (1).

Once the k ants have constructed the graphs, we update the pheromone scores on the edges after evaluating the ants performance by using a reward function. We do so by calculating the realized diameter and clustering coefficient, and

---

Algorithm 2. Layered ACO Graph Construction

Require: $n, m, C_{bounds}, D_{bounds}, T$ iterations, K ants
1: Initialize $\tau_{ij} \leftarrow 1, \forall (i,j) \in \mathcal{E}_{avail}$
2: **for** $t = 1 \ldots T$ **do**
3:     **for** $k = 1 \ldots K$ **do**
4:         Construct G_k by sampling m edges $e \in \mathcal{E}_{avail}$ with $p_e \propto \tau_e$
5:         Evaluate R_k using $\text{gcc}(G_k)$ and $\hat{D}(G_k)$
6:     **end for**
7:     $\tau_e \leftarrow (1 - \rho)\tau_e + \sum_{a \in S_{elite}} R_a W_e^a$ ▷ Update via Eq. 1
8: **end for**
9: **return** $\text{argmax}_{G_k}(R_k)$

---

defining the reward function corresponding to the ℓ-th ant's graph as follows:

$$R_k = \begin{cases} \frac{\text{diam}_{\text{valid}}}{\varepsilon + |C^\star - \text{gcc}(G_k)|} & \text{if } \hat{D} \leq D_{max}, \\ \frac{\text{diam}_{\text{invalid}}}{\varepsilon + |C^\star - \text{gcc}(G_k)|} & \text{otherwise}, \end{cases}$$

where $C^\star$ is $\frac{\text{gcc}_{\min} + \text{gcc}_{\max}}{2}$, $\hat{D}$ is the estimation of the diameter acquired by doing a double sweep BFS, and $\text{diam}_{\text{valid}}$, and $\text{diam}_{\text{invalid}}$ are constants used to reward ants that produce graphs with valid diameters. In our implementation, we use 1 and 0.1 for those constants. This reward function is used to update the pheromones on the edges to boost the formation and dissolution of triangles as follows.

Pheromone Score Update. We employ an elitist pheromone update strategy to make sure that the ants who get closer to valid graphs can steer the others to look for solutions. This means that once all the k graphs have been constructed we rank them based on the graphs reward score, and new pheromones are updated based on the elite ants, or, in other words, the graphs associated with the highest fitness values.

To guide the search, we use the fact that the formation of intra-layer edges boosts triangle generation, whereas formation of inter-layer edges shrinks the number of triangles. We use the parameter ρ for pheromone evaporation rate. We implemented $\rho = 0.1$. The pheromone update is given by $\tau_e \leftarrow (1 - \rho)\tau_e + \sum_{a \in S_{\text{elite}}} R_a \cdot W_e^a$ where W_e^a modulates triangle formation based on the target C^*:

$$W_e^a = \begin{cases} B & \text{if } \text{gcc}(G_a) < C^* \text{ and } e \text{ is intra-layer}, \\ & \text{or } \text{gcc}(G_a) > C^* \text{ and } e \text{ is inter-layer}, \\ H & \text{otherwise}, \end{cases} \tag{2}$$

where parameters B and H correspond to boosting and hindering edge formation within or between layers. In our implementation, $B = 2$ and $H = 0.5$. The formal description of the procedure is presented in Algorithm 2.

3.3 Hybrid Framework: From ACO to MCMC

We propose a hybrid strategy that leverages the complementary strengths of ACO and MCMC approaches. We first utilize the ACO algorithm to generate a set of distinct, feasible graph instances satisfying the target requirements n, m, $\mathrm{gcc_{min}}$, $\mathrm{gcc_{max}}$, $\mathrm{diam_{min}}$ and $\mathrm{diam_{max}}$. Unlike random graph generation with prescribed number of edges, which may fail to locate a feasible region in highly constrained spaces, ACO acts as a guided global search to provide valid starting points. By seeding the sampler with topologically diverse solutions from ACO, we ensure the MCMC explores multiple distinct regions in the solution space, thereby generating more representative graph ensemble.

4 Experimental Results

In this section we will report some results on our ACO-MCMC hybrid approach. All code and data for reproducing results are available online[1].

4.1 Success Ratio and Structural Diversity

First we demonstrate the effectiveness of our ACO-MCMC framework for generating structurally diverse graphs. We evaluate the *success ratio* and *structural diversity* for given pairs of diam and gcc for a graph on 40 nodes with various density. Figure 2 shows the success ratio and structural diversity for a fixed edge density.

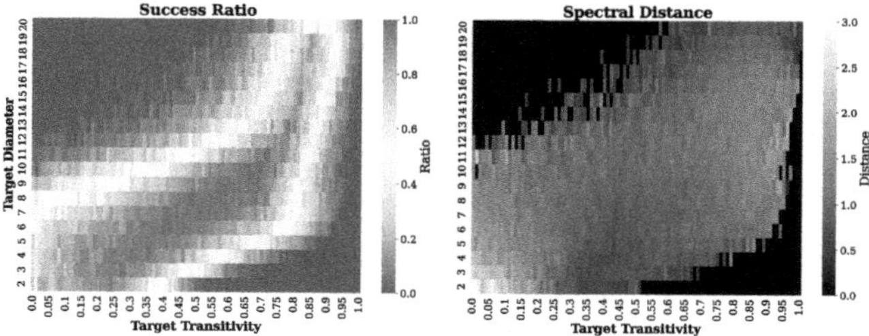

Fig. 2. Success ratio (left) and spectral distance (right) for graphs with edge density 0.2.

For each set of parameters, 100 instances of ACO were run with the input parameters of the number of nodes, edges, gcc and diam. Each instance had 40 ants looking for solutions. *Success ratio* was calculated as the fraction of trials successfully finding graphs satisfying the given constraints.

To quantify the *structural diversity* of the generated graph ensembles, we use the *spectral distance* of the normalized Laplacian [8,19], normalized by the number of nodes. Let G be a graph obtained and let $\boldsymbol{\lambda}(G) = (\lambda_1, \lambda_2, \dots, \lambda_N)$ denote

---

[1] https://github.com/ferenczid/constrained_graph_generation.

the sequence of its normalized Laplacian eigenvalues sorted in non-decreasing order. The spectral distance of G and G' is $d_{\text{spectral}}(G, G') = \sqrt{\frac{\sum_{i=1}^{N}(\lambda_i - \lambda_i')^2}{N}}$.

For a given set of constraints, we generate an ensemble of L valid graphs, denoted as $\mathcal{G} = \{G_1, G_2, \ldots, G_L\}$. To quantify the overall functional diversity of this ensemble, we calculate the mean pairwise spectral distance: $\mathcal{D}_{\text{ensemble}}(\mathcal{G}) = \frac{\sum_{1 \leq i < j \leq L} d_{\text{spectral}}(G_i, G_j)}{\binom{L}{2}}$. This metric represents the average structural variation within the solution space located by the algorithm. A lower value indicates graphs that are structurally similar, where high values show there are structurally different graphs satisfying the constraints [18].

4.2 Difference Between MCMC and Hybrid MCMC

Next, we demonstrate the practical potential of our proposed hybrid framework by testing both, pure MCMC and hybrid MCMC, and measuring the structural difference of the seed and the output graphs of the MCMC and the hybrid MCMC.

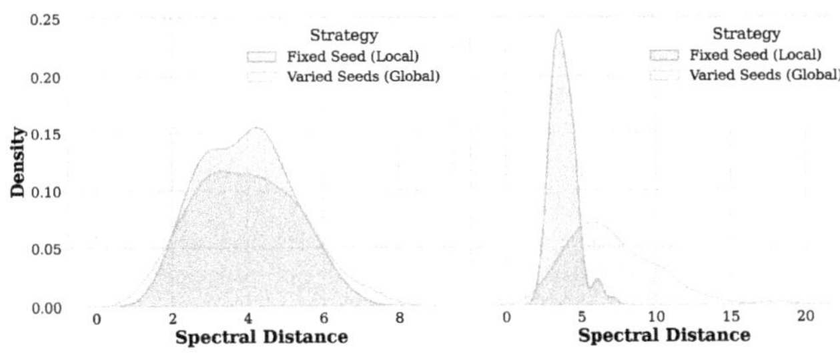

Fig. 3. Estimated density functions of the spectral distance (drift from seed). **Left:** ($n = 40$, $m = 78$, diam $= 12$, gcc $= 0.35$) Both methods find structurally similar solutions. **Right:** ($n = 40$, $m = 195$, diam $= 4$, gcc $= 0.4$) Varied seeds allow for more versatile sample.

As shown in Fig. 3 (**Left**), when the feasible space is heavily constrained, both methods converge to similar structures and their distributions overlap, indicating that standard MCMC is sufficient when the target topology is unique. However, in the case, where the constraints allow for a rich variety of valid graphs (**Right**)a clear divergence appears. While both methods find valid solutions, the standard MCMC remains trapped in the local neighborhood of its initialization (narrow peak). In contrast, the hybrid approach successfully samples from the broader solution space, capturing a much richer set of graphs.

5 Conclusion and Future Work

In this work, we developed and tested an efficient graph generation framework capable to keep in control clustering coefficient and diameter. While this framework already serves as a practical tool for generating valid graphs under given constraints, there are open questions that can be further investigated:

1. Is it possible to theoretically characterize graphs that can be reached from a seed doing edge swaps, while maintaining the constraints for clustering and the diameter?
2. How do competing constraints on local transitivity (clustering) and global path lengths (diameter) interact to shape the overall topology of the graph?
3. Alternatively, could soft-constraint MCMC methods serve as a viable, albeit computationally less efficient, alternative to our guided ACO initialization?

References

1. Aingworth, D., Chekuri, C., Indyk, P., Motwani, R.: Fast estimation of diameter and shortest paths (without matrix multiplication). SIAM J. Comput. (1999). https://doi.org/10.1137/S0097539796303421
2. Alstott, J., Klymko, C., Pyzza, P.B., Radcliffe, M.: Local rewiring algorithms to increase clustering and grow a small world. J. Complex Netw. (2018). https://doi.org/10.1093/comnet/cny032
3. Blum, C.: Ant colony optimization: introduction and recent trends. Phys. Life Rev. (2005). https://doi.org/10.1016/j.plrev.2005.10.001
4. Bollobás, B.: Random Graphs. Cambridge Studies in Advanced Mathematics. Cambridge University Press (2001)
5. Brooks, S., Gelman, A., Jones, G., Meng, X.L.: Handbook of Markov chain Monte Carlo. CRC Press (2011). https://doi.org/10.1201/b10905
6. Dorigo, M., Birattari, M., Stutzle, T.: Ant colony optimization. IEEE Comput. Intell. Mag. (2006). https://doi.org/10.1109/MCI.2006.329691
7. Earl, D.J., Deem, M.W.: Parallel tempering: theory, applications, and new perspectives. Phys. Chem. Chem. Phys. (2005). https://doi.org/10.1039/B509983H
8. Gu, J., Hua, B., Liu, S.: Spectral distances on graphs. Discret. Appl. Math. (2015). https://doi.org/10.1016/j.dam.2015.04.011
9. Hofstad, R.v.d.: Random Graphs and Complex Networks. Cambridge Series in Statistical and Probabilistic Mathematics. Cambridge University Press (2016)
10. Magnien, C., Latapy, M., Habib, M.: Fast computation of empirically tight bounds for the diameter of massive graphs. J. Exper. Algorith. (2009) https://doi.org/10.1145/1412228.1455266
11. Maslov, S., Sneppen, K.: Specificity and stability in topology of protein networks. Science (2002). https://doi.org/10.1126/science.1065103
12. Molloy, M., Reed, B.: A critical point for random graphs with a given degree sequence. Random Struct. Algorit (1995). https://doi.org/10.1002/rsa.3240060204, https://onlinelibrary.wiley.com/doi/abs/10.1002/rsa.3240060204
13. Newman, M.E.J.: The structure and function of complex networks. SIAM Rev. (2003). https://doi.org/10.1137/S003614450342480
14. Newman, M.: Networks (July 2018). https://doi.org/10.1093/oso/9780198805090.001.0001
15. Robert, C.P., Casella, G.: Monte Carlo Statistical Methods. Springer Texts in Statistics. Springer, New York, NY, 2 edn. (2004). https://doi.org/10.1007/978-1-4757-4145-2

16. Sambridge, M.: A parallel tempering algorithm for probabilistic sampling and multimodal optimization. Geophys. J. Inter. (2014)
17. Watts, D.J., Strogatz, S.H.: Collective dynamics of 'small-world' networks. Nature (1998). https://doi.org/10.1038/30918
18. Wills, P., Meyer, F.G.: Metrics for graph comparison: a practitioner's guide. PLoS ONE (2020). https://doi.org/10.1371/journal.pone.0228728
19. Wilson, R.C., Zhu, P.: A study of graph spectra for comparing graphs and trees. Pattern Recogn. (2008). https://doi.org/10.1016/j.patcog.2008.03.011

Evaluating the Effectiveness and Stability of the Constrained Hybrid Metaheuristic Algorithm in Probabilistic Neural Networks Training

Szymon Kucharczyk[1,3]($\boxtimes$) , Piotr A. Kowalski[1,2] , and Jacek Mańdziuk[4,5]

[1] Faculty of Physics and Applied Computer Science, AGH University of Krakow, Krakow, Poland
{kucharcz,pkowal}@agh.edu.pl

[2] Systems Research Institute, Polish Academy of Sciences, Warsaw, Poland

[3] AGH Doctoral School, AGH University of Krakow, Krakow, Poland

[4] Faculty of Mathematics and Information Science, Warsaw University of Technology, Warsaw, Poland
jacek.mandziuk@pw.edu.pl

[5] Faculty of Computer Science, AGH University of Krakow, Krakow, Poland

Abstract. Probabilistic Neural Networks (PNNs) are memory-based networks that have been used successfully for classification and regression tasks. Training of PNNs may be performed by analytical methods, e.g., plug-in or by heuristic methods, e.g., Particle Swarm Optimization. Heuristic methods are superior to traditional PNN training techniques because of their nonparametric behavior, independence of the PNN kernel selection, and ability to optimize method parameters for a given problem. One of the recently proposed training algorithms - *constrained Hybrid Metaheuristic* (cHM), overperformed other analytical and heuristic procedures on a variety of datasets. Here, we present a further evaluation of the cHM method for training PNNs for classification tasks. In particular, we study its effectiveness and stability with different hyperparameters across 10 datasets. The results show that the cHM training procedure is generally stable and the parameter selection does not significantly impact the PNN training accuracy for 8 of 10 tested datasets.

Keywords: Probabilistic Neural Networks · learning procedure · metaheuristic · hybrid metaheuristic · synergy · hyperparameter optimization

P. Neumann et al. (Eds.): ICCS 2026, LNCS 16784, pp. 558–566, 2026.
https://doi.org/10.1007/978-3-032-29924-6_52

1   Introduction

Probabilistic Neural Networks constitute a family of neural models that explicitly embed probabilistic reasoning into learning, making them well-suited for classification and regression tasks [18]. Their core idea is to approximate class-conditional probability distributions from data, usually through kernel density estimation (KDE), and then assign a label by selecting the class that maximizes the estimated likelihood. In contrast to conventional neural networks that learn decision boundaries via iterative weight optimization (e.g., backpropagation), PNNs assess how probable it is that a given input originates from each class distribution and make decisions directly from these distributional comparisons.

PNNs are valued in settings where uncertainty and noise are intrinsic, because probability distributions naturally express ambiguity and support robust decisions. At the same time, their probabilistic structure promotes interpretability by linking outputs to explicit density estimates and prototype contributions, which aligns well with explainability requirements [9] and uncertainty-aware modelling [8]. Despite remaining computational challenges, continued work on optimization and hybridization indicates that PNNs are likely to remain a relevant component of explainable and probabilistic AI.

1.1   Hyperparameter Optimization

Hyperparameter optimization (HPO) is a critical factor in metaheuristic algorithms. Not only does it provide control over the behavior of the algorithm, but it also helps maximize metaheuristic performance for a given problem [3]. The HPO techniques for metaheuristics can be divided into three categories. Simple generate-evaluate methods generate candidate hyperparameter sets and evaluate them all. Iterative generate-evaluate methods perform the generation and evaluation phases repeatedly, testing a new set of hyperparameters in each iteration. A different approach to HPO uses hyperheuristic methods that rely on self-adaptation and hybridization of a few algorithms, aiming at their optimal selection and parameterization. Popular approaches of this type include self-adaptation and hybridization of the Particle Swarm Optimization (PSO) [14,15]. Also, probabilistic models have become very popular in the area of HPO thanks to their ability to model uncertainty in the objective function [1,17].

In this work, the first type of HPO was selected, particularly a GridSearch optimization [2]. This brute-force technique starts with a definition of all possible parameter values to test. Next, the Cartesian product C of all these parameters is produced. Then, the GridSearch algorithm evaluates all parameters from C in the same way. In the end, the evaluation run with the highest performance metric is considered to be the optimal value of the hyperparameters for the given algorithm. Generally, this method can suffer from the curse of dimensionality [2] when the parts of the Cartesian product are large. However, for this study, the parameter set space was selected to omit the issue and test a reasonable space of possible cHM parameter values.

1.2 Motivation and Contribution

The cHM algorithm [7] demonstrated superior performance in PNN training, surpassing both single metaheuristics and traditional statistical methods in terms of accuracy. As a computational intelligence approach, cHM's performance can be further enhanced through HPO. Investigating the impact of HPO on this algorithm offers valuable insights into optimal parameter selection. Moreover, such an analysis shows the algorithm's stability across varying hyperparameter configurations when applied to diverse datasets.

While this study investigates the cHM parameterizations across multiple datasets, it does not aim to compare the computational cost or predictive accuracy of the proposed approach with other PNN training techniques, including conventional and heuristic methods. Instead, the analysis concentrates on the internal parameters of the hybrid method and examines their impact on the overall performance.

The main contributions of this paper are three-fold: **(1)** We conduct a thorough HPO for the cHM method across 10 datasets; **(2)** The best cHM parameters for each dataset are proposed; **(3)** The dependence of the cHM algorithm on the number of iterations, probing, and fit constraints is analyzed.

1.3 Related Work

The training process of PNNs, particularly in determining smoothing parameters, can be divided into two main categories, each with distinct characteristics. The first category includes deterministic methods, e.g. the plug-in [19] procedure. These approaches focus on minimizing the error between the estimated and probability density functions, ensuring that the estimated density closely matches the actual data distribution. As deterministic methods, they consistently produce the same results for the same input data and are particularly effective when the primary objective is accurate density estimation. The second category comprises non-deterministic approaches, including meta-heuristic algorithms like Genetic Algorithms, PSO, Simulated Annealing (SA) and constrained Hybrid Metaheuristic algorithm, as well as reinforcement learning [11] techniques. These methods are tailored to optimize classification performance by adjusting the smoothing parameter to maximize class separability. Although less stable than statistical methods, they offer greater flexibility and the potential to achieve superior results in individual training runs, especially in complex classification tasks where optimal class distinction is crucial. By leveraging their adaptability, non-deterministic methods can outperform statistical techniques under specific conditions. They can deliver exceptional classification accuracy when carefully tuned, making them valuable in scenarios where class separability is a priority [7,10].

2 Methods

When using heuristics, particularly swarm-based algorithms, to train PNNs, each individual within the population is represented as a vector of proposed smoothing parameters. Specifically, an individual corresponds to a vector that contains parameters necessary to configure a PNN for a given dataset [10].

2.1 Constrained Hybrid Metaheuristic

Figure 1 presents the flow diagram of the PNN training with the cHM algorithm. Generally, the training algorithm combines k single (inner) metaheuristics with a shared population to ensemble them into one hybrid training method [7]. It consists of 2 stages: probing and fit. Before the cHM algorithm starts, its internal parameters are initialized:

- $maxFE_{probing}$ ($maxFE_p$) - number of maximum cost function evaluations during the probing phase [20]. This parameter is incremented for each individual for each test sample in the dataset.
- $maxFE_{fit}$ ($maxFE_f$) - maximal number of cost function evaluations during the fit phase [20]. The incrementation strategy is similar to the $maxFE_p$ one.
- n - number of probing and fit phases.
- Random initialization of the population θ, the same for each inner metaheuristic.

Next, the algorithm is executed for n iterations. Firstly, the probing phase is run. In this step, each kth metaheuristic is used to train a PNN until the number of cost function evaluations does not exceed the $maxFE_p$ criteria for each of the k methods. After probing, the population θ_{best} from the best-performing method, in terms of the cost function value, is passed to the fit phase. In the fit phase, the metaheuristic that produced θ_{best} is used for further PNN training. The training continues until the number of cost function evaluations does not exceed the $maxFE_f$ or the PNN training convergence condition is met. In the end, after n probing and fit phases, the best individual from the best population is taken as a final smoothing parameter vector for the PNN construction [7].

In this work, a group of five metaheuristic methods is evaluated as the inner-optimization methods of the cHM algorithm: PSO [5], the Bat algorithm (BAT) [12], Bacterial Foraging Optimization (BFO) [16], SA [6], and the Flower Pollination Algorithm (FPA) [10]. These global optimization techniques are well-established in the literature [13]. Following [7], we adopted the standard versions of these metaheuristics.

2.2 Datasets and Experiment Parameters

In this work, PNNs are constructed using the Cauchy kernel, incorporating distinct smoothing parameters for each feature vector within the dataset. The cHM algorithm is utilized to train the PNNs for classification tasks. The cHM method is initialized with a randomly generated population of individuals, where each individual represents a set of smoothing parameters required for building the PNN. The initial population comprises 20 individuals with parameter values constrained to real numbers in the range [0,10]. The same population is employed

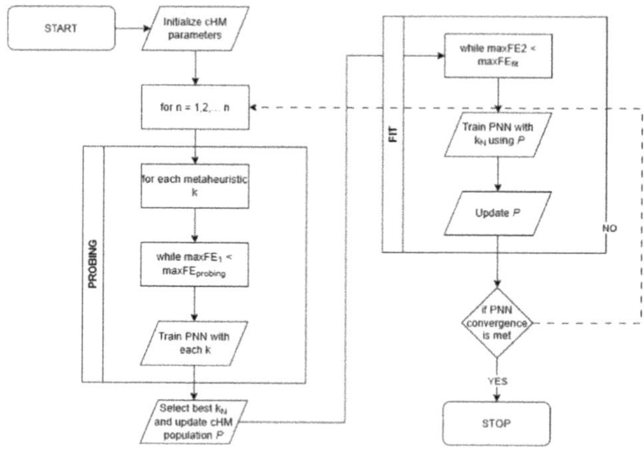

Fig. 1. Block diagram of PNN training using the cHM algorithm.

to initialize each inner optimizer within the cHM procedure. Following [7], the error rate is used as the cost function.

When training PNNs using computational intelligence techniques, the smoothing parameter values during optimization must be constrained due to PNN architecture requirements. The possible values for these parameters are restricted to the interval [0,10000] of real numbers. If a smoothing parameter is found to be negative, the reflection technique [4] is used to ensure that the parameter value is adjusted to be within the permissible positive range.

The specific parameters of the cHM algorithm are summarized in Sect. 3, while the parameters used for each metaheuristic within the cHM framework are detailed in [7]. The cost function convergence threshold is set to $1e-8$.

The performance of PNN training with the cHM algorithm is evaluated on 10 well-known datasets taken UCI repository. Each dataset is stratified into train and test subsets, with the size of the test set comprising 20% of the total dataset. The training process is repeated 10 times for each experiment configuration, for each dataset, enabling the calculation of cumulative (average) metrics, including accuracy, precision, and recall.

3   Experimental Evaluation

The main focus of this research is performing the hyperparameter optimization of cHM for PNN training for various classification tasks. The cHM with different sets of algorithm parameters is used to train PNN and evaluate its performance for classification tasks. The $maxFE_p$ and $maxFE_f$ values for HPO are established proportionally to population size and training set cardinality [7].

3.1 HPO

Table 1 demonstrates $maxFE_p$ and $maxFE_f$ parameter ranges used in the cHM for HPO for each dataset. The value of cHM n was taken from the set of [3,4,5] for each dataset. This gives a sample of 48 parameter sets for each dataset, tested for PNN training using the cHM algorithm (4 probing values * 4 fit values * 3 n values).

In Table 1, the results of the HPO experiment are summarized. For each dataset, the cHM parameters with the highest average accuracy value from 10 runs are presented. To exemplify, the table presents the maximum test accuracy metric from the algorithm run with the highest average test accuracy for given cHM hyperparameters. In addition, Table 1 shows the ratio of $maxFE$'s probing and fit constraints together with the n value for the best run. Generally, cHM usually converged after 3 or 4 iterations, except for the Banknote dataset, where cHM performed best with 5 iterations. The results also indicate that there is no obvious choice for the probing and fit maximum number of function evaluation constraints ($maxFE_p$ and $maxFE_f$). The mean value of the probing/fit (p/f) ratio was 0.291, and the median was 0.3. The ratio distribution suggests there is no clear indication of an optimal ratio value. The detailed results of the correlation between individual cHM parameters and PNN accuracy performance on the test set are presented in Sect. 3.2.

Table 2(a) presents accuracy, precision, and recall metrics on average for all 10 experiment repetitions for all hyperparameters. In addition, the average standard deviation of each metric value is presented. For Iris, Wine, Cancer, ILPD, Parkinson and Climate datasets the standard deviation of each metric was smaller than 10% of the average metric value over all HPO runs. It may indicate that the cHM has similar training performance with various hyperparameters for these datasets. For the Glass, Ecoli, Heart and Banknote datasets, the average standard deviation across all HPO runs was significantly higher. This may imply the impact of cHM hyperparameters and algorithm randomness on the PNN training performance. The results for these three datasets require further studies of parameter selection for these datasets.

3.2 cHM Parameters Impact on PNN Training Performance

To determine the dependence of cHM hyperparameters on the performance of PNN training, Pearson and Spearman correlation coefficients were calculated to evaluate the linear and monotonic relationship between variables. For this purpose, $maxFE_p$, $maxFE_f$ and n were assumed to be independent of each other. The correlation coefficients were calculated separately for each dataset, with a degree of freedom equal to 46, which comes from $n_{samples} - 2$. Pearson's α and Spearman's $p - value$ were set to 0.05. The t_s and t_c stand for T-statistics statistical and critical values for the Pearson correlation, respectively. The p_s represents a p value for the Spearman correlation. The null hypothesis stated that there is a relationship between each parameter and the average test accuracy metric value for PNN trained with the cHM algorithm. If the absolute value of t_s

Table 1. HPO experiment. Tested and finally selected parameter values with the corresponding optimization results. The $maxFE_p$ and $maxFE_f$ values are in thousands of feature evaluations, e.g., 48 equals 48 000 FE.

Dataset	Ranges		Selected cHM parameters			Performance			Ratio
	$maxFE_p$	$maxFE_f$	$maxFE_p$	$maxFE_f$	n	avg acc	avg prec	avg recall	pf_ratio
Iris	[24, 48, 72, 120]	[120, 240, 480, 720]	72000	240000	3	0.937	0.938	0.937	0.3
Cancer	[91, 182, 273, 455]	[455, 910, 1820, 2730]	273000	910000	4	0.959	0.957	0.954	0.3
Wine	[28.4, 56.8, 85.2, 142]	[142, 284, 568, 852]	85200	284000	3	0.892	0.897	0.893	0.3
ILPD	[92.6, 185.2, 277.8, 463]	[463, 926, 1852, 2778]	185200	1852000	3	0.668	0.604	0.611	0.1
Glass	[34.2, 68.4, 102.6, 171]	[171, 342, 684, 1026]	171000	684000	4	0.588	0.576	0.504	0.25
Parkinson	[31.2, 62.4, 93.6, 156]	[156, 312, 624, 936]	31200	312000	4	0.931	0.905	0.917	0.1
Ecoli	[53, 106, 159, 265]	[265, 530, 1060, 1590]	265000	530000	4	0.742	0.648	0.526	0.5
Heart	[47.4, 94.8, 142.2, 237]	[237, 474, 948, 1422]	237000	1422000	4	0.442	0.290	0.251	0.167
Climate	[86.4, 172.8, 259.2, 432]	[432, 864, 1728, 2592]	259200	432000	3	0.858	0.505	0.504	0.6
Banknote	[219.4, 438.8, 658.2, 1097]	[1097, 2194, 4388, 6582]	2194000	1097000	5	0.997	0.996	0.997	0.5

Table 2. (a) Test set performance metrics from HPO. (b) Correlation results between cHM parameters (n and $maxFE_p$) and average test accuracy of trained PNN. $t_c = 2.013$ was used in all experiments.

(a)

Dataset	Accuracy		Precision		Recall	
	Mean	Std	Mean	Std	Mean	Std
Iris	0.916	0.027	0.918	0.026	0.916	0.027
Cancer	0.948	0.010	0.948	0.010	0.941	0.012
Wine	0.831	0.084	0.840	0.078	0.833	0.083
ILPD	0.650	0.022	0.587	0.025	0.594	0.028
Glass	0.529	0.088	0.488	0.121	0.434	0.096
Parkinson	0.911	0.033	0.879	0.042	0.900	0.043
Ecoli	0.702	0.079	0.576	0.135	0.455	0.088
Heart	0.401	0.049	0.246	0.043	0.217	0.035
Climate	0.849	0.014	0.489	0.036	0.492	0.033
Banknote	0.984	0.028	0.984	0.028	0.985	0.028

(b)

Dataset	n				$maxFE_p$			
	$corr_p$	t_s	$corr_s$	p_s	$corr_p$	t_s	$corr_s$	p_s
Iris	-0.065	-0.444	-0.033	0.826	-0.224	-1.561	-0.175	0.233
Cancer	0.183	1.263	0.23	0.115	-0.024	-0.166	-0.032	0.830
Wine	-0.267	-1.881	-0.268	0.065	-0.042	-0.286	-0.023	0.877
ILPD	-0.136	-0.932	-0.114	0.439	-0.116	-0.789	-0.125	0.399
Glass	0.146	1.004	0.172	0.242	0.239	1.671	0.256	0.079
Parkinson	-0.328	-2.354	-0.310	0.032	-0.300	-2.134	-0.333	0.021
Ecoli	-0.155	-1.063	-0.168	0.255	0.124	0.844	0.136	0.357
Heart	0.019	0.126	0.066	0.654	0.132	0.903	0.044	0.764
Climate	0.202	1.399	0.182	0.216	-0.082	-0.555	-0.093	0.529
Banknote	-0.006	-0.042	-0.060	0.686	0.364	2.653	0.315	0.029

was higher than t_c, the null hypothesis cannot be rejected, and there might be a linear relationship between variables according to the Pearson correlation theory. If p_s is lower than $p-value$ for the Spearman correlation, the null hypothesis may not be rejected, and the examined variables might have a monotonic relationship.

Table 2(b) demonstrates the correlation coefficients of Pearson $corr_p$ and Spearman $corr_s$ between the cHM parameter n and the average test accuracy of the PNN trained with the cHM method. The results indicate that there might be a relationship between the cHMs n value and the average test accuracy of PNN classification for the Parkinson dataset. For other datasets, calculations did not show significant evidence to assume such a relationship. Similarly, Table 2 b) presents that a relationship between the average test accuracy metric of PNN and the cHMs $maxFE_p$ for Parkinson and Banknote datasets cannot be rejected.

4   Conclusions

In this paper, Hyperparameter Optimization of the cHM algorithm for PNN training is conducted on 10 classification datasets. Although no clear optimal values for the probing and fit constraints are identified, the best performance is typically achieved within 3–4 iterations (n). The parameters $maxFE_p$ and $maxFE_f$ should be selected based on dataset characteristics, using Table 1 or via dedicated HPO. The results in this table indicate low metric variability, confirming the robustness of the cHM algorithm across different parameter settings. Correlation analysis (Table 2 b)) revealed potential relationships between cHM parameters and performance only for the Parkinson and Banknote datasets. Future work may include evaluating the impact of varying the number of inner optimizers and improving population transfer between cHM phases.

Acknowledgments. SK and PK were partially supported by the program, Excellence Initiative research university" for the AGH University of Krakow and by a Grant for Statutory Activity from the Faculty of Physics and Applied Computer Science of the AGH. JM was partially supported by the National Science Centre, Poland, grant number 2023/49/B/ST6/01404.

References

1. Arsenault, B.: Learning to optimize. Articulon (2018). https://articulon.bradleyarsenault.me/article/learning-to-optimize
2. Feurer, M., Hutte, F.: Chapter 1. Hyperparameter Optimization. Springer (2019)
3. Huang, C., Li, Y., Yao, X.: A survey of automatic parameter tuning methods for metaheuristics. IEEE TEVC **24**(2), 201–216 (2020)
4. Innocente, M., Sienz, J.: Constraint-handling techniques for particle swarm optimization algorithms (Jan 2021). https://doi.org/10.48550/arXiv.2101.10933
5. Kennedy, J., Eberhart, R.: Particle swarm optimization. In: Proceedings of ICNN 1995. vol. 4, pp. 1942–1948 (1995)
6. Kirkpatrick, S., Gelatt, C., Vecchi, M.: Optimization by simulated annealing. Science (New York) **220**, 671–80 (1983)
7. Kowalski, P.A., Kucharczyk, S., Mańdziuk, J.: Constrained hybrid metaheuristic algorithm for probabilistic neural networks learning. Inform. Sci. **713**, 122185 (2025). https://doi.org/10.1016/j.ins.2025.122185
8. Kowalski, P.A., Kulczycki, P.: Interval probabilistic neural network. Neural Comput. Appl. **28**, 817–834 (2017)
9. Kowalski, P.A., Kusy, M.: Determining significance of input neurons for probabilistic neural network by sensitivity analysis procedure. Comput. Intell. **34**(3), 895–916 (2018). https://doi.org/10.1111/coin.12149
10. Kowalski, P.A., Wadas, K.: Triggering probabilistic neural networks with flower pollination algorithm. Comput. Intell. Mat. Tackling Complex Problems (2019)
11. Kusy, M., Zajdel, R.: Application of reinforcement learning algorithms for the adaptive computation of the smoothing parameter for probabilistic neural network. IEEE Trans. Neural Netw. Learn. Syst. **9**(26), 2163–2175 (2015)

12. Naik S.M., Jagannath R.P.K., Kuppili, V.: Bat algorithm-based weighted laplacian probabilistic neural network. Neural Comput & Applic **32**, 1157–1171 (2020)
13. Okulewicz, M., Mańdziuk, J.: The impact of particular components of the PSO-based algorithm solving the dynamic vehicle routing problem. Appl. Soft Comput. **58**, 586–604 (2017). https://doi.org/10.1016/j.asoc.2017.04.070
14. Okulewicz, M., Zaborski, M., Mańdziuk, J.: Generalized self-adapting particle swarm optimization algorithm with archive of samples (2020). https://arxiv.org/abs/2002.12485
15. Okulewicz, M., Zaborski, M., Mańdziuk, J.: Self-adapting particle swarm optimization for continuous black box optimization. Appl. Soft Comput. **131**, 109722 (2022). https://doi.org/10.1016/j.asoc.2022.109722
16. Passino, K.: Biomimicry of bacterial foraging for distributed optimization and control. IEEE Control Systems Mag. **22**(3), 52-67 (2002). https://doi.org/10.1109/MCS.2002.1004010
17. Sieradzki, S., Mańdziuk, J.: Modified adaptive tree-structured parzen estimator for hyperparameter optimization (2025). https://arxiv.org/abs/2502.00871
18. Specht, D.F.: Probabilistic neural networks. Neural Netw. **3**(1), 109–118 (1990)
19. Wand, M.P., Jones, M.C., et al.: Multivariate plug-in bandwidth selection. Comput. Stat. **9**(2), 97–116 (1994)
20. Wu, G., Mallipeddi, R., Suganthan, P.: Problem definitions and evaluation criteria for the cec 2017 competition and special session on constrained single objective real-parameter optimization (Oct 2016)

Three-Dimensional Collocation-Based Robust Variational Physics Informed Neural Networks

Tomasz Służalec$^{(\boxtimes)}$, Marcin Łoś , and Maciej Paszyński

AGH University of Krakow, Krakow, Poland
{sluzalec,los,paszynsk}@agh.edu.pl

Abstract. Physics Informed Neural Networks (PINNs) are an increasingly popular approach to utilizing tools and infrastructure developed for neural network training to solve PDEs. While the mainstream approach is based on strong formulations, Variational PINNs (VPINNs) have been proposed to tackle problems with lower regularity. Their issues with robustness, which manifest as a disconnect between the value of the loss function used for training and the error in the relevant Sobolev norm , can be alleviated by employing Robust Variational PINNs (RVPINNs) at the expense of efficiency due to the cost of integrating terms involving the neural network and factorizing the Gram matrix. Collocation-based Robust Variational PINNs (CRVPINN) aim to regain the efficiency of PINNs while retaining robustness by applying the RVPINN framework to variational formulations based on discrete grids and finite difference approximations.Here, we extend the CRVPINN method to 3D and validate it on Poisson and advection-diffusion problems.

Keywords: Collocation method · Robust loss · Physics Informed Neural Networks · Advection-diffusion problem

1 Introduction

The rapid development of deep learning has significantly influenced numerical methods for solving Partial Differential Equations (PDEs) (see, e.g., [3,5]). Physics-Informed Neural Networks (PINNs) [7] incorporate physical constraints into neural network training by minimizing strong-form residuals at collocation points. While flexible and mesh-free, classical PINNs often suffer from stability and convergence issues, which become more pronounced in three-dimensional problems due to increased computational costs and ill-conditioning. Variational Physics-Informed Neural Networks (VPINNs) [4] address some of these limitations by constructing loss functions based on weak formulations. However, the original VPINN framework lacks robustness at the discrete level. Robust VPINNs (RVPINNs) [8] resolve this issue by introducing Gram-matrix-weighted norms that ensure consistency between discrete and continuous formulations. Despite their theoretical soundness, RVPINNs require costly numerical integration and dense matrix operations, limiting their scalability in higher

P. Neumann et al. (Eds.): ICCS 2026, LNCS 16784, pp. 567–574, 2026.
https://doi.org/10.1007/978-3-032-29924-6_53

dimensions. In [12], we introduced Collocation-Based Robust Variational PINNs (CRVPINNs), combining point-collocation with a Gram-matrix-weighted loss and LU-based solver strategy. The method was validated in two spatial dimensions on Laplace, advectiondiffusion, Stokes, NavierStokes, and linear elasticity problems, demonstrating improved efficiency while preserving robustness.

We extend the CRVPINN framework to 3D PDEs. By discretizing the weak formulation directly at collocation points, we obtain a sparse Gram matrix resembling finite-difference operators [10]. Its one-time LU factorization enables efficient evaluation of the robust loss via forward and backward substitutions, yielding a scalable and stable formulation suitable for 3D problems.

2 Mathematical Formulation of 3D CRVPINN

We extend the CRVPINN method [12] to 3D. Let us consider the unit cube $\Omega = (0, 1)^3$ and a set of uniformly distributed collocation points

$$\Omega_h := \{(ih, jh, kh) : 0 \le i, j, k \le N\}, \tag{1}$$

where $h = 1/N$ is the point spacing for some fixed grid size N. Our discrete formulations will be built using subspaces of the space of real functions on Ω_h:

$$D_h := \{u \colon \Omega_h \to \mathbb{R}\} \cong \mathbb{R}^{(N+1)^3}. \tag{2}$$

Mimicking the continuous theory, we can endow it with a scalar product and its induced norm:

$$(u, v)_h := h^3 \sum_{\boldsymbol{x} \in \Omega_h} u(\boldsymbol{x})v(\boldsymbol{x}), \qquad \|u\|_h^2 := (u, u)_h. \tag{3}$$

These make D_h a $(N+1)^3$-dimensional Hilbert space with a natural orthogonal basis $\{\delta^{ijk}\}$ given by

$$\delta^{ijk}(\boldsymbol{x}) = \begin{cases} 1 & \text{if } \boldsymbol{x} = (ih, jh, kh) \\ 0 & \text{otherwise.} \end{cases} \tag{4}$$

To simplify notation, we shall write u_{ijk} to denote $u(ih, jh, kh)$. Derivatives are replaced with finite difference approximations:

$$\nabla^+ u_{ijk} := \left(\nabla_x^+ u_{ijk}, \nabla_y^+ u_{ijk}, \nabla_z^+ u_{ijk}\right), \quad \nabla^- u_{ijk} := \left(\nabla_x^- u_{ijk}, \nabla_y^- u_{ijk}, \nabla_z^- u_{ijk}\right)$$

$$Dcu_{ijk} := \left(\nabla_x^c u_{ijk}, \nabla_y^c u_{ijk}, \nabla_z^c u_{ijk}\right) \tag{5}$$

where

$$\begin{aligned}
\nabla_x^+ u_{ijk} &= \frac{u_{i+1,j,k} - u_{ijk}}{h}, & \nabla_x^- u_{ijk} &= \frac{u_{ijk} - u_{i-1,j,k}}{h}, \\
\nabla_y^+ u_{ijk} &= \frac{u_{i,j+1,k} - u_{ijk}}{h}, & \nabla_y^- u_{ijk} &= \frac{u_{ijk} - u_{i,j-1,k}}{h}, \\
\nabla_z^+ u_{ijk} &= \frac{u_{i,j,k+1} - u_{ijk}}{h}, & \nabla_z^- u_{ijk} &= \frac{u_{ijk} - u_{i,j,k-1}}{h}, \\
\nabla_\alpha^c u &= \frac{1}{2}\left(\nabla_\alpha^+ u + \nabla_\alpha^- u\right)
\end{aligned} \tag{6}$$

for these indices (i, j, k) for which the right-hand side is defined, and zero otherwise. We can define a degenerate scalar product and a corresponding seminorm, mimicking the continuous H_0^1 concepts:

$$(u, v)_{\nabla, h} := \left(\nabla_x^+ u, \nabla_x^+ v\right)_h + \left(\nabla_y^+ u, \nabla_y^+ v\right)_h + \left(\nabla_z^+ u, \nabla_z^+ v\right)_h$$
$$\|u\|_{\nabla, h}^2 := (u, u)_{\nabla, h} = \left\|\nabla_x^+ u\right\|_{\nabla, h}^2 + \left\|\nabla_y^+ u\right\|_{\nabla, h}^2 + \left\|\nabla_z^+ u\right\|_{\nabla, h}^2 . \tag{7}$$

When restricted to the subspace

$$D_{0,h} := \left\{ u \in D_h : u|_{\partial \Omega_h} = 0 \right\}, \quad \partial \Omega_h := \partial \Omega \cap \Omega_h \tag{8}$$

of functions that vanish on the discrete boundary points, these two become a scalar product and a norm, respectively.

Advection-Diffusion formulation. In our numerical examples, we solve the advection-diffusion equations of the form

$$-\epsilon \Delta u + \beta \cdot \nabla u = f \tag{9}$$

with Dirichlet boundary conditions. The corresponding discrete problem posed in D_h spaces can be formulated as: find $u \in D_{0,h}$ such that

$$-\epsilon \Delta_h u + \beta \cdot \nabla^c u = f \tag{10}$$

where $\nabla^c = \frac{1}{2}(\nabla^+ + \nabla^-)$ is the central difference operator. By forming $(\cdot, \cdot)_h$-product with testing functions $v \in D_{0,h}$, we obtain a discrete variational formulation: find $u \in D_{0,h}$ such that

$$\underbrace{\epsilon \left(\nabla^+ u, \nabla^+ v\right)_h + (\beta \cdot \nabla^c u, v)_h}_{b(u,v)} = \underbrace{(f, v)_h}_{l(v)} \tag{11}$$

holds for all $v \in D_{0,h}$. We can prove that the above problem is well-posed by showing that b is bounded and coercive with respect to the $\|\cdot\|_{\nabla, h}$ norm and invoking the Lax-Milgram theorem [1].

Collocation Variational Physics Informed Neural Networks. In the PINN approach, the neural network is used as the direct representation of the solution of a PDE. We seek to solve scalar problems posed on a three-dimensional domain, so our neural network accepts a vector (x, y, z) as input and outputs a single value:

$$u_\theta(x, y, z) = NN(x, y, z) = \sigma_n(A_n \sigma_{n-1}(\cdots \sigma_1(A_1 \begin{bmatrix} x \\ y \\ z \end{bmatrix} + \beta_1) \cdots) + \beta_n) \tag{12}$$

where A are layer weights, σ are nonlinear activation functions, and β are biases. Following the CRVPINN approach introduced in [12], we train the neural network by minimizing a loss function constructed as the norm of the Riesz representative of the residual of the variational formulation from Eq. (11). More precisely, the loss function is defined as

$$\mathcal{L}(\theta) = \|r(\theta)\|_{\nabla, h}^2 \tag{13}$$

where $r(\theta) \in D_{0,h}$ is the unique element such that $(r(\theta), v)_{\nabla,h} = b(u_\theta, v) - l(v)$ for all $v \in D_{0,h}$. Applying the theory from [9] to the variational formulation Eq. (11), we obtain the following bounds on the true error in terms of value of the loss function. A practical way of evaluating the robust loss is by computing $\mathcal{L}(\theta) = r(\theta)^T G r(\theta) = \mathrm{RES}(\theta)^T G^{-1} \mathrm{RES}(\theta)$. The following theorem highlights what robustness means here.

Theorem 1 (Robustness). *Let the loss function $\mathcal{L}$ be given by Eq. (13). Then*

$$\frac{1}{\mu}\sqrt{\mathcal{L}(\theta)} \leq \|u_\theta - u_{EXACT}\|_{\nabla,h} \leq \frac{1}{\alpha}\sqrt{\mathcal{L}(\theta)}, \tag{14}$$

where u_{EXACT} denotes the exact solution of the variational formulation Eq. (11), and μ, α are the boundedness and coercivity constants of b.

Let $r(\theta)$ denote the vector of coefficients of $r(\theta)$, and $\mathrm{RES}(\theta)$ denote the vector of values of $b(u_\theta, v) - l(v)$, where v ranges over the basis functions of $D_{0,h}$. We can compute $r(\theta)$ by solving

$$G r(\theta) = \mathrm{RES}(\theta) \tag{15}$$

where G is the Gram matrix of the scalar product that makes b bounded and coercive. In the case of advection-diffusion equations, $(\cdot, \cdot)_{\nabla,h}$ satisfies that condition, so we employ the Gram matrix of this scalar product in our numerical tests. Since

$$\begin{aligned}
\left(u, \delta^{ijk}\right)_{\nabla,h} &= \left(\nabla_x^+ u, \nabla_x^+ \delta^{ijk}\right)_h = -\left(\nabla_x^- \left(\nabla_x^+ u\right), \delta^{ijk}\right)_h \\
&= -\left(\Delta_h u, \delta^{ijk}\right)_h = -h^3 \left(\Delta_h u\right)_{ijk} \\
&= h\big[6u_{ijk} - (u_{i+1,j,k} + u_{i-1,j,k} + u_{i,j+1,k} \\
&\quad + u_{i,j-1,k} + u_{i,j,k+1} + u_{i,j,k-1})\big]
\end{aligned} \tag{16}$$

the entries of the Gram matrix can be computed as

$$G_{ijk}^{pqr} = h \begin{cases}
6 & \text{if } (i,j,k) = (p,q,r) \\
-1 & \text{if } p = i \pm 1, \ (q,r) = (j,k) \\
-1 & \text{if } q = j \pm 1, \ (p,r) = (i,k) \\
-1 & \text{if } r = k \pm 1, \ (p,q) = (i,j) \\
0 & \text{otherwise}
\end{cases} \tag{17}$$

Then, the loss function can be computed as

$$\mathcal{L}(\theta) = r(\theta)^T G r(\theta) = \mathrm{RES}(\theta)^T G^{-1} \mathrm{RES}(\theta) \tag{18}$$

To achieve efficient evaluation, we assemble the Gram matrix and compute its Cholesky factorization before the training process. Since the matrix does not change during training, this is a one-time upfront cost. Furthermore, since G

is symmetric and positive definite, factorizing it is easier than factorizing the matrix of the bilinear form b.

Three-Dimensional Laplace Problem with Sine Functions as the Right Hand Side

In the strong formulation, we seek a solution u on $\Omega \subset (0,1)^3$ such that

$$- \Delta u = f \tag{19}$$

In our examples, we will calculate the manufactured solution with Dirichlet boundary conditions. For a given $u(x,y,z) = \sin(2\pi x)\sin(2\pi y)\sin(2\pi z)$, we obtain the right hand side

$$f(x,y,z) = -\Delta u(x,y,z) = -12\pi^2 \sin(2\pi x)\sin(2\pi y)\sin(2\pi z) \tag{20}$$

Then our residual in the CRVPINN is a vector defined as follows:

$$\mathrm{RES}(\Theta)_{ijk} = \Delta u(\boldsymbol{x}_{ijk}) + f(\boldsymbol{x}_{ijk}), \quad 0 < i,j,k < N. \tag{21}$$

The last layer of the neural net is the calculation presented in [11], which enforces Dirichlet boundary conditions. The loss in the CRVPINN is calculated as (18).

Three-Dimensional Laplace Problem with Exp-Sin-Sin as the Right-Hand Side. The second model problem taken into account is related to the Laplace problem Eq. (19). We construct the manufactured solution that includes the sine and exponential functions $u(x,y,z) = -e^{\pi(x-2y)}sin(2\pi x)sin(\pi y)sin(\pi\ t)$. The interpretation is that we have a peak spot with high values in one corner of the cube. Then we can calculate the right hand side of the problem, $f = \Delta u$, namely

$$f = e^{\pi(x-2y)}\pi^2(4\cos(\pi y)\sin(2\pi x) + (-4\cos(2\pi x) + \sin(2\pi x))\sin(\pi y))\sin(\pi z) \tag{22}$$

Then, the residual is defined this way

$$\mathrm{RES}(\Theta)_{ijk} = \Delta u(\boldsymbol{x}_{ijk}) + f(\boldsymbol{x}_{ijk}), \quad 0 < i,j,k < N. \tag{23}$$

The computation of the CRVPINN loss is as follows (18).

Eriksson-Johnson Model Problem. [2]. We consider the advection vector in the y direction; then $\beta = [0,1,0]$, $\epsilon = 0.1$, and our formula in 3D is as follows:

$$\frac{\partial u}{\partial y} + \epsilon \frac{\partial^2 u}{\partial x^2} + \epsilon \frac{\partial^2 u}{\partial y^2} + \epsilon \frac{\partial^2 u}{\partial y^2} = 0 \tag{24}$$

We also define the specific boundary conditions. There are zero Dirichlet boundary conditions on 5 planes, and there is a source of pollution on one plane.

$$f_3 = \begin{cases} \sin(\pi x)\sin(\pi y), & \text{on} \quad (x,y,0) \quad x \in (0,1), y \in (0,1) \\ 0, & \text{on} \quad (x,0,z),(0,y,z) \quad x,y,z \in (0,1) \\ 0, & \text{on} \quad (1,y,z),(x,1,z),(x,y,1) \quad x,y,z \in (0,1) \end{cases} \tag{25}$$

We introduce the shift for the boundary conditions.

$$u_{\text{shift}}(x, y, z) = \sin(\pi x)(1 - y)\sin(\pi z) \qquad (26)$$

We can clearly see that $u(x, y, z) - u_{\text{shift}}(x, y, z) = 0$ on $\partial\Omega$. We will find a solution for the shifted u, namely $NN(x, t, z) = u(x, y, z) - u_{\text{shift}}(x, y, z)$, so our neural net approximating the solution can be enforced to have zero Dirichlet boundary conditions [11]. Now we can define the residual for $0 < i, j, k < N$,

$$\text{RES}(\Theta)_{ijk} = \frac{\partial u}{\partial y}(\boldsymbol{x}_{ijk}) - \epsilon \Delta u(\boldsymbol{x}_{ijk}) + \frac{\partial u_{\text{shift}}}{\partial y}(\boldsymbol{x}_{ijk}) - \epsilon \Delta u_{\text{shift}}(\boldsymbol{x}_{ijk}). \qquad (27)$$

Our loss for this problem also comes in the form of (18).The exact solution to this problem is as follows.

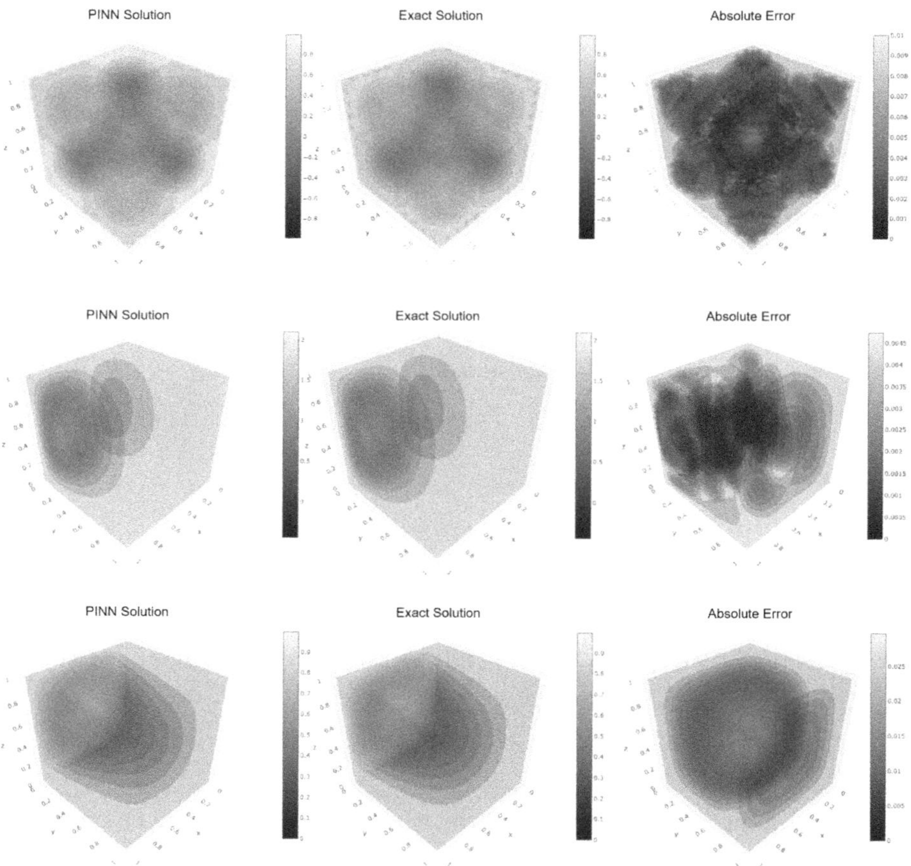

Fig. 1. First row: Laplace problem with sin-sin-sin. Second row: Laplace problem with sin-exp-sin. Third row: Eriksson-Johnson problem. First solumn: CRVPINN solution. Second column: Exact solution. Third column: point-wise error.

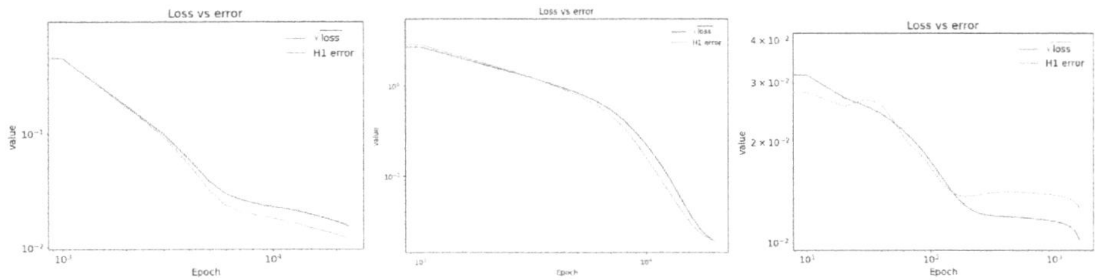

Fig. 2. Convergence of training for the Laplace problem with sin-sin-sin, the Laplace problem with sin-exp-sin, and the Eriksson-Johnson problem. Comparison of the square root of the robust loss and the H^1 norm of the solution (see Theorem 1).

$$u_{\text{exact}}(x,y,z) = \frac{e^{\alpha_1(1-y)} - e^{\alpha_2(1-y)}}{e^{-\alpha_1} - e^{-\alpha_2}} \sin(\pi x) \sin(\pi y) \tag{28}$$

where $\alpha_1 = \frac{1-\sqrt{1+(4\pi\epsilon)^2}}{4\epsilon}$, $\quad \alpha_2 = \frac{1+\sqrt{1+(4\pi\epsilon)^2}}{4\epsilon}$.

3   Numerical Results

The solution was obtained by our CRVPINN code written in python and pytorch. We employ a fully connected neural network with 2 layers and 100 neurons per layer. The input to the neural network is (x,y,z); the output is $u(x,y,z)$. We selected the activation function according to [6]. The last layer applied the pinning technique to obtain specific boundary conditions [11]. We use the Adam optimizer and a different number of epochs in our numerical experiments. Our code can be run on Google Colab Pro with an A100 graphics card to perform fast GPU computations. For the first problem, we used $20 \times 20 \times 20$ mesh; for the second and third problems, we used $40 \times 40 \times 40$ mesh. To obtain higher accuracy, we need to either increase the number of collocation points or consider non-uniform adaptive distributions, particularly for the Eriksson-Johnson problem (Fig. 1 and 2).

4   Conclusions

We extended the Collocation Robust Variational Physics-Informed Neural Network framework to 3D problems. The proposed approach preserves the computational efficiency of standard PINNs while significantly improving robustness through a carefully designed loss function. Numerical experiments confirm that the resulting loss provides a reliable indicator of the true discretization error. The proposed methodology is general and can be applied to a wide range of three-dimensional PDEs. For each new problem, the key step is the design of a suitable inner product that reflects the structure of the weak formulation. This positions CRVPINNs as a robust and flexible alternative to standard PINNs, closely related in spirit to residual minimization and PetrovGalerkin techniques, while remaining well suited for high-dimensional problems.

Acknowledgments. This work has been supported by the National Science Centre, Poland grant no. 2025/57/B/ST6/00058.

References

1. Ciarlet, P.G.: The finite element method for elliptic problems. No. v. 4 in Studies in mathematics and its applications, North-Holland Pub. Co. ; sole distributors for the U.S.A. and Canada, Elsevier North-Holland, Amsterdam; New York : New York (1978)
2. Eriksson, K., Johnson, C.: Adaptive streamline diffusion finite element methods for stationary convection-diffusion problems. Math. Comput. **60**(201), 167–188 (1993)
3. Hinton, G., et al.: Deep neural networks for acoustic modeling in speech recognition: the shared views of four research groups. IEEE Signal Processing Mag. **29**(6), 82–97 (2012)
4. Kharazmi, E., Zhang, Z., Karniadakis, G.E.: Variational physics-informed neural networks for solving partial differential equations. arXiv preprint arXiv:1912.00873 (2019)
5. Krizhevsky, A., Sutskever, I., Hinton, G.E.: Imagenet classification with deep convolutional neural networks. Commun. ACM **60**(6), 84–90 (2017)
6. Maczuga, P., Paszyński, M.: Influence of activation functions on the convergence of physics-informed neural networks for 1d wave equation. In: International Conference on Computational Science, pp. 74–88. Springer (2023). https://doi.org/10.1007/978-3-031-35995-8_6
7. Raissi, M., Perdikaris, P., Karniadakis, G.E.: Physics-informed neural networks: a deep learning framework for solving forward and inverse problems involving nonlinear partial differential equations. J. Comput. Phys. **378**, 686–707 (2019)
8. Rojas, S., Maczuga, P., Muñoz-Matute, J., Pardo, D., Paszyński, M.: Robust variational physics-informed neural networks. Comput. Methods Appl. Mech. Eng. **425**, 116904 (2024)
9. Rojas, S., Maczuga, P., Muñoz-Matute, J., Pardo, D., Paszyński, M.: Robust variational physics-informed neural networks. Comput. Methods Appli. Mech. Eng. **425**, 116904 (2024)
10. Shin, D., Strikwerda, J.C.: Inf-sup conditions for finite-difference approximations of the stokes equations. ANZIAM J. **39**(1), 121–134 (1997)
11. Sun, L., Gao, H., Pan, S., Wang, J.X.: Surrogate modeling for fluid flows based on physics-constrained deep learning without simulation data. Comput. Methods Appl. Mech. Eng. **361**, 112732 (2020)
12. Łoś, M., Służalec, T., Maczuga, P., Vilkha, A., Uriarte, C., Paszyński, M.: Collocation-based robust variational physics-informed neural networks (CRVPINNs). Comput. Struct. **316**, 107839 (2025)

HuSc3D: Human Sculpture Dataset for 3D Object Reconstruction

Weronika Smolak-Dyżewska[1,2(✉)] [iD], Dawid Malarz[1,3] [iD],
Grzegorz Wilczyński[1,2,3] [iD], Rafał Tobiasz[1,2,3] [iD], Joanna Waczyńska[1,2,3] [iD],
Piotr Borycki[1,2,3] [iD], and Przemysław Spurek[1,3] [iD]

[1] Faculty of Mathematics and Computer Science, Jagiellonian University,
Kraków, Poland
[2] Doctoral School of Exact and Natural Sciences, Jagiellonian University,
Kraków, Poland
`weronika.smolak@doctoral.uj.edu.pl`
[3] IDEAS Research Institute, Warsaw, Poland

Abstract. 3D scene reconstruction from 2D images is important tasks in computer graphics. Unfortunately, existing datasets and benchmarks concentrate on idealized synthetic or meticulously captured realistic data. Such benchmarks fail to convey the inherent complexities encountered in newly acquired real-world scenes. In such scenes the background is often dynamic, and by popular usage of cell phone cameras, there might be discrepancies in, e.g., white balance. To address this gap, we present HuSc3D, a novel dataset specifically designed for rigorous benchmarking of 3D reconstruction models under realistic acquisition challenges. Our dataset features six highly detailed, fully white sculptures characterized by intricate perforations and minimal textural variation. Furthermore, the number of images per scene varies significantly, introducing the additional challenge of limited training data for some instances alongside scenes with a standard number of views. By evaluating 3D reconstruction methods on this diverse dataset, we demonstrate the distinctiveness of HuSc3D in effectively differentiating model performance, particularly highlighting the sensitivity of methods to fine geometric details, color ambiguity, and varying data availability limitations often masked by more conventional datasets. The project page is available here.

Keywords: Gaussian Splatting · NeRF · Benchmark · Novel View Synthesis

1 Introduction

The burgeoning field of 3D scene reconstruction has witnessed remarkable advancements, largely propelled by novel neural representations such as Neural Radiance Fields (NeRF) [1] and, more recently, 3D Gaussian Splatting (3DGS) [2]. These methods have demonstrated impressive capabilities in generating photorealistic novel views and detailed 3D geometries from collections of 2D

P. Neumann et al. (Eds.): ICCS 2026, LNCS 16784, pp. 575–582, 2026.
https://doi.org/10.1007/978-3-032-29924-6_54

images. Consequently, a significant body of research now focuses on improving the fidelity, speed, and robustness of these techniques. Central to this progress is the availability of diverse and challenging datasets for training and, critically, for benchmarking the performance of these algorithms. However, majority of existing datasets, while valuable, present a somewhat sanitized view of the data acquisition process. Synthetic datasets, by their nature, offer perfect camera poses and controlled environments. Even datasets captured in the real world often undergo meticulous curation, extensive calibration, or are captured under studio-like conditions, resulting in data that is cleaner and more consistent than what an average user might produce. This discrepancy is particularly relevant as methods like 3DGS become more accessible, inviting users to capture scenes spontaneously with readily available devices like smartphones. Such "in-the-wild" captures, often intended for casual 3D reconstruction, inherently possess a different set of challenges not fully represented by current benchmarks. To address this gap, we introduce HuSc3D dataset which consists of 6 scenes of white sculptures. The dataset was made by three different methods and showcases several challenges that the average user encounters when starting with the reconstruction task. Our dataset introduces several real-world challenges, including a low number of COLMAP-matched images [3,4], resulting in limited training data, variations in automatic white balance (AWB) typical of smartphone video capture, dynamic background elements (e.g., passing people in public spaces), and objects with intricate geometry but low contrast and minimal texture relative to their surroundings.

2   Related Works

Reconstructing 3D scenes from 2D images is a central problem in computer vision and graphics. Recent advances have been driven by learning-based approaches, particularly Neural Radiance Fields (NeRF) [1] and 3D Gaussian Splatting (3DGS) [2], along with their many extensions [5–14]. Progress in this area is closely tied to the availability of benchmarking datasets.

While numerous datasets exist supporting progress in 3D reconstruction, most are either synthetic or rely on professionally acquired real-world data. Here, we highlight widely recognized benchmarks that represent key data types and challenges, providing context for the gap addressed by HuSc3D. Synthetic datasets such as NeRF-Synthetic [1] offer fully controlled environments with perfect camera parameters and ground truth geometry. While useful for development, they omit real-world issues like calibration errors, noisy sensors, lighting variation, and dynamic elements—factors emphasized by HuSc3D. Among real-world datasets, Mip-NeRF 360 [5] focuses on large-scale, unbounded scenes with high-fidelity 360° captures. In contrast, HuSc3D targets object-centric challenges involving difficult materials (e.g., low-texture or white surfaces) and consumer-grade capture artifacts such as white balance inconsistencies. The LLFF dataset [18] addresses sparse, forward-facing views from handheld cameras. While HuSc3D also includes sparse inputs, it extends this to 360° settings with additional photometric and texture-related challenges. CO3D [19] represents large-scale, category-centric datasets with diverse multi-view object sequences. Rather than focusing on category generalization, HuSc3D emphasizes reconstruction of particularly challenging objects under everyday capture conditions. Finally, datasets like DeepBlending [20] focus on controlled indoor scenes with artificial lighting and room-scale reconstruction, differing from the object-centric focus of HuSc3D.

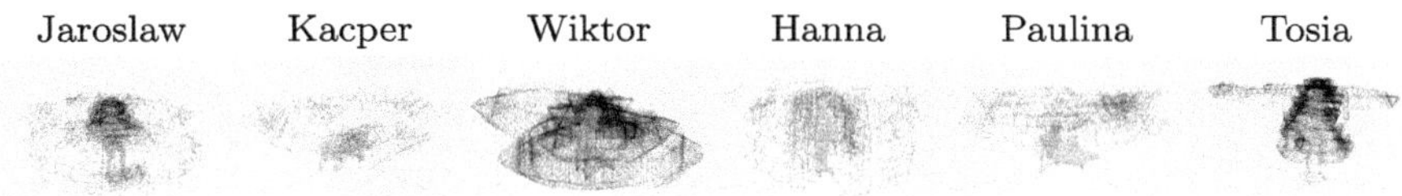

Fig. 1. Visualisation of cameras in scenes in HuSc3D. The visualisation was made in Blender [15] using addons Photogrammetry-based Framework [16] and Kiri [17].

3   HuSc3D Dataset

Data Acquisition and Challenges. The HuSc3D dataset consists of six scenes, each featuring a different sculpture made by the Polish sculptor Paweł Althamer. The dataset was acquired in the Foksal Gallery Foundation headquarters. Captured sculptures were made in 2012 and are a part of a Almech project. All sculptures are white with multiple perforations. Among the dataset there are three ways of capturing the data with camera positions presented in Fig. 1.

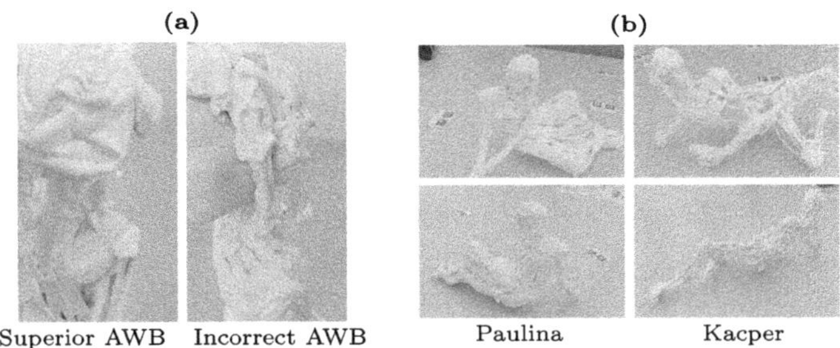

Fig. 2. (a) Example of variety in AWB in Tosia scene. **(b)** Examples of Paulina and Kacper scenes' images.

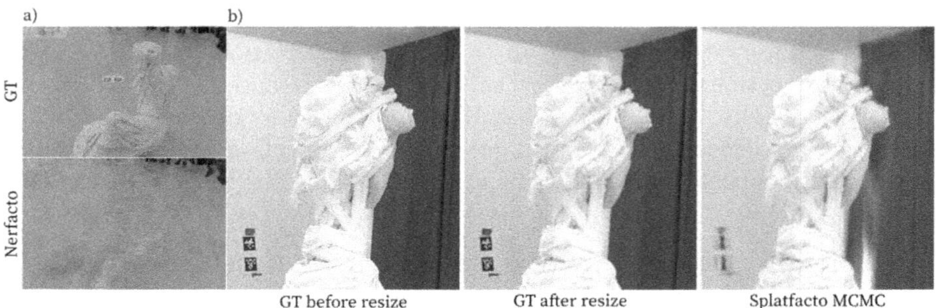

Fig. 3. (a) In scenes with low training samples (Paulina) methods based on NeRF struggle with reconstruction. (b) The necessary 8x downsizing of input images (Hanna) causes substantial detail loss, hindering satisfactory reconstruction.

Kacper and Paulina Scenes. To simulate sparse-view challenges, the Kacper and Paulina scenes use images captured with a Nikon D7000 and fixed camera settings. After COLMAP-based preprocessing, the final sets contain only 66 (Kacper) and 104 (Paulina) images (see Fig. 2b). This limited data makes high-fidelity reconstruction difficult, especially for detailed objects. Methods like NeRF are particularly sensitive to this sparsity, yielding the weakest results compared to approaches such as Splatfacto-MCMC (see Table 1 and Fig. 3a).

Tosia and Wiktor Scenes. To simulate common mobile capture issues, two scenes were recorded using a Samsung Galaxy S24 Ultra, yielding 680 and 596 images by extracting every 20th frame. A key challenge is photometric inconsistency caused by automatic white balance (AWB), which introduces varying color casts (e.g., reddish tint) across frames. This reflects real-world conditions where on-device processing affects data quality. The Tosia scene contains 13.2% affected images, while Wiktor has 28.4%. Although these inconsistencies are easily noticeable to humans (see Fig. 2a), they typically require preprocessing for reconstruction algorithms.

Jarosław and Hanna Scenes. Two scenes in HuSc3D highlight a key limitation in modern 3D reconstruction: handling ultra-high-resolution images. Captured with a Samsung Galaxy S24 Ultra in PRO mode (fixed ISO, aperture, shutter), the datasets include 348 (Jarosław) and 190 (Hanna) images at 6000×8000 px resolution. While rich in detail, their use is constrained by computational cost—requiring 8× downscaling, which removes fine details. These scenes therefore act as a stress test for methods to either process high-resolution data efficiently or remain robust to information loss. Even top-performing methods like Splatfacto-MCMC show noticeable detail degradation (see Fig. 3b).

4 Experiments

To benchmark HuSc3D, six widely used 3D reconstruction methods were evaluated: 2DGS [13], Mip-Splatting [21], NeRF (Nerfacto, Nerfstudio [22]), 3DGS (Splatfacto, Nerfstudio), 3DGS-MCMC

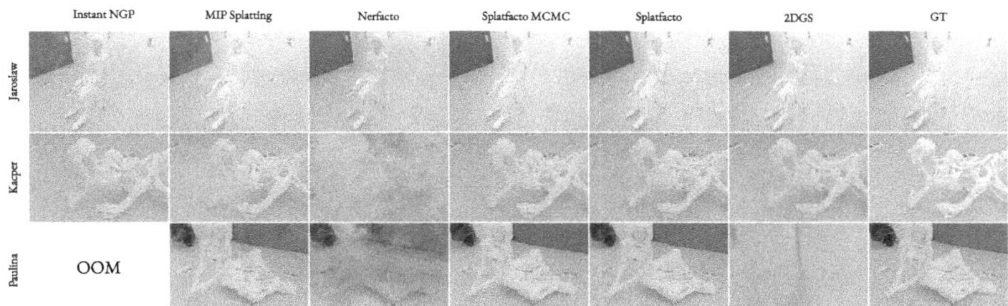

Fig. 4. Qualitative comparison. The majority of methods struggled on scenes with sparse number of training views (Kacper and Paulina).

(Splatfacto-MCMC, Nerfstudio) [23], and Instant-NGP [24] (Nerfstudio). These represent key approaches in the field, spanning explicit point-based and implicit volumetric methods.

Experimental Setup. Reconstruction quality and efficiency were evaluated using PSNR, SSIM, LPIPS, training time, and FPS.

For all methods we used publicly available implementations with minimal changes. 2DGS and Mip-Splatting follow their original repositories and default settings, while Nerfacto, Splatfacto, Splatfacto-MCMC, and In-stant-NGP are run via Nerfstudio with default configurations. Images were downsampled by 4× (8× for Hanna and Jarosław). Experiments run on an NVIDIA RTX 4090 (256 GB RAM, Ubuntu 24.04). Following 3DGS protocol, 12.5% of images are held out for testing, and all metrics are computed on this subset.

Quantitative Results. The quantitative performance on the HuSc3D dataset is presented in Table 1. The superior performance of Gaussian Splatting (GS) methods (2DGS, Mip-Splatting, Splatfacto, Splatfacto-MCMC) in both reconstruction quality and rendering speed suggests that explicit, point-based representations are more robust to the challenges in HuSc3D. In particular, Splatfacto-MCMC achieved the best metrics. In contrast, NeRF-based methods (Nerfacto, Instant-NGP) struggled more significantly. Nerfacto showed consistently lower fidelity, while Instant-NGP encountered memory limitations on multiple scenes. These issues likely stem from sensitivity to dynamic backgrounds, limited training views, and photometric inconsistencies such as white balance shifts, which are further exacerbated by the texture-poor nature of the objects.

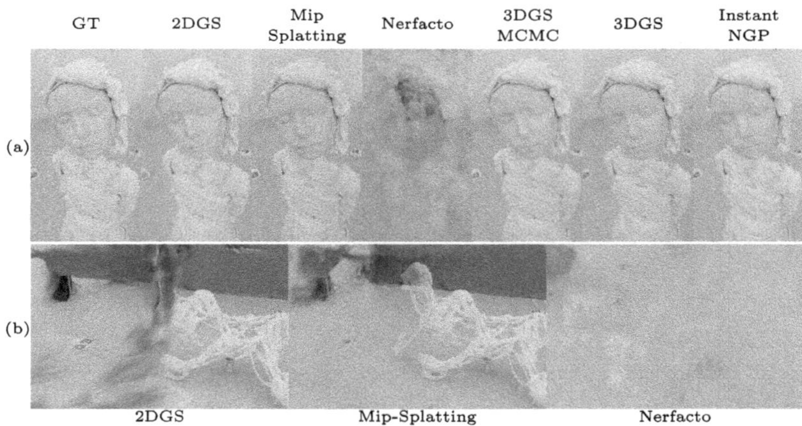

Fig. 5. (a) Qualitative results. Instant-NGP and Nerfacto favor the dataset's average white balance (WB), causing errors or blur, while 3DGS methods successfully reconstruct sudden WB shifts. **(b)** Significant artifacts in sparse views. 3DGS - Splatfacto

Table 1. Quantitative results across HuSc3D. Best scores per metric are bolded. Time (mm:sec). *Instant-NGP training failed with OOM for Hanna and Paulina scenes.

Method	SSIM ↑	PSNR ↑	LPIPS ↓	Time ↓	FPS ↑
2DGS	0.920	29.96	0.222	10:21	187.17
Mip-Splatting	0.930	30.62	0.192	11:29	**191.74**
Nerfacto	0.807	21.98	0.359	12:12	1.39
Splatfacto	0.944	31.38	0.136	**7:38**	165.71
Splatfacto-MCMC	**0.953**	**32.45**	**0.109**	16:06	82.34
Instant-NGP	0.908*	27.435*	0.231*	9:55*	1.23*

Qualitative Results. Qualitative results are presented in Figs. 4 and 5(a). It represents renders made on test set with different methods. Even though, Splatfacto-MCMC achieved the best results both qualitatively and quantitatively, it still could misses intricate details as previously mentioned in Fig. 3. Multiple methods failed at reconstructing correctly Paulina and Kacper scenes with sparse views. For fair comparison, we used the same frame throughout every method, however, multiple methods failed to correctly reconstruct every point of view in testing sets creating a significant amount of artifacts located on the object of interest. The methods that had at least one frame failed were 2DGS, Mip-Splatting, Nerfacto (which failed on almost every image). Additionally, Instant-NGP OOM on Paulina scene and on multiple renders in Kacper. We showcased these exemplary problematic frames in Fig. 5(b).

5 Conclusion

HuSc3D is a novel dataset addressing the limitations of existing 3D reconstruction benchmarks. While previous datasets often rely on idealized synthetic or meticulously captured data, HuSc3D focuses on realistic challenges faced by non-expert users. Given recent advancements in reconstruction methodologies, we believe the field is now equipped to tackle these real-world complexities.

Limitations and Future Work. The dataset size is the biggest limitation of HuSc3D. Future Work could include more sculptures, presumably from different artists. Additionally, every scene could contain captures showcasing every combination of the mentioned challenges.

Acknowledgments. We are deeply grateful to the amazing artist Paweł Althamer for its wonderful art and his curtosy in enabling us to scan and share his work. We also want to thank Foksal Gallery Foundation for providing us with space for scanning, a warm welcome, and helping in contacting the artist. The work of W. Smolak-Dyżewska, D. Malarz, G. Wilczyński and P. Spurek was supported by the project *Effective Rendering of 3D Objects Using Gaussian Splatting in an Augmented Reality Environment* (FENG.02.02-IP.05-0114/23), carried out under the First Team programme of the Foundation for Polish Science and co-financed by the European Union through the European Funds for Smart Economy 20212027 (FENG). The work of P. Borycki was supported by the National Centre of Science (Poland) Grant No. 2025/57/N/ST6/04389. The work of J. Waczyńska was supported by the National Centre of Science (Poland) Grant No. 2025/57/N/ST6/04390.

References

1. Mildenhall, B., Srinivasan, P.P., Tancik, M., Barron, J.T., Ramamoorthi, R., Ng, R.: Nerf: representing scenes as neural radiance fields for view synthesis. In: ECCV (2020)
2. Kerbl, B., Kopanas, G., Leimkühler, T., Drettakis, G.: 3D gaussian splatting for real-time radiance field rendering. ACM Trans. Graph. **42**(4) (2023)
3. Schönberger, J.L., Zheng, E., Pollefeys, M., Frahm, M.: Pixelwise view selection for unstructured multi-view stereo. In: European Conference on Computer Vision (ECCV) (2016)
4. Schönberger, J.L., Frahm, J.M.: Structure-from-motion revisited. In: Conference on Computer Vision and Pattern Recognition (CVPR) (2016)
5. Mildenhall, B., Verbin, D., Pratul, P., Srinivasan, P., Hedman, R., Martin-Brualla, R., Barron, J.T.: MultiNeRF: a code release for Mip-NeRF. In: Ref-NeRF, and RawNeRF, vol. 360 (2022)
6. Verbin, D., Hedman, P., Mildenhall, B., Zickler, T., Barron, J.T., Srinivasan, P.P.: Ref-NeRF: structured view-dependent appearance for neural radiance fields. In: CVPR (2022)
7. Pumarola, A., Corona, E., Pons-Moll, G., Moreno-Noguer, F.: D-nerf: neural radiance fields for dynamic scenes. In: Proceedings of the IEEE/CVF Conference on Computer Vision and Pattern Recognition (2020)

8. Hong, Y., Peng, B., Xiao, H., Liu, L., Zhang, J.: Headnerf: a real-time nerf-based parametric head model. In: Proceedings of the IEEE/CVF Conference on Computer Vision and Pattern Recognition (CVPR), pp. 20374–20384 (2022)

9. Deng, K., Liu, A., Zhu, J.Y., Ramanan, D.: Depth-supervised nerf: fewer views and faster training for free. In: Proceedings of the IEEE/CVF Conference on Computer Vision and Pattern Recognition (CVPR), pp. 12882–12891 (2022)

10. Wu, G., et al.: 4D gaussian splatting for real-time dynamic scene rendering. arXiv preprint arXiv:2310.08528 (2023)

11. Huang, Y.H., Sun, Y.T., Yang, Z., Lyu, X., Cao, Y.P., Qi, X.: SC-GS: sparse-controlled gaussian splatting for editable dynamic scenes. arXiv preprint arXiv:2312.14937 (2023)

12. Waczyńska, J., Borycki, P., Kaleta, J., Tadeja, S., Spurek, P.: D-MiSo: editing dynamic 3D scenes using Multi-Gaussians soup. arXiv preprint arXiv:2405.14276 (2024)

13. Huang, B., Yu, Z., Chen, A., Geiger, A., Gao, S.: 2d Gaussian splatting for geometrically accurate radiance fields. In: SIGGRAPH 2024 Conference Papers, Association for Computing Machinery (2024)

14. Malarz, D., Smolak-Dyżewska, W., Tabor, J., Tadeja, S., Spurek, P.: Gaussian splatting with nerf-based color and opacity. Comput. Vis. Image Underst. **251**, 104273 (2025)

15. Blender Online Community: Blender - A 3D Modelling and Rendering Package. Blender Foundation, Stichting Blender Foundation, Amsterdam (2018)

16. Bullinger, S., Bodensteiner, C., Arens, M.: A photogrammetry-based framework to facilitate image-based modeling and automatic camera tracking. In: International Conference on Computer Graphics Theory and Applications (2021)

17. Kiri-Innovation: 3DGS render blender addon by KIRI engine (2025). https://github.com/Kiri-Innovation/3dgs-render-blender-addon

18. Mildenhall, B., et al.: Local light field fusion: practical view synthesis with prescriptive sampling guidelines. ACM Trans. Graph. (TOG) (2019)

19. Reizenstein, J., Shapovalov, R., Henzler, P., Sbordone, L., Labatut, P., Novotny, D.: Common objects in 3D: large-scale learning and evaluation of real-life 3D category reconstruction. In: International Conference on Computer Vision (2021)

20. Hedman, P., Philip, J., Price, T., Frahm, J.M., Drettakis, G., Brostow, G.: Deep blending for free-viewpoint image-based rendering. ACM Trans. Graph. (SIGGRAPH Asia Conference Proceedings) **37**(6) (2018)

21. Yu, Z., Sattler, T., Geiger, A.: Gaussian opacity fields: efficient high-quality compact surface reconstruction in unbounded scenes. arXiv:2404.10772 (2024)

22. Tancik, M., et al.: Nerfstudio: a modular framework for neural radiance field development. In: ACM SIGGRAPH 2023 Conference Proceedings, SIGGRAPH '23 (2023)

23. Kheradmand, S., et al.: 3D Gaussian splatting as markov chain Monte Carlo. In: Advances in Neural Information Processing Systems (NeurIPS) (2024). Spotlight Presentation

24. Müller, T., Evans, A., Schied, C., Keller, A.: Instant neural graphics primitives with a multiresolution hash encoding. ACM Trans. Graph. **41**(4), 102:1–102:15 (2022)

Proactive Forecasting with a Digital Twin in Emergency Departments: Preserving Key Performance Indicators Values

Mercedes Planas[1]([✉])[iD], Eva Bruballa[1][iD], Maria Harita[2][iD], Alvaro Wong[2][iD], Dolores Rexachs[2][iD], and Francisco Epelde[3][iD]

[1] Escoles Universitàries Gimbernat, Computer Science School, Universitat Autònoma de Barcelona, Sant Cugat del Vallès, Barcelona, Spain
{merce.planas,eva.bruballa}@eug.es
[2] Computer Architecture and Operating System Department, Universitat Autònoma de Barcelona, Barcelona, Spain
{MariaDeLosAngeles.Harita,alvaro.wong,dolores.rexachs}@uab.cat
[3] Internal Medicine Department, Parc Taulí Hospital Universitari. Institut d'Investigació i Innovació Parc Taulí (I3PT-CERCA). Universitat Autònoma de Barcelona, Sabadell, Barcelona, Spain
fepelde@tauli.cat

Abstract. Efficient management of hospital Emergency Departments (EDs) is essential to prevent service saturation or bottlenecks caused by unexpected patient inflows and resource limitations. This work proposes a Digital Twin (DT) framework that simulates ED operations to anticipate performance degradation and support proactive decision-making. The DT operates faster than the real system, enabling exploration of future operational scenarios and evaluation of corrective staffing strategies. A heuristic optimization method is used to identify personnel configurations that preserve Key Performance Indicators (KPIs) under disruptive demand conditions while respecting resource constraints. Results show that the proposed DT supports early detection of KPI degradation risks and enables timely staffing adaptation to maintain ED operational performance.

Keywords: Decision Support · Digital Twin · Emergency Department · Optimization · Simulation · Prevention · Key Performance Indicators

1 Introduction

EDs are critical hospital units characterized by high variability in patient inflow, complex resource interactions, and strong dependence on staffing availability. These factors make maintaining service quality and operational efficiency particularly challenging, especially under unexpected demand surges.

Traditional ED management relies on reactive decision-making once performance degradation becomes visible. In contrast, DT technology enables proactive

P. Neumann et al. (Eds.): ICCS 2026, LNCS 16784, pp. 583–591, 2026.
https://doi.org/10.1007/978-3-032-29924-6_55

control by replicating system behavior and forecasting future operational conditions through accelerated simulation. Figure 1 illustrates the transition from traditional reactive management to a DT-based predictive control loop for ED operation.

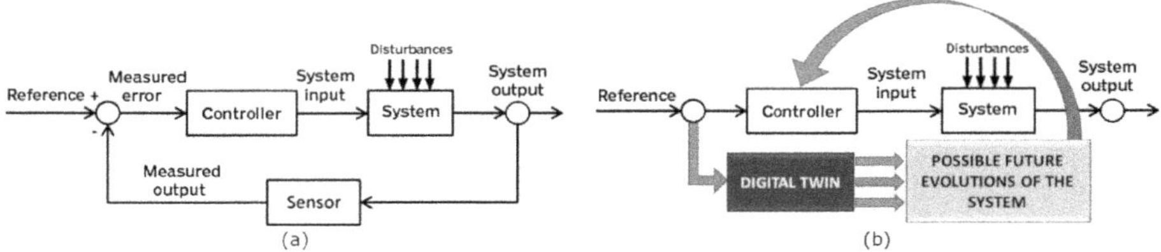

Fig. 1. (a) Feedback control loop. (b) Digital twin-based control.

DT technology is increasingly used in healthcare as a predictive decision-support framework for complex systems. Existing applications include medical device monitoring and organ-level modeling [7,11], although they mainly focus on patient-specific scenarios rather than hospital operations. DT-based solutions have also been applied to hospital workflow optimization and emergency resource planning [2,3,10]. However, these approaches typically rely on descriptive simulation and do not support proactive control under dynamic demand conditions.

Although agent-based simulation has proven effective for modeling ED dynamics [5,6,9], the integration of DT-based predictive modeling with staffing adaptation driven by optimization remains limited.

This work proposes a DT-based framework that anticipates KPI degradation and evaluates corrective staffing configurations before disruptions affect the real system. Suitable configurations are identified using the Monte Carlo Clustering Search Algorithm (MCSA), a stochastic sampling-based heuristic optimization method integrated within the DT environment to evaluate alternative staffing strategies and mitigate performance degradation proactively.

2   Management of the ED Through a DT

The objective of this research is to improve ED management using a DT that simulates its operations to anticipate its behavior.

2.1   ED Simulator

The DT relies on a stochastic agent-based ED simulator developed by the High Performance Computing for Efficient Applications and Simulation (HPC4EAS) research group at the Universitat Autònoma de Barcelona (UAB) and calibrated using historical data from Hospital Parc Taulí in Sabadell [4,5]. Its stochastic formulation enables realistic representation of patient flow variability and supports the evaluation of alternative staffing configurations under varying arrival patterns and resource constraints.

The validity of the proposed DT is ensured through calibration and validation of the underlying agent-based modeling and simulation (ABMS) ED simulator framework using historical operational data. Model outputs were compared with observed KPI values to verify consistency between simulated and real system behavior. In addition, periodic data updates allow recalibration when deviations are detected, maintaining alignment between the physical ED and its digital counterpart over time.

2.2   Model Inputs and Outputs

To support decision-making, the ED model considers key input parameters including patient inflow classified according to the Spanish Triage System [8], physical resources (e.g., beds, laboratories, and test units), and healthcare staffing composition. Patients are treated in two care areas based on triage priority: Area A (levels 1–3) and Area B (levels 4–5). Staffing configurations account for both the number of professionals and their experience level (junior and senior), which influences service times and system performance.

System performance is evaluated through several KPIs [12], including Length of Stay (LoS), Length of Waiting Time (LoW), Patient Attention Time (PaT), and staffing occupation indicators. Among these, LoS is used as the primary indicator of operational performance due to its relevance for ED efficiency and service quality. The simulator provides LoS estimates by triage level $i \in \{1, 2, 3, 4, 5\}$; in this work, the overall average LoS is used as a global efficiency indicator to compare operational scenarios.

2.3   Digital Twin Operation

The ED receives patients classified by triage level and operates under target KPI conditions. As shown in Fig. 2, the DT is configured with the same healthcare staff (HS) and physical resource (PR) parameters as the real system and receives identical patient inflow data updated dynamically over time.

The proposed system maintains continuous correspondence between the physical ED and its digital replica through calibrated simulation models and operational inputs. Unlike a standalone simulation model, the DT preserves synchronization with the physical ED through periodic data updates and recalibration mechanisms. This enables the DT not only to reproduce system behavior but also to anticipate performance deviations and evaluate corrective actions before their implementation in the real environment, acting as a predictive decision-support layer within the ED management loop.

By executing simulations faster than real time to explore alternative future scenarios, the DT enables early identification of staffing configurations that preserve target KPI values. Due to the multidimensional interaction among

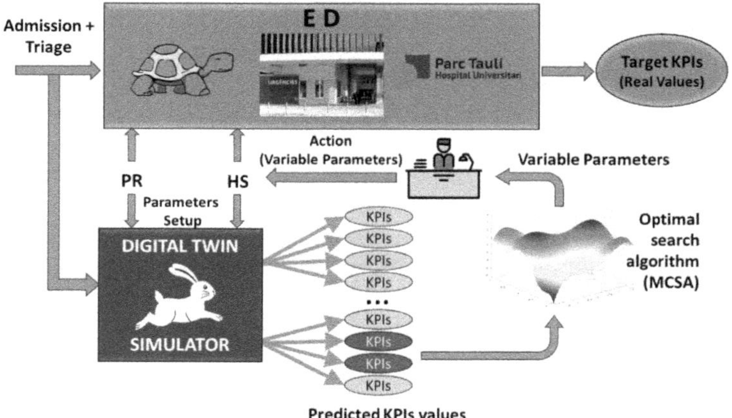

Fig. 2. Operation of the ED Digital Twin.

decision parameters, the search process is performed using a heuristic optimization method based on Monte Carlo sampling, referred to as MCSA [1], which efficiently explores the configuration space through stochastic sampling and simulation-based evaluation without exhaustive enumeration.

3 Monte Carlo Clustering Search Algorithm

To identify suitable medical staffing configurations in the ED, the MCSA heuristic optimization method is employed. MCSA alternates between exploration and intensification phases, exploring the multidimensional configuration space through stochastic sampling combined with simulation-based evaluation of candidate solutions using the ABMS simulator.

The method can be interpreted as a stochastic simulation-based optimization approach that combines Monte Carlo sampling with clustering-driven intensification. Candidate staffing configurations are evaluated using the ED simulator model, and the search is iteratively biased towards high-performing regions of the solution space identified through clustering, enabling efficient identification of suitable configurations without exhaustive enumeration.

The algorithm iteratively evaluates staffing configurations according to their impact on KPIs (e.g., mean LoS) and refines the search until convergence is achieved. From a computational perspective, the method scales with the dimensionality of the configuration space, and since candidate evaluations are independent, it is naturally parallelizable through concurrent simulation runs.

4 DT Integration for Predictive Optimization in ED

4.1 Predictive Simulation and Disruption Management

As a first step, the proposed framework identifies staffing adjustments required to prevent abnormal operating conditions and avoid ED saturation. As illustrated in

Fig. 3, the system is periodically monitored at one-hour intervals, and predictive simulations are executed on the DT to detect potential deviations from target KPI values. When performance degradation is anticipated, the MCSA heuristic algorithm is applied to identify suitable staffing configurations. The selected configuration is then validated through simulation to ensure that KPI levels remain within acceptable limits.

At each monitoring interval, predicted KPI values obtained from the DT are compared with observed values from the real ED. When deviations exceed a predefined threshold, a recalibration process is triggered by updating model input parameters using recent operational data, ensuring continuous alignment between the digital and physical systems.

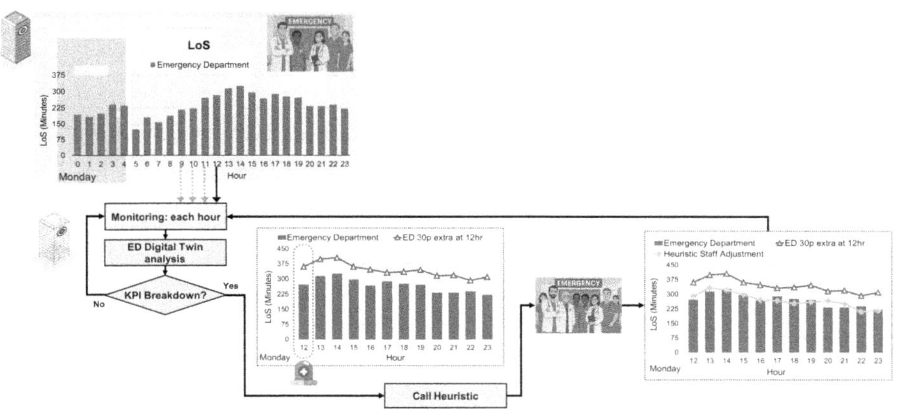

Fig. 3. Predictive Simulation and Disruption Management Process.

4.2   Intervention Window

Once the appropriate staffing adjustments have been identified, the intervention window is defined as the time available to implement corrective actions before performance degradation affects the real ED. This window is estimated by simulating disturbance scenarios with increased patient inflow and monitoring the evolution of the LoS over time (Fig. 4(a)).

As shown in Fig. 4(b), a noticeable deviation in LoS appears between the second and third hour after the disturbance, defining the available intervention window. Early identification of this interval enables timely corrective actions to stabilize system performance and prevent service disruptions.

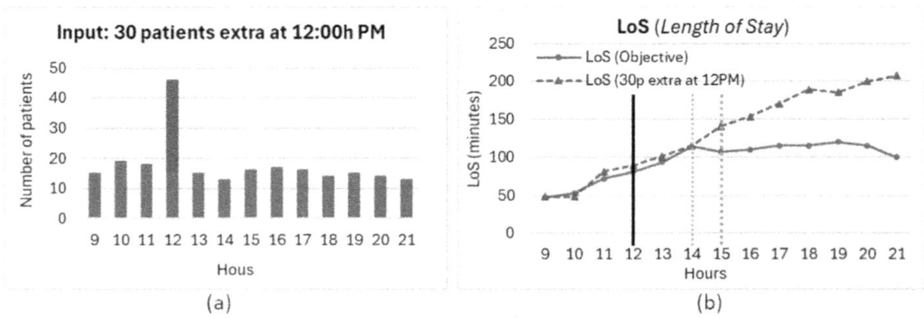

Fig. 4. (a) Scenario: Surge of 30 additional patients at 12:00 PM. (b) Comparison of LoS values between the target and the scenario with additional patients at 12:00 PM.

5   Advanced Management Case ED/DT

To maintain ED operation within the target range of the selected KPI (LoS) under unusual patient inflow conditions, the proposed strategy adjusts staffing configurations through targeted temporary reinforcement of healthcare personnel. The operational parameters considered in this case study are summarized in Table 1.

Table 1. Initial and optimized staffing configuration for the ED (SD: Senior doctor, JD: Junior doctor, SN: Senior nurse, JN: Junior nurse)

	Area A		Area B	
Role	Initial	Optimized	Initial	Optimized
JN	2	2	5	6
SN	3	3	7	4
JD	2	2	5	3
SD	3	7	2	7

In the initial phase, the DT is configured to replicate the operational conditions of the ED. Disturbance scenarios are generated by injecting additional patients at specific hours; as an illustrative example, a surge of 30 extra patients at 12:00 p.m. on a Monday is considered. Simulation results show that this disturbance produces a significant increase in average LoS beyond the target threshold, indicating a potential overload situation.

To mitigate this effect, the MCSA heuristic method identifies a feasible staffing reconfiguration under realistic resource constraints (Table 1). The updated configuration is then evaluated through simulation using the DT. As shown in Fig. 5, the adjusted staffing plan restores the average LoS to the target range.

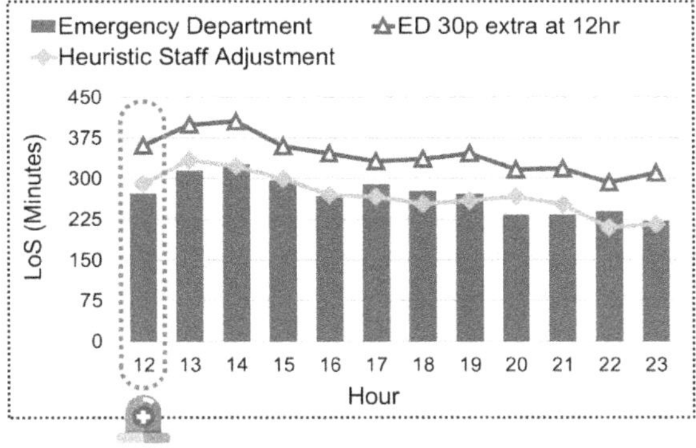

Fig. 5. Comparison of Scenario LoS, Target LoS, and LoS after staffing adjustment.

These results highlight the capability of the DT framework to anticipate performance degradation and support proactive staffing adjustments before disruptions affect the real ED.

The results demonstrate that the proposed DT supports proactive staffing optimization and provides insight into system behavior under varying demand conditions, enabling corrective actions before performance degradation affects the real ED.

6   Conclusion

This work demonstrates the potential of DT technology to support proactive management of hospital EDs by anticipating performance degradation and evaluating corrective staffing strategies through accelerated simulation. The integration of the MCSA heuristic method enables efficient identification of staffing configurations that preserve service quality under disruptive patient inflow conditions.

A key contribution of this study is the definition of the intervention window, identified as the critical 2–3-hour period following a disturbance, during which corrective actions can be applied before system performance deteriorates.

Results also highlight the need to balance KPI improvement with operational feasibility, since configurations that minimize LoS may not always correspond to the most efficient use of resources. The DT environment enables validation of alternative staffing strategies before implementation, reducing operational risk and supporting informed decision-making.

Overall, the proposed DT-based framework provides an effective predictive decision-support tool for improving resilience and operational efficiency in Emergency Departments.

7 Future Work and Ethical Considerations

Future work will focus on extending the DT with additional system parameters and KPIs to better capture the interactions affecting ED performance, as well as validating the proposed framework in different hospital environments to assess its generalizability. Further research will also address the integration of real-time operational data streams to improve model calibration and support continuous alignment between the physical ED and its digital counterpart.

From an ethical perspective, the use of hospital operational data requires strict compliance with data protection regulations such as General Data Protection Regulation (GDPR). Although the proposed DT does not rely on individual patient identification, ensuring transparency in model assumptions and preventing bias in decision-support recommendations remain essential for responsible deployment in clinical environments.

Acknowledgments. This research has been supported by the Agencia Estatal de Investigación (AEI), Spain and the Fondo Europeo de Desarrollo Regional (FEDER) UE under contract PID2023-147955NB-I00.

References

1. Harita, M., Wong, A., Suppi, R., Rexachs, D., Luque, E.: A metaheuristic search algorithm based on sampling and clustering. IEEE Access **12**, 15493–15508 (2024). https://doi.org/10.1109/ACCESS.2024.3354714
2. Hu, X., Cao, H., Shi, J., Dai, Y., Dai, W.: Study of hospital emergency resource scheduling based on digital twin technology. In: Proceedings of the 2021 IEEE 2nd International Conference on Information Technology, Big Data and Artificial Intelligence (ICIBA), vol. 2, pp. 1059–1063. IEEE, Chongqing, China (2021)
3. Karakra, A., Fontanili, F., Lamine, E., Lamothe, J.: Hospit'win: a predictive simulation-based digital twin for patients pathways in hospital. In: Proceedings of the 2019 IEEE EMBS International Conference on Biomedical and Health Informatics (BHI), pp. 1–4. IEEE, Chicago, IL, USA (2019)
4. Liu, Z.: Modeling and simulation for healthcare operations management using high performance computing and agent-based model. Ph.D. thesis, Barcelona, Spain (2016)
5. Liu, Z., Rexachs, D., Epelde, F., Luque, E.: An agent-based model for quantitatively analyzing and predicting the complex behavior of emergency departments. J. Comput. Sci. **21**, 11–23 (2017)
6. Liu, Z., Rexachs, D., Luque, E., Epelde, F., Cabrera, E.: Simulating the micro-level behavior of emergency department for macro-level features prediction. In: 2015 Winter Simulation Conference (WSC), pp. 171–182 (2015). https://doi.org/10.1109/WSC.2015.7408162
7. Martinez-Velazquez, R., Gamez, R., El Saddik, A.: Cardio twin: a digital twin of the human heart running on the edge. In: Proceedings of the IEEE International Symposium on Medical Measurements and Applications (MeMeA), pp. 1–6. IEEE, Istanbul, Turkey (2019)

8. Ministerio de Sanidad, Servicios Sociales e Igualdad: Unidad de urgencias hospitalaria: Estándares y recomendaciones (2011). https://www.sanidad.gob.es/areas/calidadAsistencial/excelenciaClinica/docs/UUH.pdf. Accessed Dec 2025

9. Moyaux, T., Liu, Y., Bouleux, G., Cheutet, V.: An agent-based architecture of the digital twin for an emergency department. Sustainability **15**(4), 3412 (2023). https://doi.org/10.3390/su15043412

10. Siemens Healthineers: From digital twin to improved patient experience (2025). https://www.siemens-healthineers.com/perspectives/mso-digital-twin-mater.html. Accessed Dec. 2025

11. Subramanian, K.: Digital twin for drug discovery and development–the virtual liver. J. Indian Inst. Sci. **100**, 653–662 (2020)

12. Welch, S.J., Asplin, B.R., Stone-Griffith, S., Davidson, S.J., Augustine, J., Schuur, J.: Emergency department benchmarking alliance. Emergency department operational metrics, measures and definitions: results of the second performance measures and benchmarking summit. Ann. Emerg. Med. **58**(1), 33–40 (2011). https://doi.org/10.1016/j.annemergmed.2010.08.040

Author Index

© The Editor(s) (if applicable) and The Author(s), under exclusive license
to Springer Nature Switzerland AG 2026
P. Neumann et al. (Eds.): ICCS 2026, LNCS 16784, pp. 593–596, 2026.
https://doi.org/10.1007/978-3-032-29924-6

GPSR Compliance
The European Union's (EU) General Product Safety Regulation (GPSR) is a set
of rules that requires consumer products to be safe and our obligations to
ensure this.

If you have any concerns about our products, you can contact us on

ProductSafety@springernature.com

In case Publisher is established outside the EU, the EU authorized
representative is:

Springer Nature Customer Service Center GmbH
Europaplatz 3
69115 Heidelberg, Germany